British Slave

The Sugar Colonies and the Great Experiment
1830–1865

BRITISH SLAVE EMANCIPATION

The Sugar Colonies and the Great Experiment
1830–1865

WILLIAM A. GREEN

CLARENDON PRESS · OXFORD

Oxford University Press, Great Clarendon Street, Oxford OX2 6DP

Oxford New York
Athens Auckland Bangkok Bogota Bombay
Buenos Aires Calcutta Cape Town Dar es Salaam
Delhi Florence Hong Kong Istanbul Karachi
Kuala Lumpur Madras Madrid Melbourne
Mexico City Nairobi Paris Singapore
Taipei Tokyo Toronto Warsaw
and associated companies in
Berlin Ibadan

Oxford is a trade mark of Oxford University Press

Published in the United States by
Oxford University Press Inc., New York

First published 1976
First issued in paperback 1991

British Library Cataloguing in Publication Data
Data available

Library of Congress Cataloging in Publication Data
Data applied for

ISBN 0-19-820278-4

7 9 10 8 6

Printed in Great Britain
on acid-free paper by
Biddles Ltd., Guildford and King's Lynn

Preface

I T has been nearly forty years since William Law Mathieson published the final book in his three-volume survey of the West Indies between 1823 and 1865. Since that time, two generations of scholars have combed British and colonial archives, seeking fresh answers to new questions and exploring untrodden avenues of Caribbean history. Excellent studies have appeared on individual sugar colonies or specific estates, with Jamaica—as usual—attracting primary attention. This book attempts a new comprehensive assessment of the British West Indies in the mid-nineteenth century, welding together in a single narrative the diverse experiences of more than a dozen sugar colonies. Though their similarities were far greater than their differences, the dependencies of Great Britain that swept in a wide arc from Jamaica through the Lesser Antilles to British Guiana were marked by numerous structural, institutional, and social variations. This variety lends fascination and intrigue to the history of the Caribbean, but it complicates the work of scholars who set out to synthesize imperial history in the West Indies. Historians cannot avoid generalizations, for their task requires that they render the enormously complicated affairs of former generations comprehensible to their own. Generalizations arise from the accumulation of particular evidence, but in a study of this kind it is not profitable to offer citations from a large number of colonies to verify all judgements of a general character. Points are made by illustrative examples rather than by reference to numerous similar cases. The reader should be aware, however, that in the British West Indies there were exceptions to most rules. Where divergences were significant they are examined in the text; where they were more interesting than important they commonly receive treatment in footnotes.

The book is produced in two parts. The first, an examination of the salient aspects of West Indian life on the eve of emancipation, serves two purposes. As an introduction to the principal portion of the study dealing with the development of the British Caribbean, 1834–65, it provides clarity to various aspects of society, economy, and government that might otherwise appear confused or abstruse. At the same time, Part I is intended to stand on its own as a cross-sectional assessment of the sugar colonies and their relations with the mother country at a vital watershed in their history.

The inspiration of this study is as much imperial as it is West Indian. My aim has been to examine the manner in which the Colonial Office managed the sensitive and tangled problems associated with slavery and its abolition and to ascertain how closely developments in the colonies coincided with the aspirations and expectations of the imperial power. The book might well have been subtitled 'A Study in Imperial Policy', for my objectives as well as my documentation have led in that direction.

No scholar can hope to acknowledge all those who have aided his researches, enlightened his thinking, and tolerated his irritabilities and idiosyncrasies during the long but happily toilsome effort of preparing a book. To the many scholars whose works and advice I have relied upon and built upon, I am deeply indebted. I am extremely grateful to numerous people at the Public Record Office, whose cordiality and efficiency rendered my research there immensely pleasant and rewarding. Especially, I owe thanks to Mr. Leslie Seed of the P.R.O. for the many extraordinary services he has rendered me. The archivists at the London Missionary Society, the Baptist Missionary Society, and the Methodist Missionary Society have been most helpful to me. Also, I extend my appreciation to the editors of the *Journal of African History* and *The Economic History Review* for permitting me to reproduce sections of articles I have published in those journals. I wish to thank the Revd. and Mrs. Herbert McGie of Kingston, Jamaica, for their great hospitality during my research visit in that island. The cost of my research has been aided by the National Endowment for the Humanities and by the Batchelor Fellowships distributed by Holy Cross College. For this assistance, I am truly grateful. The Administrators at Holy Cross have consistently offered me time and encouragement to complete this book, and I appreciate the confidence they have displayed in me. To my mother, Mrs. June R. Green, who has performed many typing services for me, and to Mrs. Pearl M. Jolicoeur who typed the final manuscript I extend enormous thanks.

Throughout the eight years I have devoted to this book my wife has borne many sacrifices. She has managed our large family for months at a time while I ventured abroad; she has read and commented intelligently on every part of the manuscript; and she has encouraged me, inspired me, and endured my preoccupations and occasional reclusiveness. In the hope that this book is worthy of her, I dedicate it to Karin.

Holden, Massachusetts

Contents

List of Tables

List of Illustrations

List of Illustrations

PART I

THE SUGAR COLONIES ON THE
EVE OF EMANCIPATION

CHAPTER 1

West Indian Society

THE British West Indian colonies were organized to produce wealth, not contentment. Blacks were in bondage to whites, the whites to cupidity. As Governor Henry Light observed, the great majority of European colonists 'left Great Britain very young, without education, rarely of any position in Society—having only one object that of making money as rapidly as possible'.[1] If this was not entirely desirable, it was altogether natural. What sane man, asked the *Guiana Chronicle*, would emigrate to a tropical colony which merely afforded him what he might enjoy in a temperate country?[2] No matter how long a Briton remained in the Caribbean or how successful his tenure there, he referred to England, not to the colonies, as 'home'.[3]

Society in the West Indies was rigidly segmented: 'The inhabitants of this colony', declared the Jamaica Assembly in 1797, 'consist of four classes; whites, free people of colour having special privileges granted by private acts, free people of colour not possessing such privileges, and slaves. . . .'[4] Europeans dominated all aspects of society, and, unlike the blacks, preserved most of their own cultural and social institutions. Africans, on the other hand, had been subjected to forced creolization: their traditional living habits, their labour patterns, their language, and their family relations had undergone drastic change in order to accommodate white planters

[1] Light to Russell, 19 Apr. 1840, C.O. 111/167. no. 53.

[2] *The Guiana Chronicle*, 15 Mar. 1839.

[3] Anthony Trollope discovered that third-generation Jamaicans who had never left the colony referred to England as home. See his *The West Indies and the Spanish Main* (New York, 1860), pp. 100–1. These sentiments were moderated in Barbados where a strong local patriotism developed among resident proprietors.

[4] Quoted in Edward Brathwaite, *The Development of Creole Society in Jamaica, 1770–1820* (Oxford, 1971), p. 105.

and satisfy the requirements of the plantation economy. By 1830 a full generation after the abolition of the slave trade, people who had personal memories of Africa, probably did not exceed 25 per cent of the whole black population, and their numbers were swiftly shrinking.[5] Although African cultural legacies remained—among them, slash and burn methods of cultivation, obeah, African burial practices and folklore— uprooted blacks forged new customs in response to their Caribbean environment and assimilated much of the dominant culture.

White West Indians considered themselves remote components of metropolitan society, not members of a distinctive colonial culture. Nevertheless, a 'frontier' spirit pervaded the islands, and the whites—like their counterparts in Canada and Australia—exhibited a strong democratic demeanour.[6] The European pedigree of the Caribbean élite was generally undistinguished, and leading men in the islands were separated from young, impoverished newcomers only by their pecuniary successes or their proven ability to endure the vicissitudes of the climate. Informality was the rule; privacy was almost unknown; and crudity was commonplace. White society in the Caribbean assumed a far greater creole quality than whites themselves were prepared to admit, but British West Indians could not develop a profound local identity like that which had emerged in the thirteen mainland colonies. The Caribbean colonies were small, isolated, and weak. In time of war, they relied on the Royal Navy for defence; at all times they required the presence of the British Army to help discourage and reduce slave insurrections. The population was predominantly black, and a large portion of the white minority was dispersed among

[5] Brathwaite determined that 36 per cent of the Jamaican slave population in 1817 was African born. This figure is roughly corroborated by Higman and Craton. who estimate the percentage to be 37 and 38 respectively. See, Michael Craton, 'Jamaican Slave Mortality: Fresh Light from Worthy Park, Longville and the Tharp Estates', *Journal of Caribbean History*, III (1971), 15; and, B. W. Higman, 'Slave Population and Economy in Jamaica at the Time of Emancipation' (Unpublished Ph.D. Dissertation, University of the West Indies, 1970), p. 168. Compared to Barbados or the Leeward colonies, the Jamaica estimates are very high, and there is little doubt that even in Jamaica the figure had fallen to around 25 per cent by 1834.

[6] Henry Nelson Coleridge, *Six Months in the West Indies in 1825* (London, 1826), p. 294.

hundreds of separate estates. Schemes designed to increase the ratio of whites to blacks by attracting European settlers and encouraging agricultural diversity consistently failed.[7] Emigrants from Europe, deterred by the slave system, ventured to North America. The high price of sugar in comparison with other agricultural products, the planters' financial dependence on metropolitan merchants, and a variety of other factors—many of them beyond the colonists' control—precluded agricultural diversification.

In lieu of settlers, the West Indies attracted adventurers—men seeking rapid social advancement. Because their commitment to the islands was mainly economic, they tended to view the colonies as large staple-producing factories. When the plantation economy languished, as it did after 1820, whites left the islands in large numbers: Jamaica's European population fell by half, from about 30,000 to 15,000 between 1820 and 1834.[8]

Even those whites who were second and third generation West Indians had a remarkable rootlessness about them. The private gardens, monuments, minor adornments, and institutions which men of wealth and power have commonly created to demonstrate their social status were exceedingly rare in the Caribbean colonies. Europeans took their personal pleasures and exhibited their munificence in transitory, not permanent, objects—in such things as elaborate dining, not in the establishment of elegant homes. The West Indies had nothing to compare with the pretentious *ante bellum* mansions of the American South. Indeed, great houses on the estates were usually small dwellings of rude construction which contrasted sharply with adjacent, well-built stone sugar factories. Economic productivity had permanence in the West Indies; the individual tenure of Europeans did not. White planters and merchants who fought tirelessly to preserve the legislative independence of their assemblies against the inroads of Parliament—a struggle of monumental importance to their economic interests—commonly retired to England when their finances permitted. It may be true that most small white landowners, pen-keepers,

---

[7] Brathwaite, *Creole Society*, pp. 86–92.

[8] Gisela Eisner, *Jamaica, 1830–1930: A Study in Economic Growth* (Manchester, 1961), p. 127.

estate overseers, physicians, artisans, petty merchants, printers, and the like—men whose numbers greatly exceeded those of the wealthy proprietors and merchants—lived out their lives in the colonies and adopted the creole habits which variously amused and repelled metropolitan visitors. But few of those lesser whites relinquished the hope that they or their white progeny would some day accumulate the means to return comfortably to Britain. Surrounded by an overwhelming majority of blacks whom they exploited, disdained, and perpetually feared, and dependent upon the mother country for their economic livelihood, physical safety, and cultural models, white West Indians did not develop a separate and singular Caribbean identity.

The transient ethos of the Europeans and their overriding economic focus was reflected in the meagre quality of community life. Public facilities were limited to the barest requirements of God and government. Buildings for local courts and legislatures, jails for incorrigible rogues or slaves whose crimes exceeded the disciplinary prerogatives of their masters, and Anglican church buildings constituted, in most colonies, the outer limit of public accommodation. Jails were notoriously decrepit; there were no public baths, no museums, and excepting the well-designed capital of Trinidad, there were no public parks or exercise grounds. Community hospitals and welfare agencies were rare or unindulged luxuries. Europeans were expected to remain self-reliant; slaves secured medical treatment on the plantations and were maintained in old age by their masters and friends. Welfare in the colonies, as in the mother country, was an object of private initiative, and only those communities with a substantial nucleus of European residents were able to organize charitable institutions.

Overland communications were deplorable. Roads in the wet and mountainous Windward Islands were too hazardous to accommodate carriages.[9] Carriage roads did not exist in Dominica, and many remotely situated planters gained access to the principal port by dug-out canoe.[10] During six months of

---

[9] John Davy, *The West Indies, Before and Since Slave Emancipation* (London, 1854), pp. 229–78; F. W. N. Bayley, *Four Years Residence in the West Indies* (London, 1833), p. 484.

[10] Joseph Sturge and Thomas Harvey, *The West Indies in 1837* (London, 1838), p. 94; *Sketches and Recollections of the West Indies, by a Resident* (London, 1828), p. 62.

the year when rains were common in Trinidad, most of the
roads were impassable.[11] Tobago possessed little more than
bridle-paths, and many of those were overgrown.[12] Although a
few roads penetrated Jamaica's mountainous interior, long
distance travel was normally undertaken on horseback.
Bridges were few and invariably bad. Torrential rains caused
sudden flooding, making passage over mountain trails hazardous.[13] Contemporary observers frequently measured the level
of civil development in a colony by the quantity of carriages
possessed by its inhabitants, and in this regard the small,
relatively flat islands of Barbados and Antigua excelled.

Intellectual life was not esteemed in the West Indies. Life
was consumed by issues of an agricultural nature—the weather,
the harvest, the price of sugar—and there was too little time
and too much heat for the assiduous cultivation of mental
faculties not relevant to the planting life. As one rhymester
commented,

> It is all about sugar, molasses and rum,
> Till your ears are confounded, your senses struck dumb;
> And the penkeeper joins with his innocent prattle,
> Which is all about pastures, and fences, and cattle.[14]

Literary societies were organized in several communities,[15] but
the general apathy of colonists towards books and literature
was evinced by the paucity of booksellers in the Caribbean and
by the successive failure of every attempt—whether in Jamaica,
Barbados, Antigua, Grenada, or Demerara—to initiate a local
monthly magazine devoted to literature and science.[16] For the
majority of colonists reading was confined to the local press.
Most colonies possessed two newspapers—Jamaica, for reasons
of size, and Barbados, by virtue of its large European population,

---

[11] Harris to Grey, 12 May 1848, C.O. 295/161, no. 46.

[12] Davy, *The West Indies*, p. 260.

[13] Anton V. Long, *Jamaica and the New Order, 1827–1847* (Mona, Jamaica, 1956),
pp. 72–3.

[14] Quoted in Thomas Jelly, *A Brief Enquiry into the Condition of Jamaica* (London,
1847), p. 41.

[15] Bridgetown, St. John's, New Amsterdam, Kingston, and St. Kitts: each had
private literary societies and modest collections, mostly of light reading.

[16] Bayley, *Four Years Residence*, p. 32; Sir Robert Schomburgk, *The History of
Barbados* (London, 1848), p. 26; John Stewart, *An Account of Jamaica and Its Inhabitants* (London, 1808), pp. 171–3.

maintained several more. These weekly or bi-weekly newspapers were devoted primarily to commercial topics: to shipping news; to data on imports, exports, and the state of the London market; and to advertisements by ships' captains seeking cargo and merchants seeking customers. World news was quoted directly from the pages of month-old European and American journals, and local news was conveyed with a tone of scurrility calculated to enliven the monotony of colonial life, outrage the governor, and insult the editor of a competing newspaper.[17]

Towns served as merchandising depots for hinterland estates. Professional men, important merchants, planters whose estates lay near the metropolis, and of course the governor and subordinate government officers resided in or adjacent to the colonial ports.[18] European women were visible in the towns, and as a rule the local garrison produced a few military officers to enliven society. Located beside natural harbours or indented bays on the leeward coasts, the towns were both hot and poorly ventilated. Aside from their magnificent natural settings they offered no pretensions to beauty: streets were unlit and unclean; buildings were disorderly; and with few exceptions the towns bore an aspect of general neglect and community indifference.[19] The extraordinary rate at which building materials deteriorated in the tropics contributed a tired and haggard look to most houses. Roofs constructed of heavy wooden shingles required major repair within five years; buildings needed substantial restoration every ten years; and paint lasted only a short time under the alternating assaults of heavy rains and broiling sun.[20]

By common estimate of contemporary travellers, the capital

[17] In language typical of his colleagues, the Governor of Trinidad referred to the local press as teeming 'with libels upon nearly every Public Functionary of the Island . . .' Hill to Stanley, 8 Jan. 1834, C.O. 295/101, no. 3.

[18] Jamaica was an exception to this general rule. Her capital, Spanish Town, was located 13 miles from the principal port. Kingston possessed few white residents. Moneyed Europeans lived at pens in the Liguenea Mountains where they could avoid the heat and dust of the town. Stewart, *Account of Jamaica*, p. 11.

[19] Rows of well-constructed buildings would be interrupted by tiny hovels, likened by one observer to 'bird cages' or by vacant lots which became depositories for trash and filth. Trelawny Wentworth, *The West India Sketch Book* (London, 1834), II, 2, 157–8; MacLeod to Russell, 20 Aug. 1840, C.O. 295/130, no. 51.

[20] Daniel McKinnen, *A Tour Through the British West Indies in the Years 1802 and 1803* (London, 1804), p. 14; MacLeod to Russell, 9 Sept. 1840, C.O. 295/131, no. 59.

towns of Antigua, Barbados, and Trinidad were clearly superior to the numerous collection of drab and stagnant ports which served the smaller Leeward and Windward Islands. Roseau, Dominica, evoked such adjectives as desolate, decadent, apathetic. Grass grew luxuriantly between the stones of its main street, and one visitor mused, 'All is silent, and soft and lifeless like a city in the Arabian Nights . . .'[21] Castries, St. Lucia, was situated within a fine natural harbour, but Bayley considered it 'one of the dirtiest looking holes [he] ever witnessed.'[22] The capitals of St. Vincent and Grenada were quaint but ramshackle.[23] Four ports in the Lesser Antilles were not equipped with careenages,[24] and passengers were obliged to endure a thorough drenching when landing on the beach in open boats.

For all its size and importance, Kingston, the principal port of Jamaica, offered neither beauty, comfort, nor convenience.[25] Houses, churches, wharves, and stores wore the perpetual look of decay. The city was unornamented by trees; its central square was a desert of sand; streets were unpaved, narrow, filthy, and one to three feet lower in the centre than at the edges—the result of torrents of rain water rushing down its inclined causeways to the harbour. As elsewhere in the Caribbean, in Kingston roads had no pavements. In dry weather pedestrians were forced to elbow their way amid wheelbarrows, carriages, gigs, and horsemen upon a surface of hot sand; in wet weather, they walked on the raised edges of a watercourse.

Trading establishments in the port towns varied in character from dingy little shops, six feet square, in which a customer was unable to stand erect, to the great merchant houses which supplied the sugar plantations. The former were operated by free black or coloured women who retailed a variety of provisions, candles, and cottons to the slaves. A number of middling stores, commonly owned by Scotsmen or Jews.[26] sold a variety of dry

[21] Coleridge, *Six Months*, p. 152.   [22] Bayley, *Four Years Residence*, p. 161.
[23] R. R. Madden, *A Twelvemonth's Residence in the West Indies* (Philadelphia, 1835), I, 43; Bayley, *Four Years Residence*, pp. 190–3.
[24] These were Kingstown, Roseau, Plymouth, and Basseterre.
[25] For contemporary descriptions of Kingston, see McKinnon, *Tour*, pp. 83–4; John Bigelow, *Jamaica in 1850* (London, 1851), pp. 10–16; William G. Sewell, *The Ordeal of Free Labor in the British West Indies* (New York, 1862), pp. 174–5; Trollope, *West Indies*, pp. 15–18.
[26] In the 1830s it was estimated that the Jewish population of Jamaica was 5,000, most of whom were engaged in shopkeeping. The Assembly adjourned over

goods from tin pots to high fashion. Large merchant houses were located at the harbour-sides. They contained articles of every description—salt fish, grain, rice, tobacco, wine, pitch, tar, tools, lumber—anything which might form a staple of sale to the estates. Enterprising merchants made handsome profits on goods imported from Britain and America. Prices were fixed at the highest figure which traffic would bear, a practice dictated in part by the need to compensate for the default of some customers. If a storekeeper cornered the market on a product for which there was considerable demand, he exacted his own price without fearing a diminution of business.[27] As a result, the cost of basic necessities in the West Indies was twice what it was in England, a fact which weighed heavily on underpaid overseers and free tradesmen.[28]

Public entertainment in the islands was limited and occasional. For the most part, white colonists sought amusements among themselves: dining with convivial company; drinking, frequently to excess; gambling at billiards or dice; and wenching. Travellers from abroad were received with unstinting hospitality. They offered a welcome break in the monotony of plantation life and afforded an occasion for lavish dining. Tables laden with turtle, mutton, fowl, ham, ducks, and guinea birds, a variety of local fruits and vegetables, as well as puddings, sweets, and Madeira lent credence to Lady Nugent's jibe that Caribbean colonists ate like cormorants and drank like porpoises.[29] Ceremonious dining was a common form of entertainment in colonies where few alternatives existed. All attempts to sustain local theatre failed.[30] Staged entertainment was con-

the Jewish holiday of Yom Kippur in 1849, an action which attests to the wealth and influence of that community. Anton Long, *Jamaica*, pp. 17–18.

[27] Stewart, *Account of Jamaica*, pp. 148–9. A merchant in Falmouth told a Scots minister, '. . . there are so many rogues in this country, who never pay their debts, that honest men like you must pay double, or we could not live.' Hope Masterton Waddell, *Twenty-nine Years in the West Indies and Central Africa* (London, 1863), p. 31.

[28] Smyth to Stanley, 3 May 1834, C.O. 111/131, no. 112. A London *Times* correspondent writing from Berbice in November 1834 noted: 'The price of everything is extravagant, at least 50–100 per cent higher than in England.'

[29] Frank Cundall, ed., *Lady Nugent's Journal* (London, 1934), p. 108. Lady Nugent, wife of the governor, 1801–5, has left one of the most valuable journals dealing with white society in Jamaica.

[30] Henry H. Breen, *St. Lucia: Historical, Statistical, and Descriptive* (London, 1844), pp. 270–1; Bayley, *Four Years Residence*, p. 582; Mrs. Flanders, *Antigua and the Antiguans* (London, 1844), II, 211–12; Bigelow, *Jamaica*, pp. 53–4.

fined largely to the visitations of itinerant minstrels, dwarfs, puppeteers, jugglers, and other circus performers.[31]

European women rarely ventured to those colonies which lacked a considerable body of resident proprietors, or to those where civic amenities were especially meagre, where roads were bad and estates remote. A clergyman in Tobago observed that during four years in that colony his wife had seen only one other white woman cross her threshold.[32] European females who did reside in the colonies, especially Creole women born and raised in the islands, were described as listless, uninformed, and lacking in the arts of conversation.[33] Lady Nugent commented, 'Mrs. C. is a perfect Creole, says little, and drawls out that little, and has not an idea beyond her own Penn.'[34] In the absence or paucity of European women, white males commonly cohabited with black or coloured concubines.

FREE PEOPLE OF COLOUR

The coloured population occupied an insecure middle ground between the dominant whites and servile blacks, scorned socially by the former and despised by the latter. That they were designated a 'middle class' indicates the extent to which race, not occupation or education, determined social rank.[35] Rigid racial gradations fixed by Europeans were readily adopted by the people of colour as marks of caste distinguishing them from Negro slaves, and in the degree of their colour, from one another.[36] The patronizing demeanour of whites towards

[31] On 16 August 1841 the *Jamaica Despatch* advertised the arrival of a trained 'Ourang Outang' who would dress himself with shirt and trousers, eat with a fork and spoon, wash his face and hands, smoke a Spanish cigar, leap through a hoop, dance with a dog, play the organ, and ride horseback.

[32] Davy, *The West Indies*, p. 247.

[33] Bryan Edwards, *The History, Civil and Commercial, of the British Colonies in the West Indies* (London, 1801), 3rd ed., II, 12–14; Stewart, *Account of Jamaica*, p. 156.

[34] Cundall, *Nugent's Journal*, p. 72.

[35] Hall has used the analogy of an isosceles triangle to characterize West Indian Society. The tiny apex of the triangle would represent Europeans; the small middle section, free coloured people; the large base area, the slaves. Rigid lines separated the segments from one another so that even the poorest white could never fall below his base line. A free coloured person could enjoy mobility within his segment. African extraction prevented him from moving into the white apex, and his freedom kept him above the slave segment. Douglas Hall, 'Jamaica', in David W. Cohen and Jack P. Greene, eds., *Neither Slave Nor Free: Freedmen of African Descent in the Slave Societies of the New World* (Baltimore, 1972), p. 195.

[36] Each degree by which a person receded from pure negro origins had its own

coloureds was reproduced, in turn, in the demeanour of coloureds toward blacks.[37]

The free coloured population had been growing rapidly
since the late eighteenth century. In Grenada, free non-whites
increased from 1,125 (4·7 per cent of the population) in 1788
to 3,786 (15·6 per cent of the whole) in 1829.[38] Their number
rose in Trinidad from about 4,500 to 17,000 in the first 30
years of the century.[39] Similarly, in Barbados free coloureds
doubled their number between 1787 and 1829.[40] In the last
years of slavery Barbados was the only colony in which whites
outnumbered free coloureds (see Table 1).

Manumission accounted for much of the increase in the free
coloured population. In addition to the growth of liberal
sentiments among masters, the process of whitening which
occurred among racially mixed bondsmen over several generations produced more people who, in the judgement of European
slave-owners, were deserving of manumission. That manumission was frequently conferred upon women as a reward for
sexual favours is indicated by the disproportionately large
percentage of women among free coloureds. In Antigua, for
example, they comprised 58 per cent of the free coloured
population in 1821;[41] in Jamaica there were twice as many
females as males among the adult free coloured population in
1825.[42] Although it is impossible to determine with certainty
what portion of the slave population was of mixed race, a

designation. A mulatto was the offspring of a black and a white; a sambo of a black
and a mulatto; a quadroon, of a mulatto and a white; and a mustee of a quadroon
and a white. Although distinctions continued beyond this level, the child of a
mustee and a white was declared free at birth if by chance his mother was a slave.

[37] Some European writers contended that blacks abhorred being the slaves of
coloured masters on account of their harsh and imperious bearing. A. C. Car-
michael, *Domestic Manners and Social Conditions of the White, Coloured, and Negro
Population of the West Indies* (London, 1834), I, 75; John Stewart, *A View of the
Past and Present State of the Island of Jamaica* (Edinburgh, 1823), pp. 331–2; Edwards,
History, Civil and Commercial, II, 24–5.

[38] R. Montgomery Martin, *History of the West Indies* (London, 1836), I, 267–8.

[39] Ibid., I, 215; enclosure in Hill to Glenelg, 13 Mar. 1836, C.O. 295/110, no. 34.

[40] Schomburgk, *History of Barbados*, pp. 86–7.

[41] Flanders, *Antigua*, I, 284.

[42] Report of Persons Deputed to Commissioners of Legal Enquiry by People of
Color, Dec. 1825, C.O. 318/76, Commissioners of Enquiry in the West Indies.
Manumission figures for Barbados in the mid 1820s indicate that about two-thirds
of the slaves manumitted were female. Handler and Sio, 'Barbados' in Cohen and
Greene, eds., *Neither Slave nor Free*, p. 222.

TABLE I

Selected West Indian Populations, c. 1830

Colony	Date	White	Free coloured and free black*	Slave
Antigua[a]	1821	1,980	4,066	30,985
Berbice[b]	1833	570	1,651	19,320
Barbados[c]	1829	14,959	5,146	82,902
Dominica[d]	1832	791	4,077	14,387
Demerara and[e]				
Essequebo	1829	3,006	6,360	69,467
Grenada[f]	1829	801	3,786	24,145
Jamaica[g]	1834	15,000	45,000	311,070
Montserrat[h]	1828	315	818	6,247
Trinidad[i]	1831	3,212	17,148	21,210

Sources: [a] R. Montgomery Martin, *History of the West Indies* (London, 1836), II, 311; [b] Henry Dalton, *The History of British Guiana* (London, 1855), II, 539; [c] Sir Richard Schomburgk, *The History of Barbados* (London, 1848), pp. 86–7; [d] Martin, II, 283–5; [e] Dalton, II, 538; [f] Martin, I, 267–8; [g] Gisella Eisner, *Jamaica, 1830–1930: A Study in Economic Growth* (Manchester, 1961), p. 127; [h] Martin, I, 215; [i] Enclosure, Hill to Glenelg, 13 Mar. 1836, C.O. 295/110, no. 34.

* Since colonial statistics, such as they were, grouped free blacks and free coloureds together for census purposes it is impossible to determine precisely what percentage of this group was of pure African origin. In her study on Jamaica, Gisella Eisner has determined that only 5,000 or 11 per cent of the free non-white population of that island was black. This percentage would seem a fairly safe estimate in view of the preferences afforded to coloureds in the slave system, but a report before legal commissioners of inquiry in 1825 made by deputies of the coloured population declared that the free black population of Jamaica was between 9,000 and 10,000. The actual number of free blacks probably lay somewhere in between these two figures. One should assume that at least 15 per cent of the numbers listed in this column represent free blacks. Barbados, as always, would be an exception. In detailed tables covering the Barbados population in the early nineteenth century, Handler and Sio have determined that coloured people constituted 53·2 per cent of the free non-white population and blacks, 46·7 per cent. See their 'Barbados' in Cohen and Greene, eds., *Neither Slave Nor Free*, p. 221.

rough calculation can be made by comparing post-emancipation census figures with statistics obtained before abolition. The 1844 census[43] of Jamaica numbered the black population at 293,128, a figure 17,942 lower than the recorded slave population in 1834. The same census determined that the coloured

[43] Census figures enclosed in Elgin to Stanley, 7 Nov. 1844, C.O. 137/280, no. 128.

population was 68,520 or 23,520 larger than the declared non-
white free population in 1834. Allowing some latitude for error
and remembering that a portion of the free non-white population
before 1834 was black, one might assume that between 20,000
and 25,000 Jamaicans of mixed ancestry were slaves on the eve
of emancipation.[44] This means that well over half of the
coloured population had achieved freedom in Jamaica before
slavery had been abolished. In Barbados, this was not the case.
The Barbados census of 1851[45] recorded a coloured population
of 30,059. Since free people of colour were fewer than 3,000 in
1829, it must be assumed that the overwhelming majority of
coloured people in that island remained enslaved until 1834.

Poverty weighed heavily on most of the coloured population.
In material respects, domestic slaves on the estates were more
comfortable than most town-dwelling free coloured people. A
report written by representatives of the coloured population in
1825 declared that of the 28,800 free people of colour then
resident in Jamaica (free blacks were excluded from this statement) 400 could be considered rich, 5,500 in moderate circumstances, while 22,900 were poor. The richest 400 were estimated
to hold £4,075,000, in property; the poorest 22,900 people
were thought to possess property worth £4,675,000; while the
total value of property held by the free coloured population
was considered to be about £15,000,000 (see Table 2).

Concentrating in the towns, the free coloured population
compensated for the gradual retirement of whites from the
West Indies during the early nineteenth century. The poorest
among them engaged in huckstering and petty retail traffic,
selling water vessels, salt fish, guinea corn, assorted fruits, and
various trifles.[46] In Jamaica, coloured youngsters supplied the

---

[44] Eisner (p. 152) estimated the coloured slave population to be 23,000 in 1834.
This is challenged by Higman who contends, on the basis of his survey of the
coloured slave population on 10 properties, that coloured people comprised 10 to
11 per cent of Jamaica's slaves—about 34,000—in 1832. B. W. Higman, 'Slave
Population and Economy in Jamaica', p. 135. I incline toward the lower figure,
but even if Higman is correct, the majority of Jamaica's coloured people were
free before 1834.

[45] Census figures enclosed in Hamilton to Pakington, 13 April 1852, C.O.
28/176, no. 20. The Barbados census of 1844 did not divide the population by race.

[46] Bayley, *Four Years Residence*, p. 61. Free coloured pedlars commonly exchanged
their wares for rum and sugar stolen from the estates by slaves. Matthew Gregory
Lewis, *Journal of a West India Proprietor* (London, 1834), pp. 347-8.

TABLE 2

Distribution of Wealth among Free Coloured Population of Jamaica, 1825

Value of Property £	Number of Persons Holding Property
100,000	5
50,000	10
25,000	25
12,500	60
7,000	100
5,000	200
2,500	500
1,500	1,000
1,000	4,000
500 or less	22,900

Source: Report of Persons Deputed to Commissioners of Legal Enquiry by People of Color, December 1825, C.O. 318/76.

community with wild fowl, wild hogs, turtles, crab, and fish.[47] More established coloured retailers maintained stores dealing in a variety of dry goods; others retailed spirits from grog shops. In some ports, coloured men were among the most opulent merchants.[48] Free coloured men assumed a leading position in the craft trades as coopers, carpenters, cabinetmakers, smiths, shoemakers, masons, and tailors.[49] In Jamaica they enjoyed a virtual monopoly of pimento production, and in Jamaica and Dominica they cultivated coffee, frequently on a large scale.[50] Indeed, Dominican coloured people owned 22 per cent of the island's slave population in 1820.[51] On no occasion would a free man of colour work in cane fields: to perform agricultural labour in the company of slaves constituted an intolerable

[47] Long, *Jamaica*, p. 6.
[48] Breen, *St. Lucia*, pp. 166–7; Carmichael, *Domestic Manners*, I, 79.
[49] *Sketches and Recollections*, p. 230; Breen, *St. Lucia*, pp. 166–7; Davy, *The West Indies*, p. 80.
[50] Long, *Jamaica*, p. 6; *Sketches and Recollections*, p. 229.
[51] Coloureds in Dominica produced 1,492 cwt. of sugar, 55 puncheons of rum, and 1,862 cwt. of coffee compared with the production by whites of 46,739 cwt. of sugar, 1,972 puncheons of rum, and 7,878 cwt. of coffee. Commissioners of Enquiry in the West Indies, Dominica, C.O. 318/76.

degradation.[52] Literate men of colour held clerkships in large merchant houses, professional offices, or in minor government services; those with the best education had penetrated the professions. In 1829 Robert Osborn and Edward Jordan established *The Watchman and Jamaica Free Press*,[53] a bi-weekly newspaper in Kingston; the *Chronicle* of Grenada, one of the best papers in the Lesser Antilles, was owned and edited by a man of colour, as was the *Weekly Register* of Antigua.[54] The extensive capital required for the development of sugar property prevented all but a few men of colour from securing large plantations,[55] and coloured men were not widely employed on the estates in supervisory positions. Deficiency laws which imposed taxes upon the owners of plantation property who did not maintain a prescribed ratio of whites to blacks rendered the employment of coloured overseers burdensome.

For the coloured population, social and occupational conditions differed from colony to colony. In a community like Barbados, where there was a substantial white resident population, men of colour were subjected to unequal competition with white colonists for superior employment. Where the European population was insignificant people of colour enjoyed ready access to the trades and secured leading places in medicine as well as merchandising.[56] Caste distinctions were most

[52] Sel. Comm. on the Extinction of Slavery, P.P. 1831–2 XX (721), evidence of the Revd. John Barry. Coloured people who remained slaves were rarely compelled to perform field labour. Lewis, *Journal*, p. 74.

[53] In 1832 the name of this paper was changed to the *Jamaica Watchman*, and in 1838 these two journalists began publication of *The Morning Journal*, a daily paper which preserved the spirit of the defunct *Watchman*. For a brief biographical sketch of Edward Jordan, see W. Adolphe Roberts, *Six Great Jamaicans* (Kingston, 1912), pp. 3–24.

[54] Robson Lowe, *The Codrington Correspondence, 1743–1851* (London, 1951), pp. 70–2. Henry Loving, owner of the *Weekly Register* was born a slave and manumitted at age nine. In 1832 he testified before the House of Commons Select Committee on the Extinction of Slavery.

[55] A notable exception was St. Luce Philip, owner of three plantations in Trinidad, including Philippine Estate, one of the finest in the island. He was a physician, educated at the Medical College of Edinburgh, but he devoted most of his attention to sugar culture. Philip was the only man of colour serving in the Privy Council in Trinidad in the years immediately following emancipation. George Truman, John Jackson, Thomas B. Longstreth, *Narrative of a Visit to the West Indies in 1840 and 1841* (Philadelphia, 1844), pp. 92–3; MacLeod to Russell, 20 April 1844, C.O. 295/134, no. 85.

[56] Breen, *St. Lucia*, pp. 166–7; Bayley, *Four Years Residence*, p. 449.

rigid in colonies possessing the lowest ratio of whites to non-whites, and were most relaxed in islands where Europeans were few. Colour prejudice was most intense in Barbados where the lineage of every free person underwent microscopic scrutiny to ascertain whether he bore the slightest trace of African ancestry.[57] Long after emancipation, Sewell observed that well-educated people having Anglo-Saxon features and complexion could be entirely excluded from white society because of the presence of colour in their family background.[58] Samuel Prescod, a well-educated, liberal journalist and leader of the free coloured community bore 'no distinguishing marks of negro complexion', yet as a young man he had been ejected from the Barbados House of Assembly for merely observing its proceedings.[59] The colour bar assumed an orthodoxy so powerful that those who dissented from the prevailing spirit were intimidated from voicing their objection for fear of social ostracism, a punishment of no small consequence in a tiny community thousands of miles from the mother country.[60]

In Antigua, where planters were reputed to have exhibited unusual liberality toward their slaves, colour prejudice remained a firm fixture. Excluded from interment in the picturesque Anglican churchyard which overlooked the port of St. John's, the bodies of deceased coloured people were buried beside a country road where white criminals and suicides commonly found their ignominious interment.[61] Even the bell used to toll the death of a coloured person was inferior in size and quality to that which announced the death of a white colonist.[62]

Until the final years of slavery free people of colour were subjected to a variety of civil and political disabilities. They were excluded from juries and were ineligible for the most elevated colonial government positions. They could neither vote for assemblymen nor be elected themselves to the assemblies.[63] Educated or otherwise distinguished free coloured

[57] Sturge and Harvey, West Indies, p. 154; Sewell, Ordeal, pp. 67–8; Trollope, West Indies, pp. 211–12.   [58] Sewell, Ordeal, pp. 67–8.
[59] Handler and Sio, 'Barbados' in Cohen and Greene, eds., Neither Slave nor Free, pp. 248–9.   [60] Sturge and Harvey, West Indies, p. 155.
[61] Coleridge, Six Months, p. 256.   [62] Flanders, Antigua, II, 179.
[63] First Report of Commissioners of Enquiry into the Administration of Criminal and Civil Justice in the West Indies, P.P. 1826–7 XXIV (559), pp. 114–15.

people who enjoyed the favour of whites and the endorsement of powerful men could petition their colonial legislatures for special Privilege Acts which, at a cost to them of about £100 currency, would eliminate all or some of their individual disabilities.[64] Although such enactments occurred frequently,[65] they affected the lives of a scant minority of the coloured population, and the great mass of disenfranchized coloured people raised a crusade during the 1820s to abolish all disability laws. The language which the free coloured leadership employed to persuade white legislators of their merits and deserts provides a valuable insight into their economic position and emotional identity. In a petition written in 1823, free coloured people in Grenada declared themselves 'true and loyal Englishmen' committed to the same values as the whites and separated from them only by the accident of colour:

The people of Colour comprise by far the greatest part of the Free population, and possess no small portion of the Property in this Colony, particularly in the Capital, where at least two-thirds are owned by Persons of this Class.

While the White Man who emigrates to the Colony generally returns to Europe so soon as he has realized a Competency, the Coloured Man on the contrary is attached to the Soil in which his Family and Friends reside, forming in his Class the most powerful check to the numerous Slave Population, and from his attachment to the *British* Constitution, always ready and willing if necessary to sacrifice his Life and Property in defense of that *Constitution*.[66]

The argument of free coloureds that they constituted 'the most powerful check to the numerous Slave Population' was their trump card in dealing with a dwindling European élite. A threat made in 1823 by a group of Jamaican coloured men to withhold their services from the militia in time of martial law created grave consternation.[67] On this point, the petitioners in Grenada were explicit:

---

[64] Ibid.; Manchester to Bathurst, 8 Jan. 1827, C.O. 137/165, no. 78.

[65] Petitions for special privileges were made for 200 people in Jamaica between 1823 and 1830. Hall, 'Jamaica', in Cohen and Greene, eds., *Neither Slave Nor Free*, p. 201.

[66] Petition from Free Colored People to Henry Maddocks and Fortunatus Dwarris, Esquires, His Majesty's Commissioners of Inquiry into the Administration of Justice in the Colonies, 1823, C.O. 318/76.

[67] Brathwaite, *Creole Society*, p. 198.

In a Government where the Slave Population so considerably out-numbers the free Population, we humbly conceive it would be a prudent policy to extinguish as much as possible all feelings of jealousy that may exist between the Free Classes, it being their mutual interest to be unanimous, having but one object in view the maintenance of the Security of these Colonies from Foreign as well as internal Enemies (from either of which, it is our earnest prayer that God may ever defend them).[68]

Although the 'internal Enemies' to which this memorial referred were unruly slaves, the campaign for civil equality which people of colour waged against the white establishment eventually brought them into alliance with anti-slavery forces. By no means, however, were coloured West Indians of one mind on the slavery question. Many of the most enlightened people of colour[69] favoured emancipation, but many others ranging in status from prosperous coffee-planters to unmarried women who maintained themselves exclusively on the earnings of a few urban slaves were economically threatened by it and, in many cases, ideologically opposed to it. Writing of Barbados four years after abolition, Thome and Kimball declared that 'the colored people . . . have been far in the background in the cause of abolition, and even now, the majority of them are either indifferent, or actually hostile to emancipation.'[70]

By 1832 all civil disabilities applying to free people of colour had been removed, but the colour bar remained a fixture of day to day life. Astute Europeans appreciated that people of colour would play a very important—in some cases, dominant—role in the future life of the colonies; and, increasingly, steps were taken, usually at the initiative of governors, to bring distinguish-ed coloured people into contact with white society. In 1836 the Governor of Trinidad announced, with undisguised relief, that 'without offending society' his wife had introduced 'for the first time some highly respected married ladies of Colour to a Christmas Ball'.[71] Such endeavours were not always successful.

---

[68] Petition from Free Colored People, 1823, C.O. 318/76.

[69] The first coloured members of the Jamaica Assembly supported abolition. Long, *Jamaica*, p. 16.

[70] J. A. Thome and J. H. Kimball, *Emancipation in the West Indies* (New York, 1838), p. 74, quoted in Handler and Sio, 'Barbados' in Cohen and Greene, eds., *Neither Slave Nor Free*, p. 246.

[71] Hill to Glenelg, private, 11 Jan. 1836, C.O. 295/110.

When Sir Lionel Smith, Governor of Barbados, invited a coloured gentleman to his table, a white guest fled the room in high dudgeon.[72] It was reported that even in Dominica where the paucity of whites had narrowed racial divisions, wealthy men of colour who entertained the Governor or European planters at dinner never sat down at the table themselves until asked.[73]

Marriage between whites and non-whites continued to be considered anathema by Europeans, and the courageous few who undertook such unions courted instant social ostracism. At the same time, informal liaisons between white men and coloured women were commonplace, not only for single adult males but also for resident married proprietors and their adolescent sons.[74] The white somatic preference which was inculcated in the status mentality of West Indians induced coloured women to favour concubinage with white men above marriage to men of mixed origins. More importantly, concubinage[75] conferred valuable economic advantages for women of colour. The concubine of a planter or town merchant enjoyed relatively comfortable living in a great house or town residence. She consumed better food, enjoyed more fashionable dress; not infrequently, she was awarded the services of slaves whom she could hire out as craftsmen, washerwomen, or peddlers.[76] On the death of her keeper, a concubine and her children would be likely to inherit some, possibly all, of a deceased European's property, including his slaves.[77] The children of a concubine would be of lighter complexion than she, and in a society which placed a premium upon European somatic properties this would entitle her offspring to greater social and economic opportunities. Furthermore, it was not uncommon for wealthy white fathers to exhibit strong paternal affection towards their

[72] Sturge and Harvey, *West Indies*, Appendix xxxiv.

[73] *Sketches and Recollections*, p. 232.

[74] Stewart, *Account of Jamaica*, pp. 154–5.

[75] For contemporary descriptions of West Indian concubinage, see Waller, *A Voyage in the West Indies*, pp. 19–21, 93–4; Sylvester Hovey, *Letters from the West Indies* (New York, 1838), pp. 68–70; Bayley, *Four Years Residence*; Edwards, *History, Civil and Commercial*, II, 25–6; Carmichael, *Domestic Manners*, I, 91–3; Flanders, *Antigua*, II, 180–1; Sel. Comm. on Extinction of Slavery, P.P. 1831–2 XX (721), evidence of John Barry, Wesleyan Missionary.

[76] Long, *Jamaica*, p. 6.

[77] Cundall, ed., *Nugent's Journal*, p. 298; Lewis, *Journal*, p. 402.

illegitimate progeny and to secure them some education either by instructing the children themselves, providing them some rudimentary training in the colonies, or by sending them to school in England.[78] In view of the less bountiful and less glamorous alternatives to concubinage, there is nothing mysterious about its popularity and pervasiveness.

Sexual licence was among the most distinctive characteristics of British Caribbean society. Simon Taylor, the richest planter in Jamaica, a bachelor and owner of several estates, was said to possess a numerous coloured family on each of them.[79] J. B. Moreton, the polemical detractor of the planters, claimed that attorneys kept concubines on all their estates, obliging overseers to pamper and indulge them 'like goddesses'.[80] Men who lived in open adultery with coloured mistresses suffered neither public derision nor, in many cases, the rebuke of their wives and families; indeed, white women deemed 'respectable' owned and mongered coloured and black prostitutes in the port towns.[81]

West Indian concubinage was uniformly deplored as licentious and immoral by English travellers, clergymen, government officers, and abolitionists. The asperity of their condemnation was not always merited. Concubinage, though it implied an unequal relation between partners, offered rewards to both parties and frequently produced strong and lasting ties of affection. The system was most indecorous because of the hypocrisy of pursuing it concurrently with a formal colour bar. European critics abhorred concubinage because it rarely led to marriage and therefore violated the precepts of Christian morality. In fact, concubinage was a natural product of the transient status of Europeans. Men who conceived it possible that they would retire with some wealth to England could not take a non-European wife and family with them lest they forfeit

[78] Flanders, *Antigua*, II, 178; Carmichael, *Domestic Manners*, I, 91–3; Stewart, *Account of Jamaica*, p. 200.

[79] Cundall, ed., *Nugent's Journal*, p. 93.

[80] J. B. Moreton, *Manners and Customs of the West India Islands* (London, 1790), p. 77, quoted in Brathwaite, *Creole Society*, p. 137.

[81] Officers arriving in Barbados were advised by white matrons to secure concubines as a means of reducing their expenses and increasing their comforts. Waller knew a 'respectable' European lady of fifty years—a virgin by his estimate—who owned a 17-year-old mulatto girl whom she let out to officers of the garrison for 12 dollars a month. See his *Voyage in the West Indies*, pp. 20–1, 93–4.

the social advancement which it had been their object to achieve by going to the West Indies in the first place. Furthermore, it was unreasonable to assess the moral qualities of Caribbean life by the standards in vogue in England where a settled society produced equal numbers of men and women considered to be of similar rank and background. If concubinage was immoral, it was also the inevitable result of a peculiar social environment. It may be assumed that scandalized British moralists were as violently offended by the custom of interracial sex as they were by the defiance of matrimonial conventions.

Within their own class free people of colour were widely differentiated by education, occupation, wealth, and somatic properties. As a group they aspired to equal status with whites, and they embraced the cultural values, social conventions, behavioural patterns, modes of speech, and in many cases the prejudices of the European élite. To demonstrate their worthiness, free coloured people emphatically differentiated themselves from the slaves whom they frequently owned and toward whom they exhibited a haughty superiority. This behaviour provoked rancour in the bondsmen and smug curiosity among whites, but it did not erode the social barrier which separated white from coloured, for no measure of individual achievement or gentility in a man of colour could erase the mark of caste which ensued from his African ancestry.

SLAVE SOCIETY

The society of slaves—like that of whites and people of colour—was stratified in terms of occupation and origins. Creole slaves believed themselves superior to those of African birth. They quarrelled with them, humiliated them socially, and taunted them with such epithets as 'salt water' or 'Willyforce' Negroes.[82] The Africans themselves were divided socially along tribal lines although such distinctions were wearing thin by 1830. The really important divisions within the slave segment were based on occupation. Occupation, in turn, was a function of colour as well as intelligence, reliability, and physical dexterity.

[82] Coleridge, *Six Months*, pp. 261–3; Bayley, *Four Years Residence*, pp. 456–7; Flanders, *Antigua*, II, 50; Carmichael, *Domestic Manners*, I, 113–19, 201, 252; Patterson, *Slavery*, p. 146.

Domestic servants,[83] artisans, and drivers formed a slave élite and were sharply differentiated in wealth, status, and privilege from the mass of field slaves. Since masters often considered it indelicate for slaves with European ancestry to perform field-work in the company of pure Negroes, domestic positions were arrogated to coloured bondsmen—one reason, perhaps, for the excessive number of domestics in West Indian households.[84] The tasks of domestics were light; their physical accommodations and material rewards were superior to those of the field hands; and domestics were respectfully addressed by other slaves as 'mister' and 'ma'am'.

By serving in the household, a domestic sacrificed some of the independence allowed field hands in their cottages and grounds, but this was more than compensated by the better food (frequently from the master's table), candles, soap, sugar, and other objects and comforts which attended life at the great house. The children of domestics received better treatment than those of field slaves, and were often raised in the company of white youths. The relative ease, affluence, and status of household slaves is best illustrated by reference to the direst punishment which might befall them—demotion to the field gang.

Artisans and drivers, designated headmen,[85] lived and worked at a distance from the great house, but they enjoyed an esteem among field slaves which was rarely conferred on domestics. Each estate possessed a head carpenter, cooper, mason, smith, potter, boilerman, clarifier, and distiller, as well as assistants and apprentices in these trades. Such slaves were valued more highly than field hands[86] and by general estimate the chief boilerman and the driver of the great gang were the most valuable slaves on an estate—men whom managers were advised to treat with care and respect. Head artisans were exempt from field-work, although in slack periods they might

[83] Domestics included butlers, coachmen, stable crew, cooks, storekeepers, maids, cleaning women, washerwomen, and seamstresses.

[84] It was not uncommon for the household staff to number 20 or 30 out of a plantation population of 300 slaves.

[85] The term distinguished those who worked with their heads from the ordinary field slaves who toiled with their bodies.

[86] J. Harry Bennett, *Bondsmen and Bishops: Slavery and Apprenticeship on the Codrington Plantations of Barbados, 1710–1838* (Los Angeles and Berkeley, 1958), p. 16.

be hired off the plantation or employed outside their own speciality to assist other tradesmen. Craftsmen were permitted to fabricate items for sale, to work additional hours for pay, and to hire themselves out on free days. A carpenter on one Codrington plantation in Antigua kept a horse and gig, was married to a free woman, owned a hearse and acquired virtually all of the funeral business in the area.[87] Although slave codes forbade bondsmen to own horses, these laws were generally neglected and head slaves kept large numbers of horses and cattle on their masters' properties. Young overseers arriving in Jamaica frequently bought their riding-horses from head slaves.[88] In 1837 the abolitionist Joseph Sturge was entertained by the head Negro of a cattle pen who served his guest Madeira in a comfortable, well furnished house and related how in the time of slavery he had owned nine slaves, twenty head of cattle and seventy sheep.[89] Field Negroes zealously aspired to learn a trade, but artisan jobs on the plantations were few and when coloured slaves were present and able they were generally awarded preference in these occupations.[90]

Of the 480 slaves at Worthy Park, Jamaica in 1795, the 25 who were designated headmen received an inordinate share of the estate's allowances.[91] They absorbed a quarter of the annual rum allocation as well as exceptional food and clothing allotments. At Codrington in Barbados, drivers were given annual bonuses of £20.[92] Artisans were exempt from ignominious forms of punishment; they received better care in time of sickness and greater assistance in the building and repair of their houses.[93] Their dwellings were larger and more elaborate than those of field hands, frequently having plank floors, respectable furniture, bed linens, mosquito netting, dishes, decanters, and even wine glasses.

[87] Lowe, *The Codrington Correspondence*, p. 73.

[88] Alexander Barclay, *A Practical View of the Present State of Slavery in the West Indies* (London, 1826), p. 273; Lewis, *Journal*, pp. 201–2; Madden, *Twelvemonth's Residence*, p. 106.

[89] Sturge and Harvey, *West Indies*, p. 186.

[90] Elsa Goveia, *Slave Society in the British Leeward Islands at the End of the Eighteenth Century* (New Haven, 1965), p. 232.

[91] Michael Craton and James Walvin, *A Jamaican Plantation: The History of Worthy Park 1670–1970* (Toronto, 1970), p. 141.

[92] Bennett, *Bondsmen and Bishops*, p. 18.

[93] Ibid.

In return for these advantages, headmen marshalled and controlled the slave population during and after work hours. They established informal tribunals in slave villages, judging disputes between bondsmen and assigning fines for irregular behaviour.[94] Their authority was readily acknowledged by field slaves, but their practical loyalty to the masters who were the fount of their privileges was seldom forsaken. According to an observer in Barbados, the plantation system in that colony had produced so great a merger of interest between headmen and planters that the former would sacrifice their lives to defend the personal safety and property of their masters.[95]

At the bottom of the plantation hierarchy, field slaves performed the hard, relentless labour of cane cultivation, receiving a mere subsistence in return. Because they lacked economic incentives, their service was thoroughly regimented through a gang system which facilitated maximum supervision. On a typical estate in the final years of slavery bondsmen worked about 280 days a year.[96] Sundays were free; Christmas holidays occupied three days and Good Friday one; half of each Saturday out of crop belonged to the slaves; and bad weather and sickness accounted for an average of sixteen work-free days a year. Slaves awoke in darkness and laboured until sunset, enjoying only a half hour break for breakfast and a two hour pause at midday. During five or six months of the year when crop was taken and sugar boiled, they worked shifts throughout alternate nights. On short-handed estates having only two shifts, a slave might labour nineteen hours one day and thirteen the next.[97]

Plantation slaves lived in small villages adjacent to the sugar works. Cottages[98] were small and simple, usually about 15 by 20 feet, commonly comprised of wattle and daub and thatched

---

[94] Patterson, *Slavery*, pp. 230–1.
[95] Bennett, *Bondsmen and Bishops*, p. 18.
[96] Papers on the Abolition of Slavery, C.O. 318/117.
[97] Sel. Comm. on Extinction of Slavery, P.P. 1831–2 XX (721), evidence of Robt. Scott, 5006–10.
[98] For a description of the slaves' living situation, see Wentworth, *Sketch Book*, II, 216–18; Bayley, *Four Years Residence*, pp. 90–2; Carmichael, *Domestic Manners*, I, 128–36; Stewart, *Account of Jamaica*, p. 231; Flanders, *Antigua*, II, 131; Edwards, *History, Civil and Commercial*, II, 163–5.

with leaves of pimento or cocoa-nut trees. Floors were dirt; furnishings were sparse. Meals were taken in a surrounding yard, where there was usually a tiny garden producing yams and vegetables and an enclosure for poultry, goats or pigs. Orange, banana, calabash, and cocoa-nut trees provided shade and fruit for the villagers.

The means by which plantation slaves were provisioned varied according to climate and topography. In Jamaica, the Windwards, and Trinidad, where there were extensive vacant areas or mountain lands unsuited to the cultivation of sugar, individual slaves were allotted portions of the backlands for raising a variety of provisions—yams, cassava, other root crops, beans, limas, peas, pumpkins, melons, and maize. To a large extent slaves were expected to maintain themselves on the produce of these grounds except, of course, in time of natural calamity when proprietors purchased food to supplement their diet. In Jamaica the extent of provision areas was generous,[99] but in many cases the grounds were miles away from estate villages and hiking to the uplands to attend the crops was extremely taxing on frail or aged slaves. In the Leeward Islands and Barbados unoccupied land was scarce and provision grounds, where allowed, were small and relatively unproductive.[100]

Bondage did not preclude the exercise of individual economic initiative, and most slaves supplemented their meagre plantation allowances by engaging in a variety of individual enterprises. Where the provision ground system prevailed, they exploited their lands for saleable food products. Everywhere they engaged in petty manufactures, raised poultry and small livestock, collected fruit, firewood, and other commodities.

[99] In dry weather districts like Vere, at a distance from the mountains, frequency of drought rendered cultivation of plantains and other vegetables precarious, and provision ground was not given to slaves. Guinea corn, cultivated by routine slave labour, constituted the basic provision crop. Cynric R. Williams, *A Tour Through the Island of Jamaica, from the Western to the Eastern End, in the Year 1823* (London, 1827), pp. 197–8.

[100] Goveia, *Slave Society*, p. 136; Coleridge, *Six Months*, p. 137. In these colonies, slaves normally maintained small plots adjacent to their houses, but these were all too often infertile. Generally estates raised enough provisions under regular labour routines to sustain their slaves for several months, but during the remainder of the year they were dependent upon food imports from Europe and North America. Bennett, *Bondsmen and Bishops*, p. 37.

The central focus of slave enterprise was the Negro market held once a week in every town or port throughout the Caribbean. Pine tarts, pickled peppers, every variety of fruit and vegetable; beef, mutton, pork, goat, live pigs, and other stock; hot soups, biscuits, cakes, candles, cloth, baskets, wicker-chairs, bed mats and odds and ends of lumber—all the accumulation and manufactures of the slaves were hawked amid a tumult of human voices and the bleat, squealing, and crowing of livestock. In Jamaica women walked as much as twenty-five miles during the night, bearing produce on their heads, in order to procure a favourable location for the opening of the market.[101] These markets provided field slaves the means to vary their diet, to obtain finer clothing than the coarse oznaburgs allotted by the planters, to secure small luxuries and to enjoy the thrill and excitement of a modest but colourful commerce.

Slavery was a diverse institution in the West Indies.[102] It was more rigorous on sugar estates than on cattle pens or plantations producing secondary crops. In the towns, harbour pilots, longshoremen, prostitutes, and petty hawkers were most commonly slaves.[103] They enjoyed considerable independence but were obliged to turn over a fixed portion of their weekly incomes to their owners. Gangs of slaves owned by men having no plantation property were hired out to short-handed estates to perform specific functions. These jobbing slaves were assigned the most arduous tasks without the compensating advantages of provision grounds, medical care, a stable environment, or even a dry place to sleep at night.[104] The lowest of all slaves were those few who were owned by other bondsmen. They worked

---

[101] Sel. Comm. on Extinction of Slavery, P.P. 1831–2 XX (721), evidence of John Barry.

[102] While the description of slavery in this chapter applies most heavily to estate slavery, a substantial portion of the slave population in the British West Indies did not reside directly on sugar estates—though, to be sure, many of the slaves who lived elsewhere functioned indirectly in the maintenance of a sugar economy. In Jamaica in 1832, only about half of the slave population actually resided on sugar estates. See, Higman, 'Slave Population and Economy in Jamaica', p. 255.

[103] Bayley, *Four Years Residence*, p. 61; Lewis, *Journal*, p. 402. For a discussion of the free movement of town slaves, see Goveia, *Slave Society*, p. 230.

[104] Stewart, *Account of Jamaica*, pp. 110, 146. By 1830 the shortage of slaves occasioned by the abolition of the slave trade had reduced the size and number of jobbing gangs, and jobbing slaves were being bought up by short-handed estate owners.

their owners' grounds, carried provisions to market, and endured the unmitigated contempt of the whole society.[105]

In the West Indies, social, religious, and educational matters were subordinated to and delimited by economic needs. That Africans were deprived of their cultural heritage was considered unexceptionable, even meritorious, by Europeans, who deemed the culture of Africa unworthy. At the same time, white planters made no attempt to compensate for this deprivation by cultivating in their slaves an appreciation for European institutions. Christian missionaries appeared in the West Indies in increasing numbers after 1800, but most planters discouraged the dissemination of Christian doctrine, forbade marriage, and restricted the slaves' social and recreational prerogatives in the interest of preserving a disciplined, subordinate slave labour force. The creole culture which gradually arose among West Indian slaves was neither European nor African. It comprised an eclectic blending of various African customs, pragmatic adjustments to harsh Caribbean circumstances, and selective borrowings from the dominant European culture.

A paucity of records precludes any reliable estimate of the number of slaves who had adopted some form of Christianity by 1830. It may be assumed, however, that neither native preachers representing various Afro-Christian cults nor orthodox missionaries of all denominations had drawn more than a fraction of the whole West Indian slave population to their fold. Writing from the west coast of Demerara in 1814, John Wray of the London Missionary Society declared that over a stretch of twenty-seven miles there were forty estates having above 8,000 slaves without a single place of worship or a minister to offer instruction.[106] The situation was somewhat better in the Windwards and Jamaica and vastly better in the Leeward Islands where Methodists and Moravians, between them, claimed a following of about 20,000 slaves in the final years of the eighteenth century.[107]

---

[105] Patterson, *Slavery*, p. 224.

[106] Diary of John Wray, 21 Feb. 1814, *L.M.S. Papers*.

[107] Goveia, *Slave Society*, pp. 281, 298. Neither Moravians nor Methodists made significant inroads among the slaves of Jamaica. Although by 1831 the Methodists had 11 circuits, 19 ministers, and nearly 13,000 members in Jamaica, Methodism was, in the main, the special denomination of free people of colour. W. J. Gardner, *A History of Jamaica from its Discovery By Christopher Columbus to the Present Time*

Despite the inroads of Christianity, few West Indian slaves entirely shed the spiritual attitudes of their forebears. Belief in obeah, a form of witchcraft transmitted from Africa, was almost universal, and many slaves who submitted to Christian baptism did so only because they believed it a superior form of magic which protected them from obeah.[108] For pleasure or for hire, the obeah man (or woman)—usually of African birth—practised his black arts to cause injury or to protect his clients from the depredations of others. These practitioners were skilled in the administration of poison, a capability which gave credence to their claim, generally accepted by slaves, that they caused the death of their victim by catching their shadows.[109] The terrifying influence of obeah had dwindled somewhat by 1830 as a result of the declining number of African born slaves and the increasing impact of missionary teaching, but it remained a subject of alarm to planters who frequently reported that slaves who thought themselves bewitched would languish and die for no ostensible reason other than their fatalistic contention, 'I'm obeahed—I know I'll go dead.'[110] Furthermore, obeah was used to inspire solidarity in time of rebellion. Slaves were sworn to the fetish, and oathtakers, whether willing or reluctant, were assured that magical powers would protect them from Europeans. Many a slave was driven to insurrection by

(London, 1873), p. 361. Jamaican slaves were most receptive to English Baptists whose missions, established after 1814, capitalized on the groundwork laid by a full generation of Native Baptists. See, Philip Curtin, *Two Jamaicas: The Role of Ideas in a Tropical Colony* (Cambridge, Mass., 1955), pp. 33–4, and Patterson, *Slavery*, pp. 210–12.

[108] Lewis, *Journal*, p. 374; Waddell, *Twenty-nine Years*, p. 23.

[109] Barclay, *State of Slavery*, pp. 190–1.

[110] European planters and missionaries marvelled at, and probably grossly exaggerated, the effects of fatalism among slaves. Bryan Edwards claimed that one Jamaican planter lost 100 slaves over 15 years to the awful wrath of an aged Dahomean obeah woman. See his *History, Civil and Commercial*, II, 114–17. Madden declared, 'Hundreds have died of the mere terror of being under the ban of death.' See *A Twelvemonth's Residence*, II, 74. Mrs. Carmichael who fully appreciated that obeah men were skilled at the use of poison contended, nevertheless, that in one instance 15 people died in the course of several months simply from the belief that they were under a witch's spell. See her *Domestic Manners*, I, 254. On 2 Nov. 1813, the Missionary, John Wray, wrote, 'It is impossible to describe the influence these men [obeah men] detain over the minds of the Negroes. As soon as they suspect obeah is put upon them, they give themselves up for lost and pine away . . . and it is beyond the power of medicine to save them.' *Diary of John Wray*, entry 2 Nov. 1813, L.M.S.

the terror of obeah, and this union of witchcraft and rebellion induced white legislatures to declare the practice of obeah punishable by death.[111]

Myalism was a form of anti-witchcraft also derived from West Africa which slaves employed to counteract the evil effects of obeah. Myalism was organized on a cult basis, not on the individual level of practitioner and client, and its ceremonies involved various ritual dances. Myal men were skilled in the use of herbs, and after slavery they were often resorted to by black freedmen to cure somatic illnesses as well as to offset the effects of obeah.[112]

The entertainments of slaves, though basically African in character, had acquired a European overlay by 1830. Music and dancing were principal diversions,[113] and despite successive enactments of restrictive legislation, weekend or holiday dances remained the most significant form of organized recreation enjoyed by West Indian slaves for nearly two centuries. Such dances, continuous affairs often lasting into the morning hours, provided a central focus for ancillary entertainments—drinking, festive eating, even gambling. The forms of dance—rhythmic, supple, seductive, and sometimes frenzied—were distinctively African, as were most of the accompanying instruments: rattles made from calabashes or gourds, various log drums, stone clappers, log xylophones, banjo-like stringed instruments and even conch shells which produced a trumpeting sound. In the eighteenth century European instruments, especially the violin and tambourine, came into use, and negro fiddlers adopted a repertoire sufficiently diverse to enable them to provide the instrumental accompaniment at European balls.[114]

White missionaries had a considerable impact on the musical entertainment of slaves. They laid siege to the loud, spontaneous

[111] Madden, *A Twelvemonth's Residence*, II, 73; Edwards, *History, Civil and Commercial*, II, 112–14. The slaves' extraordinary fear of obeah practitioners made the latter's detection extremely difficult, and chances of conviction were small except in extreme cases. Waddell, *Twenty-nine Years*, p. 138; Stewart, *Present State of Jamaica*, p. 278.

[112] Patterson, *Slavery*, pp. 182–95.

[113] For the contents of this paragraph, I am indebted to Jerome S. Handler and Charlotte J. Frisbie, 'Aspect of Slave Life in Barbados and its Cultural Context', *Caribbean Studies*, XI (1972), 5–40.

[114] John Williamson, *Medical and Miscellaneous Observations Relative to the West India Islands* (Edinburgh, 1817), I, 43.

qualities of African vocal music which they condemned as heathenish, and in time their slave congregations were singing European hymns in wholly 'agreeable' fashion. Believing the African dance form profane and lascivious, missionaries discouraged the traditional Sunday and holiday dances, and by 1830 these festivities were clearly in decline. The agent of the London Missionary Society in British Guiana congratulated himself that on the estate where he resided Christmas holidays were celebrated with due decorum in contrast to the passion and noise which emitted from neighbouring properties.[115] Writing in 1832, the Bishop of Barbados observed, 'The disorderly and demoralizing dances on the Lord's day, formerly so common in this colony, are at present of comparatively rare occurrence.'[116]

Fancy dress was a particular passion of the slaves and, in this, European influences were pervasive. Pro-slavery authors described the finery which slaves displayed in elaborate detail, always noting that weekend and holiday festivities produced an array of neat waistcoats, linen trousers, ties, dresses, and jewellery, which would have evoked the envy of English working people. These observations were confirmed by missionaries like William Knibb, the inveterate enemy of the Jamaica planters, who characterized the slaves' weekend attire as 'desperately fine'. The men, he declared, were 'profound dandies' and the women dressed 'in white, with an abundance of lace'.[117]

In fact, the material comforts and apparent happiness of the slaves,[118] even field slaves, disarmed Knibb, who upon his arrival in Jamaica was predisposed to regard the island as a 'land of sin, disease, and death, where Satan reigns with awful power . . .'[119] He acknowledged that the slaves had 'temporal comforts in profusion', adding that the evil of slavery was

---

[115] *Diary of John Wray*, 28 Dec. 1813, L.M.S.

[116] Quoted in Handler and Frisbie, 'Aspects of Slave Life', p. 40.

[117] Knibb to Miss Spurrier, 13 Sept. 1825, *B.M.S. Papers*.

[118] In a letter to a Bristol printer, Knibb wrote, 'When I first beheld a slave, my feelings sunk within me, nor could his smiling face dissipate the gloom which overspread mine, for the idea that a person could be happy in a state of slavery seemed to me one of its most *accursed fruits*.' Knibb to A. J. Fuller, 19 Feb. 1825, *B.M.S. Papers*.

[119] Knibb to Mrs. S. Nichols, March 1826, *B.M.S. Papers*.

moral not physical. 'At their dances', he wrote, 'they have con-
fectionary of every kind, and wine of every description, many
of them will not drink rum as it is mean.'[120] With few exceptions, metropolitan travellers supported the planters' claim
that West Indian slaves possessed material comforts which surpassed those of most British labourers.[121] An anti-slavery
author, Henry Coleridge, rendered a common verdict: 'the
slaves in general do labour much less, do eat and drink much
more, have much more ready money, dress much more gaily,
and are treated with more kindness and attention, when sick,
than nine-tenths of all the people of Great Britain under the
condition of tradesmen, farmers and domestic servants.'[122]

CONCLUSION

Society in the West Indies on the eve of emancipation was
something more than a monstrous system of unmitigated exploitation, as Patterson[123] has asserted, and it was something
less than the 'coherent whole' described by Goveia.[124] Europeans
used the slaves for economic gain; they despised their cultural
origins, and to a large extent they remained ignorant of their
attitudes and affairs. A witness before the House of Commons
committee on slavery who spent thirteen years in Jamaica and
lived at the door of hundreds of slaves admitted to knowing
nothing of them or of what they thought.[125] The rebellion of
1831 caught him wholly unaware. Nevertheless, the common
humanity of master and slave produced a social condition

[120] Knibb to Miss Spurrier, 13 Sept. 1825, *B.M.S. Papers.*

[121] Waller, *Voyage*, p. 91; Stewart, *Account of Jamaica*, p. 218; Bayley, *Four Years
Residence*, p. 342. Lady Nugent who went to Jamaica from Ireland said of the slaves,
'I wish the poor Irish were half as well off.' See, Cundall, ed., *Nugent's Journal*,
p. 74. Williamson expressed identical sentiments in his *Medical and Miscellaneous
Observations*, I, 135. One planter, noted for his benevolence, wrote '. . . if I were . .
asked whether I chose to enter life anew as an English labourer or a Jamaica
negro, I should have no hesitation preferring the latter.' See, Lewis, *Journal*, p. 101.
'I have great doubts', wrote Cynric Williams, 'whether the labouring people of
England enjoy as much even under the most favourable circumstances: as for those
of Ireland, poor souls! it is almost idle to mention them, except to contrast their
squalid misery with the comparatively epicurean plenty of the negro slave.' See
his *Tour Through the Island of Jamaica*, p. 98.

[122] Henry Nelson Coleridge, *Six Months*, p. 313.

[123] Patterson, *Slavery*, pp. 9–10.

[124] Goveia, *Slave Society*, pp. 249–50.

[125] Sel. Comm. on the Extinction of Slavery, P.P. 1831–2 XX (721), evidence
of Wm. Taylor, 257.

which was vastly more lenient than the laws which encompassed it. A British commission studying civil and criminal justice in the colonies in the 1820s reported that slaves were, in general, mildly treated; that rigorous aspects of old slave codes were *never* put in execution'; that the treatment of slaves by an increasing majority of the whites was prompted by 'humane and enlightened' sentiments.[126] Slaves maintained property, often in considerable quantity, and they engaged in a vigorous internal marketing system. Even on isolated estates where brutal masters might impose a sadistic tyranny, the slaves had means of reprisal, if not redress: accidents could occur; the mill could break; cane fields might burn; carriages could become disabled and stock hobbled. There was no equality between master and slave in the British West Indies, but there was, most decidedly, a mutually accepted *modus operandi*.

West Indian society was erected on the principles of inequality and subordination, with race being the main determinant of status. The slaves, most of whom had limited intercourse with whites or free coloured people, had their own clearly differentiated social structure. Free people of colour, mainly townsmen, rejected any identity with the slaves. They aspired to union with the whites but were denied acceptance by the dominant group. The whites possessed a transient ethos. They used the slaves economically; they exploited coloured people sexually; and they viewed both subordinate castes with supercilious contempt.

Both Africans and Europeans were subject to creolization in the West Indies, but a uniform creole culture did not evolve. Cultural changes were especially apparent among slaves, largely as a result of their bondage. Change was less apparent among whites, most of whom considered modifications in their living habits to be temporary adjustments to an alien climate and a slave economy. European participation in the system of concubinage may be considered a function of creolization, but most aspects of the Caribbean social and economic structure did not differ from the European pattern as much as many authors have implied. In many respects, the structure of the estate system was similar to the organization of property in

[126] First Report of the Commissioner of Inquiry into the Administration of Civil and Criminal Justice in the West Indies, P.P. 1825 XV (517), pp. 14–15.

England and Ireland where the bulk of the land, having undergone enclosure, was owned by a tiny minority of great landlords, often absentees, and worked by a large population of
impoverished agricultural wage labourers. With a few exceptions, the political and judicial systems in the colonies were
English. English was the common language of most colonies.
Even the Established Church, for what it was worth, reinforced
the European identity of whites.

Despite varying degrees of creolization among Africans and
Europeans the several segments of West Indian society did not
cohere. The principles of inequality and subordination which
determined all social distinctions were divisive, not cohesive.[127]
Perhaps the well known retort of slaves in addressing people of
colour best illustrates the point: 'you brown man hab no
country . . . only de neger and buckra hab country'. Buckra's
country, his often referred to 'home', was England. For better
or for worse, the slaves' country was the West Indies. But the
people of colour who identified culturally with England were
bound physically to the islands. Division, impermanence, insecurity, and exploitation remained the touchstones of colonial
life.

[127] Madden observed that 'the ignorance of the negro, the arrogance of the
brown man, and the pride and prejudice of the white will continue for some time
to baffle the endeavor to amalgamate their interests.' See, Madden, *A Twelvemonth's Residence*, I, 14.

CHAPTER 2

The Plantation Economy

SUGAR dominated the Caribbean economy. It was the principal product of all West India colonies and the only product of some. Plantations formed the basic social and economic units in the islands, providing the main focus of identity and community allegiance for the labouring people. Colonial revenue depended on the well-being of sugar estates; colonial courts, legislatures, and parish vestries were controlled by sugar planters; the militia was officered by them; and the public calendar was regulated by the seasonal requirements of sugar production.

By 1830 the West Indian sugar economy was in jeopardy. Planters in the older colonies confronted mounting competition in the protected home market as a result of Britain's acquisition of foreign sugar colonies during the Napoleonic wars. Between 1830 and 1834, 46 per cent of the colonial sugar entering the United Kingdom was being produced in recently annexed dependencies[1] (see Table 3). As the supply of colonial sugar increased, prices fell. More importantly, the basic cornerstones of the West Indian economic system—slave labour and the monopoly of the home market—were under attack from a formidable phalanx of humanitarian societies and competing commercial interests.

Although preferential duties continued to prevail against the sugar of British India, that arrangement was vigorously challenged by the East India lobby. During the early years of the century, India had supplied England with cotton piece goods, but the rise of Manchester textiles undermined India's cotton industry, and by 1833 she was importing over £1,500,000

[1] Much of this competition was arising from Mauritius where sugar exports increased an amazing 1,200 per cent in the two decades after the war. In 1825 Parliament abolished the 10s. per cwt. penalty paid by Mauritius planters in the British market, equalizing their duties with those of the Caribbean colonists. *6 Geo. IV. cap. 76.*

TABLE 3

Sugar Production in the Ceded Colonies, 1815–1834
(tons)*

Year	British Guiana	Trinidad	Tobago	St. Lucia	Mauritius	Average Annual Production of the Ceded Colonies	Average Annual Production of the old British Colonies	Percentage Produced in Ceded Colonies
1815–19	20,084	7,196	6,377	3,201	2,687	39,545	141,457	22%
1820–4	30,753	8,257	5,850	3,563	9,634	58,057	131,115	31%
1825–9	51,084	11,616	5,664	4,121†	18,365	90,250	124,181	42%
1830–4	55,910	14,702	4,883	3,175	30,945	109,615	126,328	46%

Source: Computations made from Noel Deerr, *The History of Sugar* (London, 1949), I, pp. 193–203.

* Figures are given in English long tons. Mauritius figures have been converted from metric tons to English long tons.
† The figure for 1827 is missing.

worth of English cottons.[2] India required new articles of export
to pay for her expanding imports, and sugar was among her
most promising products. West Indians had long claimed
preference against East Indian sugar on the grounds that
British navigation laws had precluded free access to the American market for plantation supplies. When this access was
belatedly granted in 1830, the logical justification for West
Indian preference vanished. The discriminating duty on East
Indian muscovado was halved in 1830 and abolished in 1836.[3]

In spite of these adjustments, British sugar growers were
protected in the home market by a differential duty against
foreign producers amounting to 42s. a cwt. Preferential duties
of this type were a fixture of the old colonial system. Since the
time when highly integrated mercantile empires ruled the
Atlantic basin, preferential duties had compensated producers
of raw materials in the colonies for restrictions imposed on their
trade and manufacture by the mother country. By 1830,
however, colonial preference was becoming a costly burden for
metropolitan manufacturers and consumers. The growth of
Britain's metallurgical and textile industries afforded her a
commanding position in world commerce and made her the
principal beneficiary of free, or less restricted trade. In many
respects the Empire was an expensive source of raw materials,
and neither the lightly populated, remote temperate colonies
nor the depressed slave colonies offered sufficient allurement as
outlets for the rapidly accumulating capital of the mother
country.

Increasingly, trade and investment were flowing beyond the
confines of empire. The independent republics of Latin
America offered a valuable market for British manufactures, a
rich harvest for traders, and a tempting, although perilous,
area for investment.[4] The United States was supplying 80 per
cent of England's rapidly expanding cotton imports, and British
goods constituted 43 per cent of America's imports.[5] London
had become the money market for all forms of American securi-
ties. The expansion of British exports to most countries depended

[2] *Hansard*, 3rd Series, XXVIII, 22 June 1835, pp. 960–1.
[3] *6 & 7 Wm. IV. cap. 26.*
[4] Arthur D. Gayer, W. W. Rostow, and Anna Jacobson Schwartz, *The Growth
and Fluctuation of the British Economy, 1790–1850* (Oxford, 1953).
[5] Leland H. Jenks, *The Migration of British Capital to 1875* (New York, 1927), p. 67.

upon Britain's ability to absorb their raw materials in payment for refined products.[6] In this respect, colonial monopolies of the home market constituted a vexing obstacle. In a single year fifty-one ships trading from Liverpool to Rio de Janeiro returned in ballast because they were unable to load Brazilian sugar or coffee for the British market.[7] To think imperialistically was to think restrictively. In rising numbers, shipowners, sugar-refiners, London financiers, and northern industrialists denounced the system of preferential tariffs.

The colonial monopoly was partially circumvented in 1828 in the interest of Britain's badly depressed sugar-refiners. Until that year, the prohibitive tariff on foreign sugar had obliged refiners to purchase higher-priced colonial and East Indian sugar, a requirement which increased their production costs and hazarded the saleability of their sugar in European markets. Some European countries, hoping to stimulate their own refining industries, had established protective tariffs, impeding the import of British refined sugar. The Government countered by admitting foreign muscovado into the United Kingdom at the colonial rate of duty on the condition that it was to be refined exclusively for export purposes.[8] This action was not sufficient to reverse a widening depression in the industry. In 1833 two-thirds of the refining trade was in a state of near paralysis.[9] Parliament responded by passing an Act which admitted, duty free, all sugar—British and foreign—to be refined exclusively for export purposes.[10]

Attacks upon the preferential system alarmed West Indians. World production of sugar was rising dramatically in the early nineteenth century, and the surplus British colonial sugar being marketed in Europe confronted ruinous competition. Continental markets were increasingly dominated by inexpensive Cuban and Brazilian sugars. Brazil was a major sugar exporter, and Cuba—with vast tracts of virgin soil and large estates—was on

---

[6] R. C. O. Matthews, 'The Trade Cycle in Britain, 1790–1850' in Derek H. Aldroft and Peter Fearon, *British Economic Fluctuations, 1790–1939* (London, 1972), pp. 122–3.

[7] G. R. Mellor, *British Imperial Trusteeship* (London, 1951), p. 110.

[8] *Geo. IV. cap. 93.*

[9] Eric Williams, *Capitalism and Slavery* (Chapel Hill, 1944), p. 165.

[10] *3 & 4 Wm. IV. cap. 61.* This Act received the royal signature on the same day as the Act abolishing slavery.

the way to becoming the world's leading producer. Exports from Havana increased from 140,000 cases in 1800 to 245,000 in 1825, three-quarters of which was being sold in Europe.[11] The sugar industries of these states were consistently invigorated by the importation of African slaves, most of whom were male and in the prime of life.[12] No such recruits swelled the British Caribbean labour force after 1807, the year in which Parliament abolished the slave trade. By 1830 only 44 per cent of the slaves in the British West Indies were considered effective caneworkers, whereas in Cuba effective agricultural slaves were estimated to be 64 per cent of the whole servile population.[13]

Although foreign sugar was excluded from the United Kingdom, the price of sugar in Britain was greatly affected by prices prevailing in Europe. This would remain the case as long as the surplus production of the British colonies had to be sold overseas. After the Napoleonic wars, prices fell sharply. This decline shattered the morale of Caribbean growers whose hopes had been buoyed by a leap in price after the collapse of the Continental System. The wholesale price of Caribbean muscovado rose from 40s. per cwt. in 1811 to 72s. in 1814, bringing temporary prosperity to planters who had slogged through the difficult war years. Their rapture subsided with the steady slide of prices. The average wholesale price reached 31s. in 1822; by 1831 it was below 24s. (see Appendix 1). At the latter rate, sugar grown on inferior, poorly situated British colonial plantations was selling below the cost of bringing it to market. The poorest estates in the British Caribbean were generally located in older colonies, where soil exhaustion occasioned disproportionately heavy expenditures on labour and

[11] Select Committee on the State of the West India Colonies, P.P. 1831-2 XX (381), Appendix 1. In addition at least 20,000 cases of sugar were being exported from the Cuban ports of Matanzas and Trinidad.

[12] Philip D. Curtin, *The Atlantic Slave Trade: A Census* (Madison, 1969). Curtin estimates that between 1808 and 1865, 572,000 slaves were imported into Cuba and 56,900 into Puerto Rico. By his assessment, Brazil was the largest single importer, admitting over 1,145,000 slaves between 1811 and 1860. The French colonies imported about 96,000 slaves during the nineteenth century. Drawing from Cuban census data, it appears that in 1827 the sex ratio among slaves in that island was 1,768 males to 1,000 females. Incoming slave cargoes contained two to five males for every female.

[13] Report of the Select Committee on the State of the West India Colonies, P.P. 1831-2 XX (381).

fertilizer. In the newer colonies, notably Trinidad and Guiana, well capitalized planters remained competitive. The land in these latter dependencies was extremely fertile; virgin soil was abundant; and the productivity of slaves was exceptionally high.[14] Over the long term, however, Trinidad and Guiana confronted serious labour shortages. Their slave populations were declining, and individual attempts to offset the labour problem by acquiring bondsmen from worn-out properties in the Lesser Antilles were blocked by an Act of Parliament in 1824[15] forbidding the intercolonial migration of slaves.

During the half-century preceding emancipation the rate of sugar duties rose in inverse proportion to profits. In 1787 the duty on one cwt. of colonial muscovado was a mere 12s. 4d., but this rate was periodically revised upward to aid the payment of British war debts. During the 15 years after Waterloo the duty fluctuated between 27s. and 30s.; it came to rest at 24s. in 1830 (see Appendix 2). At the latter rate, the duty was roughly equivalent to the wholesale price of the product. Fifty years earlier the tax was only 30 per cent of the wholesale value of sugar. It was a moot point whether the tax was borne by the planters or consumers, and colonial and metropolitan sentiments differed diametrically on this issue. In vain the planters argued that a reduction in the rate of duty would stimulate wider domestic consumption, soak up their surpluses, and provide them an increased return.

Credit was a vital part of the West Indian plantation system. It had always been essential that the planters enjoy some financial cushion against a sudden collapse of the market or the

[14] A crude and imperfect estimate of slave productivity can be obtained by dividing the average annual production of sugar in various colonies for the period 1824–33 by the number of agricultural slaves liberated in those colonies in 1834. These figures indicate that in Barbados, the oldest of the British colonies, roughly 560 pounds of sugar per slave were produced per annum; in St. Kitts, 760 pounds; in Antigua, 800 pounds. The general figure for the colonies as a whole was 760 pounds per praedial slave (a slave employed as an agricultural labourer). In the newer colonies the figures were sharply higher: for Trinidad, 1,780 pounds per slave per annum; for British Guiana, 1,760 pounds per annum. On John Gladstone's Vreedenhoop Estate in Demerara an output of 2,000 pounds per slave per annum was achieved. See, S. G. Checkland, *The Gladstones: A Family Biography, 1764–1851* (Cambridge, 1971), p. 268.

[15] 5 Geo. IV. cap. 113. Between January 1822 and Dec. 1824 nearly 2,500 slaves had been transported to Trinidad. C.O. 318/117, *Comparative State of the Increase and Decrease of the Slave Population.*

accidents of drought, hurricane, or insurrection. Regardless of
the operational efficiency of the plantations, natural calamities
occurred periodically in the colonies and credit was needed
to restore damaged property. Traditionally, the source of credit
for the planter was his merchant agent in Britain who received
sugar on consignment and shipped out to the colonies whatever
items were required for the operation of an estate and the
comfort of the planter. Merchants who made mortgage and
other loans to the planters insisted on terms commensurate
with their risks. In addition to an interest payment of 5 or 6 per
cent, a planter was obliged to consign all his sugar to his merchant, and to ship his cargoes in the merchant's vessels.[16] This
relation reduced the planter to fiscal peonage. The merchant
could sell the planter's sugar when the market was sated and
prices low. He could charge a high price for supplies shipped
to the colony even though he was able to purchase those
supplies for cash in Britain at a discount of 10 to 12 per cent.
The merchant had the assurance of two-way freights for his
ships, and in the West India trade a merchant vessel of 400 tons
costing £6,000 might, with good fortune, clear £40,000 in ten
years.[17] West India merchants were the leading underwriters at
Lloyds, and in many cases they insured both their vessels and
cargoes at the planters' expense.

As Table 4 indicates, commercial charges on the shipment
and sale of colonial sugar were numerous and heavy. In that
example, the selling price of a cargo of Trinidad muscovado
was £2,011 4s. 7d. £1,085 or more than half of that amount,
represented the duty paid on 919 cwt.[18] In the United Kingdom, duty was paid on sugar before it was put up for sale, a
practice which applied to no other large article of import—
neither tea nor coffee. The merchant's commission, paid by
the planter, was charged on the amount of duty as well as on

[16] Lowell Joseph Ragatz, *The Fall of the Planter Class in the British Caribbean,
1763-1833* (New York, 1928), pp. 100-2; R. W. Beachey, *The British West Indies
Sugar Industry in the Late Nineteenth Century* (Oxford, 1957), p. 19; T. W. Jackson to
Sir Charles Metcalfe, 6 May 1842, enclosed in Elgin to Stanley, 6 June 1842,
C.O. 137/263, no. 6.

[17] R. R. Madden, *A Twelvemonth's Residence*, II, 156.

[18] Sugar duties were paid on the weight of sugar upon its arrival in port, but
planters were paid only on the amount of sugar actually delivered to buyers. In
the interval between the landing of the sugar and its subsequent sale there was an
inevitable loss by drainage.

the price of the sugar. This commission regularly amounted to
2½ per cent of the gross sale. In addition, the merchant charged
the planter interest—usually 5 per cent—on cash he had
advanced for the payment of freight and duties.[19] After duties,
the cargo of Trinidad muscovado under consideration realized
£926; but £366—or nearly 40 per cent of that—was deducted
for commercial charges, leaving the planter only £560. Except
for the merchant's and broker's commissions, commercial
charges were levied on a flat rate. When sugar prices were low,

TABLE 4

Commercial Charges on a Cargo of Trinidad Muscovado, c. 1830

Cargo: 64 hogsheads, landed net weight of 919 cwt.
Selling Price: £2,011.4s.7d. at net weight of 904 cwt.

	£	s.	d.		£	s.	d.
Freight	229	14	10				
Primage	1	12	0				
Pierage	1	4	0				
Trade	1	12	0				
Total	234	2	10	234	2	10
Interest on freight and duty,							
¼ per cent on gross sales					10	1	3
Insurance from fire, 1s. premium, 2s. duty					3	1	0
Landing: waiters, ¼d. per cask						2	8
Dock rate, 8d. per cwt.					30	12	8
Samples, 6d. per cask					1	12	0
Insurage on 640, 25s. premium, duty 5s.					9	12	0
Stamp					10	0
Commission on Insurance					3	4	0
Brokerage on Sales					10	1	2
Commission on Sales					50	5	10
TOTAL COMMERCIAL CHARGES					353	5	5
Guarantee, if required, ¼ per cent on insurance					3	4	0
Guarantee, if required, gross sales, ¼ per cent					10	1	2
					366	10	7

Source: Sel. Comm. on West India Colonies, P.P. 1831–2 XX (381), evidence of
Charles Marryat, merchant and proprietor of estates in Grenada, Trinidad, St.
Lucia.

[19] Sel. Comm. on West India Colonies, P.P. 1831–2 XX (381), QQ 668, 1432;
Sel. Comm. on Sugar and Coffee Planting, P.P. 1847–8 XXIII (206), evidence of
H. N. Browne.

as in this case, they absorbed a substantial portion of the receipts.

In time of high prices and general prosperity planter indebtedness was a balm to the business of West India merchants who accumulated interest as well as commissions. The temptation to loan money on the security of plantation property (loans which entitled merchant creditors to a monopoly of their clients' commission business) led inevitably to a perilous over-extension of credit when prices fell and the value of estates depreciated. In 1830 many West India plantations were over-laden with debt, and merchants who held the bulk of those debts were, themselves, deeply involved with other merchants, bill-brokers, and London bankers who had provided them with much of the capital used to make loans to the planters. Writing from the Colonial Office in 1832, James Stephen determined that the planters' credit was so exhausted that no prudent person would advance a shilling on the security of West Indian estates.[20] In fact, the situation was more complicated than that. Merchants who held mortgages on properties that were in default as a result of low sugar prices could not hastily foreclose lest they acquire estates which could neither be borrowed against nor resold at a profit.[21] In these circumstances the merchants' only alternative was to offer their beleaguered clients revised, though onerous, mortgage terms or to extend them limited credit at high interest on the security of slaves, crops, or other property. It was in the interests of hard pressed mortgagees to keep the estates afloat and in their debtors' hands, hoping for an upturn in market prices. Merchants whose assets were tied up in unproductive and depreciated West India property frequently went to the wall. In the dismal year

[20] James Stephen, memo., 22 Mar. 1832, C.O. 320/1.

[21] No one wanted heavily burdened West Indian estates. Wary Britons would not put up the necessary cash to buy them, and wealthy West Indians perceived that as long as estates remained in the hands of absentees they would have to be employed as attorneys. Under prevailing circumstances, the latter usually preferred the certainty of salaries and commissions to the risks of ownership. Henry Taylor, memo, Jan. 1833, C.O. 318/117; Sel. Comm. on West India Colonies, P.P. 1831–2 XX (381), evidence of Macdonnell, Colville, Oliver, Colquhoun; Mrs. Flanders, *Antigua*, II, 156–7; Sylvester Hovey, *Letters from the West Indies* (New York, 1838), p. 75. When the proprietor of Worthy Park, Jamaica, died in 1835 he directed his trustees to sell whatever portion of his property would be necessary to fulfill his bequests. The trustees, besieged by over 20 creditors and encumbrancers, found the property incapable of sale. Craton and Walvin, *Jamaican Plantation*, p. 188.

1831, ten West India houses failed; in the preceding forty years, sixty others had become insolvent.[22] Clearly, the prosperity of the mercantile community rested squarely upon that of the planters.

In the face of mounting difficulties, proprietors cut back on maintenance costs. Buildings and equipment deteriorated and the quantity of stock declined. The acquisition of essential stock and horses offers a fairly reliable index of the purchasing power of the planters in this period. In Jamaica the average importation of horses and cattle for the three years 1820–2 was 1,620 and 1,386 respectively; between 1825 and 1828, these averages had fallen to 557 horses and 74 cattle.[23] Even on comparatively profitable estates maintenance expenditures were reduced. Profits taken from the joint properties of Llandovery and Flat Point in the Parish of St. Ann, Jamaica, averaged £5,187 per year during the period 1816 to 1831, but they were secured at considerable cost to the capital inventory of these estates. The quantity of livestock diminished from 429 to 316 animals during the final six years of that period. In the same six years, the slave population declined from 399 to 362—a dead loss of human property amounting, at the very least, to £1,600.[24] During the six year period from 1816 to 1821, the proprietor of these plantations spent an average of £5,752 a year on supplies; in the six years preceding 1831, the average outlay for supplies dropped to £3,238.[25]

The crisis in the West Indies was not confined to sugar. If anything, planters of secondary crops were worse off than the sugar-planters. By 1830 coffee and cocoa were the only important secondary crops. American competition had undermined West Indian cotton-growers. Indigo, ginger, and arrowroot were insignificant items of export. Pimento represented only 3 per cent of the exports of Jamaica, and its production was confined to that island.

---

[22] Richard B. Sheridan, 'The West Indies Sugar Crisis, 1830–1833', *Journal of Economic History*, XXI (1961), 542–4.

[23] *Votes of the Jamaica Assembly.*

[24] This figure is based on the average value of Jamaican slaves established for compensation purposes by the Commissioners of Compensation, July 1835, C.O. 318/117.

[25] Papers on the Abolition of Slavery relative to the Trust Estates of William White, C.O. 318/117.

Grenada exported some cocoa, but Trinidad was the only important producer of that crop. The mountain regions of northern Trinidad contained scores of cocoa plantations which had been settled in the early nineteenth century by French and Spanish planters.[26] These planters possessed little capital and maintained few slaves. For labour they relied on free peons who migrated to the island from the adjacent continent. In 1827, Trinidad exported over 3,500,000 lb. of cocoa valued at £57,850, but a substantial fall in prices, beginning in that year and continuing through the next several decades, brought ruin to the planters. Cocoa production in Trinidad vastly exceeded the trifling demand of Great Britain. Even the British Army and Navy eschewed the purchase of the colonial product in favour of a superior quality cocoa produced in South America.[27] Spain was the principal European market for cocoa, but both Spanish and British navigation laws impeded the export of colonial cocoa to that quarter. Spanish ships were discouraged from visiting ports in Trinidad, and Trinidad cocoa transported to Spain in British ships paid a duty three times the price of the product when sold in the colonial market. As a result, Trinidad planters were obliged to ship their cocoa to Spain through Cuba and Puerto Rico, where cargoes were landed, bonded, and re-shipped in Spanish vessels.[28] This was a vexatious, tedious, and costly process.

In 1832 coffee constituted 18 per cent of the value of Jamaica's exports and 32 per cent of those of Dominica.[29] Elsewhere its production was insignificant, except in the district of Berbice, British Guiana. Coffee exports from these areas had risen sharply after 1808 when duties were moderated in the home market, but soil exhaustion occasioned by the insufficient use of fertilizer was overtaking many properties. The abandonment of worn out coffee plantations had already begun in Jamaica; emancipation would accelerate the process.

Cattle farms, called pens, were abundant in the Caribbean. They were economically dependent on the sugar estates to

---

[26] Donald Wood, *Trinidad in Transition* (Oxford, 1968), p. 34.
[27] James Stephen, minute, 25 May 1840, bound in C.O. 295/130, no. 37.
[28] Memorial of the Cultivators of Cocoa, enclosed in MacLeod to Russell, 11 July 1840, C.O. 295/130, no. 37.
[29] Martin, *History of the West Indies*, I, 122–3; II, 286.

which they marketed their animals, and in many cases they were owned by the proprietors of sugar property. Independent pen keepers, like the planters of secondary crops, were politically and socially insignificant. They resided on the fringes of the dominant productive system, occupying lands not suited for sugar cultivation, benefiting from the prosperity of sugar planters, and suffering indirectly from their losses.

On the whole, prospects for the British West Indian economy were unfavourable. An extensive thinning out of plantation properties, primarily those having inferior soil or other physical liabilities which inflated production costs, was inevitable whether or not slavery was abolished. Nevertheless, there were districts in the older colonies and extensive areas in the newer dependencies where prospects were still promising if the planters could command adequate labour, refine their techniques, and minimize their indebtedness. The West Indies would produce no more nabobs in the style of the eighteenth century, but on a selective basis they could offer opportunities for speculative investment where it was not unreasonable to anticipate annual returns of 5–10 per cent on capital ventured.[30] This was certainly the view of John Gladstone, a shrewd self-made businessman who invested £336,000, three-fifths of his extensive fortune, in the West Indies, principally in Demerara, during the years preceding emancipation.[31] Sugar property still possessed a curious fascination. Because of its paramount importance to the remainder of this study, a brief examination of the character and operation of West Indian estates is warranted.

Sugar estates were comprehensive units of production,

---

[30] The diverse character of the British West India colonies in terms of soil fertility, size of estates, and prospects for profit (as evidenced, for example, in the differences between Nevis, St. Vincent, and Trinidad or British Guiana) call in question the general conclusion reached by the sociologist M. G. Smith who, from an assessment of a few standard contemporary writings, argues that by 1820 the sugar system had become so uneconomical that its preservation was predicted more upon consideration for the social status of the planter class than for reasons of an economic nature. While Smith's conclusion may be valid for some areas of the British West Indies or for particular districts of large colonies, it does not merit approval as a general thesis. See, M. G. Smith, *The Plural Society in the British West Indies* (Berkeley and Los Angeles, 1965), Chap. 5.

[31] Checkland, *Gladstones*, p. 263.

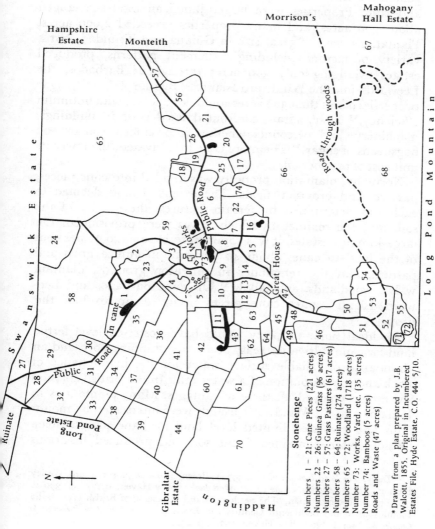

A Plan of Hyde Estate, Trelawny, Jamaica*

Stonehenge

Numbers 1 – 21: Cane Pieces (221 acres)
Numbers 22 – 26: Guinea Grass (96 acres)
Numbers 27 – 57: Grass Pastures (617 acres)
Numbers 58 – 64: Ruinate (274 acres)
Numbers 65 – 72: Woodland (1718 acres)
Number 73: Works, Yard, etc. (35 acres)
Number 74: Bamboos (5 acres)
Roads and Waste (47 acres)

*Drawn from a plan prepared by J.B.
Walcott, 1855. Original in Incumbered
Estates File, Hyde Estate, C.O. 444 5/10.

Hampshire Estate

Monteith

Morrison's

Mahogany Hall Estate

Swanswick Estate

Ruinate

Public Road

Long Pond Estate

Gibraltar Estate

Haddington

Long Pond Mountain

Great House

Works

Public Road

In cane

Road through woods

engaging both in agriculture and manufacture. They planted, cultivated, reaped, processed, and packaged their cane, generating three export products: muscovado sugar, molasses, and rum. Properties were large. Jamaican estates averaged about 900 acres, and many properties exceeded 2,000 acres. Plantations were of great size in Guiana and Trinidad, but a variety of factors, including settlement patterns, produced estates averaging only 300 acres throughout Barbados, the Leewards, and the Windward Islands.[32] By rule of thumb, sugar properties of less than 300 acres could not operate with optimum efficiency.[33] Every estate confronted fixed costs in buildings, machinery, and personnel whether it produced 100 or 200 hogsheads of sugar.[34] The more cane it cultivated, the lower its unit cost of production.

Normally, plantation property was divided into cane pieces, pasture, and provision fields. The extent of land devoted to each was determined by terrain features, the quality of the soil, and the manner by which slaves were provisioned. On large Jamaica estates, it was common to have 20 to 30 per cent of the land in cane, about 40 per cent in guinea grass and pasture, and the remainder in provision grounds, plantain walks, woodlands, and fallow.[35] On some Barbados and Leeward Island estates cane pieces occupied up to half the property.[36]

An ideal sugar property would have possessed level fertile land for cane cultivation, easy access to a shipping port, and an abundance of reliable surface water for the maintenance of stock and the propulsion of a water mill. In the British colonies few estates enjoyed all these advantages. Many plantations in Jamaica and the Windward Islands were intersected by mountains and possessed limited level land for cane pieces. Steep hillsides often contained fertile soil and produced luxurious

[32] Davy, The West Indies, pp. 180, 397–8; Breen, St. Lucia, p. 317; Frank Wesley Pitman, The Development of the British West Indies (New Haven, 1917), pp. 370–2.

[33] Frank Wesley Pitman, 'The Settlement and Financing of British West India Plantations in the Eighteenth Century', in Essays in Colonial History Presented to Charles McLean Andrews (New Haven, 1931), p. 258.

[34] Edwards, History, Civil and Commercial, II, 296.

[35] Stewart, Account of Jamaica, p. 108.

[36] Davy, The West Indies, pp. 112–13, 446. The estates of St. Kitts, normally 300 acres, had an average of 130 acres suited to cane cultivation.

canes, but oxen could not draw carts on the hillsides during the harvest, and canes had to be transported to the mill on the backs of mules or donkeys.[37] Neither the plough nor other implements were adaptable to mountain cultivation. In the Leeward Islands, the shortage of surface water was a serious problem; conversely, an excess of surface water plagued both Guiana and Trinidad. In the tidal lowlands of British Guiana the high cost of maintaining dykes, dams, and sluices restricted sugar cultivation to heavily capitalized proprietors. Although estates in Barbados and the Leewards enjoyed easy access to ports, some Jamaica properties were separated by 30 miles of gutted and hazardous road from the nearest shipping point.[38] Occasionally, Trinidad planters living only six miles from San Fernando were unable to transport their sugar to port because an early onset of rains rendered the roads impassable.[39]

Regularity was a vital ingredient in good cane husbandry. Planting occurred in autumn after the heaviest rains of summer and the danger of hurricanes had passed. Before the arrival of dry weather, young plants had risen to shade the ground. Weeding began when the canes reached a height of twenty inches. Manuring followed, and thereafter the plant was stripped. Stripping involved the removal of dried leaves and their placement on the earth around the cane plants. This process, performed several times during the growth of the plant, preserved surface moisture and exposed growing canes to the full influence of the sun. Plants matured in twelve to eighteen months,[40] and canes planted in the fall were ready for crop

---

[37] Sturge and Harvey, *The West Indies*, p. 121. The difficulty of this form of cartage may be appreciated when it is acknowledged that an acre or two of cane producing three hogsheads of sugar would yield 60 to 80 tons of vegetable matter. Jelly, *A Brief Encounter*, p. 49.

[38] Craton and Walvin, *Jamaican Plantation*, pp. 173–4; Memorial of the Proprietors and other Inhabitants of Clarendon, enclosed in C. E. Grey to Earl Grey, 25 Mar. 1847, C.O. 137/291, no. 27.

[39] Subcommittee of the Agricultural and Immigration Society of Trinidad, evidence of Horatio Huggins, March 1841, enclosed in MacLeod to Russell, 20 Aug. 1841, C.O. 295/134, no. 85.

[40] The rate at which canes matured varied. Ratoons ripened about two months earlier than plant canes. In Barbados, plant canes required as much as 18 months; in Trinidad, 15 to 18 months. On the coastal estates of British Guiana, they ripened in 14 months, but on river estates they required 16 months. See, Davy, *The West Indies*, pp. 319–20, 360–1; also Otis P. Sharkey, *The Economic Geography of Barbados* (New York, 1939), p. 39.

(the West Indian term for harvest) at the beginning of the second year. This was vitally important. The period from January to April was the driest of the year in the West Indies. In dry weather, fuel burnt most readily; manufacture was easily performed; and hogsheads of sugar could be conveyed to port with minimal burden to draft animals and least danger of accident. Crop occupied four to six months, but on well regulated estates the harvest ended before the arrival of heavy summer rains and the renewed peril of hurricane. Cane lands cropped during the spring were devoted to provisions or fallowed until fall planting.[41] Although variants of this schedule prevailed in different sectors of the Caribbean, the emphasis on regularity was the same. Bryan Edwards warned, '. . . there is not a greater error in the system of planting than to make sugar or to plant canes, in improper seasons of the year . . .'[42]

The sugar crop of a plantation was produced either from plant canes or ratoons. Plant canes grew from cuttings taken from the upper joints of mature cane. Ratoons, on the other hand, constituted the new growths which sprouted naturally from the roots of harvested cane plants. Ratoons yielded less saccharine juice than cane plants, and as a rule their yield diminished each year.[43] Where ratooning was possible cane pieces were kept in ratoons until they ceased to be remunerative. At that point they were grubbed up and replaced by plants. Ratoons precluded the arduous preparation of new land; they required less care than plants; and, consequently, they afforded a valuable saving in time and labour. The ability of land to sustain ratoons was considered a measure of its natural fertility. In Barbados and St. Kitts ratoons seldom

[41] With the advent of fast maturing Otaheite cane, planters in St. Kitts and Nevis who did not normally ratoon their cane eliminated the fallow period and replanted fields immediately after crop had been taken. Seasonal regularity was thereby forsaken and mills worked throughout most of the year. This schedule, possible in the Leeward colonies because of their lower level of rainfall, was not practical elsewhere. See, Goveia, *Slave Society*, pp. 127–8; Davy, *The West Indies*, p. 453.

[42] Edwards, *History, Civil and Commercial*, II, 252.

[43] On Cornwall Estate, Jamaica, plant canes yielded an average of two hogsheads per acre, ratoons, one. Lewis, *Journal*, p. 88. At Seville Estate, a mediocre property in St. Ann's, the following yields were achieved over a 4-year period on a cane piece of 10 acres: plants, 23 hogsheads of 18 cwt.; first ratoons, 21; second ratoons, 12; third ratoons, 13. Report of the Royal Agricultural Society accompanying the return of John Woolfreys, 1 May 1845, enclosed in Elgin to Stanley, 2 Sept. 1845, C.O. 137/284, no. 79.

paid beyond a single year, and many planters relied exclusively upon plant canes.[44] In Jamaica, estates in the parish of Vere produced primarily from ratoons. The better estates in St. Thomas in the East ratooned for ten years; most properties in the western parishes maintained them half that time; but, in some districts of Jamaica ratoons scarcely paid at all.[45] The great natural fertility of Trinidad and Guiana permitted ratooning for up to twenty years.[46]

Because sugar was a seasonal crop, the number of slaves required to operate an estate was determined by the extraordinary demand for labour at harvest time when sugar was cut, milled, boiled, cured, packaged, and transported to port. These functions, when added to regular agricultural tasks, strained and fatigued the manpower resources of every plantation. Since planters were compelled to retain a full complement of slaves in the peak season, they were obliged to tolerate a degree of labour redundancy during other periods of the year. Rather than invest in costly agricultural machinery to magnify the extent of that redundancy, planters tended to rely on the manual labour of slaves whose maintenance costs they were obliged to bear whether or not they were fully employed.

English critics considered the planters' reliance on hand tools and manual labour manifest evidence of their rigid conservatism and unconscionable abuse of slaves. The planters, on the other hand, valued the careful and precise work achieved by close manual labour, and they believed that the maintenance of steady year-round work routines was essential to the preservation of a disciplined labour force.[47] In this regard, slaves rein-

[44] Sel. Comm. on the West India Colonies, P.P. 1842 XIII (479), evidence of Carrington, Sharpe, Estridge.

[45] Lewis, *Journal*, p. 213; Sel. Comm. on West India Colonies, P.P. 1842 XIII (479), evidence of McCornock; Elgin to Stanley, 17 Apr. 1844, C.O. 137/279, no. 62.

[46] Subcommittee of the Agricultural and Immigration Society of Trinidad, evidence of Richard Darling, Aug. 1841, enclosed in MacLeod to Russell, 20 Aug. 1841, C.O. 295/134, no. 85; Sel. Comm. on West India Colonies, P.P. 1842 XIII (479), evidence of Campbell. The extent to which ratoons were employed varied from estate to estate. Peter Rose, a Demerara planter, claimed that he maintained ratoons only four years. Sel. Comm. on West India Colonies, P.P. 1831–2 XX (381), Q. 1740.

[47] The proposition that mechanization has been or will be the decisive factor in advancing the rate of agricultural output is challenged in E. J. T. Collins' 'Harvest Technology and Labour Supply in Britain, 1790–1870', *The Economic*

forced the planters' preferences. They resisted innovations in
either the tools or techniques employed in West Indian agriculture. The heavy hand-hoe was the dominant agricultural
implement in West Africa, and Caribbean slaves exhibited
remarkable dexterity in its use. Shovels and scythes were contemptuously disdained in favour of hoes and bills, and, if the
anecdotal recordings of some contemporary authors can be
believed, slaves even resisted the use of wheelbarrows as devices
for hauling manure, preferring the traditional wicker baskets
which they carried on their heads.[48] While some aspects of
West Indian agriculture may have been judged wasteful of
human labour by the criteria employed in assessing the efficiency of free English farming, the plantation system was
effective in producing the maximum exportable product with
the greatest measure of social control under conditions dictated
by a tropical environment and slave labour.

   In the contemporary debate on the efficiency of Caribbean
slave agriculture, much attention was focused upon the use
of the plough. No implement was so heartily recommended to
the planters. In England, a remarkable variety of ploughs was
in service, and treatises dealing with their relative merits were
commonplace.[49] Nevertheless, in the West Indies, most planters continued to open their land by the ancient and toilsome
practice of cane holing.[50] Opponents of this practice asserted

History Review, 2nd ser. XXII (1969), 453–73. Collins begins his article with a
quotation from J. Wrightson (1910) which most West India planters would have
endorsed: 'Manual labour is superior to any application of unconscious power, on
account of its intelligence, as shown in selection, variation in force, delicacy of
touch, and adaptation to every minute difference in the material acted upon ... It
is therefore well to pause before substituting machines, when men are available
and wages are not too high.' Collins doubts whether, historically, 'economic
growth in agriculture has been at all closely correlated with either machines or
other high-cost technological inputs' (453). He concludes that intermediate hand
tool technology, as an alternative to mechanization in agriculture, had the advantages 'of simplicity, cheapness, and easy maintenance ... of operational flexibility
... [and] of being able to offer satisfactory labour savings without creating serious
technological redundancy...' (472).

   [48] Wentworth, Sketch Book, II, 68–9; Hovey, Letters from the West Indies, p. 66.
   [49] G. E. Fussell, The Farmers Tools, 1500–1900 (London, 1952), pp. 35–73.
   [50] Holing was considered the most arduous work on a sugar estate. Land designated for holing was subdivided into hundreds of squares, each about 4 feet wide
(16 square feet), which were marked off by rows of wooden pegs. A gang of slaves
was lined up on the first row of pegs, usually one slave to a square. By the use of
his hoe, each slave excavated a hole about 2½ feet broad at the top, 15 inches wide

that a number of cattle, several ploughmen, and a plough could perform the labour of three dozen slaves in a single day. The plough had been tried in Jamaica before 1774, and it was subsequently introduced in all the colonies.[51] Only a few planters adopted it on a regular basis, and in most cases they employed it to loosen stiff clay soils in order to minimize the work of cane holing.[52]

When the abolition of the British slave trade, in 1807, occasioned a steady decline in the effective labouring population of the colonies, proprietors exhibited increasing interest in conserving their existing supplies of labour. Many absentees unsolicitedly shipped ploughs out to their estates[53] only to discover that in spite of shrinking labour resources practical planters commonly rejected their use. Rejection occurred for a variety of reasons. Many planters thought ploughing over-exposed the soil, causing desiccation and a loss of fertility.[54] This was a real problem in the tropics. Where consistent planting had exhausted the natural fertility of the soil and supplementary fertilizer was in short supply, the planters had good reason for concern. In Barbados, ploughs had been adopted widely before 1820, but a period of dry seasons and low crops during the following decade persuaded planters to revert exclusively to the hoe.[55] On some estates cane fields were not suited to ploughing. The land was either too hilly, too stony, or too heavy. The Nevis legislature determined in 1789 that only 400 of that island's 8,000 cane acres were fit for ploughing.[56] In the Windward Islands and Dominica most of the cultivation and many of the best canes were located on steep hillsides. Tree stumps prevented the use of ploughs in many flat lands. When these lands had been cleared, the shortage of labour had pre-

at the bottom, and 5–8 inches in depth. Upon completing the first hole, the slave stepped back to the next row of pegs and started opening the second.

[51] Noel Deerr, *The History of Sugar* (London, 1950), II, 353–4.

[52] On Jamaican estates managed by William Taylor, a slave would be expected to dig 90 cane holes a day in unploughed land and 120 in land loosened by the plough. Sel. Comm. on the Extinction of Slavery, P.P. 1831–2 XX (721), QQ 61–83.

[53] Sel. Comm. on the West India Colonies, P.P. 1842 XXII (479), evidence of McCornock.

[54] Ibid., evidence of Estridge.

[55] Davy, *The West Indies*, pp. 113–14.

[56] Richard Pares, *A West India Fortune* (London, 1950), p. 111.

cluded the removal of stumps.[57] In Trinidad, a wet heavy soil capable of pulling the shoes off horses compounded the stump problem and made ploughing, for the most part, unrewarding.[58] Guiana estates were rifled with surface drains and canals. To effect proper drainage the land had to be ploughed at right angles to the drains, but these ubiquitous obstacles were too wide for the passage of cattle and plough.[59] In both Guiana and Trinidad, opportunities for the employment of ploughs were further limited by the universal use of ratoons.

The great economies made by the use of the plough in Europe and the United States depended on a powerful and efficient draft animal. No such beast was available to West Indians. Neither the light creole horse nor the mule was suitable, and powerful draft horses had severe acclimatization problems.[60] Attempts to introduce the draft horse to Jamaica failed;[61] in Barbados the mortality rate of horses of all species was about 25 per cent of the whole stock per year.[62] Having experimented with the plough and horse-hoe, one innovating Antigua planter declared that the 'stiff lands in this hot climate require more strength of cattle than we are able to maintain . . . for if these strong soils are either too wet or too dry (as is generally the case), ploughing is impracticable.'[63]

The breakage of costly agricultural equipment was both commonplace and maddening. Unlike European peasants, West Indian slaves had little or no experience with animal-drawn machinery and no rooted respect for its worth. Ironically, slaves tended to perceive the plough as an intrusion upon the traditional relation between man and the soil. They exhibited little aptitude as ploughmen, and the planters generally concluded that no success would attend the introduction of

---

[57] Carmichael, *Domestic Manners*, II, 165–7.

[58] Subcommittee of the Agricultural and Immigration Society of Trinidad, July 1841, enclosed in MacLeod to Russell, 20 Aug. 1841, C.O. 295/134, no. 85; Sel. Comm. on West India Colonies, P.P. 1842 XIII (479), evidence of Bushe and Church.

[59] Sel. Comm., Ibid., evidence of Campbell.

[60] George E. Cumper, 'Labor Demand and Supply in the Jamaica Sugar Industry, 1830–1950', *Social and Economic Studies*, II (1954), 63.

[61] Jelly, *A Brief Enquiry*, p. 48.

[62] Schomburgk, *History of Barbados*, p. 165.

[63] Quoted in Richard B. Sheridan, 'Samuel Martin, Innovating Sugar Planter of Antigua, 1750–1776', *Agricultural History*, XXXIV (1960), 135.

animal-drawn equipment until European ploughmen were brought out to the islands.[64] A progressive Jamaica proprietor who insisted that animal power be substituted for the labour of slaves in opening the land suffered a common disappointment:

I impressed this wish of mine upon the minds of my agents with all my power; but the only result has been the creating of a very considerable additional expense in the purchase of ploughs, oxen, and farming implements; the awkwardness, and still more the obstinacy, of the few negroes, whose services were indispensable, was not to be overcome: they broke plough after plough, and ruined beast after beast, till the attempt was abandoned in despair.[65]

There was wide variation in the use of fertilizers in the British West Indies, but in only a few districts did this aspect of husbandry receive the attention it deserved. In Trinidad and Guiana where labour was scarce and the illusion of inexhaustible natural fertility still prevailed, there was little or no use of fertilizer.[66] Greatest care was rendered in the Leewards and Barbados where natural fertility had long been exhausted. The movable cattle pen was the most common system of manuring, but pens alone were not sufficient. One hundred cattle penned every day and night throughout a year could prepare only 18 acres for planting.[67] Cattle pens were supplemented by a rich compost which was prepared from dung taken from horse and mule stables, from the dregs of the still house, and from coal and vegetable ashes removed from the boiling house.[68] An abundance of healthy stock was vitally important to a sugar plantation, for in addition to providing manure, stock carted canes from the fields to the mill, carried sugar from the curing house to port, and, where necessary, powered a grinding mill. Edwards determined that a 900 acre Jamaica estate could not be administered prudently with fewer than 80

---

[64] Carmichael, *Domestic Manners*, II, 265–8. In Antigua as elsewhere, Scottish ploughmen were brought out to the colony under indenture. Report of Privy Council, enclosed in MacGregor to Spring Rice, 2 Dec. 1834, C.O. 7/39, no. 245.

[65] Lewis, *Journal*, p. 325.

[66] Burnley correspondence, Nov. 1835, C.O. 295/109; Subcommittee of the Agricultural and Immigration Society of Trinidad, evidence of Darling, May 1841, enclosed in MacLeod to Russell, 20 August 1841, C.O. 295/134, no. 85.

[67] Jelly, *A Brief Enquiry*, p. 60.

[68] Stewart, *Account of Jamaica*, p. 113; Edwards, *History, Civil and Commercial*, II, 253–7.

steers and 60 mules.[69] The value of animal manure depended upon the quality of pasture land and fodder available to the stock. In Antigua and Barbados, pasturage was insufficient and supplementary grasses for fodder were not produced in adequate quantity.[70] Consequently, both cattle and manure were of low quality. In the Leewards some compensation was provided by burying pigeon pea plants in the ground in advance of planting the cane. The peas provided a food crop for the slaves and served as a valuable green dressing for cane.[71] Sorghum was similarly employed in Barbados.[72] But, during the era of slavery, imported fertilizer received too little use. Guano was not widely employed in Jamaica before 1844, nor did Barbados or the Windward colonies import it in large quantity until after emancipation. Cays lying off the coasts of Jamaica and Antigua possessed deposits of guano, but these were not commercially exploited until the 1850s when the arrival of American guano diggers aroused the colonists and provoked a mild international dispute over possession of the cays.[73]

Every West Indian estate milled its own sugar cane by employing wind, water, or animal power. All three propulsion systems possessed deficiencies. The grinding power of windmills was irregular. A prolonged lull could bring the manufacturing process to a standstill, causing canes already cut to sour, and throwing the harvest into July when rains were probable and hurricanes possible. The initial cost of an iron water wheel and the masonry aqueduct needed to convey water was high, and water wheels enjoyed no immunity from the capriciousness of nature. Sugar grinding occurred during the driest part of the year, and drought conditions often depleted the water sources used to power the giant wheels. Estates employing cattle mills required a large number of draft animals. Cattle mills ground slowly and were extremely taxing on the animals used to turn them.

[69] Ibid., II, 295.

[70] Goveia, *Slave Society*, p. 117; MacGregor to Stanley, 5 May 1834, C.O. 7/38, no. 99; Reid to Grey, 24 May 1848, C.O. 28/168, no. 39.

[71] Sel. Comm. on West India Colonies, P.P. 1842 XIII (479), evidence of Estridge; Davy, *The West Indies*, p. 447.

[72] MacGregor to Russell, 15 Sept. 1840, C.O. 28/135.

[73] Douglas Hall, *Free Jamaica*, 1838–65 (New Haven, 1959), p. 114; Beachey, *West Indies Sugar Industry*, p. 88.

The type of power employed on the estates depended upon environmental conditions. In Barbados and the Leewards where easterly winds were quite reliable, wind mills were a predominant feature of the landscape. Whenever it was feasible, estates in Jamaica and those in the well-watered Windward Islands employed water mills. Only when conditions required it, as in Trinidad where winds along the western plain were irregular, and water lay in sluggish rivers or tidal marshes, did planters resort to cattle mills. By no means were rude cattle mills the typical crushing device of the West India plantations as one West Indian historian has asserted.[74]

Many contemporary critics contended that steam power offered a milling panacea which West Indians blindly rejected. On the contrary, steam was introduced in the British West Indies around 1810,[75] and British colonists remained well ahead of their French and Brazilian competitors in this aspect of sugar technology.[76] The engineering of steam devices was primitive in the early nineteenth century and steam engines were just as liable to be disabled as windmills. A windmill would resume grinding with the renewal of a breeze, but steam engines broken by the careless treatment of slave operators required the repair services of skilled machinists. Spare parts were unobtainable in the West Indies. Foundries were located in most large Caribbean ports, but distances between the mills and the towns made the repair process tedious, time-consuming, and costly. In the mid-century, when superior steam equipment was made available, and repair facilities were commonplace, the planters of Trinidad and Guiana uniformly adopted these engines. The later actions of Trinidad planters did not indicate a superior willingness to innovate any more than their earlier employment of animal power exhibited a woeful conservatism. Topography and wind conditions had precluded any effective alternative to animal power in Trinidad until the arrival of dependable steam engines and adequate repair facilities.[77]

[74] Ragatz, *Fall of the Planter Class*, pp. 61–3. For a critique of Ragatz's assessment of West Indian milling operations, see W. A. Green, 'The Planter Class and British West Indian Sugar Production, Before and After Emancipation', *The Economic History Review*, 2nd ser. XXVI (1973), 451–3.

[75] Pares, *West India Fortune*, p. 115. [76] Deerr, *History of Sugar*, II, 552–4.

[77] In 1841 the proprietor of a foundry in Port of Spain submitted an advertisement to the local newspaper recommending his establishment in these terms:

The West Indies produced a raw brown sugar called mus-covado. Juice extracted from the cane was transferred from the mill to the factory and boiled in a succession of heavy copper receptacles. When the heated sugar was about to crystallize, it was removed from the last of the coppers and transferred to wooden trays for cooling. Thereafter it was packed into hogs-heads, and the hogsheads were mounted on open beams in an adjacent curing house. The bottom of each hogshead was rifled with bore holes so that molasses which drained freely from the sugar could be collected in a cistern at the bottom of the curing house. After twelve to fifteen days, the contents of the hogsheads were rammed down with heavy mallets, and the containers were filled to the brim. They were headed by a cooper, marked with the name of the estate, and carted to port for shipment to England.

This process was crude and wasteful, but British mercantile restrictions, not the conservatism of the planters, inhibited the introduction of more sophisticated manufacturing tech-niques and equipment. In order to protect metropolitan sugar refiners, the British Government established a prohibitive duty of £8 8s. per cwt. on refined sugar.[78] In 1833 Charles Bean, proprietor of Richmond Estate in British Guiana, acquired a vacuum pan at very high cost in order to enhance the quality of his product. Sugar boiling by the vacuum process was of special value in British Guiana where excessive humidity reduced the

'. . . in this Island the Planter may now, with confidence, erect a Steam Engine, that paragon of power and science, without that former natural dread that if anything broke or went wrong how could it be replaced or repaired.' *Port of Spain Gazette*, 16 April. 1841.

[78] Although the declining slave population and the eroded fiscal position of the planters precluded the development of a refining competence on most estates after 1815, before that time many proprietors could have enlarged their manufacturing units, adding necessary facilities and equipment for the production of a more refined product. An average hundredweight of colonial muscovado yielded about 70 pounds of pure product and 28 pounds of molasses. West Indian plantations were equipped to distil molasses into rum, and with each hogshead of raw sugar shipped from the colonies the planters were losing enough molasses to produce four gallons of rum. In addition, drainage of molasses occurred during the sea voyage to Britain, causing as much as 16 per cent reduction in the weight of a hogshead over the transit period. This was dead loss to the growers. At the price of sugar current in 1830 the drainage loss to Jamaica planters alone amounted to about £600,000. Report from the Sel. Comm. on Sugar and Coffee Planting, P.P. 1847–8 XXIII (245), Appendix no. 8.

ignition quality of fuel, prevented brisk boiling by the open pan process, and caused the production of an inordinately high ratio of molasses to sugar.[79] The better quality product obtained from the vacuum process on Richmond Estate was refused admission to the British market at the rate of duty charged on muscovado.[80] Rather than pay the outrageous tariff on refined sugar, Bean returned his shipment to Demerara for sale in the colony. Not until 1845 were penal duties lifted on superior forms of British plantation sugar.

Most British West Indian properties were owned by absentees.[81] They were managed by local agents, called attorneys, who purchased supplies, ordered goods from England, handled shipping details in the colonial port, and, ostensibly, supervised the agricultural management of the estates. Attorneys were commonly drawn from a small coterie of merchants, lawyers, and successful planters, many of whom made attorneyship a profession.[82] A single attorney might supervise fifteen separate estates and have jurisdiction over several thousand slaves.[83] Normally he received a commission of 5 or 6 per cent on the net produce of each property, and he enjoyed the privilege of house and board in addition to the services of slaves, horses, and gig at whichever estate he chose to reside.[84] Attorneys frequently fared better than their distant employers. Their commission came off the top after the basic operating costs of the property were met, and in lean years there was little or nothing left to the owner. The system was wasteful and liable to abuse. Some attorneys lived extravagantly at their employers'

[79] Beachey, *West Indies Sugar Industry*, p. 67.

[80] Bean to Smyth, 7 Feb. 1834, enclosed in Smyth to Stanley, Feb. 1834, C.O. 111/131, no. 78; Stewart to Lefevre, 17 June 1834, C.O. 111/134, Treasury correspondence.

[81] In 1832 540 of 646 sugar estates in Jamaica were owned by absentees. Richard B. Sheridan, 'Simon Taylor, Sugar Tycoon of Jamaica, 1740–1813', *Agricultural History*, XLV (1971), p. 287.

[82] Frequently, attorneys were proprietors of one or more estates of their own. In some cases, a man would serve as manager and attorney on one estate while acting as attorney for several others. Sel. Comm. on the West India Colonies, P.P. 1842 XIII (479), evidence of T. McCornock.

[83] William Shand, a Jamaica proprietor and attorney, claimed to have had 18,000 slaves under his charge at one time. Sel. Comm. on Slavery, P.P. 1842 XX (721), 6394.

[84] Thomas Roughley, *The Jamaica Planter's Guide* (London, 1823), pp. 8–11. A Demerara planter indicated that attorneys' commissions could vary from 2½ to 10 per cent. Sel. Comm. on the West India Colonies, P.P. 1831–2 XX (381), 1613.

expense, and those who were colonial merchants often over-stocked estates with supplies of low quality from their own stores while charging the highest market price. Attorneys who doubled as merchants were able to secure six to twelve months credit on goods shipped from Europe; but they charged their absentee employers, to whom they sold those supplies from the date of delivery, adding an interest rate of 5 per cent per annum until payment was made. In settling accounts with tradesmen or jobbers, unscrupulous attorneys could make out receipts for more money than they actually paid, pocketing the difference. The tradesmen did not suffer. They inflated their prices 15 to 30 per cent in anticipation of the graft of attorneys. In selling estate rum locally, an attorney could purchase the product at a very low price through a silent partner, then resell it for its actual value. Self-seeking attorneys might favour the interests of a mortgagee over those of the owner, calculating that a mortgagee who was becoming powerful in a colony might have the means of advancing his influence, wealth, and authority by affording him the management of other estates.[85]

The practical day by day administration of a sugar estate was vested in a salaried manager[86] whose responsibilities were both diverse and exacting. His expertise was expected to cover planting in all its varied dimensions, the maintenance of stock and the repair of tools, carriages, mill, and buildings. He supervised the grinding and manufacturing process, curing and packaging sugar, and the distillation of rum. He maintained the daily log of estate business and kept small accounts. Concurrently, he superintended the well-being of slaves, mediated in their disputes, and administered rewards and punishments. He was an agricultural expert, an industrial foreman, a social psychologist, and a jurist—all in one—and there is little

[85] An indictment of absentee proprietorship appears in Roughley's *The Jamaica Planter's Guide*, pp. 3–21. The classic modern statement is Ragatz, 'Absentee Landlordism in the British Caribbean, 1750–1833', *Agricultural History*, X (1931). There is a valuable report by Major James Fagan enclosed in a private dispatch, Harris to Grey, 20 Jan. 1847, C.O. 295/156. Some long standing attitudes have been challenged in Douglas Hall's 'Absentee Proprietorship in the British West Indies, to About 1850', *The Jamaican Historical Review*, X (1964), 15–35.

[86] In Jamaica, as distinct from the Lesser Antilles, managers were referred to as overseers. Their subordinates, called overseers in the other colonies, assumed the title 'book-keepers' although they kept no books and were in some cases scarcely literate. In this book the terminology of the Lesser Antilles is employed.

wonder that managers could scarcely be found who were not deficient in one or more categories of responsibility. For his varied services, a manager received between £150 and £300 a year. If the owner or attorney did not reside on the property, he occupied the great house and supplemented his income with a variety of allowances. The nature and extent of those allowances differed from estate to estate according to the whim of the proprietor and the bargaining talent of the manager.[87] They usually involved the use of domestic servants and a horse, as well as the privilege of maintaining a few pigs, poultry, and a garden on the property. Allowances of rum, sugar, and salt provisions were at the disposal of the manager to the extent of his needs.[88] With little fear of detection, a cunning manager was able to maintain more stock than his contract permitted and to employ plantation slaves to raise his own poultry and attend his gardens. To one degree or another all managers deceived their absentee employers. Those who were prudent laid away small savings without jeopardizing their reputations and future prospects.

Beneath the manager, one or more white overseers were employed at miserably low wages of £50 to £75 sterling a year with modest allowances of food and primitive lodging.[89] Overseers were recruited, almost indiscriminately, from the body of needy young adventurers, a great portion of whom were Scotsmen, who arrived each year in Caribbean ports seeking a reversal of their fortunes.[96] Knowledge of sugar culture was no pre-requisite for employment, nor could an employer offering paltry wages, hard labour, and an austere environment expect knowledge or experience from his recruits. The Caribbean overseer endured a voluntary slavery nearly as drudging and considerably more lonely than that of the slaves he supervised. He

[87] Goveia, *Slave Society*, pp. 208–10; Carmichael, *Domestic Manners*, I, 61–2; Davy, *The West Indies*, pp. 132–3.

[88] Pares, *West India Fortune*, pp. 18–19.

[89] Craton and Walvin, *Jamaican Plantation*, pp. 145–7; F. W. N. Bayley, *Four Year's Residence*, p. 84.

[9c] Flanders, *Antigua*, II, 194; Stewart, *Account of Jamaica*, p. 196. Lady Nugent, wife of a Jamaica governor, noted that almost all the agents, attorneys, merchants and shopkeepers of Kingston and its environs were Scotsmen. Cundall, *Nugent's Journal*, p. 40. Henry Breen wrote that a substantial portion of the young men engaging as overseers in St. Lucia were Scotsmen or Irishmen. See his, *St. Lucia*, pp. 159–60.

rose before dawn and observed the work of bondsmen throughout the day, frequently varying the location of his surveillance
from one gang to another, from the field to the mill to the boil-
ing-house. He distributed stores and equipment; he observed
the repair of tools, machines, and buildings; and he supervised
the treatment of stock and the transport of produce to port. In
crop an overseer was required to sit up and watch the slaves
boiling sugar throughout every second or third night. His
entertainment was limited to meals taken at the great house in
his manager's company, where he might consume the less
desirable pieces of chicken, a single glass of his host's wine, and
a head full of jokes and tales at which he felt obliged to laugh.[91]
If an overseer survived his initial years of exposure to sun and
rain, and if he merited the commendation of his superior, he
was likely to secure a managerial position with its relative comforts and its attendant prospects for saving.

Management of estates by paid agents was clearly inferior
to management by permanently resident, temperate, and thrifty
proprietors.[92] But all aspects of the colonial system militated
against resident proprietorship. The acquisition of a sugar
estate with its complement of slaves required extensive capital.
Englishmen who had access to such capital were unwilling to
exile themselves to tropical colonies, and those who earned it
in the West Indies were disposed to retire to Britain to spend it.
When absentee proprietorship became a common practice,
well-founded Caribbean estates were producing enough income
to maintain their trans-Atlantic owners in high style.[93] Although
it was prudent for a proprietor to make occasional visits to the
West Indies to survey the condition of his estate, there was little
reason for him to reside permanently in a portion of the world
where white men were reputed to wilt beneath a torrid sun,
to suffer inordinately from disease, and to die prematurely.
Cynric Williams observed quite correctly that absentees con-

[91] For a colourful account of this type of relation, see *The Traveller's Guide to
Madeira and the West Indies* (Haddington, 1815), pp. 102–4.
[92] R. R. Madden determined that most Jamaica proprietors would save above
£800 a year by maintaining active residence in the island. See his *Twelvemonth
Residence*, I, 164–5.
[93] For an interesting parallel to West Indian landownership, see David Large,
'The Wealth of the Greater Irish Landowners', *Irish Historical Studies*, XV (1967),
21–45.

sidered the sugar colonies 'a sort of infernal region, a purgatory, through which they must occasionally toil to enjoy the Elysian fields of Scotland or Mary-le-bone.'[94]

The common practice of primogeniture reinforced the pattern of absenteeism. Since West India planters who lived in the colonies often educated their children in England, there was always the possibility that an heir, tempted by the comforts of English life, would object to permanent residence in the West Indies. The second sons of Caribbean planters who were sent to England for education frequently remained there, took up employment, raised children, and severed direct relations with the family plantations until, at the death of a father or brother, properties devolved on them by inheritance. Rather than abandon their lives and friends in England, they employed attorneys to manage their estates. In many cases absentees inherited their properties from other absentees, or from relations in the colonies whom they had never known.

There was no easy alternative to West Indian absenteeism. The recommendation, often repeated in the lean years before emancipation, that absentees should assume residence on their Caribbean properties was impractical. Most absentees had never lived in the West Indies. They possessed no agricultural expertise; they had no experience in the management of slaves; and they had little capacity to withstand the rigours of the West Indian environment. During the nineteenth century, West India merchants in England, the principal mortgagees for sugar estates, acquired ownership of many properties. For them there was no alternative to absentee proprietorship. Furthermore, absentees frequently owned property in several colonies. The Codringtons owned the island of Barbuda, had five estates in Antigua, and others in Barbados; John Gladstone held estates in Jamaica and Guiana. Even if these proprietors had chosen to assume residence in the colonies—which, indeed, is hardly conceivable—to which colony or estate would they have gone?

Whatever the flaws of absentee proprietorship, a converse model to the pattern of British absenteeism was not without liabilities. The permanent residence in the colonies of proprietors whose wealth would have been sufficient to establish them

[94] Cynric R. Williams, *Tour Through the Island of Jamaica*, pp. 136–7.

as absentees might have lent distinction to colonial society, talent to colonial government and jurisprudence, and creative genius to colonial arts and letters. But such an élite in a slave society would have constituted a much more rigid agrarian aristocracy than the one which actually arose. Where the size of the resident proprietary was greatest, namely Barbados, the intensity of the colour bar was strongest.[95]

In the final years of slavery, the West Indies were more thoroughly committed to sugar than they had ever been. The agricultural diversity characteristic of the Windward Islands in the eighteenth century had given way to sugar. Cotton was no longer exported from Barbados, the Leewards, or Jamaica. It constituted less than 2 per cent of the exports of Guiana. The few remaining secondary staples were depressed, and there was no new crop, mineral, or industry rising to challenge the paramount importance of sugar or to relieve the islands of their profound dependence upon it. The beleaguered systems of trade and labour which had enthroned King Sugar were on the verge of extinction. It remained to be seen whether the sugar economy would survive their demise.

[95] Sturge and Harvey, *West Indies*, p. 154; Sewell, *Ordeal of Free Labor*, p. 67.

CHAPTER 3

Law and Government

GREAT Britain possessed fourteen sugar colonies in tropical America.[1] Six of them were originally settled by Englishmen; the remaining eight were secured by conquest, beginning with Cromwell's acquisition of Jamaica in 1655. A system of representative or assembly government initially established in the reign of Charles II prevailed in eleven colonies. Trinidad, St. Lucia, and British Guiana—prizes of the protracted conflict with revolutionary and Napoleonic France —were governed under an authoritarian system which reserved all legislative initiative to the Crown or its representative in the colony.

The legislative colonies[2] were bicameral in structure. In those colonies real political power resided in the lower houses of government, the assemblies. During the century and a half preceding emancipation, West Indian assemblies had systematically encroached upon executive authority in order to protect their interests against the corruption and negligence of the British Government. This corruption had been most apparent in the ancient system of patronage whereby many of the most important colonial appointments made in England were delegated to incompetent and idle deputies in the colonies at rates of pay which allowed English absentees the highest possible rent from their offices.[3] Until 1823 the British Government expressed few scruples about the slave system of the Caribbean colonies. It willingly or inadvertently conceded local power to

---

[1] In addition, Britain possessed the Bahamas, Bermuda, British Honduras, the Cayman Islands, and Turks and Caicos Islands. None of these were sugar exporting colonies, and their histories are not encompassed by this study.

[2] Barbados, Jamaica, Antigua, St. Kitts, Nevis, Montserrat, the Virgin Islands, Dominica, Tobago, Grenada, and St. Vincent.

[3] Stewart, *Account of Jamaica*, pp. 38–9; Brathwaite, *Creole Society*, p. 13. As late as the 1840s the office of Island Secretary in Jamaica was held by a deputy of Charles Greville, the English appointee. Metcalfe to Stanley, 6 Mar. 1842, C.O. 137/262, no. 94.

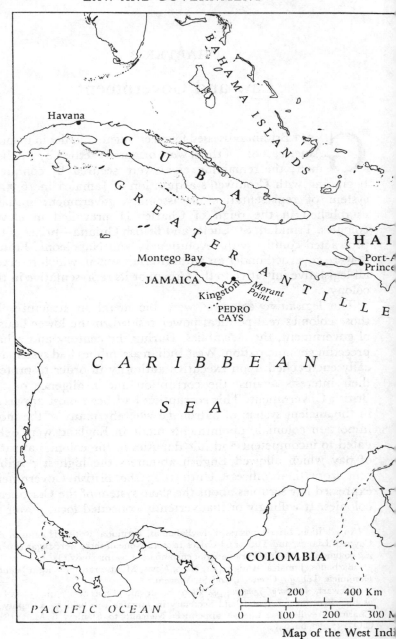

Map of the West Indi

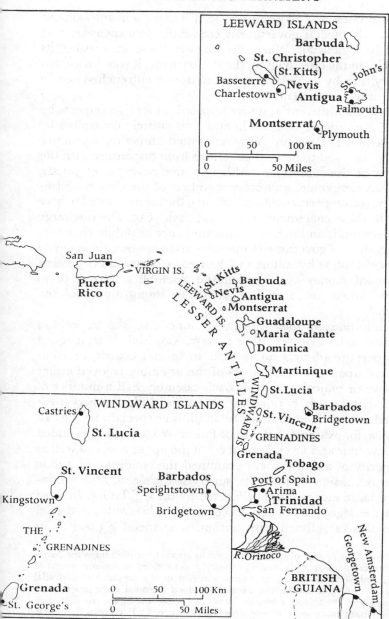

nd British Guiana, 1830

the assemblies, and having done so it found their autonomous exercise of colonial government convenient, inexpensive, and mutually beneficial. When the Crown chose to reassert its authority in the late 1820s on the slavery issue, it was obstructed at every turn by a thickly woven and deeply entrenched system of assembly government.

Except the differential duties imposed on foreign imports by Acts of Parliament, colonial finance was entirely controlled by the assemblies. Revenue Acts were voted annually, a practice initially designed to prevent governors from dispensing with the services of the assemblies. Although the payment of jurists, Anglican clergymen, and other members of the civil establishment rested on permanent enactments, the money raised to give effect to those enactments was voted each year. The discharge of interest on island debts, the maintenance of public charities, the payment of government annuities and pensions, the security of deposits made by suitors in Chancery Courts—all depended on annual money votes which the assemblies were able to suspend when provoked by policies or importunities of the Crown.[4]

In addition to their legislative functions, the assemblies possessed extensive executive powers. Colonial Acts assigned all important administrative tasks to special boards, or commissions, upon which members of the assembly enjoyed either exclusive or majority control. Each assembly had a number of permanent boards performing executive duties; others were created when the need arose to administer special projects. In Jamaica, for example, a Board of Public Works, which included the Governor and several members of the upper house as well as a majority of assemblymen, examined the condition of public structures, assigned contracts, supervised projects, and administered large money grants allocated by the legislature. In 1844 when the legislature voted to construct a lazaretto, a special board was established with authority to spend £3,000 at its

----

[4] Although a stoppage of supplies wrought its greatest hardship upon the colonists themselves, not upon the mother country, it constituted an embarrassment to the imperial Government, the open acknowledgement of a breakdown in colonial affairs. Rather than endure the discomfort which attended such proceedings, governors and councillors normally humoured their assemblies, passing their most important enactments without strenuous objection. C. E. Grey to Earl Grey, 7 May 1849, Confidential, C.O. 137/302.

own discretion on the project. Hospitals, asylums, lighthouses, prisons, schools, charities, and a variety of other public institutions were administered in the same manner.[5] The most powerful of the government boards was the Commission of Public Accounts. It recommended ways and means, appointed tax collectors and regulated their activities; it appropriated money under direction of the assembly, scrutinized the work of the treasurer (a Crown appointee), and, in a haphazard fashion, performed a public audit. The board functioned whether or not the legislature was in session, and it was not affected by dissolution or prorogation. In Jamaica, Commissioners of Public Accounts were drawn exclusively from the Assembly. Elsewhere the board was a joint legislative organ: in Barbados, members of the upper house occupied four seats, assemblymen six; in St. Vincent, assemblymen held four of six seats; in Tobago, five of seven.[6]

Each colonial assembly had a commission of correspondence which maintained communication with an agent in London. Agents were responsible for diplomatic liaison with the Colonial Office and political lobbying in Parliament. In time of crisis, they convened meetings of absentees and conducted propaganda campaigns in their behalf.[7] Their correspondence with British ministers was extensive, and letters defending the policies of their constituents were commonly written with a view to publication in the *Parliamentary Papers*.[8] During the 1820s and 1830s, agents appeared regularly at the Colonial Office to advocate the views of their assemblies on disputed issues and to support Acts of the colonies which arrived in London for confirmation. As a medium of communication between the assemblies and the Secretary of State, they encroached upon the legitimate

[5] On some occasions, members of boards did not hold seats in either house of the legislature. Four of eleven men appointed to the board which administered the public hospital in Kingston were merely inhabitants of the city.

[6] Colebrooke to Newcastle, 20 Mar. 1854, C.O. 28/180, with enclosure.

[7] During the Jamaica constitution crisis of 1839, William Burge, the Colonial Agent, called meetings of absentees and merchants interested in Jamaica, and organized the parliamentary campaign against the Melbourne government's attempt to suspend the constitution of the colony. Burge to Commission of Correspondence, 1 Apr. 1879, enclosed in Smith to Normanby, 11 May 1839, private, C.O. 137/238.

[8] Publication was assured whenever a member of Parliament having West Indian connections presented a motion to that effect in Parliament.

functions of colonial governor. James Stephen, Permanent Under-Secretary for the colonies, was keenly aware of this, and he counselled his political superiors to avoid embracing colonial agents as regular avenues of communication with the assemblies. To do that, he argued, would be 'little else than to transfer the administration of . . . Affairs . . . from the Governor to the Committee of Correspondence'.[9]

In the Lesser Antilles assemblies were perpetually in session. Members lived only a few miles from the seat of government, and they met for a few hours once or twice a month as it suited their convenience.[10] This was not possible in a large island like Jamaica where the Assembly was convened for protracted annual sessions. Meetings commenced in Spanish Town during October and generally concluded before Christmas in order to permit planters to return to their estates for the beginning of crop. After emancipation, the length of legislative sessions in Jamaica increased, and the legislature commonly returned to the capital after a Christmas recess. This worked a hardship on planter members who were obliged to be at their estates for the start of crop, and it contributed to the rising influence of the town party. There was no uniformity in the duration of Caribbean legislatures. Elections occurred in Barbados and Nevis every year; the Montserrat House sat indefinitely; and the Jamaica Assembly, like that of Antigua, was elected septennially.[11]

The upper houses in the legislative colonies—the councils— combined executive and legislative functions. They rendered judgement on all Acts passed by the assemblies, but they did not possess the right to amend fiscal measures. Although councils in the Lesser Antilles retained the privilege of originating Bills which were not designed to raise supplies or to dispose of public

[9] Stephen's minute, bound in Burge to Russell, 6 Feb. 1840, C.O. 137/252. Emancipation rendered the imperial Government more solicitous of the interest of the whole West Indian population. Because colonial agents really only represented the planter élite, they were regarded with suspicion, and the Colonial Office was compelled by political circumstances to maintain a cool official bearing towards them. Visitations at Downing Street by colonial agents were discouraged, and by the mid-forties the agency system was largely defunct.

[10] Wood to Stephen, 22 Apr. 1847, C.O. 323/62 Law Officer's Reports; Colebrooke to Grey, 27 Apr. 1849, C.O. 28/170, no. 20.

[11] Hume Wrong, *Government of the West Indies* (Oxford, 1925), p. 38.

money,[12] the upper house in Jamaica was deprived the ability to originate any measure whatever.[13]

In their executive capacity councils constituted privy councils, bound by secrecy and expected to render advice to their governors on request. To a large extent, however, this latter role had become a meaningless formality. During the prolonged controversy over slavery and in the difficult years that followed emancipation, councils were swayed by public feeling and were often seriously at odds with their executive officers. On one occasion, the Governor of Barbados declared his Council more violent, recalcitrant, and obstructive than the Assembly.[14] Councillors who were drawn from the planter élite were commonly linked by political, social, or family ties with parties in the assembly, and this connection made it impossible for governors to rely upon their confidence.[15] Furthermore, it was difficult to assemble the full privy council on short notice, especially in peak agricultural seasons. In Jamaica, only a few councillors lived in Spanish Town, and during most of the year it was difficult to secure a quorum of five members.[16] In practice, West India governors rarely solicited the advice of their privy councils except when such a gesture served their political interests.[17]

Governors in the legislative colonies were severely constrained in their conduct of office. They had veto power over colonial

[12] Schomburgk, *History of Barbados*, p. 207.

[13] Theoretically, the Jamaica Legislative Council had not relinquished its right to originate Bills, but in practise it was intimidated from doing so by the Assembly's refusal to entertain any measures saving its own. C. E. Grey to Earl Grey, 9 Mar. 1849, C.O. 137/302, no. 32. Between 1679 and 1769, the Council in Jamaica originated 34 Bills, 3 of which passed the Assembly. Between 1769 and 1832 it failed to originate any measures. When the Council tried to revive its powers of initiative in 1832, the Assembly resisted it successfully. W. L. Burn, *Emancipation and Apprenticeship in the British West Indies* (London, 1937), p. 150.

[14] Smith to Lefevre, 31 May 1834, confidential, C.O. 28/113.

[15] Smith to Glenelg, 6 July 1835, confidential, C.O. 28/115. The Jamaica Legislative Council was weaker constitutionally than its counterparts in the Lesser Antilles. As a rule its outlook was more akin to the views of the Governor and less bound to those of the Assembly than pertained in the councils of the smaller islands.

[16] C. E. Grey to Earl Grey, 9 Mar. 1850, C.O. 137/306, no. 25.

[17] In spite of the favourable relations between Sir Charles Metcalfe and both houses of the Jamaican legislature, Metcalfe used his Privy Council only on matters of form, relying for advice almost exclusively on his private secretary. Metcalfe to Stanley, 2 Mar. 1842, separate, C.O. 137/262.

legislation, but they exercised that veto with great caution lest they incur the retaliation of assemblymen who could neglect issues of importance to the British Government or refuse to vote supplies for public services. Governors had no agents in the assemblies through whom they could pursue a coherent legislative policy.[18] Political actions, taken by a governor, which appeared to threaten the jealously guarded independence of an assembly, were invariably construed as breaches of that body's privilege. When Henry Barkly, the newly appointed Governor of Jamaica, dispatched a special message to the Assembly suggesting the postponement of a legislative action, he was publicly ignored and privately reproached.[19] Had he not been new to the office and popular with assemblymen, he would have been declared in breach of privilege, and the Assembly would have suspended its business until Barkly had submitted an appropriate apology.

Until the late 1820s colonial governors were selected with little regard for merit. They received no important direction or supervision from London, and they were expected to accommodate their attitudes and their activities to the requirements of the planters.[20] Emancipation changed that. The labour of governors increased several-fold, and the situation called for men of energy and vision. Notwithstanding that, the Colonial Office had great difficulty filling minor West Indian appointments with qualified men,[21] and it was often compelled to

[18] In some of the Lesser Antilles, governors used public officers who concurrently held seats in the assemblies as informal media for conveying their views to the assemblymen. This practice assured executives a fair hearing, but it did not provide them significant political leverage since the public officers who served as their spokesmen were expected to exercise complete independence from Government House in their capacity as legislators. Howard Aston Rogers, 'The Fall of the Old Representative System in the Leeward and Windward Islands, 1854–1877' (Unpublished Ph.D. Dissertation, University of Southern California, 1970), pp. 50–1.

[19] Barkly to Sir George Grey, 18 Sept. 1854, C.O. 137/324, no. 101.

[20] The burdens of office were light; indeed, the Duke of Manchester, who held the government of Jamaica during most of the period between 1808 and 1828, was utterly indolent. James Stephen remarked of him: 'I do not believe that during all that time he wrote for himself a single Dispatch, or did for himself a single act as Governor, beyond acts of mere ceremony. A colonist, Mr. Bullock, was the real Governor, and of course Lord Bathurst was never warned to distrust the motives or conduct of the Assembly.' Stephen to G. W. Hope, 16 Sept. 1841, bound in C.O. 137/256, no. 234.

[21] Earl Grey, *The Colonial Policy of Lord John Russell's Administration* (London, 1853), I, 41.

solicit nominations for those assignments from the Army.[22] Since deserving executives were commonly promoted from minor to major posts in the Caribbean, a substantial number of governors and lieutenant-governors administering the colonies at any time were senior half-pay officers. Their authoritarian bearing was oddly disproportionate to their limited powers, and in time of great tension many of them lacked the tact, subtlety, and flexibility required to preserve harmony in government. In general, however, the colonies were well served in the emancipation period. This was especially true of Jamaica. The island had traditionally commanded the services of a nobleman, and as late as 1828 its Governor described it as the most valuable colony in the Empire[23]—a statement which fairly reflected the lingering, though incorrect, popular image of Jamaica. In the first two decades of the free era—a period which coincided with the final years of Jamaica's prominence—the colony was governed by men of great ability and distinction, including the Marquis of Sligo, Sir Charles Metcalfe, Lord Elgin, and Sir Charles Edward Grey.

In the legislative colonies, as in England, only a small percentage of the citizenry possessed the franchise or met qualifications for membership in the legislature. Fewer than 2,000 people voted in Jamaica in the elections of 1838.[24] Even after post-emancipation franchise reforms had been enacted, the number of qualified electors in the colonies was small. A few merchants, lawyers, and medical practitioners secured seats in the Jamaica Assembly before 1840, but planters dominated colonial government in the thirties and forties. Barbados merchants petitioned that they were totally unrepresented in their Assembly.[25] In 1837, twenty-two of twenty-five Antigua assemblymen, and all but one of the island's councillors, were planters.[26]

The old legislative system had many defects. Even in Jamaica where it was most highly refined, committees which conducted public inquiries in advance of drafting legislation usually made only the most superficial investigations of local problems. Because time and manpower were in short supply, the assemblies

[22] Hill to Russell, 12 Sept. 1840. *Russell Papers*, PRO 30 22/3E.
[23] Keane to Murray, 21 Nov. 1828, C.O. 137/167, no. 27.
[24] Smith to Glenelg, 25 Dec. 1838, C.O. 137/230, no. 214.
[25] Smith to Spring Rice, 14 July 1834, C.O. 28/113, no. 23.
[26] Sturge and Harvey, *The West Indies*, appendix viii.

copied much of their legislation directly from British statutes. Jobbing was commonplace in the public boards. Commissioners were able to award contracts to friendly parties or to surrogates who acted in their own behalf. In smaller islands, boards met once a month on the same day as the assemblies convened. Business was tardy, payments were perpetually in arrears, and the sickness or prolonged absence of a key member could delay indefinitely the actions of a board. Commissioners of public accounts were often guilty of favouritism. While they scrutinized the records of one creditor, they permitted those of friends to pass unnoticed.[27] Because they administered the collection of taxes they were able to afford relief to favoured taxpayers or collectors; and, indeed, tax collection was a shoddy and irregular business in most of the sugar islands. Once accounts were passed, nothing short of a resolution by a majority of the board could occasion their revision. In Barbados where the Assembly was elected every year and new boards were created with equal regularity, it was virtually impossible to re-examine past transactions.[28]

To judge the old legislative system in terms of its checks and balances, or of the latitude it offered for corruption, is to distort its essential purpose. There was no balance in West Indian government, nor was balance intended. Opportunities for corruption were legion because the system was founded on the mutual trust of members of the colonial élite who managed it in their own interest. Assemblymen and commissioners served without pay, sometimes with distinction, dedication, and personal sacrifice. In the smallest and most sparsely populated islands where assemblies were a mere burlesque, the conduct of public affairs commonly devolved upon one or two conscientious men who prepared Bills, engineered their passage, and dominated important commissions.[29] Elsewhere, the compre-

[27] MacDonnell to Colebrooke, 1 Dec. 1853, enclosed in C.O. 28/179 Windward Islands, no. 8.
[28] C. E. Grey to Stanley, 15 July 1843, C.O. 28/157, no. 52.
[29] Sir William Colebrooke commented on this, as did Stephen, in the minute written in the margins of Taylor's memorandum, 25 Nov. 1840, bound in C.O. 28/138. Stephen claimed: 'When I read a volume even of West India Acts on matters remote from local prejudices, I am almost continually surprised to find how well they are prepared, being as they are the result of unrequited labour, and pure public spirit! I have always supposed that in reality I was reading the work of some one man, whose fortune had led him to a scene affording no other scope

hensive services rendered by assemblymen reduced the cost of government and superceded the need for a colonial bureaucracy. If the Governors of Jamaica, the Windward Islands, and the Leeward Islands in 1840 are to be believed, planters who conducted their own affairs endured higher taxes and were more willing to invest in public welfare projects than their counterparts in the Crown colonies.[30] If corruption were a feature of the legislative system it was no more rife and certainly less grand than political corruption in the mother country.

The quality of assembly government varied from one colony to another depending upon the prosperity of the islands and their capacity to attract able, intelligent, public-spirited men. Good public service depended on a positive public spirit, and the spirit of West Indian communities hinged on their economic well-being. When the property of the governing élite was endangered or seriously devalued, their commitment to the public welfare was impaired. The assembly system worked well in Jamaica during the early forties when the planters expressed some confidence in their economic prospects. It faltered badly after free trade shattered their fortunes. In Barbados, where prosperity was preserved with only temporary setbacks, the colonists maintained a consistently scrupulous and energetic assembly government.[31] In the poorest legislative colonies, economic decay systematically diluted the élite rendering their government negligent, utterly languid, and in some cases farcical.

In contrast to the anomalies of the legislative system, Crown colony government was straightforward and authoritarian.[32] The term, Crown colony, designated a constitutional arrange-

for considerable talents and mental activity. I believe that almost every Colony has some such man who is the real Legislator on all subjects beyond the range of prejudices of the place, and the passions of the day; and it seems to me that almost all the good legislation of the world is the result exactly of this system.'

[30] Henry Taylor reviewed the sentiments of Governors Metcalfe, MacGregor and Colebrooke in a lengthy memorandum, 25 Nov. 1840, bound in C.O. 28/138.

[31] Writing in 1853, Colebrooke declared that Barbados was blessed by an active system of boards which conducted their affairs speedily and reliably. The Board of Lunacy, for example, had sent a local physician to England to study the conduct of asylums there. Colebrooke to Newcastle, 22 Dec. 1853, C.O. 28/179 Windward Islands, 8.

[32] Trinidad and St. Lucia might be called conventional Crown colonies. British Guiana, while subject to the legislative initiative of the Crown, possessed a unique constitution.

ment by which legislative initiative was reserved to the Crown. It did not connote a uniform organization of state. The advent of Crown colony government at the end of the eighteenth century reflected an important change in the character of the British Empire. British victories in the French wars had produced a harvest of new dependencies inhabited by alien people and administered under systems of law which differed fundamentally from those employed in the mother country. The administration of such diverse lands as Ceylon, Mauritius, the Cape of Good Hope, Guiana, and Trinidad, where the loyalties of the people commonly differed from those of the rulers, required firm executive authority and rendered the immediate application of legislative government and English legal institutions neither possible nor desirable.

Trinidad and St. Lucia possessed similar political institutions. Although they had no assembly, each possessed a small legislative council comprising an equal number of official and unofficial members. Official members were the most prominent office holders in the colony: the Chief Justice, the Colonial Secretary, Attorney-General, Treasurer, Solicitor-General, and Collector of Customs.[33] Unofficial members were private citizens, nominated by the Governor and appointed by the Crown. They were selected from the most respectable planters and merchants in the colony, men having substantial economic investments in the staple industry.[34] The Governor sat in the Council and enjoyed a double vote. He organized the business of the Council and initiated all legislation; however, he was not permitted to propose measures involving an outlay of public money without prior sanction of the Secretary of State.[35]

[33] Mein to MacGregor, 4 Aug. 1839, C.O. 295/126, no. 37; Breen, *St. Lucia*, p. 389.

[34] Murray to Sir George Grey, 30 Oct. 1835, C.O. 295/109. Planters were preferred to merchants. The sentiments of the *Guiana Chronicle* would have been echoed in Trinidad and St. Lucia: 'All men of sense and information agree in acknowledging, that in such a Colony as British Guiana, the Agricultural Interest ought to have a decided preponderance in the Local Legislature. . . . We have no manufacture, properly so called: it is our Agricultural classes who consume the bulk of our Imports. Our Merchants would be nothing or next to nothing if our staples failed. Therefore, the Planting Interest ought to have a majority of votes in any Legislature, of any form, that can be granted us.' *The Guiana Chronicle* XXIV, no. 3, 354, 22 May 1839.

[35] Minutes by James Stephen, 6 Jan. 1841, 17 Aug. 1841, 20 Aug. 1841, and 29 Dec. 1841, bound in C.O. 295/133 and C.O. 295/134.

Councillors were expected to advise the Governor and draft legislation proposed by him. The Governor was not required to accept their advice, nor were the councillors compelled to endorse legislation recommended by the Crown. Although official members normally voted with the Governor, affording him a majority, the system did not always function so securely. In the absence of suitable alternatives, well-educated colonial planters were selected for high government office. Their presence in the council gave additional power to the planting interest. In 1836 the Chief Justice of Trinidad complained that the appointment of two planters to the offices of Colonial Secretary and Attorney-General gave the planting interest 'perfect control of the Council upon all questions', in which the planters' well-being was at variance with that of the community at large.[36] Still, the Crown maintained the upper hand, for it possessed the power to legislate for the Crown colonies by Orders in Council. The Orders could not be abrogated or amended by colonial Ordinances. Although it preferred to use its legislative power abstemiously,[37] the Crown imposed far-reaching alterations in the slave codes of Crown colonies by Order in Council, and after 1838 it promulgated the most important measures of social legislation in the same manner.[38]

The constitution of British Guiana, while nearly as authoritarian as those of Trinidad and St. Lucia, had a number of unique features. Although Guiana's legislative council, called the Court of Policy, possessed an equal number of official and unofficial members, the unofficial members were chosen by a curious electoral procedure.[39] Colonists who enjoyed the franchise—which in times of slavery meant the possession of twenty-five slaves—elected seven persons to a College of Electors (Keizers). This body nominated persons to the Court of Policy; as vacancies occurred, the Court of Policy made its

[36] Scotland to Sir George Grey, 20 Sept. 1836, C.O. 295/113 (Scotland Correspondence).

[37] Drafts of a letter to W. H. Burnley, 15 Feb. 1836, C.O. 295/109 (Burnley correspondence).

[38] As a means of abbreviating the review of colonial Ordinances, Orders in Council were used to amend legislation which originated in the Crown colonies. Rather than disallow a colonial Ordinance, explaining the deficiencies of the measure and recommending specific changes, the Colonial Office merely altered the colonial measure to suit itself and promulgated it by Order in Council.

[39] P.P. 1840 XXXIV (404), pp. 3–5.

own choice from among those nominated by the College of Electors. In addition to the Court of Policy, a small group of financial representatives were chosen by election to work in conjunction with the Court to determine the means by which colonial revenue was to be raised. This joint group was called the Combined Court. Although questions concerning the amount of revenue to be levied were theoretically reserved to the Court of Policy, a practice grew up after 1812 whereby the Combined Court determined both the ways and means and the amount of revenue to be raised in the colony. Since the unofficial members of the Combined Court outnumbered the official members, the planter element in the Combined Court had the decisive voice in granting supplies to the colonial Government.[40] This power provided the planting interest a degree of leverage not enjoyed by their counterparts in Trinidad and St. Lucia. During two protracted crisis in the 1840s the Combined Court withheld supplies, and the perennial threat that they might do so obliged the Colonial Office to treat the Guiana planters with considerable deference.[41]

The judicial apparatus of the West India colonies was neither uniform nor efficient. Crown colonies retained the judicial systems of their former rulers. In St. Lucia the system was French; in Trinidad, Spanish. The legal system in British Guiana was Roman Dutch. Although English common law had provided a uniform denominator in the legislative colonies, island legislatures had modified and moulded the courts to satisfy local requirements, causing an infinite variety of distinctions between the several Caribbean colonies. Law courts bore the same titles in all colonies, but their compositions, jurisdictions, and proceedings differed widely.[42]

With rare exception, judges in British Caribbean courts were planters and public men who possessed no legal training. Their

[40] Light to Normanby, 1 May 1839, C.O. 111/163, no. 77.

[41] In 1835 and 1840, governors from adjacent colonies were ordered to British Guiana to mediate between the Governor of the colony and his Combined Court in order to secure the annual supplies. In 1848 and again in 1849 the Combined Court refused to grant supplies for 11 months.

[42] Third Report of the Commissioner of Enquiry into the Administration of Civil and Criminal Justice in the West Indies, 5 Oct. 1826, P.P. 1826–7 XXIV (36), p. 110.

ignorance of the law and their failure to observe regular procedures in court produced the most capricious and inequitable
results.[43] Writing in 1825, Henry Nelson Coleridge considered
the judges of Barbados well-intentioned and conspicuous for
their integrity, but, he added, 'They neither comprehend the
extent, nor are agreed upon the validity of the laws which they
are called upon to interpret; they adhere to no fixed principles;
they are bound by no precedents.'[44] In each colony, a small
pool of persons served as jurors. Because in many colonies there
were no lawyers to preside over juries, the jurists became judges
of law as well as of fact. Decisions of the courts were woefully
lacking in consistency. This undermined confidence in the
system; it impaired the dignity of the bench and promoted
dissension in the community.

Inferior courts which handled the bulk of criminal justice
were dominated by white planters. In Antigua, for example,
only three of thirty-three justices of the peace were men
of colour.[45] Almost all of the eighty-two J.P.s appointed by the
Governor of British Guiana in 1834 were planters.[46] Throughout the islands, unpaid planter justices exercised duties similar
to those performed by their counterparts in England. Governors
of the legislative colonies appointed a number of justices of the
peace for each parish. By virtue of this appointment, J.P.s—
drawn from the most worthy and respectable members of
colonial society—occupied a seat in the parish vestry, a local
governing body which levied taxes and appropriated revenue
for poor relief, public hospitals, and the maintenance of roads
and bridges. In their judicial capacity, J.P.s possessed a summary power to deal with minor criminal offences and violations
of the slave code. As a rule, procedures were informal. Judgements were rendered by individual J.P.s in the parlour of a great
house, and punishment, if it involved the 'cat', followed swiftly
in the yard outside. The principal court of the J.P.s, the Quarter
Sessions, comprised a panel of magistrates. It was held four
times a year and had concurrent jurisdiction with Supreme

[43] First Report of the Commissioner of Enquiry into the Administration of Civil
and Criminal Justice in the West Indies, 16 May 1825, P.P. 1825 XV (517),
pp. 54–5.
[44] Coleridge, Six Months, pp. 295–6.
[45] Sturge and Harvey, The West Indies, appendix x.
[46] Smyth to Stanley, 2 July 1834, C.O. 111/132, no. 136.

Criminal Courts on all cases which did not involve the possibility of capital punishment or transportation.[47]

In a review of jurisprudence in Jamaica, R. R. Madden, a severe critic of the system, declared that blacks received fair and impartial justice in superior as well as inferior tribunals when both parties in the case were black. Madden believed that Chief Justice Sir Joshua Rowe exhibited a bias in favour of blacks and that 'the same crimes with which Negroes stood charged in [the] colony would be visited in England with far greater rigour.'[48] But, argued Madden, white juries and white justices of the peace swiftly abandoned their impartiality when whites were pitted against blacks in court.

In London, West Indian affairs were administered through one of four geographically determined departments of the Colonial Office. A few clerks performed most of the routine labour of the department under the supervision of a senior clerk who was responsible to the Permanent Under-Secretary of State, the highest ranking civil servant in the office. At the summit of the official pyramid were two members of Parliament representing the political party in power, the Secretary of State and his Parliamentary Under-Secretary.

The burden of work in the West Indian Department increased dramatically during the emancipation controversy. Before 1830 correspondence from the colonies was barren of any description which would afford either a public servant or scholar a satisfactory notion about conditions in the West Indies. Each year, the whole annual correspondence of Jamaica fit neatly into a single volume of the public records. By the mid-thirties, however, yearly correspondence from that island was filling four to six volumes, and an equivalent increase was being sustained from every other Caribbean colony.

Most correspondence from the West Indies did not proceed beyond the Senior Clerk or Permanent Under-Secretary. Draft replies to routine letters were undertaken at a low level and sent up the chain for the Secretary of State's signature. The

---

[47] First Report of the Commissioners of Enquiry into the Administration of Criminal and Civil Justice in the West Indies, 29 June 1827, P.P. 1826–7 XXIV (559), p. 113.

[48] Madden, *A Twelvemonth's Residence*, II, 76–7.

Permanent Under-Secretary, James Stephen, exercised an exceptional amount of authority during Lord Glenelg's administration, 1835–1839, and until the latter year he directed the disposition of incoming dispatches of the greatest importance. The minutes which he attached to those dispatches were commonly transformed verbatim into out-letters to colonial governors. On delicate political matters, Stephen called upon the Parliamentary Under-Secretary to draft correspondence. Secretaries of State rarely drafted dispatches, though Earl Grey's profuse memoranda often served, with little change of language, as a basis for official correspondence.

The management of colonial legislation was a more complicated business. Each year the legislation of nineteen slave or former slave colonies arrived in London for review and decision. Stephen, whose task it was to report upon this multitude of legislation, confessed that to 'shape a consistent and steady course through such a maze would . . . baffle any degree of diligence and clearsightedness . . .'[49] Colonial Acts required delicate treatment. Governors who had approved them were prone to consider their rejection a form of reproach to themselves. Rejection was commonly construed as an insult to colonial assemblies, an offence which assumed exaggerated significance in Caribbean states where the disallowance of Acts was frequently applauded by the politically disfranchised black or coloured majority.

Colonial Acts traversed a tortuous route from their initial passage through a local assembly to their final disposition by Order in Council. The colonial governor constituted the first hurdle. If he rejected an Act, it went no further. If he assented to it, he dispatched the Act along with his attorney-general's analysis of it to the Colonial Office. In cases of particular sensitivity a governor might offer an analytical comment of his own, suggesting reasons why the Act should be allowed, or

[49] Stephen to Labouchere, 13 Apr. 1839, C.O. 28/127. James Stephen was Legal Adviser at the Colonial Office from 1813 to 1846. In 1839 he commented, 'On rough estimate I take at 21,000 the number of Laws on which in my time I have had to report my opinion.' Stephen to Vernon Smith, 17 Oct. 1839, C.O. 318/148. Lord John Russell marvelled at his grasp of colonial legislation, declaring that there was 'no chance of our having anyone to follow Mr. Stephen in his comprehensive view of the legislation of our colonies'. Russell memorandum, 19 Oct. 1839, C.O. 318/148.

indicating why he had been obliged to approve it in spite of certain deficiencies. Acts which fell within the province of the Board of Trade were transferred to that office for decision. All other measures passed under the scrutiny of the Legal Adviser of the Colonial Office who reviewed them in reports addressed directly to the Secretary of State. Acts which involved matters of concern to the Treasury, the Ordinance Department, the Home Office, or any other agency of government were referred to those departments for comment. In describing the system to a colleague, Stephen observed: 'Four or five copies must be made of all the Titles, and about as many letters must pass between different Departments, each of which approaches the subject reluctantly, and stands in need of continual flapping . . .''[50] When advice had been gathered from various departments and a decision on the Act was rendered at the Colonial Office, the measure was sent to the Lord President to be laid before the King in Council. The King in Council referred it to a Committee of the Privy Council whose membership was identical to that of the Board of Trade, although by a legal fiction the two boards were considered separate and distinct.[51] The Privy Council normally accepted the advice of the Colonial Office and reported accordingly to the King in Council. Thereupon, orders were drawn up in the Council Office and sent to the Colonial Office for transmission to the colonies. If the Act were approved, the Order in Council "left it to its operation" which, technically speaking, was not an assent to the law but rather an intimation that the King did not intend to exercise his prerogative of disallowance. On many occasions, however, Acts of the colonial legislatures were passed with suspending clauses which declared that they would not take effect unless specifically confirmed by the Sovereign. If such an Act were approved, the King was obliged to perform a legislative function, issuing an Order in Council which 'specifically confirmed and finally enacted' the measure.[52] Unless an Act having a suspending

---

[50] Stephen to Vernon Smith, 17 Oct. 1839, C.O. 318/148.

[51] The Secretary of State for the Colonies was a member of the Committee of the Privy Council, but in order to save himself the inconvenience of attending it, he dispatched a minute to the Committee stating his opinion of the Act in question and acknowledging the views of whatever other departments had been consulted in the course of deliberations on the Act.

[52] An explicit statement of this process is provided in a memorandum by James

clause was confirmed within a period of three years, it was effectively disallowed.

The system was much simpler in the case of Crown colonies. Measures produced by the nominative legislatures, always termed Ordinances, could be confirmed in part, rejected in part, or confirmed with amendments. The ultimate decision on Ordinances rested with the Secretary of State, and the elaborate arrangements undertaken for Acts of the assemblies were entirely dispensed with.[53] When imperial authorities chose to amend a colonial Ordinance, the Secretary of State sent a draft of a legislative order to the Lord President for the consideration of the King in Council. The draft was referred to the Law Officers of the Crown, and subject to their revisions, it was promulgated as an Order in Council.

The most vexing problem associated with colonial legislation was the agonizing delay occasioned by consultation between the Colonial Office and other departments. The Treasury and Board of Trade were the worst offenders. They engaged in petty jurisdictional disputes, and colonial business referred to them commonly suffered delays of two to four months—occasionally of a year.[54] The Treasury assumed increasing control over all government spending during the 1830s, and items of colonial expenditure involving the smallest denominations required their approval. The Board of Trade's dilatory review of revenue Acts provoked great embarrassment at the Colonial Office. When reviewing a Barbados Act in 1845 involving the imposition of export and import duties, Stephen wrote:

Stephen, dated 1839, which appears in the *Russell Papers*, PRO 30 22/3C; also, Stephen to Hope, 6 Sept. 1841, C.O. 323/56, Law Officer's Reports. For a scholarly treatment of the process of review, see D. B. Swinfen, *Imperial Control of Colonial Legislation* (Oxford, 1970), pp. 11–20.

[53] The process of review, including reports to the Secretary of State, undertaken by the legal counsel were not required in the case of Ordinances passed by Crown colony legislatures, the members of which were nominees of the Crown. In practice, Stephen did review Crown colony Ordinances, but rather in the capacity of Permanent Under-Secretary than of legal counsel, and his reports on them were submitted to the Parliamentary Under-Secretary in the form of minutes on regular dispatches rather than to the Secretary of State in the manner of formal reports. Memorandum, Stephen to Hope, 3 June 1842, bound in C.O. 295/136, no. 45.

[54] Paul Knaplund, 'Mr. Oversecretary Stephen', *Journal of Modern History*, I (1929), p. 45.

This Act is passed in amendment and continuation of a similar Act of the year 1843, which, however, is still under the consideration of the Board of Trade. . . . the effect of such delays is nothing less than to abdicate the authority over the commercial Legislation of the Empire at large which Parliament has so repeatedly asserted and reserved to the Crown.[55]

Throughout the mid-century, the annoying decentralization of authority, the overlapping jurisdiction of departments, and the consequent protraction of colonial business constituted a continuing obstacle to efficient colonial administration.[56]

Notwithstanding these difficulties, West Indian affairs were generally well managed within the Colonial Office. After 1825, Caribbean matters were handled principally by Henry Taylor, Senior Clerk, and James Stephen, Legal Adviser of the office from 1813 to 1846 and Permanent Under-Secretary between 1836 and 1847. Both men possessed extraordinary intellectual endowments and great literary acumen. Stephen was a shy, nervous, deeply sensitive, and utterly precise man. Son of a leading abolitionist,[57] he was raised in the bosom of the Clapham sect and married to the daughter[58] of one of its members. He was the most gifted, industrious, and dedicated member of the office, but his family connections and strong personal convictions rendered his services controversial. The West India planters regarded Stephen a natural enemy, and twice during 1829–30 Wellington objected to his drafting of slavery Ordinances, asserting that his work was biased in favour of the slaves.

In spite of his anti-slavery views, Stephen deplored the declamatory excesses of abolitionists. He was reluctant to afford the emissaries of Exeter Hall interviews at Downing Street, and he advised the staff to abstain from communicating with anti-slavery leaders, fearing that such exchanges would be

---

[55] Stephen to Stanley, 20 Mar. 1845, C.O. 323/60, Law Officer's Reports.

[56] Swinfen, *Colonial Legislation*, pp. 33–5.

[57] Stephen's father, James Stephen, Sr., wrote a two volume study *The Slavery of the West India Colonies Delineated* (London, 1824) which being based on slave law as opposed to social practice in the islands, was a searing but grossly distorted assessment of West Indian slavery. Stephen's brother, George, was a leading figure in the Agency Committee, the most radical segment of the anti-slavery movement in the years immediately preceding emancipation.

[58] Stephen married Jane Catherine Venn, daughter of John Venn, who was Rector of Clapham and one of the founders of the Church Missionary Society.

either fruitless or pernicious.[59] Nevertheless, Stephen's own associations with Exeter Hall—his father made a final ceremonial appearance there in 1832—were more profound than he cared to admit. In his approach to West Indian policy he bore the unmistakable mark of the missionary idealist, being deeply suspicious of the planters, revolted by their social behaviour, and vexed by a system of rule which provided them undiluted control over the apparatus of local government.

Stephen doubted both the willingness and the capacity of the planters to initiate meaningful social reform. He also questioned the economic soundness of the sugar colonies under a system of free labour. Writing in 1840, he declared himself no believer in the future prosperity of Jamaica: 'I am convinced that the inevitable tendency of things is toward the substitution of small holdings and a Peasantry living on detached Plots of Land, for the old system of large Plantations.'[60] This prospect caused him far less alarm than any of his political superiors, and in contrast to some of them, he remained obdurately opposed to infringing the personal liberty of labouring people as a means of preserving the existence of the plantations. His comment upon Barbados, a colony possessing a large and firmly intrenched resident proprietary, sheds light on his expectations: 'I look to the assertion of an absolute supremacy by the People of Colour, as an inevitable and not very distant event. The policy of the Government shd I think be directed to the object of divesting their success, when at length obtained, of the character of a triumph, with its attendant persecutions.'[61]

Stephen's most trusted lieutenant and firm friend, Henry Taylor, held the post of Senior Clerk in the West India Department until 1872. Taylor was a pragmatist, not a philosopher,

[59] Anti-Slavery Society Papers, C.O. 137/252; Stephen to Grey, 21 Sept. 1838, C.O. 318/141. Stephen was contemptuous of the ignorance exhibited by many of the lobbyists who took West Indian business under their particular patronage, and he was especially annoyed by the long, often inaccurate memorials received from 'bodies of unknown and irresponsible men'. In reply to one such memorial written by Samuel Prescod, liberal anti-slavery figure in Barbados, Stephen commented: 'A petition for the redress of grievances from the hands of a man who writes a newspaper, and who declaims at Exeter Hall can hardly be expected to confine itself within the bounds of what is practical and to the purpose.' Stephen to Vernon Smith, 25 July 1840, bound in C.O. 28/134, no. 55.

[60] Minute by Stephen, bound with Burge to Russell, 8 Sept. 1840, C.O. 137/252.

[61] Stephen to George Grey, 18 Aug. 1835, bound in C.O. 28/115.

and as such he provided a moderating influence upon Stephen which the Permanent Under-Secretary recognized and appreciated. Garrulous and straightforward, Taylor was spared the agonizing complications of Stephen's introverted personality. He abhorred the prejudices and persecutions of the planters, but he was not driven by the passionate solicitude for Caribbean blacks which dominated the sentiments and occasionally warped the judgement of James Stephen.

Taylor was the most worthy and distinguished of the senior clerks. Although Gladstone and others considered offering him a colonial government or promoting him out of the office, he discouraged those invitations, and in 1847 he rejected an offer to succeed Stephen as Permanent Under-Secretary in order to retain sufficient leisure time for his private literary endeavours.[62] He placed the highest premium on efficiency, and he manifested an invaluable capacity to render sound judgement in the shortest time with a minimal exchange of minutes and memoranda.

During the latter part of his career, Taylor was beset by an asthmatic condition which forced him to perform almost all his official work at home. He rarely spent more than an hour a day at Downing Street, remaining altogether absent for extended periods. The daily administration of the West India Department during the 1850s passed to Charles Cox, a man of modest abilities who later became Senior Clerk in the Australian section. Although this arrangement was awkward, it was readily endured as a means of retaining Taylor's services, for, as Herman Merivale, Stephen's successor, observed: 'Mr. Taylor's powers of judgment, experience, and most of all of writing, are what they always were, quite unrivalled in this office.'[63]

It has been asserted that the great need of the Colonial Office in the 1830s was for able men,[64] a charge which gains authority by Stephen's description of drones of little talent

---

[62] Henry Taylor, *Autobiography* (London, 1885), I, 233–5. A friend of Wordsworth and Southey, Taylor is principally remembered for his *Philip van Artevelde*, a highly popular poetic drama published in 1834. Two years later he produced *The Statesman*, an important contribution to nineteenth-century political theory.

[63] Merivale to Newcastle, 29 Sept. 1859, *Newcastle Papers*, 10,897.

[64] J. C. Beaglehole, 'The Colonial Office, 1782–1854', *Historical Studies*, I (1941), 183.

and no industry who inhabited the shabby precincts of 14 Downing Street as a result of the patronage of important people. This condition should evoke no wonderment. The duties of a minor clerk were routine and painfully dull; or in Huskisson's words, 'nugatory and contemptible'. As a rule, gifted men who required intellectual challenge and stimulation either succeeded rapidly to positions of authority, like Taylor, or departed the office in favour of more interesting careers, as in the case of James Spedding and the future Cardinal Manning.[65] Spedding was a friend of Taylor's who joined the Colonial Office in 1835 to help relieve the mounting pressure of correspondence in the West India section. His acute power of analysis swiftly won the respect of Stephen who described his intellect as 'always serene, always in motion . . . a most clear-sighted and equitable judge of men and things . . .'[66] Spedding produced superb memoranda on a wide variety of colonial problems and he assumed the task of reviewing the quarterly reports of West Indian magistrates, abstracting vital data and analysing social and economic developments for the Secretary of State. Spedding resigned his position in 1841 to devote the remainder of his life to research on the philosophy and life of Bacon. Although Stephen recommended him as a permanent consultant to the Colonial Office, and at Taylor's suggestion he was offered the position of Permanent Under-Secretary in 1847, he never returned to the office which for six years had rewarded his exceptional services at the meagre rate of £150 a year.

When the slavery question subsided, colonial affairs received comparatively little notice in the Cabinet, the Parliament, or the press. The office of Secretary of State held no allurement for experienced ministers at the height of their careers. Nevertheless, gifted and distinguished figures, who, by the fortunes of politics stood at the fringes of power, occasionally assumed the seals of office. Lord Stanley, a renegade Whig, was offered the Colonial Office by Peel in 1841 as a reward for his parliamentary opposition to Melbourne; and Earl Grey, whose maverick

---

[65] Commenting on the adversity of men who relied for their livelihood on government service, Stephen said: 'You may write off the first joint of your fingers for them, and then you may write off the second joint, and all that they will say of you is, "What a remarkably short-fingered man!"' Taylor, *Autobiography*, I, 235.

[66] Caroline Emelia Stephen, *James Stephen, Letters with Biographical Notes* (London, 1906), p. 100.

qualities had cast a shadow over his natural talents and damaged his standing among the Whigs, took the colonial ministry during Russell's first Government. Russell himself administered the Empire between 1839 and 1841 after performing the more exalted services of Home Secretary and leader of the House of Commons. His case constitutes the lone exception to the rule that the most prominent and powerful statesmen of the mid-century abjured the administration of the colonies.

During prolonged periods, colonial affairs received little guidance from the men who occupied the ministry. Some of them, including Russell, arrived at Downing Street woefully and admittedly ignorant of the dependencies they administered. The dilatory habits of Lord Glenelg in the thirties, and the rapid succession of ministers during the fifties—eight in seven years—enhanced the importance of the permanent staff without affording them the power or leisure to generate a comprehensive and forceful colonial policy.

Glenelg was unfit by temperament to preside over a government department. Kindly, unoffending, honest, and contemplative, he lacked an active and assertive spirit. He was overwhelmed and intimidated by the complexity of his office, and he had neither the will nor the energy to surmount his trepidation. His weakness was partly redeemed by the industry of his Parliamentary Under-Secretary, Sir George Grey, but during the troubled years of his administration, 1835 to 1839, when colonial affairs required a firm hand and clear direction, they secured neither. The magnitude of Canadian, South African, and West Indian problems which Glenelg confronted would have baffled the intelligence, exhausted the spirit, and injured the reputation of the most able of ministers. His shortcomings cannot be assigned to his failure to conciliate the colonists or to erect a viable strategy for the governance of empire. Events were moving too swiftly for that. Rather, Glenelg is culpable because he brought neither energy nor resourcefulness to the conduct of imperial affairs. In all the prodigous quantity of West Indian correspondence, minutes, and memoranda collected in the public records, Glenelg's hand is scarcely evident, and we have only Stephen's witness to assure us that he was constantly consulted on matters of signal importance. Glenelg was an embarrassment to his own party. Howick criticized his drifting administration with unrelenting vigour, and in February 1839 Lord John Russell threatened to resign from the cabinet unless Glenelg was relieved of office,[67] a threat which had its intended effect.

Within seven months of Glenelg's resignation, Russell became Secretary of State. His manner was firm and decisive; the permanent staff admired him; and Stephen commended his 'dominant soul'. But his education in colonial affairs was scarcely finished before the Whigs fell from power and the office was transferred to Lord Stanley. An orator of rare ability, Stanley possessed the combative instincts of a party politician. He lacked the qualities of a philosophical statesman and he derived little pleasure from his labours at the Colonial Office. He had no patience with the sentimentality of Exeter Hall, but he nourished a sentimental devotion to the old imperial system which, he believed, conferred wealth, power, and prestige upon the mother country. Authoritarian in outlook, he expressed less solicitude for the individual liberty of West India freedmen than for the plight of hard pressed planters whose economic survival was crucial to Stanley's concept of empire. Taylor disliked him, thinking him cold, haughty, and vain—a talented but dissembling politician who, though wilfully independent, exploited the intellectual prowess of his subordinates without due expressions of gratitude. Stephen described him 'a stupendous glacier', and like Taylor he resented Stanley's offhanded and neglectful treatment, although this neglect stemmed in part from their fundamental policy differences.

The most energetic and purposeful Colonial Secretary of the mid-century and the man who held the office for the longest single term, 1846–52, was Earl Grey. Grey was the perfect antithesis of Glenelg. He possessed an enormous aptitude for business and was attentive to every detail of his office. His ubiquitous, often lengthy, notations on correspondence and his extensive memoranda on questions of great and small significance enrich the public records and afford clear evidence of his extraordinary command of colonial affairs. Courteous and candid with his subordinates, he merited their admiration and

[67] Russell to Melbourne, 2 Feb. 1839, *Russell Papers*, PRO 30 22/3C.

inspired in them an industry and diligence which mirrored his own. His commendable vigour was partly offset by his over-zealous, self-confident dogmatism. Unlike Glenelg, whose distrust of general rules and simple solutions formed an impediment to action, Grey exuded a fierce decisiveness based on his excessive attachment to doctrinal beliefs. He was an ardent free-trader, intolerant of opposing views and indifferent to exceptional cases which failed to conform to his rigid principles of political economy. He had the naive belief that all people, regardless of social or cultural differences, responded to the same stimuli that inspired the cupidity and generated the industry of Europeans. In his correspondence with West Indian governors he persistently recommended tax plans and other policies which, though feasible in Europe, were positively unworkable in the Caribbean. Whatever his deficiencies, Grey brought clarity, strength, and cohesion to the conduct of West Indian policy, an achievement unequalled by his predecessors and dissipated by his numerous successors.

By no stretch of the imagination did the Colonial Office rule the Empire. Power was diffused between Westminster and the dependencies. The British Government could recommend legislative action; it could reject colonial measures which it disapproved; and, as evidenced in the Act for the abolition of slavery, the Secretary of State could carry an extraordinary measure of great magnitude through Parliament requiring a major alteration of colonial institutions. But initiative in ordinary legislation was vested in the colonial assemblies. They were able, at their own risk, to reject the advice of the Secretary of State or to modify his recommendations to satisfy their own requirements. They claimed a far greater knowledge of local conditions than the staff at Downing Street, an assertion which imperial authorities readily acknowledged and normally took into consideration when reviewing colonial Acts. Furthermore, the colonists employed numerous devices to exert their will in defiance of the objectives of the Colonial Office. They passed measures without suspending clauses, the effects of which were irreversible. For example, in 1823 the Jamaica Assembly passed an Act which empowered local commissioners to sell slaves attached to the Governor's residence. Lacking a suspending clause, the Act became immediately effective and the slaves were sold. Although Stephen and the Colonial Secretary strongly disapproved the action, preferring to retire the government slaves, they had little recourse but to allow the measure, since disallowance after a considerable lapse of time would have annulled the contracts of sale and imposed on the Government of Jamaica the onerous and complicated burden of locating the slaves in question and refunding money to those who had purchased the slaves.[68]

On many occasions, colonial assemblies deliberately delayed the passage of vital enactments until the last moment so that a governor, regardless of his opposition to some elements of that legislation, could not veto it. An objectionable Barbados Police Act was passed at the eleventh hour in 1834, purposely, the Governor declared, 'to force [his] consent, rather than leave the Town without a Police . . .'[69] Colonial assemblies were in the habit of passing annual Acts which, in view of the time required for their review and referral in London, could not be disallowed with effect. In the West Indies, where the civil code exercised during slavery was gradually moderated by the advice of the Colonial Office, the Secretary of State was reluctant to disallow Acts which did not inculcate all the reforms he desired lest his rejection of them revive more severe earlier laws or leave the colonies without any law at all. The impotence of the Secretary of State in many cases of West Indian legislation is aptly summarized by a comment of Henry Taylor's made in reference to a dubious Jamaica measure involving the organization of a general police force: 'The [imperial] Gov't seems to me to be without power in this matter. The previous act was annual and if this were refused there wd be none. This act is annual also and the Assembly will no doubt do as they please in future years.'[70]

---

[68] Manchester to Bathurst, 3 Apr. 1827, with minute by Stephen, C.O. 137/165, no. 4.

[69] Smith to Spring Rice, 26 Aug. 1834, C.O. 28/113, no. 34.

[70] Henry Taylor's marginal notation on Wood to Stephen, 23 July 1847, C.O. 323/62, Law Officer's Reports. Even in the Crown colonies it was possible for a governor in collusion with the colonists to avoid the censure of the Secretary of State. In 1840, Acting Governor Mein discovered five Ordinances which his predecessors in Trinidad had not referred to London. Mein to Russell, Mar. 1840, C.O. 295/129, nos. 2, 5. In this case, there is no evidence that Sir George Hill, Mein's predecessor, had deliberately deceived the Colonial Office; rather it appears the failure to submit these Ordinances was a matter of oversight.

Lord John Russell abhorred the indignity of badgering assemblymen 'who did not choose to listen, and whom you cannot compel to alter their course'.[71] In concurring with Russell's sentiments, Stephen set out the alternatives available to the Colonial Office.

they who govern must rule either by power, by motives addressed to mass interests . . . or by argumentation addressed to their understandings. The Government of this country is without either of the two first resources, when applying to a West India Assembly for improvements in their Laws. The alternative is between argumentative Despatches, dogmatic Despatches and absolute silence.[72]

Before and immediately after emancipation, the administration of colonial laws remained in the hands of unpaid local magistrates who were mainly planters or salaried public officers who had spent many years in the colonies and inculcated the prejudices of the European élite. The labouring population was rural, dispersed, and ignorant of the fine details of the law; consequently, evasion or neglect of justice was achieved with facility by men of property and power. In many instances, Stephen's careful scrutiny of colonial Acts was little more than an academic exercise.

It is a problem, admitting of no intelligible solution, [he declared] how wise and safe laws shall be made for the government of a Society in which confidence cannot be reposed in the judicial administrators of the Law . . . Whether it is better that good Laws should be made to be executed by bad Judges, or that a country possessing bad Judges should remain destitute of such Laws, might seem to be the alternative in which the choice is to be made . . .[73]

The Colonial Office was equipped to supervise the affairs of the colonies, not to govern them. The permanent staff was occupied by routine business—the perpetual, often onerous, duty of 'getting off the mails'—and they possessed neither the time, the machinery, nor the depth of personnel to assert and maintain the initiative in colonial government. Political officers came and went, often with such disquieting speed that they left no mark by which their administrations could be dis-

---

[71] Minute, L. J. Russell, 10 Dec. 1839, bound in C.O. 28/128, no. 102.

[72] Minute, Stephen, 11 Dec. 1839, bound in C.O. 28/128, no. 102.

[73] Stephen to Normanby, 11 Apr. 1839, C.O. 323/54, Law Officer's Reports.

tinguished. The most esteemed and competent Colonial Secretaries were deeply involved in Cabinet affairs, and their political Under-Secretaries had extensive parliamentary duties to perform. Stephen and Taylor lamented the absence of any instrumentality by which the Colonial Office could pursue far-sighted philosophical government for the Empire. In 1839 Stephen proposed the creation of a formal consultative body comprised of men conspicuous for their knowledge of imperial affairs who could study matters of utility for the colonies, propose strategies for the conduct of colonial government, and advise the Secretary of State on matters of extreme delicacy.[74] Failing that, he suggested that the Colonial Office employ on the permanent staff one or two men of proven competence who could devote their attention to deliberating on the complex problems which confronted the Empire. He was disappointed on both counts. The Colonial Office continued, as before, to respond to colonial problems as they arose, making policy in the shadow of emergency without any clear conception of where that policy would lead.

Had the Colonial Office developed a contemplative dimension, it could not have overcome the two key obstacles to the exercise of philosophical colonial government: the perennial commitment of successive ministries to economy in government, and the ignorance and unreliability of Parliament on matters relating to the Empire. The Treasury elevated economy to the status of religion limiting the latitude of colonial ministers to initiate reforms, to sustain programmes of economic value for the dependencies, or to employ meritorious public servants in sufficient numbers to exert effective control over local affairs. As one Secretary of State observed, colonial projects which were important enough to warrant Cabinet consideration usually required monetary support, and that always involved a collision with the Chancellor of the Exchequer.[75] Because the West India colonies maintained fifteen separate public establishments for a composite population which, had it occupied a single unbroken continental tract, could have been administered by one set of functionaries, their cost to the public service

---

[74] Stephen to Vernon Smith, 4 Oct. 1839, *Russell Papers* PRO 22/3C.
[75] Colin Clifford Eldridge, 'The Colonial Policy of the Fifth Duke of Newcastle' (Unpublished Ph.D. Dissertation, University of Nottingham, 1966).

was considered extravagant. Projects that involved additional outlay were decidedly unwelcome.

Measures necessitating a fundamental restructuring of colonial institutions required the consent of Parliament, a body which took little interest in colonial affairs. With few exceptions, M.P.s—like the member who referred to the 'island' of British Guiana—were ignorant of the dependencies and not anxious to be informed.[76] The colonies had no representation in the House of Commons, and debates on colonial issues were commonly conducted before half-empty, somnolent houses. Henry Taylor declared that it was virtually impossible to obtain Parliament's consent to a strong colonial measure until the evil which that measure was intended to check had assumed such vast and dangerous proportions that it provoked a loud and sustained cry for action.[77] On the other hand, the unreliability of Parliament when finally roused to action rendered the Colonial Office exceedingly reluctant to solicit its intervention to correct abuses in the colonies. The department's attitude was reinforced by its bitter defeat in 1839 when a politically inspired House of Commons repudiated the Government's attempt to suspend the Jamaica constitution and precipitated the resignation of Lord Melbourne. Wary of a capricious Parliament and constrained by the Treasury, the Colonial Office was in no position to afford dynamic leadership to the Empire.

The institutions of West Indian law and government, forged in the era of slavery, were controlled by a thin European élite and administered in their interest. Generations of neglect by the British Government had strengthened the grip of planter oligarchs and permitted their usurpation of executive power. This élite initiated legislation, controlled the purse, dominated the courts, and defied the King's representatives at will. The planters had endless opportunities for corruption for their system was founded on the mutual trust of oligarchs. Although

---

[76] The colonists were aware of British ignorance concerning the dependencies. A letter appeared in the *Guiana Chronicle*, 8 Mar. 1839 stating, 'British Guiana is only very partially known even to the better informed classes of society at home and in many of the rural districts not even by name'.

[77] Taylor's draft of a confidential dispatch which, though not sent, is bound in C. E. Grey to Earl Grey, Confidential, 21 Feb. 1849, C.O. 137/301.

the colonies produced numerous worthy and dedicated men whose service to the proprietary interest was balanced in so far as slavery permitted by a sincere paternalistic commitment to the welfare of the whole community, the psychology of the oligarchs—even the most fair-minded—was shaped by slavery. Their social, political, and racial prejudices reinforced their economic interests. The massive changes which emancipation wrought in the structure of West Indian society were not attended by significant changes in the character of colonial courts and governments. Nor could such changes have been achieved in view of the constitutional arrangements between London and the Caribbean and the emphasis placed by both parties on economy in government. Freedom was grafted upon an exclusive system which was ill-equipped in sentiment and character to administer a free society.

PART II

THE GREAT EXPERIMENT, 1830–1865

CHAPTER 4

Emancipation

THE abolition of slavery in the British Empire was the
first major act of emancipation in modern times. It was not
achieved without great difficulty, but in contrast to Brazil
or the United States, political and economic circumstances
prevailing within the British Empire facilitated the work of
abolitionists. British slavery, unlike that of the large American
states, was confined to colonies, and its abolition posed no significant threat to the well-being or prosperity of the metropolitan community. It was possible for abolitionists and their allies
to argue that the trade of Britain was not increased, the wealth
of her citizenry not enlarged, and the extent of her power not
enhanced by the presence of slavery in the West Indies. In the
United States the national abolition of slavery by peaceful
legislative means would have required a constitutional amendment ratified by three-fourths of the states—an impossibility
where half the states in 1830 supported slavery. In Britain
abolition merely required an Act of Parliament. Parliament
continued to claim the right to legislate for the Empire. Though
it had been reluctant to exercise that right after 1778, it had
not formally relinquished it. In view of this, British abolitionists
pursued a clear and singular strategy: they admonished
Parliament to abolish colonial slavery by legislative action.
Their campaign was waged on moral grounds, and the debate
over slavery which occupied British attention for a full decade
was as colourful as it was intense. Since that debate has received
extensive treatment from other historians,[1] it will occupy our
attention only briefly. The main purpose of this chapter is to
examine political developments between London and the
Caribbean colonies during the slavery controversy and to
focus upon the main social and economic objectives which

---

[1] Detailed treatments may be found in William Law Mathieson, *British Slavery
and Its Abolition, 1823–1838* (London, 1926) and Ragatz, *Fall of the Planter Class*.

emancipationists—whether private citizens or government officials—hoped to achieve as a result of the abolition of British slavery.

When the Society for the Mitigation and Gradual Abolition of Slavery Throughout the British Dominions was formed in 1823, its membership comprised only five Lords and fourteen members of the House of Commons.[2] Against these few stood the West India interest, the most powerful non-political pressure group in Parliament with at least 56 M.P.s having a personal interest in slavery.[3] To that point, the anti-slavery movement had suffered considerable frustration. The abolition of the slave trade in 1807 had not produced the amelioration of slavery predicted by the Saints,[4] that is, the steady transformation of chattel slaves into benign and improving serfs. A campaign to institute slave registration in the colonies had taken five years to bear fruit.[5] There was little public interest in the slavery question; the Tory Government had discouraged further controversy on the issue; and Wilberforce, the venerated leader of the movement, weak with age and infirmity, was unable to direct another parliamentary campaign. When, after a year's deliberation, Sir Fowell Buxton accepted the mantle of leadership from Wilberforce, it is little wonder that his position on the slavery question was marked by moderation.

Gradualism dominated anti-slavery counsels in the 1820s. When Buxton raised the slavery issue in Parliament on 15 May

[2] Sir Reginald Coupland, *The British Anti-Slavery Movement* (New York, 1964), p. 121.

[3] Dr. Lushington counted this number in the House of Commons. See, Mathieson, *British Slavery and Abolition*, p. 118.

[4] Humanitarians (often Evangelicals or Quakers with their intellectual roots in the Clapham Sect) who had initiated the campaign to abolish the slave trade and continued to crusade against slavery and other forms of oppression in the colonies were labelled 'Saints' by contemporaries. Though the term was conceived as one of mild derision, it has had lasting quality. In this book, the term will be used frequently to designate anti-slavery forces in Britain.

[5] In 1812 James Stephen, Sr., obtained support of the Clapham group to press for a measure introducing a general registration of slaves. If all slaves were registered, he perceived, illicit importations from Africa could be more easily controlled. Wilberforce first pressed a Registration Bill in Parliament in 1815. The Government opposed parliamentary enactment of the measure, and with some difficulty commended the plan to West Indian legislatures. By 1820 Slave Registration Acts had been passed in all the Caribbean colonies, and a central registry for maintaining colonial registers was set up in London by Act of Parliament.

1823, he declared himself opposed to 'sudden emancipation'; instead he recommended 'such preparatory steps, such measures of precaution, as, by slow degrees, and in a course of years, first fitting and qualifying the slaves for the enjoyment of freedom shall gently conduct us to the annihilation of slavery'.[6] The protracted controversy over slave registration had convinced abolitionists that colonial legislatures would not willingly reform the system of slavery. The Saints did not oppose oligarchic government in the Caribbean, but they did demand that Parliament impose reforms on colonial society and prepare the slaves for freedom. It was just such a use of parliamentary prerogative that the Tory Ministry wished to avoid. Since the American War of Independence, Parliament had demurred from legislating upon domestic affairs in the colonies, and, as we have seen, West Indian legislatures had gradually assumed a practical autonomy over the conduct of local government. This arrangement—being simple, convenient, and inexpensive —pleased metropolitan Ministers as well as the colonists. George Canning, Tory leader in the House of Commons, was no friend of the plantocracy. But he was unwilling to abrogate existing constitutional arrangements with the colonies, and he was determined to maintain Government—as opposed to parliamentary—control over the amelioration of slavery.[7] When he failed to discourage the Saints from bringing the slavery issue before Parliament, he took steps to neutralize their effect. Government Ministers met representatives of the West India interest privately to work out a mutually satisfactory approach to the problem. It was determined that the Ministry would press its own measures of amelioration, outmanoeuvring the Saints and keeping matters under the Government's direction. In turn, the West Indians agreed to accept 'a progressive improvement in the characters of the slave population, such as may prepare them for equal rights and privileges, as enjoyed by others of His Majesty's subjects'.[8] When Buxton introduced

---

[6] Charles Buxton, ed., *Memoirs of Sir Thomas Fowell Buxton, Bart.* (London, 1866), p. 138.

[7] Canning is reported to have said: 'By proposing some regulations we may keep the matter in our own hands and proceed in it with caution and prudence, but if we are once in a minority all would be lost.' Quoted in Murray, *West Indies Government*, p. 128.

[8] Ibid.

resolutions in the House calling for the gradual elimination of slavery, Canning was prepared to counter with resolutions of his own. Canning's resolutions were calculated to appease the Saints without fully satisfying them.[9] Under the circumstances, however, Buxton had little choice but to withdraw his motion. Canning's resolutions—enjoying the pre-arranged support of West Indian members—passed the House unopposed. Having made slave amelioration a responsibility of the Ministry, not of Parliament, Canning committed the Government to a policy of working with the West Indians, exhorting reform from them rather than imposing it upon them.

The most crucial of Canning's resolutions declared the House of Commons anxious for emancipation 'at the earliest period that shall be compatible with the well-being of the slaves themselves, with the safety of the colonies, and with a fair and equitable consideration of the interests of private property'.[10] Canning offered no timetable for the implementation of reform, and the Saints were fearful lest the phrases 'the safety of the colonies' and 'the interests of private property' serve as a pretext for inordinate delay. Canning was not interested in delay, but he was determined to avoid a constitutional imbroglio with the Caribbean colonies. The most basic issue dividing the Government and the Saints was one of trust. Buxton, Brougham, and Wilberforce insisted that colonial legislatures could not be trusted to enact progressive reforms on behalf of the slaves; Canning—being assured the co-operation of the metropolitan West India interest—believed that patient exhortation with Caribbean legislatures would produce the desired effect.

Within the month, Lord Bathurst, the Secretary of State, ironed out an amelioration plan in consultation with a sub-committee of the Society of West India Planters and Merchants. Because religion was considered 'the foundation of every beneficial change in the slave's character and future condition',[11]

---

[9] Buxton had proposed two points: first, that slave children born after a certain date be declared free; second, that amelioration take effect in the existing slave community. His first point would have systematically brought an end to slavery. Buxton, *Memoirs*, pp. 138–40.

[10] The full text of the Canning Resolutions is printed in Frank J. Klingberg, *The Anti-Slavery Movement in England* (New Haven, 1926), p. 199.

[11] This language appears in Bathurst's Circular Letter, 28 May 1823, C.O. 854/1. The letter is quoted in Mary Reckord's 'The Colonial Office and the Abolition of Slavery', *The Historical Journal*, XIV (1971), 723.

it was determined that slaves should receive religious instruction. Impediments to moral development were to be removed; slave marriage was to be legalized and encouraged; slave families were not to be separated by sale. Brutal or unseemly practices were to be abandoned. It was recommended that the driving whip be removed from the field, that women be relieved the indignity of whipping, and that a limit of twenty-five lashes be established for male slaves. Sunday markets were considered a desecration of the Sabbath, and it was desired that markets be held on other days. It was recommended that under certain conditions slave evidence be admitted in court. Means were to be provided to ensure the rights of slaves to property, and it was urged that bondsmen be accorded the privilege of purchasing their own manumisson as a reward for thrift and industry. Circular letters conveying these recommendations were dispatched to the colonies in May and July. Concurrently, the West India body sent letters to the legislative assemblies advocating the implementation of these reforms.

Before examining the evolution of amelioration policy, some mention of the historiography of the subject is in order. Histories of the anti-slavery campaign, 1823–33, have tended to convey three important, but somewhat misleading impressions.[12] First, it has been contended that West Indian legislatures reacted with truculent and persistent intransigence to the Government's amelioration plan. Second, the imperial Government has been criticized for a dilatory and feeble prosecution of reform. Finally, the Anti-Slavery Society has been credited with applying consistent and steadily mounting pressure on imperial authorities, finally obliging them to produce a Bill for emancipation. In part, this view of the period emerges from the sentimental bias of early writers; more importantly, it reflects a heavy dependence on abolitionist literature and biography and an uncritical approach to those sources. More balanced studies[13] of the period have begun to

---

[12] The works referred to include Coupland, *British Anti-Slavery Movement* (1933): Klingberg, *Anti-Slavery Movement in England* (1926); Ernest M. Howse, *Saints in Politics: The Clapham Sect and the Growth of Freedom* (London, 1952); and, to a lesser extent, Mathieson, *British Slavery and Abolition* (1926).

[13] Clearly the best and most comprehensive study of the slavery question in British government is D. J. Murray's, *The West Indies and the Development of Colonial*

appear, but a thorough treatment of the anti-slavery movement which perceptively comprehends Caribbean aspects of
the problem has yet to be published. Within the limited scope
of this chapter some attempt will be made to modify conventional interpretations.

West Indian assemblies responded to amelioration with outspoken indignation. Their rage that the British Government
was infringing their legislative prerogative and undermining
their property was heightened by a fear that trans-Atlantic
interference in the slave system would provoke insurrection. A
slave rebellion erupted in Demerara in August 1823, and shortly
thereafter distraught Jamaica planters executed eleven slaves
who were alleged to have engaged in insurrectionary plots.
In the first year, amelioration made almost no headway.
Nevertheless, the imperial Government persisted in its policy
of admonishing the legislative colonies to undertake reform. In
Trinidad, where the Crown possessed legislative initiative, it
promulgated an Order in Council in 1824 embodying the full
weight of its amelioration programme. The Trinidad Order
in Council served three purposes. It established a practical
experiment for the conduct of amelioration; it offered a model
for emulation by the legislative colonies; and it served notice
on the planters that the British Government meant business.

The argument of the planters against the amelioration plan—
apart from the venomous tone of their proceedings—was
predictable. Amelioration, they claimed, would reduce their
productivity and undermine the value of estate property. This
was an inevitable consequence of curtailing the exercise—or, as
important, the threat of the exercise—of corporal punishment
over refractory bondsmen. The shifting of Sunday markets to
another day and the prohibition of labour on the Sabbath
would decrease the total working time on estates. A change in
the slaves' market day might disrupt long established commercial routines, and alienate bondsmen who had no ingrained

Government (1965). Balanced and penetrating analyses of aspects of the anti-slavery
movement are presented in several articles by David Brion Davis: 'James Cropper
and the British Anti-Slavery Movement, 1821–1823', *The Journal of Negro History*,
XLV (1960), 241–58; *'James Cropper and the British Anti-Slavery Movement, 1823–33'*,
ibid., XLVI (1961), 154–73; 'The Emergence of Immediatism in British and
American Antislavery Thought', *The Mississippi Valley Historical Review*, XLIX
(1962), 209–30.

respect for the Sabbath. The prospect that slaves would obtain
the right to purchase their freedom was especially threatening
to the planters. The bondsmen most likely to secure manumission were those who were indispensable to the welfare of the
estates—drivers and artisans whose role in the slave community
provided internal discipline and regularity to the plantations
and whose special status and supplementary incomes would
facilitate their securing manumission. What especially galled
West India planters was that the metropolitan nation, having
consistently affirmed the legality of slave property, and having
long maintained in its own commercial interest a colonial
system based very heavily on slavery, was demanding that they
—the planters—sacrifice their property and prospects without
a firm promise of compensation. Provide a formula for compensation, they argued; then amelioration could be fairly
entertained.

The British Government was unwilling to contemplate
compensation at that point, but the planters—despite their
vocal opposition—did undertake amelioration. In no colony
did they entirely meet the Government's expectations, but
neither did any colonial legislature ignore the admonitions of
Westminster.[14] Manumission was the most pervasive problem,
and only the Bahamas—islands which did not produce major
agricultural staples under a plantation system—adopted the
entire programme of compulsory manumission recommended
by the Crown. Demerara conceded to the Colonial Office on
most points, but the Demerara planters—already short-handed
—balked at compulsory manumission.[15] For many years, the
right of slaves to possess private property had been universally
recognized in the colonies, but colonial enactments on this
matter rarely met the standards advocated by the British
Government. By and large, the assemblies constrained the
exercise of corporal punishment by masters, imposing a limit
of twenty-five stripes on male offenders. In some islands—e.g.
St. Vincent and Grenada—the whip was removed from the field,
but as a rule women remained subject to corporal punishment.

[14] A detailed review of the process of amelioration in the legislative colonies
appears in an undated Colonial Office memorandum, C.O. 318/117.
[15] Murray, *West Indies Government*, pp. 135–8. Compulsory manumission was
imposed on all the Crown colonies by Order in Council in 1829.

The principle that slaves should be entitled to give evidence in court was generally conceded, but except in Grenada and Tobago colonial legislatures hedged and qualified the practical application of that privilege. In Barbados, for example, a slave's testimony could not be admitted until he produced a certificate of competence from an Anglican clergyman and a statement from his owner confirming his credibility. Even then, the slave's testimony was deemed acceptable only when it was confirmed by circumstantial evidence. Slavery was not an ennobling institution: deceit and prevarication were commonplace among bondsmen, and the planters feared that by granting their slaves uninhibited liberty to bear witness they would merely provide them with a licence for perjury.

The Government's recommendation that slaves be given religious instruction and that slave marriages be legalized—seemingly innocent and wholesome projects—evoked unexpected opposition where sectarian rivalries had produced bitter political hostility. Except in Barbados, dissenters performed most of the pastoral services for slaves. This act did not constitute a serious problem in the Leeward Islands where Christianity, much of it being Methodist or Moravian, had already penetrated a large segment of the slave community. But in Jamaica where particular groups of dissenting missionaries were openly hostile to slavery and generally suspected of undermining the authority of the masters, the Government's desire that religious teachers have easy access to bondsmen aroused substantial opposition.

Although the progress of amelioration was chequered, the response of colonial governments was not uniformly refractory. Nor could it have been. Colonial assemblymen were capable of strong language in reference to their abolitionist tormentors or the British Government, but they clearly acknowledged that a policy of utter obstinacy might provoke direct parliamentary action and destroy what remained of their legislative independence. Even if they did not satisfy all the expectations of their official antagonists, they were obliged to compromise on amelioration without immediate hope of compensation. Anti-slavery forces, on the other hand, regarded the amelioration programme manifestly moral and not subject to compromise. The qualified response of West Indian legislatures was deemed unworthy and recalcitrant. The Saints' disgust for the planters was only equalled by their disappointment in the King's Ministers whom they accused of faint-heartedness in their conduct of amelioration.

The Government's position was an awkward one. It had not the will and possibly not the power to govern the colonies by force.[16] Even had it imposed law in the Caribbean, it could not guarantee, without extraordinary expense, the effective enforcement of that law. The administration of law in the colonies was vested in planters who interpreted the law according to their own views of what was right.[17] Unless the Government was willing to sacrifice the European framework of colonial society—which it was not—it could not hope to achieve a swift and effective implementation of the amelioration programme by coercion. Successive British Ministries staunchly maintained that the long term interest of colonial society required that reform emanate—or, at least, appear to emanate —from colonial legislatures rather than the Crown. Peel succinctly expressed the Government's view in 1824: was it not better, he asked, 'for the sake of the slave himself to conciliate than to estrange those authorities, without whose assistance it was impossible to do anything important in his favour?'[18]

For eight years the British Government walked a tightrope between the Saints and the colonists, satisfying neither side and suffering abuse from both. By no means was the Government neutral on the slavery question. It was committed to emancipation, and it pressed amelioration to the narrowest tolerance which reasonable working relations with the colonies would permit. After 1824 Colonial Office correspondence was almost entirely devoted to amelioration, to the civil rights of free coloured people, to the maltreatment of slaves or missionaries, and to requests for additional information on conditions and institutions in the colonies. The Colonial Office played a vital educational and propagandist role in the interest of emancipation, relentlessly exposing abuses of the planters and thereby undermining the attempts of West Indians to justify slavery. Cases involving the maltreatment of slaves were reviewed with meticulous care by James Stephen, and official

[16] Ibid., p. 132.   [17] See chapter III, pp. 13–16.
[18] Murray, *West Indies Government*, p. 132.

correspondence relating to such cases was invariably printed for Parliament. Many years later, Henry Taylor recalled:

we knew what we were about. We had established protectors of slaves in the few colonies in which we had legislative power; they made their half-yearly reports in which every outrage and enormity perpetrated on the slaves was duly detailed . . . we wrote despatches in answer . . . distinctly marking each atrocity, and bringing its salient points into the light; we laid the reports and despatches before Parliament as fast as they were received and written; Zachary Macaulay forthwith transferred them to the pages of his 'Monthly Anti-Slavery Reporter,' by which they were circulated far and wide through the country.[19]

It became increasingly difficult for colonists to conceal acts of brutality toward bondsmen. Slaves informed missionaries of cases of maltreatment. Missionaries notified their superiors in Britain, and their superiors appealed to the Colonial Office for investigation. In many cases inquiries pursued by the Secretary of State in response to charges made by anti-slavery spokesmen proved false or vastly exaggerated, but the effect of their vigilance was manifest. Magistrates in the colonies, aware of the ubiquitous presence of abolitionist's agents, exhibited increasing scrupulosity in their treatment of cases of brutality. In 1831 a junior magistrate in the parish of Port Royal, Jamaica, charged the Custos[20] of the parish with improper treatment of slaves.[21] The case was given full publicity in the *Parliamentary Papers*, and the Custos, Mr. John Jackson, was suspended from the magistracy.[22]

Imperial authorities were firm without being rigid in their review of colonial reform measures. While they never forgot that their mission was to persuade, cajole, and admonish the colonists to reform, they were not always sympathetic to particular local difficulties. The firmness of the Colonial Office as well as its limited tolerance for special problems is evident in the treatment given Jamaica's Consolidated Slave Act. The Act,

[19] Taylor, *Autobiography*. I, 122–3.

[20] A Custos Rotolorum was the principal magistrate of a parish. Appointed by the Governor with the confirmation of the Crown, he presided over the parish vestry.

[21] Belmore to Goderich, 8 July 1831, C.O. 137/178, no. 70.

[22] Belmore to Goderich, 31 Aug. 1831, C.O. 137/179, no. 84.

incorporating a number of desirable reforms, passed the legislature in 1826. Stephen produced a report of ninety-seven
pages, offering a minute examination of the Act, pointing out
its flaws, and indicating where protection was absent and where
it was thin or transparent.[23] Although the measure was a
substantial improvement over Jamaica's Consolidated Slave
Act of 1816, William Huskisson, Colonial Secretary, disallowed
it on the grounds that it constituted an inadequate response to
the Trinidad Order in Council of 1824 which spelled out the
imperial Government's expectations for amelioration. Most
instructive, however, is the particular emphasis which Huskisson rendered in a dispatch to the Governor in March 1828. He
announced that had the Jamaican Act been satisfactory in every
other detail, he would not have confirmed it because it contained clauses restricting religious liberty.[24] The most objectionable of those clauses, number 83, stated that preaching by
superstitious slaves without permission from their owners and
from the quarter sessions of their parishes, was punishable by
whipping or imprisonment with hard labour. Stephen and
Huskisson regarded this clause an intolerable violation of
religious liberty. Their passionate objection to it indicated their
inflexible position on matters involving the religious instruction of slaves; it also exposed their ignorance of the particular
colonial problem to which clause 83 was addressed.

Huskisson was concerned with correct principles. The Jamaica
Assembly, never over-zealous in its defence of non-conformist
sects, had a special grievance against slave preachers. Many
black preachers travelled about the countryside holding
meetings at night, harping on hell-fire and the devil, bewildering and terrifying their audiences, and making off at the end of
their performances with a goodly portion of their listeners'
money.[25] Liberal missionaries readily acknowledged that many
independent slave preachers led 'very unholy lives'.[26] Planters
regarded clause 83 an essential protection for the health of their
bondsmen, for in the past, credulous slaves influenced by
dissembling black preachers had been driven to lunacy—some

[23] Stephen to Goderich, 5 May 1827, C.O. 323/44, Law Officer's Reports.
[24] Papers Relating to the Consolidated Slave Act, C.O. 137/165.
[25] Ibid.
[26] Sel. Comm. on Slavery, P.P. 1831-2, XX (721), evidence of Knibb, 3945.

planters claimed death—by their exaggerated fear of the devil.[27]

Controversies like this one poisoned relations between planters and the Colonial Office. West Indians considered imperial authorities to be intellectual captives of the Anti-Slavery Society, ignorant of conditions in the colonies and incompetent to render judgement on their legislation. In turn, the Colonial Office personnel regarded the planters stubborn and ungenerous. Angered by disallowance of the Consolidated Slave Act, the Jamaica Assembly declared that it would not adopt measures which it considered incompatible with the best interest of the island merely to gratify the government of Great Britain. The planters punctuated this declaration by passing the same Act again, changing only the dates which appeared on the published document. It was rejected out of hand by the Acting Governor.[28]

In confrontations like this the Colonial Office held high cards. West Indian assemblymen could parade their anger, but they were obliged to constrain their defiance lest they provoke the imperial parliament into overt measures that would nullify their autonomy. Given sufficient time to lick their wounds and recover their equilibrium, colonists generally responded to the persistent pressures of the Colonial Office. In 1829, the Jamaica Assembly produced an improved Slave Act although the religious restrictions which had rendered the former measure unacceptable remained intact. It was vetoed by the Secretary of State, who issued a strong rebuke to the Governor for having signed it. In 1831 the Earl of Belmore, reeling from a succession of admonitions, sent home an acceptable measure shorn of the offending clauses restricting the preaching of slaves. Patience and exhortation had finally borne fruit, but it had taken five years for the Assembly to produce a satisfactory Slave Act.

During the late twenties, it was Stephen and Taylor at the Colonial Office, not the Saints, who principally exerted pressure on the planters. The anti-slavery movement was plunged in lethargy during 1826–7: the London Committee of the Anti-

---

[27] Lewis, *Journal*, p. 174.
[28] Keane to Murray, 11 Dec. 1828, C.O. 137/167, no. 30.
[29] Belmore to Goderich, 19 Feb. 1831, C.O. 137/178, no. 4.

Slavery Society met infrequently, and when it did meet it was preoccupied by details of little significance.[30] During 1826 Buxton was deeply involved in the Mauritius slave trade question; in May 1827 he was seized with apoplexy and was lost to the movement for a year.[31] Brougham was prevented from reviving the slavery issue in Parliament in 1828 by a prolonged illness. During that year, Lushington devoted himself to achieving equality for free coloured people in the Caribbean. When Buxton's health was restored, he trained his attention upon the Mauritius problem and the status of Hottentots in South Africa. He was at odds with Brougham and alienated from young radicals in the movement. To a large degree, the anti-slavery cause was in disarray in the late twenties, its leadership uncertain and its focus blurred.

Notwithstanding that, the movement had continued to accumulate popular support. Dissenters had grown increasingly hostile to the planters as a result of the exposure of the latters' maltreatment of colonial missionaries. East Indian merchants had joined the attack against West India colonists in hope of undermining the system of tariff preferences that thwarted their own commercial interests. After Catholic emancipation, Daniel O'Connell took a strong stance against slavery and influenced the Irish vote accordingly. Furthermore, the literary organs of the movement had achieved a cumulative effect, gaining thousands of adherents in towns and villages throughout the United Kingdom.

The years 1830–1 served as a watershed for the anti-slavery movement. The impatience of abolitionists (especially young recruits with limited political experience) over the slow progress of amelioration became manifest at a meeting of the Anti-Slavery Society in May 1830, when a young member rose from the floor and amid a tumult of cheers demanded an end to temporizing measures: the time had arrived, he declared, to proclaim that slavery shall cease.[32] From that point, the movement gathered momentum, and by 1831 it was being swept along by an unprecedented sense of urgency. An Agency Committee representing the more strident radical side of the

[30] Davis, 'James Cropper and the British Anti-Slavery Movement, 1823–33', p. 162.
[31] Buxton, *Memoirs*, p. 200.   [32] Ibid., pp. 260–1.

movement[33] was created to generate greater public involvement in the question by canvassing the nation, employing itinerant speakers, and promoting debate. While the Agency Committee's tactics often violated the sensibilities of the old leadership, its impact was immediate: the number of affiliated anti-slavery societies rose from 200 to 1,300 in a single year.[34]

The Government was not unconscious of the rising tide of anti-slavery immediatism, but it continued to affirm a gradualist policy. In 1831 the Secretary of State assured the colonists that the mother country did not intend to 'disturb by abrupt and hasty measures the present relations of society in the colonies', or to abandon that 'course of progressive improvement, which has had for its avowed object, the ultimate extinction of Slavery . . .'[35] In November, however, the Government dispatched a new Order in Council to the Crown colonies, extending the programme of reform; its terms were commended to the legislative assemblies for their guidance. Reaction in the old colonies was predictably hostile. The Jamaica Assembly declared that any further amelioration would have to emanate from colonial bodies, and throughout the Lesser Antilles every assembly refused to entertain the Order.[36] Once again, an impasse had been reached between the mother country and her legislative colonies which only time and further persuasion could have relieved. But time was made short and persuasion rendered futile by the insurrection which erupted in Jamaica at Christmas in 1831.

It was the Jamaican rebellion, not the new vigour of the anti-slavery movement, that proved the decisive factor in precipitating emancipation. Sugar estates in western parishes were burned and pillaged; whites fled *en masse* to the coastal ports; and, with customary severity, the insurrection was put down by regular troops and militia. Its origins lay in that tangled skein of colonial intemperance, slave ignorance, and

[33] For a reinterpretation of the role of the Agency Committee in the anti-slavery movement, see Davis, 'James Cropper and the British Anti-Slavery Movement, 1823–33', pp. 165–8.

[34] Coupland, *British Anti-Slavery Movement*, p. 137.

[35] Extract from Goderich's dispatch, enclosed in Belmore to Goderich, 4 Aug. 1831, C.O. 137/179, no. 76.

[36] Memorandum on the reaction of legislative colonies to Order in Council of 2 Nov. 1831, C.O. 318/117.

missionary zeal which had, during a decade of mutual frustration, created volcanic conditions in the island. The slaves were alarmed by public threats that planters would seek union with the United States rather than submit to emancipation.[37] For years, information concerning the abolitionist movement and parliamentary proceedings on the slavery question had reached the plantations in highly embellished form through black servants who eavesdropped at dinner conversations and public meetings of the planters, or through free coloured sympathizers who communicated the contents of newspapers and incendiary pamphlets to the slaves.[38] A few dissenting clergymen, sympathetic to the slaves, employed indiscreet language in prayers and sermons before illiterate, excitable, impatient, and frustrated people.[39] During 1831 a notion gained currency among slaves that the King had granted emancipation but that planters were conspiring to withhold it.[40] When insurrection broke out, William Knibb, Baptist missionary and ardent opponent of the planters, had no success in convincing rebellious slaves in St. James that no 'free law' had come for them.[41] Before peace was restored in February 1832, twelve whites had died, several hundred slaves had perished in skirmishes with troops and by public execution, and property estimated at £1,500,000 was laid waste.[42] Black men were flogged to death in the streets of Montego Bay: one of them, a Baptist slave, was reported to have expired after receiving 500 lashes.[43] Incensed white colonists tore down the chapels of dissenting ministers and organized the Colonial Church Union to defend the two orthodoxies of the colony—Anglicanism and slavery. In Great Britain news of the rebellion and the desperate

[37] Sel. Comm. on Slavery, P.P. 1831–2, XX (721), evidence of Vice Admiral Charles Fleming. Hope Masterton Waddell, Presbyterian missionary, wrote of the 'wild revilings of the colonists against abolitionists, saints, missionaries, and their threats to join America, and wade in the blood of their slaves, rather than free them...' See his *Twenty-Nine Years*, p. 68.

[38] Barclay, *State of Slavery*, pp. 243–4; Carmichael, *Domestic Manners*, II, 192.

[39] Waddell admitted 'It was easy most unintentionally to err in that respect, and to say things in a slave congregation fit only for a free one'. *Twenty-Nine Years*, p. 68.

[40] Proclamation to Rebellious Slaves, 2 Jan. 1832, C.O. 137/181; Gardner, *History of Jamaica*, pp. 272–3.

[41] Sel. Comm. on Slavery, P.P. 1831–2, XX (721), evidence of Knibb, 3902.

[42] Report of a Committee of the Jamaica House of Assembly, C.O. 137/181.

[43] Sel. Comm. on Slavery, P.P. 1831–2, XX (721), evidence of Knibb, 3611–15.

excesses of the Colonial Church Union aroused fear and disgust. A House of Commons committee was created to examine the slavery question. One of its principal objectives was to determine whether the danger of rebellion and its ugly consequences would not be gravely magnified by withholding, any longer, freedom from the slaves.[44]

Evidence produced by the select committee had great impact at the Colonial Office. Both Taylor and Howick, the Parliamentary Under-Secretary, concluded that the peace of Jamaica could only be preserved by the immediate abolition of slavery.[45] Stephen was afraid that embittered planters, motivated by reckless passion, might provoke further incidents in their determination to escape concessions to the Crown.[46] If further inspiration was needed to commit the Government to decisive action, the reform of Parliament provided it.[47]

The Reform Act which widened the franchise and revised parliamentary districts became law in June 1832. During the election that followed, political activism by the Anti-Slavery Society was so successful that the reformed House of Commons, assembled in early 1833, was virtually divested of West Indian members.[48] The result was anticipated at the Colonial Office. Taylor pointed out that if the Government did not assert its authority and sponsor a Bill to abolish slavery, the reformed Parliament, in response to intense public demand, would carry through its own measure of emancipation affording neither compensation to the planters nor security for the future well-being of the colonies.[49] In December the Colonial Office circu-

[44] Report of the Sel. Comm. on Slavery, P.P. 1831–2, XX (721).

[45] Taylor Memorandum, Jan. 1833, Papers on the Abolition of Slavery, C.O. 318/117; Murray, West Indies Government, p. 194.

[46] Stephen was always gravely suspicious of the planters. In a memorandum written shortly after the Jamaican insurrection he suggested that the planters had, by intentionally disregarding the rebellious sentiments of the slaves, permitted the revolt to occur in order to verify their earlier prophesies that imperial interventionism would provoke a slave rebellion. Stephen Memorandum, 22 Mar. 1832, bound in C.O. 320/1, no. 4.

[47] Reckord, 'The Colonial Office and Abolition', p. 734; Temperley, British Antislavery, p. 16.

[48] Debates in Parliament—Session 1833—On the Resolutions and Bill for the Abolition of Slavery in the British Colonies (London, 1834), p. 104.

[49] Taylor Memorandum, Jan. 1833, Papers on the Abolition of Slavery, C.O. 318/117. In a private meeting with representatives of the West India party, Viscount Howick, Parliamentary Under-Secretary and the commanding figure at the

lated a paper to members of the Cabinet declaring that the
policy of amelioration had run its course and that the constant
peril of insurrection rendered full emancipation necessary.[50]
Still, there was much hesitation. The King suspected that
emancipation might cost Britain her Caribbean colonies,[51] and
the Prime Minister was reluctant to move. But when Sir Fowell
Buxton, acting independently, declared his intention to bring
an abolition measure before the Commons, the Government
was compelled to respond. Emancipation had become a legislative certainty, and if the Government wished to retain control
over the process it was obliged to produce its own Bill. Accordingly, Buxton was informed that the Ministry intended to
introduce a safe and satisfactory measure for emancipation.

Drafting a Bill proved no easy task. Indeed, four plans were
formulated at the Colonial Office before a satisfactory measure
was obtained. No member of the Colonial Office doubted that
slavery should and must end, but neither did anyone express
optimism regarding the probable results of emancipation.
Fears dominated expectations. The fear that emancipation
might provoke bloodshed was only exceeded by the conviction
that a withholding of freedom would probably produce even
greater bloodshed. The only modern precedent for a massive
measure of emancipation was Haiti where decades of economic
stagnation had followed a period of butchery. Haiti was not a
fair precedent, but its example lingered menacingly in the
minds of men who formulated plans for British emancipation.[52]
It was feared that freedmen might not distinguish between the
planters' property in slaves and the planters' property in land.
Many of them, it was known, expected to benefit from a general
redistribution of estate lands when slavery ended. There was
anxiety lest the freedmen would discontinue estate labour and

Colonial Office, warned that unless abolition could be secured by amicable
arrangement between the Government and the West India body, it would be
achieved by direct vote of the Parliament or by an insurrection of the slaves. To an
uncertain member of his own party Howick urged: '. . . do you think, supposing the
negroes not to be sufficiently prepared, that either they or the people of this
country will wait, or that it can be left safely to any party but the Govt to effect
the change . . . which must take place?' Howick to Russell, 8 Dec. 1832, bound in
C.O. 318/116.
   [50] Outline of Plans for the Abolition of Slavery, C.O. 320/8.
   [51] Burn, *Emancipation and Apprenticeship*, p. 104.
   [52] Taylor, *Autobiography*, I, 124.

succumb to an indolent barbarism. In bondage they had satisfied most of their food requirements by working in provision
grounds one day a week. Why, asked Henry Taylor, should
they labour for wages on sugar plantations when their small
needs were so easily satisfied?[53] There was fear that the sugar
estates would be thrown up, that Europeans would leave the
islands, that civic amenities, modest as they were, would
decline or disappear. Each of the four plans for emancipation
drafted at the Colonial Office in 1833 were designed to prevent
the realization of these fears, it being the profound belief of
both the Government and the abolitionists that an active
plantation economy should be preserved.

Henry Taylor, the author of one plan, proposed a system
by which slaves could purchase their freedom by instalments.[54]
He recommended that the British Government buy a slave's
freedom on two days of every week. The slave, he argued,
could employ those days to earn enough money to purchase his
freedom for the remaining days of the week. Underlying this
plan was a notion that by working in his own interest a slave
would acquire personal initiative and habits of industry. These,
Taylor hoped, would inspire him to labour for wages on the
plantations when his freedom was secured. Taylor's concept
had obvious flaws. Although a strong male slave could achieve
total freedom in a little more than three years, the weak and
infirm would suffer an unmerited prolongation of their bondage. Furthermore, the plan was complicated, and as its author
later observed, 'When there is a popular cry for anything, it
can only be satisfied by something broad and simple and almost
as inarticulate as the cry itself.'

The problem of drafting a satisfactory emancipation Bill
was complicated by the divergent character of the colonies,
especially in terms of the density of their populations and the
availability of unoccupied arable land. In Barbados, Antigua,
and St. Kitts, there was an abundant population and little or
no vacant land for peasant settlement. There, it was anticipated,
the freedmen would have to work for wages or starve. Elsewhere,
there were vast tracts of vacant land beckoning the freedmen.

[53] Taylor Memorandum, Jan. 1833, Papers on the Abolition of Slavery, C.O.
318/117.
[54] Taylor, *Autobiography*, I, 127.

Trinidad and British Guiana already suffered from labour shortages, and in the former colony only 43,000 acres out of an estimated 1,300,000 were under cultivation.[55] In the Windwards and Dominica there were over 100 square miles of uncultivated mountain land, some of which—like the Charib country of St. Vincent—was among the most fertile in the islands. Jamaica possessed extensive mountain regions capable of sustaining a large portion of her black population.

Lord Howick addressed himself to the land problem with his customary energy and certainty of conviction. Howick was a convert to Wakefield's concept that the development and maintenance of colonial industries that required the combined exertions of a large number of people could not be achieved unless colonial land was withheld from settlers by the artificial device of high taxes and high upset prices.[56] With unflinching confidence in his views he pursued a plan for Caribbean land and labour which, however consistent with the progressive theories of his time, disregarded the temperament of the black population and the essential realities of West Indian geography and government. Howick was prepared to restrict freedom in the interest of productivity, declaring that unless freedmen were prevented from occupying vacant lands, the colonies would regress to a primitive state.[57] He proposed a heavy tax on all land in the colonies which had not been used for the production of export staples. This plan constituted a subsidy to the estates and a penalty on prospective peasant proprietors. Crown lands were to be grudgingly alienated; squatting would be rigorously prosecuted; and peasant settlers would be required to pay taxes on their lands before they brought them into cultivation. His objective, plainly stated, was to induce the freedmen to perform wage labour on the estates by replacing the fear of the whip by the fear of starvation.

Lord Brougham, a spokesman of the abolitionist movement, took strong exception to the Howick plan.[58] A delegation from the West India Planters and Merchants was cool toward it,

[55] Evidence of Martin Sorsano, Surveyor General, before a sub-committee of the Agricultural and Immigration Society of Trinidad, July 1841, enclosed in C.O. 295/134, no. 85.
[56] Outline of Plans for the Abolition of Slavery, C.O. 320/8.
[57] Ibid.
[58] Burn, *Emancipation and Apprenticeship*, pp. 110–11.

and after two months of deliberation, it was rejected by the Cabinet. This decision was warmly endorsed by Lord Mulgrave, the Governor of Jamaica, who described Howick's scheme as 'perfectly visionary and impracticable'.[59] In Jamaica and other colonies, Mulgrave argued, there was no accurate land survey distinguishing private property from Crown lands, and a land tax could not be levied until such information was available. Furthermore, colonial governments did not possess the bureaucratic machinery or the quality of personnel to collect such taxes and to treat the citizenry equitably. Even if they had, they could not have laid effective distraints on free blacks who refused to pay.[60]

In March Edward Stanley (later fourteenth Earl of Derby) replaced Goderich as Secretary of State for the Colonies, and shortly thereafter he introduced an Abolition Bill, largely his own creation, in the House of Commons. Stanley's proposal satisfied neither the anti-slavery party nor the West Indians. It too was shelved, but the Bill contained two features which were to be retained in the emancipation measure which subsequently passed: a transitional period of apprenticeship and monetary compensation for the planters. The Bill declared the slaves to be legally free, but it required them to continue to labour for their former masters without remuneration for $7\frac{1}{2}$ hours a day, six days a week, for up to 12 years.[61] Throughout this extended period, the slaves—designated apprentices— would receive their customary allowances. Each apprentice would undergo an appraisal, and apprentices would be encouraged to work for wages for at least $2\frac{1}{2}$ hours a day in order to accumulate the means of purchasing their freedom before the end of the 12-year transitional period. To compensate planters for their losses of slave property, Stanley recommended that the British Government either loan or give the West Indians £15,000,000. The nature of that transaction he left to the discretion of Parliament.

In the debates that followed, West Indians asserted that

---

[59] Quoted in Murray, *West Indies Government*, p. 196. Mulgrave was the only Caribbean governor who saw the Howick plan.

[60] Wilbur D. Jones, 'Lord Mulgrave's Administration in Jamaica, 1832–1833', *The Journal of Negro History*, XLVIII (1963), 52–3.

[61] *Debates in Parliament—Session 1833*, p. 68 ff.

£15,000,000 was an inadequate compensation for losses which might entail the whole capital invested in Caribbean estates.[62] Parliamentary spokesmen of the Anti-Slavery Society did not balk at the principle of compensation;[63] but, having demanded immediate abolition, they took strong exception to the concept of apprenticeship. A majority of both Houses agreed with Stanley that a sudden release of slaves from the obligation to perform labour might devastate the sugar estates and lead freedmen in brief time to adopt the 'primitive habits of savage life'.[64] Nevertheless, there was considerable opposition to a 12-year transitional period. Stanley's most persistent critic was Lord Howick, whose departure from the Colonial Office shortly after the rejection of his own scheme afforded him licence to criticize the Government's Bill and to advocate the principles upon which he had based his own approach to emancipation.[65] Howick opposed any transitional apprenticeship. Predictably, the debates isolated extreme views and created a framework for compromise. The final abolition measure, drafted by James Stephen in a 48-hour ordeal which seriously undermined his health, reduced the term of apprenticeship from 12 to 6 years and increased the level of compensation from £15,000,000 to £20,000,000.

£20,000,000 was a prodigious, almost incredible, sum for a British Parliament, preoccupied with economy, to award to any party. Members of Parliament were shocked by their own extravagance.[66] So was the Colonial Office. For nearly a

---

[62] Ibid., p. 431. Labour was the critical factor without which all other forms of property held by Europeans in the West Indies might be rendered useless. The slaves constituted one portion of the whole property of West India proprietors, but the planters appreciated that without adequate labour—and they doubted the adequacy of free labour—their land, buildings, and machinery would cease to have much value.

[63] See p. 406, n. 1.

[64] *Debates in Parliament—Session 1833*, p. 76. This phrase was employed by Stanley in support of his plan of apprenticeship.

[65] Ibid., pp. 84–5, 94–7.

[66] The staggering nature of the compensation proposal evoked, in one instance, a giddy hilarity in the House of Commons. On the night the House passed the resolution favouring a £20,000,000 grant, a curious exchange took place. Sir Alexander Baring, member of the famous banking family, expressed his bewilderment that M.P.s who normally haggled over £500 salary votes could readily approve a grant of £20,000,000. His astonishment evoked laughs from many members. 'Gentlemen may laugh,' he responded, 'but voting away £20,000,000 is not laughing matter, and I am surprised at the levity the House manifests upon the subject.' His remark only produced another round of laughter. Ibid., p. 501.

decade the Colonial Office had operated under the assumption
that Parliament was more concerned about reducing expenditures than alleviating the condition of slaves.[67] When drafting
his extensive memorandum recommending emancipation,
Henry Taylor determined that £20,000,000 would constitute a
just indemnity for the slave owners, but neither he nor Stephen
dreamed that Parliament would grant such a sum.[68] On 27
February, Cobbett told the House of Commons that he would
never consent to any scheme that would take 'an additional
farthing from the pockets of the English, Irish, or Scotch
people'.[69] This remark appeared to typify opinions held by a
large segment of the population, most notably an increasingly
vocal element of the anti-slavery movement. As late as 13
March, Howick believed that Parliament would reject any
abolition Bill which contemplated a loan of £15,000,000 to the
West Indians. He thought the House of Commons unwilling to
consider a compensatory gift of any size, asserting that a loan
of £7,500,000 would be the maximum amount which could
be obtained to indemnify the planters.[70] Why, then, by mid-
summer, did large majorities in both Houses vote an outright
grant of £20,000,000?

As E. L. Woodward has observed, the central problems in
British government after the Napoleonic wars involved the
defence of private property.[71] The Government of Britain was
controlled by great landowners who regarded property a hall-
mark of patriotism: those who had it possessed a vested interest
in the state and its security; those who did not were considered
vulnerable to seditious influences. Dangerous influences were
thought to be abroad in British society. The Captain Swing
disorders in 1830 produced widespread alarm, as did the tension
and turmoil aroused by the question of parliamentary reform.
In fact, the reform of Parliament was a strategic concession

---

[67] Murray, *West Indies Government*, p. 141.

[68] Taylor Memorandum, Jan. 1833, Papers on the Abolition of Slavery, C.O.
318/117; also, Taylor, *Autobiography*, I, 127.

[69] *Hansard*, XV, 3rd series, 1179, 27 Feb. 1833.

[70] Colonial Office Memorandum, 13 Mar. 1833, C.O. 318/117. This document
was signed by Howick, although it was not written in his hand. The views recorded
in the above text are certainly Howick's; they are taken from marginal notes
made by him on the memorandum.

[71] E. L. Woodward, *The Age of Reform, 1815–1870* (Oxford, 1962), p. 56.

taken in defence of property, and after the Reform Act the security of property became a heightened and anxious question among the governing élite. Any Act of Parliament that would confiscate millions of pounds in private property without adequate compensation would set an ominous precedent which might be used against the landowning class. Members of Parliament interested in preserving a respect for the rights of property would have been recklessly denying their own interest by abolishing slavery without indemnity to the planters. Henry Taylor was explicit on this point:

The decision on the Slavery Question would affect the course of other political opinions and events, add force to popular influence, and by inspiring in the public mind an increased consciousness of instability and change, with a redoubled disregard of the right of property, accelerate the progress of the movement party, and probably tend to precipitate the policy of the Government upon the vital questions of popular interest, which may be considered as the necessary *sequela* of the Reform Bill.[72]

In defending the principle of compensation, Stanley argued that on no other basis could emancipation be achieved in a manner consistent with honesty and justice.[73] He might have added self-interest.

On 1 August 1834 slavery was legally ended. All freedmen above the age of 6 were to be classified as either agricultural or domestic servants on the basis of the type of labour which they had performed 12 months before the passage of the Abolition Act. For agricultural workers, the apprenticeship was to continue for six years, to 1840, but domestics were to receive complete freedom on 1 August 1838. Apprentices were permitted to purchase their discharge before the end of the transitional period, and employers were compelled to accept a fair payment. The amount of that payment was to be determined by an impartial appraisal of the labour value of the involved apprentices. The planters were obliged to provide their workers with legally established allowances of food, clothing, lodging, and medical attendance. In exchange, the apprentices were compelled to perform 45 hours of unpaid labour per week for

---

[72] Taylor Memorandum, Jan. 1833, Papers on the Abolition of Slavery, C.O. 318/117.

[73] *Hansard*, XVIII, 3rd series, 584–7, 11 June 1833.

their former owners. Children under six years of age were declared totally free and were entrusted to the care of their mothers. If a mother suffered destitution and was unable to provide for her child, the youngster was liable to indenture on the estate of his residence until he reached the age of 21. A body of 100 special magistrates was created to superintend the conduct of apprenticeship and to adjudicate all disputes between masters and servants.[74]

During the early months of 1833, when the Colonial Office was labouring to produce an acceptable emancipation measure, it held firmly to the view that interference by the imperial Parliament in the legislative affairs of the colonies should be confined to what was strictly necessary.[75] The Act abolishing slavery affirmed the prerogative of the British Parliament to legislate upon matters involving the domestic affairs of the colonies, but the Act preserved the formalities which had long persisted between the imperial Government and its Caribbean dependencies. Although the Act of Parliament established the basic framework for emancipation, it reserved to the colonial legislatures the task of preparing the terms upon which the apprenticeship system would be regulated. Local assemblies were assigned the responsibility for framing rules for the classification of apprentices, for the appraisement of those who wished to purchase their freedom, for the maintenance of discipline among apprentices, and for the prevention of indolence and vagrancy. They were also directed to establish regulations to guide the conduct of planters, to assure that they provided allowances of requisite quality to their labourers, that they observed the 45-hour limit imposed on the apprentices' time, and that they were punished for acts of cruelty toward their servants. As an inducement to speedy enactment of this legislation, the Act of Parliament declared that no compensation payments would be made in a colony until its legislature had produced an emancipation Act in conformity with the framework of the imperial measure, incorporating rules and regulations which were acceptable to the Crown.

Jamaica responded with remarkable alacrity, producing a measure in December 1833 which speedily received confirma-

---

[74] *3 & 4 Wm. IV c. 73.*
[75] Colonial Office Memorandum, 13 Mar. 1833, C.O. 318/117.

tion by the Secretary of State. That confirmation, freeing compensation funds to the Jamaica planters, produced a serious rupture at the Colonial Office between Stanley and Stephen. Stephen reviewed colonial emancipation Acts with a highly critical eye, noting every variance from either the letter or the spirit of the original measure,[76] and he was highly critical of the Jamaica Act.[77] Time and again he accused the Jamaican legislators of inspecific use of language, failure to define terms, vagueness, and oversight. He found an inequality between the liability of apprentices and the liability of masters. Apprentices were subject to being whipped for rendering false accusation against their masters; planters guilty of such perjury were not obliged to indemnify wrongly accused apprentices. No attempt had been made to determine the nature of the whip to be used in punishments, nor was there any stipulation which would prevent the imprisonment of apprentices in improper places. Although Stephen found little in the Jamaica Act which con-stituted flagrant opposition to the spirit of the imperial measure, he suspected that once the planters received their compensation money they would interpret the vague terms of the Jamaica Act in a manner decidedly hostile to the interests of the appren-tices.

Stanley took a different view. Convinced that the good will of the planters was vital to the successful operation of apprentice-ship, he assumed a liberal posture toward them, hoping that they would respond in kind by amending the deficiencies which the Colonial Office pointed out in the Jamaica Act. In this situation Stanley confronted a dilemma which would repeatedly arise in relations between Downing Street and Jamaica during the ensuing three decades. Should the British Government rigorously assert its authority in a delicate colonial question and accept the risk of alienating the colonial élite? Or, should the Secretary of State conciliate the planters at the risk of compromising the British Government's role as trustee for the labouring class? Stephen held to the former course. Stanley, confident that conciliation would succeed better than domina-tion in protecting the interests of the freedmen, adopted the

---

[76] Stephen to Grant, 30 Apr. 1835, C.O. 323/51, Law Officer's Reports.
[77] Stephen to Stanley, 31 Jan. 1834, C.O. 323/50, Law Officer's Reports.

latter.[78] It is difficult to fault or favour either view. Although Stanley's conciliation failed, a forcible policy was equally liable to failure. Probably Stanley's position was better calculated to bear fruit than Stephen's, but in his liberality Stanley exceeded his authority. Stephen was quick to inform him of this. In reviewing the Barbados Emancipation Act, Stephen pointed out some of the same defects he had criticized, without avail, in the Jamaica Law, adding the following comment:

My judgment was and is, that the King in Council has no right to assent to a colonial enactment directly repugnant to a British Act of Parliament. Trifling as the particular contradiction may be, it is no trifling principle which is involved in the assumption by the King's Privy Council of the right to advise His Majesty to sanction that which Parliament have expressly forbidden.[79]

On the whole, the passage of emancipation laws in the colonies was not a serious problem. Compensation was withheld from the Barbados planters until mid-1835, but St. Kitts produced a wholly satisfactory measure on the first try, and most colonial assemblies proved co-operative.[80] In the Crown colonies, the British Government imposed its own terms by Orders in Council. Antigua and Bermuda produced the only surprises, rejecting the system of apprenticeship and conferring immediate and total freedom on the slaves.

During the summer of 1833, Antigua planters had assembled to discuss Stanley's Emancipation Bill, and with few exceptions they considered the apprenticeship plan more damaging than full emancipation.[81] To a large extent Antigua proprietors maintained their slaves on imported provisions. Under the apprenticeship system their maintenance costs would have remained stable while the amount of labour performed by their workers would have diminished by 25 per cent. Having the dual advantages of a dense population and a comparatively

---

[78] Reviewing his decision several years later, Stanley commented that he was the first Secretary of State who had refused to transfer Stephen's reports on colonial Acts into dispatches to the governors. Professor Paul Knaplund referred to the rupture between Stanley and Stephen as the 'most nerve shattering experience' of Stephen's official life. See his, 'Sir James Stephen: the Friend of the Negroes', *The Journal of Negro History*, XXV (1950), 380.

[79] Stephen to Stanley, 24 May 1834, C.O. 323/50, Law Officer's Reports.

[80] Smith to Glenelg, 22 Aug. 1835, C.O. 28/116, no. 33.

[81] Lowe, *Codrington Correspondence*, p. 73.

large body of resident proprietors, the Antigua planters were disposed to gamble in favour of full freedom.[82] At the Colonial Office, the Antigua Emancipation Act produced mixed sentiments of pleasure and anxiety, for it was feared that total emancipation in that island would seriously jeopardize the peaceful conduct of apprenticeship in other colonies.[83]

After numerous setbacks and occasional periods of inactivity, the anti-slavery movement had created a political environment conducive to emancipation. It had marshalled public opinion, flooded Parliament with petitions, and provided East India merchants and other commercial opponents of the West Indian monopoly a platform from which they could attack the colonial regime. The gathering strength of the anti-slavery movement in Britain emboldened West Indian slaves and rendered their servitude—however ameliorated—increasingly intolerable. Missionaries who ventured to the Caribbean during the decade of anti-slavery agitation were but thinly disguised agents of that cause. Their presence aroused angry indignation from the planters while giving encouragement to bondsmen. The rising expectations of the slaves coupled with their persistent frustrations produced a major slave rebellion in Jamaica in 1831, and that event galvanized sentiment at the Colonial Office in favour of immediate abolition.

Until 1832 the British Government had pursued a policy of cautious but firm gradualism on the slavery question. It did not want to destroy the working relation with the legislative colonies that allowed planters to exercise responsibility over their own internal affairs. Even though the autonomy of the local assemblies was eroded during the decade following the Canning Resolutions, the imperial Government maintained existing arrangements by permitting colonists to enact their

---

[82] MacGregor to Stanley, 5 May 1834, C.O. 7/38, no. 99.

[83] Stephen to Spring Rice, 16 July 1834, C.O. 323/50, Law Officer's Reports. Stephen thought the apprentices in other islands would force planters to abandon apprenticeship. In Montserrat, a Bill to abolish apprenticeship was defeated in the Assembly by one vote during 1835. Like their counterparts in Antigua, the Montserrat planters were motivated by self-interest. A hurricane followed by drought had ruined provision grounds and confronted many planters with the costly prospect of subsidizing their apprentices with imported foodstuffs. See, Sturge and Harvey, *West Indies*, pp. 81–2.

own emancipation measures in response to the model Act passed at Westminster.

Although abolition imperilled prevailing social and economic institutions in the Caribbean, most emancipators—both government and private—hoped to avoid any significant alterations in the plantation system of agriculture or the hierarchical character of society. In fact, the preservation of those conditions was considered vital to the successful evolution of a free society. In Britain society was extremely hierarchical, and the gradations of West Indian society, founded on race and cultural identity, were quite acceptable to people who believed Africa a continent of darkness and her people the products of savagery.[84] Enlightened British paternalism could best succeed, it was thought, under a hierarchical system, and it was the conviction of missionaries, metropolitan abolitionists, and government officers alike that a powerful paternal guidance was necessary to uplift the slaves—to provide them religious instruction, to encourage Christian morality, to institute European marriage customs, and to extinguish obeah, myalism, and other African cultural remnants.

From one point of view the British would judge the progress of emancipation in terms of the extent to which the Christian religion and European cultural patterns penetrated the newly liberated population. Economically, they would assess it according to the health and vigour of the sugar estates. The plantations, it was thought, provided a cohesive, stable, and orderly living environment which would facilitate the establishment and maintenance of churches, schools, and social and medical services. A decline of the plantations might jeopardize social order by precipitating the dispersal of labouring people, impairing the work of British paternalists, and perpetuating African cultural relics that abolitionists and missionaries hoped to eliminate.

Of wider importance, perhaps, was the effect which abolitionists expected British emancipation to have upon the world. The West Indies were considered a testing ground for the maxim that free labour could produce tropical staples at lower cost and with greater efficiency than slave labour. Abolitionists sought

[84] Philip D. Curtin, *The Image of Africa: British Ideas and Action, 1780–1850* (Madison, 1964).

the destruction of slavery in every quarter of the globe, and they believed, as Buxton remarked in 1834, that the most effective way to attack American slavery was to make a show-piece of the British West Indies.[85] When slave masters were forced to concede the superiority of free labour in the production of sugar, then, argued the abolitionists, both slavery and the heinous African slave trade would cease. In their view, West Indian freedmen were morally obliged to labour diligently on the sugar estates. Their failure to do so would cripple the economy of the free West Indies and prolong the bondage of millions of slaves throughout the hemisphere.

In his opening comments on the Emancipation Bill, Stanley described British abolition as a 'mighty experiment'. Could 800,000 slaves in 19 colonies be set free without violence? Once free, would they sustain a plantation economy and its related institutions. These were momentous questions evoking the interest of people throughout the Atlantic basin. Before they could be put to the test, however, the freedmen were compelled to serve a painful and troubled apprenticeship.

[85] Temperley, *British Antislavery*, p. 76. As late as 1840, a delegate at the international anti-slavery convention predicted 'that under an improved economy and management, the extended cultivation of sugar in the rich soils of Demerara and other colonies by free labour, would speedily enable British merchants to undersell the sugar planters of Brazil and Cuba, so as to drive all slave-grown sugar out of the markets of the world'. *Proceedings of the General Anti-Slavery Convention* (London, 1841), pp. 396–8.

CHAPTER 5

The Apprenticeship

FOR most Britons, Jamaica was synonymous with the West Indies. It was the principal sugar colony; it possessed nearly half of Britain's Caribbean slaves; and it was larger than the combined British islands of the Lesser Antilles. During the preceding century it had produced the wealthiest, most ostentatious class of absentee proprietors. Its Assembly was the most powerful legislative body in the Caribbean, its planters the most outspoken and assertive. Political faction was most rife and public controversy most virulent in that island. Relations between whites and blacks were more inflamed and dangerous there than anywhere else in the British Caribbean. The Governor of the colony exerted less influence upon local society and politics than any other West Indian executive, and by virtue of its size and importance, Jamaica carried most of the legislative colonies with it on every significant controversial question.

At the best of times imperial policy was devised to meet the requirements of Jamaica; in the worst of times it was contrived to break the resistance of that colony. The anti-slavery party concentrated its attention upon Jamaica.[1] The House of Commons Committee on slavery drew almost all of its evidence from Jamaican sources. Henry Taylor's valuable Colonial Office memorandum recommending the abolition of slavery treated the problem solely in terms of Jamaica.[2] To an inordinate degree, public debate and parliamentary inquiry on the course

---

[1] This condition continued to prevail after the apprenticeship ended. Speaking at the General Anti-Slavery Convention in London, in June 1840, Samuel Prescod, a representative from Barbados, declared: 'We have heard a great deal of Jamaica, but I beg you to remember, that that colony comprises only about half of our emancipated population. I am aware, that in Jamaica the great experiment of freedom must principally be worked out . . . But as abolitionists . . . we have as much to do with the smallest as with the largest colony.' *Proceedings of the General Anti-Slavery Convention* (London, 1841), p. 403.

[2] Taylor Memorandum, Jan. 1833, C.O. 318/117.

of the apprenticeship focused upon that island, and the decision to abandon the apprenticeship system two years ahead of schedule, in 1838, was taken in response to conditions prevailing there.

Until recently, Jamaica has dominated the attention of West Indian historians, and in some cases Caribbean history has been written solely in terms of that colony. This tendency is evident in W. L. Burn's *Emancipation and Apprenticeship in the British West Indies*, the outstanding work of scholarship on the apprenticeship period. Burn produced a penetrating study of Jamaica, with only scattered references to other colonies. He excused this orientation with the comment, correct in itself, that 'it was on the assumption that Jamaica represented the norm that the apprenticeship system was devised'.[3] On the contrary, Jamaica was a caricature, not a likeness, of the other island communities—the extraordinary, not the typical, West India colony. Without ignoring that island, this chapter will attempt to complement Burn's study by affording special attention to other major West India colonies: Barbados, British Guiana, and Trinidad.

Theoretically, apprenticeship offered important strategic advantages to the European establishment. It afforded missionaries additional time to mould the thinking of the apprentices, to encourage habits of industry, to build churches, and to establish stable social patterns that would induce freedmen to remain in settled estate villages when the system ended. It allowed time for the orderly preparation of a legal system to supersede discarded slave codes. It provided sufficient time for the establishment of colonial banking institutions that could meet the needs of a free plantation economy, and it offered the Treasury an opportunity to rectify serious monetary problems and supply the colonists with enough coinage to pay the wages of free workers. Moreover, apprenticeship gave the planters a brief period before the onset of full freedom to introduce new equipment, to experiment with new techniques, and to revise methods of labour management. In essence, it was an interval intended to facilitate the creation of social and economic machinery that would perpetuate the established order after 1840.

In practice, few of the strategic advantages offered by

[3] Burn, *Emancipation and Apprenticeship*, p. 10.

apprenticeship were realized. A spirit of reconciliation and compromise so necessary to the success of the plan did not arise among various parties who had quarrelled bitterly before 1834. In labour relations, most planting attorneys and managers were unable to overcome their habitual reliance on force and intimidation. Perceiving this, missionaries and their philanthropic allies in Britain maintained an uncompromising, self-righteous approach to colonial society and government, perpetuating the breach between themselves and the planters and antagonizing imperial authorities. Before the British Government could mature its legal and monetary arrangements for the free society, a wave of popular indignation in Britain, aroused and organized by anti-slavery groups, forced the premature abolition of the apprenticeship system.

Neither slaves nor planters were consoled by apprenticeship. The former wanted complete freedom.[4] The latter, resenting their loss of arbitrary power, feared the disintegration of a social system which had provided them the highest rank and authority. The Governor of Barbados expressed little confidence in the planter's adaptability, denouncing their 'unbending spirit . . . and the tenacity with which they cling to arbitrary power over the Negroes'.[5] His colleague in Guiana claimed that planters were prone to declare their apprentices insubordinate in cases where other men, unaccustomed to slavery, would have found them faultless.[6] Clearly, colonial planters, threatened socially as well as economically, opposed emancipation with far greater stridency than absentee proprietors who were, in most cases, quietly grateful for both the transitional apprenticeship and the receipt of monetary compensation. Absentees had observed

[4] When slavery ended, hundreds of St. Kitts apprentices refused to submit to further coerced labour. Martial law was called, and militiamen swept the highlands driving runaways back to the estates. There was a small incident in Montserrat requiring the assemblage of militiamen, and a disorder arose in the Essequebo district of British Guiana. For a short time, pandemonium broke out in Port of Spain to which hundreds of slaves had repaired to demonstrate their opposition to apprenticeship. None of these incidents ended tragically; labourers returned to the field, unwilling to risk the fruits of freedom which, however delayed, were within sight. J. Cox to J. Beecham, 13 Aug. 1834, *Methodist Missionary Society Papers*; MacGregor to Spring Rice, 19 Aug. 1834, C.O. 239/37, no. 167; William A. Green, 'The Apprenticeship in British Guiana, 1834–1838', *Caribbean Studies*, IX (1969), 50; Hill to Spring Rice, 7 Aug. 1834, C.O. 295/103, no. 7.

[5] Smith to Spring Rice, 28 July 1834, C.O. 28/113, no. 6.

[6] Smyth to Spring Rice, 9 Aug. 1834, C.O. 111/132, no. 14.

first hand the force of British abolitionism; they knew the futility of resistance. The value of their estates had plummeted in anticipation of abolition, and the fact of emancipation, bearing with it the grant of compensation, appeared less harmful to their short term financial interests than a prolongation of the slavery question.

Generalizations concerning labour relations during apprenticeship should be approached with caution; nevertheless, one might conclude with safety that a majority of colonial planters took an exacting, rather than conciliatory, approach to their apprentices. Insisting that people who demanded their freedom should be deprived the 'indulgences of slavery', some planters defied the spirit of the Emancipation Act by withholding customary privileges not specifically required by statute. In slave times, women who had borne six children were universally exempted from field labour. Many of these women were recalled to the field when apprenticeship began.[7] In Jamaica it had been routine for slaves to receive weekly allowances of herrings and salt fish, and at the end of harvest and at Christmas they were granted oatmeal, flour, sugar, rum, and additional clothing. The extent of these allowances had always varied from estate to estate, but after 1 August 1834 some planters abandoned them altogether. During slavery, older men had guarded provision grounds to prevent them from being plundered by stray animals or thieves. During apprenticeship, watchmen were often assigned jobs of greater value to estate owners. Likewise, elderly women who had attended field hands as cooks and water carriers during slavery were given more productive employment.[8] Where these indulgences were continued, apprentices were usually expected to pay for them by performing additional work.

Planters took a hard line on issues involving the preservation of their labour forces, especially the classification of apprentices and the valuation of those who wished to purchase their freedom. Since apprenticeship for non-praedials (slaves not normally engaged in agricultural labour) was scheduled to end two years before field workers were to be freed, planters often misrepresented the status of non-praedials in the hope of

[7] Sturge and Harvey, *The West Indies*, p. 347.
[8] Madden, *A Twelvemonth's Residence*, II, 182–7.

retaining their services for the extended period. Insubordinate domestics were threatened with demotion to the field. Tradesmen complained that masters compelled them to perform agricultural labour in order to register them as field hands.[9] In 1837 the Lt. Governor of Grenada observed that planters obstinately persisted in classifying all slaves as praedials.[10] The Law Officers of the Crown to whom this matter was referred declared that craftsmen must be classified as non-praedials in spite of the planters' insistence that their labour was an essential part of the system of production.[11] An Order in Council to this effect was issued for the Crown colonies in April 1838. Under intensive pressure from London the legislative assemblies adopted a similar approach,[12] but not before thousands of apprentices had been permanently alienated from their masters and anti-slavery zealots had made improper classification a symbol of planter intransigence.

Abolition Acts entitled apprentices to buy their freedom at a fair valuation of the unexpired term of their apprenticeship, but planters commonly impeded this procedure by rendering exorbitant appraisements upon their servants. Since appraisement tribunals normally comprised two planters in addition to an independent judge, biased decisions were the rule.[13] Colonial governors and missionaries denounced unfair valuations, but the British Government deferred action on the question until the spring of 1838 when apprenticeship was nearing its conclusion.

The system of valuations penalized industrious apprentices. Value was determined by a labourer's age, strength, skills, and general worth. Strong, accomplished, reliable apprentices, the people most likely to seek appraisement were valued much

[9] W. J. Brittain, S.M., to H. E. F. Young, 22 Oct. 1835, enclosed in Smyth to Glenelg, 13 Nov. 1835, C.O. 111/140, no. 79.

[10] C. Doyle to MacGregor, 13 Nov. 1837, enclosed in MacGregor to Glenelg, 30 Dec. 1837, C.O. 28/120, no. 292.

[11] R. M. Rolfe and J. Campbell to Glenelg, 22 Mar. 1838, C.O. 318/133.

[12] In Barbados, for example, 1,166 apprentices were transferred from praedial to non-praedial status in the eleven months preceding June 1838. MacGregor to Glenelg, 14 June 1838, C.O. 28/123, no. 141.

[13] In Jamaica, for example, the members of an appraisement tribunal included the nearest stipendiary magistrate, a planter justice nominated by the master, and a third planter justice agreeable to the stipendiary and the master's nominee. Madden, *A Twelvemonth's Residence*, II, 148.

more highly than their idle or unproductive counterparts, and the inflated valuations which planters placed on them bore no relation to the wages offered for the extra work they performed. Domestics and tradesmen constituted a large percentage of those seeking manumission by purchase. Women were more numerous than men.[14] In all colonies the number of apprentices who appealed for valuation was relatively low, and as the time for freedom approached, the incentive to expend one's savings to purchase a premature release diminished. Wisely, most working people who accumulated money saved it for the purchase of house, land, or stock upon the commencement of freedom.

The Emancipation Act freed all children under six years of age, but it permitted mothers who suffered destitution to indenture their free children on estates until they attained the age of 21. In colonies where apprentices produced their own food from provision grounds, the care and sustenance of small children was not a problem. The situation was dramatically different in Barbados where apprentices were sustained largely upon food distributed to them by their masters. Interpreting the Emancipation Act with self-serving rigidity, Barbados planters refused to supply customary allowances to the island's 14,000 free children. An appeal by Governor Sir Lionel Smith to the humane instincts of assemblymen, a group already bristling over their capitulation on the slavery question, proved unavailing.[15] The apprentices were equally intransigent. Magnificently adamant, they refused to indenture their children, asserting that they would prefer to see them starve than to bind them for fifteen years or more to the estates.[16] Although individual planters repented their conduct on this question, the mistreatment of the young remained a persistent issue until 1837

[14] Of all apprentices discharged into freedom in Barbados in 1837 (467 by appraisement, 282 by agreement, 429 voluntarily, 16 by sentences of magistrates), 466 were men, 712 women. Non-praedials numbered 775, praedials 403. Enclosure in MacGregor to Glenelg, 12 Mar. 1838, C.O. 28/122, no. 44. In the rural districts of Trinidad, few apprentices sought freedom by purchase. In Port of Spain, 90 apprentices secured manumission through appraisement in the first two years of apprenticeship. Of those, 61 were non-praedials and 60 were women. Enclosure in Hill to Glenelg, Oct. 1836, C.O. 295/112, no. 127.

[15] Smith to Spring Rice, 30 Sept. 1834, C.O. 28/114, no. 37.

[16] Smith to Spring Rice, confidential, 25 Aug. 1834, C.O. 28/113.

when the Assembly, at long last, passed an Act providing adequate allowances to free children.[17]

In spite of these tribulations, working conditions improved during apprenticeship. The hours of coerced labour were reduced and in most colonies the loss of customary allowances was offset by the opportunity for extra wage labour. Figures recorded early in apprenticeship indicated that extra work for hire was being performed on 70 per cent of Jamaica's estates.[18] In Trinidad, about half the apprentices engaged in extra wage labour.[19] Since sugar-boiling continued for most of the year in British Guiana, there was ample opportunity for extra work at wages up to 2s. 2d. a day.[20] Task work—that is, the performance of specifically assigned tasks rather than the conduct of service for a particular duration of time—was the common medium of labour in Trinidad and Guiana. During apprenticeship, task workers normally completed their day's assignment by one or two p.m., having commenced labour shortly after dawn and having taken an hour's rest at breakfast. Diligent men could perform two tasks a day, one for their masters and one for wages.

Punishments were mitigated during apprenticeship, and in some colonies the whip was entirely abandoned. Where it was not retired, it was allowed only as a form of judicial punishment. In January 1838 Lord Glenelg expressed concern that the whip was being used with undue liberality by magistrates in Trinidad, but records indicate that during the preceding five months the number of whippings had averaged only twenty-nine per month for the whole colony.[21] It was common knowledge that military punishments were much more severe than those inflicted upon apprentices. Since both soldiers and apprentices were subject to rigid discipline for a term of years, comparisons between them are not unreasonable and do, in fact, provide some perspective on the times. In 1838 a Jamaica trooper of the West India Regiment was sentenced to transportation for life for having offered violence to a superior officer.

[17] Stephen to Glenelg, 11 May 1837, Law Officer's Reports, C.O. 323/52.
[18] Burn, *Emancipation and Apprenticeship*, p. 271.
[19] Reports of Stipendiary Magistrates, enclosed in Hill to Glenelg, 12 Oct. 1836, C.O. 295/112, no. 130.
[20] Reports of Stipendiary Magistrates, enclosed in C.O. 111/138, 111/139, 111/140, 111/145.
[21] Hill to Glenelg, 30 Mar. 1838, C.O. 295/120, no. 25.

Six others with similar crimes received fourteen years transportation, and two men were transported for life for desertion and theft of regimental stores. In many cases, these sentences were imposed in full knowledge that the guilty soldiers were drunk when committing their crimes—rum being considered by the Governor of Jamaica, himself, a well-nigh irresistible temptation in that 'vicious country'.[22] Where the whip was still in service, a threat of violence by an apprentice upon his master would likely have earned him fifteen to thirty-nine stripes; everywhere it would have been cause for a brief imprisonment. Even insolence by an apprentice toward his superiors could serve as a sufficient cause for whipping when a presiding magistrate was in collusion with local planters. By the same token, a degree of leniency was exercised toward apprentices which was not evident during slavery and was certainly not manifest in military tribunals. For example, two apprentices who were caught stealing plantains in British Guiana and who threatened an estate constable with a gun were fined merely a guinea each. Local newspapers deplored such leniency. Commenting on this case, the *Guiana Chronicle* argued that such 'was the decision of a Special Magistrate in this colony for crimes which in Europe would have been visited with transportation, or hard labour in the Hulks'.[23]

Protection for apprentices against overwork, maltreatment, and abuse was vested in a body of independent stipendiary magistrates (distinguished by their name from unpaid local justices of the peace). They were appointed and paid by the Crown and dispatched to the West Indies to enforce the terms of the Emancipation Act upon all parties. Stipendiary magistrates became the sole arbiters in minor disputes between employers and apprentices. They ascertained that allowances demanded by law were being paid, that apprentices were submitting to the regular discipline of the estates and that the latter were working their required time. They inspected plantation hospitals and lock-ups, as well as public prisons; they sat on appraisement tribunals; and they reviewed complaints involving the classification of apprentices. To an immense degree, the equitable functioning of the apprenticeship depend-

Special magi- [margin annotation]

---

[22] Smith to Glenelg, 27 Feb. 1838, C.O. 137/226, no. 33.
[23] *The Guiana Chronicle*, 21 Mar. 1838.

ed upon the propriety and efficiency of the stipendiary magistrates (hereafter referred to as S.M.s).

The concept of the stipendiary magistracy was sensible and uncomplicated, and it is hard to imagine by what other means the apprenticeship could have been administered. In practice, however, the British Government was responsible for mismanagement of this vital agency and for a callous and niggardly treatment of the magistrates. The Emancipation Act authorized the appointment of 100 stipendiaries. This number was ludicrously inadequate, and although it was subsequently expanded after vigorous representations from the colonial governors, the size of the magistracy was never equal to the demands placed upon it. Furthermore, when the apprenticeship commenced, fewer than half of the allotted magistrates had arrived in the West Indies. Nevis, Montserrat, and Tobago were without any. Only one S.M. had landed in the tense colony of St. Kitts, and one in Grenada. Two magistrates were present in Trinidad, but one of those was so ill that his services were useless. The other had arrived on 31 July when anti-apprenticeship disturbances were beginning in Port of Spain, and he perished from sickness and general fatigue six weeks later.[24] A Wesleyan missionary in St. Kitts asserted that the strike of apprentices which had occasioned the declaration of martial law in that colony during August might have been averted had the magistrates, whose arrival was anxiously awaited by the blacks, appeared in time to tour the island and confer with leaders of the resistance.[25]

By terms of the Emancipation Act, S.M.s received only £300 in salary a year, a niggardly display of imperial meanness, especially in view of the £20,000,000 compensation awarded the planters. In a single voice, colonial governors declared that stipendiaries could barely subsist and could not perform their duties on such meagre incomes.[26] The work of an S.M. carried him from one estate to another in all types of weather and over every variety of terrain. He required at least two horses, tack,

[24] Hill to Spring Rice, 30 July 1834, C.O. 295/106, no. 6; Hill to Spring Rice, 15 Sept. 1834, C.O. 295/103.
[25] J. Cox to MacGregor, 18 Aug. 1834, enclosed in MacGregor to Spring Rice, 19 Aug. 1834, C.O. 239/37, no. 167.
[26] Smyth to Stanley, 24 June 1834, C.O. 111/132, no. 135; Smith to Stanley, 5 July 1834, C.O. 28/113, no. 22.

and in some colonies a gig, in addition to the normal para-phernalia of a respectable household. The cost of living in the colonies was much higher than in Britain; indeed, minor appointments on large Guiana estates carried salaries of £300 as well as additional benefits of equal value, but no one expected the subordinate planters who received that income to maintain the appearance of respectability. The case of Captain James Grady, a magistrate commissioned to British Guiana, offers insight into the enormous difficulties which poorly paid S.M.s confronted.[27] Brady was given jurisdiction over two parishes on the left bank of the Demerara River where cultivation extended for sixty miles. Only twenty miles of his district was passable by road, and then only in dry periods; the rest of the area had to be traversed by water. There was no police estab-lishment to assist him in his responsibility for 7,000 apprentices. He could find no decent place to live that he could afford, and rather than follow the example of other stipendiaries who were swiftly sinking into debt to local planters, he resigned his com-mission and returned to England. When the Governors of Guiana, Barbados, and Jamaica all appealed for a supplemen-tary income to enable stipendiaries to meet the costs of horses and house rent, the Treasury relented, offering up to £150 a year in allowances.[28]

Without question, the parsimony of the British Government impaired the health and efficiency of its agents. It undermined their morale, reduced their independence, and in some cases it vitiated their dedication to duty. Death and disease stalked the magistracy. A few days before his death, Magistrate Everard told a colleague in Jamaica that he frequently fell asleep on his horse from sheer fatigue.[29] 'Seasoning fever' was commonly contracted by magistrates newly arrived from Europe. By October 1834 one stipendiary in British Guiana had died from fever, and the rest had suffered or were suffering from it.[30] Guiana magistrates declared that from the great extent of their districts and the duties required of them they obtained too

---

[27] Brady to Spring Rice, 29 Aug. 1834, C.O. 111/134.
[28] Smyth to Stanley, 24 June 1834, C.O. 111/132, no. 135; Smith to Stanley, 5 July 1834, C.O. 28/113, no. 22; Burn, *Emancipation and Apprenticeship*, p. 216; Spring Rice to Smyth, 18 Sept. 1834, C.O. 112/18, no. 26.
[29] Madden, *A Twelvemonth's Residence*, II, 180.
[30] Smyth to Spring Rice, 13 Oct. 1834, C.O. 111/133, no. 30.

little rest and had no time for leisure.[31] Writing from eastern
Trinidad, a stipendiary was able to find no words to describe
the horror of his circumstances: 'It is a dreary waste', he declared, 'and should your Memorialist be obliged to remain here
long, he fears he will become a perfect invalid and unfit to
hold any situation'.[32] One of the most graphic portraits of
human misery was penned by E. D. Baynes, a magistrate in
Jamaica. In three and a half years he incurred charges of £500
for medical care; four of his eight children died; and he suffered
persistent persecutions and harassment. The duties of a stipendiary magistrate, he claimed, were the 'most dangerous, and
the most difficult, and . . . the most thankless, that have ever
fallen to the lot of any magistracy'.[33]

An S.M. was expected to visit all the estates in his district
at frequent and established intervals or upon special summons
to hear the complaints of both masters and apprentices. Stipendiaries had no clerks or assistants. They recorded each
judicial action themselves and wrote periodic reports to their
governors on subjects varying from agricultural conditions to
education. The desperate loneliness of their labours; the penury
of their existence; the physical strain and sheer tiredness they
suffered—all these factors endangered the judicial equity of
the magistrates and caused many of them to become planters'
men. Imagine, if you will, the feelings of an indisposed, middle-
aged English magistrate at the end of a ten-mile ride through
blistering heat over rough colonial roads. For several days he
may have ridden the circuit of his estates; several more would
pass before he could return to his family and the bare comforts
of a stipendiary's house. Should he accept the hospitality of an
estate manager who cordially proffered a meal, Madeira,

[31] Memorial of Stipendiary Magistrates, enclosed in Light to Russell, 15 Nov.
1839, C.O. 111/166, no. 184. S.M.s dreaded an early death in the tropics, which
would leave their families destitute. In some cases, their widows were unable to pay
for passage back to England after their husband's deaths. Captain William Gray,
an S.M. who had lost an eye in military service, died in Trinidad as a result of
the movement of a ball which he had received in 1814 during the American war.
To compensate his indigent family, the Treasury awarded his widow a mere
£100. C.O. 295/134, no. 17.

[32] Memorial of John Scott, enclosed in MacLeod to Russell, 8 Mar. 1841, C.O.
295/133, no. 21.

[33] E. D. Baynes to S. R. Warren, 10 Jan. 1838, enclosed in Smith to Glenelg,
8 Mar. 1838, C.O. 137/226, no. 43.

tobacco, and a clean bed? Should he relieve his loneliness in the company of men with whom he shared an identity of customs, language, and national loyalty, knowing that on the morrow he must assess their government of the apprentices? Or, should he press on to a shabby inn, if such an inn existed, or string his hammock in a local church or lock-up? This situation is not merely a literary contrivance; it represents, quite fairly, the dilemma which stipendiary magistrates consistently confronted while conducting their duties. Human frailties being what they are, magistrates usually accepted the hospitality of the planters. But having dined at a planter's table and having absorbed an earful of woes, a magistrate compromised his neutrality. Even if his judicial assessment was not influenced by his relation with the planter, apprentices were bound to question his impartiality. Too often, the appearance of justice was sacrificed even when justice was done.[34]

The successful conduct of a magistrate's commission required more than a keen sense of judicial equity, physical strength, courage, and dedication to duty. It required a capacity for delicate diplomacy and patient persuasion. Magistrates who perceived their function as that of cold, aloof, and incorruptible arbitrators satisfied neither the masters nor apprentices. Incorruptibility was vital, but the job demanded immense subtlety, flexibility, and a willingness to examine each situation in a spirit of conciliation. On the estates, a basic, often crude, common sense was essential. A magistrate had to win the confidence of both masters and apprentices on the strength of his own character and by a timely mixture of stern rebuke and good-natured cajolery. Few men commissioned to the Caribbean possessed these varied attributes. Some began their service predisposed to favour the planters; a smaller number were openly partial to the apprentices; but no matter how equitable or meritorious a magistrate's conduct, he was liable to slanderous attack. In the colonies, the S.M.s were frequently assailed as paid servants of the Anti-Slavery Society. In Britain, they were

[34] In the larger colonies, S.M.s could not have avoided some dependence on the planters for food and shelter. In the interior of the colonies towns were few; estates or waste land occupied whole districts; inns were also few. Stipendiaries were not disposed to secure their nights' lodgings in the cottages of apprentices, and had they done so, their impartiality would simply have been compromised on the other side.

ridiculed as 'servile defendants and purchased instruments of the planters'.[35]

Planters lavishly patronized co-operative magistrates and severely abused negrophiles. Richard Hill, a coloured justice whose leniency with Jamaica apprentices rendered his service ineffectual, was referred to as the 'black viper' by violent elements in the planter class.[36] Justices who were accused, rightly or wrongly, of favouring the apprentices were reviled, insulted, and even attacked; they were denied the rudiments of hospitality on some estates and occasionally prosecuted in colonial courts. In four years E. D. Baynes was prosecuted three times. The most zealous of the Guiana stipendiaries, J. A. Allen, was successfully sued for 7,000 guilders (approximately £465, or more than a year's pay and allowances) in a case of assault in which the expenses of the prosecution were paid by planters who bore witness against him.[37] Even when the magistrates won court cases, they were obliged to pay attorney's fees. George Ross, a Guiana S.M., was successful in two cases brought against him in 1836–7, but his attorney's fees amounted to £250. When the lawyer sued him for this amount, Ross was in danger of having his salary stopped, his books and furniture sold at auction, and himself thrown in the colonial jail.[38] Claims which S.M.s made on the British Government for the payment of legal fees and fines imposed upon them by prejudiced and vindictive colonial courts became a sore subject at the Treasury. In 1837 the Treasury warned stipendiaries that the British Government would no longer indemnify magistrates for the cost of a legal action unless it was clear beyond any doubt that, in the action in question, they had been properly engaged in the conduct of their duties.[39] In view of the poverty of the magistrates and the insecurity of their position, such a warning, coupled with the unfriendly nature of colonial courts, discouraged them from too zealous a defence of the rights of apprentices.

[35] E. D. Baynes to S. R. Warren, 10 Jan. 1838, enclosed Smith to Glenelg, 8 Mar. 1838, C.O. 137/226, no. 43.
[36] John Joseph Gurney, *A Winter in the West Indies Described in Familiar Letters to Henry Clay of Kentucky* (London, 1840), p. 113.
[37] Smyth to Glenelg, 8 Jan. 1838, C.O. 111/153, no. 3.
[38] Light to Glenelg, 6 Oct. 1838, C.O. 111/156, no. 71.
[39] Circular to S.M.s, Jan. 1837, C.O. 137/230.

Although the Colonial Office assured Parliament that it would closely control appointments to the stipendiary magistracy, avoiding anyone who might have been implicated in the controversy over slavery or any member of colonial society with compromising connections, it failed to do so. It underestimated by about one-third the number of magistrates actually needed in the colonies, and during the first year of apprenticeship the Secretary of State was forced to fill a large number of places vacated by justices who died, resigned, or retired from ill health. Labouring under intense pressure with entire districts unpatrolled, colonial governors hastened to appoint local residents to fill gaps in the magistracy. As a rule the Colonial Secretary, having difficulty finding suitable English replacements at the salary offered, confirmed local appointments. This was especially true in Trinidad where most apprentices spoke a patois French and many others spoke Spanish. At the very least, knowledge of French was a necessary qualification for magistrates in that island, but most of the men sent out from England could not speak the languages of the apprentices.[40] When replacements were needed, the Colonial Office welcomed the appointment of local people having the requisite linguistic skills in spite of their questionable connections.[41]

Colonial governors were responsible for administering the stipendiary magistracy, but the extent of executive supervision and discipline differed from colony to colony according to size and terrain. In the larger colonies, stipendiaries who were guilty of consistently administering unreasonable and harsh, but not brutally harsh, punishments on apprentices were able to avoid detection by their governors for long periods. On the other hand, atrocious punishment of apprentices for trifling acts of insubordination rarely went undetected. When it

[40] Hill to Glenelg, 9 Feb. 1836, C.O. 295/110, no. 25.
[41] During the period 1835–8 four local appointments were made in Trinidad. One of the appointees was connected by marriage to fashionable society in Port of Spain where he served; a second was the brother of a leading member of the colonial bar; a third was the son of a former slave, who held part ownership in a heavily mortgaged estate. Perhaps the most extraordinary Trinidad magistrate, a Colonial Office appointee, was Benito Fernandez, a Spaniard who was unable to read or speak English well enough to communicate with his colleagues or administer the laws correctly. Hill to Glenelg, 9 Feb. 1836, C.O. 295/110, no. 25; MacLeod to Russell, 15 Mar. 1841, C.O. 295/133, no. 24; MacLeod to Stanley, 19 Jan. 1842, private, C.O. 295/136.

occurred, the records of a guilty magistrate were closely examined to determine whether the notorious incident was part of a general pattern. The most difficult cases for governors to handle were those involving S.M.s who barely remained within the limits of tolerable behaviour. If a stipendiary was indolent, often unjust, excessively friendly with planters, and inclined to drink too much,[42] a governor would remonstrate with him, but rarely would he seek his dismissal until the disquieting pattern of his behaviour had become absolutely repugnant.[43] Dismissals involved replacements, and suitable unprejudiced replacements were extremely difficult to find.

An outrageous act of injustice toward apprentices was more likely to occasion dismissal than a history of undue leniency. In fact, Lord Sligo resigned as Governor of Jamaica in March 1836 because the Colonial Office refused to dismiss a notoriously lenient and insubordinate magistrate whom he had suspended.[44] W. L. Burn determined the number and cause of dismissals in Jamaica during apprenticeship: three were for general uselessness; three for consistent and undue leniency toward apprentices; and seventeen for excessive harshness toward apprentices.[45]

In view of the inadequate number of S.M.s assigned to the colonies, the great distances they travelled, the withering climate and the loneliness they endured, the prevalence of disease, and the parsimony of the imperial Treasury, it is remarkable that the magistrates succeeded as well as they did in preserving order and dispensing justice. In every colony the planters received them with suspicion and hostility, and governors invariably set high ethical standards of performance which took too little account of the torments and temptations that beset the stipendiaries. Admittedly, their work was uneven, and some executives considered the magistracy no more than a necessary evil protecting apprentices from the more dangerous

[42] Drunkenness was a serious problem among S.M.s, but rarely a cause for dismissal. A dispatch from Jamaica in 1838 declared that two justices had died from habitual drunkenness, and that two or three others were expected to perish from the same cause. No action to dismiss the latter was suggested. Smith to Glenelg, 27 Feb. 1838, C.O. 137/226, no. 32.

[43] See p. 406, n. 2.

[44] Burn, *Emancipation and Apprenticeship*, p. 232.

[45] Ibid., p. 262.

jurisdiction of planter justices. In Britain, critics of the apprenticeship selected singular instances of cruelty and injustice committed by individual stipendiaries and cast a plague upon the entire magistracy. At best it was an imperfect body, inclined by circumstances to favour the interests of the planters over the well-being of apprentices, but in the last analysis the tribute of James Spedding who read and summarized the reports of S.M.s at the Colonial Office is perhaps most fitting:

> taking them as a body of men—who have to ride two or three hundred miles and dispose of five or six hundred complaints every month, and to receive only £450 a year—we must say that they have discharged their most important, but at the same time most difficult, laborious, harassing, and thankless duties, with a degree of zeal, ability, and integrity which deserves some other reward than these idle aspersions.[46]

As representatives of the reforming British Government, West India governors, like stipendiary magistrates, were expected to serve as agents of conciliation, it being the belief of metropolitan authorities that apprenticeship could not succeed unless leading members of the planter élite were induced to co-operate. Of the five principal West India executives who governed during this period—Lord Sligo, Jamaica; Sir Lionel Smith, Barbados and Jamaica; Sir Murray MacGregor, Antigua and Barbados; Sir James C. Smyth, Guiana; and Sir George Hill, Trinidad—four were military officers and three died at their posts.[47] Hill was clearly the least competent of the number. Although well-intentioned he lacked both industry and resolve, and at the time of his death the Secretary of State was preparing to relieve him of office.[48] The remaining four possessed energy, integrity, and firm commitment to justice. They were able administrators, but too often they possessed little political skill, subtlety, and tact. The administrations of Sligo and Smith foundered upon bad relations with their legislatures. At British Guiana, Smyth overcame similar difficulties by exploiting the extensive power afforded him by the Guiana constitution. MacGregor's relations with the planters

---

[46] James Spedding, *Reviews and Discussions, Literary, Political, and Historical, Not Relating to Bacon* (London, 1879), p. 62.

[47] Hill, Smyth, and MacGregor died in the colonies.

[48] Normanby to Russell, 22 Sept. 1838, *Russell Papers*, PRO 30 22/3D.

of Antigua were abrasive, but his administration of Barbados proved both cordial and productive.

Jamaica was easily the most troubled colony. The Marquis of Sligo, a high-spirited and industrious adventurer, owner of colonial property, and father of eight children, arrived in the island in April 1834. During his two years in Spanish Town, he encountered the full wrath and obstructionism of an Assembly determined to exploit its privileges against the new order. With little unequivocal support or direction from a train of Secretaries of State, all of whom were as perplexed as he about the best mode of administering the colony, Sligo tried to pursue an equitable policy, fulfilling the spirit of the Emancipation Act while respecting the rights and privileges of the Assembly. He found these objectives incompatible. During the final year of his tenure, he was driven to the conviction that humanity and justice would require the displacement of the Jamaica Assembly in favour of the legislative supremacy of Parliament.[49]

Sligo was followed in Jamaica by Sir Lionel Smith, whose prior administration of Barbados, a much different colony, had been marred by bitter strife with the legislature. Rather than dwell upon Smith's trials in Jamaica—a subject ably treated by W. L. Burn—it would be more profitable, and perhaps more instructive, to examine his administration of Barbados. The history of Smith's governorship in the smaller island affords valuable insight into the nature of political conflict during apprenticeship. Smith was a forceful, imperious, often inflexible man, in whose character the salient qualities of a commanding general dominated the more subtle skills of a politician. He approached the government of a proud and old legislative colony with the rigid, even pompous, bearing of a soldier, demanding subordination to his own superior sense of justice and humanity. He was intolerant of opposition, even when it was moderate in tone, and those who defied his will were scathingly denounced for their violence and insolence. Scornful of local prejudices and mildly contemptuous of colonial society, Smith neither coveted nor sought popularity with the planters. He was an authoritarian figure, a warrior in the cause of human justice, and a much admired and utterly trusted servant of

---

[49] Sligo's predecessor, Lord Mulgrave, had arrived at the same conclusion. See, Jones, 'Lord Mulgrave's Administration', pp. 48–9.

several Secretaries of State. But, his talents were not well suited to the successful management of proud and self-conscious colonists in a period of great tension between the Crown and its Caribbean dependencies.

In the smaller legislative colonies, Councils and Assemblies were dominated by a few powerful individuals who influenced the votes of a majority and managed the progress of legislation. Unless a governor achieved a working arrangement with these powerful figures, he was bound, in his legislative objectives, to confront incessant and insurmountable obstacles. Smith had no talent for subtle manipulation. As Governor of Barbados he demanded the subordination of men who had grown accustomed to subordinating their governors, and consequently his relations with both branches of the legislature were marked by open conflict. The Governor took refuge in self-righteousness; the political atmosphere of the colony was poisoned; and both parties were driven to assert extreme positions. To a large extent, the obduracy of the Barbados legislature, which exhibited itself in such damaging terms as its initial refusal to extend allowances to free children, transcended social questions and legislative issues and took the form of a determined opposition to the domineering spirit of the Governor himself.

Smith's most serious altercations were with his Council, a body whose hostility to the Governor exceeded that of the Assembly.[50] Of the twelve men who served in it, seven were described by Smith as violently opposed to the King's Government.[51] The opposition was led by Renn Hamden, a planter whose influence was equally powerful in the Assembly. Smith made no demonstrative effort to conciliate Hamden and his colleagues; rather he abused his opponents in confidential dispatches to London, and recommended that they be dismissed from office by the Secretary of State. Glenelg refused, being opposed to any action which might initiate a constitutional crisis at a time when the Government's principal objective was to reconcile warring factions.[52]

Smith's quarrel with the Council reflected a similar dispute with the Assembly where members resisted incursions by the

[50] Smith to Lefevre, 31 May 1834, confidential, C.O. 28/113.
[51] Smith to Aberdeen, 28 May 1835, confidential, C.O. 28/115.
[52] Glenelg to Smith, 31 Aug. 1835, confidential, C.O. 29/33.

executive upon their traditional constitutional prerogatives. They claimed to enjoy a status in their own island equivalent to that of Parliament in England, and they justified their competence to manage their own affairs, to determine local franchise laws, and to advise upon police and judicial appointments on the basis of their long experience of local conditions and needs.[53] Smith considered these assertions no more than ridiculous pretensions, evidence of the conceit and magnified self-esteem of narrow-minded and dangerously conservative people.[54] Smith insisted that the structure of colonial government and politics required substantial modification in response to changes in the social order, that the prerogatives which the planters had exercised over slaves dare not be permitted them in a society of free men. Barbados, like other Caribbean colonies, suffered a crisis of trust. The colonists thought themselves worthy of trust; the Governor did not. Regrettably, Smith made no attempt to conceal his sentiments, and no basis for compromise was developed.

The differences which persisted between the Governor and the legislature were more than a matter of style, but style was important. The planters had to be weaned gently, patiently, and persuasively from the exercise of their traditional powers. This was possible, for there were in the Barbados men of good character, fair mind, and great ability. R. Bowcher Clarke was among them. Clarke was Solicitor-General under Smith's Government, a native of the island, an ally by marriage to opposition members of the Council, and, according to the Governor, the 'active Instrument of that disloyal body in the House of Assembly'.[55] Smith repeatedly denounced Clarke to the Secretary of State, but a review of Clarke's long career in Barbados where he rendered exceptional service to subsequent governors, was knighted, and made Chief Justice of that island and St. Lucia suggests that Sir Lionel's difficulties were, in some measure at least, of his own making.

A comparison between Smith's tenure at Barbados and that

[53] Memorial of House of Assembly to Lord Aberdeen, enclosed in Smith to Aberdeen, 28 Apr. 1835, C.O. 28/115, no. 18.
[54] Smith to Aberdeen, 28 Apr. 1835, C.O. 28/115, no. 18; Smith to Aberdeen, 9 May 1835, C.O. 28/115, no. 23.
[55] Smith to Aberdeen, 9 May 1835, confidential, C.O. 28/115.

of his successor, Sir Murray MacGregor, tends to confirm this judgement. MacGregor was neither formidable nor austere. His language was conciliatory, and his declining health obliged him to rely for assistance upon the most able members of colonial society. At his best, MacGregor lacked Smith's unyielding sense of justice and intense dedication to his work. His correspondence was uninspired, offering limited analysis of colonial affairs and none of those passionate passages which enlivened his predecessor's dispatches. At the same time, MacGregor confronted none of the animus which Smith had encountered, either from individuals or the legislature, and his administration was distinguished by the production of liberal and remedial legislation. He referred to Bowcher Clarke, Smith's hated adversary, as a zealous and assiduous law officer, 'amiable, talented, and incapable of countenancing any design calculated to prove oppressive in its operation to the labouring population of his country'.[56] This may have been an overstatement, but when apprenticeship had ended, MacGregor commended Clarke for having afforded invaluable service in actively supporting measures promoted by the British Government.[57] Similarly, he complimented the Barbados legislature for its 'liberal and confiding manner'.[58] MacGregor was ill, irritated by what he considered a low rate of salary, and inclined to scold his correspondents at the Colonial Office with acid or sarcastic comment; but he was not blindly naïve. The success of his administration at Barbados was partly a matter of time. When he assumed the Government, the apprenticeship system was working well on the estates and the worst fears of the planters had been dismissed. Nevertheless, the sharp contrast between his administration and that of Sir Lionel Smith strongly suggests that Smith failed to perceive and exploit those essential opportunities for compromise and conciliation which, under

[56] MacGregor to Glenelg, 1 May 1837, C.O. 28/119, no. 88.

[57] MacGregor to Normanby, 7 Aug. 1839, C.O. 28/138, no. 83. In May 1838 MacGregor wrote: 'On Mr. Clark's professional ability and zeal, I am perfectly disposed to rely, I entertain towards him sentiments of personal regard, and have been frequently indebted to him for the manner in which he has exerted himself, in the transaction of public business. But as Solicitor-General, this Gentleman receives no salary, and before, and ever since, my arrival in Barbados, he has acted as Attorney General . . . besides having to prosecute his private practice.' MacGregor to Glenelg, 12 May 1838, C.O. 28/122, no. 110.

[58] MacGregor to Glenelg, 28 June 1838, C.O. 28/123, no. 154.

different management, could have rendered relations between an old and proud plantocracy and a reforming British Government both cordial and productive.

Even in the Crown colonies where executive authority confronted few constitutional impediments, governors who failed to exercise their extensive power with caution and moderation provoked intense opposition and imperilled the operation of apprenticeship. This was the case of Sir James C. Smyth whose arbitrary and overbearing demeanour aroused violent hostility among the Guiana planters. Smyth was a tough, quick-tempered, and authoritarian major general in the Royal Engineers. In a former assignment he had alienated the Commander in Chief by his peremptory and injudicious treatment of a subordinate officer, and he continued to exhibit so little regard for military etiquette that the Colonial Secretary was obliged to intercept correspondence from the Lt.-Governor which would normally have reached the Horse Guards in order to protect Smyth from causing himself irreparable damage.[59] He was an indefatigable worker; he was candid almost to a fault; and he produced a rich correspondence, offering a comprehensive and detailed analysis of conditions in the colony. Smyth assiduously cultivated the confidence of the apprenticed labourers, regarding himself as their trustee and protector.[60] But he callously, even contemptuously, piqued the planters by his arbitrary and arrogant display of authority. His suspension of the High Sheriff on grounds of his having permitted the flogging of women and having peculated from colonial funds proved hasty and intemperate when a subsequent inquiry cleared that officer of the charges.[61] In February 1835 he abruptly dismissed two special justices of the peace for having exceeded their authority in a case involving a strike of workers at La Penitence Estate.[62] The justices were widely respected planters, and one of them, Peter Rose,[63] had held a

[59] Taylor to Gladstone, memo, n.d., C.O. 111/136; Stephen to Sir George Grey, minute, bound in C.O. 111/146, no. 223.
[60] Smyth to Stanley, 10 Mar. 1834, C.O. 111/113, no. 92.
[61] Stephen to Lefevre, 21 Jan. 1834, bound in C.O. 111/134; also C.O. 111/137, no. 28.
[62] Smyth to Aberdeen, 4 Mar. 1835, C.O. 111/136, no. 15.
[63] In 1817 Rose had been elected to the College of Kiezers and Financial Representatives, a job he held until his departure for England in 1818. He was renamed

succession of high legislative and judicial offices in the colony during a twenty-year residence. The magistrates' actions at La Penitence deserved public censure, but their dismissal only exacerbated the tense relations which prevailed between the planters and the Lt.-Governor.

Smyth was justified in exercising great vigilance to protect the apprentices, for the planters exhibited too many old prejudices and too little forbearance in their relations with the workers. But the manner and methods of the Lt.-Governor deeply humiliated individual white colonists and angered the rest. When apprentices expressed their satisfaction at these developments they were branded insubordinate by the planters, who consistently complained of a growing contempt for law and authority in the colony. In December 1834 a remonstrance, bearing thirty-five pages of signatures was dispatched to the Colonial Secretary denouncing Smyth's arbitrary conduct.[64] The alienation of the colonial members of the Court of Policy was so complete that there was some anxiety that the Combined Court would refuse to enact a revenue measure, thereby provoking a constitutional crisis. To prevent that eventuality, and to conciliate the colonial party, the Secretary of State directed Sir Lionel Smith, who was technically Smyth's superior, to visit Guiana, to assume temporary command of the Government, and to negotiate a revenue Act.

Sir Lionel was not a diplomat, but diplomacy was unnecessary in this situation. The Guiana planters were mainly interested in demonstrating their antipathy to Lt.-Governor Smyth, not in provoking a constitutional confrontation. They speedily produced a revenue measure for the visiting executive that was similar in its terms to the one they had denied Sir James Smyth. Assuming the role of arbiter, Lord Aberdeen censured Smyth, advising him to moderate his behaviour and declaring that the interests of the apprentices could not be served by alienating the planters.[65] Sir Lionel's mission was a

to this body on his return in 1826, and re-elected in 1829. In 1830 he was appointed a member of the Court of Criminal and Civil Justice; also in 1830 he became Deputy Fiscal (sheriff), enjoying the rank of Major in the colonial militia. He was elected to the Court of Policy in Feb. 1835.

[64] Memorial of Planters, enclosed in Smyth to Spring Rice, 29 Dec. 1834, C.O. 111/133, no. 53.

[65] Aberdeen to Smyth, 3 Apr. 1835, private, C.O. 112/18.

watershed in Smyth's administration. Political relations gradually improved, and by mid-1837 only two of Smyth's original antagonists remained in the Court of Policy. Having reasserted his authority, the Governor exercised it with greater moderation and, in consequence, with noteworthy success. The final years of apprenticeship in British Guiana were highly productive of Ordinances designed to safeguard the operation of the system and to establish regulations for the ensuing free society. Smyth remained a fearless humanitarian, using the extraordinary power of his office to ensure that the apprentices received justice with mercy, but his experiences in office pointed up the limitations of high-handed policy, even in the most authoritarian of executive offices.

Throughout the apprenticeship period, West Indian affairs were monitored with critical scrutiny by the anti-slavery party in Britain. Apprenticeship was little more than a mitigated form of slavery, and during the parliamentary debates on emancipation in 1833 abolitionists had vehemently opposed adoption of the system. When, under the force of circumstances, Buxton had reluctantly acceded to the apprenticeship plan, he was bitterly denounced by radical members of his own movement. From the outset, then, the Saints viewed apprenticeship in the most hostile terms, and they committed themselves with characteristic zeal to exposing weakness and abuses in the system. In June 1835 Buxton returned to the fray, accusing the Jamaica legislature of denying elementary liberties to the apprentices.[66] Stipendiary magistrates, he insisted, were biased in favour of the planters, and he documented his assertion by reference to a case of magisterial injustice in St. Kitts. Buxton urged the formation of a select committee to investigate the operation of apprenticeship, and he recommended that compensation payments be withheld from the planters until the committee could report its findings. Sir George Grey, Parliamentary Under-Secretary, assured the House that the apprenticeship was functioning well and that any specific complaints produced by Buxton and his friends would be promptly investigated.[67] Confronting an unsympathetic House, Buxton withdrew his motion for a committee, but he returned to the

[66] *Hansard*, XXVII, 3rd series, 918–36, 19 June 1835.
[67] Ibid., 938–51.

same theme in March 1836. By that time the anti-slavery party was conducting large public meetings in protest against abuses in the colonies. On 22 March Buxton complained of excessive use of corporal punishment by stipendiary magistrates in Jamaica.[68] Again, he appealed for a select committee to study the system. On this occasion, the Government approved his motion, but Sir George Grey warned the House against distorted assertions about the apprenticeship being circulated by its opponents. In the same debate, Gladstone chided the Saints for complaining that Caribbean apprentices were compelled to work eight hours a day at a time when the President of the Board of Trade was recommending a Bill to compel British children twelve years of age to perform factory labour for twelve hours a day.[69]

The Select Committee formed to study apprenticeship comprised fifteen members. Buxton, O'Connell, Lushington, and Johnson represented anti-slavery opinion; and Lord Sandon, a proprietor of sugar property, Patrick Stewart, the agent for Tobago, and William Gladstone defended the planters' position. Government evidence was largely based on Lord Sligo's public correspondence from Jamaica, which was considerably more optimistic in tone than his private correspondence to Glenelg. The apprenticeship system achieved its greatest success in Jamaica in 1836 at the time of the inquiry, and elsewhere it was functioning quite well. Consequently, in spite of the contradictory nature of much of the evidence produced before the committee, that body offered a reasonably optimistic statement on the future prospects of the system.

The Saints were disappointed, but they assiduously studied the Acts of colonial legislatures printed with the committee's evidence as a basis for a further public attack on the despised system.[70] In October 1836 four anti-slavery leaders—Joseph Sturge, John Scoble, William Lloyd, and Thomas Harvey— sailed for the Caribbean to secure first hand evidence on the operation of apprenticeship. Scoble and Lloyd visited British

---

[68] *Hansard*, XXXII, 3rd series, 450–67, 22 Mar. 1836.

[69] Ibid., 486–9.

[70] *Colonial Laws as Examined by a Committee of the House of Commons in the Year 1836, Exhibiting Some of the Principal Discrepancies Between Those Laws and the Imperial Act of Abolition* (London, 1837).

Guiana; Sturge and Harvey travelled among the Lesser Antilles, arriving ultimately in Jamaica. On their return to Britain,
the latter published a densely detailed and well argued
condemnation of apprenticeship, *The West Indies in 1837*, which
supported the fundamental propositions of the anti-slavery
party without a flagrant tone of bias. The authors determined
that blacks in Dominica had gained nothing from apprenticeship,[71] that Montserrat was being destroyed by the system. The
Barbados apprenticeship, they asserted, was unduly severe,
and stipendiaries there were 'without a single exception,
accustomed to share the hospitality of the planters'.[72] The
authors devoted half their space to Jamaica, complimenting
neither Sir Lionel Smith nor the bulk of the stipendiaries whose
function, they seemed to feel, was confined to coercing blacks
and maintaining the authority of the whites.[73] Antigua received
rapturous praise for having rejected apprenticeship, but the
sharp contrast drawn between Antigua and the apprenticeship
colonies was decidedly strained.

John Scoble gathered evidence from British Guiana, and
in 1837 he produced a table of punishments inflicted upon
apprentices in Jamaica, Guiana, Barbados, Grenada, and St.
Lucia during the first twenty-two months of the system, charging that about 350,000 stripes had been administered.[74] Delegations from the Anti-Slavery Society called at the Colonial
Office criticizing the apprenticeship,[75] and Buxton and others
wrote to Grey and Glenelg making specific accusations against
individual stipendiaries or other public figures in the Caribbean.[76]

---

[71] Sturge and Harvey, *The West Indies*, appendix xxi.

[72] Ibid., p. 132.

[73] Ibid., pp. 367–8. The authors commended S.M.s known for partiality toward
apprentices even when they were notoriously lazy, as in the case of Stephen Bourne,
S.M., in Jamaica.

[74] Robert Stokes, Secretary to the Anti-Slavery Society, to James Stephen, 21
Sept. 1837, with enclosed article by John Scoble from *The Patriot* newspaper,
C.O. 318/128.

[75] Memorandum of Representations to The Right Honourable Lord Glenelg
by a Deputation of the Committee of the Anti-Slavery Society, 1 Dec. 1837, C.O.
318/128.

[76] On one occasion, Buxton informed Sir George Grey that R. Bowcher Clarke
was endeavouring to achieve the forcible indenture of free children in Barbados.
It was discovered upon inquiry that Clarke was engaged in preparing legislation
to assure the extension of allowances to free children. Much admonished by his

Without exception, colonial governors were wary of the Saints and much discomforted by their activities. In 1836 a copy of *The Philanthropist* newspaper reached Barbados, bearing a quotation involving the use of the whip from a dispatch of Sir Lionel Smith's which had been printed for Parliament. The quotation, taken out of context, misrepresented Smith, but it received wide circulation in the colonial press and aggravated the Governor's difficulties with the legislature.[77] Sir Lionel expressed a heated contempt for 'these foolish philanthropists', and as Governor of Jamaica during Sturge's tour of the colony he wrote Glenelg, 'After Mr. Sturge's treasonable speeches, nothing I think can disturb the good sense of the Negroes and their disposition to Patience and Quiet'.[78] John Scoble's tour of British Guiana aroused heated enmity of the planters and added to the trials of Sir James C. Smyth. The Lt.-Governor gave Scoble free access to official documents, facilitated his visits to every part of the colony, and promptly investigated all complaints made by him. But Smyth believed Scoble's zeal more certain than his judgement: '. . . the good which might be gained by the observations of a judicious and impartial traveller, is, in the case of Mr. Scoble, neutralized by the haste with which he arrives at his conclusion, and but too frequently upon erroneous and inaccurate information.'[79] When Scoble returned to England, he described Smyth as a man easily deceived, if not controlled, by the planters—a charge which the latter would have found bewildering if not humorous. In his frequent speeches to anti-apprenticeship audiences Scoble employed a repertoire of distressing stories about the oppressions of the planters, including some which had been proven false or highly exaggerated.[80]

In late 1837 the anti-slavery party intensified its campaign to abolish apprenticeship. Delegations from all parts of the United Kingdom converged at Exeter Hall for a five-day

fault, Buxton penned a formal apology to Clarke. Buxton to Grey, n.d., C.O. 28/131; copy of letter, Buxton to Solicitor General of Barbados, 26 June 1837, C.O. 28/121.

[77] Smith to Glenelg, 18 Mar. 1836, separate, C.O. 28/117.

[78] Smith to Glenelg, 15 Apr. 1838, private, C.O. 137/227.

[79] Smyth to Glenelg, 8 Aug. 1837, C.O. 111/150, no. 363.

[80] Memo by G. Barrow concerning Scoble's allegations against local authorities in British Guiana, bound in C.O. 111/165, no. 133.

meeting in mid-November. At the end of their deliberations, the delegates marched to Downing Street to deliver a petition calling for a speedy end to coerced labour in the British colonies. An attempt was made by the Central Negro Emancipation Committee,[81] the organization created to spearhead the anti-apprenticeship campaign, to accumulate petitions from Caribbean apprentices. A. L. Palmer, Secretary to the Committee, wrote to the editor of the Barbados *New Times*, asking him to draft and circulate petitions stating the apprentices' grievances and declaring their desire to be free.[82] The editor declined, and Sir Murray MacGregor denounced the scheme as an irresponsible incitement to violence. On 20 February Lord Brougham delivered a long, luxuriantly phrased speech in the House of Lords berating the planters and calling for legislation to terminate the apprenticeship.[83] Brougham's flamboyant style concealed a very imperfect knowledge of West Indian affairs, but his impact was immense. In February and March the Government received a host of petitions declaring that Caribbean blacks had suffered an aggravation of their miseries during apprenticeship, that the system was incapable of protecting their interests, and that the labouring people had amply demonstrated their capacity for unlimited freedom.[84]

The Government was embarrassed and distressed. In November 1837 Glenelg had written a circular letter to the colonial governors, applauding the operation of apprenticeship and stating that in the main its results had justified the hopes of the Ministry. He was aware, of course, that many abuses still persisted in the colonies, and in response to Brougham's attack, Glenelg announced the Ministry's willingness to correct faults and improve the operation of apprenticeship by parliamentary enactments.[85] He declared, however, that the Government was not prepared to violate its contract with the colonists by a premature abolition, for they believed that the vast majority of

---

[81] For a statement of abolitionist politics on the apprenticeship question, see Temperley, *British Antislavery*, pp. 35–41.

[82] MacGregor to Glenelg, 6 Feb. 1838, C.O. 28/122, no. 26.

[83] *Hansard*, XL, 3rd series, 1284–1316, 20 Feb. 1838.

[84] Memorials of Liverpool Anti-Slavery Society, of Delegates of Anti-Slavery Bodies at Exeter Hall, of the Committee of the London Anti-Slavery Society, etc., C.O. 318/134; Temperley, *British Antislavery*, p. 39.

[85] *Hansard*, XL, 3rd series, 1329–1341, 20 Feb. 1838.

colonists had fulfilled their obligations to the apprentices, and that an abrupt termination of the system would dislocate colonial society and endanger the Government's long range goals for the free population.

The Colonial Office was worried that anti-apprenticeship agitation would provoke violence in the colonies, especially after non-praedials received their freedom in August 1838. Anti-apprenticeship proceedings in Britain were reported in great detail in the colonial press, and there was clear evidence that the conduct of apprentices and their relations with the planters were suffering under its effect.[86] In March Glenelg prepared a Bill to Amend the Abolition of Slavery Act. It was designed to satisfy the most persistent grievances of the anti-apprenticeship forces—the regulation of working hours, the right of apprentices to receive all customary allowances, the total abolition of flogging, the regulation of appraisements, and the right of stipendiaries to declare the freedom of apprentices who received brutal treatment from their masters.[87] Although the measure passed into law on 11 April 1838, it did not derail the popular campaign for immediate abolition. The zeal of the Saints was unrelenting, and Glenelg lamented that it was impossible 'to possess the public mind with just and moderate views'. At the beginning of April he warned colonial governors that an intensification of anti-apprenticeship agitation would undoubtedly misrepresent and discolour their most meritorious public proceedings, and in referring to these circumstances, he advised them to endeavour to bring the apprenticeship to an early end.[88]

In its public posture, the Ministry remained firmly opposed to the abolition of apprenticeship. On 22 May a lean House of Commons narrowly endorsed a private member's resolution calling for the immediate elimination of the system,[89] but within a week Sir George Grey had obtained a majority of seventy-two votes for a contrary resolution sustaining the original six-year

---

[86] MacGregor to Glenelg, 1 Jan. 1838, C.O. 28/122, no. 1. As early as January 1838, the *Royal Gazette* of British Guiana, reviewing the Exeter Hall meetings and developments in Parliament, warned its readers that the continuance of apprenticeship beyond August 1838 was doubtful.

[87] Circular, private and confidential, 1 Mar. 1838, C.O. 854/2, no. 38.

[88] Circular, private and confidential, 2 Apr. 1838, C.O. 854/2, no. 41.

[89] Parliamentary Memo, *Russell Papers*, n.d., PRO 22/3C.

term.[90] By this time, however, Parliament had ceased to dominate the question. Copies of the Government's Bill for the reform of apprenticeship had begun to circulate in the West Indies in early April. Apart from the fact that Parliament's enactment of that measure would further erode the legislative autonomy of the colonies, the Bill called for an increase in the power of colonial executives and stipendiary magistrates at the expense of the assemblies and planter justices. Moreover, it envisaged a sweeping reduction in the planters' authority over apprentices. Recognizing the mounting influence of anti-apprenticeship forces in Britain—250 petitions favouring abolition had reached Parliament by April—the planters could not be certain that the Ministry would not be compelled to terminate apprenticeship before 1840 even if the colonies adopted the Government's reform measures. What the planters could be certain of was that abolitionists would systematically increase their agitation against apprenticeship both in England and the colonies. In sum, the planters were obliged to consider whether by perpetuating apprenticeship they were not risking more than they could gain. This was certainly the concern of Sir Murray MacGregor. Fearing the disquieting effects of anti-apprenticeship agitation, he had urged the Barbados Assembly as early as January to abolish the apprenticeship on 1 August 1838.[91] Subsequently, he made similar recommendations to his Lt.-Governors in the Windward Islands. Although reactions from the planters to these initiatives ranged from a grudging willingness to consider the matter to blatant hostility, MacGregor and his subordinate executives persuasively pressed their case. By mid-April, the Barbados Council had acceded to the Governor's position,[92] and on 16 May the Assembly, impressed by a disclosure of Glenelg's private views, agreed to abolition.[93] It was a bitter pill for the planters to swallow. They considered themselves callously maligned by the anti-slavery party and badly mistreated by the British Government, but they correctly perceived that under prevailing circumstances abolition was a lesser evil than remedial legislation and a perpetuation of

---

[90] Circular, 31 May 1838, C.O. 318/132.
[91] MacGregor to Glenelg, 1 Feb. 1838, C.O. 28/122, no. 22.
[92] MacGregor to Glenelg, 12 Apr. 1838, C.O. 28/122, no. 77.
[93] MacGregor to Glenelg, 16 May 1838, C.O. 28/122, no. 133.

abolitionist agitation. By June all the Leeward colonies and
St. Vincent had passed Acts declaring an end to apprenticeship
on 1 August.[94]

These developments thrust immense pressure upon planters
in Trinidad, Guiana, and Jamaica, where there was strong
opposition to any alteration in the duration of apprenticeship.
Sir George Hill acknowledged that the Trinidad planters
could not preserve a system of coerced labour when neighbouring colonies had eliminated it, but he met obdurate opposition
from his Council.[95] In July Hill toured the colony to inform
praedial apprentices that they were legally required to serve
another two years, but he was angrily received by blacks who
declared that Parliament had made them free, that 'the planters
had altered the papers', and that on no account would they
work beyond 1 August.[96] Some planters left the colony in fear
of violence, and the distraught Lt.-Governor appealed to
Glenelg to promulgate an Order in Council abolishing coerced
labour.[97] In the last week of July a majority of the Council
were persuaded to abandon their resistance, and a colonial
measure was finally enacted over the opposition of at least two
official members of the Council.[98]

A similar trial occurred in British Guiana. As early as March
1836 Sir James Smyth had reacted with alarm to reports of
public meetings in England which condemned apprenticeship.
Smyth insisted that Guiana apprentices were adequately protected, that apprenticeship was advantageous to planters and
labourers alike, and that an abbreviation of the system would
be injurious to the long term interests of the colony.[99] News that
the Barbados Assembly had abolished apprenticeship sent a
shock wave through the colony. The Acting Governor (Sir

---

[94] Circular, 27 June 1838, C.O. 854/2, no. 62. The most thorough analysis of
the process of abolishing apprenticeship is Woodville K. Marshall's 'The Termination of the Apprenticeship in Barbados and the Windward Islands: an Essay in
Colonial Administration and Politics', *The Journal of Caribbean History*, II (1971),
1–45.

[95] Hill to Glenelg, June and July 1838, C.O. 295/121, nos. 59, 66, 121.

[96] Hill to Glenelg, 21 July 1838, C.O. 295/121, no. 79.

[97] Hill to Glenelg, 22 July 1838, private, C.O. 295/121, The Colonial Office
did draft an Order in Council to end apprenticeship, but it was not sent until
September and had no effect upon the outcome of the crisis.

[98] Hill to Glenelg, 26 July 1838, private, C.O. 295/121.

[99] Smyth to Glenelg, 19 Mar. 1838, C.O. 111/144, no. 133.

James C. Smyth had died in March 1838) regretted the imposition caused by that measure, arguing that the Guiana apprentices were as well off as any peasantry in the world.[100] The proprietary body was hotly divided on the issue, and when one of their number, Michael McTurk, brought an abolition measure before the Court of Policy on 20 June, both he and the Court of Policy were besieged with opposing petitions. The *Royal Gazette* stridently deplored abolition, but the *Guiana Chronicle*, after years of belabouring abolitionists, liberals, and the Governor alike, argued that further resistance was futile and concession necessary. That concession became the first public act of the new Governor, Henry Light, who arrived in Georgetown on 26 June after a service of thirteen months in Dominica.

The Jamaica Assembly also bowed before the superior power of Exeter Hall, but its submission was distinguished by an unparalleled expression of rage. Glenelg's advice that Jamaica shorten its apprenticeship was received simultaneously with the news that such measures were already in contemplation in the lesser islands and that some absentee proprietors had ordered a full manumission of apprentices on their estates.[101] The Council saw no alternative to abolition. Nor did the Assembly, but its unpredictable character inspired Sir Lionel Smith to write a wildly emotional dispatch to Glenelg declaring the assemblymen ignorant, violent, 'mad', and likely to provoke an insurrection 'for the pleasure of destroying the Negroes and Missionaries'.[102] The apprentices expected their freedom. Smith expected violence, and he asked the British Government to dispatch a naval vessel to the island to dampen the resistance of the planters.[103] The Assembly's deliberations were noisy and confused, but an Act was produced in mid-June ending the apprenticeship. Within a week the Assembly sent home a savagely worded remonstrance, venting its pent-up rage at Parliament, the Colonial Office, and the anti-slavery party.[104]

[100] Bunbury to Glenelg, 15 May 1838, C.O. 111/154, no. 62.
[101] Smith to Glenelg, 17 May 1838, C.O. 137/228, no. 98.
[102] Smith to Glenelg, 17 May 1838, private, C.O. 137/228.
[103] Smith to Glenelg, 1 June 1838, private, C.O. 137/228.
[104] This remonstrance was so bitter that it is worth quoting at length. Having declared that it was unreasonable and unnatural for the British Parliament to presume to legislate for colonies of which the parliamentarians were woefully

On 1 August Sir Lionel Smith, standing on the portico of King's House in Spanish Town, addressed his congratulations to an assembly of several thousand freedmen. The day passed in worship and jubilation, unmarked by the violence so fearfully forecast by the Governor.

The abbreviation of apprenticeship was a punitive development which fell indiscriminately upon all planters regardless of their conduct during the apprenticeship. Planters who had complied with the spirit and letter of the Emancipation Act received no compensation for having forfeited the coerced labour of praedial apprentices for two years. That colonial assemblies abandoned the system by their own legislative actions should not be construed as an eagerness for abolition. In the Leewards and Barbados, apprenticeship was abolished because the losses which the planters anticipated by an early termination were more tolerable than the pain and peril of pursuing the system in the face of anti-apprenticeship agitation. The decision of these colonies to terminate the system made it incumbent upon others to follow, for once apprenticeship began to topple, apprentices throughout the Caribbean refused to work beyond 1 August 1838. The use of force to compel further labour would have proved self-defeating, especially in view of numerous individual acts of manumission which occurred in all colonies without respect to measures taken by local legislatures.

In no regard did apprenticeship fulfil the strategic expectations of its authors. The spirit of reconciliation and compromise upon which the success of apprenticeship depended was not

---

ignorant, it continued: 'This House does not dread a comparison with the Commons of England in the success of their legislation. Our laws have not been defied, as by the Irish opponents of tithes; murders are not committed in our island by companies of armed men in open day; nor do bands prowl about at night setting fire to barns and ricks of corn . . . Our courts are never occupied with the obscenities which disgrace England . . . nor have we ever known an instance of parents putting their infant families to death, to save them from the protracted sufferings of starvation . . . nor is it under our laws that wretches commit suicide to escape the refuge which is provided for worn-out and aged industry. We have no Corn Laws to add to the wealth of the rich, nor Poor Laws to imprison, under pretence of maintaining, the poor. We cannot, as the English Parliament does, boast of a pauper law which has taken millions from the necessities of the destitute, to add to the luxuries of the wealthy.' Enclosed in Smith to Glenelg, 23 June 1838, C.O. 137/228, no. 121.

forthcoming, and in retrospect it appears naïve that anyone should have expected it to. The apprenticeship brought no immediate environmental or personnel changes on the estates. The same setting, the same tasks, the same planters persisted from slavery to apprenticeship with no break in continuity to allow old grudges to subside or new habits to develop. Imperial high-handedness could not induce the planters to co-operate in the system. That required patience, persuasion, and compromise. But a tactful, compromising policy toward the white élite inevitably involved the British Government in a reluctant toleration of abuses which were considered unendurable by missionaries and their metropolitan allies. Anti-slavery forces demanded an immediate and thorough reform in the spirit and practice of Caribbean labour relations. They dramatized injustices, maligned their opponents, and discredited governors whose approach to reform was less fervid than their own, showing little appreciation for the complex political relations prevailing in the colonies and the multiple pressures operating upon West Indian executives. Their successful campaign to abolish apprenticeship caught the British Government unprepared with either the monetary or legal reforms deemed necessary for a properly structured free society. Throughout the apprenticeship years, the Government was short-sighted in its parsimonious management of the stipendiary magistracy, the most critical agency of law enforcement in the system. Additional magistrates, more carefully selected, with higher pay and greater independence, might have reduced some of the tensions of the system and given the Saints fewer reasons to condemn it. In spite of its defects, apprenticeship did produce better working conditions and a moderation of discipline for the labouring people, and it offered the planters a valuable cushion between slavery and full freedom. In all respects, however, the system failed to establish the firm foundation for a free society which its proponents had intended.

CHAPTER 6

Forming a Free Society

THE early abolition of apprenticeship imposed an immense burden upon the Colonial Office and precipitated a constitutional crisis in Jamaica which humiliated the Secretary of State and caused the momentary demise of Lord Melbourne's Government. In response to a recommendation of the Select Committee on Apprenticeship, the Colonial Office had deliberately delayed its overhaul of the legal machinery of the Caribbean colonies until the final scheduled years of apprenticeship, 1839–40.[1] Before that time, the Secretary of State merely studied the character of colonial law and initiated preliminary consultations with colonial governments regarding the nature and extent of forthcoming reforms. Slave codes had to be rooted out and replaced by a new body of law. Since the planters needed specie in unprecedented quantities to pay the wages of free workers, currency reform was required. Financial institutions had to be established to facilitate currency exchange and to meet the increasing demand for short term credits. If an independent magistracy was to be preserved, judicial reform was imperative. The political future of the emancipated people, their access to the franchise and to public office had to be decided. An expanded police establishment was needed for domestic security, and firm decisions had to be made on the future of colonial militias and the disposition of Crown land.

In August 1838 none of these objects had been accomplished. The abolition of apprenticeship transformed the Government's schedule for reform into a precipitate and exasperating rush for new laws and new institutions. Under time pressure, the Colonial Office abandoned its policy of consulting with Caribbean governments and resorted to authoritarian methods which produced a head-on collision with colonial oligarchs. This

---

[1] Circular, 6 Nov. 1837, C.O. 854/2, no. 29; draft circular, not sent, 26 July 1838, C.O. 318/141.

confrontation took the form of a constitutional struggle, but the principal issue at stake was the control of labour.

Submissive and disciplined labour was the pivot upon which the whole apparatus of planter power depended. West Indian oligarchs intended to perpetuate their exclusive control over the political, judicial, and law-enforcement machinery of the colonies as a means of regulating the lives and labours of former slaves. Imperial authorities, like the planters, were afraid that freedmen might abjure estate labour. They too wanted to maintain plantation agriculture, and they conceded that élitist government was inevitable where the majority of people were illiterate and imbued with the vices of slavery. However, during the Glenelg years the Colonial Office exercised a sincere trusteeship for the emancipated class. Where the planters were determined to preserve their own power at some cost to the freedmen's liberty, Glenelg and Stephen were prepared to curb the authority of the planters in the interest of freedmen's liberty.

Upon the abolition of apprenticeship, West Indian legislatures immediately dismantled their slave codes and drafted new legislation covering every aspect of colonial life. Downing Street was inundated with colonial Acts in the summer of 1838. No two of these Acts were alike and most of them were in conflict with principles upon which the Colonial Office intended to base legislation for the free society.[2] Never before in the history of the Empire had so large a group of colonies been forced to submit so important a body of legislation for approval at one time, and the Secretary of State was determined to achieve a high degree of uniformity in the philosophy and structure of colonial statutes. Consequently he disallowed the bulk of the Acts transmitted to London in 1838 and drew up a series of Orders in Council as well as explicit instructions for colonial legislatures on the most sensitive legislative topics—contracts, vagrancy, Crown land, poor laws, and the disposition of police and militia. The Orders in Council[3] became law in the Crown colonies. Together with other instructions, they were circulated to the legislative colonies as models for the use of assemblies in their revision of previously disallowed measures. West India

[2] Stephen to Grey, 21 Aug. 1838, C.O. 318/141.
[3] Orders in Council dealt with contracts, vagrancy, marriage, Crown land.

governors were told to withhold assent from Acts of the colonial assemblies which did not conform to the models devised by imperial authorities.[4]

Colonial assemblymen protested this imperial interference in their legislative autonomy. They were especially angered by Glenelg's insistence that vagrancy and contract laws, which the planters intended to use to head off the withdrawal of freedmen from plantation service, must be more lenient than those of the mother country.[5] Resistance was strongest in Jamaica. Jamaican oligarchs had fiercely resented the early termination of apprenticeship. Their uncompensated loss of two years of coerced labour was complicated by severe economic problems. One of the colony's chief sources of revenue—the poll-tax on apprentices—had been withdrawn before alternative means of income could become established. In August 1838 there was not enough coin in the island to pay the wages of free workers, and the colonial treasury was empty. The Assembly's most important legislation for the free society had been disallowed, and the self-esteem of the planters was deeply wounded by the incessant ridicule and abuse they endured in public discourse, in the press, and in the Parliament of the mother country. When, in August, the imperial Parliament passed a West India Prisons Act providing a blueprint for the reform and regulation of those institutions, the Jamaica Assembly considered it the last straw. It declared the measure an intolerable invasion of the Assembly's legislative prerogatives and announced a moratorium on public business until the Prisons Act was withdrawn.[6] The crisis which ensued—perhaps the most important political event in the British Caribbean during the mid-century—dramatically affected the character of West Indian law and stabilized the constitutional structure of the colonies for the ensuing three decades.

The West India Prisons Act was the product of a lengthy

[4] Circular, 15 Sept. 1838, C.O. 854/2, no. 82.
[5] Stephen provided the justification for this: 'The large powers which in England are confided to the Magistracy for the punishment of Vagrants are kept in check by many circumstances which have no existence in the West Indies, and the identical Law, which in the Mother Country may be nothing more than a necessary security against crime, may in the colony become the ready instrument of oppression.' Stephen to Glenelg, 22 Aug. 1838, C.O. 323/53, Law Officer's Reports.
[6] Smith to Glenelg, 12 Nov. 1838, C.O. 137/230, no. 193.

inquiry into the state of British Caribbean prisons undertaken by Captain J. W. Pringle during the winter of 1837–8. Commissioned by the Melbourne Government, Pringle toured the colonies examining jail facilities, the administration of prisons, the health and well-being of inmates, and modes of prison punishment. His reports, although devoid of polemics, confirmed the observations of numerous travellers who had condemned West Indian prison facilities as insanitary, decaying, ill-provided, and reeking with the stench of human excrement.[7] In the common jails of Jamaica, for example, classification of prisoners normally involved only the separation of men and women at night: convicted parties, untried persons, males, females, and debtors shared common facilities. Personal cleanliness was not enforced; neither clothing nor bedding was provided; and inmates slept on bare boards. Road gangs persisted in all the colonies with men and women working fettered together. In many jails, security was lax, escapes were frequent. A British commissioner, who visited the Dominica jail several years before Pringle, discovered the outer door of the lock-up open and the inner door off the hinges. Ascending a staircase leading from the prison yard, he found a filthy room covered by a decayed and leaky roof in which there reposed a lone debtor too languid to make his escape.[8]

Prison reform was overdue, and the colonists knew it. When society had been divided between masters and slaves, the masters had administered most discipline independently and had exhibited very little concern for the condition of public jails. Freedom changed that. The planter élite was prepared to repair or rebuild facilities; in Barbados they had already begun.[9]

[7] Reports on West Indian Prisons, P.P. 1837–8, XL (596) (596–II). In 1825 Coleridge visited jails throughout the Lesser Antilles, declaring all but two (Port of Spain and Kingstown) to be disgraceful. The jail in Montserrat, he observed, 'is the ruinous remnant of an old fort, a sort of parcus clausus where no man of common humanity would imprison a transgressing donkey'. See his *Six Months*, p. 183.

[8] Second Report of the Commissioner of Inquiry into the Administration of Civil and Criminal Justice in the West Indies, P.P. 1826, XXVI (276).

[9] Barbados had undertaken prison construction and reform of its own volition in 1835–6, and the extent of those reforms evoked uncustomary commendation from John Scoble, the most contumacious of the travelling Saints who visited Barbados on two occasions. MacGregor to Glenelg, 13 Dec. 1838, C.O. 28/124, no. 340.

Everywhere they deemed the Prisons Act a humiliating and ungracious measure calculated to paralyse their independent initiative. Rightly or wrongly, Caribbean oligarchs considered themselves undeserving of the suspicion and contempt which the Act symbolized.

The Governor of Jamaica, Sir Lionel Smith, already at odds with the planters, was isolated and nonplussed by the Assembly's adamant refusal to conduct public business. All but two coloured members of that body had 'gone over to the Enemy', and the leaders of the coloured population, Messrs. Osborn and Jordan, had placed their newspaper, *The Morning Journal*, firmly behind the Assembly.[10] With their political star ascending, coloured members were no more willing than planters to surrender the colony's legislative autonomy. The Council was feeble, and the Attorney-General, long alienated from the Governor, offered him no support. Smith dissolved the Assembly on 3 November, but that action merely raised the political temperature by allowing contenders for seats in the new House to outstrip one another in vociferous denunciation of the British Government.

When the House reassembled in December, having been returned by an electorate of only 1,796 voters, it reaffirmed its position. The Governor had only 800 soldiers to preserve tranquillity in a colony of 350,000 people.[11] Overwrought by his difficulties, Smith calumniated his opponents and wildly exaggerated their intentions. In January he expressed fear that the island militia would assemble under order of its own officers —'all Planters, and the very People, who are burning with malignant hatred against the Blacks'—and brutalize the emancipated people.[12] Smith could see no way out of the crisis saving a radical alteration of the Jamaica constitution which would dispense with 'that insane Body', the Assembly.[13]

Smith's views were unequivocally endorsed at the Colonial Office by Henry Taylor who had prepared a lengthy memorandum in October 1838 recommending the universal adoption of Crown colony government in the West Indies.[14] In Taylor's

---

[10] Smith to Glenelg, 13 Oct. 1838, confidential, C.O. 137/230.
[11] Smith to Glenelg, 8 Jan. 1839, C.O. 137/237, no. 16.
[12] Smith to Glenelg, 16 Jan. 1839, C.O. 137/237, no. 20.   [13] Ibid.
[14] Taylor, *Autobiography* I, 249–57.

view, it was futile to attempt a vast social and economic experiment through constitutional apparatus devised to govern a slave society. He believed West Indian legislatures unfit to educate and uplift the emancipated people. Parliament, he thought, should eliminate assembly government in the Caribbean and assert its responsibility to legislate for the colonies. It was a matter of fair representation. The blacks had no property and no knowledge; they were not represented by the few coloured members of West Indian assemblies who tended to identify more strongly with the planter élite. It was only fitting, Taylor argued, that Her Majesty's Government assert its trusteeship by stepping in to protect the interests of the majority.

Stephen was impressed by Taylor's logic, but his fundamental preference for representative institutions—even dubious colonial ones—rendered him less sanguine than Taylor about the prospects of a Crown colony system. Glenelg shrank from radical measures, and the Cabinet, conscious of political realities, determined to suspend the Jamaica constitution for a period of five years rather than permanently abolish the Assembly. A Bill to this effect was brought before Parliament on 6 April. By that time, Lord Glenelg, having forfeited the confidence of his colleagues by his inert manner had been nudged from office. His successor, the Marquis of Normanby, who as Lord Mulgrave had governed Jamaica in 1833–4, was considered a better foil for the troublesome Lord Brougham whose attacks on Glenelg in the House of Lords[15] had been a source of embarrassment to the Whigs.

The Jamaica question became a parliamentary hornet's nest. One year before, in 1838, the British Government had suspended the constitution of Lower Canada. The Government's decision to send Lord Durham, a Radical, to Lower Canada as High Commissioner did not reduce the clamour of parliamentary Radicals who vigorously denounced the suspension measure.[16] The Jamaica Bill widened the breach between the Whigs and Radicals, the latter being ardent—though undiscriminating—advocates of constitutional liberty.

---

[15] Trowbridge Harris Ford, 'The Era of Lord Brougham', (unpublished Ph.D. Dissertation, Columbia University, 1967), pp. 181–2, 193–4, 201–2.
[16] Elie Halevy, *The Triumph of Reform, 1830–1841* (New York, 1950), p. 237.

As leader of the opposition, Peel exhibited considerable ignorance of West Indian conditions, but under Gladstone's persuasion he declared the Jamaica issue a matter of grave constitutional principle.[17] It was a dubious policy, he argued, to suspend a colonial constitution in every session of Parliament. Would not such action unhinge the confidence of colonists throughout the Empire? Lord Brougham, whose solicitous concern for the welfare of Caribbean blacks was only exceeded by his burning resentment against Melbourne for having excluded him from his second Ministry, lent his voice to the opposition. Wellington argued with curious logic that if the suspension measure passed no white man could continue in Jamaica.[18] William Burge, the Agent of the colony whose annual salary of £1,500 depended upon a retention of the Assembly, rallied Jamaica absentees against the Government, but by no means was he able to secure unanimous support. Lords Seaford and Sligo[19]—the first a traditional champion of the planters, the second a recent Governor of Jamaica— voiced their disapprobation of the Assembly. Anti-slavery societies and missionary and religious bodies supported suspension.[20] Captain J. W. Pringle, whose investigation of West India prisons had initiated the controversy, wrote a stinging rebuke of the Jamaica Assembly and vehemently endorsed the Melbourne Cabinet.[21] When the Commons voted on 6 May, ten Radicals defected from the Government, and the suspension Bill passed by a mere five votes. It was not enough. Not only did the narrow margin preclude any overt action against the Jamaica Assembly, it convinced Melbourne that he could not honourably continue in office.

Melbourne's resignation proved little more than a gesture. When the Queen refused to relinquish her Whig ladies-in-waiting, Peel—whose party formed a minority in the House— declined to form a government. Melbourne returned to office.

---

[17] Long, *Jamaica*, pp. 39–40.

[18] Spelding, *Reviews and Discussions*, p. 118.

[19] (Lord Sligo), *A Letter to the Marquis of Normanby* (London, 1839).

[20] Central Negro Emancipation Committee to Normanby, 27 Mar. 1839, C.O. 318/143; Correspondence of Protestant Society for the Protection of Religious Liberty, C.O. 137/245.

[21] Capt. J. W. Pringle, R.E., *The West Indian Colonies. Remarks on Their Present State and Future Prospects* (London, 1839), pp. 17–18.

A second Jamaica measure was prepared, but its terms merely gave the colonial Governor power to perpetuate annual laws which the legislature had allowed to lapse. This diluted Bill, designed to mitigate the financial chaos occasioned by a withholding of supplies, passed the House of Commons in June 1839 by a margin of only ten votes.

Failing to gain firm support for their Jamaican policy in Parliament, the Government had no choice but to conciliate the planters. Since all West Indian legislatures shared the successes or failures of the Jamaica Assembly, the Government's conciliatory policy ramified across the Caribbean. In June the governorship of Jamaica was offered to Sir Charles Metcalfe, a courageous and gifted politician who had spent the preceding thirty-eight years in India working his way up from company writer to Provisional Governor-General. Restless in his retirement in England, Metcalfe welcomed the call to duty in Jamaica. He was given wide latitude for constructive conciliation by Lord John Russell, the new Secretary of State. Russell believed that 'no improvement in legislation, and no ability in government, [could] secure to the island prosperity and peace unless a better spirit [could] be infused into the various orders of society'.[22] During his two years in Jamaica, Metcalfe assiduously cultivated that 'better spirit' between the British Government and the Jamaica oligarchs. Achieving reconciliation between freedmen and planters was a more formidable task.

The main fact of life in the free West Indies was that black labourers were unwilling to remain submissive and disciplined cane workers. When the planters tried to coerce them into performing regular estate work, many of them withdrew from the estates. Except in Barbados and the Leeward Islands, there was plenty of vacant land for peasant settlement. Even the remote portions of active estates offered sufficient seclusion for squatters to erect huts and plant provisions. Thrifty freedmen could save enough from their wages to purchase freeholds, and planters, threatened by the withdrawal of workers and desperately in need of working capital, sold backland portions of their properties in hope that peasant buyers would continue to

---

[22] Draft, Russell to Metcalfe, 27 Sept. 1839, C.O. 137/240.

afford some labour to the plantations. Proprietors who threw up the cultivation of staples willingly sold plantation property to freedmen as a means of recovering a portion of their losses. When missionaries discovered that the dispersal of freedmen was breaking up their congregations, they bought derelict plantations for subdivision among their parishioners,[23] in some cases using funds contributed for that purpose by British philanthropists.[24] In Jamaica, the Baptist Western Union established 3,300 freeholders on the land during the first four years of freedom at a cost to the people of £38,450.[25]

The development of free villages was already in progress when Sir Charles Metcalfe arrived in Jamaica. In another four years there would be 20,000 new freeholders in the island,[26] and by 1846 the labouring population residing on the estates would be only a third of what it had been in the final years of slavery.[27] The flight from the plantations and the irregular work of the freedmen who stayed behind caused officials in London to fear that the plantation system might collapse. In reaction to that danger, the Colonial Office modified its approach to West Indian affairs. The priorities of Glenelg and Stephen—namely, protecting the liberty of freedmen against encroachments from the planters—were supplanted by an official determination to reinforce the planters and preserve plantation agriculture. Sir Charles Metcalfe became a powerful advocate of that policy.

Three weeks after his arrival in Jamaica, Metcalfe identified a source of tension which, in his judgement, impaired the reconciliation of classes. Baptist missionaries, he claimed, were sowing distrust and resentment between planters and labourers. They prevented work settlements and they alone among the sectarians had become deeply embroiled in politics, enlarging

[23] This was true of Methodists, Moravians, and Presbyterians as well as Baptists. The comment of a Presbyterian was characteristic of missionary thinking: 'Averse to lose my people . . . by their dispersion through the interior, I proposed to purchase a run of mountain land, and divide it among them, that they might keep together, and form the nucleus of a new mission station.' Waddell, *Twenty-Nine Years*, p. 152.

[24] Long, *Jamaica*, pp. 49–50.

[25] Sel. Comm. on the West India Colonies, P.P. 1852, XIII (479), evidence of Knibb, 5999–6000.

[26] Eisner, *Jamaica, 1830–1930*, p. 220.

[27] Report of a Committee of the Jamaica Assembly, enclosed in C. E. Grey to Earl Grey, 7 Feb. 1846, C.O. 137/295, no. 17.

their own influence by their abusive and inflammatory decla-
mation of the planters.[28] Though they had not created the
animosity between freedmen and planters, Metcalfe thought
they had encouraged and exploited it. By arousing disaffection
among a poor and ignorant people they were, in his view, planting the seeds of insurrection.[29]

Although one wonders at the hasty nature of Metcalfe's
judgement, his rebuke of the missionaries evoked a resounding
echo from all sectors of the European community, including
other sectarian groups. Scots missionaries prepared a nine-
point remonstrance declaring the Baptists preoccupied with
numbers, neglectful of discipline, tolerant of superstition, and
guilty of deceit and simony.[30] Edward Holland, a London
missionary, referred to the 'God-insulting, Hell-invented, and
soul-destroying practices' of the Baptists whom he, in common
with his puritanical colleagues, passionately despised.[31] Some
allegations against the Baptists were well founded. Their outspoken hostility toward the planters had enhanced their
popularity with the freedmen and occasioned a widespread
demand for Baptist schools and chapels. By 1841 the Baptist
preacher in Spanish Town had been instrumental in forming
seventeen stations, some of which had become centres for
launching other stations.[32] Vastly over-extended, Baptist
missionaries provided only the most superficial surveillance over
the religious activities of thousands of adherents. Since their
principal source of strength was political, they were compelled
by circumstances and reputation to pursue a policy of political
activism while consolidating their spiritual harvest.[33]

No action was better calculated to endear Metcalfe to the
Jamaican oligarchy than his denunciation of the Baptists.

---

[28] Metcalfe to Normanby, 16 Oct. 1839, C.O. 137/240, no. 8.
[29] Metcalfe to Russell, 13 Apr. 1840, C.O. 137/240, no. 56.
[30] Waddell, *Twenty-Nine Years*, Appendix I, pp. 661–3.
[31] Edward Holland to Arthur Tidman, 27 July 1842, *L.M.S. Papers, Jamaica*.
[32] Edward Bean Underhill, *Life of James Mursell Phillippo* (London, 1881),
pp. 174–5.
[33] Metcalfe was most critical on this point. He declared that Baptists would swiftly
lose their enormous following if they did not continually impress the freedmen
that they were being oppressed and that the Baptists were the only party to whom
they could turn to relieve that oppression: '. . . the Baptist missionaries require
agitation for the support of their influence and the continuance of their pecuniary
resources . . .' Metcalfe to Russell, 13 Apr. 1840, C.O. 137/248, no. 56.

Nor was any action more indicative of his own political philosophy. While the Baptists were determined to achieve equal social standing for their clients, Metcalfe favoured the perpetuation of a privileged paternalistic white ruling class which would exercise wide-ranging judicial as well as political power in a manner similar to that obtaining in rural England. He considered his government an experiment. Could he inculcate in the planter oligarchy so genuine a sense of responsibility for the whole of society that their power could be preserved without jeopardizing the civil rights of the emancipated people?[34] He believed he could. But he knew he could not succeed unless the British Government was prepared to exhibit confidence in him and in the oligarchy he was trying to reform.

The Colonial Office was sceptical, if not pessimistic, but having failed to suspend the Jamaica constitution, the Government had no choice but to support Metcalfe.[35] As for the Baptists, only Stephen lamented their discomforture. Vernon Smith, the Parliamentary Under-Secretary, considered them dangerous, narrow-minded fanatics,[36] and his sentiments were quietly shared by Russell.

In pursuing his objectives Metcalfe employed a style and strategy diametrically different from that of his predecessor. Magnanimous rather than contentious, trusting rather than suspicious, he cultivated the best qualities of the Jamaica oligarchs. By crediting their public spirit, and expressing confidence in their political judgement, he helped to restore their self-esteem. He denied categorically the assertion of Sir Lionel Smith that the planters were intent upon reducing the labouring people to a state of slavery, and he attacked the excesses and ignorance of the anti-slavery press.[37] In his correspondence, he appealed to the Secretary of State to 'discard from [his] mind the idea that the Legislature of the Island [had] any affection

[34] Metcalfe to Russell, 30 Mar. 1840, C.O. 137/248, no. 50.
[35] Minute by Vernon Smith, bound in Metcalfe to Russell, 16 Apr. 1840, C.O. 137/251, no. 62.
[36] Minute by Vernon Smith in Metcalfe to Russell, 1 May 1840, C.O. 137/249, no. 76.
[37] Copy of a speech by Sir Charles Metcalfe to the Jamaica House of Assembly, enclosed in Metcalfe to Russell, 16 Apr. 1840, C.O. 137/251, no. 62.

for Oppression and Injustice . . . give us credit', he asked, 'for an honest desire to perform our Duty faithfully . . .'[38]

One aspect of that duty involved the re-enactment of legislation which had been disallowed by Lord Glenelg in the early months of freedom. Assured by Metcalfe that no people were more fiercely independent or less likely to submit to oppression than Jamaican freedmen,[39] the Colonial Office agreed to modify its guidelines on labour legislation. The Jamaica Vagrancy Act of 1840 provides a case in point. Glenelg had insisted that Jamaica pass a measure more lenient than the English statute and that all legislation involving relations between employers and freedmen be administered solely under the jurisdiction of stipendiary magistrates. The new Jamaica Act met neither of these conditions: it was just as stringent as the English law and it declared that ordinary planter justices were as competent as stipendiary magistrates to administer the law.[40] Metcalfe endorsed the Act, and Russell, after some trepidation, approved it.

Anti-slavery groups were outraged by this and similar concessions. For years they had served as watchdogs over colonial legislation. Every enactment of the assemblies was scrutinized by dedicated committeemen who bedevilled the Colonial Office with visitations and remonstrances, alerting the Department to inadequacies or excesses in colonial Acts. The societies dispatched energetic travellers to the colonies to investigate the progress of freedom and to organize local watchdog committees. A Colonial Union of the Coloured Classes was created in Barbados and the Windward Islands to 'watch the framing of laws in the several colonies'.[41] The persistence of their petitions and the rigidity of their views exasperated officials at the Colonial Office. Even James Stephen, whose family connections and private views rendered him the natural ally of the Saints, ultimately renounced a hard-line policy toward West Indian legislatures.

Stephen's conversion to conciliation was dictated more by pragmatism than by a desire to reinforce the planters. The

---

[38] Metcalfe to Russell, 11 June 1840, C.O. 137/249, no. 86.
[39] Metcalfe to Russell, 21 Dec. 1839, C.O. 137/240, no. 31.
[40] Stephen to Russell, 25 Apr. 1840, C.O. 323/55, Law Officer's Reports.
[41] Enclosure, MacGregor to Russell, 1 May 1840, C.O. 28/134, no. 44.

Jamaica constitution crisis had proven that for the time being the assemblies could neither be destroyed nor significantly enfeebled. Stephen believed that in spite of Metcalfe's able guidance legislation in Jamaica would continue to gratify the interests of the European élite at the expense of black freedmen; but, after all, he conceded, laws everywhere were written by the rich in behalf of the rich, and it was unreasonable to upbraid the oligarchs of Jamaica for practices which were commonplace in Parliament.[42] In view of prevailing arrangements, Stephen conceded that the British Government would accomplish more good for all elements of West Indian society by propitiating the assemblies and coaxing their members to amend faulty enactments than it could achieve by rejecting bad measures at the cost of protracted quarrels with colonial oligarchs. This approach, adopted during Lord John Russell's administration, was affirmed by Lord Stanley who returned to Downing Street as Peel's Colonial Secretary in 1841.[43]

Jamaica was the pace-setter. As difficulties increased on the estates, concessions made to the Jamaica planters on labour legislation were extended to their counterparts elsewhere in the Caribbean. In 1843 Lord Stanley authorized Crown colony governments to alter and amend the 1838 Orders in Council on contracts and vagrancy, and he sent them copies of the Jamaica Acts for use as models.[44] Stiff labour legislation was psychologically important to the planters, but it had limited practical effect on labour relations. Although freedmen may not have been regular and disciplined cane-workers, neither were they aimless vagrants who could be compelled to work lest they be thrown in jail. Contract laws, however rigorous, were largely ineffectual. Even freedmen who lived on the estates refused to work under contract, and the planters had no satisfactory means of forcing them to.

The imperial Government's policy of conciliating the assemblies encompassed every aspect of colonial legislation—the franchise, use of fire-arms, the organization of police, militias,

---

[42] Stephen to G. W. Hope, 16 Sept. 1841, enclosed in C.O. 137/256, no. 234.

[43] Draft, Stanley to Metcalfe, 27 Sept. 1841, bound in Metcalfe to Russell, 2 Aug. 1841, C.O. 137/256, no. 234.

[44] MacLeod to Stanley, 3 Feb. 1845, C.O. 295/146, no. 13. The tightening of labour legislation in the planters' behalf was recommended in the thirteenth resolution of the 1842 Select Committee on the West India colonies.

and colonial judiciaries. On every issue the British Government retreated from positions it had taken during the initial year of freedom, conceding points of principle and positions of power to the planter élites.

Colonial franchise was a highly sensitive topic. West Indian governments were dominated by elected assemblies, and narrow franchises served as the cornerstones of white oligarchic power. The franchise had always been restricted to free men, and until the last years of slavery it had been generally reserved for Europeans. Property qualifications for the franchise during slavery were low—normally around £10 annual freehold value. Emancipation threatened, in time, to inundate the electorate with numerous black and coloured voters. To preclude that, assemblymen throughout the Caribbean revised franchise laws, raising property qualifications for new voters while preventing the disfranchisement of old voters who could not meet the new property qualifications. This transparent attempt to exclude blacks and coloureds from voting while retaining the franchise for poor whites was rejected by Glenelg on the ground that such tactics would divide the colonies into opposing racial camps, provoke revolt, and infringe the national honour of England by frustrating the freedmen's just expectations for political as well as personal freedom.[45]

The Government's high-minded approach was bitterly contested by the planters, and nowhere was it fought with more success than in Barbados. From 1835 to 1841 the Barbados legislature, supported by successive governors, tried to tighten the island's franchise law. Stephen battled them at Downing Street, but by the end of 1841, Lord Stanley, engulfed in a climate of conciliation and persuaded by the persistent remonstrances of the colonial legislature, rejected the counsel of his Permanent Under-Secretary and approved a complicated and restrictive law which had the effect of preserving a uniformly white Barbados Assembly throughout the mid-century. As late as 1857 the total number of registered voters in Barbados (population exceeding 135,000) was only 1,350, and the ten rural parishes had less than 700 of them.[46] Similar concessions on the franchise question in other colonies produced equally

[45] Stephen to Glenelg, 22 Feb. 1837, C.O. 323/52, Law Officer's Reports.
[46] Hincks to Labouchere, 6 June 1857, C.O. 28/187, no. 28.

disproportionate ratios between population and electors. In 1854 Grenada (population 32,600) had 191 electors; St. Vincent (population 30,125) had 273; and Tobago (population 14,500) possessed 135.[47] In the 1863 election for the Jamaica Assembly only 1,457 votes were cast out of a population numbering above 440,000.[48]

Had the British Government succeeded in suspending the Jamaica constitution it would probably have eliminated that island's militia and used its enhanced power to impose uniform institutions for law enforcement throughout the colonies. Having failed to subdue the Assembly, the Government was obliged to concede to the perpetuation of planter dominated militia forces although the principal purpose for those bodies—the reduction of slave rebellions—had ceased to exist. Rather than provoke confrontations with Caribbean oligarchs, the Colonial Office reluctantly confirmed rigorous fire-arms laws which were contrived to keep weapons out of the hands of freedmen. Furthermore, it was obliged to discard its plan for colonial police establishments in favour of diverse arrangements produced by the separate colonial governments.[49]

The reform of colonial judiciaries was a serious problem in the West Indies. In 1836, Parliament passed a West India Judiciature Act[50] providing for two circuit court systems in the Lesser Antilles, each possessing three experienced judges. Regrettably, this attempt to improve the professional quality of colonial high courts failed to resolve the two ubiquitous problems of West India justice—money and personnel. It made no provision for the payment of judges, and its authors failed to appreciate the difficulty of procuring qualified and experienced jurists who would exile themselves to the Caribbean. Since colonies were confronting increasing public costs after emancipation, they refused to pay for the enlarged judicial apparatus envisaged by the Act. The British Treasury was equally unwilling to incur the cost of circuit courts on the colonists' behalf, and the Act remained a dead letter.

The concept of circuit courts appealed more to officials in

[47] Colebrooke to Newcastle, 20 Mar. 1854, C.O. 28/180, no. 15.
[48] Eyre to Cardwell, 19 Dec. 1864, C.O. 137/385, no. 303.
[49] Stephen to Normanby, 29 May 1839, C.O. 324/54, Law Officer's Reports.
[50] 6 & 7 Wm. IV. C. 17.

London than it did to colonists in the islands. Environmental problems were very great. Transport by sea was uncertain; delays and accidents were inevitable. Frequent circuits were necessary since the climate demanded alacrity in gaol delivery. The diversity of laws in the separate colonies and the presence of a French legal system in St. Lucia and Spanish remnants in Trinidad posed serious difficulties for transient judges. Furthermore, the several colonies were prone to quarrel over their portions of the cost and proceeds of any circuit arrangement. In view of financial stringency, imperial penury, and the pragmatic difficulties of a circuit system, sweeping reform of West Indian judiciaries was not feasible in the early years of freedom. For the most part, the colonies were obliged to make the best use of existing personnel.

At the lowest judicial level where the greatest volume of business was handled, existing personnel were either stipendiary magistrates or ordinary justices of the peace. The stipendiaries, whose commissions were scheduled to expire at the close of apprenticeship, were retained after 1838 as a temporary expedient. Until some satisfactory reform of West India judiciaries had been achieved, Lord Glenelg believed that ordinary magistrates should remain subordinate to the stipendiaries and that the latter should regulate the affairs of colonial police, inspect prisons, supervise the apprenticeship of children, administer poor laws and immigration, and preside over Courts of Quarter Session.[51] Glenelg's policy, manifesting grave distrust of the ordinary magistracy, was nullified by Jamaica's successful defiance of the home Government.

In the wake of the constitutional crisis, Sir Charles Metcalfe strengthened the planters' position by declaring that a colonial magistracy divided into two hostile and competing parties was inimical to the interests of justice. He assured the Secretary of State that the planter justices were worthy of trust and that if the stipendiaries were diminished in number, or withdrawn from Jamaica, the liberty of the emancipated people would suffer no impairment. Since the British Government could not abolish the ordinary magistracy and since some action was

---

[51] Memorandum on the Necessity of Making Provision for the Continued Employment of a Stipendiary Magistracy, 20 Nov. 1838, C.O. 318/141.

necessary to ease tension between that group and the stipendiaries, the Secretary of State agreed to diminish both the number and jurisdiction of Jamaica's stipendiary magistrates provided that some form of improved tribunals be established.[52] Improved tribunals were created in both Jamaica and Barbados. Barbados devised a compromise system whereby ordinary magistrates assumed full responsibility for summary justice, but an Appeal Court, comprising three stipendiaries, acquired the power to review all decisions which affected the emancipated population.[53] Initially, the Colonial Office objected to the Barbados measure on the grounds that several stipendiary magistrates would be discharged and the remaining ones would be relieved of direct involvement with the freedmen. But the home Government's opposition to the plan weakened as its position on the Jamaica constitution question deteriorated. When the Barbados Assembly willingly eliminated the costs and complications associated with applications by freedmen to the Appeal Court, the Secretary of State confirmed the plan. In time, the Colonial Office became an advocate of the Barbados system.[54] The Barbados plan was recommended to Jamaica, but that colony preferred to upgrade its nine Courts of Quarter Session by the appointment of chairmen who were barristers with English or Jamaican experience. These improved courts were given appellate jurisdiction over the decisions of ordinary or stipendiary magistrates who shared responsibility for summary justice.[55]

Reforms undertaken in Jamaica and Barbados could not be emulated in the less developed colonies. A recommendation that the Windward colonies reduce their number of stipendiaries, create strong local magistracies, and establish appeal courts on the Barbados model met vehement opposition from lieutenant governors. Since there were few resident proprietors in the

[52] Russell to Metcalfe, 29 Jan. 1840, C.O. 138/62, no. 51.
[53] Stephen to Normanby, 18 May 1839, C.O. 323/54, Law Officer's Reports.
[54] It was under continuous pressure from the Treasury to terminate or greatly reduce the stipendiary magistracy, and it finally resolved, as Stephen conceded, that there was no 'safe middle point between the entire abolition of the judicial powers of the ordinary Magistrates and the entrusting them with whatever was necessary to render those powers effectual'. Stephen to Russell, 14 Apr. 1841, C.O. 323/56, Law Officer's Reports.
[55] Stephen to Russell, 5 June 1840, C.O. 323/55, Law Officer's Reports.

Windwards, a reduction of the stipendiary magistracy would have placed virtually all summary jurisdiction in the hands of managers of estates in whom the freedmen reposed no confidence. The Lieutenant Governor of Tobago declared that if the stipendiaries were withdrawn blacks would conclude that the British Government took no interest in their welfare. Such action, he predicted, would cause the abandonment of half the estates.[56] Similarly, the Executive Officer in Grenada warned that if the stipendiary magistrates were removed, the black population would emigrate in massive numbers to Trinidad.[57] The Colonial Office had no choice but to retain the stipendiaries under existing arrangements.

When apprenticeship ended the financial machinery needed to sustain a free labour plantation economy was inadequate. Planters required much larger advances than they were accustomed to receiving from British merchant firms in order to pay the wages of free workers. Merchant houses did not have sufficient capital to meet the planters' demands, and the precarious economic situation in the colonies deterred those who had not been associated with the West Indies from investing there. Banking institutions which could issue paper currency, extend credit to the estates, exchange bills, and provide facilities for the maintenance of accounts and the payment of interest were desperately needed. The Colonial Bank of London, incorporated in 1836, established offices in most of the colonies during 1837, and at the same time local banks were formed in Jamaica and British Guiana. The limited credit facilities and high charges of the Colonial Bank encouraged a group of Barbados colonists to found the West India Bank in 1839 which quickly established branch offices throughout the Lesser Antilles. In the same year, the Planters' Bank was formed in Jamaica, principally by local people, to provide swift and easy credit to the estates.

Need triumphed over caution in the formation of several of these institutions. Except for the Colonial and West India

[56] Darling to C. E. Grey, 12 Aug. 1842, enclosed in C.O. 28/156, Windward Islands, no. 6.
[57] Doyle to C. E. Grey, 15 Nov. 1842, enclosed in C.O. 28/156, Windward Islands, no. 6.

Banks, both of which secured royal charters, financial institutions in the Caribbean were subject to few restrictions. By November 1838 the Bank of Jamaica, a local affair, had incurred liabilities amounting to £458,145 (currency) although its paid-up capital was only £56,000 (currency).[58] Similarly, the Planters' Bank assumed unsecured liabilities which vastly exceeded its assets.[59] As long as confidence was retained in these institutions, their notes—although generally depreciated and often not convertible into specie—served as a basis for local exchange.

Foreign exchange was a more difficult problem. The British Government had never managed to regulate or control the flow of money from its Caribbean dependencies where monetary conditions were among the most confused and complex in the world. Money contracts and government accounts were expressed in terms of a nominal currency in designations of pounds, shillings, and pence. But the nominal currency of the islands varied in value from colony to colony, and all nominal currencies differed from British sterling.[60] Regardless of the terms in which money of account was expressed, the silver dollar was the commodity intended to be conveyed in every contract of purchase or sale, for the circulating medium in the islands was, almost exclusively, dollars and doubloons of Spanish, Mexican, or South American origin.

During 1825–6, the Treasury had introduced a new silver coinage from Britain in hope of displacing foreign coins, but it simultaneously declared that so long as the Spanish dollar remained a necessary medium for the payment of British troops,

[58] Calvert to Grey, 20 Nov. 1838, C.O. 137/234.

[59] Hall, *Free Jamaica*, p. 113.

[60] All nominal currencies had reference to the dollar and doubloon with 16 silver dollars being declared by law equivalent to one gold doubloon. The relative values of the several denominations of currency in three of the most important colonies were as follows:

	Jamaica			Barbados			Trinidad		
	£	s.	d.	£	s.	d.	£	s.	d.
1 Doubloon	5	6	8 currency	5	0	0 currency	8	0	0 currency
1 Silver Dollar	0	6	8 currency	0	6	3 currency	0	10	0 currency
1 English Shilling	0	1	8 currency	0	1	6 currency			

Data on West India currency has been gathered from two extensive minutes prepared for the Treasury and bound in C.O. 854/2.

it should have an exchange value of 4s. 4d. Relative to the rate of exchange prevailing in London, this constituted an undervaluation of British silver of about 2d. in the dollar, and it rendered the retention of British silver in the colonies for the purpose of internal exchange virtually impossible. British silver and the dollar could not remain in concurrent circulation because colonists were unwilling to discharge their debts in the undervalued coins, and as soon as British silver was issued, it was remitted to London in favour of bills on the Treasury.

The difficulties created by the disappearance of British silver were compounded by a similar outflow of dollars. In European and North American markets, the relative value of silver dollars to gold doubloons was about 15·3 to 1, but in the British West Indies the doubloon was declared by law to be the equivalent of sixteen dollars. In terms of the world market, the doubloon was overvalued in the West Indies by about five per cent. Payments into the colonies were rendered in doubloons, the overvalued coins, and dollars were speedily withdrawn. American merchants, whose percentage of Caribbean trade was rapidly increasing, almost always exchanged their goods for specie, and they invariably demanded payment in dollars. As a result, the colonies were stripped of a convenient circulating medium, and gold became the basis of money in the British Caribbean. Attempts to prevent the escape of dollars by mutilating coins, cutting and plugging them, bore little success, and throughout the islands colonists were obliged to pay a heavy premium to obtain silver.

The dollar drain created severe problems. The Colonial Bank was obliged by its charter to redeem its notes in silver dollars of recognized weight and fineness while at the same time it was compelled to accept payments in doubloons. The bank was at risk because individuals dealing with it had the advantage of dual standard, and the drain of dollars from the islands prevented the bank from issuing notes (redeemable in dollars) in large amounts.[61] This necessary tightening of credit and the related shortage of dollars had a deleterious effect on planters who required an enormous amount of specie in small denominations for wage payments to free labourers. An attempt

[61] Memorandum of Anthony Cummins, manager of the Colonial Bank, 14 Mar. 1838, enclosed in C.O. 295/120, no. 37.

by one governor to alter exchange rates in order to keep silver in circulation was angrily denounced by the imperial Treasury which jealously guarded its exclusive prerogative to adjust currency values.[62]

The Treasury exercised its prerogative slowly. When apprenticeship prematurely ended, it was still engaged in a study of the West India currency problem. Its inordinantly delayed decision to curb the dollar drain by bringing the rate of exchange between the dollar and doubloon to 15·3 to 1—the rate prevailing in the world market—was not taken until September 1838.[63]

Without exception, the West India colonies launched their free labour experiment with a critical shortage of specie. In Jamaica silver was sold at a premium of 10 per cent. Cheques were being written for as little as a shilling,[64] and the demand for coin occasioned a run on the colony's banks. The Bank of Jamaica had promised to redeem its notes[65] in silver or Island cheques (notes issued by the Island Treasury on the credit of the colonial Government). Being unable to produce silver on demand, the bank paid its note-holders in Island cheques. But this served little purpose. The colonial Treasury was empty and, consequently, government secured cheques could not be converted into specie. On the eve of total emancipation, Sir Lionel Smith grimly announced that Jamaica was bankrupt.[66]

What Smith meant was that the Jamaica Treasury had momentarily run dry, and that new revenue was needed to restore island credit and meet the higher expenses of a free society. Since colonial governments fell heir to a wide array of responsibilities formerly borne by the masters of slaves, the cost of government rose sharply after emancipation. In Barbados, for example, public expenditure doubled between 1835 and 1840. During those years public outlay on the civil and judicial establishment trebled; prison costs doubled; and the amount

---

[62] A. G. Spearman to Stephen, 27 July 1836, C.O. 323/222.

[63] See p. 407, n. 3.

[64] Sel. Comm. on the West India Colonies, P.P. 1842, XIII (479), evidence of William Knibb, 6137.

[65] Bank of Jamaica notes were the only bank notes circulating in Jamaica at that point, the Colonial Bank having withheld its distribution of notes in that colony. Smith to Glenelg, 15 Feb. 1839, C.O. 137/237, no. 43.

[66] Smith to Glenelg, 8 July 1838, private, C.O. 137/228.

spent on police magistrates rose by 61 per cent.[67] The Barbados case was similar to that of Jamaica. Both colonies had possessed a substantial free population prior to 1834, and consequently both had maintained public facilities to accommodate that group. In British Guiana, on the other hand, there had been a comparatively small free population in the slavery period, and increases in public outlay after apprenticeship were greater. In 1833 the government of British Guiana spent only £812 on police and gaols and £1,820 on health and hospitals. By 1840 these figures had risen to £27,796 and £11,114 respectively. The total public expenditure in those years increased from £53,996 to £125,209.[68]

New taxes were needed to supplant the head-tax on slaves and apprentices which had formed the basic source of colonial revenue before 1838. At the outset of freedom, the Colonial Office believed that the landed interest should continue to bear the burden of taxation, that estate property and the staple exports of the colonies should produce the additional revenue needed in the free society.[69] The landed interest, already heavily burdened, rejected this approach and resorted to higher import duties to meet expanded public responsibilities. Import duties offered a dual advantage to the oligarchs. They shifted the weight of taxation from the proprietors to the freedmen, the latter being obliged to pay higher rates on the purchase of ordinary necessities of life. By raising the cost of necessities, these duties were expected to stimulate the freedmen to perform wage work on the estates.

The struggle between imperial authorities and colonists over methods of taxation was decided in Jamaica. All parties in that island—including the Baptists[70]—agreed that the proprietary body suffered a grievous tax burden. Parish revenue was primarily based on land and stock, and in Jamaica the amount of revenue collected for parish purposes exceeded the general colonial income by more than three and a half times.[71]

---

[67] Abstract of returns from Blue Books of Windward Islands, C.O. 28/174.

[68] Michael Moohr, 'The Economic Impact of Slave Emancipation in British Guiana, 1832–1852', *The Economic History Review*, XXV (1972), 593.

[69] Draft, Russell to Light, 30 Nov. 1839, C.O. 111/163.

[70] Sel. Comm. on the West India Colonies, P.P. 1842, XIII (479), evidence of William Knibb, 6230–40.

[71] Metcalfe to Stanley 24 and 27 Dec. 1841, C.O. 137/257, nos. 30, 32.

In St. Mary's parish, plantation property paid £20,000 taxes on a computed annual income of £62,000. Merchants in the parish who earned £30,000 paid only £150 in taxes.[72] Estates were taxed on 6 per cent of their valuation on the presumption that 6 per cent was a reasonable annual income for sugar property. The tax was collected whether or not the estate made a profit. In addition, property owners paid export duties amounting to 1*d.* per cwt. on sugar, ¼*d.* per gallon on rum, and 3*d.* per cwt. on coffee and ginger.[73]

The determination of Jamaican oligarchs to raise necessary revenue by import duties extended to British as well as foreign imports. The colonies had always been permitted to raise revenue by taxing foreign imports provided that those imposts did not have the effect of regulating trade by exacting differential duties. Colonial governments had been forbidden, however, to tax British imports. In the autumn of 1839 Jamaica challenged that prohibition, and Sir Charles Metcalfe reluctantly endorsed the colonial position, noting that import levies on British goods were a lesser evil than the further burdening of sugar properties which were already deteriorating under the vicissitudes of free labour.[74] When similar pressures arose from Guiana and other colonies, the Colonial Office and Board of Trade conceded to the West Indians, sanctioning the imposition of 3 per cent tariffs on British imports. Jamaica got by with a 5 per cent duty on British goods,[75] but the Colonial Office firmly rejected the colony's attempt to establish differential duties in 1843.[76] By the mid-forties, two-thirds of the revenue raised in Jamaica for island purposes (as opposed to parish purposes) was derived from import duties, and a similar dependence on import taxes prevailed throughout the Caribbean.[77]

[72] Report of Stipendiary Magistrate Fyfe, St. Mary's, Oct. 1842, enclosed in C.O. 137/264, no. 64.
[73] Long, *Jamaica*, p. 68.
[74] Metcalfe to Russell, 1 Nov. 1839, C.O. 137/240, no. 16.
[75] Minute of Russell, bound in Metcalfe to Russell, 29 Dec. 1840, C.O. 137/250, no. 154.
[76] Stanley to Elgin, 1 May 1843, bound in C.O. 137/273, no. 77.
[77] In British Guiana, property and income taxes (direct taxes) had produced 76·5 per cent of the central government's revenue in 1833. By 1845, customs duties and excise taxes were bringing in 74·3 per cent of the vastly enlarged revenue, and direct taxes were producing a mere 4·5 per cent. Moohr, op. cit., p. 605.

West Indian oligarchs consistently advocated the use of capitation taxes to repair roads which during slave times had been maintained by labour levies on the plantations. Capitation taxes fell equally on every male head. The planters argued that roadways were as important to freedmen who carried provisions to market as they were to sugar-growers. Furthermore, easy communications were vital to the extension of civilization in the islands.[78] Everyone benefited from that, they asserted, and consequently everyone should share equally in the maintenance of roads and bridges. These arguments were vigorously countered at the Colonial Office by James Stephen who believed that capitation taxes, once permitted, would be used to so excessive an extent that public burdens would be systematically transferred from the proprietors to the freedmen in order to render the latter's habitual labour essential to their subsistence.[79] Rather than establish a dangerous precedent, every Secretary of State from Glenelg to Stanley disapproved the use of capitation taxes, however modest their levy.

When Earl Grey assumed the seals of office in 1846 imperial policy changed. Deploring the actions of freedmen who withdrew from estate labour or performed it irregularly, Grey advocated a system of taxation which would weigh heavily on the labouring class while it relieved pressure on the owners of estate property. He advised colonial governments to reduce export levies on staple products,[80] and he criticized West India import taxes on the grounds that high duties on the necessities of life, especially on foodstuffs, merely raised the cost of these items and encouraged the freedmen to abandon estate labour in favour of the production and sale of provisions. Contrary to all his predecessors, Grey advocated heavy capitation taxes which would force freedmen to perform steady wage work in order to satisfy the tax collector. Those who could not pay, he argued, should be forced to labour on the roads or be hired out in gangs to the planters.[81]

[78] Report of Mr. Edward Jackson, enclosed in Hill to Glenelg, 26 July 1837, C.O. 295/115, no. 49.

[79] Stephen to Stanley, 31 Dec. 1842, C.O. 323/51, Law Officer's Report.

[80] Earl Grey, *The Colonial Policy of Lord John Russell's Administration* (London, 1835), I, 111, 367–89; Minute by Grey which became the basis of an out-letter, bound in C. E. Grey to Earl Grey, 6 Nov. 1847, C.O. 137–293, no. 106.

[81] Minute by Earl Grey, bound in Harris to Grey, 21 Feb. 1848, C.O. 295/160, no. 21.

Earl Grey represented the final stage in a decade of changing imperial attitudes. Glenelg and Stephen had been exceedingly solicitous of the freedmen. They distrusted the planters and discountenanced measures and procedures which might remotely lead to the discomfiture or oppression of the labouring class. When the Jamaica proprietors stood their ground in the constitution crisis, Lord John Russell was obliged to conciliate them. His successor, Lord Stanley, was sympathetic to the planter class, and his sympathies were reinforced by evidence collected from the colonial governors and parliamentary inquiries which indicated that freedmen were enjoying luxuries and independence beyond those of the English peasantry while the planters were sinking swiftly to ruin. The minutes and memoranda of Henry Taylor provide a barometer for official thinking. Taylor had identified with the Stephen-Glenelg policy in the early stages of freedom, but by 1846 his sympathies had come to rest with the planters. In that year, Taylor spurned Anti-Slavery Society complaints that planters were shifting the burden of taxation˙ to the freedmen. He declared that the freedmen had too much money and too much spare time, that they misappropriated both their money and their time, and that they should endure heavier taxation to relieve the hard pressed landed interest.[82]

In every category of legislation the imperial Government modified its initial formula for the free society in order to accommodate the needs of an increasingly distressed planter class. On the question of immigration—a subject given detailed treatment in a subsequent chapter—the Colonial Office withdrew its objection and permitted labour migration from West Africa in 1841 and from India in 1845. The duration of labour contracts for immigrants was increased in response to appeals from the colonies, and during Grey's administration of the Colonial Office the imperial Government offered financial and technical assistance to the largest colonies to increase the rate of immigration. Vagrancy legislation and laws concerning the collection of rents were stiffened.[83] Stronger measures were approved to combat squatting by freedmen on vacant Crown

----

[82] Memorandum by Henry Taylor, 15 Feb. 1846, C.O. 318/169.
[83] Ibid.

land.[84] And, as seen earlier, concessions were made to the planters perpetuating their control over the political, judicial, and law-enforcement machinery of the colonies.

Although the planters retained the appurtenances of power, their authority was constrained in practice. The central fact of life in most West India colonies was that the proprietors and managers of plantations needed the services of wage labourers much more than the labourers needed or wanted plantations. In all their actions, planter oligarchs were held in check by that reality. Motives which compelled English labourers to strive long hours for their livelihoods in cool northern latitudes did not operate in the Caribbean. The needs of former slaves could be easily satisfied: land was plentiful and productive; fuel was unnecessary; and clothing was relished for style, not warmth. Stringent labour legislation designed to evoke steady wage work from Caribbean freedmen could only have had marginal effects among people who were capable of supporting themselves without resort to daily wages. To prevent squatting on Crown land or derelict estates the colonies required enforcement machinery vastly beyond their means; indeed, Henry Taylor commented that nothing short of hanging malefactors could have controlled squatting.[85] Earl Grey's doctrinaire faith in discriminatory taxation was not applicable in the free West Indies. The emancipated people would not tolerate excessive capitation taxes or distraints upon their property and no colonial government had the manpower or audacity to try to collect oppressive imposts of that kind.[86] The judicial power of the planters, fearfully conceded by the Colonial Office, provided little leverage for disciplining unresponsive labourers. A planter justice who rendered oppressive judgements was subject to retaliation by freedmen who could quit his estate in favour of another. Even the militia, the ultimate instrument of planter power so staunchly defended in the early days of freedom, became a limp imposter by 1850. The tranquillity of the islands during the 1840s dispelled the Europeans' fear of violence, and

[84] Harris to Grey, 17 Aug. 1848, C.O. 295/164, no. 90.
[85] Minute by Henry Taylor, 28 Sept. 1857, bound in C.O. 28/187, no. 42.
[86] Harris to Grey, 15 May 1848, C.O. 295/161, no. 47. Attempts to collect a tax on hereditaments in St. Mary's parish, Jamaica, led to serious altercations between freedmen and collectors in which a collector and police constable were beaten. C. E. Grey to Earl Grey, 20 Oct. 1848, C.O. 137/299, no. 91.

the militias—having no vital function to perform—wilted in morale, numbers, and prestige.[87]

The peace of the islands represented an outstanding achievement. All elements of West Indian society exercised commendable restraint in the early years of freedom. The planters, though exasperated by the erosion of estate property, recognized the limits of their authority. The freedmen, often irritated and harassed, appreciated their economic power and behaved with circumspection. The Jamaica constitution crisis was a regrettable, but instructive, event. It sobered the imperial Government, whose prejudices against colonial oligarchs were exaggerated, and it led to a period of productive conciliation between the Colonial Office and the assemblies. The moderation exhibited by the pace-setting Jamaica Assembly in the 1840s was due in large measure to the skilful diplomacy of Sir Charles Metcalfe and his successor, Lord Elgin. Although Metcalfe brought out the best in the Jamaica planters, his high-minded paternalism was not suited to an environment in which the working people were strong individualists and the élite class was teetering on the edge of economic disaster. For the short term, his policy was the only practicable approach to the Assembly, and, without doubt, it worked. Lord Elgin found the Assembly cordial, zealous, anxious to please the Crown and intent on meeting the heavy responsibilities which freedom imposed upon the island.[88] As long as protective duties lasted and the price of sugar offered some promise of profit to the planters, West India oligarchs exuded a cautious optimism and worked amicably with their governors and the Colonial Office. When economic disaster ripped the colonies in the late forties, that optimism and amicability—indeed, most of the old planter class itself—was extinguished.

The material well-being of the freedmen improved dramatically in the years after emancipation. Imports to the British West Indies increased in response to the demands of freedmen whose wages gave them access to luxuries they had not savoured during slavery. Internal commerce rose sharply: shops shot up

[87] Elgin to Stanley, 14 Jan. 1846, C.O. 137/287, no. 17; Hamilton to Pakington, 13 Apr. 1852, C.O. 28/176, no. 20.

[88] Elgin to Stanley, 21 Mar. 1843, C.O. 137/273, no. 99; Elgin to Stanley, 23 June 1843, C.O. 137/274, no. 131; Elgin to Stanley, Jan. 1844, C.O. 137/278, no. 2.

in remote districts and hucksters relentlessly plied their trade in clothing, foodstuffs, liquors, and tobacco. A measure of prosperity was extended to tens of thousands who had never possessed it; however, the sugar estates, upon which the money economy and the traditional social and political apparatus of the West Indian colonies rested, gradually deteriorated.

Contemporary Britons considered commerce a vital factor in the development of civilization, and the Colonial Office expressed great satisfaction that freedmen were rapidly acquiring a taste for the products of European industry. But anxiety mounted in Downing Street lest the prosperity of the freedmen prove the undoing of the planters. Sugar plantations were considered the pivot upon which all civil and economic development in the Caribbean depended, and the hierarchical structure of society produced by the estate system appealed to the paternal and élitist instincts of the English ruling class. Finding a workable arrangement which permitted the survival of the plantation system without sacrificing the liberty of freedmen was clearly the most difficult and elusive problem of the free society.

CHAPTER 7

Free Labour and the Plantation Economy

FOR many years abolitionists had argued that free labour could produce tropical staples more cheaply than slave labour. By proving that dictum in the free West Indies they hoped to precipitate the destruction of the slave trade and slavery throughout the Atlantic region. John Gurney, a Quaker abolitionist, told a Jamaican audience that the eyes of slave-owners throughout the Americas were fixed on the British Caribbean: it was vain, he argued, to appeal to their morality; they must be shown that free labour was more profitable than slave labour.[1] Another abolitionist scolded the freedmen of Guiana: 'You strengthen the fetters of the slave in other lands, by giving colour to the charge, that if not compelled by force to labour as he is, he would be as idle as you are.'[2] James Stephen was convinced that a decrease in the profits of free-labour sugar would reinforce the slave system in other countries.[3] In an address to the Jamaica legislature, Lord Elgin remarked that the British West India colonies were destined to exercise an influence upon humanity disproportionate to their territorial extent. They were, he declared, 'the theatre of a great experiment, the issue of which may affect the doom of thousands now in bondage, and of millions yet unborn'.[4] These words may seem strangely melodramatic, but they constituted an article of faith for a generation of Britons who con-

[1] Gurney, *Winter in the West Indies*, pp. 113, 240–4. In the Introduction to his book, Gurney urged abolitionists 'to promote, by their influence over the emancipated negroes, a steady attention to the cultivation of the staple articles of these and other islands . . . for the sake of the slaves in the Brazils, in Cuba, and Porto Rico, and far above all, for the safety of untold multitudes in benighted Africa—let them direct their energies to the extension of the cultivation of sugar and coffee.'

[2] A lecture Delivered to the Masters and Labourers of British Guiana by Captain Charles Stuart, Berbice, 1839, C.O. 111/165.

[3] Stephen to Stanley, 3 Nov. 1841, bound in C.O. 295/135, Correspondence of the Colonial Land and Emigration Commissioners.

[4] Address to the Legislature, 25 Oct. 1842, enclosed in Elgin to Stanley, 25 Oct. 1842, C.O. 137/263, no. 40.

ceived the abolition of slavery in the sugar colonies a test of monumental significance for the rest of the world. In light of these sentiments it is the purpose of this chapter to assess the effects of emancipation upon the productive system of the Caribbean plantations during the first decade of freedom.

In freedom, as in slavery, labour was the principal factor determining the cost of sugar production. Natural fertility, proximity to shipping points, and regular terrain capable of accommodating modern implements of husbandry were vital assets, the lack of which would imperil a plantation's survival. But profitability depended above all else on an abundant supply of reliable cheap labour.

In the free West Indies, the supply as well as the quality of labour was mainly determined by two factors: population density and the availability of arable land—that is, land useful for the cultivation of provisions as well as staples. Where the ratio of people to arable land was high—as in Barbados, St. Kitts, and Antigua—estate labour was comparatively plentiful. Where the ratio was low—as in Jamaica, Trinidad, and British Guiana—estate labour was scarce. Table 5 offers a statement of population per square mile in the eight most productive sugar islands during the post-apprenticeship period, distinguishing between colonies having high, medium, and low population densities. Although the table does not reflect with precision the ratio of population to arable land, the geographical configuration of these colonies permits us to assume that such figures would not alter significantly the tabular breakdown. The most important sugar islands (along with British Guiana, the lone continental colony) fall into either the high or low density categories. Because differences in population density coincided with distinctions which arose in the supply and quality of estate labour, the terms high density and low density will be employed repeatedly in this study.

In high density colonies, sugar planters controlled virtually all arable land. Because the provision ground system had not been widely employed in Antigua and Barbados during slavery, the emancipated population in those islands had not assumed the character of a proto-peasantry. In low and medium density colonies, where provision grounds had been commonplace, slaves had developed a strong attachment to independent land

TABLE 5

Population Density of Slaves in Eight
Caribbean Sugar Islands, 1834

Colony	Slave Population	Square Miles	Slaves per Square Mile
High Density Colonies			
Barbados	83,150	166	500
Antigua	29,121	108	269
St. Kitts	19,780	63	314
Medium Density Colonies			
Grenada	23,638	133	177
St. Vincent	22,226	140	159
*Low Density Colonies**			
Jamaica	311,070	4,207	74
Trinidad	20,657	1,754	12
St. Lucia	13,291	233	57

Source (for Slave Population): House of Commons Papers, 16 Mar. 1838, n. 215, bound in C.O. 137/280.

* British Guiana is not included in this table because the continental extent of that colony would render any computation of slaves per square mile meaningless. However, the population land ratio in the fertile coastal strip of the colony would require that British Guiana be considered a low density colony.

holding. Their natural desire to pursue peasant agriculture after emancipation was further heightened by the increasingly seasonal nature of free labour sugar production. After 1838 the planters—being compelled to trim labour costs—introduced machinery and new techniques which dramatically reduced the number of hands employed out of crop. An attorney for numerous Jamaican estates declared that the labour requirements of most plantations declined about 30 per cent when crop ended.[5] At Hill-Side, one of his properties, year-round employment was given to only 50 or 60 persons, whereas up to 120 were needed

[5] Evidence of L. McKinnon before a Committee of the Jamaica Assembly, *Votes of the Jamaica Assembly*, 1845, Appendix LXVI. In defiance of known weather patterns and at risk to both the quality and quantity of his sugar, a manager could alter his schedule of agricultural operations, pushing ahead the preparation of land and other processes to a time of year when labour was relatively abundant. This might reduce the variation in employment figures between crop and inter-crop periods to about 20 per cent. Craton and Walvin, *Jamaican Plantation*, p. 216.

during crop.[6] Given this employment pattern, planters could not assure all freedmen year-long income security, and those workers who had access to arable land were well advised to pursue the cultivation of ground provisions. The busiest time in the provision grounds coincided with crop time on the estates.[7] When forced to choose between their own and their employers' crops, the freedmen quite naturally favoured their own. In simple terms, the seasonal character of sugar production combined with the propensity of the freedmen to pursue peasant agriculture on accessible fertile lands rendered it impossible for most planters in the low density colonies to command an abundant pool of reliable estate labourers during peak demand periods.[8]

In all seasons, irregularity of estate labour was a chronic problem for the planters. When the provision grounds were productive, freedmen in the low density colonies could sustain their lives at a customary level without resort to consistent wage work. Because estate labour supplemented their independent livelihoods providing income for the purchase of land, household items, or luxuries, they worked for wages in order to accumulate money for particular purchases. When their consumer goals were satisfied, they retired from estate work until a new demand for income arose. In some cases, freedmen worked three or four days a week, commonly at task work which, when superficially completed, required merely five hours' time.[9] In other cases they laboured consistently for several

[6] Evidence of R. Fothergill, ibid.

[7] This was the case even where sugar was made year-round, as in St. Mary's, Jamaica. The most important month in the plantation schedule in that parish was August, but planters could not secure adequate labour at any reasonable price during that month. Evidence of John Dillon before a Committee of the Jamaica Assembly, *Votes of the Jamaica Assembly*, 1845, Appendix LXVI.

[8] Crop was a crisis time for reasons other than the heavier demand for labour to cut and manufacture cane. It was very costly to neglect agriculture at that period, a time when plants set out in the fall were at an early stage of growth. One planter commented: 'In early stages of the cane, there is no plant that suffers so much from the presence of weeds and the want of air; if you can cultivate your fields highly and keep the cane perfectly clean . . . one plant throws out a dozen shoots in the place of three or four, or five, and every succeeding shoot is large and more juicy than the previous one, till in a well cleared and well manured field the row is perfectly full of those succulent shoots.' Sel. Comm. on Sugar and Coffee Planting, P.P. 1847–8, XIII (184), evidence of A. Geddes.

[9] Task work was commonly performed out of crop. During crop labourers worked by the day. Metcalfe to Normanby, 16 Oct. 1839, C.O. 137/240, no. 8; MacLeod

weeks, then disappeared from the field for a week or more. Employers were unable to determine what number of people would appear for work on a given day, and consequently their planning of estate routines—a vital factor in the efficient and economical operation of sugar property—was impaired. At crop time, employers were at the mercy of labourers. Every estate required a fixed number of workmen each day to perform the essential tasks of cutting, hauling, grinding, and boiling cane. If too few labourers turned out for work, the manufacturing operation was liable to falter, or to cease altogether. The sudden refusal of a fireman or boilerman to continue labour might result in the loss of canes already cut and carried to the mill. On many occasions freedmen struck work while canes lay cut and rotting in the field, exposing planters to an either-or situation: either they meet the workers demands or lose their crops.[10] During Christmas and New Year holidays when crop was ready to commence, labourers remained idle for two or three weeks, and no measure of persuasion could induce them to abbreviate their festivities.[11] Edward D. Baynes, President of Montserrat and a former stipendiary magistrate in Jamaica who suffered intense vilification for his alleged partiality to freedmen, considered it a fact known to everyone that labourers did not afford the proprietors 'half a day's honest labour' for their pay, noting that the real cost of free labour was more than double the stipulated rate of wages.[12]

to Stanley, 28 May 1842, C.O. 295/136, no. 60; evidence of F. Maxwell before the Subcommittee of the Agricultural and Immigration Society of Trinidad, enclosed in C.O. 295/134, no. 85; Sel. Comm. on the West India Colonies, P.P. 1842, XIII (479), evidence of M. Campbell, 1955–62.

[10] Report of T. Abbot, S.M., enclosed in Metcalfe to Russell, 20 Oct. 1840, C.O. 137/250, no. 118; Report of A. Fyfe, S.M., enclosed in Elgin to Stanley, 27 Feb. 1845, C.O. 137/283, no. 23; Sel. Comm. on Sugar and Coffee Planting, P.P. 1847–8, XXIII (123), evidence of Lord Howard de Walden, 4544–51; Edward Henry Stanley, *Claims and Resources of the West India Colonies; a Letter to the Rt. Hon. W. E. Gladstone* (London, 1850), p. 58.

[11] Report of T. McCornock, Custos of St. Thomas, March 1842, enclosed in Elgin to Stanley, 6 June 1842, C.O. 137/263, no. 6. This extended Christmas holiday was especially damaging to coffee planters whose crop ripened around that time: '. . . a great sacrifice of property takes place from the loss of coffee, which falls to the ground, from want of hands to pick it during the period of two or three weeks, when no wages, however extravagant, can obtain their labour, this too being the period when the ripening of the coffee is the most general.' Evidence of H. F. Leslie before a committee of the Jamaica Assembly, enclosed in C.O. 137/295.

[12] P.P. 1847–8, XLV (399), p. 109. While an S.M. in Jamaica, Baynes had

Negligence was as costly to the planters as irregularity. The abuse of equipment, destruction of carts, and the brutalization of draft animals increased in the free period.[13] Fires caused by negligence were common.[14] Inadequate weeding and sloppy work in boiling houses impaired the quality of plantation sugar, but managers were commonly afraid to upbraid negligent workmen for fear of losing their services during crop.[15] In the first two years of the free period the quality of sugar produced on one of Trinidad's best estates depreciated 5s. a cwt., the equivalent of £1,200 sterling a year.[16] H. M. Grant, an attorney for eight St. Vincent estates, listed the consequences of inadequate and inefficient labour which he encountered:

A decrease in the extent of cultivation, causing a diminution in the quantity of produce raised; less care in the mode of cultivation, causing a decrease in the average return per acre; the necessity of planting at unfavorable periods of the year, in order to increase as much as possible the present small quantity of plant canes . . . inability to manufacture sugar from the canes at the best yielding season, which causes a loss of quantity and quality; inability to carry on agriculture and manufacture at the same time, so that it is very difficult to keep up a regularity of system; loss in the quantity of juice of the cane, from the necessity of cutting it some days previous to commencing to make sugar.[17]

Wage rates varied in relation to the availability of labour. Contemporary evidence on West Indian wage rates, though fairly plentiful, must be used cautiously because of wide-ranging

published the *West Indian* newspaper which had encouraged freedmen to hold out for equitable wages and advised them to resist ejectment on the grounds that no power could simultaneously evict 300,000 people from their cottages. Burge to Glenelg, 23 Oct. 1838, C.O. 137/233.

[13] Jelly, *A Brief Enquiry*, p. xiii.

[14] In one issue, 14 Apr. 1846, the *Falmouth Post* reported fires at seven estates, mostly caused by careless workers.

[15] Referring to the Trinidad planter, the Governor of the island wrote: '. . . tho' he is suffering continued annoyance from the carelessness, the idleness and the waste of his property which he sees ever going on, yet for the sake of some little peace and quiet he is obliged almost to cringe to those whose vices he can scarcely endure, and to permit much in order to save himself from greater loss and discomfort.' Harris to Grey, 21 Feb. 1848, C.O. 295/160, no. 21.

[16] Sel. Comm. on the West India Colonies, P.P. 1842, XIII (479), evidence of W. H. Burnley, 715, 1058.

[17] Ibid., evidence of Grant.

differences in payment practices and currency values.[18] Apart from seasonal fluctuations, the rates of monetary payments were determined by the workers' places of domicile, the jobs they performed, and the extent of food and other allowances (including, in some colonies, houses and grounds) they received. In general terms, however, the price of labour was lowest and its efficiency greatest in the high density colonies where competition for pay and allowances was most keen. In Barbados, Antigua, and St. Kitts, first-class labourers commonly worked by the day, a period of nine hours. During the early forties they earned about a shilling a day, sometimes less, plus allowances of rum, salt meat, and provisions.[19]

Attempts by Jamaica planters to establish equally low wage rates were frustrated by Baptist missionaries and others who successfully induced workers to hold out for 1s. 6d. a day, the value at which ordinary field work had been assessed in appraisement proceedings conducted during the apprenticeship.[20] In Trinidad and British Guiana where labour shortages were especially grave, freedmen earned 1s. 8d. to 2s. 1d. a task, and able bodied workmen could perform two, sometimes three, tasks a day.[21] Plantation labour was most abundantly rewarded

[18] For a table indicating daily wages for first class field workers in 14 West India colonies, 1839–50, see W. Emanuel Riviere, 'Labour Shortage in the British West Indies After Emancipation', *The Journal of Caribbean History*, IV, (1972), pp. 29–30. Riviere's table only accounts for monetary remuneration; it does not—nor given the problem of sources, could it—take into account comparative currency values or the extent to which money payments were, on average, supplemented by allowances.

[19] Grey to Stanley, 19 Apr. 1842, C.O. 28/143, no. 12; Sel. Comm. on the West India Colonies, P.P. 1842, XIII (479), evidence of Sharpe, Carrington, Nugent, and Estridge; Flanders, *Antigua*, II, 75–6.

[20] Sel. Comm. on the West India Colonies, P.P. 1842, XIII (479), evidence of W. Knibb, 5974–90. This is a case of the planters' chickens coming home to roost. The rate of 1s. 6d. established during apprenticeship was deliberately inflated to discourage apprentices from purchasing their freedom. After apprenticeship the planters were forced to accept that rate as the basis for wages, a costly result of earlier inequities.

[21] Freedmen who immigrated to Trinidad from the United States commonly performed three tasks a day, but most native Trinidad freedmen refused to undertake more than a single daily task or four tasks a week. Evidence of St. Luce Philip before the Subcommittee of the Agricultural and Immigration Society of Trinidad, 22 Mar. 1841, enclosed in MacLeod to Russell, 20 Aug. 1841, C.O. 295/134, no. 85; MacLeod to Stanley, 28 May 1842, C.O. 295/136, no. 60; George Barrow's minute on the stipendiary magistrates' reports, bound in C.O. 295/133, no. 69.

in Trinidad.[22] During the early years of freedom, field-workers in that island received daily allowances of salt fish, plantains, rice, flour, and rum in addition to wages.[23] On Trinidad properties freedmen enjoyed the use of cottages and provision grounds without payment of rent. Nevertheless, the quality of labour in Trinidad was notoriously bad, and planters were reputedly willing to hire villains of any description short of murderers.[24] Because workers had no fear for their jobs, they had no inducement to perform them well.

During the early years of freedom concerted efforts by the planters to trim wages failed. The first general attempts at wage reduction occurred at the beginning of 1842 after a year in which the average wholesale price for muscovado in London had fallen 16s. a cwt. Under extreme pressure to curtail costs, the planters of St. Mary's parish, Jamaica, reduced wages 33 per cent, but a strike of workers which threatened to nullify the prospects of a large crop shattered the unanimity of the employers, forcing wages to return to the pre-strike level.[25] A similar failure occurred in Trinidad.[26] In British Guiana, pro-

[22] In view of the allowances granted West Indian freedmen, wage rates in the low density colonies did not compare badly to payments made to agricultural wage earners in Britain and the United States. On average, both British and American farm workers earned about 2s. 6d. a day in the 1830s. See, Donald R. Adams, 'Some Evidence on English and American Wage Rates, 1790–1830', *The Journal of Economic History*, XXX (1970), pp. 505–7. To ascertain accurately the relative well being of British or American as opposed to Caribbean wage workers it would be necessary to determine the value of allowances enjoyed by each, and to account for the savings made by West Indians as a result of climatic conditions which rendered the costs associated with life in cold climates superfluous. Consideration must be given to the higher cost of consumer goods in the West Indies, and some account should be taken of the opportunities for additional income provided West India freedmen through assiduous exploitation of the task-work system and their provision grounds.

[23] Mein to Normanby, 18 May 1839, C.O. 295/125, no. 36; Cadett to Russell, 25 Sept. 1839, C.O. 295/127; Sel. Comm. on the West India Colonies, P.P. 1842, XIII (479), evidence of Burnley and Bushe.

[24] MacLeod to Stanley, 5 Aug. 1845, C.O. 295/147, no. 58.

[25] Report of W. Marlton, S.M., enclosed in C.O. 137/263, no. 6.

[26] During the period 1842–5 numerous attempts were made to lower wages in Trinidad, but the competition for labour prevented employers from maintaining a solid front against the workers. A reduction of about 25 per cent was achieved at the end of crop in 1844 after a strike lasting six weeks halted work in some districts. When crop commenced the following year, wage rates had climbed back to their former level. Reports of S.M.s, enclosed in MacLeod to Stanley, 6 Jan. 1845, C.O. 295/146, no. 5. In 1845 most freedmen were earning 1s. 8d. a task and 2s. 1d. *per diem* for a decreased quantity of labour. Houses and grounds re-

prietors promulgated a rigid code of conduct for estate labour in a desperate effort to cut production costs. By terms of their 'Rules and Regulations' wages were reduced and allowances eliminated; labourers who failed to complete assigned tasks were expected to forfeit their pay; those who absented them- selves from work were held liable to fine. Freedmen were afford- ed no guarantee of the use of provision grounds, nor were they permitted to raise stock, other than feathered creatures, without permission of their managers. Those who refused to submit to this code were held liable to ejectment from their estate cottages. An absentee proprietor described these regulations as the attempt of drowning men to grasp a straw,[27] but the freedmen considered them a blueprint for re-enslavement, and a labour strike of six weeks duration ensued. Although many freedmen voluntarily left the plantations during the strike, the threatened ejectments did not materialize. As the Governor observed, it was not difficult to evict a few idle workmen, 'but who is to eject some twenty thousand, and having done so where are they to go?'[28] In time, the planters conceded, unable to continue a fruitless struggle which had already reduced their pool of workers and impaired the quality of their growing crop. Sir Charles Metcalfe's observation on the labour situation in Jamaica was equally applicable to Guiana and to all low-density colonies:

The real difficulty with regard to the prosperity of the Proprietors appears . . . to consist in the means possessed by the labourer of comfortable subsistence, independent of labour for wages. He may have recourse to the latter for the sake of money, or handsome clothing, or luxuries; but he is hardly ever reduced to it from absolute necessity. The usual order of things prevailing in other countries is thereby reversed in this; and it is here no favour to give employment, but an assumed and almost acknowledged favour to give labour.[29]

Interest in scientific agriculture spread rapidly in the early years of freedom. Throughout the Caribbean, agricultural

mained rent free, and some employers continued granting allowances. MacLeod to Stanley, 19 Apr. 1845, C.O. 295/146, no. 26.

[27] Sel. Comm. on the West India Colonies. P.P. 1842, XIII (479), evidence of H. Barkly, 2563.

[28] Light to Stanley, 21 Jan. 1842, C.O. 111/189, no. 18.

[29] Metcalfe to Russell, 14 Nov. 1839, C.O. 137/240, no. 22.

societies were established to facilitate the exchange of information on all aspects of sugar production and to encourage the
improvement of agrarian skills. Lord Elgin established a Royal
Agricultural Society in Jamaica,[30] and small associations were
formed in separate parishes. Agricultural shows, held periodically, featured exhibitions of stock as well as competition in
the use of ploughs and harrows. Money prizes were awarded
to managers who produced the largest crop on the smallest
acreage, to those who devised new cultivating implements, and
to others who made successful innovations in the manufacturing
process.[31] In many colonies awards were extended for the best
essays on agricultural topics—on the management of estate
land, on diseases of the cane or cane pests, or on various aspects
of animal husbandry. Soil chemistry evoked great interest, and
special attention was given to experiments with imported
fertilizer, notably guano. The Westmoreland Agricultural
Society divided its parish into eight districts according to soil
types, and meetings were held, in turn, at an estate in each
district.[32] Similar 'preambulatory' meetings were conducted in
Barbados where the formation of district societies preceded the
establishment of a general agricultural association.[33] In December 1843 an agricultural meeting in St. Catherine attracted
planters from nearly two-thirds of Jamaica's estates,[34] and three
years later 5,000 people from all parts of the island attended
the Cornwall County agricultural show at Montpelier
Estate.[35]

Changes in agricultural patterns and techniques occurred
everywhere in the British West Indies. The extent of those
changes was determined by need, natural conditions, and the
supply of labour, as a review of developments in the four most

[30] Elgin to Stanley, 22 Feb. 1844, C.O. 137/278, no. 30.

[31] In February 1846, the Trelawny Agricultural Society was offering the following prizes: a silver cup, value £25, to the overseer who made the largest crop from
the smallest cane field; a silver cup, £20 value, to the overseer who most successfully applied artificial manure; a silver cup, value £20, to the overseer who obtained the largest return from a field of not less than 5 acres, cultivated with the
least manual labour; a silver cup, £20 value, for the overseer showing improved
apparatus, or improved systems for manufacturing sugar or distilling rum.

[32] Elgin to Stanley, 17 Apr. 1844, C.O. 137/279, no. 62.

[33] Schomburgk, *History of Barbados*, p. 133.

[34] Elgin to Stanley, 20 Dec. 1843, C.O. 137/275, no. 197.

[35] *The Falmouth Post*, 1 Sept. 1846.

important sugar exporting colonies indicates. The most significant change in Barbados involved land use. In slave times the
island was self supporting in provisions, and it exported surplus
foodstuffs to neighbouring colonies. After emancipation, when
the wage labour system relieved masters of direct personal
responsibility for the sustenance of their workers, Barbados
planters reduced their commitment to foodstuffs in favour of
heavy speculation in sugar. Thousands of acres formerly
planted in provisions were converted to cane, and by 1845 two-
thirds of the colony's food was being imported.[36] If landless
freedmen were to eat, they had to earn wages on the estates
to buy imported foodstuffs. By the fifties well over half the total
acreage in the island was committed to sugar, and even the
working people preferred to use their small cottage plots for
growing the cash crop.[37] A similar though more limited expansion of cane acreage occurred in Antigua after emancipation.[38]
By contrast, planters in low density colonies were usually
obliged to reduce their cane acreage because they could not
command enough labour at an acceptable cost to harvest all
the land formerly devoted to cane.

Barbados planters were distinguished by their care in cultivation, but they were slow to adopt animal-drawn farm implements. They possessed ample cheap labour to perpetuate their
garden-type cultivation, and neither freedmen nor planters
were anxious to change—the former because animal-drawn
implements deprived them of wage work, the latter because
the use of ploughs and harrows was thought to have a desiccat-
ing effect on tropical soils. Not until the 1850s did the plough
receive much use, and even then its adoption was far from
universal.[39] In other areas, however, the Barbados planters
were quick to innovate. The natural fertility of their soil had

---

[36] Davy, *The West Indies*, p. 127; Henry Taylor, minute, 1 Nov. 1845, bound in
C.O. 28/162, no. 56; Colebrooke to Pakington, 2 Jan. 1853, C.O. 28/178, no. 2.

[37] Of the 106,500 acres in Barbados, approximately 55,000 were estate held cane
pieces. Much of the additional 20,000 acres owned by small proprietors or used
in labourers, allotments was planted in cane. The remaining 31,500 was in pasture,
road, town, or other acreage not arable. Hincks to Lytton, 1 Sept. 1858, C.O.
28/188, no. 48.

[38] Davy, *The West Indies*, pp. 396–7.

[39] Ibid., p. 114; Reports of police magistrates, enclosed in Grey to Stanley,
19 Apr. 1842, no. 12; Sel. Comm. on the West India Colonies, P.P. 1842, XIII
(479), evidence of Carrington, Sharpe.

been exhausted by two centuries of planting. A light, easily conveyed fertilizer which could be applied with minimal use of labour was desperately needed to augment the limited supply of animal manure in the island. The artificial fertilizer industry was in its infancy in the thirties and forties: both England and the Caribbean colonies imported bone dust, but bones were low in nitrogen and their rich phosphate content was very slowly released. In 1841 Peruvian guano was introduced in England,[40] and experiments with this light fertilizer possessing high nitrogen and substantial phosphate content were quickly initiated in the West Indies. Barbados planters led all others in the use of guano, and by the mid-fifties they were dressing the soil with an average of £50,000 worth of guano a year.[41] High fertilization, combined with an expansion of cane acreage, enabled Barbados proprietors to more than double their sugar exports in the first three decades of freedom, an achievement not equalled elsewhere in the Caribbean.

In Trinidad conditions were very different. Virgin land abounded and great natural fertility permitted the ratooning of cane for ten to twenty years. On the other hand, labour was both scarce and expensive. Trinidad estates were located on level or gently sloping land, but the soil of the island tended to be wet and heavy, and the extensive use of ratoons as well as the presence of tree stumps in cane pieces—left there because the scarcity of labour had prevented their removal—generally prevented the use of the plough. The colony's planters devised methods of producing sugar which limited their liabilities, exploited their assets, and permitted large crops to be produced by a small number of labourers. Canes were ratooned for long periods, and every year half the canes of an estate were harvested. Because the canes grew thick and tall for a period of two years, a considerable amount of weeding was avoided. Manuring was rarely done. Each year as some ratoons went

---

[40] W. H. Mathew, 'Peru and the British Guano Market, 1840–1870', *Economic History Review*, 2nd ser., XXIII (1970), 112–13.

[41] Hincks to Labouchere, 6 June 1857, C.O. 28/187, no. 28; Walker to Newcastle, 27 Sept. 1859, C.O. 28/189, no. 66. Using London prices as a base, £50,000 would have purchased about 4,000 tons of guano. But, the price of guano advertised in Jamaica in 1846—£7 a ton—was much lower. If the Jamaica price is used as a base then consumption of guano in Barbados was closer to 7,000 tons a year.

out of production a few additional acres of virgin land were planted in cane.[42] This system was crude, and it produced inferior sugar. Trinidad estates were ramshackle affairs in the early years of the free period: their cane pieces lacked the groomed appearance of Barbados fields; buildings and works were in a perpetual state of decay; negligence was apparent in the profusion of broken tools, wheels, and boilers which littered the plantations; and livestock was neglected, ill fed, feeble, and sickly.[43] On the strength of the island's natural fertility, Trinidad planters sustained their sugar exports during the initial decade of freedom, but they did so at considerable cost to the quality of their product and the physical condition of their properties. The low supply, high cost, and poor performance of labour precluded important technological innovations in the agriculture of the island.

During the apprenticeship years, there was a commendable spirit of enterprise in British Guiana. Capital derived from the compensation fund was generously invested in steam engines for sugar mills; elevators were installed to convey cut canes to mill houses from punts which had transported them from the field; megass-carriers were adopted for transferring the refuse of squeezed canes to storehouses.[44] A steam-propelled canal excavator was patented in 1836. It was designed to discharge silt from the numerous canals which traversed Guiana plantations—an operation which was extremely hateful to labourers who stood waist-deep in water shovelling the mud to adjoining banks—but the device was badly underpowered and the high cost of developing a workable machine forced the abandonment of the project.[45] Alexander Macrae developed a novel steam driven plough which was dragged across the land on a rope suspended between punts located on opposite sides of a cane piece, but this device proved too awkward for general service.[46]

[42] Sel. Comm. on the West India Colonies, P.P. 1842, XIII (479), evidence of R. H. Church.
[43] Davy, The West Indies, pp. 318–20.
[44] Sel. Comm. on the West India Colonies, P.P. 1842, XIII (479), evidence of H. Barkly, 2534–6.
[45] The Guiana Times, 18 Jan. 1841; Smyth to Glenelg, 13 June 1836, C.O. 111/145, no. 172.
[46] Sel. Comm. on the West India Colonies, P.P. 1842, XIII (479), evidence of M. Campbell, 2069–72.

The intricate network of surface drains which laced Guiana estates precluded the use of orthodox animal drawn agricultural implements, and planters were forced to rely on expensive manual labour to perform all field operations. The extent of water retained in the soil—especially water which held a large quantity of saline matter in solution—damaged the quality and colour of Guiana sugar.[47] In the mid-1840s, the planters launched an experiment in sub-surface drainage in hope of eliminating open drains and rendering the land suitable for labour-saving implements. Dr. John Shier, an agricultural chemist employed by the colony, was granted a section of La Penitence Estate which he cleared and fitted with underground tile drains. A steam engine was employed to extract excess water from the tiles, and the land was ploughed and planted. The first canes grown under these conditions were large and healthy, and their yield per acre was twice that of canes produced on neighbouring fields [48] The planters were elated. Referring to a recent Act of Parliament[49] which committed the British Government to assist agricultural interests in the mother country, the Court of Policy petitioned the Crown for monetary assistance to undertake large scale drainage of colonial land [50] The Secretary of State, constrained by economic difficulties in Europe and by his own dogmatic *laissez-faire* principles, refused to consider a loan for agricultural improvements. Grey informed Governor Light that undertakings of that kind should most properly be 'gradually effected by individual exertion'.[51]

In response to Grey's recommendation, a group of Berbice planters formed a company for the purpose of introducing a further five-year experiment in sub-surface drainage.[52] This endeavour—although endorsed by a committee of absentees in London—was defeated by the planters' inability to raise sufficient capital. In effect this failure proved fortuitous, for during

[47] Petition of the Combined Court of British Guiana to the House of Commons, 3 June 1847, P.P. 1847–8, XXIII (167), Appendix to the Third Report from the Sel. Comm. on Sugar and Coffee Planting.

[48] Dalton, *History of British Guiana*, I, 501.

[49] 9 & 10 Vict. C. 101.

[50] Extract of minutes of the Combined Court, 1 Mar. 1847, P.P. 1847–8, XXIII (167), Appendix to the Third Report from the Sel. Comm. on Sugar and Coffee Planting.

[51] Grey to Light, 14 Apr. 1847, Ibid.

[52] P.P. 1847–8, XLVI (749).

the second and third year of Shier's experiment, his crops were deeply disappointing. Underground tiles became choked with roots; the canes grew weakly; many of them rotted; and their yield was sharply diminished.[53] Although British Guiana continued to lead the colonies in the use of advanced milling and boiling equipment, the mode of cultivation in the colony remained what it had been in the time of slavery. Davy declared that in rudeness it even surpassed Trinidad, noting that weeds grew thick among the cane and that the only implements of husbandry in use were the shovel, hoe, and cutlass.[54] This rudeness was not occasioned by stubborn conservatism or inadequate enterprise on the part of the planters; rather, it resulted from a shortage of labour, the low efficiency of that which existed, and the ubiquitous drainage problems of Guiana estates.

Agriculture by implement was enthusiastically adopted in Jamaica. The plough gained universal service on level and gently undulating cane fields which were free of obstructions. Local craftsmen improved on light-weight European and American ploughs by developing rugged, deep-cutting implements, tailored to the soil requirements of individual estates.[55] Harrows of various types were introduced in the 1840s, but they were received with less enthusiasm and were employed more sparingly than the plough. This device was not serviceable in stiff or stony tropical soil, nor was it useful in hard, sloping ground where it was liable to slide into a row of cane, cutting up sprouts and damaging roots. As a weeding implement it was not as effective as the hand-hoe, and consequently it had to be employed frequently. Imaginative planters modified conventional harrows to meet their specific requirements, adding scarifying tools and mould-boards which thrust the earth onto the roots of young plants as a means of smothering weeds.[56] In the Liguanea Plain where the soil was light, and the plough

---

[53] At the end of the century another attempt was made to effect underground drainage with the same discouraging results. See, Beachey, *British West Indies Sugar Industry*, p. 97.

[54] Davy, *The West Indies*, p. 359.

[55] Where the land was heavy and compact, the plough was used to loosen and pulverize the soil, permitting more luxurious cane growth.

[56] Weeds growing on the cane rows could only be safely and effectively controlled by the hand hoe.

and harrow were fully and productively employed, planters reduced the annual cost of cultivation from £6 or £7 per acre to £2 or £3.[57] Similar economies were reported in St. Dorothy.[58] A Hanover planter conserved the labour of twenty-two first-class workers, reducing his tillage costs £2 per acre by adopting the plough.[59]

In the free period as in slavery the extent of cultivation on an estate was regulated by a planter's capacity to harvest and manufacture his cane. Although the introduction of animal-powered implements afforded the best situated estates the technical capacity to expand sugar cultivation, expansion was prevented by labour shortages at crop, and the absence of any alternative to manual labour in cutting cane. In fact, many planters reduced their sugar acreage, confining cultivation to their richest soil. These reductions were always acts of necessity, not policy, since an estate's overhead costs—including salaries, taxes, buildings, and machinery—remained fairly stable whether it produced 100 or 300 hogsheads of sugar. There was no satisfactory way to compensate for a decline in sugar acreage, but vigorous efforts were made through intensive manuring and a revision of techniques to gain the greatest possible yield from the land in cultivation.[60]

On many estates, the distance between cane plants was lengthened from 4½ feet to 6 feet.[61] Although this permitted more abundant weed growth in the early life of the cane, wider banks were cleaned by the use of animal powered implements. Because each plant was allowed greater space, a larger number of healthy shoots could be obtained from fewer cane tops, and consequently labour costs sustained in securing and planting

[57] Elgin to Stanley, 20 May 1843, C.O. 137/274, no. 125.

[58] Report of W. A. Bell, S.M., enclosed in Metcalfe to Russell, 6 May 1841, C.O. 137/255, no. 214.

[59] Report of R. Chamberlain, S.M., enclosed in Elgin to Stanley, 26 June 1844, C.O. 137/279, no. 80.

[60] Fly penning and basket dunging remained the principal modes of fertilization in Jamaica, but guano quickly gained popularity. Initially there was fear that guano affected the quality of sugar, producing a greasy substance in the liquor. Experiments conducted with guano produced varying results, but in most cases sugar yields were substantially increased. See, for example, Report of David Ewart, Dec. 1845, enclosed in C.O. 137/287, no. 2.

[61] The technique of wider planting was introduced in many West India colonies after emancipation. Colebrook to Grey, 25 Mar. 1850, C.O. 28/172, no. 16.

cane tops was reduced. Furthermore, canes received more sunlight; they grew rapidly, matured more quickly, and stooled out, covering the adjacent soil. The task of trashing—a form of labour for which there was no mechanical device—was thereby diminished, and cutting was made somewhat easier. The introduction of implemental tillage rendered the maintenance of low-yielding ratoons inefficient and unprofitable on estates having level, easily worked land and a fair prospect of good seasons. New plants promising much higher yield could be set out at comparatively small cost at a time of year when labour was generally available.[62]

Implemental tillage and improved techniques permitted savings to the planters, but they offered no panacea for the ills which beset the plantations in the free period. The cost of cultivation represented only a modest portion of the total expenses of a sugar estate, and those expenses were only partially reduced by the substitution of animal power. At Seville Estate, Jamaica, where soil conditions prevented the use of the harrow and rendered the plough only partially serviceable, labour costs incurred in all agricultural functions formed slightly more than 38 per cent of the estate's labour bill for 1844. In relation to the whole annual expenses of the estate, the cost of cultivation constituted merely 22 per cent (see Table 6). By the most extensive use of machinery the manager of Worthy Park trimmed his number of field labourers by 75 per cent, but the cost of labour in cultivating the land was merely halved. More skilled workers were needed to wield ploughs and harrows, and their wages were higher than those of ordinary field workers.[63]

Worthy Park Estate offers an outstanding example of the perils associated with the employment of sophisticated machinery in the West Indies in lieu of human labour. Between 1843 and 1847, gross annual expenditures on the estate rose from £5,542 to £18,856. Most of the increase represented investments in farm implements, factory equipment, a steam-powered mill, and a movable light railway several miles in

[62] Evidence of George Price before a committee of the House of Assembly appointed to enquire into the state of agriculture in Jamaica, *Votes of the Jamaica Assembly*, 1845, Appendix LXVI.

[63] Ibid.

TABLE 6

Annual Costs Incurred at Seville Estate, St. Ann, Jamaica, 1844

Expenses	£	s.	d.
Labour			
Cane Cultivation	316	16	1½
Manuring	125	0	3
Manufacturing Sugar	348	7	10½
Manufacturing Rum	36	13	7½
Tradesmen	106	12	4½
Maintenance of Cattle and Pastures	79	17	0
Maintenance of Fences and Stone Walls	38	13	0
Overlookers, Rangers, etc.	25	7	3
Domestics and Provisions	54	0	6
Repairing the High Road	3	14	9
Miscellaneous	56	9	3
Total	1,191	12	0
Contingencies (Salaries, Taxes, Supplies)	1,016	13	7
Total Cost of Estate Operation	2,208	5	7
Deduct Receipt of Rents	215	4	6
Total Expended	1,993	1	1

Source: Abstract of a Return to the Royal Agricultural Society, enclosed in Report of John Woolfreys, magistrate, 1 May 1845, bound in C.O. 137/284, no. 79.

length which was employed to transfer cane to the factory. With these devices the progressive manager of the property hoped to increase his output from about 230 hogsheads in 1843 to 875 hogsheads in 1846. Regrettably, his rails proved too light to provide adequate balance for heavy laden tram carts, and they rusted in the wet soil. The new mill sent from England had numerous constructional defects and broke down at the height of crop, causing a loss of £8,000. The estate's yield in 1846 was 302 hogsheads; in 1847 it fell to 266 hogsheads, far short of the anticipated 875.[64]

During the difficult years of adjustment in Jamaica, Lord Elgin repeatedly commended the planters for their vigorous pursuit of progressive agricultural methods. Most assuredly, there were recalcitrant managers who resisted innovation, but

[64] Craton and Walvin, *Jamaican Plantation*, pp. 220–2.

the reports of stipendiary magistrates are filled with praise for the greater number who, as David Ewart asserted, manifested 'the most judicious and vigorous efforts . . . to improve cultivation'.[65] In 1845 one of the most independent magistrates in the island reported 'astonishing improvement' in the character of cultivation, noting that the Jamaica planter had earned the title 'agriculturist'.[66]

This title was earned in the face of overwhelming natural misfortunes. During the first eight years of freedom, Jamaica suffered five years of prolonged and paralysing drought. In the parish of Vere, one crop in three was virtually destroyed, and planters expressed fear that the island had sustained a dramatic change of climate. Drought devastated herds, reducing the quantity and value of their manure.[67] Without rain it was impossible to assess with desired accuracy the value of supplementary fertilizers, and there is little doubt that the transformation in agricultural techniques—however commendable—was both delayed and stunted by this unprecedented succession of dry years. Stipendiary magistrates bewailed the hardship of the planters, reporting extraordinary scenes of distress. Twickenham Park, a large, partly irrigated plantation in St. Catherine, which combined sugar production with cattle ranching, made no crop in 1846, and ponds which supplied its stock dried up during a period of eight months when no rain fell.[68] At Dawkins Caymanas, where various ploughs and harrows, a megass elevator, and a variety of artificial fertilizers were in use, only 21 hogsheads of sugar out of an anticipated 200 were produced.[69] Streams disappeared and wells ran dry in Clarendon, preventing the manufacture of cane. When rains returned the cane grew luxuriantly, but subterranean cavities remained dry. During 1845, a favourable year, one Vere property did not have enough water in its wells to supply a steam engine, and the estate's manager was obliged to haul water in puncheons from the River Ninho, a distance of five miles, to keep the engine

[65] Report of D. Ewart, May 1844, enclosed in C.O. 137/279, no. 80.
[66] Report of H. Pringle, June 1845, enclosed in C.O. 137/284, no. 79.
[67] Reports of stipendiary magistrates, enclosed in Elgin to Stanley, 26 June 1844, C.O. 137/279, no. 80.
[68] Report of W. Ramsay, 1846, enclosed in C.O. 137/289, no. 17.
[69] Ibid.

going.[70] The effect of drought upon the cost of production on five Vere estates may be seen in Table 7.

It was an undeserved twist of fate which crippled the Jamaica planters during the trying years of transition, eroding their assets, undermining their credit, and testing beyond measure their self-confidence and composure. The drought of 1846 was in its final debilitating stages when news reached the island that the British Parliament had passed the Sugar Duties Act, establishing a schedule by which the preferential tariff for colonial muscovado would be systematically eliminated by 1851. This was a crowning blow to a planter class already dispirited by its misfortunes. During the succeeding two decades the island's sugar industry sustained a decline unparalleled in the British Caribbean.

Dramatic innovations in the manufacture of sugar were not common in the West Indies following emancipation. The centrifugal was developed in 1837 as a quick and efficient means of separating molasses from sugar after boiling, but it required heavier motive power than most estates possessed, and saving in British Guiana, its adoption in the colonies was delayed until later in the century.[71] The vacuum pan received wide attention in Guiana during the forties and fifties, but several factors inhibited its use in the islands. Many planters, especially those of Jamaica, were enjoying a very considerable return on their rum; consequently they placed great emphasis on the production of a rich molasses. The vacuum pan generated a poor grade of molasses, capable of producing only a low quality rum. The cost of establishing a vacuum pan factory was prodigious. In 1846 a vacuum pan was introduced at Retreat Estate in Westmoreland, Jamaica, at a cost of £3,000.[72] That amount was greater than the total annual expenses of most Caribbean properties. Even in British Guiana it was considered imprudent to adopt this equipment on estates making less than 500 hogsheads a year,[73] and there were probably not half a dozen island plantations capable of yielding such a crop.

Steam engines were installed on many estates which had

[70] Report of H. Pringle, June 1845, enclosed in C.O. 137/284, no. 79.
[71] Beachey, *British West Indies Sugar Industry*, pp. 72–3.
[72] Hall, *Free Jamaica*, p. 92.
[73] Barkly to Newcastle, 26 May 1854, C.O. 137/323, no. 73.

TABLE 7

Cost of Sugar Production on Five Vere Estates, 1844–1847

Estate	Year	Weather	Total Expenses £ s. d.	Sugar (cwt.)	Rum	Cost of Sugar per cwt. After Deducting Rum £ s. d.
Salt Savanna	1844	Drought	2,098 19 10	130	1	16 0 11
	1845	Good	2,447 19 2	943	27¼	2 7 11
	1846	Drought	2,427 18 2	569	16½	3 18 3
	1847	Good	2,650 0 0	2,831	80	0 9 7
Hill Side	1844	Drought	3,040 11 6	231	6	12 18 5
	1845	Good	2,485 11 6½	1,980	60	0 18 1
	1846	Drought	2,642 14 10	992	23	2 5 3
	1847	Good	3,000 0 0	2,755	112	0 8 9¾
Brazaletto	1844	Drought	2,648 9 1	214	3	12 4 0
	1845	Good	1,991 9 6¼	1,122	29	1 8 6
	1846	Drought	2,017 19 5	267	12	6 19 10
	1847	Good	2,633 3 7	1,716	41	1 3 0
Halse Hall	1844	Drought	2,533 18 0	212	5½	11 10 3½
	1845	Good	2,405 14 2½	2,416	57	0 14 4½
	1846	Drought	2,448 9 8½	1,003	38	1 19 5
	1847	Good	3,352 10 0	2,904	88	0 13 4½
Moreland	1844	Drought	3,135 8 3½	660	19	4 9 9
	1845	Good	2,516 12 4½	2,508	57	0 14 10
	1846	Drought	3,598 10 7	1,881	72	1 8 8
	1847	Good	4,370 0 0	3,943	90	0 14 10

Source: Report of a Committee of the Jamaica Assembly, 1847, enclosed in C.O. 137/295, no. 17.

previously employed cattle or windmills. In Trinidad and Guiana the transition to steam was almost universal.[74] By 1846 33 steam engines were employed in St. Kitts, and this mode of power was rapidly replacing the windmill.[75] According to a local almanac printed in 1849, 23 out of the 63 mills operating in Tobago were steam-driven.[76] One hundred and eight of Jamaica's 300 estates were milling by steam in 1854; water mills were in use on 125 other properties.[77] In the Windward Islands, water mills continued to predominate. Barbados and Antigua retained their windmills, the former because strong easterly winds were most reliable over the island during crop, the latter because a severe shortage of fresh water inhibited the introduction of steam power.

Most planters who possessed properly functioning wind or water mills could not justify a change to steam power under the straitened economic circumstances of the free period. The manufacture of sugar required balance between the milling and boiling operations. An efficient steam system speeded the process of grinding and permitted estates with an abundance of labour to plant more canes and to harvest them with greater alacrity. The rate at which steam milling produced cane juice usually exceeded the receptive capacity of boiling houses which had been geared to other power systems.[78] If steam was to be used efficiently, the boiling house required major renovation. Proprietors of large estates having cattle mills—especially those of Trinidad and British Guiana—were well-advised to invest in steam engines. But most planters in the Lesser Antilles occupying estates of 350 acres or less could not anticipate production increases that would compensate for the cost of a steam-powered mill and new boiling equipment.

The abolition of slavery obliged the planters to reconsider the entire concept of a unitary, self-contained sugar estate, and it occasioned among them an increased interest in the prospect of using central factories for the processing of raw cane. Theoretically, centrals would have relieved the planters

[74] Sewell, *Ordeal of Free Labor*, p. 138.

[75] Davy, *The West Indies*, p. 454.

[76] Ibid., p. 259.

[77] Report of R. Hill, 25 Jan. 1856, enclosed in C.O. 137/330, no. 35; Hall, *Free Jamaica*, p. 71.

[78] See p. 407, n. 4.

of their excruciating anxieties over labour during crop, and would have permitted them to cultivate more cane with greater care. The French had erected six centrals—two at Martinique, one in Maria Galante, and three in Guadaloupe—after the earthquake of 1843 had shattered a large percentage of the mills located on those islands.[79] Although the French factories produced little or no profit, their existence offered a challenge to British colonists. During the late forties two attempts were made to establish central factories in Jamaica, both of them unsuccessful. The Colonial Office refused to endorse one of the plans because of an indiscretion committed by its promoter.[80] The second project failed by virtue of its inability to attract capital—a common problem in a community haunted by the Sugar Duties Act and suffering the lowest prices for its principal staple since 1831.

In the best of times the introduction of centrals would have been fraught with problems. Many planters believed that central factories would exercise a monopoly position, placing the cultivator at the mercy of the manufacturer. Those who specialized in a particular brand of rum would have been prevented from doing so under a system of central manufacture. Merchants who held mortgages on West India property might have been reluctant to permit central factories a prior claim on their clients' cane. The poor quality of colonial roads and the high cost of wainage required the introduction of a new and easy form of transport, linking the central mill with its dependent estates. It took 20 tons of cane to produce a single ton of muscovado, and no group of estates possessed either the stock or carts to carry this enormous weight of vegetation the greater distances required by central mills.[81] The construction of railways or tramways was an essential preliminary to the establishment of central factories, and their cost complicated the fundamental problem before which all others become insignificant—the difficulty of raising capital.

Apart from the formation of central factories, railroads offered immense advantages to colonists whose estates lay at

---

[79] H. C. Cobbe to Colebrooke, 28 July 1853, enclosed in C.O. 28/179, no. 57.
[80] Gordon Correspondence, C.O. 137/294; Hall, *Free Jamaica*, p. 77.
[81] Sel. Comm. on Sugar and Coffee Planting, P.P. 1847–8, XXIII (184), evidence of O. Pell.

some distance from shipping points. The cost of conveying hogsheads of sugar weighing up to a ton over gutted roads constituted a heavy expense to the planters. Stock was exhausted and frequently destroyed; carts were battered; and thieves occasionally intercepted wagons, pilfering sugar and rum.[82] A stipendiary magistrate in Jamaica, writing in 1842, declared: 'Some idea ought to be formed of the expense entailed on the community by the badness of these roads from the number of waggons or carriages . . . to be seen lying broken throughout the country.'[83] For Jamaica planters in St. Thomas in the Vale, St. John, or upper Clarendon whose properties lay 20 to 30 miles from the sea, for Trinidad planters whose sugar was occasionally confined to the estates by an early onset of rains which rendered road traffic impossible, and for Guiana proprietors who conveyed their sugar to Georgetown harbour in small schooners, railways appeared to offer great savings, if not the best hope for survival.

In the first decade after emancipation, numerous railway schemes were projected in the four major West Indian colonies. Two lines were actually built, one in Jamaica and another in British Guiana. The Demerara and East Coast Railway was contemplated in 1838 but construction did not start until 1846.[84] Swampy soil adjacent to the coast, coupled with the need to bridge numerous canals created engineering problems, and construction ceased in 1848 as a result of economic depression. Only a loan guaranteed by the British Government permitted a resumption of work.[85] By 1852, 16 miles of track had been laid at an expense of £230,000—a cost per mile nearly three times the original estimate.[86]

In 1846 the Barbados legislature passed an Act permitting a British firm to establish a railway between Speightstown and

[82] Memorial of the Proprietors and other Inhabitants of Clarendon, enclosed in C. E. Grey to Earl Grey, 25 Mar. 1847, C.O. 137/291, no. 27. The cost of conveying sugar from upper Clarendon to port, barring mishap, was about £2 per hogshead.

[83] Report of Grant, enclosed in Elgin to Stanley, 28 Dec. 1842, C.O. 137/264, no. 64.

[84] The Guiana Chronicle, 12 Oct. 1838; Rogers to Grey, 17 Nov. 1846, C.O. 323/61.

[85] This loan of £250,000 raised in England was intended primarily to support the cost of immigration, but some of the money was used to extend the railway.

[86] Dalton, History of British Guiana, II, pp. 64–5.

Bridgetown which was expected to dominate haulage on the entire leeward side of the island.[87] In preceding years, however, the legislature had appropriated £12,500 to the repair of roads. When the post-1846 financial crisis forced a withdrawal of the railway project, the colony's 200 miles of public roads which 'would have done credit to any part of England' continued to afford its planters the greatest ease of haulage in the British Caribbean.[88]

The most interesting and instructive case of railway speculation occurred in Trinidad where two firms—the Trinidad, Great Eastern, and South Western Railway, and the Trinidad Railway Company—competed for the right to establish a trunk line between Port of Spain and San Fernando. From the outset the Trinidad Railway Company, its provisional committee dominated by West India merchants and absentee proprietors,[89] gained favourable attention in the Legislative Council. By late 1846 deposits had been paid on almost 95 per cent of its shares, some of them having been subscribed by resident proprietors.[90] The company had intended to use native hardwoods for rails, but a detailed survey of the projected line exposed the inexpedience of a 'cheap' railway, and it was determined that 90 miles of railway, two piers, plus a maintenance structure at Port of Spain would cost £1,000,000 sterling.[91] Apprehensive that traffic on the railroad—expected to include 80 per cent of the island's sugar crop—would not repay the enormous expense of construction, the company's directors implored the Legislative Council to guarantee the stockholders a 5 per cent annual dividend on capital invested in the line. The company's terms were hard. They insisted that the Government grant a wide tract of Crown land on either side of the rail line, land

---

[87] Rogers to Grey, 26 Sept. 1846, C.O. 323/61.

[88] Schomburgk, *History of Barbados*, pp. 184–5.

[89] Henry Barkly, James Cavan, William Eccles, John Irving, Alexander Mac-Gregor, and Charles Marryat were among the committeemen who had long-standing interests in West India property. The provisional committee of the competing railway firm listed 44 names which in many cases were those of company directors of railroad firms in England and the Empire. A third railway company, projecting a line from Port of Spain to Arima, made its appearance in 1848, but this area was not heavily planted in sugar and the company's reliability was suspected. It received little attention. C.O. 295/165, Miscellaneous Offices.

[90] C.O. 295/148, Railway Companies.

[91] Harris to Gladstone, 21 May 1846, C.O. 295/151, no. 14.

which having afforded timber for rail ties could subsequently be sold by the company for profit. The Council offered to guarantee an annual dividend of 5 per cent, but it refused to grant an unbroken swath of Crown land for fear of conceding too much power to the company. Instead, the Council offered alternate sections of land to the railway, insisting that the intervening lots remain Crown land to be sold by the Government at the increased value they would enjoy as a result of the presence of the line. The proceeds of those sales were to be used by the Government to finance labour immigration. Most importantly, however, the Council demanded that the company import to the colony, at its own expense, an amount of labour equal to that needed to build the line.[92]

The labour question was crucial. Planters were convinced that their labourers—already too few—would abandon the estates in favour of construction work on the railway. Furthermore, it was thought that the railway would enable moneyed interests in England to open new sugar properties, further depleting the working population on older estates. There was massive opposition to the company's demands among leading planters and members of the Council,[93] and a memorial with fifteen pages of signatures reached the Governor from smaller planters who feared being overwhelmed and destroyed by a railway monopoly.[94]

The project was abandoned in mid-1847. The company declared that under the conditions stipulated by the Trinidad Government it could not lure enough capital to build the line.[95] Competing projects had arisen in Britain to attract the interest of investors; moreover, the East India Company was offering a guaranteed annual dividend of 5 per cent plus additional advantages to parties who would build railways in India. Lord Harris, the Governor of Trinidad, was disappointed but

[92] John R. Reid to Earl Grey, 26 Dec. 1846, C.O. 295/154.

[93] John Losh and P. A. Ganteaume, legislative councillors, presented a memorial against the company's proposals. Another memorial was submitted by William Harding Burnley, the best known and most articulate Trinidad proprietor who had long supported the concept of rail lines in the colony. A public meeting of planters in Naparima upbraided the Council for having guaranteed a 5 per cent dividend. Harris to Grey, 21 June 1847, C.O. 295/157, no. 58.

[94] Harris to Grey, 17 July 1847, C.O. 295/157, no. 66.

[95] Reid to Grey, 13 Aug. 1847, C.O. 295/159, Railroad Company correspondence.

sympathetic to the anxieties of the colonists. The Secretary of State, Earl Grey, expressed considerable agitation at the colonists' opposition to a scheme which he considered of utmost advantage to the island.[96]

It is difficult to assess the rights and wrongs of the case. Earl Grey was always partial to grand designs like the railway project; he was vitally interested in increasing the volume of exports and reducing production costs, but he had too little patience with the particular tribulations of the great mass of colonists who considered the Trinidad Railway Company a titan whose onerous exactations were more likely to destroy than to benefit them. The colonists were asked to assume all the risks—to guarantee a 5 per cent annual profit to a company whose construction costs may have exceeded £1,000,000 at a time when the sugar market was in a perilously depressed state and to sacrifice manpower from their meagre labour resources to permit construction of the line. The first of these they might have tolerated; the latter they could not.

The first British West Indian railway was opened in 1845 between Kingston and Spanish Town. Financed by a Lancashire consortium, the line extended a distance of 12 miles at a cost of £7,000 a mile.[97] Its immediate success inspired other schemes, the most significant being the Jamaica South Midland Junction Railway. This railway was expected to join the Jamaica Railway Company's line and proceed through Vere to Clarendon Park Estate on the fringe of the Manchester uplands—a distance of 34 miles at a projected cost of £400,000.[98] In 1845 an Act passed the Jamaica legislature permitting construction of another line through Bog Walk into St. Thomas in the Vale, with the option of continuing on to the north coast.[99] Another enabling Act passed in 1847 for establishing a railway across the northern parishes from Annotto Bay to Montego Bay which was expected to acquire virtually all the haulage traffic for that part of the island.[100] Two tramway projects were conceived for the purpose of linking upper Clarendon with the

[96] Draft, Grey to Harris, 1 Sept. 1847, bound in C.O. 295/157, no. 57.
[97] *Votes of the Jamaica Assembly*, 1845, Appendix III.
[98] Ibid., Appendix XXXI.
[99] Elgin to Stanley, 6 Jan. 1846, C.O. 137/287, no. 6, with enclosure.
[100] C. E. Grey to Earl Grey, 15 May 1847, C.O. 137/292, no. 44, with enclosure.

south coast,[101] and in 1845 proprietors in the Plantain Garden River district contemplated a form of rail conveyance to connect their estates with shipping wharves.[102] There was no shortage of initiative in Jamaica concerning the formation of rail connections, but all these projects collapsed for lack of capital before a single tie was laid.

Scarcity of capital was a perpetual problem for the planters. West Indian proprietors had received a substantial infusion of capital in the late thirties through slave compensation payments. But those payments, amounting to about £21 per slave or between 44 and 49 per cent of the property value of the whole slave population,[103] were used for the most part to relieve or extinguish the massive indebtedness that had accumulated on Caribbean property.[104] Since West Indian merchants were the leading creditors of the planters, much of the compensation money passed swiftly into their hands. A much smaller share was used to restore estate property that had deteriorated in the last years of slavery. Although the transfer of compensation funds from the planters to their metropolitan creditors may have increased the credit worthiness of the former while it enhanced the lending power of the latter, the dubious future of free-labour sugar production caused metropolitan lenders to proceed with caution in extending credit to West Indian clients. In the long term, capital could only be attracted to the colonies by the promise of respectable earnings, not by force of habit or patriotic sentiments. Developments in the British West Indian sugar industry in the first decade of freedom did not inspire confidence in British investors.

---

[101] Elgin to Stanley, 6 Jan. 1846, C.O. 137/287, no. 6, with enclosure; C. E. Grey to Earl Grey, 25 Mar. 1847, C.O. 137/291, no. 27, with enclosure.

[102] Report of R. Daly, July 1845, enclosed in C.O. 137/284, no. 79.

[103] It is generally conceded that the compensation grant amounted to 44 per cent of the appraised value of the slaves. Fogel and Engerman have determined that the cash subsidy came to £21 3s. per slave, that the actual value of the average slave was £43 2s. and that compensation paid to the planters was, therefore, 49 per cent of the estimated actual value of the Caribbean slaves. Robert William Fogel and Stanley L. Engerman, 'Philanthropy at Bargain Prices: Notes on the Economics of Gradual Emancipation', *The Journal of Legal Studies*, III (1974), 395–6.

[104] Richard A. Lobdell, 'Patterns of Investment and Sources of Credit in the British West Indian Sugar Industry, 1838–97', *Journal of Caribbean History*, IV (1972), 36.

Data collected by colonial governors, travellers, stipendiary magistrates, and investigating committees in England and the colonies left little doubt that in colonies with low population density free-labour sugar production had entailed higher production costs, lower output, and reduced profits. For our material on this subject we are confined very largely to evidence offered by planters who were intent on dramatizing their difficulties, and it is necessary to make some allowance for exaggeration. At the same time, private estate records which have undergone careful scrutiny[105] as well as the generous files of the encumbered estates courts maintained at the Public Record Office confirm the basic position taken by the planters in their public testimony.

One of the most reliable proprietors to testify before the Select Committee on Sugar and Coffee Planting in 1847-8 was Henry Barkly, a member of Parliament, future Governor of British Guiana and Jamaica, and owner of Highbury Estate in the former colony. According to Barkly, his property had produced 616 hogsheads of sugar in 1834, and between 1826 and 1838 it earned an average annual income of £5,080, or 8·4 per cent a year on a capital investment of £60,000. In the first nine years of freedom, the average yield of the estate fell to 250 hogsheads a year (see Table 8), and during that period the property lost a total of £6,170, an average annual loss of £685.[106]

Other Guiana planters offered corroborative testimony. G. H. Loxdale claimed that he sustained an increase in production costs from 6s. per cwt. in 1837 to 25s. 5d. in 1844.[107] Mungo Campbell and Matthew Higgins recorded similar increases (see Table 9).[108]

---

[105] Craton and Walvin, *Jamaican Plantation*, ch. IX.   [106] See p. 407, n. 5.

[107] Sel. Comm. on Sugar and Coffee Planting, P.P. 1847-8, XXIII (206), evidence of G. H. Loxdale.

[108] The low cost figures which these proprietors claim to have enjoyed during the slavery period may be misleading. In determining their pre-emancipation production costs, planters failed to account for the depreciation of slave property by death, disease, or old age. It is not likely that proprietors in British Guiana produced sugar in the slave period at an average cost much lower than that of the slave masters of Cuba, whose expenses for cultivating and manufacturing sugar, without considering interest on invested or borrowed capital, seem to have averaged about 11s. or 12s. a hundredweight. These latter figures are derived from the reports of British consuls in Cuba who conveyed information on the sugar industry to Lord Palmerston. Appendix to the Seventh Report from the Sel. Comm. on Sugar and Coffee Planting, P.P. 1847-8, XXIII (245).

TABLE 8

Cost of Sugar Production at Highbury Estate,
British Guiana, 1831–1847

Years	Hogsheads (ave.)	cwt. (ave.)	Cost of Production (per cwt.)
			s. d.
1831			
1832	457	7,000	6 8
1833			
1835			
1836	505	8,122	6 1
1837			
1839			
1840	238	3,454	40 3
1841			
1842			
1843	250	3,750	30 7
1844			
1845			
1846	269	4,055	25 10
1847			

Source: Sel. Comm. on Sugar and Coffee Planting, P.P. 1847–8, XXIII (206), evidence of H. Barkly.

TABLE 9

Cost of Sugar Production on Twelve British Guiana
Estates, 1831–1841

Estate	1831–3 (ave.)		1835–7 (ave.)		1839–41 (ave.)	
	s.	d.	s.	d.	s.	d.
Endeavour[a]	9	6	8	8	31	1
Aurora[a]	5	4	7	3	26	10
Enterprise[a]	3	2	5	5	26	9
Nine Other Properties[b]	6	6½	8	2	24	11

Sources: [a]Sel. Comm. on the West India Colonies, P.P. 1842, XIII (479), evidence of M. Campbell; [b]Sel. Comm. on Sugar and Coffee Planting, P.P. 1847–8, XXIII (184), evidence of M. Higgins.

At the end of apprenticeship, 206 estates were being cultivated in Trinidad; 193 remained in 1848. The Governor reported that during the first decade of freedom 159 of the colony's estates had been run at a loss.[109] This figure, possibly exaggerated, did not imply that Trinidad proprietors were unable to meet necessary annual expenses without new infusions of capital—although that was certainly true in some cases. Rather it meant that after necessary expenses had been deducted from income, insufficient money remained to cover the cost of property maintenance. The resulting deterioration of physical property, causing a reduction in the market value of estates, led planters to conclude that after 10 years of free labour, losses exceeded gains. The Governor claimed that no sugar had been made in free Trinidad for less than 12s. 6d. a cwt. and that the average cost of production in 1847 was between 16s. and 20s.[110] His figures were supported by Lord George Bentinck, Chairman of the Select Committee on Sugar and Coffee Planting, who estimated the average cost of production in Trinidad to be 18s. 9d. on sugar, which, being of inferior quality, sold below the average London price.[111]

The most extensive study of production costs was undertaken in 1847 by a committee of the Jamaica Assembly which examined 43 proprietors and estate attorneys, some of whom managed 10 to 16 properties. The committee determined that the average cost of producing sugar by free labour in Jamaica was 22s. 7½d.[112] This figure reflected the high cost of successive years of drought. Since the passage of the Act abolishing slavery, 140 sugar estates had been abandoned. Most of those properties were poorly situated; many had been devastated by drought; others—like 11 estates abandoned in upper Clarendon —were 'miserable worthless places' thrown up in consequence of being plunged in debt long before the abolition of slavery.[113] Terrain, soil, and climatic conditions varied much more in Jamaica than in other colonies; consequently the range of

[109] Harris to Grey, 19 June 1848, C.O. 295/162, no. 71.
[110] Harris to Grey, 21 Feb. 1848, C.O. 295/160, no. 21.
[111] Proceedings of the Sel. Comm. on Sugar and Coffee Planting, P.P. 1847–8, XXIII, p. xvi.
[112] Report of a committee of the Jamaica Assembly, enclosed in C. E. Grey to Earl Grey, 7 Feb. 1848, C.O. 137/295, no. 17.
[113] Report of H. Pringle, 1 June 1845, enclosed in C.O. 137/284, no. 79.

production costs recorded on the estates was greater. At Golden Grove, where the soil was 10 to 12 feet deep, where 10th ratoons occasionally yielded 1½ tons of sugar per acre, and where 604 hogsheads were made in 1845, the cost of production in the free period did not exceed 14s. a cwt.[114]

Throughout the free period, Barbados estates retained their profitability. Although properties were small—usually making less than 100 hogsheads—and although the planters relied on manual labour and wind power, they generally held their production expenses around 15s. a cwt. On some estates unit costs were as low as 10s.[115] Thomas Jelly lamented that many Jamaican estates of between 1,000 and 5,000 acres were valued at merely one-sixth or one-eighth that of small Barbados properties. The reason, he correctly observed, was the density of the Barbados population and the consequent efficiency and reliability of her wage labourers. Writing of Jamaica, Jelly remarked, 'Could we suddenly annihilate two-thirds of the island, and translate the whole population into the County of Cornwall, the value of land would be immediately quadrupled, not because it would yield a greater interest, but because a steady supply of labour would increase the security of capital.'[116]

If Lord George Bentinck was correct in determining that 21s. per cwt. was the average cost of producing sugar in the British West Indies,[117] then the cost of marketing that product with the additional 8s. charge imposed by English merchants was 29s. per cwt. From 1843 to 1846 the London price for Caribbean muscovado held remarkably firm between 32s. and 35s. This narrow margin of profit prevented any significant renovation of property or capital accumulation for most planters.

[114] Evidence of T. McCornock before a committee of the Jamaica Assembly, *Votes of the Jamaica Assembly*, 1845, Appendix LXVI; Sel. Comm. on Sugar and Coffee Planting, P.P. 1847–8, XXIII (206), evidence of P. Borthwick.

[115] There is extensive evidence on Mt. Clapham estate in the official correspondence of Barbados. The cost of production on that property in 1842 was 12s. 11d. per cwt.; in 1846, it was 10s. 8½d. Reid to Grey, 8 Mar. 1848, C.O. 28/168, no. 21.

[116] Jelly, *A Brief Enquiry*, p. 34.

[117] Bentinck accumulated a remarkable knowledge of the sugar industry as chairman of the 1847–8 select committee. He assessed the average cost of production, colony by colony, as follows: Barbados, 15s. 6½d.; Antigua, St. Kitts, and Grenada, 17s. to 18s.; St. Vincent, 19s. 2½d.; Jamaica, 22s. 7½d.; Guiana, 25s.; Trinidad, 18s. 9d. Proceedings of the Sel. Comm. on Sugar and Coffee Planting, P.P. 1847–8, XXIII, p. xvi.

Only the most profitable estates could have hoped to approach the 8 to 10 per cent return on capital which planters deemed necessary to compensate them for the grave risks involved in sugar production—namely volatile market prices and the perpetual danger of natural disaster.[118]

Conditions were considerably worse on plantations producing secondary crops. Soil exhaustion had begun to take its toll of Jamaica's coffee exports before the slaves were set free (see Table 10). Between 1832 and 1847, 465 Jamaican

TABLE 10

Average Annual Export of Coffee from Jamaica, 1824–1843

Years	Total Exports £	Annual Average £
1824–28	117,240,000	23,448,000
1829–33	88,226,000	17,645,000
1834–38	64,260,000	12,412,000
1839–43	37,060,000	7,412,000

Source: Tabular Return of Exports from Jamaica, enclosed in C.O. 137/287.

coffee properties were abandoned.[119] The higher cost of free labour merely accelerated the collapse of the plantations, for the wages paid to free workers formed a much higher portion of the expenses of a coffee plantation than of a sugar estate. At Pleasant Hill, a typical Manchester property which suffered speedy decline in the free period, wages constituted nearly 80 per cent of the annual cost of production.[120] Without exception, planters considered free labourers casual and careless. When crops were bounteous and the trees were laden with

[118] Ten per cent was a figure commonly used by planters. As late as 1858 Governor Hincks of Barbados commented, 'no one would buy an estate and run the risk of markets without expecting to realize from 8 to 10 per cent for his money'. Hincks to Lytton, 10 July 1858, C.O. 28/188, Windward Islands, No. 3.

[119] Report of a committee of the Jamaica Assembly, enclosed in C. E. Grey to Earl Grey, 7 Feb. 1848, C.O. 137/295, no. 17.

[120] Between 1842 and 1846 the wage bill at Pleasant Hill amounted to £2,287; the whole expenses of the estate, including English supplies, came to £2,872. Evidence of R. Lewis before a committee of the Jamaica Assembly, enclosed in C. E. Grey to Earl Grey, 7 Feb. 1848, C.O. 137/295, no. 17.

berries there was no difficulty procuring workmen who by assiduous effort could pick up to three bushels a day at one shilling a bushel. When the crop was scanty, however, the work was tedious and planters had great difficulty securing ample labour. William Lowe, a proprietor of two Jamaican plantations and the manager of two others, claimed that he lost about 15 per cent of his crop in lean years because the labourers refused to pick the coffee trees thoroughly.[121] An average price for colonial coffee cannot be established because of the sharply varying market values of different grades, but some appreciation of the impact of rising costs may be seen in Table 11 which

TABLE 11

Cost of Producing Coffee on Plantations of Charles Jopp,
St. Andrew, Jamaica, 1830–1846

Years	Average Price (per lb.) d.	Total Production (lb.)	Total Cost of Production £ s. d.	Cost of Production (per lb.) d.
1830–3	6½	475,566	5,797 12 3	2¾
1834–7	10¼	489,918	7,283 7 5	3½
1838–43	10½	520,714	17,250 6 8¼	7¾
1844–6	7	192,660	7,637 14 7	9½

Source: Evidence of Charles Jopp before a committee of the Jamaica Assembly, enclosed in C.O. 137/295, no. 17.

offers statistics on several plantations in St. Andrew owned by Charles Jopp. By the mid-'forties coffee property was unsaleable in Jamaica except when divided into small parcels for transfer to freedmen. Plantations which produced a high quality coffee exhibited the greatest lasting power, but by the late 1850s coffee cultivation had passed very largely to black and coloured farmers who supplied an inferior product for the American trade.

The cocoa-planters of Trinidad who suffered persistent depression in the 1830s were further injured by the elimination of compulsory labour. In the slave period, free peons who had

[121] Evidence of W. Lowe, ibid.

disdained cane labour in the company of bondsmen supplied labour at very low cost to the numerous cocoa plantations of northern Trinidad. The abolition of slavery thrust cocoa planters into an unequal competition for peon labour with sugar planters who offered high wages and allowances and whose properties were no longer degraded by the presence of slaves. By necessity, wages rose sharply on the cocoa plantations, but they remained below that of the sugar estates—a condition which precipitated a drain of manpower.[122] By 1842 cocoa-planters claimed a deficiency of 2,000 workers, a monumental shortage when it is perceived that the whole manpower requirement of the cocoa industry was only 6,000 workmen.[123]

A reduction in cocoa prices from between $13 and $19 a fanega (110 lb) in the early 1820's to $6 a fanega in 1841 provoked the abandonment of many plantations. In the latter year, a well-established, debt-free cocoa property, which might have cost $30,000 (about £6,000) to develop, could have been expected to earn a gross revenue of $1,800 on the sale of 300 fanega of cocoa. But the production costs of that plantation would have absorbed $1,722, leaving the proprietor a mere $80 in revenue.[124] Realistically, there were no more than six properties in Trinidad producing that large a crop, and most plantations were heavily mortgaged, incapable of obtaining further credit, and desperately short-handed. A reduction of the cocoa duty in Britain from 2d. to 1d. per lb. in 1844 offered little relief to colonial planters because of the small consumption of the product in Britain. High tariffs and navigation laws impaired the easy export of Trinidadian cocoa to Spain, the largest European market. The Board of Trade offered little encouragement to depressed planters, acknowledging that their principal hope of salvation lay in the 'acceptance of enlightened

---

[122] On the principal cocoa plantations where labourers were afforded a house and provision ground the maximum wage rate was 30 cents (1s. 3d.) a day— 20 cents below the common rate paid on sugar properties. Some cocoa planters paid wages equivalent to those offered on sugar estates, but they provided neither houses, grounds, nor allowances. This and other data on the cocoa plantations is derived from a Memorial of Cocoa Planters, enclosed in MacLeod to Stanley, 10 June 1842, C.O. 295/136, no. 62.

[123] Reviewing reports from the stipendiary magistrates in 1844, Henry Taylor acknowledged, 'the Cocoa Plantations are deserted . . .' Minute by Taylor, bound in MacLeod to Stanley, 6 July 1844, C.O. 295/143, no. 53.

[124] See p. 408, n. 6.

commercial policy by Spain'—a dubious prospect.[125] Successive
governors lamented the impoverishment of cocoa-planters.
Henry MacLeod believed that a prosperous cocoa industry
could have provided energetic freedmen and coloured men
who had not the capital to engage in sugar-planting a means of
elevating their social status by acquiring a small acreage and
a few hundred cocoa trees.[126] Not only were they discouraged
from such endeavour, the old Spanish settlers who formed the
only class of small proprietors in the island were being systematically destroyed.

For the West India colonies there was no ready alternative
to sugar as a commodity suited to large scale production capable
of attracting the capital of metropolitan investors. Ginger,
pimento, and arrowroot promised insignificant return, and
when substantial numbers of small planters began cultivating
these crops, the market for them was quickly glutted and
prices fell sharply.[127] There was scattered interest in cotton, and
during 1841 a specimen of Sea Island cotton experimentally
produced in Jamaica by Mr. H. Gourges was sent to a committee of brokers in Liverpool who found it 'Clean and well
got up, but rather speckled with brown and dead bits'.[128] Had
West Indians been able to produce a cotton of extraordinary
quality for a selective market, there might have been some
value in proceeding with the crop. But the absolute dominance
of low cost, slave-grown American cotton in the British market
rendered large-scale production by Caribbean planters altogether unsound. The Board of Trade, motivated by *laissez-faire*
principles, was unwilling to encourage by special initiative or
protection any new colonial ventures, and in response to a
recommendation that the silkworm be introduced in the West
Indies their Lordships advised that silk was 'one of those
enterprises which they would always leave to the free choice,

[125] C.O. 295/154, Board of Trade Papers.
[126] MacLeod to Russell, 11 July 1840, C.O. 295/130, no. 37; MacLeod to
Stanley, 31 Dec. 1841, C.O. 295/134, no. 29.
[127] Ginger was a scourging crop which quickly exhausted soil. Growers were
continually obliged to bring new lands into cultivation. Small estates in St. Vincent
developed arrowroot cultivation during the crisis which followed the Sugar Duties
Act, but as exports increased from 300,000 to 490,000 pounds in the period
between 1847 and 1851, the price of the product diminished from 3s. 6d. a pound
to 6d. a pound. See Davy, *The West Indies*, pp. 187–8.
[128] Correspondence from the Board of Trade, bound in C.O. 137–256, no. 4.

and to the voluntary exertions of private individuals—unbiased by any attempts on the part of Government to afford them assistance'.[129] An American, Samuel Whitmarsh, established a mulberry plantation, silk factory, and small settlement of thirty white labourers in St. Ann parish, Jamaica in 1840, but a variety of accidents, drought, the impatience of investors at the early unprofitability of the enterprise forced its demise by 1845.[130] Stephen Bourne, a stipendiary magistrate who formed a household school of industry sent home a specimen of hemp made from the stalk of plantain and banana trees, but the master rope maker at Deptford found it weak and unserviceable.[131] Discoveries of copper ore aroused keen interest in Jamaica, and throughout the mid-century prospecting and speculation were commonplace. A few mines were opened, but since Jamaica had no coal for smelting purposes it was essential that she have veins of rich ore to compensate for the great cost of transporting it to England.[132] Regrettably, she had not, and by 1860 mining ventures had withdrawn from the island.

As late as 1846 a West Indian newspaper repeated the old arguments of the abolitionists: 'as soon as we can produce sugar more plentifully and cheaper . . . than the Spaniards, Dutch, French, and Portuguese . . . then—and not until then—will these nations set themselves to abolish slavery.'[133] There was little evidence, however, that the free sugar colonies were in reach of this objective. Prosperity was evident in Barbados, and the St. Kitts and Antigua planters had suffered only modest increases in the cost of production.[134] But throughout the low-density colonies scores of plantations were in imminent peril of collapse despite a widespread conversion to scientific agriculture and the use of animal-drawn farm implements. In those colonies, the planters chastised freedmen for failing to perform careful continuous labour, but in fact the planters did not, and

---

[129] J. Murray to Glenelg, 7 May 1838, C.O. 323/224, Board of Trade correspondence with James Stephen, 1 Nov. 1838, C.O. 318/132.

[130] Hall, *Free Jamaica*, pp. 129–37.

[131] Metcalfe to Russell, 10 Mar. 1841, C.O. 137/255, no. 202.

[132] Murchison to Vernon Smith, 6 Mar. 1841, C.O. 137/259; Hall, *Free Jamaica*, pp. 137–51.

[133] *The Falmouth Post*, 21 July 1846.

[134] Sel. Comm. on Sugar and Coffee Planting, P.P. 1847–8, XXIII (184), evidence of O. Pell.

could not, offer the workers continuous employment. Freedmen having access to arable land for cultivating provisions or minor staples enjoyed enhanced prosperity. They pursued their own self-interest without deliberately undermining the estates, but the short supply, irregularity, and high cost of their labour curtailed or eliminated plantation profits and discouraged capital investment. Rail and tramway projects which might have reduced shipping costs and enhanced the competitive position of many proprietors fell through because the bleak economic forecast for the plantations discouraged investment. The progressive dissolution of the estates, the decline of staple exports, the reduction in tax revenue, and the contraction of the money supply jeopardized the economic well-being of all elements of West Indian society and threatened to retard the development of civil institutions. This would become increasingly manifest in the late forties when changes in imperial tariffs and economic depression wrought havoc throughout the British Caribbean.

CHAPTER 8

The Impact of Free Trade

THE CRISIS YEARS, 1846-1850

ON 25 June 1846, after five months of acrimonious debate, Sir Robert Peel's Bill eliminating the English Corn Laws passed its third reading in the House of Commons. This landmark victory for the free trade interest was the first decisive step in dismantling an imperial system of trade and navigation which had, in its various complexions, lasted for two centuries. The anguish it evoked is well known. Outraged Tory protectionists avenged themselves upon their embattled leader, forced his resignation, and precipitated the disintegration of the party. Power was delivered to a Whig Government which swiftly extended the principles of the Manchester School to the Empire. In August Lord John Russell carried the Sugar Duties Act with a comfortable majority of 130. This measure contemplated the immediate reduction of duties on all foreign sugar—both free and slave grown—to 21s. The differential tax on the foreign product was to be systematically reduced by 1s. 6d. a year until by 1851 the duties on all sugar entering the United Kingdom would be equalized.

The favoured position of West Indian sugar in the home market had been consistently attacked and partially eroded during the preceding decade. As each passing year separated the British people from their initial enthusiastic commitment to the great experiment, the high cost and dwindling supply of colonial sugar had become less tolerable. In the first three years of the free period, the average annual export of West Indian sugar declined 30 per cent, from about 185,000 tons a year during apprenticeship to 127,000 tons.[1] The *per capita* consumption of sugar in the United Kingdom fell from 20 lb. in 1830 to 15 lb. in 1840,[2] and in the latter year, the price of

[1] Deerr, *History of Sugar*, II, 193-203, 377.
[2] Memorandum, n.d., *Russell Papers*, PRO 30/22/4A.

the product reached its highest level since 1818. With no surplus sugar to be marketed in Europe, West India planters were enjoying the full effect of their monopoly. Between 1836 and 1845 the pre-duty price of Caribbean muscovado was 12s. 4d. above its foreign competition; from 1821 to 1830, when excess colonial sugar had been shipped overseas, it had sold at a premium of only 6d.[3] In an attempt to supply more sugar to British consumers while continuing to exclude the slave grown staple, Peel reduced the rate of duty on foreign free grown sugar in 1844 and again in 1845 (see Appendix 2). His actions failed to mollify ardent free-traders who considered any form of imperial preference beneficial to the colonies at England's expense. In their view, the industrial prowess of Great Britain enabled her merchants to compete favourably in any market, and the reciprocal protection they received in colonial ports was of no significance.[4] Conversely, the protective duties which obliged the British to buy high cost colonial rather than cheap slave-grown sugar constituted a weighty annual tribute on the mother country. In 1841 British consumers could have saved over £4,000,000 had they been permitted to buy slave-grown sugar at the same rate of duty levied on the colonial staple,[5] and the lower price of the foreign product would undoubtedly have encouraged larger domestic sales, rendering an increased tariff revenue to the state (see Table 12).[6]

The West India interest naturally opposed every modification of differential duties on foreign sugar, and the Sugar Duties Act evoked a massive barrage of protests and a unanimous

---

[3] Philip D. Curtin, 'Sugar Duties and West Indian Prosperity', *Journal of Economic History*, XIV (1954), 159–60.

[4] Klaus E. Knorr, *British Colonial Theories, 1570–1850* (Toronto, 1944), p. 319.

[5] The average cost of British colonial sugar, excluding duty, in 1841 was 39s. 8d. Cuban sugar marketed at 21s. 6d., Brazilian at 20s. 9d. The United Kingdom imported 2,260,000 cwt. from the West Indies and 2,020,000 cwt. from India and Mauritius, giving a total of 4,280,000 cwt. British consumers paid approximately £8,500,000 for that sugar, excluding tax—about twice what they would have paid for the foreign slave-grown product. West India planters mistakenly referred to the £4,000,000 raised from duties on colonial sugar as revenue furnished the mother country. On the contrary, had foreign sugar been admitted at the colonial rate of duty, the home government would have earned at least as much revenue as it did from the tax on the protected colonial product.

[6] Sugar was a product for which there was considerable price-elasticity of demand. See, R. C. O. Matthews, *A Study in Trade-Cycle History: Economic Fluctuations in Britain, 1833–1842* (Cambridge, 1954), p. 18.

TABLE 12

Comparative Sugar Prices, 1841–1846
(per cwt.)

Year	British West Indian		Cuban		Brazilian	
	s.	d.	s.	d.	s.	d.
1841	39	8	21	6	20	9
1842	36	11	20	1	18	3
1843	33	9	21	2	17	2
1844	33	8	21	8	17	0
1845	32	11	26	4	20	5
1846	34	5	24	6	19	11

Sources: P.P. 1847–8, LVIII (422); P.P. 1866, LXVI (193).

cry of ruin. No previous action of the British Parliament—
neither the abolition of the slave trade nor of slavery itself—
aroused such universal despair.[7] In the former encounters with
the British Government, West India planters had borne the
villains' image, being traders and masters of slaves. But in
1846 they were the defenders of free labour engaged in a fateful
competition with the forces of slavery. However incongruously,
they denounced Russell and the Whigs for sacrificing morality
to mammon. In this they were joined by the Saints who warned
the nation that the Sugar Duties Act would enrich the slave
states and expand the Atlantic slave trade.[8] West Indians
claimed that free trade in sugar would precipitate the abandonment of colonial estates and provide Brazilian and Cuban

[7] Stephen Cave, *A Few Words on the Encouragement Given to Slavery and the Slave
Trade by Recent Measures, and Chiefly the Sugar Bill of 1846* (London, 1846); Bigelow,
Jamaica in 1850, p. 45.

[8] The Saints had consistently opposed any relaxation of the prohibitive duties
on slave-grown sugar. In 1841 Buxton advised Russell that if the people were
informed that foreign sugar could only be obtained through the 'medium of the
Slave Trade—they would not call upon the Government to instigate such crime
. . .' Letter of Sir T. F. Buxton, 31 Mar. 1841, *Russell Papers*, PRO 30/22/4A;
C. Duncan Rice, 'Humanity Sold for Sugar! The British Abolitionist Response to
Free Trade in Slave Grown Sugar', *Historical Journal*, XIII (1970), 410.

planters a *de facto* monopoly of British and European markets.[9] The ruin of the planters, they argued, would be accompanied by an irrevocable social and economic regression among the freedmen.[10]

The most compelling and articulate defence of the West Indian position was stated by James Matthew Higgins, an absentee proprietor of several Guiana estates, who frequently contributed articles to *The Times* under the pseudonym Jacob Omnium.[11] Although an admirer of Cobden and a selective advocate of his movement, Higgins asserted that the West Indies constituted a special case and that sugar could not conform to the rigid principles of free trade. By abolishing slavery and compensating the planters, taxing her subjects and aggravating relations with slave-holding and slave trading states, and by maintaining a naval squadron on the African coast to police illicit slave traffic to Cuba and Brazil, Britain had committed herself to a moral position that was incompatible with the indiscriminate free-trade maxim of buying in the cheapest market. With trenchant sarcasm he taunted his adversaries:

Let slavery be considered as a practice which humanity condemns, and which civilization must eventually abolish, but which cannot be permitted to enter into the calculations of a great commercial people. Let the coast squadron be immediately recalled, and the Bights thrown open to the sugar-growers of all nations to procure their labourers on the easiest terms. Let them make as much sugar as they can, each for itself, and let the agency by which this article is produced be as much a matter of indifference as in the case of any other article, and then may sugar fairly be subjected to the operations of free trade.[12]

Although Britain had destroyed her colonies to gratify her morality, denouncing theft to save her honour, she was prepared, Higgins lamented, to live on stolen goods to save her

<hr>

[9] S. Cave, Chairman of West India Committee, to Earl Grey, 16 July 1846, C.P. 318/196.

[10] Memorandum of Acting Committee of West India Planters and Merchants, 25 Oct. 1847, C.O. 318/170.

[11] *History of the Times* (London, 1939), II, 108. The 10 articles written by Higgins for *The Times* were subsequently published together under the title, *The Real Bearings of the West India Question as Expounded by the Most Intelligent Free-Trader of the Day.*

[12] *The Times*, 17 Jan. 1848.

pockets: 'We ruin our colonies because slavery is so horrible, and buy our sugar at Brazil because slave produce is so cheap.'[13]

While fighting to retain protection, West Indians sought compensation for the Sugar Duties Act. They implored the imperial Government to use more vigorous means to destroy the slave trade which was feeding over 40,000 Africans into Brazil each year.[14] Citing the principles of free trade, they demanded unrestricted access to the coast of Africa to procure free-labour immigrants.[15] Under the protective system West Indian sugar and molasses had been excluded from the breweries and distilleries of the mother country. Numerous petitions were dispatched urging the removal of these restrictions as well as the duty on rum which penalized that product in competition with domestic spirits.[16] The colonists appealed for the abolition of the Navigation Acts which obliged them to use British ships to transport their products. Freight costs from the island colonies averaged between £4 and £4 15s. a ton compared with £2 15s. from Cuba.[17] By employing American

[13] Ibid.

[14] Curtin, *The Atlantic Slave Trade*, p. 234. Memorials enclosed in C.O. 28/169, no. 12; C.O. 28/170, no. 12. In 1849, David Turnbull (author of *Travels in the West. Cuba with Notices of Porto Rico, 1840*) organized a mass movement in Jamaica, gathering petitions calling for vigorous steps to force Cuba and Brazil out of the slave trade. Commentary on a series of well attended meetings held throughout the island appears in *The Jamaica Movement, for Promoting the Enforcement of the Slave-Trade Treaties, and the Suppression of the Slave Trade* (New York, reprint, 1969). Jamaica's Governor, C. E. Grey, recommended, somewhat preposterously, that a joint stock company be formed with one-third of its directors appointed by the Crown for the purpose of buying up the colonies of Portugal and other African territories as a means of destroying the slave trade and regulating voluntary emigration to the British West Indies. C. E. Grey to Earl Grey, 21 May 1849, C.O. 137/302.

[15] Memorial of Jamaica Proprietors and Merchants, bound in Davidson Correspondence, C.O. 137/294; Harris to Grey, 4 Sept. 1846, C.O. 295/151, no. 58; Correspondence with West India Committee, C.O. 318/169.

[16] West India Agents to Earl Grey, 15 Feb. 1847, C.O. 318/170; Memorial of Planters of St. Thomas in the East, C.O. 137/289, no. 51; Memorial of West India Planters and Merchants, C.O. 318/170; Memorial of a Public Meeting in Trinidad, C.O. 295/152, no. 73. Equalization of taxes on rum and English spirits would still allow the metropolitan distillers an advantage; Caribbean rum was subject to heavy freight charges and to the dual problems of evaporation and leakage *en route* to Europe.

[17] The average freight for Jamaica, Antigua, and St. Kitts in 1847 was £4 6s. od.; Schomburgk estimated that freights from Barbados ran around £4. Sel. Comm. on Sugar and Coffee Planting, P.P. 1847-8, XXIII (184), (206), evidence of Geddes, Bell, Pickwood, Miles.

vessels, planters believed they could reduce their freight charges
and secure staves and provisions at cheaper rates.[18]

Their petitions were only partially satisfied. They were not
permitted free access to the coast of Africa, but labour re-
cruiting was allowed on the Kroo coast adjacent to Sierra
Leone. The Government offered positive encouragement to free
African immigration, guaranteeing loans to the principal importing colonies and arranging with the Admiralty for the use
of a steam vessel (see Chapter 9). The tax on rum was lowered,
not eliminated. In keeping with the principles of free trade,
colonists were given full liberty to regulate their own customs
duties, to abolish restrictions on foreign goods and to eliminate
differential duties which favoured the mother country. After
heated controversy, the Navigation Acts were removed on
1 January 1850.

While these issues were being mooted and resolved, Europe
and the western world sustained a paralyzing economic crisis.
Its effects magnified the problems occasioned by the Sugar
Duties Act. The depression sharply reduced the demand for
sugar and discouraged speculative buying. Ironically, in 1847
the West India colonies produced a bumper crop, 50,000 tons
or 23 per cent above their annual average for the preceding
eight years. Foreign imports, attracted to Britain by the reduced
tariff, rose by 38 per cent, adding to the oversupply and con-
tributing to a sharp decline in prices.[19] The *Gazette* price
dropped from 37s. in February to 22s. 6d. in November. For
the next eight years the price hovered between 22s. and 26s. a
cwt, rendering estates with production costs above 12s. or 14s.
perennially unprofitable.

The fall in prices bankrupted 48 West India merchant
houses.[20] Caribbean planters were unable to redeem bills drawn
on insolvent British companies in exchange for consignments of
sugar already shipped. Losses were immense. Even the most
stable merchant firms refused to extend further credit to West
Indian clients.[21] Deprived of their regular source of capital,

---

[18] Memorial, enclosed in C. E. Grey to Earl Grey, 6 Apr. 1847, C.O. 137/291,
no. 29.

[19] First Report from the Sel. Comm. on Sugar and Coffee Planting, P.P. 1847–8,
XXIII (123), Appendix 2.

[20] Craton and Walvin, *Jamaican Plantation*, p. 223.

[21] Peter Rose, spokesman of the Guiana planters, declared '. . . there is not a

planters defaulted on wage payments and short term obligations to local banks. The West India Bank, its headquarters in Barbados with branch offices in seven other colonies, suspended cash payments in December 1847.[22] The Planters' Bank of Jamaica followed suit in 1848.[23]

Estate values collapsed. Whole plantations changed hands for 20 per cent of the value which their buildings and machinery would have brought in prosperous communities enjoying confidence in the future. Bog Estate, Jamaica, thought to have been worth £80,000 during slavery, sold for £500 in 1849.[24] Windsor Forest in British Guiana, valued at £85,000 during slavery and resold without slaves in 1840 for £45,000, was executed in 1849 for just under £2,000.[25] Plantation Vive la Force in the same colony was purchased for £50,000 in 1822, resold for £24,000 in 1840, and again in 1849 for a mere £625.[26] The Attorney General of Trinidad, speaking in 1848, graphically described the situation in that colony:

. . . 64 petitions of insolvency have been filed; estate after estate thrown upon the market, and no purchaser found. Even where there has been no insolvency, many estates have been abandoned from the inability to raise money on the faith of the coming crop . . . Within the last few weeks Jordan Hill estate . . . with a crop of 450 to 500 hogsheads on the ground, and on which about £1,500 were expended last year, in laying down tram roads . . . has been sold for £4,000. This sale has taken place, not under an insolvency or bankruptcy, nor to meet the pressure of creditors, but by persons of wealth and respectability; and men here wonder, not at the sacrifice of the vendors so much as at the rashness of the purchaser.[27]

merchant who would advance a farthing on the best estate in Jamaica, Trinidad, or British Guiana . . .' Court of Policy, enclosure 2 in Light to Grey, 31 Mar. 1848, P.P. 1847–8, XLVI (749); Memorial of Jamaica Proprietors, enclosed in C. E. Grey to Earl Grey, 22 Dec. 1847, C.O. 137/293, no. 125; Harris to Grey, 18 Sept. 1847, C.O. 295/157, no. 81.

[22] Reid to Grey, 7 Dec. 1847, C.O. 28/167, no. 80.

[23] Correspondence on the Planters' Bank crisis appears in C.O. 137/297, nos. 75, 96, 107, Aug. to Dec. 1848: Hall, *Free Jamaica*, pp. 112–14.

[24] Hon. E. Stanley, *Claims and Resources of the West India Colonies: A Letter to the Rt. Hon. W. E. Gladstone, M.P.* (London, 1850), p. 29.

[25] There were numerous listings of devalued Guiana properties. See, Dr. W. Ranken, 'Thoughts on British Guiana', published in 1847 and extracted for printing in the Appendix to the Fifth Report from the Select Committee on Sugar and Coffee Planting. Also, Dalton, *History of British Guiana*, II, Appendix.

[26] Barkly to Grey, 4 June 1849, C.O. 111/226, no. 93.

[27] Quoted in Davy, *The West Indies*, pp. 313–14. In the period before emancipation, Jordan Hill afforded its owner an average annual profit of £3,000.

Where banks stopped payment, colonial governments suffered heavy losses. West Indian governments commonly banked surplus revenue in local institutions, and the money of account held by government departments consisted very largely of local bank notes.[28] Furthermore, taxes could not be collected in full because colonists had little or no money with which to pay them. In December 1847 several vessels lay at anchor in Port of Spain unable to sail or discharge cargo as a result of the inability of the colony's merchants to pay customs duties.[29] The Government of Trinidad failed to pay the salaries of public employees during the final quarter of 1847, and salaries were only partially paid in Barbados.[30]

The labouring people were hard hit. Some of them had hoarded bank notes only to find them worthless. The elimination of credit to the estates caused protracted delays or the total cessation of wage payments. Workers resisted all attempts to reduce wage levels, denouncing such measures as deceitful means of subjecting them to bondage. In Jamaica a rumour spread throughout the colony that 'Buckra' was going to turn the island over to Cuba or the United States to accomplish their permanent re-enslavement. White and coloured colonists feared rebellion; the Governor reinforced his police as well as the garrison and requested that a steamship of war be dispatched to the island.[31]

Jamaica was spared an incident, but a confrontation between labour and management occurred in British Guiana. In January 1848 hard pressed planters announced a 25 per cent reduction in wage levels, but the freedmen refused to tolerate the cuts in spite of assurances by the Governor, magistrates, and missionaries that planters could not maintain their former schedule of payments without absolute ruin to themselves.[32] Blacks struck work, remaining idle for up to three months. The only estate labour performed during the initial weeks of the

[28] Reid to Grey, 7 Dec. 1848, C.O. 28/167, no. 80.
[29] Harris to Grey, 11 Dec. 1847, C.O. 295/158, no. 106.
[30] Harris to Grey, 6 Dec. 1847, C.O. 295/158, no. 101; Light to Grey, private, 20 June 1848, C.O. 111/253.
[31] Enclosure in C. E. Grey to Earl Grey, 7 July 1848, C.O. 137/299, no. 64; C. E. Grey to Earl Grey, 22 July 1848, C.O. 137/299, no. 68.
[32] Light to Grey, 18 Jan. 1848, private, C.O. 111/249; Light to Grey, 6 Mar. 1848, C.O. 111/251, no. 41.

year was accomplished by Portuguese and Indian immigrants who suffered both intimidation and physical violence at the hands of striking freedmen. Portuguese homes and shops were plundered, and after one such incident in Berbice, sixty-six people were arrested and another lay dead, slain by a hard-pressed and terrified shopkeeper.[33] Incendiary fires occurred throughout the colony: arsonists destroyed megass buildings at Palmyra, Montrose, Melville, and Blairmont during January; and on at least two occasions the houses of Europeans were set fire to at night.[34] In this confrontation, the adamant and necessitous planters prevailed, and by April freedmen had generally resumed work at reduced wages, retaining the use of their houses and grounds free of rent.

The West India crisis crippled resident proprietors, a class whose numbers and influence had increased during the early years of the free period.[35] In the best sugar districts, there had been much speculation in estate land. The most daring white colonists in British Guiana, for example, had assumed mortgages amounting to 60 or 80 per cent of the sale value of estates, promising to liquidate their debts in five or six years.[36] In principle, the Colonial Office heartily approved the growth of a resident proprietary. Earl Grey frequently commented on the evils of absenteeism, and he expected the Sugar Duties Act to remedy that 'vicious arrangement': '. . . the stimulus of foreign competitn will compel the proprietors either to reside & personally superintend the management of their estates, or to let them for fixed money rents to persons havg an individual interest in their successful cultivatn.'[37]

Grey's views offered little comfort to resident proprietors whose anguish was dramatically illustrated by the suicide of Thomas McCornock, one of the most intelligent and distinguished proprietors of Jamaica, a popular resident of forty years, manager of Golden Grove, owner of Stanton Estate, and Custos

---

[33] Light to Grey, 4 Apr. 1848, C.O. 111/252, no. 60.
[34] Light to Grey, Jan. to Mar. 1848, C.O. 111/249, nos. 17, 32, and private despatch; C.O. 111/251, no. 41.
[35] See p. 408, n. 7.
[36] Sel. Comm. on Ceylon and British Guiana, P.P. 1849, XI (297), evidence of Henry Light, 5, 6.
[37] Minute by Earl Grey, bound in Harris to Grey, 20 Jan. 1847, private, C.O. 295/156.

of St. Thomas in the East. McCornock cut his own throat in December 1848 after a period of severe mental depression and immediately following the destruction of his megass house at Stanton by the work of an incendiary.[38] A year earlier, sixteen Jamaica planters who owned nineteen estates free of debt or encumbrance and leased another thirteen declared themselves unable to cultivate for another year and incapable, without credit, of taking off the existing crop.[39] They expected to produce about 2,800 hogsheads of sugar and half as many puncheons of rum, which at existing prices would allow them a balance of £580 above their bare expenses without considering depreciation of stock, buildings, fences, and equipment. On average, this gave each planter about £36 for the year, representing an interest of ·4 per cent on an investment of £145,600. Planters whose property was mortgaged defaulted on their debts, and as the manager of the Colonial Bank in Trinidad observed, 'parties of the highest probity possessed of ample assets in houses and landed property were cruelly forced into insolvency owing to the inconvertibility of Real Estate'.[40] In May 1848, P. A. Ganteaume, a member of the Trinidad Council, resigned office for reason of insolvency.[41] Ten years before he had been free of debt and had used £6,000 in compensation money to improve his three estates. He acquired a fourth good property through his second marriage, and except for begetting twelve children, he lived without extravagance. In 1848 his liabilities amounted to £36,000. Several months later, John Losh, another member of the Council, a prominent colonial merchant and planter, resigned in similar circumstances.[42] Lord Harris was reluctant to accept his resignation lest his place in the Council could not be filled by a suitable solvent person.

Gripped by depression, colonial planters and their metropolitan allies used every device at their disposal to secure the

---

[38] *The Falmouth Post*, 19 Dec. 1848.

[39] Memorial, enclosed in C. E. Grey to Earl Grey, 22 Dec. 1847, C.O. 137/293, no. 125.

[40] Memorandum of Manager of Colonial Bank, enclosed in Harris to Grey, 5 Apr. 1848, C.O. 295/160, no. 31.

[41] Harris to Grey, 4 May 1848, C.O. 295/161, no. 42. Documentation on the Ganteaume bankruptcy appears in C. O. 295/164.

[42] Harris to Grey, 12 Aug. 1848, C.O. 295/164, no. 93. Losh was the principal partner of the Port of Spain firm of Losh, Spiers & Company which had to stop payment when the firm of Messrs. Eccles of Glasgow failed.

restoration of protective duties. Lord George Bentinck, an imperialist of the old school and leader of the protectionist element in the House of Commons, proposed and chaired the Select Committee on Sugar and Coffee Planting during 1847– 48. Minutes of evidence from this committee and documentation on the plantations fills four volumes of the Parliamentary Papers and offers a valuable mine of information on the character and condition of the sugar colonies in the 1840s. Bentinck dominated the committee, leading his witnesses and evoking a formidable mass of data to confirm his own pre-suppositions, which were 'that it is from idleness, from squatting, and from vagabondage, that the sugar plantations are deprived of their proper cultivation'.[43] Bentinck's strident pro-planter bias was moderated by other members, five of whom were firmly committed to free trade.[44] The committee's final report issued on 29 May 1848, was disappointing to Bentinck, whose death in the following September was a severe blow to protectionists throughout the Empire. While acknowledging the grinding distress of the plantation colonies, the only relief it called for was a differential duty of 10s. which would continue for a term of six years.[45]

Responding to the committee's reports, Lord John Russell offered the colonists a compromise. He proposed a small increase in the existing rate of colonial preference—from 4s. 6d. to 7s.— and agreed to postpone the date for the final equalization of duties from 1851 to 1854. To sweeten his offer he recommended that the British Government guarantee the interest on loans up to £500,000 at 4 per cent which the colonies might raise for

[43] Bentinck's resolution, 95, Proceedings of the Sel. Comm. on Sugar and Coffee Planting, P.P. 1847–8, XXIII (361).

[44] The five included Labouchere, Moffatt, Milner Gibson, Villiers, and James Wilson. Lord George Manners and Sir John Pakington voted consistently with Bentinck, as did Sir Edward Buxton who considered protection necessary as a defence against slave-producers.

[45] Eighth Report of the Sel. Comm. on Sugar and Coffee Planting, P.P. 1847–8, XXIII (361). The committee's recommendations were reinforced by advice independently offered by Caribbean governors. Sir Charles Grey of Jamaica recommended the elimination of all duty on colonial sugar and the retention of a reduced duty on foreign sugar. C. E. Grey to Earl Grey, 21 Sept. and 22 Oct. 1848, C.O. 137/293, nos. 92, 93. After a tour of Grenada and St. Vincent in early 1848, William Reid, Governor in Chief of the Windward Islands, argued that sugar production by free labour could not withstand competition on equal terms with that of slave labour, and 'that freedom should be nursed by protection for a considerable time to come'. Reid to Grey, 26 Feb. 1848, C.O. 28/168, no. 14.

the purpose of immigration, road or railroad construction, or for drainage and irrigation projects. Although approved by Parliament,[46] Russell's package was rejected by West India planters who believed that their survival depended on lasting and effective protection against slave-grown sugar. In a desperate bid to force their will on Westminster, Caribbean planters plunged headlong into open political conflict with the Westminster Government.

Their battleground was retrenchment. In Jamaica and British Guiana, legislators claimed they could not support their costly government establishments under a system of free trade, and they proceeded to reduce the salaries paid to government officers. Because the Colonial Office regarded these salaries— which did, in fact, constitute a substantial part of colonial expenses—a commitment of honour, it was bound to resist the colonists' actions. In the confrontations which ensued, West Indian legislators hoped to embarrass the Russell Government, dramatize their grievances, and wrest from a reluctant Parliament the restoration of protecting duties. In this way they were encouraged by the West India interest and by the leading financial institution in the Caribbean, the Colonial Bank.[47]

The Court of Policy of British Guiana, led by Peter Rose,[48] proprietor of Lima Estate and local manager of the Colonial Bank, demanded that government salaries in the colony be reduced by 25 per cent.[49] When the Colonial Office refused, the Combined Court, in September 1848, declared it would produce no revenue until its demands were met. Deploring this action, the Secretary of State observed that the colony's revenue came primarily from indirect taxes on the labouring class and that no

---

[46] *11 & 12 Vict. c. 130.*

[47] Governors Grey and Light made it clear to the Colonial Office that resident proprietors were acting in collusion with leading West Indians in Britain, including members of Parliament. Joseph Hume, M.P., and relative of William Hardin Burnley, the most articulate resident proprietor of Trinidad, was among their principal conspirators. Hume sat on the Committee to investigate conditions in British Guiana in 1849. Report on Governor Light's Administration, C.O. 111/253; C. E. Grey to Earl Grey, 19 June 1848, C.O. 137/296, no. 57.

[48] Rose's sugar property was in deep debt, and according to the Governor, only the salary he received from the Colonial Bank preserved his solvency. Frank, tough, and resolute, Rose dominated the planter element. He used his position as bank manager to enhance his power in a community where credit was essential.

[49] Light to Grey, 1 Jan. 1848, C.O. 111/249, no. 1.

crippling reduction in public income commensurate with the distressed position of the planter class could be anticipated.[50] The planters responded by affirming that the wealth of the community and almost every shilling of public revenue ultimately derived from the products of the soil, and that without protection the planters would be forced to abandon cultivation and cease making wage payments, rendering all revenue precarious.[51]

In hope of conciliating the colonists, Earl Grey accepted an offer by Henry Barkly to assume the governorship of British Guiana. Barkly, an M.P., Guiana absentee, former associate in a West Indian merchant firm, and a wavering free-trader, had been encouraged to offer his services by a group of London merchants interested in the colony.[52] He was warmly received in Georgetown in February 1849, but he quickly discovered that adept personal diplomacy could not resolve the controversy.[53] Fully a quarter of the plantations were in a state of insolvency; wages were in arrears; and produce was under seizure by creditors. Labourers, failing to receive their pay regularly, were departing the estates in alarming numbers. According to stipendiary magistrates, 6,500 of them left the plantations in 1849. The rivers and creeks of the colony were lined with the huts of freedmen for 50 or 60 miles, a condition which the Governor described as 'internal haemorrhage'.[54] If anything, the planters' hardships had stiffened their position: the 25 per cent reduction in government salaries demanded in December 1847 was increased to 33 per cent in July 1848 and to 50 per cent in March 1849.[55]

At the time of Barkly's arrival in the Caribbean, a Select Committee of the House of Commons was formed to investigate the Guiana situation. The committee was proposed and chaired

---

[50] Taylor minute on draft, Earl Grey to Walker, 5 Feb. 1848, bound in C.O. 111/249, no. 1. Planters paid only 1 per cent of the revenue as a separate group. Most of the colony's income came from import duties, rum and spirits taxes, hucksters licences and shop duties paid mainly by middle-class and labouring people. Report on Governor Light's Administration, C.O. 111/253.

[51] Speeches of Peter Rose and James Stuart, Combined Court, 21 Mar. 1848, enclosed in Light to Grey, 31 Mar. 1848, P.P. 1847–8, XLVI (749).

[52] Barkly to Grey, 17 Feb. 1849, confidential, C.O. 111/264.

[53] Ibid.

[54] Barkly to Grey, 17 Apr. 1850, C.O. 111/273, no. 60.

[55] Barkly to Grey, 6 May 1849, confidential, C.O. 111/265.

by a member of an absentee family, Henry James Baillie, who hoped to use it as a means of strengthening the colonists' hand. Committeemen—including Peel, Gladstone, and Disraeli—grilled Henry Light, Barkly's predecessor, in a manner more abrasive than cordial, but their final report offered little comfort to the planters. While acknowledging that great economies were essential because of the straitened position of the agricultural interest, the committee—responding to Peel's direction—confirmed the official view that government salaries could not be arbitrarily reduced for fear that such a precedent in the hands of ruling colonial élites would permanently impair the security of government offices and expose civil servants to capricious retribution for unpopular actions.[56] With all avenues of hope closed by August 1849, and some members of the Combined Court exhausted with the struggle, Barkly secured a narrow majority in favour of renewing supplies.[57] Recalcitrant members of the Court resigned, and salaries were restored at their original level.[58]

The Jamaica Assembly shared the defeat of the Guiana colonists. During 1847 and 1848 the Government of Jamaica suffered heavy deficits, and by June of the latter year the Treasury was empty.[59] When the House convened in the autumn, it refused to vote additional revenue unless the Westminster Government would consent to a measure of retrenchment consonant with the colony's reduced circumstances. Although the Assembly's main objective was the restoration of protection, Jamaicans took retrenchment seriously on its own merits. They considered it preposterous that the Chief Justice of the island should earn £3,000 while the Chief Justice of the American Supreme Court commanded a salary equivalent to £1,200, or that the President of the United States, with responsibility for a population of 20,000,000 should earn less than the Governor of their community of 400,000.[60] During

---

[56] First Report from the Select Committee on Ceylon and British Guiana, P.P. 1849, XI (297).

[57] Barkly to Grey, 16 Aug. 1849, C.O. 111/268, no. 126.

[58] Barkly to Grey, 1 Dec. 1849, C.O. 111/270, no. 174; William Law Mathieson, *British Slave Emancipation, 1838–1849* (London, 1932); p. 197.

[59] Report from Committee Appointed to Consider Reductions in Public Expenditure, enclosed in C. E. Grey to Earl Grey, 22 Dec. 1848, C.O. 137/298, no. 117.

[60] Bigelow, *Jamaica in 1850*, p. 46.

January 1849 a legislative committee including members from all political factions studied means of limiting government expenditure. Its report was swiftly transformed into a Bill calling for extensive cuts in government spending, amounting to £24,500 in addition to salary reductions between 10 and 33 per cent, the sum of which would conserve about £41,000 (up to 17 per cent of the island's general expenditures).[61] The Legislative Council, comprised in part of men whose salaries would have been affected by the Assembly's measure, rejected it, and the Governor prorogued the legislature. When the Assembly reconvened, it shrank from a full stoppage of supplies. In contrast to the all-embracing action of the Combined Court, the Jamaican Assembly passed a thin series of tax measures which permitted the maintenance of essential services while it expressly forbade the payment of salaries to public officers or Anglican clergymen.[62]

For all its venom the Jamaica Assembly could not follow the intractable course taken by the Combined Court in British Guiana. The Guiana body was comprised of white planters, who, in the circumstances of 1848–9, believed they had everything to gain and nothing to lose from a protracted confrontation with Westminster. Since they considered themselves and their estates doomed to ruin unless they secured protection, they were prepared to jeopardize the credit of the colony and all its civil institutions to get it. If they failed, they would be no worse off for the attempt, and like passengers leaving a sinking ship, they could retire from Guiana to resume their lives—however shabbily—in England. This was not the case with a large number of Jamaica assemblymen, especially coloured members, who for better or for worse, had a permanent stake in the island. They willingly joined the planters in the retrenchment battle of 1848–9, but they could not afford to pursue the struggle to the utter ruination of the colony. The defeat of the Guiana planters in August 1849 weakened resistance in Jamaica, and during the legislative session of 1849–50 the Assembly revived all important revenue enactments.[63]

In both colonies, retrenchment proceedings had received

[61] See p. 409, n. 8.
[62] C. E. Grey to Earl Grey, 27 Mar. 1849, C.O. 137/302, no. 41.
[63] C. E. Grey to Earl Grey, 5 Jan. 1850, C.O. 137/306, no. 1.

broad and vigorous public support. The political divisions and the emphasis upon colour which characterized the Jamaica Assembly during the fifties and sixties, when defeatism gripped the community, were muted at the beginning of the retrenchment battle. Members of the Jamaica legislature—whether planters or merchants, white or coloured—expressed similar aspirations regarding the future of the colony. They believed that a community of subsistence cultivators and small farmers would be inimical to the moral development and material prosperity of the island. They valued public order and the institutions of a settled and mature community, and in 1849, they contended that the acquisition and maintenance of these institutions depended on the survival of a vigorous export trade in tropical staples. Edward Jordan, newspaperman and leading coloured member of the Assembly, deplored the desolation of Kingston, its untenanted stores and houses.[64] His partner at the *Morning Chronicle*, Robert Osborn, revived the spectre of a young generation rising up with neither schools nor the rudiments of civilized life:

. . . all persons are aware that this is exclusively an agricultural country; all our wealth . . . lies in our soil . . . if our soil and its produce are not remunerative, in the name of heaven what is to become of us? . . . If property after property is to be abandoned, every man must see that we have nothing left us but to fall.[65]

To one degree or another, Jamaica's leaders were élitists, committed to the preservation of a hierarchical society which rewarded wealth, education, and good manners, and relied economically on a large lower class of agricultural wage labourers. In communion with Richard Hill, the brilliant and articulate secretary of the Stipendiary Magistrate's Department, they nursed the hope that the labouring people would learn 'to value a reliance on plantation work, and to regard the planter's good fortune, as the source of their own wealth'.[66]

---

[64] Remarks of Edward Jordan at a meeting in Kingston, 25 June 1849, quoted in (David Turnbull), *The Jamaica Movement, for Promoting the Enforcement of the Slave-Trade Treaties*, p. 236.

[65] Ibid., pp. 254–5.

[66] Report of R. Hill, 22 June 1846, enclosed in C.O. 137/289, no. 17.

THE CONTINUING STRUGGLE, 1850–1865

Free trade jeopardized the West India sugar industry; it did not destroy it. By 1865 the Caribbean colonies were producing 20,000 tons more sugar than they had in 1835. During those three decades the geographical strength of the industry shifted somewhat: the larger Leeward Islands, Barbados, Trinidad, and Guiana increased their exports while production fell by half in the Windward Islands and by 60 per cent in Jamaica. Export statistics recorded in Table 13 indicate the ebb and flow of production, although they offer no measurement of the quality of the sugar produced or the economic health of the plantations. An increasing volume of exports did not necessarily mean higher profitability. When the price of sugar fell by half, as it did between 1840 and 1848, planters were obliged to double their output in order to recover the same gross income. As will be evident in Table 14, in a single decade Barbados planters increased their production of sugar by 130 per cent to reap merely a 10 per cent expansion in gross earnings. Trinidad and Guiana were the only other West Indian colonies in which a substantially enlarged volume of exports offset in part the chronic depression in prices.

The immigration of indentured Indian labour played a decisive role in the recovery of Trinidad and Guiana after 1850. Lord John Russell's offer of an immigration loan, rejected during the retrenchment controversy, was belatedly accepted by planters in those colonies. The Guiana and Trinidad planters had not been insincere or petulant in their initial refusal of the loan. The immigration of 21,784 Asian workers to the major sugar colonies between 1845 and 1848 had proven exceedingly expensive,[67] and in the latter year colonists doubted that the estates could endure, let alone repay an immigration loan, unless protection was restored. Trinidad had expended half its revenue on Asian immigration in 1846 and 1847; indeed, the

[67] In view of the rations, medicine, and accommodations required by immigrants, the daily charge for Asian labourers in Jamaica had been about 2s. 3d. a day. Report of Richard Hill, enclosed in C. E. Grey to Earl Grey, 6 Mar. 1848, C.O. 137/296, no. 26. In Trinidad, Governor Harris determined that during the initial year of acclimatization proprietors were sustaining a dead loss of £10 per immigrant after deducting the value of their labour. Harris to Grey, 28 Dec. 1846, C.O. 295/152, no. 121.

TABLE 13

Average Annual Sugar Production in the British West Indies, 1814–1866
(tons)

Years	Antigua	Barbados	British Guiana	Dominica	Grenada	Jamaica	Montserrat
1814–23	8,346	11,622	23,237	2,089	10,880	78,518	1,548
1824–33	8,215	14,838	55,936	2,478	10,769	68,465	1,134
1834–8	8,328	20,309	51,278	1,971	8,408	54,225	762
1839–46	8,927	15,652	31,865	2,319	4,744	33,431	638
1847–56	9,858	28,622	41,790	2,821	4,687	27,474	126
1857–66	10,011	36,367	61,284	2,854	4,401	25,168	343

Years	St. Kitts	St. Lucia	St. Vincent	Tobago	Trinidad	Nevis	Virgin Is.	Total
1814–23	6,050	3,415	12,117	6,097	7,629	2,752	1,727	176,027
1824–33	4,819	3,531	12,212*	5,202	12,117	2,453	873	203,152*
1834–8	4,246	2,591	10,006	4,363	15,227	1,730	616	184,060
1839–46	5,002	2,762	6,383	2,731	15,000	1,395	328	131,177
1847–56	5,347	3,457	7,209	2,740	22,061	1,443	120	157,755
1857–66	7,978	4,627	6,934	2,820	26,564	1,699	—	191,050*

Source: Noel Deerr, History of Sugar, I, 193–203; II, 377.

* Asterisk indicates corrections made on Deerr's figures.

TABLE 14

*Sugar Production and Gross Earnings in
Barbados, 1842–1852*

Year	Hogsheads	Average Price per Hogshead	Gross Income £
1842	21,545	31	671,515
1847	32,257	20	653,980
1852	48,785	15	739,884

Source: Colebrook to Pakington, 7 June 1853, C.O. 28/178.

Governors of Trinidad and Jamaica asserted that the great cost of immigration had been the principal cause of the embarrassments sustained by their treasuries in the crisis of 1847–49.[68] Unable to recommend a further depletion of their resources at a time of unparalleled depression the governors of all the major colonies, in conformity with the views of the planters in 1848, had advised that Indian immigration be stopped. The decision to resume that immigration in 1850 was based on sheer desperation. Protective tariffs had not been restored and there appeared no other recourse by which the estates could be preserved. In spite of the vagrant habits of many Asians already introduced, their weak constitutions, and their inferior performance of some vital tasks in the production of sugar, they had proven the steadiest members of a ragged labour force and without their endeavours a large part of the crop produced in Trinidad and Guiana during 1849 could not have been harvested. For the planters, Asian immigration was an unwelcome last resort.

The reaction of colonists to the prospect of Indian immigration was an index of their commitment to plantation agriculture. In Trinidad and Guiana where legislative bodies were controlled by planters, there was no political obstacle to the

[68] Harris to Grey, 20 July 1847, C.O. 295/157, no. 68; C. E. Grey to Earl Grey, 22 Dec. 1848, C.O. 137/298, no. 117. In the decade after 1837, Jamaica spent £155,042 on immigration; £75,705 of that was spent in 1846–7. Trinidad invested £155,042 on immigration between 1838 and 1848, £83,048 was spent in 1846–7.

renewal of Indian immigration once the planters concurred in its necessity. Nor was there a quarrel over who should bear its cost. Earl Grey, his successor, colonial governors, and the planting interest agreed that unless a productive export economy was preserved the civil institutions of the colonies would disintegrate and the freedmen would suffer irreversible economic and social regression. By this logic it was considered appropriate that all elements of the population should share the cost of immigration. When the guaranteed loans were taken up by the two colonies in 1850, revenue measures enacted for their repayment fell upon the whole community.

Except for the brief period between 1860 and 1863, East Indian immigration to Jamaica was not revived.[69] The reasons for Jamaica's reticence on this question lie in a tangled medley of political, constitutional, and economic problems peculiar to that island. In the 1850s, planters did not dominate the legislature. Although the Assembly stood to a man in favour of a resumption of protecting duties, coloured members and others not directly associated with sugar property were unwilling to tax the entire community to provide indentured labour to a few large estates.[70] Asian immigration was expensive, and the colony already laboured under a £750,000 debt.[71] For social and cultural reasons the Indians were not wanted. Their introduction could not appreciably alter the population-land ratio for some time, and there was no assurance that they would remain on the estates offering dependable, disciplined labour. Even if they did, it was not clear that the plantations could survive without protection.

Jamaican society was sharply divided on the question. By the mid-fifties, vocal members of the coloured community,

[69] A rise in sugar prices in 1856–7 induced the Assembly to pass an Immigration Act in 1858. But in keeping with the attitudes of the popular party it required that the whole cost of immigration be paid by planters who hired Asians. Applications for immigrants were, consequently, few. When an Act permitting partial payment out of general funds passed in 1861, the price of sugar had fallen and the enthusiasm of the planters had abated. 4,645 Asians entered the colony between 1860 and 1863.

[70] The Governor wrote, 'the planters are in a minority at present, and the terms on which they get immigrants are so onerous that they feel they could only avail themselves of such an advantage to a very limited extent'. Barkly to H. Roberts 26 Oct. 1853, *Newcastle Papers*, 9553.

[71] C. E. Grey to Earl Grey, 31 Dec. 1851, C.O. 137/311, no. 115.

some missionaries, and some stipendiary magistrates considered the sugar régime beyond recovery, caught in an unending cost-price squeeze that would render Indian immigration an expensive social liability. Without other alternatives, they nurtured a hope that the existing population would restore the island's sinking prosperity by cultivating minor staples and foodstuffs.[72] The major planters in company with Governor Henry Barkly who had moved to Jamaica from British Guiana favoured immigration, arguing that minor staples would not bring prosperity, and that their production would be hampered by the same labour problems that plagued the sugar industry.

At best, immigration could have helped only a small percentage of Jamaica's plantations. 314 of them, fully 49 per cent of the colony's sugar estates, were thrown up between 1844 and 1854,[73] and each additional failure made survival more difficult for others. The parochial tax burdens of abandoned plantations were being shifted to remaining estates. Public roads and bridges, which in former times had traversed 10 or 20 highly cultivated estates between inland districts and the sea, were rutted, overgrown, and ruinous, making the cost of wainage disproportionately high for surviving properties.[74] Unlike the newer estates of Trinidad and Guiana, Jamaica's plantations were weighed down by complicated encumbrances which had been accumulating since the 18th century. They needed high prices as well as continuous labour to recover their equlibrium, but there was little hope that free trade would permit the former. Most Jamaican soils did not compare in natural fertility to those of the large southern colonies where savings were possible through extensive ratooning. Clearly, the Jamaican estates that collapsed before 1854 could not have been helped by Indian immigration, and many of the remaining ones were too impoverished to provide the special accommodations necessary for indentured Asians. Jamaicans confronted an awkward dilemma: they could not easily afford the cost of labour immigration, but at the same time they could ill afford the loss of their remaining sugar plantations.

[72] Barkly to Newcastle, 26 May 1854, C.O. 137/323, no. 115.
[73] Hall, *Free Jamaica*, p. 82.
[74] Report of T. W. Jackson, enclosed in Barkly to Newcastle, 21 Feb. 1854, C.O. 137/322, no. 24.

The wholesale abandonment of sugar properties endangered the economic well-being of all parties in the colony. Estates were vital markets for the peasants' food crops. When they ceased cultivation, working people who had relied heavily on wages were obliged to concentrate on raising provisions. Consequently, the market for food crops became glutted and prices fell. This had happened in north-eastern Jamaica. Of the forty-eight estates operating in Portland and St. George in 1834, only seven remained in 1854 and together they produced less than 500 hogsheads. The local provision market was dull, and in order to earn money peasants were obliged to convey their provisions by small boat to Trelawny where sugar remained the dominant crop.[75] There is little doubt that freedmen enjoyed their highest prosperity during the 1838–46 period when wages paid by over 600 sugar estates had supplemented earnings made from provisions grounds.[76] Jamaican peasants still enjoyed an adequate living in the fifties. As one missionary put it: 'necessaries of life . . . being, with trifling exceptions, of local production, men may, if they will work, eat.'[77] Although the peasants had little money, they could survive with little in good seasons by allowing their stock to gather their own subsistence, varying their crops in response to local demand, planting a little ginger, arrowroot, and coffee, or even making crude sugar for the inland market.[78] Nevertheless, the price of provisions was falling in the fifties; wage labour opportunities were shrinking; the price of imported flour, salt-fish and other necessities was rising—partly as a consequence of tariffs, although after 1861 shortages as well as inflation were occasioned by the American Civil War. Because peasants had little money, missionary chapels and schools which relied upon contributions from freedmen fell into disrepair, and Jamaican missionaries uniformly lamented the declining attendance at chapels and diminished interest in education.

A balance between the domestic and export economies of Jamaica was not achieved. The domestic product had expanded

[75] Report of C. Lake, enclosed in Barkly to Newcastle, 21 Feb. 1854, C.O. 137/322, no. 24; Report of R. Hill, 25 Jan. 1856, enclosed in Barkly to Labouchere, 6 Mar. 1856, C.O. 137/330, no. 35.

[76] Hall, *Free Jamaica*, p. 168.

[77] W. Slatyer to Tidman, 5 Feb. 1849, *L.M.S. Papers*.

[78] Hall, *Free Jamaica*, pp. 171–4.

rapidly at the expense of export staples, but it did not earn foreign credits to provide for the payment of essential imports. It did not produce the circulating medium required to elevate the economy above a barter level, and it did not sustain ancillary industries or encourage technical skills. Nor was the declining production of major staples offset by a compensating rise in the value of secondary exports. Sugar, rum, and coffee constituted 88 per cent of the value of Jamaica's exports in 1850 and 86 per cent of their value in 1865.[79] Exports of ginger fell sharply in the late 1840s and did not recover in the mid-century period (see Table 15). Pimento sales increased in the fifties, but this development offered little comfort since the indigenous and spontaneous growth of the plant indicated that nature was resuming its sway over districts in which more valuable culture had once existed.[80] When the price of pimento fell by half in the sixties, its export declined. Livestock sales remained languid. Pen-keepers who in former times had sold their cattle to the estates were delivering their animals to the butcher at severely reduced prices,[81] and the number and quality of craftsmen in the colony was shrinking as the demise of estates reduced the demand for carpenters, coopers, cartwrights, wheelwrights, and masons.

Some estimate of the sugar industry's importance to the over-all economic well-being of the colony may be ascertained from a comparison between Jamaica and Trinidad after 1850. In the latter island, the sugar plantations recovered their vigour through the employment of indentured Indian labour. Only thirteen of Trinidad's sugar properties were abandoned in the decade after 1848.[82] The influx of Indian workers permitted an extension of cultivation and thereby increased the demand for Creole labourers. In 1860 the Legislative Council determined that for every two Indians indentured to a plantation, an additional native labourer was taken into employment, normally at crop.[83] Many of these jobs were filled by over 2,000 annual

[79] Jamaica Blue Books, C.O. 142/64 and 79.

[80] Barkly to Newcastle, 26 May 1854, C.O. 137/323, no. 73.

[81] Ibid.

[82] There were 193 estates operating in 1848; 180 in 1857. It is possible that the differential may represent some consolidation.

[83] Report of Committee of Council, 7 Feb. 1860, enclosed in Keate to Newcastle, 9 Feb. 1860, C.O. 295/208, no. 24.

TABLE 15

Average Annual Export of Secondary Products from Jamaica, 1840–1864

Years	Coffee '000 (cwt.)	Logwood '000 (tons)	Ginger '000 (lb.)	Pimento '000 (lb.)
1840–4	65·9		1,739	3,084
1845–9	46·5	4·3*	692	4,732
1850–4	46·9	4·6	629	4,623
1855–9	48·5	15·1	517	9,326
1860–4	54·8	24·1	754	6,465

Sources: Tabular Return of Exports from Jamaica, C.O. 137/287; Jamaica Blue Books, 1846–9, C.O. 142, Jamaica, 1830–1930, p. 241.

* Data for 1845 are missing.

migrants from the Windward colonies where the local sugar industry was in decline and wages were comparatively low. Only a quarter of Trinidad's native freedmen deigned to perform regular estate labour, but the sugar plantations with their large contingents of immigrants afforded peasants a profitable market for their foodstuffs as well as access to wage labour. Colonial Blue Books indicate that in 1860 the cost of living in Jamaica and Trinidad was roughly equivalent whereas wage rates in the latter colony exceeded those of Jamaica by up to 40 per cent. This comparison assumes greater significance when it is remembered that in many districts of Jamaica the freedmen possessed no opportunity for wage labour as a result of the abandonment of estates.[84]

Trinidad's vigorous export economy provided higher levels of individual consumption and enabled that colony, in contrast to Jamaica, to improve its civic institutions. The stagnation of Jamaica's exports imposed an equally static condition upon her imports. During the 1850s, imports to Jamaica declined slightly while those to Trinidad rose in value by 60 per cent (see Table 16). At the end of the decade, Trinidad was importing

[84] In Jamaica, the wage rates were highest in parishes which continued to export a large amount of sugar. Reports of stipendiary magistrates, enclosed in Barkly to Newcastle, 21 Feb. 1854, C.O. 137/322, no. 4.

TABLE 16

Comparative Economic Statement, Trinidad and Jamaica, 1850–1861

Years	Colony	Annual Average Value of Imports (estimated £)	Annual Average Exports of Sugar (tons)	Annual Average Tonnage Incoming	Outgoing
1850–2	Trinidad	506,218	21,530	60,304	59,783
	Jamaica	1,061,714	28,568	104,004	104,618
1853–5	Trinidad	539,327	23,954	66,193*	66,256*
	Jamaica	594,831	23,286	91,407	88,715
1856–8	Trinidad	764,421	24,583	76,209	76,552
	Jamaica	939,229	22,152	87,817	87,287
1859–61†	Trinidad	806,977	26,644	98,425	94,970
	Jamaica	1,045,117	25,056	91,259	88,783

Sources: Jamaica Blue Books, C.O. 142; Trinidad Blue Books, C.O. 300; Deerr, History of Sugar, I, 199, 202.

* No record for tonnage for 1854.

† Population of Jamaica, 1861, census, 441,264; Population of Trinidad, 1861 census, 84,438.

goods worth about £9 10s. per person each year; Jamaica was importing goods worth approximately £2 8s. per person. The retardation of Jamaica's import trade had a damaging effect on island finance since import duties constituted the largest single source of general revenue. Revenues declined abruptly after the Sugar Duties Act—from £286,850 in 1845 to £209,400 in 1851—and they remained at a comparatively depressed level throughout the fifties.[85] Similarly, parish revenue in Jamaica which was used to maintain roads, schools, churches, and paupers fell abruptly. Until 1858 roughly 60 per cent of all parish revenue was drawn from hereditaments, an assessment

[85] Comparative Statements of Revenue and Expenditure, Votes of the Jamaica Assembly, 1845–60. For an analysis of the complex and peculiar statistics on revenue and expenditures in Jamaica, see Hall, Free Jamaica, appendix 4. Hall argues that the financial situation of the island depended very heavily on the welfare of the sugar industry.

on personal property, but the declining value of estate property, compounded by numerous abandonments, eroded the tax base upon which parochial revenue depended.

A steady increase in revenue in Trinidad enabled the legislature to finance public construction, including hospitals at Port of Spain and San Fernando, public baths, and an asylum for the insane. An underground sewerage system was initiated in the capital, and surveys were renewed for the Trinidad railway project.[86] The colony paid its debts systematically. The resident proprietary was in a healthy, though not wealthy state, and inland commerce conducted by the lower class was thriving.[87] For all its costs and inconveniences, Indian immigration had produced an economic balance between the domestic and the export product of Trinidad—the type of balance that missionaries and government officials had vainly hoped would result from the free village settlements which arose shortly after emancipation. When establishing free villages in Jamaica in the forties, William Knibb declared it his intention that villagers would share their time between the cultivation of ground crops and wage work on neighbouring estates: 'cultivation of sugar should proceed,' Knibb asserted, 'but proceed on righteous principles.'[88] It had proceeded poorly in Jamaica. In Trinidad, the sugar industry was sustained, but only by virtue of immigration.

In the Windward Islands and Nevis where planters had neither the means nor official encouragement to undertake immigration they resorted to share-cropping—the so-called *métayer* system—to stem the withdrawal of labourers and preserve their properties from abandonment.[89] By this arrangement, proprietors divided some or all of their cane lands among freedmen in small plots to be planted, cultivated, and cut by the workers in return for a percentage—usually half—of the

[86] Keate to Lytton, 4 Oct. 1858, C.O. 295/201, no. 134; Keate to Newcastle, 9 Aug. 1859, C.O. 295/205, no. 123.

[87] Keate to Lytton, 26 Sept. 1858, C.O. 295/200, no. 131.

[88] Sel. Comm. on the West India Colonies, P.P. 1842, XIII (479), evidence of W. Knibb, 6015.

[89] Davy, *The West Indies*, p. 485. Métayage was a common subject of correspondence between colonial executives and successive Secretaries of State, and its progress was carefully studied. For the Windward Islands, see W. K. Marshall, 'Métayage in the Sugar Industry of the British Windward Islands, 1838–1865', *The Jamaican Historical Review*, V (1965), 28–55.

value of the sugar raised. Planters continued to control milling and boiling procedures; they provided stock and carts for haulage; and normally they engrossed the entire production of molasses and rum. Proprietors considered the métayer system a necessary, but temporary, expedient to help them over hard times. Share-cropping was cumbersome and disputes were common. The freedmen were not progressive cultivators, and the division of cane land into small parcels precluded the introduction of new techniques and the efficient use of agricultural machinery. Métayers accused the proprietors of dishonest distribution of the proceeds of sugar. The proprietors deplored their loss of control over the labour force, the abuse of stock and equipment, the carelessness of cultivation, and the inattention given to weeding and manuring which caused deterioration in the quality of the soil. Planters having large capital investment in sugar property were unhappy with the meagre rewards of share-cropping. When the price of sugar improved temporarily in the late fifties, many of them returned to the wage labour system of production. In St. Lucia where métayage had been commonplace, the system was virtually eradicated by 1861. A return of hard times occasioned its resumption in the Windward Islands, especially in Tobago, where, despite the claim of the Royal Commission of 1883–4 that métayage was a failure, it continued to serve as the principal means of production until the end of the century.[90]

In a final effort to save the plantations, the imperial Parliament passed an Encumbered Estates Act in 1854 designed to facilitate the sale of properties laden with complicated debts.[91] Under earlier laws, properties could not be sold unless their debts were paid, but the catastrophic fall of estate values after 1846 rendered such sale impossible for plantations burdened— as hundreds of them were—by mortgages, legacies, and other charges which exceeded their market values. Even encumbrancers who possessed strong claims upon West India property were reluctant to pursue chancery suits to recover a portion of their investments for fear that court costs would

[90] Sir Daniel Morris, *Reports on the Economic Resources of the West Indies* (London, 1898), pp. 61–2; Beachey, *British West Indies Sugar Industry*, pp. 115–16.
[91] Sir Reginald J. Cust, *A Treatise on the West Indian Incumbered Estates Act* (London, 1859).

exceed the rewards of apportionment. The Encumbered Estates Act permitted any owner or encumbrancer of a West Indian plantation to initiate proceedings to have an estate sold by judicial decree through special courts which were set up in London and the participating colonies. The proceeds of such a sale were to be divided among an estate's creditors according to the wisdom of the court. The purchaser would receive his property free of liabilities under a parliamentary title.

The Encumbered Estates Act was not immediately popular in the West Indies. Most encumbrancers lived in England, and colonists correctly anticipated that the London court would handle most estate sales,[92] depriving colonial lawyers who constituted a vocal element in many Caribbean assemblies of a share in the process. More importantly, West Indians would be prevented by distance from bidding on properties sold through the London court. Resident proprietors, constituting a community of debtors, generally preferred the old chancery system which, being characterized by high foreclosure costs and delays which lasted up to forty years, protected them from their creditors and assured them of a tidy consideration if they relinquished their equity out of court under a compromise arrangement.[93] With some hesitation, St. Vincent, Tobago, and St. Kitts applied for encumbered estates courts in the late fifties; Jamaica and others followed suit in the sixties.[94] Over the whole life of these courts—they survived until 1893—382 estates were executed, 148 of them being Jamaican.[95]

Encumbered estates courts concentrated West Indian property in the hands of metropolitan merchant houses, completing a trend which had begun in the eighteenth century. By far the largest number of active estates sold through the courts were purchased by consignee merchants in London, some of whom had managed heavily encumbered plantations for many years without being able to secure legal title to them.[96] The consignee

[92] Of the 148 estates executed in Jamaica, only two were sold through the local court.
[93] Barkly to Newcastle, 26 Feb. 1854, *Newcastle Papers*, 9553.
[94] Darling to Newcastle, 9 Mar. 1961, C.O. 137/353, no. 38.
[95] Beachey, *British West Indies Sugar Industry*, pp. 6, 22–3; for a case study of the execution of a West Indian estate, see Craton and Walvin, *Jamaican Plantation*, pp. 234–8.
[96] Beachey, *British West Indies Sugar Industry*, p. 9.

lien, the covenant by which a metropolitan merchant extended credit to his West Indian client, received priority in the court, and merchants bidding on plantations were able to bid up to the amount of their lien without surrendering additional cash. There was little competition from other purchasers. All sixteen Tobago estates sold before 1868 passed to the consignee merchant, as did most of the thirty-five Antigua plantations executed by 1869.[97] The concentration of ownership occasioned by decisions of the encumbered estates courts enabled merchant proprietors to amalgamate their plantations, consolidate management, and reduce duplication. During the final third of the century the West India sugar industry shed its pattern of family ownership and began to assume its modern commercial character.

Barbados was the exception to all this. She undertook no immigration; her planters did not engage in share-cropping; and along with British Guiana, Trinidad, and St. Lucia the colony did not adopt an encumbered estates court.[98] Her high level of production caused an increase in land values during the three decades after emancipation. Abandonments did not occur. By the late fifties resident planters were engaged in intense competition to obtain property, and plantations changed hands at prices which the Governor considered exorbitant— £10,000 for an estate producing 100 hogsheads of sugar.[99] Execution sales were rare. Merely thirteen of the colony's 500 estates were brought into chancery between 1851 and 1861: the average duration of these properties in the hands of the court was four and a half months; and only one of them sold for less than its appraised value.[100]

[97] Ibid., p. 17.

[98] In Guiana and Trinidad the problem of encumbrance was not great. Trinidad estates, although heavily mortgaged, were relatively new and had not been weighed down by annuities and other charges. In Guiana, Dutch law had prevented proprietors from bequeathing estate property to their heirs, a practice which precluded the attachment of onerous family charges. St. Lucia had devised her own system of executing encumbered estates in 1833. By 1884, 76 of her plantations had been disposed by judicial sale, and in 1851 only 12 of St. Lucia's proprietors held title deeds which antedated the Emancipation Act. Breen, St. Lucia, pp. 317–18; Beachey, British West Indies Sugar Industry, pp. 2, 9–10.

[99] Walker to Newcastle, 27 Sept. 1859, C.O. 28/189, no. 66; Hincks to Newcastle, 19 Sept. 1860, C.O. 28/191, no. 46.

[100] Walker to Newcastle, 14 Mar. 1865, C.O. 28/206, no. 346.

In public finance the colony was as solvent as its estates. Revenue commonly exceeded disbursements, and deficiencies sustained in the depression of the late forties and during the cholera epidemic of the fifties were swiftly erased. The accumulation of excess revenue enabled the legislature to improve public facilities and to reduce taxes.[101] In the mid-forties, import duties on basic items of consumption used by the labouring class— dried and smoked fish, flour, and cornmeal—were reduced by 35 to 80 per cent.[102] By 1852 *ad valorem* duties on the necessities of life were 11·6 per cent in Barbados, as compared with 18·5 per cent in Trinidad, 21·2 per cent in Antigua, and 27·7 per cent in Guiana.[103] Taxes which fell upon the Barbados worker in relation to his wages were 50 per cent lower than those borne throughout the Windward Islands.[104] In combination with the island's moderate taxation, her advantageous trading position as the first port of call in the Lesser Antilles enabled her to maintain a relatively low cost of living.

Barbados proprietors derived their prosperity entirely from sugar. Production rose from 19,000 tons in 1834 to 41,000 tons in 1865.[105] By 1850 sugar and its derivatives constituted 99 per cent of the value of the colony's exports.[106] The island's planters combined the two most essential criteria of good business practice: superior management and the maintenance of quality control. Roughly 65 per cent of the island's proprietors were local residents, and Governor K. B. Hamilton, among others, applauded their industry, perseverance, skill in cultivation, and dedication to economy.[107] Nowhere in the West Indies was sugar grown with such meticulous care: every conceivable piece

[101] Barbados possessed over 200 miles of the best roads in the Caribbean. The careenage of Bridgetown was twice enlarged in this period, and water works were established to supply the city. Public buildings were improved; prison facilities built in the fifties were elaborate by West Indian standards, as was the island's judicial and police establishment. By 1861 public expenditure was twice what it had been a decade earlier. Colebrooke to Russell, 9 June 1855, C.O. 28/182, no. 46; Walker to Newcastle, 27 Sept. 1859, C.O. 28/189, no. 66; Hincks to Newcastle, 15 Oct. 1861, C.O. 28/193, no. 55.

[102] C. E. Grey to Stanley, 4 Jan. 1845, C.O. 28/161, no. 2.

[103] Hamilton to Pakington, 13 Apr. 1852, C.O. 28/176, no. 20.

[104] Enclosure in Colebrooke to Newcastle, 8 July 1853, C.O. 28/178, no. 49.

[105] Deerr, *History of Sugar*, II, 193-4.

[106] In 1849, the colony exported articles valued at £663,626; only £7,134 of that was not the product of the sugar plantations.

[107] Hamilton to Pakington, 13 Apr. 1852, C.O. 28/176, no. 20.

of land was cultivated; estates were manicured almost 'beyond what we should call perfection';[108] and weeds were 'hardly to be seen'. Most assuredly, the success of the estates was not occasioned by new technology, for as Anthony Trollope observed, 'It is certainly the fact that they do make their sugar in a very old fashioned way in Barbados . . .'[109]

The unique success of the Barbados planters may be attributed to their large and disciplined pool of wage labourers. This asset vastly offset the cost of annual replanting, the purchase of imported fertilizer, and the comparatively high unit costs of small sugar properties. It permitted the planters to exercise their skills, to expand their cultivation, and to preserve the quality of their product. Most Barbados planters earned some profit in years of lowest prices. As a uniquely solvent proprietary class they were able to attract investment capital for plantation maintenance and renovation. The colony's estates did not pass to metropolitan capitalists and throughout the century the typical Barbados proprietor remained the head of a family, not the head of a merchant company.[110]

After the Sugar Duties Act it was impossible for most planters in low density colonies, where labour was costly and unreliable, to continue cultivation without dramatically altering local conditions. In Trinidad and Guiana the planters resorted to Indian immigration on a large scale; in the Windwards, they adopted the *métayer* system. Neither of these innovations was welcome, but each sufficed to keep the estates intact. For reasons peculiar to Jamaica, that colony rejected both Asian immigration and share-cropping, and its sugar industry continued its inexorable decline throughout the period. Many of the best Caribbean properties secured by metropolitan capitalists during the crisis of the late forties or through encumbered estates courts were subsequently brought into high cultivation, richly rewarding their owners. Great Diamond, a Guiana estate purchased in 1848 for £2,000 was producing 1,800 hogsheads in 1870 and was valued above £40,000.[111] Because British

[108] Sewell, *Ordeal of Free Labor*, p. 454.
[109] Trollope, *The West Indies*, p. 207.
[110] In 1897, only 19 sugar estates in Barbados were owned by public companies.
[111] Beachey, *British West Indies Sugar Industry*, pp. 37, 120.

merchant-proprietors were able to obtain large estates of this calibre for nominal sums, they could invest more heavily in sophisticated boiling equipment, steam engines for grinding and drainage, and imported fertilizers. Superior technology was a vital factor in achieving profitability, but labour continued to be the crucial consideration in successful sugar production. The cane fields of British Guiana which had been choked with weeds in 1850 were, by virtue of Indian immigration, cultivated 'like a garden'[112] in the 1870s.

Contemporary Europeans measured economic achievement in the Caribbean in terms of gross trade figures, and on that account the free labour economy of Jamaica was considered an unmitigated disaster. Because Jamaica was the best known and most important of the former British slave colonies, pro-slavery spokesmen throughout the Americas fortified their arguments by reference to declining trade and civic impoverishment of that island.[113] Although the decline of Jamaica's staple exports was offset in large measure by a greatly expanded domestic product, cultivated and mainly consumed by peasants, the material prosperity of the peasantry was greatest during the early years of freedom, when protection prevailed and the estates were intact, buying provisions and paying respectable wages. The failure of hundreds of plantations in the late forties and fifties and the lowering of wages on those that remained reduced the peasants' money income and isolated them from the European culture group. The cost of government increased after emancipation, but estate failures reduced the quantity of taxable land, withdrew money from circulation, and occasioned a decline in taxable foreign trade, rendering it impossible for the government to achieve the revenue base needed to improve public facilities and social services. The peasants treasured their independence, but in company with all elements of the population they paid a price for the collapse of the staple industry.

[112] John Davy had found the Guiana estates strangling in weeds. The cultivation there was the least thorough in the sugar colonies. Davy, *The West Indies*, p. 359. Adamson writes that a visitor to the Ewing's estate in the seventies found the cultivation astonishingly meticulous. Adamson, *Sugar Without Slaves*, p. 181.

[113] James M. McPherson, 'Was West Indian Emancipation a Success? The Abolitionist Argument During the American Civil War', *Caribbean Studies*, IV (1964), 28–31.

CHAPTER 9

Immigration

IMMIGRATION saved the sugar economy in Trinidad and British Guiana. It produced a staggering admixture of races, languages, religions, and cultural patterns in the tiny recipient states, rendering them the most highly concentrated melting-pots in the Western Hemisphere. Immigration, or, more correctly, labour migration, was a pervasive and volatile issue throughout the British Caribbean in the mid-century. Attempts by Guyanese and Trinidadian planters to recruit labourers in the most densely populated sugar islands provoked bitter inter-colonial feuding. The immigration question added a new dimension to the anti-slave-trade activities of the Royal Navy; it revived the old controversy over the merits of Sierra Leone colony; and it affected Britain's self-appointed mission to 'civilize' Africa. Immigration intruded upon Britain's relations with foreign nations, including such diverse countries as China and the United States, and it provoked considerable soul-searching in connection with her proclaimed trusteeship for the population of India.

Interest in immigration was greatest in the largest low-density colonies—Jamaica, Trinidad, and Guiana. The labouring population in these colonies had been declining in the decade preceding the abolition of slavery, and on the eve of emancipation fewer than half the slaves were effective cane-workers. When apprenticeship ended, most women and children renounced field labour, and most men served on a reduced scale. Unless a supplementary body of cane-workers could be procured, many plantations in Trinidad and Guiana were destined to collapse. The question was where to obtain the necessary labour.

INITIAL EFFORTS TO OBTAIN IMMIGRANT LABOUR

Indirectly, the slave-trade provided one source of free labour. British naval officers occasionally landed Africans liberated from foreign slave-ships in British West Indian ports under emergency of foul weather or disease, but most slavers captured in American waters were taken to Havana or Rio to be adjudicated in Courts of Mixed Commission which, like the tribunals at Sierra Leone and Loanda, were regulated by treaties between Britain and foreign powers.[1] Despite its illegality, the slave-trade remained extensive and profitable.[2] Efforts by the Royal Navy to check the traffic failed. Swift Baltimore Clippers engaged for Cuba out-sailed the sluggish British vessels which policed the trade, and the vast length of coast on both sides of the Atlantic, coupled with the collusion of Latin American officials and African tribesmen, made the apprehension of more than a small fraction of the slave-ships impossible.[3] Patrolling efforts were concentrated in African waters, and slavers intercepted north of the line were taken to Sierra Leone where their captives were set free and maintained for a short time at British expense. The number of Africans liberated at Rio and Havana was small, but the planters of Trinidad and Guiana tried to institute systematic immigration of recaptives from those ports.[4]

In 1836, under arrangement with Spanish authorities, the British Government appointed R. R. Madden, a former stipendiary magistrate in Jamaica, to the newly created post of Superintendent of Liberated Africans at Havana. His task was to supervise the trans-shipment of 'emancipados' to free British soil. The Royal Navy moored a large hulk, the *Romney*, in Havana harbour as a reception station, and when appropriate

---

[1] Leslie Bethell, 'The Mixed Commissions for the Suppression of the Transatlantic Slave Trade in the Nineteenth Century', *Journal of African History*, VII (1966).

[2] According to Curtin's estimates, over 360,000 Africans were conveyed to the Americas in the 1830s, 126,000 going to Cuba and 212,000 to Brazil. Curtin, *The Atlantic Slave Trade*, p. 234.

[3] Christopher Lloyd, *The Navy and the Slave Trade* (London, 1949), pp. 89–90; Leslie Bethell, *Abolition of the Brazilian Slave Trade* (Cambridge, 1970), pp. 126–7.

[4] The planters' appeal to regularize this traffic was reinforced by the notorious abuse which liberated Africans received in Cuba. Let out to planters on seven-year indentures, they were either worked more brutally than slaves or transformed by surreptitious means into actual slaves. Cuban planters inserted 'emancipados' into their slave rolls under the names of deceased slaves, claiming that death had visited their indentured 'emancipados', not their slaves. Young to Smyth, 27 July 1836, enclosed in Smyth to Glenelg, 7 Aug. 1836, C.O. 111/146, no. 196; Circular, 15 Jan. 1836, C.O. 295/106; Sel. Comm. on Sugar and Coffee Planting, P.P. 1847–8, XXIII (123), evidence of Lord Palmerston, 11.

carriers could be procured, Africans were moved to Trinidad or to other British colonies expressing an interest in their services.[5] This arrangement, never very promising, provided only a trickle of immigrants for the sugar-planters. Shipping was difficult to procure, and Madden appeared predisposed to settle weak and diseased liberated Africans in the adjacent Bahama Islands.[6] In subsequent years Trinidad and Guiana appointed agents in Rio to facilitate the trans-shipment of recaptives from that port, but Rio proved as unproductive a source of immigrant labour as Havana.

Jamaica experimented with European immigrants. It was believed that Europeans could thrive in highland districts, raising provisions and supplying foodstuffs for the island's markets. By occupying the uplands, it was hoped, they would discourage freedmen from settling there; their monopolization of provision markets would oblige Negroes to seek wage labour on the sugar estates.[7] Such European immigration, the planters argued, would have the same effect for the estates as a comparable introduction of black labourers.

The scheme failed. Some of the Europeans arrived before adequate preparation was made for their reception. Lacking adequate housing, food, and medical care, they suffered wretched privation, and many of the survivors moved on to the United States.[8] The 2,371 European immigrants admitted during apprenticeship proved generally intemperate. No amount of persuasion could prevent them from moving to Kingston or to lowland districts where wages were highest. Mortality was excessive, and by 1841 Metcalfe declared European immigration a catastrophe and imposed restraints upon it.[9]

For the planters of British Guiana and Trinidad, the dense labouring populations of Barbados and the Leewards were considered fair game. Agents of the former colonies toured the

[5] Madden Correspondence, C.O. 318/127. Barbados and St. Vincent were not interested in receiving immigrants from slave-ships, the planters being concerned that such immigrants would revive obeah and barbarism in the colonies. Stephen to Spedding, 2 May 1836, C.O. 318/127; MacGregor to Russell, 22 Feb. 1840, C.O. 28/133, no. 21.

[6] The Bahama Argus, 19 Nov. 1836.

[7] Sel. Comm. on Sugar and Coffee Planting, P.P. 1847–8, XXIII (123), evidence of Lord Howard de Walden, 4519.

[8] Burn, Emancipation and Apprenticeship, p. 291.

[9] Metcalfe to Stanley, 9 Feb. 1842, C.O. 137/261, no. 72.

islands advertising the high wage rates and liberal allowances that prevailed in Guiana and Trinidad and offering cash inducements to field-workers who would emigrate there. Although planters in the high density islands—outraged by this assault on their labouring populations—passed legislation to retard emigration, more than 27,000 West Indians migrated to Trinidad and Guiana before 1849.[10] It is impossible to determine how many of them became permanent residents in the recipient states since steady seasonal migration persisted between the Lesser Antilles and the large southern colonies. Aside from Barbadians, whose outspoken loyalty for their native island alienated them from other West Indian immigrants, those who settled permanently in Trinidad and Guiana readily adjusted to their new environment. In 1847 2,600 West Indian immigrants were at work on estates in Trinidad.[11] Many more had followed the example of native freedmen, purchasing small freeholds, squatting on vacant land, or drifting to the towns.

The free Negro population of the United States attracted the attention of West India planters, and in 1839–40 agents from British Guiana, Trinidad, and Jamaica toured the eastern states seeking labour recruits. The social position of the free Negroes in America, already deplorable, promised to get worse before it improved. Laws against Negro enfranchisement in the north were becoming increasingly severe, and legislators in the slave states—anxiously recoiling from the attacks of abolitionists—threatened to expel free Negroes from southern soil. Except for the abolitionists who wanted free Negroes to remain in the United States to pursue the struggle against slavery, Americans in the north generally supported emigration.[12] West Indian agents published flattering accounts of their respective colonies,[13] and the Government of Trinidad established offices in New York, Philadelphia, and Baltimore to facilitate emigration. About a thousand people embarked for Trinidad in the

---

[10] P.P. 1844, XXXV (530), p. 64; P.P. 1847, XXXIX (496), pp. 2–3; P.P. 1866, XXVII (3697), p. 84.

[11] Harris to Grey, 21 Feb. 1848, C.O. 295/160, no. 21.

[12] The American Colonization Society had been transferring small groups of freedmen to the Liberian coast since 1821 with the general approval of the northern public.

[13] Edward Carbery, *Inducements to the Coloured People of the United States to Emigrate to British Guiana* (Boston, 1840); Alexander Barclay, *Remarks on Emigration to Jamaica: Addressed to the Coloured Class of the United States* (New York, 1840).

first half of 1840,[14] with lesser numbers departing for the other colonies. Representatives of Negro communities in the United States visited the recipient states to examine conditions there, and with few exceptions their testimony was complimentary.[15] To the colonists' dismay, however, some disenchanted emigrants returned to the United States with negative accounts of life in the Caribbean, and their reports were given wide circulation by the American Anti-Slavery Society. The rate of emigration quickly tapered off, and agents of the several West Indian colonies, meeting in New York in mid 1840, conceded that America would not provide an important source of labour.[16]

AFRICAN IMMIGRATION

Unable to procure enough immigrant labour in the Western Hemisphere and alarmed by declining productivity, Caribbean planters demanded access to Africa to recruit free labourers. The liberated Africans established in Sierra Leone by the British Government were considered a redundant and easily tapped labour force. But beginning with an appeal by the governor of Trinidad in 1835,[17] official requests for the inauguration of free labour immigration from British colonies in Africa were frigidly rejected by the British Government. Recaptives at Sierra Leone enjoyed special protection as a result of Britain's long-standing struggle against the African slave-trade. The idea of Africans migrating across the middle passage to plantations in tropical America was obnoxious to Glenelg, Stephen, and others in Downing Street, and in the first two years after apprenticeship the Colonial Office firmly rejected all West Indian emigration Acts which did not specifically exempt Africa as a source of immigrant workmen. By 1840, however, necessity had begun to dominate scruple, and even the scruples long associated with the employment of

[14] Burnley to Russell, 19 June 1840, C.O. 295/132.

[15] White to Burnley, 18 Mar. 1841, enclosed in MacLeod to Russell, 20 Aug. 1841, C.O. 295/134, no. 85.

[16] The British calculated that there were about 35,000 free Negroes between ages 24 and 35 in the U.S.A. Most of them were of mixed Afro-European ancestry, trained to domestic service or trades and unsuited to field-work. It was the barbers, hotel waiters, and small artisans who returned from Trinidad in 1840 with dreadful tales about labour in the cane fields who discouraged others from embarking for the West Indies. H. S. Fox to Aberdeen, 29 July and 27 Aug. 1843, C.O. 318/158.

[17] Hill to Aberdeen, 3 Mar. 1835, C.O. 295/106, no. 8.

recaptured Africans in the British Caribbean were being called in question.

The conventional wisdom of the English people held that American Negro slavery would collapse when free men produced sugar more cheaply than slaves. This was not happening in the West Indies: the average price of British West India sugar had risen from 33*s.* in 1838 to 49*s.* per cwt. in 1840, reflecting a sharp decline in output. The great experiment in free labour was in danger, and slave masters in Cuba, Brazil, and the United States were drawing hasty, self-justifying conclusions from the British West Indian experience. A copious and steady immigration appeared to be the only means of stemming the tide of economic disaster in the largest and most fertile British sugar colonies. If free Africans could be introduced to the colonies in large numbers, it was argued, they would increase the ratio between population and land, stiffen competition for wages, reduce the level of wage payments, improve the quality of work performed by wage earners, and permit the planters to market their sugar at lower cost. In lectures delivered at Oxford between 1839 and 1841, Herman Merivale, the future Permanent Under-Secretary for the colonies, chastised anti-slavery zealots who considered immigration a malicious device to lower the wages of freedmen. Either wages must come down, he argued, or the plantations would be destroyed, bringing economic degradation to all elements of West Indian society. 'If, all our sacrifices, all our efforts,' he observed, 'end but in the establishment of a number of commonwealths, such as Hayti now is, flourishing in contented obscurity, side by side with the portentous and brilliant opulence of slave owning and slave trading states—the best interests of humanity will have received a shock which it may take centuries to repair.'[18]

Merivale was a free-trader seeking some device to render British colonial sugar competitive without the aid of protection. But his views on immigration coincided with those of many protectionists who sincerely contended that the demise of the West Indian sugar economy would be vastly more pernicious to the welfare of Africans than the risks associated with the trans-Atlantic migration of liberated slaves. The issue posed a

---

[18] Herman Merivale, *Lectures on Colonization and Colonies* (London, 1861), p. 332.

serious moral dilemma. James Stephen, missionaries, and anti-
slavery groups believed that African immigration would stimulate a revival of obeah and other unwanted African cultural
practices in the Caribbean. If the cost of sugar produced by
British freedmen exceeded that formerly produced by British
slaves, Englishmen should endure higher prices, Stephen argued,
as a measure of national philanthropy. More importantly,
Stephen believed that the transport of free Africans to the British
West Indies, however well regulated and safeguarded, would be
misrepresented by foreign states as a disguised resumption of
the British slave-trade. Such action would encourage other
states to pursue similar practices without proper safeguards.
Britain's greatest weapon in Africa was her moral ascendancy.
In Stephen's judgement, trans-Atlantic labour migration—no
matter how legitimate its conduct—would destroy that ascendancy and expose Britain to international ridicule.[19] This fear
of ridicule might have remained the basis of British policy
had not the curious condition of Sierra Leone and the deepening
distress of the Caribbean planters dictated otherwise.

Sierra Leone had been a focus of controversy since 1808
when the British Government acquired the struggling, profitless
territory from its evangelical founders. Waste and corruption
in the colony had often been denounced[20] and the practical
value of landing recaptives at Sierra Leone was consistently
challenged by naval officers who made the bulk of their cap-
tures in the Bights and were obliged to beat six weeks and
1,000 miles to the windward to have their seizures adjudicated.[21]

---

[19] Stephen to Vernon Smith, Memo, 3 Nov. 1840, C.O. 318/148. In Feb. 1840,
Lord John Russell, subscribing to Stephen's arguments, rejected a Guiana appeal
for West African immigration on grounds that it would expose Britain to international ridicule. Russell to Light, 15 Feb. 1840, P.P. 1840, XXXIV (151),
pp. 42–4.

[20] A classic tirade against the colony is James McQueen's *The Colonial Controversy* (Glasgow, 1825). Joseph Hume, radical M.P., launched an inquiry into the
affairs of Sierra Leone in the mid-twenties, and commissioners sent to the colony
declared that villages upon which £130,000 had been spent were lying in ruins,
that church buildings stood partly finished or in various stages of disrepair, and
that corruption was rife in the Liberated African Department. Christopher Fyfe,
A History of Sierra Leone (London, 1962), p. 164.

[21] A Select Committee which studied the problem in 1830 recommended that the
Mixed Commission Court be transferred from Freetown to Fernando Po, but
evangelicals and abolitionists rallied to the defence of the old colony and the proposed change was not made.

In 1841, R. R. Madden who was commissioned to examine the condition of Britain's West African holdings produced a hastily drawn, somewhat inaccurate, but thoroughly searing document on conditions in Sierra Leone, charging inhabitants of the colony with aiding and abetting the slave-trade by reselling goods auctioned from condemned slave-ships to slavers in adjacent rivers.[22] He found the Liberated African Department riddled with inefficiency. The land was rocky and sterile; agriculture was primitive and no instruction in agrarian techniques was being offered; wages were low—only 4d. a day—and labour was redundant. Young children were apprenticed to older residents who used them in the manner of slaves, and according to Madden many of them were being kidnapped for sale up country. Madden who had spent one unhappy year as a stipendiary magistrate in Jamaica, 1834–5, endorsed the principle of free labour emigration from Sierra Leone to the West Indies as being economical for the imperial Government and beneficial to the emigrants, but he doubted that the colony could produce emigrants in the numbers sought by the planters.

Madden made his West African enquiry in the year of the ill-fated Niger expedition. The latter project, conceived by Sir Fowell Buxton and undertaken by the British Government, was intended to undermine the slave-trade in West Africa by extending "legitimate" commerce and outposts of European civilization to interior states. According to Buxton and his allies, commerce and Christianity would provide a dual antidote to slave trading and barbarism. But the Niger expedition achieved none of its purposes and within a year one-third of its personnel were lost through disease.[23] If the effort to 'civilize' Africa and terminate the slave-trade were to bear fruit, it was evident that white men, so easily decimated by fever, could not be used as agents in the cause. What was needed was a corps of competent black agents who could convey the qualities of European civilization to their fellow Africans. To qualify for this task, blacks would have to live for some time in a well ordered English or English dominated society. In this regard the British West Indies seemed to be the most satisfactory training ground.

[22] Report of Commissioner of Inquiry on the West Coast of Africa, P.P. 1842, XII (551).
[23] P.P. 1843, XXI (83); Temperley, *British Antislavery*, pp. 49–61.

Planters and colonial officials who had long advocated African immigration to the sugar colonies were cheered by the sound of new voices echoing their appeal. MacGregor Laird, a Liverpool shipbuilder who had taken a commercial expedition into the Niger in 1832,[24] advocated uninhibited government supported two-way emigration between Africa and the West Indies. Apart from generating the requisite corps of black agents, such action, he believed, would sustain the free-labour sugar economy and undermine the coerced labour systems of Cuba and Brazil which were perpetuating the slave-trade.[25] Laird represented no important vested interest and his views were too rash for a British Government sensitive to international opinion, but his denunciation of the unwarranted cost of Sierra Leone reinforced a massive body of statistics and opinion which had been accumulating since the 1820s. The British Treasury, always seeking a means of trimming public expenditures, favoured a limited policy of emigration from Sierra Leone to the sugar colonies, declaring it beneficial to Africans, West Indians, and British taxpayers alike.[26] Rather than earn 4d. a day in Sierra Leone, emigrants to Trinidad and British Guiana could obtain 2s. in daily wages, while enjoying houses, grounds, allowances, and free medical care as well as easier access to Christian education. The Treasury could comprehend no practical objection to emigration, especially in view of the prospective elimination of a £14,000 annual expenditure on the Liberated African Department at Sierra Leone.

The concept of a government sponsored trans-oceanic population movement was no longer a forbidding one. The Government had already launched migratory experiments in Canada and South Africa; in fact, the idea of state supported emigration had become a fixture of official thinking as a result of the energetic work of Wakefield and the Colonial Reformers.[27] In 1840 the Colonial Land and Emigration Com-

---

[24] MacGregor Laird and R. A. K. Oldfield, *Narrative of an Expedition into Interior Africa* (London, 1837), 2 vols.

[25] MacGregor Laird, 'Review of African Slave Trade and Its Remedy', *Westminster Review* (1840); P.P. 1842, XXI (551), Appendix 27, Emigration from Africa to the West Indies, pp. 483–5.

[26] C. E. Trevelyan to Stephen, 21 Jan. 1841, C.O. 318/151.

[27] H. J. M. Johnston, *British Emigration Policy 1815–1830: 'Shovelling out Paupers'* (Oxford, 1972); also, Knorr, *British Colonial Theories*, pp. 269–99.

mission was established to supervise the migration of British subjects.[28] An Imperial Passengers Act regulated the character of emigrant vessels, assuring passengers of adequate space, victualling, and medical care aboard ships.[29] The mentality and the machinery for large scale emigration was present in the Empire, and the economic and philosophical justification for African emigration to the West Indies so overshadowed the risks of that enterprise that Lord John Russell rejected the policies of his predecessors and the advice of his Permanent Under Secretary and inaugurated government-supervised emigration from Sierra Leone in 1841.[30]

Emigrant vessels were privately chartered, and the cost of transport was paid by the importing colonies. A government officer was appointed at Freetown to supervise emigration procedures, and regulations were adopted to prevent abuses. Emigrants had to have resided in Sierra Leone for at least six weeks, and no recaptive was permitted to embark without official consent. Provisioning and living-space aboard emigrant vessels were regulated by the Passengers Act. Surgeons, such as they were, were in attendance on each ship, and passengers received a medical examination and vaccination before embarking. Russell insisted that the sex ratio of departing Africans be at least one woman for every two men.[31]

In spite of these precautions, emigration from Africa did not go well. After an initial burst of enthusiasm, the people of Sierra Leone refused to emigrate, and three vessels chartered for Trinidad in late 1841 were obliged to leave Freetown empty.[32] Trinidad's failure to dispatch delegates to Sierra Leone from the initial emigration transport and the foundering at sea of the Jamaica brig, *Commissioner Barclay*, with several African headmen aboard provoked widespread rumours that

[28] Fred H. Hitchens, *The Colonial Land and Emigration Commission* (Philadelphia, 1931), pp. 307–9.

[29] In 1840 the British Passengers Act was extended to cover the movement of free labourers between various Caribbean dependencies. Circular 27 July 1840, C.O. 842/2.

[30] See p. 409, n. 9.

[31] Russell to Jeremie, 20 Mar. 1841, P.P. 1842 (479), p. 560. For the mechanics of African emigration to the Caribbean see Aseigbu, *Slavery and Politics* or G. W. Roberts, 'Immigration of Africans into the British Caribbean', *Population Studies*, VII (1954).

[32] MacLeod to Stanley, 14 Feb. 1842, C.O. 295/136, no. 38.

emigration was nothing more than voluntary slavery. Petty
merchants and employers in Sierra Leone encouraged these
suspicions for fear that emigration to the sugar colonies would
drain off their cheap redundant labour force, provoking a rise
in wages.[33] Other impediments arose as well. The excess of
males over females in Sierra Leone and the reluctance of the
women to emigrate impaired recruitment. The cost of passports
was more than most prospective emigrants could afford, and
those who were in debt—and that included a substantial portion of the lower class population—were prevented from leaving
the colony until their accounts were settled.[34]

As the flow of emigrants from Sierre Leone dried up, two
select committees in London pondered the problems of Britain's
African and West Indian dependencies, and in each case they
firmly endorsed the movement of Africans to the sugar colonies.[35] The Select Committee on the West India Colonies
advised the British Government to assume full control over
trans-Atlantic emigration procedures, a recommendation
strongly supported by West Indian planters, who believed that
the suspicion and reticence of liberated Africans could only be
overcome by investing emigration with the authority of the
Crown.

The new Secretary of State, Lord Stanley, adopted these
recommendations. Beginning in 1843, the Crown undertook
full responsibility for the administration of West African emigration. Transport ships, although paid for by the participating
colonies, were chartered by the imperial Government and commanded by British naval officers. Administrative impediments
to emigration were removed. Recaptives were no longer required to spend six weeks in the colony before embarking, and
incentive payments of £3 were awarded to all emigrants, partly
to relieve whatever indebtedness they suffered.[36] The require-

---

[33] Fyfe, *History of Sierra Leone*, p. 225.

[34] Report of A. David, Trinidad Agent, enclosed in Fuller to Stanley, 9 July
1842, C.O. 295/137, no. 69.

[35] Reflecting a contemporary bias toward African society, the Select Committee on the West Coast of Africa declared that 'it would be well for the African,
in every point of view, to find himself a Free Labourer in the free British West
India Colonies, enjoying there . . . higher advantages of every kind than have
fallen to the lot of the Negro race in any other portion of the globe.' Report from
the Select Committee, P.P. 1842, XI (551).

[36] Fourth General Report of the Colonial Land and Emigration Commissioners,
P.P. 1844, XXXI (178), p. 15.

ment that one-third of the emigrants be women was withdrawn,[37] and the Governor of Sierra Leone was directed, in the
most strenuous terms, to promote emigration.[38] Lest he defy his
instructions, Stanley reduced government funding to the Liberated African Department, requiring newly-landed recaptives to
live by their wits or emigrate.[39]

In spite of these changes, the new system was scarcely more
productive than the old. In two years of successive sailings
only 3,448 people could be induced to leave Sierra Leone.[40]
Since the expense of chartering emigrant ships was high and the
number of passengers low, the cost per immigrant was exorbitant. Jamaica's emigration vessel, the *Glen Huntley*, transported only forty-two Africans in her last six months of service
at an average cost of £60 per immigrant.[41] In mid-1845 Colonial officials, deeply disappointed, abandoned the system of
government transports and returned to the old practice of
paying bounties on privately conveyed African immigrants.

Emigration depended almost entirely on the recruitment of
bewildered, newly-arrived recaptives who had no knowledge of
Sierra Leone and no stake in its affairs. Although the flow of
recaptured slaves ebbed in the mid-forties, it increased for a
brief period at the end of the decade as a result of the seizures
which accompanied the expansion of the slave-trade to Cuba
and Brazil—an expansion triggered by the equalization of the
British sugar duties. As partial compensation to the planters for
the removal of protection, Lord John Russell's Government
permitted West Indians to recruit free labourers along the Kru
coast of Liberia.[42] A steamship was placed in service between

[37] Women generally outnumbered men in the sugar colonies.

[38] Stanley to MacDonald, 5 June 1843, P.P. 1844, XXXV (530).

[39] Stanley to MacDonald, 10 Feb. 1844, P.P. 1844, XXXV (530).

[40] Sixth General Report of the Colonial Land and Emigration Commissioners
(hereafter, C.L.E.C.), P.P. 1846, XXIV (706), pp. 27–8.

[41] Report of C. H. Darling, Agent General of Immigration, 28 Oct. 1845, enclosed in C.O. 137/287, no. 15.

[42] Papers Relative to Emigration from the West Coast of Africa to the West
Indies, P.P. 1847, XXXIX (191), p. 8. Recoiling from their loss of preference,
West India planters demanded free access to the whole of Africa to recruit labour,
arguing that an empire committed to free trade in plantation staples could not
logically deprive colonial planters from seeking the cheap labour they needed to
compete with slave labour producers. Kru people were favoured by British; they
frequented Sierra Leone in large numbers, participated in British ventures in the
Niger, and they did not keep slaves themselves.

West Africa and Trinidad and Guiana in 1847, and an additional ten sailing-ships were employed to carry the increased number of fresh recaptives to the Caribbean.[43] In 1848 the British Government assumed the expense of transport vessels as a means of reducing the financial burden on West India proprietors who were suffering the dual agonies of free-trade and economic depression.[44] From that year to 1850, 12,014 liberated Africans reached the West Indies, but the rate of emigration fell precipitously in the fifties as a result of the cessation of the Brazilian slave trade.[45] Over the whole 27 years of officially sponsored African emigration, 1841–67, only 36,120 Africans were conveyed to the Caribbean.[46] Of those, 16,287 were seized south of the equator, liberated at St. Helena, and removed from that barren and resourceless island to the sugar colonies.[47]

Why had African emigration been so meagre? Sierra Leone was poor and unattractive. It offered neither the wages, the accommodation, nor the material opportunities which awaited energetic immigrants in the West Indies. On the other hand, liberated Africans did not starve in Sierra Leone. Their basic needs were satisfied, and they could scrape a living by petty trade. All those who studied the problem agreed that inhabitants of the colony preferred commerce, however mean, to agriculture. West Indian agents were only interested in manual labourers, and the labour they offered was the hardest agricultural work in the tropics. Suspicion of the motives of white men, fear of exploitation, horrible recollections of earlier confinement aboard slave-ships, all these factors, compounded by the extravagant and malicious rumours about the West Indies which no contingent of well-disposed delegates could silence, discouraged emigration.[48] Having been once brutally uprooted,

[43] Eighth General Report of C.L.E.C., P.P. 1847–8, XXVI (961), p. 22. The steamer was removed from service after two voyages because of excessive disease aboard it and its slow return to Africa against prevailing trade winds.

[44] Ninth General Report of the C.L.E.C., P.P. 1849, XXII (1082), p. 20.

[45] Roberts, "Immigration of Africans', p. 251.

[46] Asiegbu, *Slavery and Politics*, p. 190.

[47] The importance of Sierra Leone as a refuge for recaptives was proportionately diminished as the focus of slave-trading moved south of the line to the Congo and Angola. In 1842 The Anglo-Portuguese Mixed Commission Court was removed from Freetown, and thereafter most Portuguese slave ships were condemned before Mixed Commissions at the Cape or Loanda or by the British Vice Admiralty Court at St. Helena. See, Bethell, *Abolition of Brazilian Slave Trade*, pp. 182–3.

[48] Reports made in 1844 and 1845 by R. G. Butts and R. Guppy, Commissioners

most Sierra Leonians were unwilling to take the enormous risks and suffer the wrenching insecurities which a trans-Atlantic migration involved.

Those who did venture to the West Indies were generally distributed in large groups among the most desirable estates. Planters hoping to employ immigrants made written application to their colonial government indicating the nature of the accommodation they could provide, the extent of medical care available, wage rates, and the availability of religious instruction.[49] Because the demand for immigrants greatly exceeded the number of arrivals, agents were in a position to select the most advantageous locations for Africans.[50] Immigrants were under no compulsion to remain on estates to which they were assigned, a condition which should have encouraged necessitous planters to treat them fairly. After five years' service in the sugar colonies they were entitled to free return passage to Sierra Leone, an opportunity which nearly 12,000 of them exploited. That so many of them returned is more an index of their attachment to Africa than a condemnation of the treatment they received at the hands of the planters. For a few, emigration to the sugar islands had been a means of accumulating the resources to sustain a more comfortable life upon returning home, a pattern of migratory behaviour familiar to Europeans. If the immigration agent at British Guiana can be believed, returnees were markedly different people from the bedraggled recaptives who had arrived in the colony. He found them more refined in habits, broadened in outlook, and considerably more conscious of their appearance. Their dress, he asserted, was superior to that of the English peasantry, and they had often amassed considerable savings. Twenty-nine returnees aboard the *Growler* in 1857 deposited £571 with the ship's commander for safekeeping. One of that number sailed with £58.[51]

of Inquiry into the Subject of Emigration from Sierra Leone to the West Indies, PP. 1847–8, XLIV (732).

[49] D. Ewart, Agent General of Immigration, to T. F. Pilgrim, 18 Aug. 1853, enclosed in C.O. 137/318, no. 88.

[50] Elgin to Stanley, 21 Nov. 1843, C.O. 137/280, no. 130; Light to Russell, 1 June 1841, P.P. 1842, XIII (479), Appendix to Report from the Sel. Comm. on the West India Colonies, pp. 566–7.

[51] A. W. Horseford to H. B. Wolseley, 24 Aug. 1847, P.P. 1847–8, XXIII (167),

The importance of African immigration to the West Indies did not lie in the numbers of people transported. In a quantitative sense, immigration from Asia was vastly more important. The significance of African immigration mainly involved attitudes and precedents. While expecting to be charged with hypocrisy by states whose ships were seized and whose slaves were transported to British Caribbean plantations, the imperial Government nevertheless justified its measures as legitimate strides in behalf of the civilization of Africans and the destruction of American slave labour régimes. Russell was prepared to "rely mainly on British honesty, and other's dishonesty . . . to strike slavery at the foundation'.[52]

In practice, the trans-shipment of Africans was not performed without the irregularities, acts of personal assault, and official negligence which accompanied every variety of Atlantic migration in the nineteenth century, whether European or non-European. The movement of recaptives seized from foreign slavers in lamentable physical condition often required hasty action not contemplated in regulations, and interpersonal relations between European conveyors and African passengers suffered from language and cultural differences that were compounded by the Europeans' strong sense of superiority. The negative aspects of the migration, even when acknowledged, could not subvert the conviction of the British that African emigration to the sugar colonies was as beneficial to recaptives as it was to planters. Even when it became apparent that the 'civilization of Africa' was not likely to be advanced perceptibly by the emigration system, the government in London could still support the programme as an essential part of its campaign to vindicate the system of free labour production in competition with the slave economies of

Appendix to the Third Report from the Sel. Comm. on Sugar and Coffee Planting, no. I, Emigration, British Guiana, no. 13.

[52] Minute of Russell, 7 Nov. 1840, C.O. 318/148. Russell's sentiments were echoed by Caribbean governors. With a *naïveté* characteristic of his age, C. E. Grey considered it a 'blessing on the negro race' that immigrants to Jamaica should exchange 'the oppressions and barbarities of their own country for the lot of a free labourer in a British colony'. C. E. Grey to Earl Grey, 7 June 1847, C.O. 137/292. From Guiana, Henry Light declared immigration an unmixed blessing for Africa, assuring the Secretary of State that civilization would flow back to that continent from the Caribbean. Light to Stanley, 3 Oct. 1841, P.P. 1843, XXXVIII (438), p. 11.

Cuba and Brazil. Having established a policy of labour migration which they could justify on moral grounds, the British moved without difficulty from African to Asian emigration.

INDIAN IMMIGRATION

Although Asian immigration had been halted after a brief trial in 1838–9,[53] the urgency of the planters and the disappointing rate of African recruitment prompted Stanley, with the concurrence of the Council of India, to revive Asiatic emigration to the sugar colonies in mid-1844. Agents were established at Calcutta and Madras, and rules were drawn up limiting departures to months in which a favourable monsoon as well as summer conditions at the Cape of Good Hope could be expected. Regulations governing the character of transport vessels and the distribution of immigrants at their destination were identical to those employed for Africans.[54] On host estates, Indians were to be accommodated in groups of twenty-five to fifty in barracks or cottages having board floors. They were assured of free medical care, adjacent provision grounds, minimum wage rates, food and clothing.[55]

The planters' jubilation at the resumption of Indian immigration was tempered only by the high cost of bringing labourers halfway around the world. Large public loans were necessary, but commissioners representing the colonies had difficulty raising money in Britain.[56] By 1846 London was feeling the initial pangs of depression, and the passage of the Sugar Duties Act in August thoroughly undermined colonial credit. Trinidad, the colony having the soundest financial position, was unable to market bonds even at a figure well below par, and it was obliged to sell £30,000 in consols—the sum of its public savings—to meet immigration expenses.[57]

The financial difficulties associated with Indian immigration were aggravated by disciplinary problems. The Colonial

---

[53] See p. 410, n. 10.

[54] Fifth General Report of the Colonial Land and Emigration Commissioners (C.L.E.C.) P.P. 1845, XXVII (617), p. 20. Regulations for Indian Emigration to the British West Indies, P.P. 1847–8, XLIV (370), pp. 5–6.

[55] MacLeod to Stanley, 18 Oct. 1844, C.O. 295/144, no. 77.

[56] Memorandum of Colonial Land and Emigration Commissioners, 30 Nov. 1846, C.O. 318/167.

[57] Harris to Grey, 28 Dec. 1846, C.O. 295/152, no. 121.

Office had consistently opposed long-term labour contracts, and refused to permit the arrangement of contracts between proprietors and immigrants before the latter entered the colonies. When Indians began to arrive in 1845, they—like Africans before them—were under no obligation to perform contract labour on the plantations, and many of them exploited their freedom by wandering aimlessly throughout the countryside. Planters and governors appealed for the establishment of mandatory three year contracts, arguing that only by such means could the high cost of Indian immigration be justified. Earl Grey refused, deploring such an invasion of the principle of free bargaining between workers and employers. He concurrently disallowed a series of Rules and Regulations prepared by Lord Harris, the Governor of Trinidad, that would have circumscribed the liberty of Indians. Having determined that Indian immigrants were 'naturally dissolute, and depraved . . . and much inclined to fall into habits of drinking, and of wandering idle about the country', Harris believed that they needed protection against the fatal consequences of their own ignorance.[58] While setting out a strict code for the proprietors, charging them with scrupulous superintendence of the physical wants of the immigrants, Harris assigned the Indians a nine-hour day and insisted that they make up every day lost by indolence or negligence. They were not to depart their home estates without a passbook which specified their destination and the duration of their leave. Among other prohibitions, they were to be discouraged from indulgence in rum. Every aspect of the employer-employee relation was thoroughly charted. Too thoroughly, thought Earl Grey, who regarded Harris's Rules and Regulations as unsuited to a condition of free labour.

On this issue, as in the case of contracts, Grey viewed labour relations in European terms, lecturing his governors against adopting programmes which contradicted the normal motivations of men and the 'experience of this and of every country in which industry flourished.'[59] He ignored the special pleas of

[58] Harris to Gladstone, 30 July 1846, C.O. 295/151, no. 34.
[59] Quoted in K. O. Lawrence, 'The Evolution of Long Term Labour Contracts in Trinidad and British Guiana, 1834–1863', *The Jamaican Historical Review*, V (1965), 19.

colonial officials, such as Governor Barkly of British Guiana, who argued that the Secretary of State would stop attributing European motivations to African and Indian immigrants if he could only see them.[60]

By 1848 the Indian labour programme was a muddle, and colonists throughout the Caribbean insisted that further immigration from that quarter cease. In every colony the causes of failure were identical: the absence of adequate control over immigrants and the massive depression which shattered the planting interest in the wake of the Sugar Duties Act. Unable to obtain advances from English merchants on the security of their burgeoning crop, many planters were incapable of paying the head-tax on Indians. They fell into arrears in wage payments to immigrants, and the Indians responded by forsaking the estates in favour of wandering and mendicancy. Many who had contracted for a single year refused to renew; others who renewed their contracts bolted the estates. Conversely, planters —like those in the southern parishes of Jamaica whose disappointment over the services of Indians was magnified by the disastrous effects of drought—were reluctant to retain Asians under the rigorous terms imposed upon them by immigration laws.[61] 'We were obliged to give the Coolies rations whether they worked or not,' said one Jamaica proprietor, 'and the consequence was that they were always pretending to be ill . . .'[62]

A vicious circle had developed: Indians had proven costly workers, and the few proprietors who had means enough to pay the taxes on immigrants were reluctant to make those outlays in view of the Asians' tendency to flee the estates. Inevitably the financial collapse of the planters and the wanderlust of the immigrants produced widespread misery and death among the Asians.

Reports dispatched from Jamaica and Trinidad on the same day in February 1848 described the horrendous consequences of Indian vagrancy.[63] The roads of the islands were strewn with

[60] Ibid.
[61] Report of Agent General of Immigration, enclosed in C. E. Grey to Earl Grey, 23 Oct. 1847, C.O. 137/293, no. 105.
[62] Sel. Comm. on Sugar and Coffee Planting, P.P. 1847-8, XIII (123), evidence of Lord Howard de Walden, 4563.
[63] Report from the Committee Appointed to Inquire into the Depressed State of Agriculture in the Island and the Cause of Such Depression, enclosed in C. E.

destitute Asians suffering a variety of diseases and the infestation of chigoes which rendered them lame and helpless. Two hospitals established for their reception in Trinidad were woefully inadequate, and the decaying remains of immigrants were frequently discovered in cane fields and woodlands throughout the colony. Sickened by their misery, Lord Harris rebuked Earl Grey for his notions about the universal motives of working people and upbraided him for disallowing the Rules and Regulations which, he believed, would have confined the Indians to the plantations and precluded their fatal wanderings. In Harris's stern judgement, the 'fatalist worshippers of Mahomet and Bramah' and the 'savages who go by the name of liberated Africans' were not, upon their arrival in the West Indies, capable of responding to the same stimuli as Europeans.[64] They 'must be treated like children,' he wrote, 'and Wayward ones too, the former from their habits and their religions, the latter from the utterly savage state in which they arrive.' Unless immigrants were subject to rigorous discipline and education, he observed, they would provide little labour for the planters and those who survived would debase the whole fabric of society.

If the idealism of the Colonial Office toward the immigrants was misplaced, colonial officials and planters who prided themselves on their pragmatism were thoroughly culpable of neglect and oversight in the early phases of Indian immigration. The most fundamental element in human relations, communication, was ignored. Except in Trinidad, where a retired Indian Army major was belatedly hired as 'coolie magistrate', there was no attempt to provide supervisory agents who could speak the language of the immigrants. Although in some well-publicized cases Asians were abused by planters, they were more generally mismanaged. The planters could not communicate with them, and they were obliged to rely on sirdars (group-leaders among the Indians) as intermediaries, even though the sirdars, often brutal and extortionate, were universally regarded as rogues and villains.

Grey to Earl Grey, 21 Feb. 1848, C.O. 137/295, no. 21; Harris to Grey, 21 Feb. 1848, C.O. 295/160, no. 21; also, Harris to Grey, 1 July 1848, C.O. 295/163, no. 75.

[64] Harris to Grey, 21 Feb. 1848, C.O. 295/160, no. 21.

When in 1851 the movement of East Indians to British Guiana and Trinidad was revived on the strength of loans guaranteed by the British Government, the new system of immigration was as rigorous in its regulatory structure as the old one had been lenient. Earl Grey conceded to a system of three year contracts, and the duration of the immigrants' industrial residence was raised from five to ten years. Upon arrival in the West Indies, Asians were required to enter a contract of service for three years, with an obligation to serve another two years under indenture unless they redeemed that obligation by payment of £2 10s. per year. The free return passage to India which the colonies had formerly provided was withdrawn; instead, at the expiry of ten years' residency, immigrants were required to contribute £7 15s. toward their return passage.[65] The substance of Lord Harris's Rules and Regulations was revived, and similar measures designed to restrict the movement of immigrants were introduced in British Guiana.[66]

In ensuing years the stringency of the indenture system was increased, and in some respects conditions among Indian labourers came to resemble those endured by Creole workers under the apprenticeship. In British Guiana labour contracts were based on a schedule of task work established in 1834. This schedule, originally designed for seasonal Negro workers, was taxing for Indians who were neither as powerful nor as durable as the blacks. Although the work programme was moderated in some measure by the planters' practice of hiring blacks to perform the heaviest and most remunerative jobs— cane-cutting and trenching—Indians were frequently forced to serve beyond the legal limit of ten hours when working indoors.[67]

The relations between masters and indentured servants was defined and circumscribed by an ever-increasing body of law, much of which gave the planters wide latitude in punishing negligent, slow, recalcitrant, tardy, or absent workers. Like the masters and servants laws framed in the early 1840s, these measures were not always enforced, but they provided em-

---

[65] Fourteenth General Report of the C.L.E.C., P.P. 1854, XXVIII (1833), p. 66; Fifteenth General Report of the C.L.E.C., P.P. 1854–5, XVII (1953), p. 52.

[66] Wood, *Trinidad in Transition*, p. 136; Adamson, *Sugar Without Slaves*, pp. 52–6.

[67] Adamson, *Sugar Without Slaves*, pp. 118–19.

ployers a disciplinary lever which they could use under special circumstances. In the indenture system, those special circumstances arose when individual labourers caused extraordinary difficulty, when exemplary punishment was deemed necessary, or when a worker's original contract of indenture expired. Whether an Indian's indenture called for three years or five—in 1863 Newcastle permitted the extension of the original contract to five years—the worker was invariably encouraged to reindenture himself to his master for all or part of his remaining industrial residence. Planters who accumulated work related charges against their indentured servants were in a position to offer clemency in exchange for reindenture.[68] In effect, rigorous laws, though irregularly enforced, provided the planters a powerful weapon over their workers.

There was a great amount of deception and injustice in the indenture system, some of it blatant but most of it subtle. Indians under contract were guaranteed the same wages paid to Creole workers. But the massive immigration of Asians precipitated a general reduction of wage levels in the free sector, with corresponding reductions among indentured people. Furthermore, planters were in the habit of confining certain tasks to Indians, a practice which relieved them from paying the wage rate prevailing in the open market.[69] Overseers and drivers who distributed money payments often cheated the field-hands by offering them less for their work than estate-managers had allocated, pocketing the difference themselves. Because drivers exercised enormous power over the daily life of indentured Indians, the least scrupulous of them were able to levy illegal distraints upon the workers—protection taxes which relieved payers of the worst work assignments.[70]

Like the apprentices before them, indentured workers had limited legal recourse against improper treatment. Stipendiary magistrates who were expected to adjudicate disputes between masters and servants had lived for many years in the colonies, and most of them, while not deliberately debasing justice, tended to view labour issues from the planters' perspective. They were alienated from the immigrants by language, religion, and customs, and they remained dependent upon the

---

[68] Ibid., p. 114.   [69] Ibid., p. 120.   [70] Ibid., p. 123.

planters for hospitality and social intercourse. The Royal Commission which studied the treatment of Indian immigrants in British Guiana in 1870 determined that the fines and sentences imposed upon indentured labourers by magistrates were unduly harsh.[71] In every detail the indenture system, though ostensibly contrived to protect labourers as well as employers, favoured the latter. It could hardly have been otherwise under a system in which both employers and regulatory agents were of one ethnic and cultural group and coerced labourers of another.

If Indians were obliged to endure a multitude of regulations proscribing their personal and territorial freedom, they were, at least, spared the famine and misery which befell millions in their homeland during the final half of the nineteenth century. Of course, one cannot justify abuses which arose in the indenture system by referring to the even greater evils which might have befallen the Indians had they remained at home. Nor can one take much consolation in the knowledge that Irish and East European immigrants to the United States in the nineteenth century endured miserable, insanitary living conditions, laboured long hours, and suffered from criminal deceptions, prejudice, and abuse without adequate protection from recognized authorities. Nevertheless, such observations do offer an element of balance in the history of immigration. In fact it is worthwhile quoting William Sewell, a journalist from New York, the port of entry for the greatest wave of immigration to cross the Atlantic. Sewell was no unbiased friend of the planters, but on observing the Indian indenture system in Trinidad, he was sufficiently impressed to characterize the Government's supervisory programme, 'perfect and complete . . . the consideration paid to the wants and comforts of the immigrant', he wrote, 'is carried to a point that many consider injurious to the planting interest.'[72]

In many respects the migration of Indians to the West Indies was not merely another bleak phase in the lives of poor and much trammelled people. As in the case of other immigrants to America, their migration, though terrifying and hard, clearly offered opportunities for self-fulfilment and material

[71] Ibid., p. 116.   [72] Sewell, *Ordeal of Free Labour*, p. 122.

gain which were not available at home. Indian immigrants to
the West Indies embarked at Madras and Calcutta. The latter
group, constituting the great majority of emigrants, were
drawn from every portion of the Gangetic Plain which stretched
1,000 miles north-west from the Bay of Bengal. Their reasons
for migrating were clear enough: grinding poverty, indebtedness and periodic famines which took millions of lives.[73] The
prospect of comparatively high wages, allowances, and medical
care in the West Indies constituted a powerful inducement to
Indian peasants who eked out a wretched existence on earnings
of $1\frac{1}{2}d$. to $2\frac{1}{2}$d, a day. That Hindus were prepared to suffer
religious defilement by travelling on the high seas, and that
people of high cast would endure pollution by contact with
lower caste beings, untouchables, and Moslems indicates with
unmistakable clarity the degree of desperation which characterized emigration from the subcontinent.

Between 1838 and 1865, 96,581 Indians were introduced
to the West Indies. About half of them went to British Guiana,
a third to Trinidad. As indicated in Table 17, a number of the
lesser colonies undertook Indian immigration on a small scale
after the indenture system had proven successful in the larger
colonies. Although most of the emigrants were lower-caste
Hindu, the majority of India's castes—numbering above
2,000—were represented at some point in the migration.
During the period covered in this study no record of caste was
kept at embarkation points. However, between 1876 and 1885,
when such records were made, 18 per cent of the Hindus leaving for Trinidad were Brahmins or of high caste, 32 per cent
were drawn from agricultural castes, 8·5 per cent were artisans,
and 41·5 per cent were considered to be of low caste.[74] Only
about a third of India's emigrants to the Caribbean were
women.[75]

Relations between Negroes and Indians in the West Indies
were generally peaceful, though not cordial. Although the
presence of thousands of Indians caused a depression in wages,
the immigrants kept the estates in cultivation, enlarging the

[73] Judith Ann Weller, *The East Indian Indenture in Trinidad* (Rio Piedras, Puerto
Rico, 1968), pp. 1–2.
[74] Wood, *Trinidad in Transition*, p. 145.
[75] Dwarka Nath, *A History of Indians in British Guiana* (London, 1950), p. 125.

TABLE 17

Immigration to the British West India Colonies, 1834–1865*

	Jamaica	Trinidad	Guiana	Dominica	St. Lucia	St. Vincent	Grenada	Antigua	St. Kitts	Nevis	Tobago	Total
Europe	3,736		402									4,138
Africa, liberated slaves	10,003	8,385	13,969	400	730	1,036	1,542		455		514	37,034
East Indies	9,195	29,254	53,652		1,535	567	2,041		337			96,581
China	472	2,048	11,839					100				14,459
Madeira	379	823	27,413			546	431	2,219	1,008	427		33,246
Cape Verde		172	819					207				1,198
Azores	91	239	164									494
Malta			264				140					404
North America	428	1,273	73									1,774
West Indies†	790	10,246	17,857					1,062	5			29,960
Unspecified			31		10	136	165					342
Total	25,094	52,440	126,483	400	2,275	2,285	4,319	3,588	1,825	427	514	219,630

Sources: Return of Number of Immigrants into the Colony of British Guiana, 1834–43, C.O. 318/162; Hill to Aberdeen, 27 Mar. 1835, C.O. 295/106, no. 9; P.P. 1843, XXXIII (136), p. 2; P.P. 1844, XXXV (530), pp. 8, 64, 102; P.P. 1847, XXXIX (496), pp. 2–3; P.P. 1866, XVII (3679), pp. 84–7; G. W. Roberts, *Immigration of Africans into the British Caribbean*, p. 259.

* This Table makes no pretension to perfect accuracy. In many cases official statistics are in conflict. Normally records were only kept on immigrants for whom a public bounty was paid. A great many immigrants were introduced to the colonies without bounty, either because the mode of their transport or the ratio of males to females on immigrant vessels was not in conformity with immigration laws. Others were conveyed to secondary West Indian ports without the knowledge of colonial officials.

† After the 1840s records were not retained concerning migration from one West India colony to another.

market for the Creoles' ground provisions, and increasing their employment opportunities during crop. There was no sustained competition for employment, and in spite of the paucity of Indian women no competition arose between Indian and Negro males for the affections of black women. Cohabitation between Indian men and Negro women was exceedingly rare. In fact, Indians exhibited no inclination to meld biologically or culturally with the Creole population. They voluntarily segregated themselves from other groups, living in separate quarters, erecting their own places of worship, and confining their quarrels largely to one another. Their language, cooking and culture remained distinctly Indian, although caste sanctions and rules of marriage broke down under the pressure of circumstances.[76] The shortage of Indian women was a source of friction among immigrant males, and the anguish occasioned by unfaithful wives was a major cause of serious crime. Between 1859 and 1863 the victims of all twenty-seven murders committed by Indians in Trinidad were wives or mistresses guilty of, or suspected of, unfaithfulness.[77]

Perhaps the most revealing illustration of the potential value of immigration to the Indians themselves is provided by a sampling of the wealth which returnees took back to India. The *Gipsy Bride* sailed for Calcutta in 1863 with 407 Indians carrying £15,000 in money and jewels.[78] This sailing was not an exceptional case. The 9,535 returnees who departed Trinidad and Guiana before 1865, took, at the lowest estimate, £145,835 in jewels and money.[79] Many Indians who remained in the sugar colonies used their savings to establish shops and businesses once their terms of indenture had ended. That thousands who had arrived penniless were able to emerge from their industrial residence with the means of establishing respectable

[76] Weller, *East Indian Indenture*, p. 77. Few of the Indians converted to Christianity. The Methodists established a mission among East Indians in Guiana, but its progress was painfully slow. By 1866 it had acquired 16 church members; in 1884 there were 48; and in 1916 there were only 117 out of an East Indian population of nearly 80,000. Findlay and Holdsworth, *History of the Methodist Missionary Society*, II, 417.

[77] Wood, *Trinidad in Transition*, p. 154; also, Nath, *Indians in British Guiana*, pp. 125–6.

[78] Twenty-third General Report of the C.L.E.C., P.P. XV (3199), p. 47.

[79] Appendix to the Twenty-sixth General Report of the C.L.E.C., P.P. 1866, XVII (3679), p. 88.

and comfortable lives in Asia or the West Indies suggests that despite the rigours of indenture, the sugar colonies offered the most durable and thrifty immigrants a measure of opportunity rarely found in the Indian sub-continent.

THE PORTUGUESE

The third most numerous immigration to the British West Indies was Portuguese, principally from the island of Madeira. The history of Madeira in the 1840s and 1850s was similar to that of Ireland. Its staple crop, the potato, became diseased. The wine crop failed during successive seasons, and the population, suffering chronic famine, was reduced to living on coarse roots, beans, and chestnuts. When thirty islanders who had migrated to Guiana in 1834–5[80] returned to Madeira in 1840 with favourable accounts of the British colony, 2,000 people immediately applied to emigrate.[81] In 1841 British Guiana, the colony which attracted the vast majority of Portuguese, admitted 4,296 Madeirans.

Wherever the Portuguese ventured in the West Indies their numbers were decimated by disease. Malaria and yellow fever diminished their ranks by $12\frac{1}{2}$ per cent in Guiana during 1841.[82] The British government hastily abolished the public bounty paid to the transporters of Portuguese immigrants, and the flow from Madeira immediately subsided. In 1845 Lord Stanley revived bounty payments under pressure from planters, and an additional 8,516 islanders emigrated to the sugar colonies in little more than twelve months. But fatalities continued to occur at an alarming rate. Of 200 Madeira immigrants who arrived in Trinidad aboard the *Senator* in May 1846, ninety-one were known dead at the end of the year.[83] In Guiana the death rate quickly reached its earlier level. This appalling situation in no way deterred Madeirans. They preferred the risks attending immigration to the West Indies to the certainty of starvation at home. In July 1847 two vessels arrived in

[80] Slightly more than 1,000 Portuguese peasants emigrated to Trinidad and Guiana in 1834–5 before Portuguese authorities terminated the process.

[81] K. O. Laurence, 'The Establishment of the Portuguese Community in British Guiana', *The Jamaican Historical Review*, V (1965), p. 52.

[82] Colonial Land and Emigration Commissioners to James Stephen, 22 Apr. 1847, P.P. 1847, XXXIX (325), p. 83.

[83] Harris to Grey, 29 Dec. 1846, C.O. 295/152, no. 122.

Demerara with passenger loads greatly exceeding the limits of
British law. The *Loyal*, which should have carried fifty-four
persons, transported 213. The vessel's master excused his action
by declaring that it had been virtually impossible to keep the
Portuguese out of his ship, and that their utterly wretched condition convinced him that it was a 'positive charity to allow
them to come'.[84] Immigration to British Guiana at government expense ceased a second time during the retrenchment
crisis of 1849. But bounties on Portuguese immigrants were renewed in 1850, and the flow of Madeirans continued steadily
until the late fifties. By 1865, 33,246 Madeirans had gone to the
sugar colonies, 27,413 of them to Guiana.[85]

The Portuguese were industrious to a fault. Lured by wages
five times greater than those in their home island, Madeirans
plunged into estate service, taxing their bodies beyond endur-
ance. They deprived themselves of adequate food and clothing
in order to lay away savings. They paid little heed to cleanliness, and in spite of the persistent warnings of planters, they
ignored the symptoms of disease until they were beyond help.
After a time, planters were reluctant to employ these head-
strong immigrants in arduous cane-work; they simply died too
easily. Lighter tasks, gardening, wood-cutting and domestic
service were considered in their case the most suitable forms of
employment.

Madeirans made their mark as merchants, not wage earners.
The situation in British Guiana was ripe for small businessmen,
and thrifty Portuguese immigrants who had secured a bit of
capital from estate service seized the opportunity. From the
earliest times, residents in Guiana had purchased their necessities from the large port-side merchant houses which conducted a high volume wholesale trade to the estates. Private
parties, unable to buy in bulk, paid high prices for goods of
every description. Because money was scarce, individual
buyers had to exercise great care in their expenditures. There
was a rapidly expanding need for small retailers who could
market bread, groceries, sugar, candles, and soap on modest

[84] P.P. 1847–8, XXIII (167) Appendix to the Third Report of the Sel. Comm. on
Sugar and Coffee Planting, no. 1, Emigration, British Guiana.

[85] Appendix to the Twenty-sixth General Report of the C.L.E.C., P.P. 1866,
XVII (3679), pp. 84–7.

credit terms and at reasonable prices. The Portuguese filled that need. Their gritty counters exhibiting everything needed to maintain a household appeared at street corners. Petty Portuguese merchants bought in bulk and sold in small quantities. Their profits were small but so were their overheads. Venturesome Madeirans rifled the countryside, setting up shops on remote estates and huckstering through the villages. In time, the most successful traders rented space in Georgetown's main commercial street and began importing goods on their own account. By the mid-fifties they either dominated or monopolized the trade in provisions, shoes, coal, shingles, and cheap cotton fabrics.[86] A few successful merchants returned to their native island with thousands of pounds in capital, and it was said that every new enterprise in Madeira was being underwritten by Demerara capital.[87]

The Portuguese were not popular with Negroes. Unlike indentured East Indians whom the freedman could playfully taunt as 'slaves', the Portuguese quickly became the creditors of black villagers. During the labour strike of 1848 Creoles drove Madeirans from the fields, assaulted traders, and pillaged a number of their shops.[88] The mounting resentment of blacks toward Portuguese was ignited again in 1856 by a violent anti-Catholic fanatic named John Orr who arrived in Georgetown after having fomented religious riots in Glasgow, Boston, and other cities in Britain and the United States. Denouncing the Pope as the Anti-Christ and his co-religionists as evil legionnaires, Orr quickly attracted a large and ugly following. Catholic Portuguese, insulted and pelted, retired from the streets, but inflamed mobs burst upon their establishments, plundering their wares, and in some cases beating defenceless shopkeepers to death. Agents of destruction fanned out into the countryside, ransacking scores of Portuguese houses and shops.[89] 200 soldiers were dispatched from Barbados; a Dutch ship of war was placed

[86] Adamson, *Sugar Without Slaves*, p. 69. Having achieved control over merchandizing, the Portuguese refused to sell items in minute quantities, a practice which alienated them from Negro buyers.

[87] Barkly to Newcastle, 22 Oct. 1853, C.O. 137/319, no. 7.

[88] Light to Grey, 4 Apr. 1848, C.O. 111/152, no. 60. After one such incident, 66 freedmen were arrested and another lay dead, slain by a hard pressed and terrified shopkeeper.

[89] Wodehouse to Labouchere, 24 Feb. 1856, C.O. 111/309, no. 16.

at the colony's disposal; and troops were landed from a French ship to suppress rioting on the western coast.[90] When the violence subsided, Portuguese victims claimed nearly $300,000 in damages.[91] This tragic and intimidating episode drew the curtain on Portuguese immigration. Only 342 people arrived from Madeira in 1857, and within a few years immigration from that quarter had entirely ceased.

CHINESE IMMIGRATION

Throughout the mid-century, immigration from China was persistently studied and periodically attempted, but numerous obstacles—moral and political—to this form of immigration rendered it relatively unimportant. Between 1852 and 1854, 2,107 Chinese were conveyed to the Caribbean on bounty by private traders. Grave troubles arose in China, however, and the immigration abruptly ceased. The anti-foreign temper of the Chinese people had erupted in riots involving one of the firms, Messrs. Tait and Co., which had arranged the transport of immigrants. The tendency of private shippers to violate treaty relations; abuses in the collection of immigrants; the notorious corruption of Chinese officials; and the representations of British merchants who were anxious lest the ill-feeling generated by emigration cause a dislocation of their trade—all of these factors contributed to the termination of Chinese immigration.[92] More decisive, however, was the inability of the British to obtain either female emigrants or adequate shipping. Sexual irregularities reported among groups of male Chinese on the sugar estates alarmed the Secretary of State, and mutinies aboard Chinese emigrant vessels bound for California and South America discouraged carriers from participating in this traffic if they could obtain any other.

In 1859 J. G. Austin, the Agent General of Immigration of British Guiana, was sent to China to reopen, on a different footing, an emigration programme which would include a substantial proportion of women. In that respect his success was marginal—only 18 per cent of 12,000 Chinese dispatched

[90] Wodehouse to Labouchere, 10 March 1856, C.O. 111/310, no. 25.
[91] Wodehouse to Labouchere, 6 Sept. 1856, C.O. 111/312, no. 115.
[92] Persia Crawford Campbell, *Chinese Coolie Emigration to Countries Within the British Empire* (London, 1923), pp. 93–105.

during the sixties were women.[93] The Chinese proved to be able cane-workers, but they commonly redeemed the final years of their indentures by money payments, left the plantations, and established shops or independent freeholds.[94] Because the cost of Chinese immigrants was high and the length of their service, in comparison with that of the Indians, relatively short, it was decided to halt further Chinese immigration in 1865.

CONCLUSION

The public cost of introducing nearly a quarter of a million immigrants to the sugar colonies over a period of thirty years was enormous. Although the mode of paying for immigration varied, the doctrine that it was beneficial to all elements of society and should be paid for, in some part at least, from general colonial revenues prevailed throughout the period. For the most part, the carriers of immigrants were given public bounties for each person legally conveyed to the receiving colonies, the size of the bounty being determined by the distance and degree of difficulty involved in the transport of labourers.[95] The cost of conveying labourers to and from India—£25 per person—imposed an exceptionally heavy drain on colonial revenues. In Trinidad, the employers of indentured labourers paid one-third the cost of transportation; the remainder was met primarily by rum taxes which fell most heavily on the labouring class.[96] General revenues, aided by an export duty which was borne by the planting interest, initially met most of the cost of Indian immigration to Guiana. In 1856 after Asian workers had restored some prosperity to the estates, employers of indentured labourers assumed two-thirds the cost of their importation. In compensation, export duties were withdrawn.[97]

Planters considered the immigration of Africans, Indians,

[93] Deerr, *History of Sugar*, II, 400.

[94] Report of the Standing Committee on Immigration, enclosed in Walker to Newcastle, 4 Aug. 1860, C.O. 295/209, no. 108.

[95] Bounties were only payable when shippers conformed to the Passengers Act and to other regulations demanded by the imperial Government, i.e. the prescribed ratio of sexes aboard immigrant ships. The following bounties were paid on immigrants to Trinidad in 1846; from Grenada, £1; Antigua, £2.18s.4d.; the United States, £6.5s.; Sierra Leone, £7.5s.10d.; Rio de Janeiro, £8.6s.8d.; Madeira, £7.5s.10d. Harris to Gladstone, 15 July 1846, C.O. 295/151, no. 27.

[96] Keate to Newcastle, 9 Feb. 1860, C.O. 295/208, no. 24.

[97] Wodehouse to Labouchere, 23 June 1856, C.O. 111/311, no. 83; Wodehouse

and Chinese necessary, not desirable. Given an alternative between the collapse of the plantations with all the social and civic ramifications which that entailed, and an immigration programme with its inherent costs, problems, and uncertainties, the Colonial Office unashamedly chose the latter. What the planters wanted most, and never got, was steady estate labour from the Creole workers. Blacks were regarded as the sturdiest and most accomplished cane-workers, but in 1858 not a quarter of all able-bodied blacks were working on estates in either British Guiana or Trinidad.[98]

In those colonies, Indians had become the backbone of the sugar industry. In 1852 only eighty Trinidadian estates applied for 2,000 immigrants, but five years later 179 estates—all but one in the colony—requested 7,000 Indians.[99] After working out their indentures most Indians recontracted for estate labour,[100] and by 1871 over 20,000 of them were engaged on plantations in Trinidad.[101] Immigration had the effect of reducing the wages paid to Creole workers, but the absence of immigration would have had the same if not a worse effect. Without Indian immigration, scores of plantations in Trinidad and British Guiana would have ceased cultivation. The demand for jobs would have risen on the surviving estates permitting their owners to lower wage payments. This is precisely what occurred in Jamaica and the Windward Islands. In Trinidad and British Guiana, Creole workers performed the harder, best paying jobs, mainly of a seasonal character, and Indian immigrants provided the consistent labour needed to keep the plantations alive. Table 18 indicates that although Creoles in Trinidad worked less than Indians they earned slightly more. That the rate of wages in that colony remained

to Lytton 17 Nov. 1848, C.O. 111/321, no. 130. For a detailed analysis of the financing of immigration in British Guiana, see Adamson, *Sugar Without Slaves*, pp. 106–9.

[98] Report of H. Mitchell, Agent General of Immigration, 1 June 1858, enclosed in Keate to Newcastle, 9 August 1859, C.O. 295/205, no. 123; Walker to Labouchere, 9 Jan. 1858, C.O. 111/319, no. 6.

[99] H. Mitchell to Johnson, 1 June 1858, enclosed in Keate to Lytton, 26 Sept. 1858, C.O. 295/200, no. 131.

[100] Apart from the subtle coercive tools which planters used to encourage Indians to reindenture, they paid a substantial bounty—$50 in British Guiana—to those who agreed to reindenture. Adamson, *Sugar Without Slaves*, p. 111.

[101] Wood, *Trinidad in Transition*, p. 158.

Table 18

State of Labour on the Trinidad Sugar Estates, March 1858

	People Resident on Estate*	Total Work Days	Total Wages Earned ($)	Average Days Worked Per Month	Average Monthly Wages ($)
Indians	5,905	115,376	34,569.39	19·5	5·85
Trinidad Creoles	3,832	64,812	22,656.52	16·9	5·91
Immigrant Creoles	4,041	71,162	25,341.91	17·6	6·27
Africans	2,885	49,285	15,479.16	17	5·36
Chinese	439	7,588	1,875.33	17·2	4·27
TOTAL	17,102	308,223	99,922.31		

Source: Report of Henry Mitchell, Agent General of Immigration, 1 June 1858, enclosed in C.O. 295/205, no. 123. Keate to Newcastle, 9 Aug. 1859.

* These statistics were taken in the height of crop season. By August or September all groups other than indented labourers had departed the fields. Creoles living on the estates did not work with regularity during the wet season. A pattern had developed whereby native and immigrant Creoles appeared in crop season to help cut and manufacture cane which had been grown under the continuous care of Asians.

abnormally high is attested by the thousands of workers from other islands who flocked annually to cut cane on Trinidadian estates.

By 1865 the success of immigration in the principal importing colonies had muted criticism of the programme. Even though abuses were frequently uncovered and heavy mortality occasionally occurred on transport ships,[102] these recurring problems did not negate the positive effects of the immigration programme. Unquestionably, the planters regarded immigrants more as units of production than human beings who should be welded into a cohesive society. The notion that the West

[102] Mortality on the transport ships from Madras was less than 2 per cent; from Calcutta it was about 6 per cent. The prevalence of cholera in Bengal and the frequency with which emigrants boarded ships in the incipient stages of illness confounded attempts to lower mortality. Interestingly, the mortality rate of Madrassees was much higher than that of immigrants from Calcutta once they had arrived in the colonies. This was attributed to the cleaner habits and greater steadiness of the Calcutta people.

Indies were colonies of exploitation, and that immigration was a necessary expedient to facilitate that exploitation, persisted throughout the mid-century. Nevertheless, the civic institutions and physical infrastructure of British Guiana and Trinidad, as well as the material well-being of a substantial portion of their inhabitants, white and non-white, were enhanced by the effects of immigration. Without it, Trinidad might well have assumed the impoverished aspect of the neighbouring Windward colonies, and whole districts of British Guiana would likely have been reclaimed by the sea.

If, in the short term, immigration is to be judged only in relation to its effects upon the immigrants, it merits cautious approval. Immigration involved great hardship and numerous indignities, but the earnings and the independence ultimately achieved by the most thrifty Portuguese, Indians, and Chinese rendered their experience in the West Indies similar in many ways to that of impoverished Europeans who ventured to America during the same period. Liberated Africans, torn from their native soil by slave-traders, found a comparatively opportune, though alien, sanctuary in the British Caribbean. Those who made their way back to Sierra Leone frequently did so with modest savings, although their return had little effect upon Britain's benevolent fantasy, the 'civilization of Africa'. Over the long term, immigration produced enormous social complexity in the recipient states. Most of the new immigrants were as different from one another as they were from the old population. They looked inward for strength and identity, exalting their own heritage and qualities while maintaining a scornful distance from others. The mutual antagonism of Negroes, Indians, and Chinese contributed to the consolidation of European power in the colonial period, and to a considerable degree cosmopolitanism still remains an impediment to social fusion in the states most affected by immigration in the nineteenth century.

CHAPTER 10

Free Society: Progress and Pitfalls

EMANCIPATION modified the class structure of the West
Indian colonies without destroying its hierarchical
character or the criteria upon which that hierarchy was
founded. Although occupation, wealth, and education were
determinators of class status, race remained the fundamental
factor. The white bias infused in the status mentality of West
Indians during slavery has survived to our own times, and it
may be presumed that the intensity of that bias was especially
strong in the years immediately following emancipation.
Describing Jamaican society in 1953, F. M. Henriques, an
anthropologist of Caribbean origins, wrote:

This 'white bias' is dependent upon the practices and behaviour of
individuals who are both consciously and unconsciously striving to
'lighten' themselves. In their minds black is associated with the
backward, primitive and undesirable qualities in man; and white
is associated with everything that is desirable. Because of his in-
escapable colour heritage the mind of the Jamaican is the seat of a
deep conflict which is exhibited in the formation of a particular
personality configuration. The individual can have little pride of
race in himself if he has the appearance of a coloured or black man,
and at the same time has the perpetual desire to identify himself
with the white man.[1]

That desire for identification was strongest among people of
colour who being generally ignorant of African culture and
repulsed by what they knew of it aspired to total identification
with the European group. To their dismay, educated and
'respectable' coloured people were not accorded full social
acceptance by whites. Their rejection occasioned deep feelings
of insecurity, but it did not induce them to seek closer relations
with blacks. In a class-conscious society identification with the

[1] F. M. Henriques, *Family and Colour in Jamaica* (London, 1953), p. 62.

lowest order was unthinkable. The values of middle- and upper-class coloured people were European, and their desire to achieve full social acceptance from the whites—though perpetually frustrated—was never abandoned.

Although whites continued to dominate society in most colonies, the rigid barriers that had divided them from coloured people were eroded in the free period. In Dominica and Montserrat coloured men quickly assumed a dominant role in the legislature. They were a powerful political element in Jamaica, and even where their inroads were less extensive—as in St. Kitts and Antigua—their rising influence provoked anxiety among the white élite. Increasingly, men of colour acquired plantation property. They held most clerkships, assumed an important place in the professions, and by the end of our period they dominated the lower and mid-ranking government positions in many colonies.[2] In numbers they constituted the largest segment of the European culture group, and, as events, in St. Vincent during 1862 and Jamaica in 1865 clearly show, they felt just as threatened by mob violence as the whites.

The Negroes were not infused with a desire for social equality. Nothing in their combined experiences had encouraged them to hope for that. Rather, they sought to reduce their dependence on the planter class, to gain release from the persistent drudgery of plantation labour. Where possible, they wanted to use the plantations rather than be used by them.

When slavery ended most freedmen on sugar estates expected to remain in their villages cultivating provisions, raising stock, and marketing their produce at a pace not previously permitted. They considered their cottages and provision grounds their own property, and they expected, as free people, to enjoy unimpeded use of them. Estate villages were the only homes the freedmen had known, and they identified profoundly with their fellow villagers. Some of them may have borne malice toward the planters, but they did not as a whole seek the destruction of the sugar plantations. Although they despised

---

[2] The increased social and economic influence of the coloured population resulted to some extent from the steady departure of white doctors, lawyers, craftsmen, and clerks. Whites continued to hold supervisory positions in the sugar industry, whether as managers or attorneys.

field labour as the badge of slavery and had no desire to work regularly for their former masters, villagers did expect to perform some plantation service as a supplement to their independent earnings.

The objectives of freedmen and planters were incompatible. If the estates were to prosper they required continuous dependable labour at crucial periods in the year. No matter how much labour saving machinery a planter might acquire, he needed a certain amount of dependable high quality labour at peak seasons if the established routines so vital to the success of sugar cultivation were to be maintained. The planters were aware that freedmen would only perform continuous plantation labour under duress. They held legal property rights to the freedmen's cottages and grounds (as opposed to customary rights of usage enjoyed by former slaves), and they exploited those rights as a means of extracting continuous labour from the ex-slaves.

Except in Trinidad and Guiana, planters charged freedmen rents for their use of cottages and grounds.[3] Rather than permit tenants to generate rent payments by marketing their own provisions, the planters insisted that rents be deducted from estate wages. This strategy obliged freedmen to work for wages on their home estates. If the working people refused to abide by the plan, they were threatened with eviction—an action which the planters presumed would throw evicted parties on the wage-labour market.

In practice, the rent-wage system varied markedly from one colony to another—indeed, from one estate to another.[4] A planter in St. James, Jamaica, declared that no two employers managed their tenants alike. Some planters charged for cottages and grounds, others only for cottages. A few employers demanded rent from every person occupying a cottage or every adult being sustained from plantation grounds. Some even charged married people less than those living out of wed-

---

[3] In Barbados, cottages were often granted rent-free on condition that freedmen work at their home estates five days a week. Those who performed less labour were fined, and the fine constituted a rent. MacGregor to Russell, 26 Oct. 1839, C.O. 28/128, no. 112.

[4] Report of stipendiary magistrates, enclosed in Metcalfe to Russell, 30 Oct. 1840, C.O. 137/250, no. 118; Sel. Comm. on the West India Colonies, P.P. 1842, XIII (479), evidence of McCornock, Lowndes, Barrett, Estridge.

lock. It is hard to arrive at a reasonably accurate average rent for any colony because of wide variations ranging from a remission of charges to tenants who worked a full week on their home estates to rents as high as 6s. 8d. per household. In Jamaica, the average would have been less than two days' wages—about 2s. a week. Elsewhere in the islands rents as well as wages would generally have been lower, but as a rule they would not have exceeded two days' wages.

The rent-wage scheme aroused a storm of protest, especially in Jamaica. Freedmen were outraged to learn that they had no legal rights to the cottages they had built and to the grounds they had cleared. Their defiance of the system provoked evictions, and evictions generated a poignant and pervasive awareness of the insecurity of cottage tenure. Some freedmen remained on the estates obdurately refusing to co-operate fully with the planters. In increasing numbers, however, Negroes began to acquire independent freeholds, labouring in cane fields until they could accumulate savings for the purchase of their own land. They were assisted in this endeavour by missionaries who were sympathetic to their plight and determined, by concerted action, to preserve the unity of their congregations. The reports of stipendiary magistrates in Jamaica during 1840 were laden with data concerning the mushrooming of free villages. James Harris asserted that the rent-wage controversy in Hanover had provoked a 'craving desire' among the free people to secure their own lands.[5] John Gurley, an S.M. in St. Elizabeth warned, '. . . should the system which has hitherto been practiced with regard to rent and the payment of wages be continued, I have no doubt the properties will soon be deserted altogether.'[6] In fear of this, Sir Charles Metcalfe urged planters to relent of their vexatious tenure arrangements, recommending that free villages be established adjacent to estates as a means of preserving the workers' access to wage-labour opportunities.[7] The planters grudgingly admitted that the rent-wage plan had not succeeded, and by the mid-forties most of them abandoned the system.

It may be, as most scholars have argued, that the planters'

[5] Report of J. Harris, enclosed in C.O. 137/248, no. 50.
[6] Report of J. Gurley, ibid.
[7] Metcalfe to Russell, 30 Mar. 1840, C.O. 137/248, no. 50.

tenure arrangements were neither moral nor practical and
that they encouraged rather than discouraged a flight of freedmen from the plantations. At the same time, it is unreasonable
to contend that planters should not have attempted to establish
tight tenure arrangements of some kind in view of the size of
their financial investment in plantation property, the need for
regular labour to keep that investment alive, and the unwilling-
ness of freedmen to perform continuous estate service. Given
the diverse aims of freedmen and planters, one party had to
prevail, and it was no more logical for the planters to have
meekly forsaken their objectives than it would have been for
the freedmen to have conceded passively to the planters' tenure
arrangements. Since the rent-wage plan was adopted everywhere except in Trinidad and Guiana (where the land-
population ratio rendered it futile), it can hardly be condemned as an irrationally conceived and clearly foredoomed
strategy. The planters were not successful in Jamaica or St.
Lucia, both low density colonies, but in islands having high or
medium population density they generally preserved the
upper hand.[8] Even in Jamaica the planters may have sacrificed less than is generally supposed by having taken a stand.
Had they imposed no charges on houses and grounds or had
they separated the collection of rents from the payment of
wages—which many of them subsequently tried to do—there
is no assurance that they would have obtained more continuous labour than they actually did in the initial years of
freedom. In the former case, they undoubtedly would have
acquired less. In the latter, freedmen could have met most or all
of their rent charges by the sale of provision crops without
resorting to field labour. Moreover, as the planters discovered,
it was sometimes as difficult and exasperating to extract rents
from Negro tenants as it was to obtain their continuous labour.
The experience of George Price at Worthy Park was probably
not uncommon. In 1840 he determined that his rentals should
produce £257 for houses and £2,570 for grounds. During 1842
he was able to recover only £49.8s.[9] The freedmen who paid
rent did little work, and all tenants, it may be presumed, care-

---

[8] W. Emanuel Riviere, 'Labour Shortage in the British West Indies After
Emancipation', *The Journal of Caribbean History*, IV (1972), 5–9.
[9] Craton and Walvin, *Jamaican Plantation*, p. 217.

fully avoided the collector. Considering the futility of trying to pry rents from his people, Price reluctantly allowed them to enjoy, rent-free, the houses and grounds they had long considered their own.

In view of developments elsewhere, there is no certainty that the rent-wage controversy in Jamaica did anything more than accelerate an inevitable retirement of freedmen from estate villages. The labouring people expressed a wish to remain in their plantation villages so long as they believed they had proprietary rights over their houses and grounds. When they were disillusioned on that score, a major factor in their attachment to the estates was removed. Moreover, those who remained in the villages were always subject to the irritating importunities of needy planters. Constant harassment, apart from any consideration of rents, tended to alienate freedmen from estate managers. Opportunities for resettlement abounded in Jamaica as a result of the abandonment of 465 coffee properties—amounting to more than 300,000 highland acres—between 1832 and 1847.[10] As time passed, and the ex-slaves learned to appreciate the full scope of their freedom, they were much more likely to shed old loyalties and seize new opportunities.

Developments in Trinidad and Guiana provide evidence of this. In those colonies freedmen residing on sugar estates received their houses and grounds without rent, and they enjoyed comparatively high allowances as well as high wages. Although they were expected to provide steady labour for the estates, they were rarely evicted if they did not.[11] Of course, those who worked irregularly were alternately scolded and threatened by the planters. Like their counterparts in Jamaica,

[10] Report of a committee of the Jamaica Assembly, enclosed in C. E. Grey to Earl Grey, 7 Feb. 1848, C.O. 137/295, no. 17.

[11] Competition for labour was so intense in Trinidad that when a notoriously insubordinate freedman was removed from one estate the proprietor of a neighbouring plantation dispatched a cart to fetch both the evicted party and his property. George Barrow, memo, bound in C.O. 295/133, no. 69. One Trinidad planter claimed that during the first four months of crop in 1839 his tenants performed only 2,884 daily tasks out of an expected 4,320, calculated on the basis of five tasks per week. During that time there was not a single eviction executed by any of the colony's stipendiary magistrates. Sel. Comm. on the West India Colonies, P.P. 1842, XIII (47), evidence of Church, 1829; Mein to Normanby, 19 May 1839, C.O. 295/125, no. 37.

they departed the estates in great numbers to inhabit yawning stretches of open land or numerous abandoned plantations. Free villages grew rapidly in the suburbs of Port of Spain and San Fernando and along the road to Arima.[12] By 1847 the available labour force in Trinidad had shrunk by nearly 40 per cent.[13] In British Guiana, the Crown Surveyor and Commissary of Population declared in 1844 that at least 19,000 freedmen had settled beyond the plantations on more than 5,000 individual holdings.[14] Four years later those figures had doubled.[15] The free village movement took hold everywhere except Barbados. It may have commenced in Jamaica under a cloud of strife, but in view of its nearly universal development—even where rent charges were not a factor—there is little reason to suppose that the rent-wage controversy did more than hasten and perhaps marginally inflate a movement which would have occurred anyway.

The Colonial Office supported free villages where their establishment was calculated to benefit the estates and opposed them where they would not. In this respect the Secretary of State was guided by the recommendations of colonial governors. Sir William Colebrooke's encouragement of free villages in the densely populated Leeward Islands was approved, and by 1846 over 9,000 Antigua labourers were residing in free communities,[16] though the modest plots they occupied did not relieve them of dependence on wage labour. The agitation of Barbados blacks in favour of free villages was opposed by colonial planters who combined to discourage the sale of land to freedmen. This attitude, endorsed by the Governor, was upheld by the Colonial Office. Spedding summed up the Government's policy: 'where the management of the planters and the nature of the country seem likely to make the peasantry prefer a dispersed unsettled life to residence on the estates . . . it is politic to encourage the formation of independent settlements [adjacent to the estates] as the best chance of saving the

---

[12] Wood, *Trinidad in Transition*, p. 49.
[13] Riviere, 'Labour Shortage After Emancipation', p. 11.
[14] Report of Crown Surveyor and Commissary of Population, C.O. 111/227.
[15] Rawle Farley, 'The Rise of Village Settlements in British Guiana', *Caribbean Quarterly*, X (1964), 58–9.
[16] Sewell, *Ordeal of Free Labour*, p. 148.

labouring community from dispersion.'[17] In Barbados, there was no place for the freedmen to take up a dispersed unsettled life, and free villages were consequently discouraged.

The development of free villages was both haphazard and planned. In the first case, individual freedmen bought random sections of waste land subdivided for the purpose by planters who needed quick capital.[18] Likewise, they obtained lots from the owners of abandoned properties who were anxious to recover some of their losses. Planned villages on the other hand were established under well defined leadership. The Presbyterian settlement at Goodwill in Jamaica is a remarkable example. Rev. George Blyth bought the land and sold it to his parishioners, reserving two acres for the residence of a minister and a half acre for a church. No gambling, no liquor store, and no 'irregular house' was permitted in the township; only members of a temperance society could possess property there; and everyone was obliged to post a £50 bond for his good behaviour which, if forfeited, would revert to the church. A committee of villagers enforced these regulations, and anyone who was regarded a nuisance by a three-quarters vote of all residents would be obliged to leave.[19] These strictures were unusually severe, but all the sectarian sponsors of free townships set aside acreage for a church and clergyman, and most of them required a degree of propriety and social awareness which could not be demanded of freeholders in the unplanned villages.

Planned villages, which in Jamaica were commonly organized by European missionaries, assumed an extraordinary character in British Guiana. There, village movements were organized on a communal, or joint stock, basis by former headmen who bought up whole estates on behalf of scores of ordinary field-workers. In November 1839 Northbrook Estate was sold to sixty-three people—many of them headmen—for $10,000.[20] Several years later, four headmen procured Den Amstel in the name of 70 field workers for $25,000; Good Hope

[17] Spedding to Stephen, 10 Jan. 1840, bound in C.O. 28/128, no. 112.
[18] See p. 410, n. 11.
[19] Blyth Correspondence, enclosed in Metcalfe to Russell, 30 Oct. 1840, C.O. 137/250, no. 118.
[20] Light to Russell, 4 Dec. 1839, P.P. 1840, XXXIV (151).

was sold on a similar basis for $50,000.[21] As a rule, the leadership which was adequate to create these villages did not suffice to preserve good order and civic co-operation. Co-operation was especially important in Guiana townships because the land was subject to flooding unless expensive and rather elaborate dykes and drainage systems were kept in good repair. Banks of mud, which had accumulated along the coast, prevented gravity drainage from cultivated lands into the sea. Planters overcame this problem by the use of steam powered pumps. But when former estate land was subdivided among freedmen, the villagers rarely possessed the organizational skills required to maintain sea walls, sluices, and trenches. The sea broke in; surface water accumulated and could not gain exit. Houses were frequently awash, and the small dykes built around individual dwellings proved of little value when over-all drainage problems were neglected. Crops were destroyed, and by the 1860s free villagers were renting land from neighbouring sugar planters for use as provision grounds.[22]

The manner in which peasant villages were established in British Guiana led to serious disputes over rights and titles. This problem was not unique to that colony,[23] but it was greatly aggravated there. In 1844 about 40 per cent of the peasants who were cultivating their own land had not received legal title to it, or, through ignorance of the law, had not officially recorded their titles.[24] This situation was complicated by the communal nature of the settlements. In some cases planters had made a single transfer of title to a headman who served as the agent for up to 200 peasants.[25] The land rights of individual members of the corporate body were never legally determined, and as years passed, deaths occurred and shifting sexual relations produced a tangled array of claims and counter-claims, rendering it impossible to sort out the rights and entitlements of contending villagers.[26]

[21] Rawle Farley, 'The Rise of the Peasantry in British Guiana', *Social and Economic Studies*, II (1954), p. 101.

[22] Adamson, *Sugar Without Slaves*, p. 59; Dalton, *History of British Guiana*, II, 6–8; Trollope, *West Indies*, p. 181.

[23] Hall, *Free Jamaica*, p. 163.

[24] Fourth Report from the Select Committee on Sugar and Coffee Planting, P.P. 1847–8, XXIII (184), Appendix 3, Hadfield to Young, pp. 174–5.

[25] Ibid.

[26] When the Demerara East Coast Railway passed through several such villages

In many cases, freedmen paid high prices for inferior land which they quickly exhausted. That poor land was subdivided into uneconomical plots caused missionary sponsors of free villages little anxiety, for during the initial stages of the free village movement they were principally interested in altering the social milieu of freedmen, not their economic habits. William Knibb noted that the plots sold to freedmen by Jamaican Baptists in the early forties were so small that their purchasers could not obtain a satisfactory livelihood without gaining some income from another source.[27] When established on freeholds, emancipated people continued to employ African methods of cultivation, clearing the land by fire and cultivating it intensively until exhausted. This practice was not a problem when cultivators could easily move on to exploit fresh lands, but very often the land available to peasants was badly depleted former coffee property. In any case, once they were established on small independent holdings, the systematic depletion of the soil was a serious hazard to their continuing prosperity. A modern geographer has concluded that Jamaican freedmen who held small parcels of land had little chance of lasting prosperity unless an alternative form of employment was developed or the demand for labour on the sugar estates expanded in relation to the growing population.[28] Neither of these occurred.

Although peasant agriculture attracted the attention of most freedmen, many were lured by the high status and high pay of the skilled trades. In brief time, the disciplinary structure of the craft trades broke down, and the quality of workmanship deteriorated. During slavery, a system of apprenticeship training similar to that prevailing in England was practised. In towns and on estates, master craftsmen—sometimes white or free coloured people—instructed and supervised slave apprentices for periods up to seven years. Emancipation interrupted the system. Proprietors lost interest in training young men

it was not possible to determine which people should be compensated for land taken by the line. Report of W. Walker, enclosed in Barkly to Grey, 21 Mar. 1849, C.O. 111/264, no. 53.

[27] Sel. Comm. on the West India Colonies, P.P. 1842, XIII (479), evidence of Knibb, 6015.

[28] E. Paget, 'Land-Use and Settlement in Jamaica', in R. W. Steel and C. A-Fisher, eds., *Geographical Essays on British Tropical Lands* (London, 1956), p. 208.

whose services they could not rely on in the future, and, as expected, when full freedom arrived in 1838 trainees bolted from the old masters and advertised themselves as independent artisans. Newcomers to the trades exhibited no interest in binding themselves to many years of training, and master craftsmen were deprived of effective control over their apprentices.[29] With a year or two of instruction in the use of tools, young men ventured into the market place competing for work with established artisans. Jobs were plentiful in the early years of freedom since the demand for new schools, churches, and public structures was unprecedented. Wages were high, but the quality of work was not. A master carpenter in Jamaica remarked that most of his young fellow tradesmen could not arrange the cutting of lumber to conserve their materials nor frame panels or window sashes competently. Deficiency in skill applied equally to the new breed of cabinet-makers, masons, shipwrights, smiths, shoemakers, and saddlers.[30] The old masters resisted the encroachment of these 'half-taught journeymen', and managed to preserve a higher rate of remuneration for their own superior skills. But when the post-emancipation boom subsided, the competitive impact of the new artisans was severely felt and the old masters suffered under-employment.[31] In the fifties artisans' wages declined along with the depression in the sugar industry. In 1858 a stipendiary magistrate in Jamaica, lamenting the gradual disappearance of the old craftsmen, wondered where the colonists would turn for high quality workmen. He had no confidence in the younger men, who, as soon as they could 'plane a board', imagined themselves 'competent and complete workmen' demanding full journeyman's wages.[32]

For all freedmen the early forties were years of buoyant hope and prosperity. Wages were high; villages were under construc-

[29] Letter to Mr. Carr, Member of the Jamaica Assembly, read in evidence before the Sel. Comm. on Sugar and Coffee Planting, P.P. 1847–8, XXIII (206), 12871.

[30] Report of Richard Hill, enclosed in Elgin to Stanley, 5 Jan. 1846, C.O. 137/287, no. 2.

[31] The best treatment of artisans in post-emancipation in Jamaica is provided in Hall's, *Free Jamaica*, pp. 215–22.

[32] Report of T. Witter Jackson, enclosed in Darling to Lytton, 25 Oct. 1858, C.O. 137/339, no. 134.

tion; and the intoxicating effects of freedom produced a bounteous confidence in the future. Long deprived of material comforts they used their high wages and independent earnings to purchase riding horses and finery which they displayed with marvellous ostentation. Sundays and holidays brought them out in full regalia. While English labourers walked to church in plain clothes, hundreds of West Indian freedmen proceeded to worship in splendid attire, mounted on horses which may have cost anything from £15 to £60. One observer counted forty-five horses in addition to seven gigs tied up outside the Scottish church in Falmouth—all the property of ex-slaves.[33] Their linen jackets and waistcoats, tall hats and broad cravats, lace-trimmed dresses, white gloves, and parasols equalled the dress of the planter class and would have given no shame to afternoon strollers in Regent Street. Their manners and polite salutations were calculated to justify their costumes and both were a subject of pride in people who viewed these pleasantries as manifest evidence of their liberation. Sir Charles Metcalfe believed the comfort, ease, and independence enjoyed by Jamaican labourers 'probably not equalled, and . . . hardly surpassed in any other Quarter of the Globe'.[34] Knibb joyously reflected that freedmen were decidedly better off than English workmen,[35] and John Gurney, the Quaker philanthropist, was cautiously pleased by the quantity of money which workers casually carried about: 'How very few of our labourers in England would be found with twenty shillings in their purse of spare money . . .'[36] A stipendiary magistrate in British Guiana wrote:

the peasantry, as a body . . . can boldly challenge comparison with the happiest and best paid labourers of the most fertile districts in England . . . The work of a labourer here is light, the time occupied

---

[33] Sel. Comm. on Sugar and Coffee Planting, P.P. 1847–8, XXIII (206), evidence of P. Borthwick, 12,906. In November 1841, Hall Pringle, the S.M. in Clarendon and Vere, wrote: 'the negroes, both males and females, are, with few exceptions, each of them in possession of a horse, and most expensive clothing, and many other superfluities . . .' Report enclosed in C.O. 137/257, no. 18. Similar observations were made throughout the island.

[34] Metcalfe to Russell, 30 Mar. 1840, C.O. 137/248, no. 50.

[35] Sel. Comm. on the West India Colonies, P.P. 1842, XIII (479), evidence of Knibb, 6158, 6275.

[36] Gurney, *A Winter in the West Indies*, pp. 103–4.

in its performance short, and the remuneration high; in England, the labourer's task is long and weary, and its remuneration small; hundreds of labourers earn daily in my district their dollar, or 4s. 2d. sterling each, by 12 o'clock at noon, having no house-rent to pay, with gratuitous schooling for their children, and when sick, medical attendance. The mower or reaper at home has to fag from sunrise to sunset, and then thankfully receives 1s. 6d. or 2s. 6d.[37]

The situation changed abruptly in the late forties and fifties. The Sugar Duties Act and the depression in the sugar industry undermined the quality of life among freedmen, repressed their enthusiasm, dampened their aspirations, and widened their separation from European influences. Freedmen who had erected villages adjacent to active plantations found themselves isolated by the abandonment of those properties. Changing circumstances were most evident in Jamaica. During the years of crisis, 1847–54, stipendiary magistrates in that colony ceased reporting on conditions in their districts. When they resumed reporting in 1854, their evaluations of social and moral conditions in the colony bore little resemblance to assessments they had made in the forties. The desire to acquire fine clothes, furniture, riding horses, and items of display which had been so evident among working people in the first flush of freedom had largely disappeared. Although people were subsisting on their small plots, they lacked easy access to money wages. Their seeming indifference to material refinements was nothing more than a practical acknowledgement that they no longer possessed the means of acquiring them. Extra efforts to increase the yield of their grounds only contributed to the glut of foodstuffs in local markets, providing no commensurate return for the additional labour expended. The people had much leisure time, but their leisure, unaccompanied by material improvement or social refinement led stipendiaries to deplore their aimlessness and 'recklessness of life'. Moral, not material, degeneracy was the pervading concern of stipendiaries, and their concern was echoed by European missionaries. A report by David Ewart best illustrates the ruling sentiment of the Jamaican magistracy:

In almost every part of the Island it has been seen that morality and Religion, have not any enduring influence upon the majority of

[37] Report of Stipendiary Magistrate, District A, Lower Demarara, in P.P. 1842, XII (551), Appendix 23.

our labouring population; that there is a shameless depravity manifested amongst the youths of both sexes, a palpable disregard of the marriage ties, total insensibility to domestic order and decency, and a general corruption of habits, arising mainly from the degraded state of the parentage of the rising generation, through which it is passing to an ignorant and depraved maturity.[38]

T. Witter Jackson, S.M. in St. Thomas in the Vale, noted that peasants had replaced planters in much of the island and that the future of Jamaica would depend upon her yeomanry. But, he warned, either the government would direct their energy into proper channels or they would become the curse of the colony.[39]

Certainly the peasantry constituted the largest portion of the emancipated class in Jamaica. Hall has classified rural freedmen under three headings: small farmers who owned land and occasionally employed labour but did not themselves work on sugar estates; peasants who possessed and cultivated small properties, but occasionally laboured on plantations; and labourers who maintained cottages and grounds on the estates and continued to work in the sugar industry.[40] By 1847, before the massive abandonment of sugar property, two-thirds of the former estate population had taken up residence beyond the plantations.[41] By 1865, Hall estimates, only about 4,000 of these people, or less than 2 per cent of the non-white male population, could be identified as small farmers with property of ten to fifty acres.[42] It is clear, therefore, that by far the greatest portion of Jamaica's rural non-white population was of the peasant class. How the government at Spanish Town, so thinly endowed with human talent and so lacking in financial resources, could have effectively channelled the energy—as Jackson put it—of so vast and dispersed a class of people is difficult to comprehend. Like his fellow magistrates, Jackson sought the moral regeneration of the peasantry through religious education and more extensive and fruitful communication with the European culture group. But it is difficult to perceive how this was to be

[38] Report of David Ewart, enclosed in Barkly to Newcastle, 21 Feb. 1854, C.O. 137/322, no. 24.
[39] Report of T. W. Jackson, ibid.
[40] Hall, Free Jamaica, p. 158.
[41] Report of a Committee of the Jamaica Assembly, 1847, enclosed in C.O. 137/295, no. 17.
[42] Hall, Free Jamaica, p. 194.

achieved without a significant and sustained up-swing in the economy. Since the amount of disposable public income in the colony depended heavily on the taxable trade generated by exports, and since there was no ready alternative to sugar as a major export commodity, there was little hope for dramatic economic recovery. The prosperity of West Indians continued to depend upon the prices received for their staple products, and after the advent of free trade, the ability of either colonial governments or individual working men to subsidize the services of missionaries, schoolmasters, medical practitioners, or other agents of social progress was extremely limited. The average annual contributions of Baptist church members, for example, fell from about 12s. in 1844 to a little over 3s. in 1859.[43] Programmes of public welfare, cautiously initiated in the early years of freedom, were commonly scrapped in the depression of the late forties. There was a revival of interest in social legislation when sugar prices turned upward in the late 1850s, but prices quickly subsided in the 1860s. By that time conditions had deteriorated among the working people, and in many colonies a distinct polarization had developed between the European and Afro-Creole culture groups.

Although it is easy and convenient to blame the planter class for this polarization, an examination of just one aspect of public welfare—medical service—offers insight into the great fissure which separated West Indian social problems from the meagre resources available to cope with them. When slavery ended, the freedmen became responsible for their own medical care. Public hospitals were needed to replace plantation infirmaries, and asylums were required for lepers and the insane. In the major colonies, hospitals were erected during the early forties. Barbados and Antigua established separate facilities for lepers and lunatics,[44] but that action was exceptional for the Lesser Antilles. The smaller islands were unable to afford new structures. Demented persons who were harmless wandered freely; violently insane people were secured in jail.[45] In Kingston,

[43] Ibid., p. 238.
[44] Grey to Stanley, 2 Nov. 1842, C.O. 28/144, no. 52; Hamilton to Pakington, 13 Apr. 1852, C.O. 28/176, no. 20; Flanders, *Antigua*, II, pp. 255–6.
[45] Hector Gavin, M.D., Medical Inspector of the West India Colonies, to the Acting Governor of Barbados, 4 Nov. 1851, enclosed in Hamilton to Grey, 7 Nov. 1851, C.O. 20/175, no. 73.

Jamaica, a public hospital with an adjacent insane asylum had existed long before emancipation, but both facilities were inadequate. The hospital was overcrowded; the asylum was a bestial place.[46] In the early forties the Jamaica Assembly undertook reform of the main institution; it voted £20,000 for the construction of a new asylum;[47] and it concurrently planned the erection of a lazaretto for lepers.[48]

In a small island, a hospital or asylum located in the principal port could render service to people from all parts of the colony. In Jamaica, on the other hand, most of the population lived in rural parishes too far from Kingston to use the main medical facilities. The closing of estate hospitals after apprenticeship, and the cessation of weekly or bi-weekly visitations from medical practitioners dramatically altered the character of medical service in country districts. Although practitioners encouraged freedmen to engage with them in a form of medical insurance, paying a fixed sum in return for regular treatment over a period of twelve months, few agreed. Instead, most of them took their business to myalists and former slaves who had served as hospital assistants. By 1842 quackery had become a major problem. Stipendiary magistrates reported that many people were dying as a result of faulty medical treatment,[49] and the Assembly responded by passing a measure restricting practice to persons qualified by education and training.[50] Although this measure may have had some effect in the towns, it was unenforceable in the country. A committee of the Assembly returned to the issue in 1845, hearing testimony from a number of physicians and clergymen who asserted that about 10 per cent of the island's blacks were suffering from yaws and were incapable of procreation.[51] Blindness and death were being caused by improper treatment of maladies. Skin infections that were easily treatable in early stages were causing great suffering as a result of neglect or wrong treatment. For every fatality

[46] A Letter to the Chairman of the Committee of Public Accounts representing the unfitness of the Present Asylum for Lunatics, written by E. N. Bancroft, M.D., enclosed in Elgin to Stanley, 11 Feb. 1843, C.O. 137/273, no. 86.
[47] Elgin to Stanley, 1 Dec. 1843, C.O. 137/275, no. 188.
[48] Elgin to Stanley, 15 Jan. 1845, C.O. 137/283, no. 15. This plan foundered in the depression of the late 1840s.
[49] Precis of S.M.s Reports by Henry Taylor, bound in C.O. 137/264, no. 64.
[50] Elgin to Stanley, 27 Jan. 1843, C.O. 137/273, no. 78.
[51] *Votes of the Jamaica Assembly*, 1845, Appendix.

attended by legitimate practitioners, twenty were not. The peasantry, it appeared, rarely resorted to European physicians until their cases had become irreversible. Medical practitioners who had enjoyed a handsome income during slavery were suffering real destitution. Many had left the colony; others were leaving. Whole districts were devoid of qualified physicians, and as a result many freedmen who might have been disposed to resort to a white practitioner were unable to do so.

An Act passed by the Assembly in late 1845 was designed to combat this problem. The island's parishes were divided into districts, and a qualified practitioner was to be assigned to each district. Dispensaries were projected for each area; clergymen, magistrates, and vestrymen who learned of sick persons were expected to refer them to the dispensaries.[52] This measure was never put into effect. The Sugar Duties Act and economic depression intervened, and the programme was abandoned in the general retrenchment of the late forties. Notwithstanding its demise, the programme is indicative of the Assembly's willingness to cope with social problems by state action. In their own way, West Indian colonists may have been more receptive to social legislation than the English. In slavery they had experienced a distorted type of welfare system which, for all its evils, had provided for the basic physical needs of the people. The responsibility of the masters to assure proper care to their bondsmen had been established in colonial law. When slavery ended and serious health problems arose, it was not unnatural or extraordinary for Jamaican oligarchs to establish some state supported machinery to cope with medical deficiencies. The regrettable aspect of the situation was that such progressive treatment of social problems was discouraged or rendered impossible by the economic collapse of the sugar industry after 1846.

The paucity of practitioners was painfully felt in the 1850s when cholera raged through Jamaica. In spite of a quarantine of vessels from Carthagena and other ports where the disease was reported in 1849, fatalities began to occur in Port Royal on October 7, 1850. A week later, deaths in that 'most filthy and ill-regulated place' were occurring at a rate of ten to twenty a

[52] Elgin to Stanley, 5 Jan. 1846, C.O. 137/287, no. 1; Elgin to Stanley, 6 May 1846, C.O. 137/288, no. 52.

day, and the disease had spread to Kingston.[53] In early November the Governor reported that 500 people had died in the vicinity of Spanish Town and that it was only 'with extreme difficulty' that the living were able to bury the dead.[54] Terrified citizenry fled from infected districts, seeking refuge in the countryside. The disease spread to every parish; towns were hardest hit, highland villages least affected. In Montego Bay, 800 bodies were interred in a single grave.[55] Although the mass upheaval occasioned by the epidemic impaired precise reporting, official sources attributed 30,000 deaths to cholera.[56]

It appeared the gods had unleashed all their wrath upon Jamaica. Cholera had arrived hard on the heels of an economic depression that had imposed privation upon planters, merchants, and labourers alike. It was to be followed by an outbreak of influenza, which was swiftly succeeded by an eighteen-month epidemic of smallpox.[57] In 1854 cholera returned, though with abated fury. In St. Thomas in the Vale, where it was reported to have caused terrible havoc,[58] there was a woeful absence of medical intelligence. A stipendiary magistrate in the district reported that an area covering 470 square miles with a population of 40,000 had only two active physicians.[59] According to that report, not 5 per cent of the people who perished in the second outbreak could have seen a European practitioner during any stage of their fatal bouts with the disease.

Cholera was not confined to Jamaica. It spread through the Lesser Antilles, striking with special horror at Barbados. Bridgetown was the scene of panic in June 1854. A month after the epidemic had begun, Governor William Colebrooke estimated that between 14,000 and 15,000 people had perished.[60]

---

[53] C. E. Grey to Earl Grey, 26 Oct. 1850, C.O. 137/307, no. 86.
[54] C. E. Grey to Earl Grey, 11 Nov. 1850, C.O. 137/307, no. 87.
[55] Barkly to Newcastle, 26 May 1854, C.O. 137/323, no. 73.
[56] C. E. Grey to Earl Grey, 31 Dec. 1851, C.O. 137/311, no. 115; Message from the House of Assembly, enclosed in C. E. Grey to Earl Grey, 28 Jan. 1852, C.O. 137/313, no. 5. The contemporary figure is corroborated by a recent survey of island statistics. Eisner, *Jamaica 1830–1930*, p. 136.
[57] Report of Central Board of Health, enclosed in Grey to Newcastle, 23 Oct. 1853, C.O. 137/318, no. 95.
[58] Barkly to Newcastle, 25 May 1854, C.O. 137/323, no. 62.
[59] Report of T. W. Jackson, enclosed in Barkly to Sir George Grey, 18 Sept. 1854, C.O. 137/324, no. 101.
[60] Colebrooke to Sir George Grey, 12 July 1854, C.O. 28/180, no. 55.

These epidemics took a heavy toll among the urban poor.[61] Most West Indian towns had received a substantial influx of country people in the years after emancipation, and the newcomers had brought their rural habits and very often their stock along with them. Thousands of tiny tenements had risen, clustered together in alleys and enclosures, unseen and unexplored by more prosperous urbanites. In port-side slums it was not uncommon for four people to inhabit a dilapidated wooden shack six by nine feet in dimension. The crowding of ramshackle dwellings obstructed sunlight and ventilation; even where air could circulate, the inhabitants closed their windows to the night for fear of intruding duppies.[62] Filth and refuse of every type abounded around and beneath these dwellings, producing the most noxious odours. Pigs poked through it in the company of an 'unprofitable multitude of idle, ill mannered, and vicious dogs'. If anything, Bridgetown was worse than Kingston. Well water in the city was contaminated and unfit for drinking. Potable water came mainly from Beckles's spring where it was sold to retailers who peddled it through the town at a half-cent a gallon. Bathing was a luxury, and there was not enough water to clean the streets or the yards, to carry sewerage, or, for that matter, to cope with fire. Surface drains conveyed fluid waste to the sea, but limestone drains readily absorbed both moisture and odour. Moveable tubs were commonly used for solid wastes. Although the people were required by law to deposit the contents of the tubs in the sea, many failed to take the trouble. Human excrement was simply thrown in the streets.[63]

The rapid, unregulated growth of West Indian towns mirrored developments in Europe and North America. Everywhere, sensible urban planning was hampered by an attach-

---

[61] This paragraph is drawn from reports on Kingston and Bridgetown. Petition of the Local Board of Health of Kingston, *Votes of the Jamaica Assembly*, 13 Dec. 1850; General Report of L. N. Samuel, Director of Public Works in Trinidad, concerning Sanitary Conditions in the City of Bridgetown, enclosed in Colebrooke to Sir George Grey, 27 Nov. 1854, C.O. 28/181, no. 74.

[62] Ghosts that appeared after dark.

[63] Readers who might presume that sanitary conditions were markedly worse in the West Indies than they were in Britain will be persuaded otherwise by a reading of Edwin Chadwick's *Report on the Sanitary Condition of the Labouring Population of Great Britain*, 1842. That report has been edited by M. W. Flinn in a new publication by the Edinburgh University Press, 1965.

ment to *laissez-faire* principles, and few governments—least of all those in the West Indies—were equipped to control urban growth and enforce residential or sanitary codes. While major social projects characteristic of the twentieth century could not have been expected of ruling colonial oligarchs, there was no legitimate excuse for a prosperous community like Barbados not having provided ample fresh water to the citizenry of its capital town before being confronted with a major epidemic. On the other hand, Barbados did react to the initial threat of cholera in 1850 by organizing a colonial Board of Health with the aid of two physicians who came out from Britain. Parochial inspectors were appointed; a general clean-up was attempted; and public vaccinators were established throughout the colony, gratuitously vaccinating 15,317 persons during 1850–1.[64] In the wake of tragedy, Barbados patriarchs established water works for the city,[65] and the comparative economic strength of that colony enabled the legislature to appropriate substantial sums for the relief of sufferers.[66] In colonies where the staple economy had been crippled, ruling classes faced their misfortunes with resigned despair. Cognizant of the enormous debt and deepening public poverty of their own island, Jamaica's Assemblymen did not vote funds for those ravaged by cholera in 1854, and they concluded their spring session without authorizing the vestries to impose taxes for that purpose.[67] Although in Barbados the public prosperity issuing from a successful plantation economy had not inspired an aggressive programme of civic construction or social reform, it did, at least, provide the means to rectify shameful conditions and afford supplication to the stricken.

Cholera and other epidemic diseases that visited the colonies in the early fifties, combined with stagnating economic conditions, produced widespread social demoralization. Everywhere hundreds of children became parentless. Indigency and crime increased. In the late fifties, Kingston teemed with vagrant and destitute children who lived by their wits, practising every form of vice.[68] The sudden deaths of freeholding peasants led

[64] Hamilton to Pakington, 13 Apr. 1852, C.O. 28/176, no. 20.
[65] Walker to Newcastle, 27 Sept. 1859, C.O. 28/189, no. 66.
[66] Colebrooke to Sir George Grey, 26 July 1854, C.O. 28/180, no. 57.
[67] Barkly to Newcastle, 25 May 1854, C.O. 137/323, no. 62.
[68] Darling to Labouchere, 11 Mar. 1858, C.O. 137/336, no. 40.

to serious and often violent strife between survivors who claimed to inherit their property.[69] Because the courts acted slowly, the strongest of the claimants commonly prevailed. The fatalism of the common people was reinforced, and they seemed no more willing to invest in the services of medical practitioners after cholera than before. Part of the reason may have been their lack of money, for it was stated by a magistrate in St. Elizabeth, Jamaica, that in 90 per cent of all cases practitioners had to institute legal proceedings to obtain a fee.[70]

Crime had not been a serious problem in the West Indies during the first decade of freedom. There were numerous assaults and petty larcenies in Trinidad and Guiana, but these were committed mainly by immigrants whom everyone regarded as the off-scourings of the island colonies. This situation changed in the late forties. Henry Barkly indicated that in one year, 1847/8, the crime rate in British Guiana rose 35 per cent.[71] A similar development occurred in Jamaica. In 1840 stipendiary magistrates reported a general absence of crime,[72] and in no year between 1839 and 1845 were there more than 1,000 criminal convictions.[73] Heinous crime remained at a fairly low level, but by the 1850s petty larceny had become a major social problem.

The most easily pilfered commodities in rural districts were growing crops. Under cover of night, stealthy thieves ravaged farms and small grounds alike, nourishing their hunger or compensating for their idleness. Correspondence from clergymen and government officials during the 1860s suggests that 'idle and dissolute young men' were the principal villains, stealing because they refused to work.[74] These reports are too common to

[69] Report of Charles Lake, enclosed in Barkly to Newcastle, 21 Feb. 1854, C.O. 137/322, no. 24.
[70] Report of C. A. H. Rumbold, enclosed in Barkly to Newcastle, 21 Feb. 1854, C.O. 137/322, no. 24.
[71] Barkly to Grey, 18 July 1849, C.O. 111/267, no. 110.
[72] Reports of S.M.s., enclosed in Metcalfe to Russell, 30 Oct. 1840, C.O. 137/250, no. 118.
[73] Elgin to Stanley, 31 Dec. 1845, C.O. 137/285, no. 108.
[74] Dr. Underhill, Secretary of the Baptists Missionary Society, and the Governor of Jamaica agreed that 'idleness and debauchery, not . . . horrible distress' occasioned most praedial larceny. Their position was endorsed by Dr. Samuel Oughton, a long-time Baptist minister, who declared in a letter to the *Jamaica Guardian* that the increase of crime resulted not so much from hunger as from 'the inveterate habits of the idleness, and the low state of moral and religious principles

ignore, especially in view of the complaints of enterprising black farmers who claimed they could not obtain adequate labour.[75] It must also be recalled that in the early years of freedom before half of Jamaica's sugar estates were abandoned freedmen were settling on quarter-acre and half-acre lots which could not adequately support them. As population grew (from 377,433 in 1844 to 441,225 in 1861),[76] and soil exhaustion took its toll, pressure on the land increased. Small freeholders who could not supplement their own productions with wage earnings were in danger of privation. The dislocations occasioned by cholera caused a decay in social ethics, and the rising price of imports during the 1860s brought about by the American Civil War, compounded by drought and crop disease, produced widespread misery. The poor people of Jamaica were stunned and angered by this concatenation of events. Whether driven by hopelessness, maliciousness, or hunger to commit depradations on the crops of their neighbours, they were paralysing and frustrating the efforts of the most industrious black farmers, some of whom had accumulated considerable acreage and had begun to export minor staples. 'If Devonshire were in Jamaica', wrote the Bishop of Kingston, 'the apple orchards would hardly continue to exist.'[77] Another clergyman reported that a proprietor who rented fifty acres in provision land received notice from his tenants that they could not continue, 'as everything they plant is either stolen or wantonly destroyed'.[78] When Governor Eyre toured the colony in 1864 he was besieged by small freeholders and farmers to do something to control praedial larceny.[79] Routine police efforts had proved unavailing. Magistrates repeatedly observed that even those few thieves who had been caught and prosecuted suffered no discredit or stigma among their peers for having been jailed.[80]

which prevail to so fearful a degree'. Eyre to Cardwell, Mar. 1865, C.O. 137/388, no. 4045.

[75] Hall, *Free Jamaica*, p. 195.

[76] Census figures, enclosed in C.O. 137/280, no. 128; C.O. 137/357, no. 168.

[77] Bishop of Kingston to Eyre, 2 Mar. 1865, enclosed in Eyre to Cardwell, 2 Mar. 1865, C.O. 137/388, no. 45.

[78] William Rowe, Archdeacon of Cornwall, to H. Austin, n.d., enclosed in Eyre to Cardwell, 19 Apr. 1865, C.O. 137/290, no. 90.

[79] Eyre to Newcastle, 10 Sept. 1864, C.O. 137/384, no. 256.

[80] Reports of Davis, Dillon, Rumbold, and Bell, enclosed in Barkly to Newcastle,

Injured freeholders, clergymen, and planters seemed to agree that the only antidote to praedial larceny was whipping, and an Act to revive corporal punishment—barred since 1840—was passed by the legislature in 1865.[81] Although strongly supported in principle by officials in Downing Street, the Act was withheld from the Privy Council as a result of the excesses which occurred during the Morant Bay episode.[82]

The cultural gap which separated Afro-Creole elements from middle- and upper-class West Indian society persisted in the free period. White and coloured leaders drew clear distinctions between European cultural patterns which they considered uplifting, and the practices derived from Africa or from slavery which they deemed debasing. The European culture group did not wish to preserve the particular habits or pageantry of the Negroes simply because they were quaint or colourful. In the West Indies, civilization was seen to be in conflict with primitivism, and the victory of the former could only be achieved, it was thought, by controlling or eradicating corrupt and debasing influences.

To the English, excessive noise evinced a lack of refinement, a primitive quality. Whether at home or in the islands, the English were, on the whole, quiet people. Black Creoles were not. Their dancing and drumming, their noisy night-long wakes, and their clamorous conduct of routine affairs irritated Europeans.[83] Perhaps nothing was more trying to the European

21 Feb. 1854, C.O. 137/322, no. 24; Eyre to Cardwell, 2 Mar. 1865, C.O. 137/388, no. 40.

[81] Eyre to Cardwell, 22 Mar. 1865, C.O. 137/388, no. 59.

[82] Fortescue, the Parliamentary Under-Secretary, expressed his view in a minute, 22 Oct. 1865: 'When thieving reaches a point at which it interferes with production, it certainly seems to me time to whip, & to whip well.' Minute bound in C.O. 137/384, no. 256. Taylor, who continued to support corporal punishment even after the Morant Bay events, expressed his reasons in a minute, 20 Apr. 1865: '. . . . a small negro freeholder and his family when they had laboured for months to cultivate their bit of ground, wd find the crop just as it arrived at maturity swept off in a night by thieves & being destitute wd themselves take to thieving as their only resource.' Minute bound in C.O. 137/388, no. 59.

[83] An example of this is house moving. When the small wooden houses occupied by blacks were removed from one location to another—a task requiring a few four wheeled trucks and a bevy of porters—the intervening march assumed the character of a parade, with loud singing and a spontaneous exchange of shouts and jests. It was splendid fun for the blacks, annoying to the whites, especially if they were engaged at worship. In Antigua, house moving was forbidden on Sunday

culture group than the annual festivals of the black poor. John Canoe marching, drumming, and revelling was a traditional Christmas exercise in Jamaica, reluctantly tolerated by the planters during slavery as an opportunity for field-hands to purge their emotions. In 1840 Hector Mitchell, the mayor of Kingston, who in company with other members of the corporation considered these revellings vulgar, damaging to public morality, and dangerous to property, banned the John Canoe celebrations. A riot ensued, and the police, beaten back by angry townsmen, were obliged to seek refuge in their station.[84] A similar attempt to ban the revellings in 1841 produced a second more serious riot in which several people lost their lives and regulars as well as a detachment from a naval vessel were called upon to restore order.[85] In the third year a proclamation by Lord Elgin banning the marches had its effect,[86] and by 1845 the Governor, in terms which typified the European attitude, declared that the 'barbarous amusements in which the lower orders were wont to indulge at Christmas' had been abandoned.[87] This, thought Elgin, was 'indicative of the progress of civilization'.

Carnival in Trinidad was equally distasteful to Protestant English colonists, but its French and Catholic origins made it impossible for the English to curb it without giving offence to their French-speaking fellow colonists. A blending of the pre-lenten pageantry of Catholic Europe and the exciting rhythms of Africa, Carnival produced a wild outburst of enthusiasm, a veritable pandemonium of noise, colour, and costumery. Masquerading encouraged licentiousness and concealed the identity of the most riotous, including those who used this saturnalia as a time for settling old grudges. Carnival occupied nearly a week of sleepless nights until 1849 when it was confined to two days. Masking was abolished with only moderate effect in the late fifties. By the sixties, uncontrolled riotousness and depravity had become so dominant an element of Carnival that

because the singing movers often drowned out the white pastors' sermons. See Flanders, *Antigua*, II, p. 133.

[84] Correspondence concerning Hector Mitchell, C.O. 137/255.

[85] Metcalfe to Stanley, 3 Jan. 1842, C.O. 137/261.

[86] Elgin to Stanley, 2 Jan. 1843, C.O. 137/273.

[87] Elgin's speech to the House of Assembly, 31 Dec. 1845, enclosed in Elgin to Stanley, 31 Dec. 1845, C.O. 137/285, no. 109.

the Archbishop of Port of Spain ignored the festivities, removing any countenance by the Catholic Church of the annual revellings of the urban poor. Carnival was never outlawed, but it failed to achieve respectability until the twentieth century.[88]

Culture conflict in the West Indies was intensified by race prejudice. Although freedmen were encouraged to embrace the mores and institutions of European society, they were given no promise of social equality. The racism of Europeans made it difficult for them to perceive of blacks as anything but a servile people, suited only to common labour and a subordinate social status. Victorians had a profound sense of place, and the appropriate place of free Negroes was deemed that of the industrious poor, striving daily in the employ of their 'betters', exhibiting thrift, temperance, and a proper deference. The more elevated coloured people tended to endorse this attitude toward blacks while aspiring, themselves, to social and political equality with whites.

In 1851 Sir Charles Grey could argue that despite a reduction of racial tension, 'old distinctions' profoundly rankled people of mixed heritage and provoked, more than anything else, the party divisions which arose in the Jamaica House of Assembly.[89] Although the Crown encouraged colonial governors to minimize racial distinctions, official prejudice was not easily overcome or concealed. Governor Henry Barkly opened an Assembly Ball in Jamaica by dancing with a lady of colour, the wife of the senior member present, but he had great difficulty inducing Lady Barkly to adopt the same courtesy with the senior assemblyman himself, Henry Franklin.[90] Governor Wodehouse in British Guiana was utterly dismayed by the difficulties of governing a colony composed of whites, coloureds, and blacks. 'The feeling on the question of colour never dies', he wrote: 'It may slumber, but can at all times be roused into a state of mischievous activity on the slightest pretext.'[91] The mischievous activities to which he referred usually involved the coloured middle class. People of colour commonly attributed their disappointments, their failure to obtain positions,

[88] Wood, *Trinidad in Transition*, pp. 243–7.
[89] C. E. Grey to Earl Grey, 31 Dec. 1851, C.O. 137/311, no. 115.
[90] Barkly to Newcastle, 10 Mar. 1854, *Newcastle Papers*, 9, 553.
[91] Wodehouse to Labouchere, 24 Feb. 1857, C.O. 111/316, no. 29.

privileges, or status to the racial exclusiveness of whites. They were extremely sensitive, Wodehouse noted, to a pejorative reflection upon any person of colour, assuming that an accusation against one was intended to embrace them all.[92] Hypersensitive and insecure they undoubtedly were, but as Donald Wood has shown in his study of race relations in Trinidad—a colony in which the colour factor was comparatively unobtrusive[93]—coloured people usually had ample reason for their suspicion and sensitivity. In 1848 there was only one coloured man holding a senior government position in Trinidad; the remaining forty positions were occupied by whites.[94] Coloured people held only fifteen of the forty-three clerkships in the government, and as a later Governor was to acknowledge, most public officers in the colony, being connected to one another by birth or marriage, were advanced through a network of patronage which excluded able and intelligent men of colour.[95]

Although white and coloured West Indians were often at loggerheads, they mutually deplored the perpetuation of a black cultural estate. The establishment of Negro villages beyond the estates had provided a geographical dimension to this cultural division, and the depression of the late forties widened it. The European cultural beach-head among the Negroes had always been fairly thin, but being unnurtured by prosperity or fruitful contact it was swiftly eroded. In Trinidad and British Guiana comparatively few sugar estates were thrown up, but the planters, unable to pay regular wages during the depression years, could not keep their workers from migrating to remote districts beyond their own or the missionaries' influence. This was especially true of liberated Africans who established villages in the interior on the basis of tribal affinities.[96] The subsequent introduction of East Indian labourers tended to stabilize

[92] Ibid.

[93] Sewell argued that attitudes toward mixed marriage were more relaxed in Trinidad than elsewhere and that the island had many 'colored planters and merchants who in mind and manner are most accomplished gentlemen'. See, *Ordeal of Free Labour*, pp. 114–15.

[94] Wood, *Trinidad in Transition*, p. 258.

[95] Ibid.

[96] Findlay and Holdsworth, *History of the Methodist Missionary Society*, II, 374. Wherever village settlements contained a body of African recaptives, missionaries complained of resurgent fetishism.

this separation since the exceptional need for black workers on the estates became a predominantly seasonal affair.

The polarization of society was pronounced in Jamaica. By the late 1850s blacks exhibited little faith in either white or coloured leadership, divorcing themselves from the political controversies that raged in the capital. The law of the island was seen as the restraining instrument of the upper classes. The stipendiary magistracy had shrunk to little more than a dozen ageing men. Most petty justice, the enforcement of labour legislation, and control over local constabularies had passed to about 270 justices of the peace, principally white and coloured men of property.[97] Although these Jamaican justices may have been committed to a fair and honourable exercise of authority, their general prejudice in favour of plantation as opposed to peasant society and their tendency to blame 'idle blacks' for the decline of the estates inevitably influenced their bearing toward the working people. In criminal cases, blacks were not inclined to testify against one another when the injured party was a European.[98] No stigma attached to criminal actions, and convicts returning from the penitentiary were often fêted as the martyrs of unjust laws.[99] In a broader sense, the peasantry expressed little or no interest in tax measures, the withholding of supplies, or even the question of immigration. Richard Hill referred to them as 'mere creatures of sensation', living a humdrum day to day existence, their public awareness extending no farther than the local market. During the constitutional crisis in Jamaica in 1854, the behaviour of the country people was unchanged: they 'enquired into nothing; talked about nothing'.[100]

Quite clearly, two Jamaicas had emerged. But was this, as Professor Curtin has argued,[101] the fault of an inflexible and reactionary planter class rigid in its approach to plantation management and colonial government and unimaginative in developing new social and economic patterns? Partially it was,

[97] Curtin, *Two Jamaicas*, p. 192.
[98] Report of W. A. Bell, enclosed in Barkly to Newcastle, 21 Feb. 1854, C.O. 137/322, no. 24; Barkly to Lord John Russell, 26 Apr. 1855, C.O. 137/326, no. 45.
[99] Reports of C. A. H. Rumbold, T. Dillon, W. A. Bell, enclosed in Barkly to Newcastle, 21 Feb. 1854, C.O. 137/322, no. 24.
[100] Report of Richard Hill, 20 Jan. 1854, enclosed in Barkly to Newcastle, 21 Feb. 1854, C.O. 137/322, no. 24.
[101] Curtin, *Two Jamaicas*.

but only partially. Although contemporary Jamaicans were prone to seek individual or class scapegoats for their mutual woes, social and cultural divisions in the colony were perpetuated and deepened more by circumstances which were beyond anyone's control than by bad or neglectful government, though Jamaica had its share of the latter. Freedmen wanted to possess their own land. As has been shown, rent-wage controversies may have accelerated their rate of departure from the estates, but as the examples of Trinidad and British Guiana show, the freedmen's quest for territorial independence was about as strong where the rent-wage issue did not arise as it was where it did. The depression of the late forties compounded by demoralizing cholera epidemics increased population dispersal, and the demise of coffee and sugar plantations isolated Negro villages which at an earlier time had been established adjacent to active estates. Meagre educational facilities and the racism of the upper classes impaired vertical mobility for Negroes and affected their attitudes toward European Jamaica. But at its best, education in that former slave community was a tender reed which required careful nurture over an extended period. Jamaica did not enjoy the benefit of time. Its social and economic foundations were shattered between 1846 and 1854 and once the population had separated into its component cultural parts, each suffering a relentless decline in prosperity, there was no effective or speedy means by which it could have been united.

The experience of Barbados was opposite that of Jamaica. The old manorial mentality persisted there. A peasantry with its rugged democratic ethos did not arise to challenge the paternalism of the old oligarchy. In Barbados the planters' contention that a well-regulated and disciplined export economy would generate superior conditions for all elements of the population was put to the test. Free villages did not arise;[102] comparatively few blacks acquired independent holdings; and the majority of them gained their livelihoods on the sugar estates, earning up to £15 a year.[103] As tenants on the estates, they paid rents

---

[102] The value of land remained extremely high—about £100 an acre. Grey to Stanley, 3 Oct. 1842, C.O. 28/144, no. 49; Colebrooke to Grey, 27 Apr. 1849, C.O. 28/170, no. 20; Colebrooke to Newcastle, 9 Nov. 1853, C.O. 28/179, no. 79.

[103] A person who worked 300 days a year at 1s. per day would earn only £15, but

commensurate to the commercial value of the land they occupied, and they assumed a further obligation to perform work on their resident estates for a specific number of days at wages below the market rate. If a tenant failed to fulfil his responsibilities, or refused to tolerate the petty tyrannies of the landlord, he could be evicted at a month's notice, his crops being taken at their appraised value.[104] Eviction was rare, the threat of it proving sufficient to preserve order, regularity and discipline on the estates. Because the freedmen had no alternative to estate service, labour relations in Barbados were the most placid in the Caribbean. Workers were encouraged to cultivate cane on rented land, and on many properties they produced twenty-five hogsheads, worth up to £400.[105] By no means, however, did they enjoy the individual freedom and leisure common to the independent peasantry in low density colonies, and their poverty provoked concern and embarrassment among the proprietors. After the cholera epidemic of 1854 the president of a local agricultural society expressed the self-reproach felt by many planters:

... after a period of 16 years, during which our peasantry have enjoyed the privileges and benefits of a free people, there have not been introduced among them, those social manners and habits and those domestic proprieties, which contribute to refine and elevate the human character, and which constitute the best enjoyments of civilized life. Indeed I am inclined to think that ... there is absolutely less of home feelings, and affections, and attachments, and less domestic comfort and even domestic cleanliness, than existed in the condition of slavery.[106]

it was the rare case when anyone would or could work that number of days. Barbados freedmen worked exceptionally hard to accumulate the means to purchase small holdings. By 1858, however, only 10,500 of 106,500 (approximate) acres were held by small proprietors. Hincks to Lytton, 1 Sept. 1858, C.O. 28/188, no. 48.

[104] Hincks to Lytton, 22 Sept. 1858, C.O. 28/188, no. 55, with enclosure from *The Liberal*, 22 Sept. 1858. Tenants commonly paid £4 an acre per annum in rent. Some of them sent substitutes to labour in the landlords' fields, occupying themselves on their own plots which might yield two or three hogsheads of sugar and two or three crops of provisions a year. The proprietor manufactured the cane in exchange for one-third the sugar and molasses and all the megass. Davy, *The West Indies*, pp. 148–50.

[105] Hincks to Lytton, 1 Sept. 1858, C.O. 28/188, no. 49.

[106] Address to the Members of the Cliff District Agricultural Society by G. E. Thomas, Oct. 1854, enclosed in Colebrooke to Russell, 9 June 1855, C.O. 28/182, no. 46.

Voluntary associations, even an association of absentees, were organized to ameliorate conditions among the labouring people.[107] They examined the question of insecure tenure, a problem which obliged workers to crowd their families into tiny wooden houses which they could easily set up on patches of estate land rented by the month and which they could just as easily carry away when their labour engagements ceased.[108] For the labouring people, these mobile arrangements constituted a serious impediment to the accumulation of the comforts of a civilized existence. While the concern of the planters may have been genuine, they did little of a practical nature to relieve the physical distress of the workers. They did not tax the land; they taxed articles consumed by the poor,[109] although admittedly those taxes were much lower than elsewhere in the British West Indies. They did not increase wages when the price of sugar rose in 1857 bringing unprecedented prosperity to the owners of estate property.[110] Instead they relied mainly on platitudes, committing themselves to the exercise of greater moral influence among their workers—an influence which usually took the form of advising them to abjure the purchase of fancy clothes and fancy funerals and to buy, instead, shingles for leaky roofs, dishes for daily use, and blankets to provide comfort for the sick. Thrift was considered a sign of civilization. What the workers needed, thought the planters, was a change of priorities, not an increase in wages.

The physical circumstances of the freedmen, not their immorality, dominated reports from Barbados. There was no reference to obeah or fear of an encroaching barbarism. The emphasis upon education as an antidote to galloping immorality was not prevalent as it was in Jamaica. The people were hard working and deferential—qualities thought appropriate for the 'lower orders' of society—and they remained among the most Europeanized working people in the Caribbean, a distinction

---

[107] C. Ready to T. D. Hill, 26 Oct. 1857, enclosed in C.O. 28/187, no. 52.

[108] Colebrooke to Newcastle, 7 June 1853, C.O. 28/178, no. 42.

[109] C. Ready to T. D. Hill, 26 Oct. 1857, enclosed in C.O. 28/187, no. 52; Walker to Newcastle, 27 Sept. 1859, C.O. 28/189, no. 66.

[110] In June 1857, Governor Hincks conjectured that the Barbados proprietors had never been more prosperous: 'estates were resold, having been held for a short period, at an advance of £5,000 to £6,000'. Hincks to Labouchere, 6 June 1857, C.O. 28/187, no. 28.

carried over from slave times.[111] There was a natural flow of attitudes and manners from whites to blacks, and blacks as well as whites expressed great pride in the island—an outspoken patriotism that was unparalleled in the West Indies and resented by colonists elsewhere.

Barbados had by far the most advanced physical and institutional infrastructure in the West Indian Colonies. The careenage of Bridgetown was twice enlarged; old wharves were rebuilt, new ones erected.[112] In addition to leper and insane asylums, the government of Barbados built, subsequently enlarged, and efficiently managed a General Hospital for Relief of the Sick Poor.[113] Its roadways were indisputably the best in the West Indies. Churches, chapels, and public buildings were kept in good repair.[114] A public jail with separate accommodation for seventy-two prisoners was erected at a cost of £28,000[115]—an elaborate facility by West Indian standards. These developments were commendable; they enhanced the quality of life in the colony and provided jobs for freedmen. But in individual terms the planters were too reluctant to share their prosperity with the working people in the form of higher wages or the selective elimination of import taxes. Public wealth and working-class poverty were the distinguishing marks of Barbados society, greatly exaggerated during the American Civil War, when high prices and dry weather produced dire shortages and civil unrest, filling the colony's jails with enfeebled people who had stolen growing crops in an attempt to survive.[116] Barbados planters had the best, perhaps the only, opportunity

[111] In 1838 Sylvester Hovey, an American professor who travelled in the West Indies at the request of the Executive Committee of the American Union for the Relief and Improvement of the Coloured Race, made a common observation that the freedmen of Barbados and Antigua were the most socially refined in the British Caribbean, a condition, Hovey thought, which derived from 'the refinement and civilization, which prevailed around them . . .' See his *Letters from the West Indies*, pp. 103, 123.

[112] Hincks to Newcastle, 15 Oct. 1861, C.O. 28/193, no. 55.

[113] Hamilton to Pakington, 13 Apr. 1852, C.O. 28/176, no. 20; Walker to Newcastle, 16 May 1863, C.O. 28/196, no. 14. Barbadian leadership was not demeaned by scandals like the one involving the General Hospital in Jamaica during the early sixties.

[114] Walker to Newcastle, 27 Sept. 1859, C.O. 28/189, no. 66.

[115] Colebrooke to Russell, 9 June 1855, C.O. 28/182, no. 46.

[116] In July 1863, there was rioting and looting on the estates; trash houses burned and cattle were mutilated. A law to revive corporal punishment for men was passed as an emergency measure. Walker to Newcastle, 25 July, 9 Aug. 1863, C.O. 28/196,

in the British Caribbean to achieve the most beneficent goals of the great experiment, the establishment of a commonwealth beneficial to proprietors and labourers alike. Regrettably, their narrow self-interest exceeded their generosity and freedmen were deprived the material prosperity essential to the growth of individual refinement.

Nowhere in the West Indies did society assume the form desired by the English proponents of emancipation in the 1830s. Free blacks embraced the superficial and material appurtenances of European society in the prosperous early years of freedom. But in Jamaica, the freedmen's assertion of economic and territorial independence and the combined impact of free trade and economic depression weakened the traditional social structure and widened the gap between European and Afro-Creole culture groups. In Barbados—and to a lesser extent in St. Kitts and Antigua—the planters, having little need to appease their workers, continued to exploit them without endeavouring sufficiently to uplift them. In Trinidad and British Guiana, black freedmen were being supplanted on the estates by East Indians; in the Windwards, private and public impoverishment precluded an improving social and civic life. In many colonies, public morality appeared at a low ebb, and petty crime with its attendant disrespect for law was increasing.

Emancipation had freed the slaves from bondage, but it could not liberate them from the hard circumstances of West Indian life. Directly or indirectly, public and private prosperity depended heavily on sugar, the only export commodity which, during the mid-century at least, was capable of linking the colonies to the commerce of the world. Those freedmen who produced it as well as those who fled its clutches were profoundly affected by the depression in sugar prices that set in after 1846. For ex-slaves, there was no clear road to progress and prosperity. What cane-workers in the high density colonies might have gained in superior civic amenities they sacrificed in personal independence and individual leisure. This pattern was simply inverted among highland peasants in Jamaica or the Windward Islands. With few exceptions, poverty had become the common condition of the labouring people by 1865.

nos. 161, 165. In 1863 more people were imprisoned in Barbados than in any previous year. Walker to Newcastle, 31 Oct. 1864, C.O. 28/199, no. 308.

CHAPTER 11

Religion and Education

APART from its intrinsic value, popular education in the West Indies, as in England, was considered an instrument of social control—a means by which the established classes could tame the multitudes, repress social barbarism, and preserve their own superior status.[1] With half the people of Great Britain illiterate, education in the mid-century remained a function of religion. People were schooled by rote or by catechism in the rudimentary precepts of the Christian faith and in their moral responsibilities to one another. The union of education and religion was even more pronounced in the West Indies where the great mass of liberated slaves had received little, if any, instruction in Christian doctrine. The Caribbean was regarded a fertile field for British missionaries, a place where the word of God must precede and envelop all other aspects of learning. In the 1820s, scores of missionaries gained a foothold in the sugar colonies, preaching to slaves on the limited sufferance of the masters. Even the Established Church changed its colours in those years. Between 1825 and 1834 the number of Anglican schools in the Lesser Antilles and British Guiana increased from 34 to 405, and the number of clergymen rose by 60 per cent;[2] concurrently, a new spirit of morality and missionary commitment infused the Established Church. Notoriously corrupt clergymen who had 'lived in open violation of the laws of God and man . . . indulging in the grossest sensuality'[3] were superseded by fresh recruits from the mother

---

[1] For modern expositions of this point, see Richard Allen Soloway, *Prelates and People: Ecclesiastical Social Thought in England, 1783–1852* (Toronto, 1969), ch. X; John Hurt, *Education in Evolution: Church, State, Society and Popular Education, 1800–1870* (London, 1971); Brian Simon, *Studies in the History of Education, 1780–1870* (London, 1960); David Wardle, *English Popular Education, 1780–1970* (Cambridge, 1970); Richard Johnson, 'Educational Policy and Social Control in Early Victorian England', *Past and Present*, no. 49 (1970), 96–119.

[2] See p. 411, n. 12.

[3] Flanders, *Antigua*, I, p. 145.

country. Missionaries became the champions of the people, scarcely concealing their repugnance to slavery. As agents of light in a sea of ignorance, they were the natural leaders and teachers of the people, a human bridge spanning the gap which separated white and black West Indians. But the task of educating and uplifting a population degraded by slavery was more formidable than the most discreet missionaries could have imagined. The people were inured to customs abhorrent to Christian society, and they possessed a legacy of African spiritual beliefs and an approach to religious matters which was more animated than reflective. The sheer physical hardship of reaching freedmen in mountainous islands with heavy seasonal rainfall became increasingly difficult after the dispersal of workers from estate villages. More important, however, was the question of funding. The construction and maintenance of schools and mission stations, as well as the subsistence of missionaries and teachers, required a steady flow of money. As in all other things, the funding of religious education in the British Caribbean depended to a large extent on the state of the sugar economy.

Metropolitan views on West Indian education were influenced by domestic English conditions. Education of the English poor had traditionally been a function of charity, not a matter for state action. But changing social and political conditions emanating from industrialization and urbanization compelled the ruling classes to devote greater attention to education as a means of protecting their status and property against attacks from angry bodies of the working poor. In 1833 the Government initiated monetary grants for the construction of school houses in England, Scotland, and Wales.[4] Six years later, under the shadow of Chartist agitation, a Committee of the Privy Council was created to supervise the distribution of public money to private educational charities.[5] Social control—the police factor—was a powerful catalyst to action. Adam Smith had acknowledged that the state would profit from widespread education which dampened the delusions, enthusiasm,

---

[4] £30,000 was granted for this purpose. After 1814, similar grants had been made for education in Ireland. John William Adamson, *English Education 1789–1902* (Cambridge, 1930), p. 34.

[5] Ibid., p. 124.

and superstition of the poor, rendering them less liable to violent disorder. A pivotal maxim of the Philosophical Radicals—the so-called 'education-mad party'—was that people filled with useful knowledge could be trusted to behave rationally. In a less doctrinaire fashion, the founders of Sunday schools, schools of industry, and evening schools had been dedicated to a similar proposition: they advocated practical piety and urged the poor to lead industrious upright lives. Indeed, such schools were considered an antidote to pauperism at a time when that condition was presumed to result from laziness, weak character, and an absence of self-respect.[6] In sum, education in the mother country, although charitable, unsystematized, poor, and piecemeal, was considered the most suitable device for reconciling working people to their lot in life. As late as 1862 a government spokesman declared that education for the poor was not intended to 'raise them above their station and business in life . . . but to . . . fit them for that business'.[7] Likewise, in the West Indies, religious instruction was deemed a noble device for uplifting the human spirit, controlling passion, and preserving the prevailing social order.

The planters were quick to recognize the disciplinary values of religious education. Those who had denied the missionaries access to their bondsmen for fear that they would arouse overt opposition to slavery welcomed the 'salutary influence' of moral and religious training once slavery had ended. James Phillippo, the Baptist missionary at Spanish Town, was asked to establish a school and chapel on virtually every plantation in his district: 'If I have had one acre of land offered me for this purpose,' he wrote, 'I have had a hundred, and in almost every case accompanied by the offer also of building materials and . . . labour.'[8] The missionaries, though generally disliked by planters, were deemed prospective allies of convenience capable of stabilizing the labouring people and inculcating in them a sense of social responsibility, thrift, and industry.[9]

[6] Charles Birchenough, *History of Elementary Education in England and Wales from 1800 to the Present Day* (London, 1930), pp. 10–11.

[7] Ibid., p. 161.   ·

[8] Edward Bean Underhill, *Life of James Mursell Phillippo* (London, 1881), p. 170. A Wesleyan in Antigua made a similar comment in 1837: 'There is not an estate in the country closed against us at this moment. We may preach on them; and we may, if we please, and *if we can*, establish schools on the same.' Robert Hawkins to J. Beecham, 28 Dec. 1837, *M.M.S. Papers*.

[9] See p. 412, n. 13.

Colonial governors hastened to enlist the missionaries as agents of public order. Sir Lionel Smith, a staunch Anglican in a colony (Barbados) dominated by the established clergy, perceived that a formal church where whites held distinct seats, where fees were demanded for marriages, funerals, and baptisms could not appeal to the freedmen. What was needed was cheap ministers and cheap places of worship: 'The object', he argued, 'is to diffuse the doctrines, and fix the belief of Christianity, and not to circumscribe its practice by any particular form of Faith.'[10] In company with other executives he appealed to the Crown for financial aid to missionaries, men who with humility and patience could carry their faith 'right into the Negro huts'.

In June 1833 the House of Commons pledged itself to assist the education of freedmen. During the next year the British Cabinet endorsed a plan for state subsidized religious and moral instruction which would enlist the services of the various 'pious' societies already engaged in charitable work in the West Indies.[11] Parliament approved a £25,000 annual subsidy for West Indian education, £20,000 of which was to be spent in general school construction and the remaining £5,000 in the creation of normal schools.[12] Because the mother country suffered a desperate shortage of trained teachers, it was essential that the colonies staff their own schools. The normal schools were conceived as non-denominational institutions capable of preparing teachers for various sectarian bodies. Agencies which accepted parliamentary funds for general school construction were expected to meet one-third the cost of the school buildings themselves.[13]

On the whole, the system worked well. In 1837 the parliamentary grant was raised to £30,000, and it remained at that figure through 1841. In the spring of 1837 C. J. Latrobe inspected schools throughout the West Indies in behalf of the British Government. His reports were generally encouraging, but he identified a number of problems. The most pervasive was the difference in attitude between planters and apprentices

---

[10] Smith to Glenelg, Confidential, 23 Aug. 1835, C.O. 28/116.
[11] Stanely Memorandum, n.d. (1834), C.O. 318/122.
[12] Grey to Stewart, 21 July 1835, C.O. 318/122, Treasury Correspondence.
[13] Grey to Campbell, draft, 31 Dec. 1835, C.O. 138/122.

concerning the purpose of education. Planters sought some method of combining practical industrial training with the cultivation of intellectual faculties, a position supported by Latrobe. But apprentices were averse to industrial training, recognizing it for what it was, a plan to persuade their children to continue in plantation service. Occasionally, territorial overlapping had occurred among missionary groups, and rivalries, sometimes unpleasant ones, had resulted. All the same Latrobe reported that education of freedmen was making rapid progress '. . . where one child went to school 10 years ago, hundreds may be enumerated; and where one man stood up in defence of the cause, 20 may be found to abet and to further it.'[14]

By far the most important private agency receiving a government educational subsidy in the West Indies was the Mico Charity. This remarkable institution, founded in the seventeenth century by Dame Jane Mico for redeeming Christian slaves from the Barbary states, had survived in profound idleness for 165 years while its assets multiplied from £2,000 to over £100,000. With Government prompting, the Charity was enlivened by additions to its Board of Trustees, and it was marshalled for the only endeavour which remotely resembled its initial purpose—the moral redemption of British West Indian slaves.[15] The Mico Charity offered exceptional flexibility. Having no natural denominational roots, it was able to approach the education of freedmen without the encumbrance of sectarian philosophy. While devoting attention to scripture and emphasizing moral and religious themes, it could operate free of chapels and preserve its non-denominational character by employing the methods of the British and Foreign School Society, the non-sectarian institution through which a substantial portion of the educational subsidy to English schools was being funnelled.[16] As a non-denominational charity, it was considered the most suitable agency for operations in colonies which had a heavy Roman Catholic population. By virtue of

[14] Quoted in Shirely C. Gordon, *A Century of West Indian Education* (London, 1963), p. 29.
[15] Mico Charity Correspondence, C.O. 318/122. The new trustees included Dr. Samuel Lushington, Sir Fowell Buxton, and James Stephen, the latter representing the British Government.
[16] Mico Charity Correspondence, C.O. 318/122.

contemporary prejudice, Catholics were not invited to participate in the parliamentary subsidy, and the Colonial Office requested the Mico Trustees to establish schools in Trinidad, Dominica, and the Windward Islands, Catholic areas where Protestant missionary activity had been comparatively slight.[17] In 1840, after five years of endeavour, the Mico Charity had established 138 day schools in the West Indies, reaching nearly 9,000 students (see Table 19). Its primary concern, however,

TABLE 19

Educational Provisions of the Mico Charity, December, 1840

Colony	Schools	Teachers	Day Students	Average Attendance	Sunday Scholars
Jamaica and Caymanas	30	40	2,541	1,796	1,897
Bahamas	19	14	712	527	388
Barbados	8	7	646	477	288
British Guiana	14	16	1,124	749	206
St. Vincent	5	8	432	350	145
Antigua and Montserrat	11	13	699	519	441
Tobago	4	5	151	131	102
Dominica	15	15	765	521	498
Grenada	5	5	331	231	153
St. Lucia	8	10	457	330	53
Trinidad	19	13	848*	848	320
Total	138	146	8,706	6,479	4,491

Source: Report of the Trustees of Lady Mico's Charity, bound in C.O. 318/156.
* Estimated.

was the founding of normal schools. Four of these, designed to lodge and board students, were set up in connection with model day schools in Jamaica, Antigua, Trinidad, and British Guiana. By December 1840, Mico normal schools had admitted 241 candidates, 158 of whom had assumed teaching appointments in schools of every religious denomination as well as in the day schools of the Mico Charity.[18]

[17] Carl Campbell, 'Denominationalism and the Mico Charity Schools in Jamaica 1835–1842', *Caribbean Studies*, X (1971), 154.
[18] *Report of the Trustees of Lady Mico's Charity* (London, 1841), bound in C.O. 318/156.

As schools mushroomed up throughout the colonies, competing missionary societies anxiously staked out spheres of influence and, not infrequently, committed themselves beyond their resources.[19] Conflicts among the societies were most intense in Jamaica.[20] The Methodists who had only one day school in the island in 1835 and the London Missionary Society and Mico Charity—the latter two having begun operations in the colony after emancipation—converged upon grounds already prospected by the Baptists. Natural competition, if not strife, between groups of missionaries was heightened by the methods used by Baptists. Pursuing a plan adopted during slavery, Baptist missionaries employed native ministers in numerous out-stations, men who lacked education and whose religious zeal was commonly tinctured by a variety of pagan beliefs. The practice of providing tickets to 'enquirers', and of totally immersing people during baptism, fired the imaginations of freedmen, giving wide vent to superstition. The correspondence of London missionaries, a strait-laced and comparatively well-educated group, teems with vociferous denunciation of the Baptists.[21] Revd. George Blyth a Presbyterian, wrote a stinging pamphlet, entitled *Remonstrances of the Presbytery of Jamaica with the Baptist Missionaries in that Island*, accusing the latter, as others did, of pandering to the superstitions of the people while extorting their money. The Baptists unhesitatingly retaliated,[22] and inter-sectarian feuds continued at a fierce level until the waning of Negro interest in Christian education, and the depression of the late forties, evoked mutual sympathy rather than discord among the diverse missionary bodies.

Pedagogical problems were exceptionally difficult in the West Indies. Children who learned to read relied on printed

[19] The cost of the Baptist mission in Jamaica leaped from £6,870 in 1840 to £9,701 in 1842 and in the same years the debt of the Baptist Missionary Society rose from £2,631 to £3,943. The mounting debt resulted principally from school and chapel construction. See, Underhill, *Life of Phillippo*, p. 202. Likewise, the expansion of Methodist facilities imposed a financial drain on the parent society. See, Findlay and Holdsworth, *History of Methodist Missionary Society*, II, pp. 322–4.

[20] These rivalries are well documented in Campbell's 'Denominationalism and the Mico Charity Schools'.

[21] Alloway to Tidman, 10 Jan. 1842; Wallbridge to Tidman, 29 Jan. 1842; Holland to Tidman, 27 July 1842; Milne to Tidman, n.d., 1842, *L.M.S. Papers, Jamaica*.

[22] *The Baptist Herald and Friend of Africa*, IV (20), 17 May 1843.

materials sent out from England, but the substance of those materials, their references to European flora and fauna, to changing seasons, and to other conditions familiar to English children, often mystified Caribbean youngsters.[23] The system of education normally employed in West Indian schools— whether Baptist, Anglican, or Mico—was monitorial. This plan, devised by Bell and Lancaster at the turn of the century, and employed respectively in National and British and Foreign schools, was entirely mechanical. Monitors who were advanced students taught, examined, promoted, and ministered to pupils under the over-all supervision of a schoolmaster.[24] The system was cheap and it offered the prospect of training large numbers of children in the mechanics of reading, writing, and simple arithmetic with very few teachers. But, if the teachers who were hastened through Mico normal schools with a few months' training[25] were limited in perspective and technique, the short-comings of their monitors were infinitely greater. The monitorial system was able to equip British children with basic techniques, and it encouraged them to be orderly and quiet. But in the West Indies where English was a quasi-foreign language for Creole children and where the religious precepts hammered at them were strange and confusing, the monitorial system had very limited utility. An inspector of schools in Jamaica reported that children who could read tolerably understood very little.[26] The massive acculturation sought through religious and moral instruction required patient personal communication between pupils and teachers. By no means, however, could the colonies or the mother country produce teachers enough to approach remotely this pedagogical ideal, and many

[23] This was especially true of British Guiana. The people knew nothing of hills, valleys, rocks, and running streams, of flocks and herds. Few of them had seen a stone, except those brought in for construction purposes. Consequently, wrote an independent missionary, they were unable to understand the most beautiful English hymns, and they could not comprehend many of the figurative sections of scripture. Charles Rattray to Tidman, 22 Feb. 1854, *L.M.S. Papers, British Guiana.*
[24] H. C. Barnard, *A Short History of English Education* (London, 1947), pp. 63–5.
[25] Report to the Jamaica Board of Education by J. F. Cargill, Inspector of Schools, enclosed in C. E. Grey to Earl Grey, 20 Sept. 1847, C.O. 137/293, no. 91. Mr. Cargill observed teachers who had spent two to six months in the Mico Normal School, whereas, he thought, 'three years would have been barely sufficient to give an intellectual ground-work with a readiness in the art of teaching.'
[26] Ibid.

of the teachers labouring in West Indian schools were woefully deficient in understanding.

When initiating the imperial grant for West Indian education, the Colonial Office urged Caribbean governments to appropriate money from their own resources to promote Negro education.[27] The Crown colonies responded fairly well. British Guiana voted approximately £2,500[28] for religious education in both 1836 and 1837. Latrobe reported that no other British colony so unhesitatingly met the wishes of the metropolitan Government.[29] At a lower level, Trinidad produced funds for education, distributing money, on application, to Anglican,[30] Catholic, and Wesleyan groups.[31] The legislative colonies were not so co-operative. Jamaica did not vote a general subsidy for education until 1844 when the imperial grant was beginning to dry up; even then, the money allotted was merely £2,000–£3,000 annually.[32] The Barbados legislature only began general educational appropriations in 1846 with a grant of £750.[33] The limited and belated nature of these subsidies reflected the colonists' pedagogical and religious biases not their opposition to educating the poor. In the older dependencies, where the Established Church gratified the conservative instincts of the planter élite, legislatures were inclined to direct public spending to Anglican schools and churches rather

[27] Grey to Stewart, 21 July 1835, C.O. 318/122. Treasury Correspondence. A circular letter to this effect was sent to the colonies on 25 Nov. 1835.

[28] Smyth to Glenelg, 11 May 1836, C.O. 111/145, no. 157; Moohr, 'Economic Impact of Emancipation', p. 593.

[29] Latrobe wrote, 'there are but few instances to be met with in which the zeal and activity of the resident Clergy or Missionaries has not been fully and frankly seconded by the good-will or munificence of gentlemen in the possession or in the charge of estates.' Latrobe to Glenelg, 14 August 1838, C.O. 318/137.

[30] The Anglican Church was comparatively feeble in Trinidad as a result of the terms of capitulation which provided for the maintenance of the religion of the capitulants.

[31] Hill to Glenelg, 25 May 1836, C.O. 295/111, no. 58; Hill to Glenelg, 5 July 1838, C.O. 295/121, no. 68; MacLeod to Russell, 7 May 1841, C.O. 295/133, no. 42; MacLeod to Stanley, 1 Dec. 1843, C.O. 295/140, no. 72.

[32] Elgin to Stanley, 15 Jan. 1845, C.O. 137/283, no. 5. Although the original approbation was only for £1,000, that amount was enlarged to £2,000 and sometimes £3,000 by additional appropriation in the Poll Tax. Also, liberal grants were made to the support of Anglican Church schools. Barkly to Labouchere, 18 Mar. 1856, C.O. 137/331, no. 47.

[33] Grey to Gladstone, 3 Aug. 1846, C.O. 28/164, no. 45; Schomburgk, *History of Barbados*, pp. 108-10.

than to competing missionary groups. In Barbados, local vestries and the colonial legislature produced £8,623 to support the Established Church in 1840, and during that year the Church spent £4,285 for religious education of the poor, exclusive of its even greater outlay for salaries to curates and chaplains who performed an educational function.[34] An Act for keeping Anglican clergymen in the rural districts was designed to provide continuous clerical supervision for parish schools. Some vestries voted money to meet teachers' salaries and to relieve the poor from paying fees for education, and in Barbados, as elsewhere, private persons liberally donated land, materials, labour, and money for the erection of schools.[35] The voluntary principle in education held high ground in the West Indies, as it did in Britain, and as long as the British Government was willing to subsidize dissenting missionary bodies, ruling elements in the legislative colonies were disposed to confine their public spending to the Established Church. When metropolitan subsidies ceased, the colonists stepped in, though rather cautiously, to fill some of the void.

The imperial grant to West Indian education ended in 1845. Five years earlier Lord John Russell had decided to reduce the subsidy by 20 per cent per annum until it ran out. It is somewhat ironic, but not incongruous, that this decision was taken by the British minister who had most distinguished himself as an advocate of extensive state-subsidized education. Between 1835 and 1841 the metropolitan Government had appropriated as much public money for West Indian education as it had for education in Great Britain[36] despite the fact that the population of the Caribbean colonies was less than one-twentieth that of the mother country. It was generally believed in England that West Indian freedmen enjoyed a higher material standard of life than the working poor of the home islands. The advance of

[34] MacGregor to Russell, 38 Jan. 1841, C.O. 28/139, no. 12. The total income for the Established Church during the year was £17,635: of that, £7,900 came from the imperial Treasury, £4,134 from the colonial Treasury; £4,489 from parochial funds, and £1,112 from a grant of the Society for the Propagation of the Gospel.
[35] T. Parry, Archdeacon, to Darling, 2 Aug. 1841, enclosed in C.O. 28/140, no. 12.
[36] In both cases the amount of the annual subsidy was £30,000. In 1842 the grant in Britain was increased by £10,000; in 1845 it rose to £75,000; and between 1848 and 1850 the yearly vote was £125,000. Adamson, *English Education*, p. 146.

technology in Britain, coupled with a widening of the franchise in 1832, created a sense of urgency regarding the education of lower class children, only 40–50 per cent of whom were receiving any form of instruction at all.[37] Russell believed it inappropriate that the working people of Great Britain should continue indefinitely to subsidize education in the sugar colonies considering, as he noted, 'how much better able the Negroes are to pay for the education of their children than our labourers'.[38] Since at that point correspondence from the colonies commonly referred to the enthusiasm with which freedmen embraced education, the Government assumed that most black parents would willingly pay a small fee to educate their children. Indeed, James Stephen observed that the Baptists, who by their own choosing had not yet received[39] any part of the imperial subsidy, had large congregations and numerous schools. By operating on the voluntary principle and insisting on payments from parents, the Baptists had shown, Stephen believed, 'that the cause of Education may prosper even after the Parliamentary Grant shall have been withdrawn.'[40] Missionary Societies were expected to maintain their usual rate of investment in colonial education after imperial subsidies ended, and it was deemed appropriate that island governments, having had a basic educational infrastructure already established, would assume some of the funding responsibilities being relinquished by the British Government.

Of all the groups working in the West Indies, none was more distressed by the withdrawal of the imperial grant than the Mico Charity. In 1840–1, the Charity had expended nearly £30,000 of its own funds in addition to the government subsidy. The Trustees declared that the institution was incapable of pursuing its West Indian programme at the existing level without a continuing government subsidy.[41] They were angry that the Government, having encouraged the Charity to overextend itself financially, would refuse to exercise enough patience and fortitude to see the seeds it had sown bear har-

[37] Ibid., p. 29.
[38] Minute by Russell on draft circular, 18 Mar. 1841, C.O. 318/152.
[39] The Baptists began receiving government aid in 1842.
[40] Minute, Stephen to Hope, 24 Sept. 1841, bound in C.O. 318/152.
[41] Trew to Stanley, 9 May 1843, C.O. 318/163.

vest.[42] The Trustees warned of a return to barbarism, of black children who were 'suffered from tender infancy to run wild, as in a state of nature—sunk in vice and ignorance, and living unblushingly in the practice of crimes too horrid to relate',[43] but their alarming testimony could not move the Government from its decision to withdraw funding. In 1842 the Charity began breaking up its schools in all sugar colonies saving the Catholic islands of Trinidad, St. Lucia, and Dominica. It chose to retain two normal schools and the attached model day schools in Jamaica and Antigua, but the remainder of its day schools were either abandoned or transferred to missionary societies.[44]

From the outset of freedom, planters had insisted that a system of education which omitted practical industrial training was ill-suited to the realities of Caribbean life. When the imperial grant ceased and colonial governments assumed greater responsibility for supporting general education, legislators placed heavy emphasis on industrial training. A stipendiary magistrate in Jamaica expressed the prevailing view:

The ability to read and write, which, in England, directs and stimulates a man's energies in his sphere of life, in Jamaica incapacitates him for any employment but that which is really above him. The consequence is, that a class of persons is produced, with only education sufficient to give them an exaggerated opinion of their own consequence, which disqualifies them for manual labour, without enabling them to obtain employment in the sphere to which they aspire.[45]

[42] Trew to Russell, 22 June 1841, C.O. 318/151; Stokes to Hope, 27 Apr. 1842, C.O. 318/156. The Charity had placed 167 teachers, 52 of them European, in some of the most backward districts of the West Indies.

[43] *Report of the Trustees of Lady Mico's Charity* (London, 1841), p. 68, bound in C.O. 318/156.

[44] The transfers were accomplished with little difficulty. Mico Charity schools had been less nondenominational than the Trustees were willing to acknowledge, for the teachers who functioned in them were drawn from one denomination or another, and hard experience had taught local administrators of the Charity to place Baptist teachers in schools located in Baptist areas and Methodist teachers in schools where the population was heavily Methodist. When the question of transfer arose, the several denominations hastened to absorb Mico schools in their respective areas. The only schools in Jamaica not transferred were those occupying rented premises. Campbell, 'Denominationalism and the Mico Charity Schools', pp. 168–72.

[45] Report of Alexander Fyfe, May 1845, enclosed in Elgin to Stanley, 2 Sept. 1845, C.O. 137/284, no. 79.

Lord Elgin offered a prize for the best essay treating the topic
of industrial education for Jamaica.[46] The parish of St.
James established a society for promoting industrial education and
promised money premiums to teachers who achieved success in
that mode of instruction.[47] The first Act in support of general
education in Jamaica appropriated £300 to establish an experimental normal school for industrial training; and an additional
£700 for existing schools, with priority being given to those
offering an industrial curriculum.[48] To the chagrin of the
assemblymen, only four of the 113 schools that applied for aid
under the Act offered any form of industrial education.[49]

It was one thing to advocate industrial training, and quite
another to implement it. Worth-while industrial education
which emphasized the union of science and agriculture required teachers who possessed a knowledge of scientific principles as well as a practical acquaintance with cane cultivation.
Such people with interest or ability in teaching were rare in
the colonies, and there was always the danger that ill-
managed industrial training would lapse into rude instruction
in the use of hoe and bill. Furthermore, it was necessary to
conquer the problem of motive. Although West Indian blacks
regarded field-work as debasing, any system of industrial training in the sugar colonies must necessarily have involved
practical work in cane culture. It was the planters' hope that
the repugnance to freedmen of cultivating sugar would be
moderated if agriculture were studied as a medium of science.[50]

No one was more enthusiastic about industrial education
than Earl Grey, the Secretary of State. At his request, Dr.
J. P. Kay-Shuttleworth, the outstanding figure in British
education, drew up a plan for West Indian industrial schools
which was circulated throughout the colonies.[51] There was no

[46] Elgin to Stanley, 23 Oct. 1844, C.O. 317/280, no. 119. Elgin received 19
essays on the subject.
[47] Report of H. Laidlaw, Nov. 1844, enclosed in Elgin to Stanley, 27 Feb. 1845,
C.O. 137/283, no. 23.
[48] Elgin to Stanley, 15 Jan. 1845, C.O. 137/283, no. 5.
[49] Report of the Board of Education, enclosed in Elgin to Stanley, 17 Dec.
1845, C.O. 137/285, no. 103.
[50] Report to the Jamaica Board of Education, enclosed in C. E. Grey to Earl
Grey, 20 Sept. 1847, C.O. 137/293, no. 91.
[51] Kay-Shuttleworth was Secretary to the Committee of the Privy Council and
the person who historians of education refer to as the founder of popular education

shortage of proposals for industrial training, but the bulk of the plans formulated were costly utopian schemes. In reality, the colonists were having a hard time maintaining the small institutions they had already established. The advent of the industrial normal school in Jamaica had coincided with the onrush of economic depression. After a year and a half, it produced only two teachers and maintained merely eight pupils. It received no funding in the economic crisis of 1848–9, and when funding was resumed (£1,000) in 1850, only three of the former pupils returned to the school, and the master promptly left in favour of holy orders in the Established Church.[52] The rocky and ill-fated early history of the industrial school which was, in itself, a mere wisp in the winds of Jamaica's broader educational problem, must have sobered practical men concerning their competence to deal with the mounting social problems of the colony.

Several converging factors in the mid-forties dampened the prospects for West Indian education. The Sugar Duties Act undermined the public spirit of the upper and middle classes, and economic depression affected the capacity of either the state or individual citizens to meet the cost of education. But even before these two hazards arose, blacks had begun to exhibit impatience with formal schooling. Missionary and magisterial correspondence which had described bulging schools and chapels in the late thirties and early forties[53] had begun to paint a different picture by 1845. Methodist membership in the sugar islands reached its peak in 1844; thereafter, it sagged steadily.[54] The Baptist missions in Jamaica, which in the bloom of their prosperity had severed their connection with the parent society, suffered increasing financial hardship from

in Britain. His proposal for the colonies was entitled *Brief Practical Suggestions on the Mode of Organizing and Conducting Day-Schools of Industry, Model Farm Schools, and Normal Schools, as Part of a System of Education for the Coloured Races of the British Colonies.*

[52] *Votes of the Jamaica Assembly*, 1851–2, Appendix XXIX.

[53] The report of Henry Britten, a Methodist in Nevis, was typical of the period immediately following emancipation: 'The market-people crowd our chapels; they almost suffocate each other and the Preacher too, the very windows being choked up by them!' Between 1833 and 1840, the number of Wesleyan missionaries increased from 54 to 85, and church membership grew by 50 per cent, from 32,000 to 48,000. In Jamaica alone, Wesleyan membership doubled in those years. Findlay and Holdsworth, *History of Methodist Missionary Society*, II, pp. 327–8.

[54] Ibid, pp. 341–2, 371–2.

the secession of whole congregations and from successive droughts which reduced the capacity of peasants to pay school and chapel fees.[55] Summarizing the reports of stipendiary magistrates, Lord Elgin asserted that black parents, having discovered that elementary book learning—tedious in itself—did not alter social status, withdrew children from school, preferring to occupy them in menial tasks at home.[56] There were other considerations as well. The burst of enthusiasm attending emancipation had passed, and the loyalty of freedmen to missionaries who had befriended them in slavery had waned. The younger generation of schoolchildren knew little or nothing of earlier loyalties, and lessons on morality taught in mission schools were directly contradicted by routine practices in peasant villages. European missionaries offered a rigorous Christianity in which there was no room for intemperance, though rum was a fixture of Caribbean consumption. Lying, quarrelling, and pilfering—habits long cultivated in slavery— were strongly denounced. Fornication was utterly condemned by the missionaries, though lifelong sexual fidelity and the concept of female virtue were alien to a black Caribbean culture moulded by slavery. Unless European education and religion could have offered tangible benefits in compensation for their excessive rigour, they could not have indefinitely attracted a people whose racial identity, social patterns, and spiritual inclinations were consistently offended by European teaching.

The financial pressure on missionary schools and chapels was magnified in the late forties. Missions fell into disrepair; schools were closed; and missionaries and teachers endured severe privation.[57] Their perpetual appeals for contributions were maddening to their parishioners who, becoming weary with the 'money story', dubbed the members of one society 'macaronihunters'. The ruination of sugar estates increased the missionaries' difficulties. Writing from British Guiana, Charles

---

[55] Long, *Jamaica*, p. 54.
[56] Elgin to Stanley, 3 Aug. 1845, confidential, C.O. 137/284.
[57] J. Cox to General Secretary, 5 Apr. 1848, *M.M.S. Papers, Antigua*; Report of W. G. Barrett, 31 Dec. 1847, *L.M.S. Papers, British Guiana*. Central mission offices in Britain encouraged their agents in the field to become self-sustaining; when they could not, missionaries were subject to official berating and chastisement. Findlay and Holdsworth, *History of Methodist Missionary Society*, II, pp. 359–60.

Rattray feared his mission would not be able to endure: the main canal was being neglected; it was filling with silt; the three or four bridges over it were falling down; and within a short time, he expected, it would be 'impossible to traverse the upper part of the district except on foot, and that through mud and rank grass . . .'[58] In his diary, James Phillippo lamented the demoralization of the Jamaica Baptists, a number of whom had left the island because their dwindling congregations could not support them.[59] An Antigua missionary believed that the Methodist establishment there would collapse if the estates fell, and he urged his superiors in London to use all their influence with the Government and Parliament to achieve a repeal of the Sugar Duties Act.[60]

Despite poverty and declining numbers, most of the mission stations hung on; but by 1850 the moral force of European missionaries was spent, their energies sapped, their influence abated. Although they tried to cultivate a 'native agency'— a corps of black pastors—to complement and ultimately supersede them in the West Indies, the most highly disciplined sectarians found few freedmen able to tolerate their rigid ethical codes.[61] The Baptists, whose discipline was comparatively lax, discovered that some native agents aggrandized the congregations of white missionaries and that others pursued practices which layered Christian ritual with pagan concepts. The chapel of James Phillippo in Spanish Town was twice the scene of violent disorder. Phillippo quarrelled with his black assistant, Thomas Dowson, and the congregation split. When one of Dowson's followers died in March 1845, Phillippo refused to permit his burial in the chapel cemetery. Dowson's people stormed the cemetery in the middle of the night, buried the corpse, and were promptly attacked by a body of Phillippo's followers. A mob grew; by morning the chapel was a scene of turmoil; and Phillippo appealed to the militia to restore order.[62] Although white missionaries in the island were perfectly divided as to which party was at fault, all of them recognized

---

[58] Rattray to Tidman, 21 Mar. 1849, *L.M.S. Papers, British Guiana.*
[59] Underhill, *Life of Phillippo*, p. 245.
[60] Cox to General Secretary, 25 Oct. 1847, *M.M.S. Papers, Antigua.*
[61] See p. 412, n. 14.
[62] Phillippo to Angus, 7 Apr. 1845, *Phillippo Papers,* Baptist Missionary Society.

that the labour of many years had been tarnished, and that the
worthiness and credibility of their Society had suffered a major
blow.[63] Six years later, a second mob stormed Phillippo's
house, destroyed his furniture, injured his wife, and might well
have killed him had the militia not arrived.[64] Revd. Samuel
Oughton, one of Phillippo's white critics, suffered a similar fate
when dissension arose in his Kingston chapel.[65]

As these events suggest, the people's interest in religion did
not diminish in the late forties and fifties; it merely changed.
While white missionaries deplored backsliding and the demise
of religious feeling, a stipendiary magistrate in Jamaica was
able to report that 'meeting houses with Black Preachers were
springing up on all sides.'[66] Black preachers became the bane of
white missionaries, invading their territories and depleting their
congregations. Whether self-appointed or briefly trained
through a European society, these black religious leaders were
invariably accused by their white competitors of ignorance,
superstition, deceitfulness, and extortion. By way of illustration,
a black catechist in the Established Church of British Guiana,
R. C. Henderson, was lured to Canada by an American freedman who was touring Demerara to raise funds for fugitive slaves.
Promptly ordained in the 'Independent Methodist Episcopal
Church of Canada', Henderson returned to Demerara preaching that blacks should cleave to their colour and abandon their
white ministers.[67] Using the theme of white persecution, his
ministry rapidly gained momentum, and in the early fifties
he returned to Canada, where he was designated Bishop with a
competence to ordain other black preachers. White missionaries were aghast. Their scarcely literate competitor had a
quick wit and a glib tongue; he had enormous appeal to the
peasantry, and he and his followers were systematically eroding the congregations of the white missionaries. One Independent, referring to Henderson, wrote:

[63] Abbott, Day, Henderson, Hewett to Angus, 10 Apr. 1845; Abbott to Angus, 22
Apr. 1845, Evants to Angus, 20 Apr. 1845; Hands to Angus, 19 Apr. 1845, B.M.S.
Papers.
[64] C. E. Grey to Earl Grey, 24 July 1851, C.O. 137/310, no. 63.
[65] Barkly to Grey, 12 Mar. 1855, C.O. 137/326, no. 24.
[66] Report of H. Kent, enclosed in Barkly to Newcastle, 21 Feb. C.O. 137/322,
no. 24.
[67] Barrett to Tidman, 4 Mar. 1846; Henderson to Tidman, 18 Jan. 1851;
Wallbridge to Tidman, 26 Jan. 1852, L.M.S. Papers, British Guiana.

. . . he panders to the prejudices, passions, and depraved tastes of the creoles, who will readily listen to such a man, especially if he has plenty to say against the whites, and particularly white ministers. These he represents as tyrants and oppressors of the people, whose aim is to enrich themselves and keep the creoles in a state of darkness, servitude and degradation.[68]

Without question, race had become an important factor in the religious loyalties of the freedmen. In fact, the issue of colour had consistently plagued the churches. Even in the thirties a splinter Methodist church had arisen in Jamaica over the alleged prejudice of white ministers toward rising men of colour.[69] The sense of cultural superiority so clearly expressed in the correspondence of white missionaries was bound to appear in their daily demeanour. Blacks resented this, and white ministers found themselves charged with racism even when discrimination was not being practised.[70]

At no time in the early decades of freedom did emancipated blacks discard their African spiritual heritage. This legacy lay barely concealed beneath a thin layer of catechetical Christianity. Even when the Christian churches were having their greatest success, in 1842, an outbreak of myalism swept through the Jamaica parishes causing the temporary desertion of estates while highly excited people searched out evil spirits by digging in the earth or assaulting persons thought to be possessed of them.[71] Interestingly, the leaders of the movement professed to be acting under the command of Jesus Christ. This merger of Christian terms and pagan belief became more commonplace as spiritual leadership passed from missionaries to uneducated native preachers.

Obeah manifested itself increasingly in the 1850s, and the Jamaica House of Assembly, without opposition, passed an Act to stiffen punishment for the persons found guilty of practising it. Revd. R. Thomas Banbury, a native of the island, wrote a

[68] Henderson to Tidman, 18 Jan. 1854, *L.M.S. Papers, British Guiana.*
[69] Findlay and Holdsworth, *History of Methodist Missionary Society,* II, 329–333.
[70] When, for example, an Independent refused to Baptize a child because he did not know the parents and was not satisfied that they comprehended the meaning of the ceremony, he was accused by the father of refusing because the parents were black. Barrett to Tidman, 15 Aug. 1846, *L.M.S. Papers, British Guiana.*
[71] Elgin to Stanley, 30 Jan. 1843, C.O. 137/273, no. 81; Waddell, *Twenty-Nine Years,* pp. 187–92.

pamphlet entitled *Jamaica Superstitions; or the Obeah Book* in which he claimed that all the black people in the colony having Christian religious connections were imbued with a belief that obeah was capable of exerting evil effects upon their minds, bodies, or properties.[72] Belief in obeah was not confined to blacks, he argued; a majority of the coloured people and some of the whites were also affected by it. Although its outward manifestations were most common in the hill country, its influence was evident everywhere. Governor Barkly declared that most of the murders committed in the three years he had been in Jamaica were attributable to the activities of obeahmen.[73]

One index of the effectiveness of Christian education in the West Indies was the readiness with which freedmen adopted the European concept of marriage. No aspect of village life disturbed missionaries so much or led to so much preaching as concubinage and sexual promiscuity. Methodists insisted on monogamy and sexual fidelity, and a breach of either often led to expulsion from the church.[74] Fornication, wrote an Independent, was the besetting sin of the colonies. Young people preferred it to religion and consequently the churches were shorn of youthful members.[75] In the early days of freedom, the threat of expulsion from a Christian church carried great force, and it was used by missionaries to influence the behaviour of freedmen. By the late forties that form of discipline was ineffectual. The incidence of marriage among freedmen, having increased rapidly during apprenticeship and the early forties, fell sharply in later years.[76] By the mid-fifties stipendiary

---

[72] This pamphlet was written around 1860 but not published until 1894. It is quoted in J. J. Williams, S.J., *Psychic Phenomena of Jamaica* (New York, 1934), pp. 92–4.

[73] At the time of his writing one such person was under sentence of death for having administered poison to a respectable person whom he had never seen but was hired to 'obeah'. Barkly to Labouchere, 9 April 1856, C.O. 137/331, no. 52.

[74] Edwards to General Secretary, 22 June 1838, *M.M.S. Papers, Nevis.*

[75] Henderson to Tidman, 2 Aug. 1847, *L.M.S. Papers, British Guiana.*

[76] Schomburgk's statistics for Barbados are typical: the number of marriages performed in 1835 were 634; 1836, 939; 1837, 980; 1838, 1,471; 1839, 1,909; 1840, 1,371; 1841, 1,120; 1842, 1,139; 1843, 1,047; 1844, 779; 1845, 651. See his *History of Barbados*, p. 89. Statistics for the parishes of Manchester, Vere, and St. Ann (Jamaica) show a great increase in marriages between 1834 and 1843; thereafter the numbers fall quickly coinciding with the declining influence of European missionaries. See, Long, *Jamaica*, p. 6, appendix D.

magistrates in Jamaica uniformly regretted that marriage ties were thoroughly disregarded by the peasantry.[77]

In the mid-fifties several stipendiary magistrates in Jamaica advocated the establishment of compulsory public education, arguing that morality among the labouring class had become so degraded that the young could only be redeemed by steady draughts of moral and religious instruction.[78] The concept of compulsory public education had been mooted in the colonies shortly after emancipation, and—though it was not adopted in England until the 1870s—the British Government had supported it in principle.[79] Nevertheless, a vast gulf separated the concept of mandatory schooling from the practical means required to accomplish it. A compulsory system would have involved state aid, state inspection, and state enforcement. To such a plan there were overwhelming philosophical, monetary, physical, and attitudinal obstacles. Taking the case of Jamaica, both the outstanding spokesmen for improved education and the bulk of the island's schoolmasters opposed a mandatory system. Richard Hill, one of the former, argued that blacks, having emerged from slavery, were fundamentally opposed to the compulsory principle and that a system of mandatory education would involve prohibitively high costs merely to enforce attendance.[80] Baptists, Independents, and some Presbyterians—advocates of the voluntary principle—had staunchly refused to accept monetary subsidies from the Jamaican Government, and even those who had (Moravians, Methodists, and Anglicans) opposed extensive government involvement in education for fear that it would lead to control.[81] Furthermore,

[77] Reports of stipendiary magistrates, enclosed in Barkly to Newcastle, 21 Feb. 1854, C.O. 137/322, no. 24.

[78] Reports of Dillon, Laidlow, Emery, and Chamberlaine, enclosed in Barkly to Newcastle, 21 Feb. 1854, C.O. 137/322, no. 24.

[79] Glenelg to Smyth, 14 Dec. 1835, C.O. 112/20, no. 64. In that dispatch, Glenelg argued that 'neither the caprice of an Employer, nor the ignorant prejudices of Parents, must be allowed to obstruct a measure which lies at the root of all Social improvement . . .' In another dispatch, Glenelg claimed that compulsory education, while not then desirable in England, was appropriate in the West Indies. Draft, Glenelg to MacGregor, 28 Nov. 1836, bound in C.O. 28/117, no. 53.

[80] Report of Richard Hill, enclosed in Barkly to Grey, 18 Sept. 1854, C.O. 137/324, no. 101.

[81] Carl Campbell, 'Social and Economic Obstacles to the Development of Popular Education in Post-Emancipation Jamaica, 1834–1865', *Journal of Caribbean History*, I (1970), 84.

after 1850 the focus of British missionary attention had moved to Africa and the East, and it was unlikely that the several societies active in the West Indies would produce the additional teachers required to support a mandatory system even if equipped with the financial means of doing so. Qualified teachers were in short supply throughout the colonies, and local normal schools could not produce the personnel to staff a compulsory public system. After 22 years the Mico institution at Kingston had produced only 201 teachers.[82] Education was expensive and no Caribbean government could justify spending the amount required for a compulsory system. Furthermore, there was no economic incentive for educating all West Indians. Emancipation had not altered the fundamental character of the colonial economy. No new industry had arisen requiring craft skills or literacy; in fact, in many colonies the demand for technical competence had subsided with the decline of the estates. In Europe and North America, advancing technology stimulated a demand for skilled workmen and educated technicians, managers and foremen. The depressed agrarian economy of the West Indies evoked no such demand. Save in the area of teaching, employment opportunities were extremely limited for lower class children who might have obtained a measure of formal education.

The same arguments employed against compulsory schooling were used to keep state grants to education at a low level. Since many sectarian groups refused in principle to accept state money, they opposed any plan which would funnel public funds to religious rivals. For their part, the labouring people exhibited decreasing interest in formal schooling. Whether disappointed by poor teaching, by the inefficiency of many schools, or by the failure to achieve social mobility through education, blacks were disposed increasingly to keep their children at home employed in their own service. In Trelawny, where there was a heavy concentration of missionary establishments, a magistrate observed in 1854 that schools were almost deserted.[83] Arguing that blacks were not using existing facilities, white planters objected to higher taxes for education.[84]

[82] S. Whitehouse to Darling, 12 Oct. 1858, enclosed in C.O. 137/339, no. 132.
[83] Campbell, 'Social and Economic Obstacles', pp. 77–86.
[84] Curtin, *Two Jamaicas*, p. 159.

Conditions had arrived at an impasse. Compassionate men could see no hope for the regeneration of society, save through more extensive moral and religious instruction, but the people marked out for regeneration had grown sour on formal education. Moreover, the vicissitudes of the economy, the attitudes of sectarian groups, and the quality and extent of human resources in the West Indies rendered high public appropriations for education impossible.

The Jamaica Government spent only about £3,000 per annum for education during the final ten years of the period treated by this study—an average of merely 1½d. per person each year.[85] An attempt to double that amount in 1856 was beaten back by planters as well as by sectarian missionaries who disapproved of the concept of state aid.[86] Baptists were the most vocal of the latter group. Since the early forties they had campaigned for the disestablishment of the Anglican Church in Jamaica, and being consistent to their principles, they denounced any plan of state support to religious bodies. By 1865 there were fewer pupils enrolled in Jamaican schools than during the final years of apprenticeship.[87]

Writing about Jamaica in 1860, Henry Taylor declared that the neglect of Negro education was an inevitable consequence of the imperial Government's failure to establish a Crown colony system at the beginning of the free period.[88] Taylor's contention is not borne out by reference to conditions in the Crown colonies. Although British Guiana maintained a comparatively high level of public support to schools, the progress

---

[85] The average annual expenditure on education increased in Jamaica after the island became a Crown colony. Expenditures doubled between 1861 and 1871 and more than doubled again in the next decade. Between 1872 and 1876, annual expenditures averaged £19,300. This figure when compared to earlier statistics is deceptive. When the Anglican Church was disestablished in 1869 the money normally spent on schools through the agency of the church was disbursed through the Government, giving the appearance of a sharper rise in educational expenditures than actually occurred. As late as 1881 nearly all adult Europeans in Jamaica could read and write; 80 per cent of the adult coloured population could read and write; but less than 10 per cent of the adult Negro population possessed these skills. For statistics on literacy and educational expenditures, see Gordon, ed., *West Indian Education*, pp. 92–3.

[86] Campbell, 'Social and Economic Obstacles', pp. 77–86.

[87] Curtin, *Two Jamaicas*, p. 159.

[88] Taylor's marginal note on Darling to Newcastle, 29 Mar. 1860, C.O. 137/349, no. 49.

of education in Trinidad was disappointing. Because the Catholic Church was firmly entrenched in that colony, the practice of distributing educational subsidies through religious bodies was abandoned in favour of a system of secular instruction. The secular plan pleased none of the competing religious groups, and because it received neither inspiration nor guidance from the Government, it made little progress. By 1870 there were fewer pupils and fewer schools than had been the case in 1846.[89]

Barbados had the most cohesive and symmetrical educational system. Being a densely peopled, prosperous community, with the population predominantly Anglican, it was the only colony in which compulsory primary education could have been seriously attempted. By 1860 every district in the island possessed a primary school, and the Government Inspector claimed that the state of education was progressing on a par with that of England.[90] This assertion was not as outrageous as it might appear. During the 1850s—a period of considerable distress in the colonies—the Government of Barbados spent more money *per capita* for education than the British Government.[91] The Central School in Bridgetown, long since established by the philanthropy of an English family, was transformed from an Anglican institution serving the poor to a teacher training school.[92] Codrington College, the oldest and most renowned institution in the West Indies, was equipped by Bishop Coleridge to offer degrees in divinity.[93] All told, Barbados had the means, the geographical compactness, and the institutional base to achieve an extremely high rate of primary school enrolments. Regrettably, it did not. Probably not more than 30 per cent of the people between ages 5 and 15 received formal day school education at any time during the period of this study,

[89] Wood, *Trinidad in Transition*, pp. 225–8.

[90] Hincks to Newcastle, 15 Oct. 1861, C.O. 28/193, no. 55.

[91] In 1850 a Board of Education was established in Barbados with an appropriation of £3,000—an amount constituting 5·2 pence per person for the year. The British subsidy for education in England, Scotland, and Wales in 1851 was £150,000, or the equivalent of 1·6 pence per person. The differential between the two figures decreased through the decade as educational subsidies in Britain grew substantially larger. Hamilton to Pakington, 13 Apr. 1852, C.O. 28/176, no. 20; Adamson, *English Education*, p. 202.

[92] Walker to Lytton, 7 Apr. 1859, C.O. 28/189, no. 24.

[93] Schomburgk, *History of Barbados*, pp. 111–23.

and in the late fifties and sixties many primary schools were poorly attended.[94] Laissez-faire was the prevailing doctrine of the age, and in view of the social control already in evidence in Barbados, planter oligarchs could see no reason for expanding educational opportunities beyond the people's natural demand for them.

Had the sectarian schoolmasters of the colonies encouraged heavier state subsidies, had the schools been more efficiently operated, had economic incentives been operating, had the black peasantry exhibited a greater interest in elementary education, and had the ruling class been convinced that heavier subsidies to charitable societies would have produced a commensurate public benefit, it would have been easier to secure higher state funding for education. But, almost everywhere existing school facilities were functioning below capacity, and many of the missionaries, in spite of their poverty, would not accept state money. A few were discouraged by failure and in some areas observers declared that the prevailing educational establishment was having little effect upon the peasant class. William Bell, a stipendiary in Jamaica, argued that the effect of moral instruction on the young was largely undone by their home environment. 'Nothing but instant separation, or an age or two,' wrote Bell, 'can alter this state of things, no better education can obviate their distressing and unhappy circumstances.'[95] Harvey and Brewin, anti-slavery writers who toured Jamaica in 1866, admitted that abolitionists had greatly underestimated the difficulty of elevating to Christian piety a people degraded by slavery.[96] Christian education had been advanced as a means of achieving individual enlightenment as well as social control. By the 1860s, there was reason to suspect that it had failed on both counts.

Missionaries grieved that their crusade among the freedmen had not been more fruitful. Phillippo considered 1842 the high

---

[94] Educational statistics from the West Indies must be used with great caution because there was usually an enormous gulf between the number of students on school rolls and the number who attended with any regularity. In 1854, before extensive expansion of school facilities, 25 per cent of the children between 5 and 15 were thought to be in attendance at school in Barbados. Colebrooke to Grey, 27 Sept. 1854, C.O. 28/180, no. 67.

[95] Report, enclosed in Barkly to Newcastle, 21 Feb. 1854, C.O. 137/322, no. 24.

[96] Thomas Harvey and William Brewin, *Jamaica in 1866* (London, 1867), p. 71.

watermark for the Baptist mission; thereafter, he thought, its influence had waned.[97] Between 1846 and 1868, membership in the Methodist Church in the West Indies fell by over 30 per cent, and during much of that period the Caribbean missions were considered an exasperating drag on the mother church.[98] The Revival which swept Jamaica in the early sixties, causing people to desert their homes and to wander in feverish excitement over the countryside, gave new but false hope to the missionaries. As the Revival veered toward myalism, with its trances, spirit-seizure, and wild dances, the sterner Christian missionaries condemned it. Their churches emptied, and by 1862 orthodox congregations were at their lowest ebb.[99]

It might be asked whether the education of freedmen could not have been entrusted to persons other than missionaries. The answer, of course, is emphatically no. It was they who commanded the loyalty of freedmen in the early days. They had established religious beach-heads in the colonies during slavery, and no other human agency was available through which instruction could have been offered. England had no normal college producing teachers until the 1840s, and the teacher training institutions established in the colonies were founded by religious bodies or were designed to prepare their graduates to teach moral and religious subjects. Religion and morality were the cornerstones of English primary education, and it is inconceivable that they would not have formed the basis for West Indian education at a time when the mass of people were pagan. Although Myalists and the leaders of various Afro-Christian cults were able to compete for the spiritual loyalty of the people, none of them conducted schools and few of them could read or write. Secular instruction would not have availed in an age of strong religious sentiment, as the failure of secular systems in Ireland and Trinidad clearly show. The task of converting and educating the freedmen was indisputably the charge of missionaries and churchmen. They laboured hard;

[97] Underhill, *Life of Phillippo*, p. 201.

[98] Findlay and Holdsworth, *History of Methodist Missionary Society*, II, pp. 359, 360, 370.

[99] B. Vickers to H. Austen, 20 Mar. 1865, enclosed in C.O. 137/390, no. 90; Findlay to Holdsworth, *History of Methodist Missionary Society*, II, p. 374; Gardner, *History of Jamaica*, p. 467; Curtin, *Two Jamaicas*, pp. 170–1.

many of them suffered great privation and personal tragedy; but their subdued brand of worship failed to satisfy the emotional needs of most freedmen and their rigid Christian morality was stifling to people whose social and cultural roots lay in Africa or in slavery.

CHAPTER 12

Colonial Politics and Constitutional Reform

Two themes dominated West Indian politics in the mid-century; economic adversity and colour. Racial distinctions, though thinly veiled, were a pervasive and compelling factor in partisan politics, although the emphasis upon race as a political motive varied widely among individuals on both sides of the colour line. In a general sense, the white plantocracy represented an established order based economically on the plantations. It was challenged politically by rising middle-class men of colour, some of whom acquired a modest amount of landed property, though most were merchants, journalists, or middle ranking office-holders. Emancipated blacks participated very little in the political process, and their interests were not well represented in colonial legislatures by either white or coloured groups, both of which maintained an essentially élitist outlook. The Colonial Office, having exhibited a strong sense of trusteeship for emancipated blacks during the initial years of freedom, gradually altered its position in light of labour crises on the estates. Notwithstanding its commitment to free trade, the British Government supported the system of plantation agriculture, and its position led inevitably to a political reinforcement of the planter class. Nowhere is this more evident than in constitutional reforms undertaken in the mid-century. Although the abortive attempt to suspend the Jamaican constitution in 1839 was intended to weaken the grip of the planters, the reforms of the fifties and the elimination of legislative government in all Caribbean colonies save one during the sixties and seventies were effected, in large part, as a means of protecting the interests of European planterdom. It is instructive that Barbados, the sugar colony in which the prosperity of the planters was not imperilled and their political domination not challenged, alone retained its ancient legislative constitution.

In colonial politics, Jamaica commands the centre of the stage. Authoritarian government in British Guiana and Trinidad offered limited latitude for politics; in Barbados, political life, though orderly, was the preserve of the planter class. In Dominica, Montserrat, and Nevis, middle-class men of colour rose quickly to dominate public affairs. But in Jamaica, where political life was comparatively complex and power was fairly evenly distributed between the principal partisan groups, the issues and circumstances which excited and divided colonial populations were most boldly manifested. Perhaps the history of Jamaican politics forms a caricature of political developments in other Caribbean colonies, but the constitutional reforms widely adopted in the West Indies during the 1850s were conceived in Jamaica, and the general demise of assembly government in the sixties and seventies was provoked, most decisively, by events which transpired in that colony. For these reasons, this chapter focuses most heavily on Jamaica.

Between 1840 and 1854 the Jamaica constitution which the Melbourne Government had tried unsuccessfully to abrogate remained a subject of continuous controversy and complaint. The powers of the Assembly were vast, those of the executive narrowly limited. Whereas in England responsible government officers prepared annual estimates for Parliament, managed the distribution of public money, and were subject to audit by a separate department of state, in Jamaica public finance was controlled entirely by the Assembly. In its dual function as a legislative organ and a Board of Public Accounts, that body levied taxes, supervised their collection, appropriated public money, and audited its own accounts. After 1847 there was no permanent revenue available to the Government except tonnage duties for support of a public hospital and a lighthouse.[1] The cost of government services, colonial debts, and the salaries of the Governor, judicial officers, Anglican clergymen, and a multitude of minor officials were paid by annual

---

[1] C. E. Grey to Earl Grey, 7 May 1849, confidential, C.O. 137/302. There was, of course, a quit rent on Crown land of 1d. per acre, but that was collected erratically and amounted to very little.

Acts of the Assembly. Even parish vestries received their power to tax through annual enactments.[2]

Apart from the Assembly's power to deny or limit funding to the Government, it executed its fiscal responsibilities unsystematically.[3] Every member of the House was entitled to propose a grant of public money, and members were inclined to gain support for their own measures by endorsing those of their colleagues.[4] These grants commonly appeared in the Poll Tax Act with little regard being taken to ascertain that the revenue could support them. Deficiencies in revenue were commonly met by the issue of island cheques, promissory notes not unlike English exchequer bills, but in difficult years these were severely depreciated, and the practice of issuing fresh cheques to pay off former ones became a risky business.

Successive Secretaries of State denounced the system in principle, lamenting the absence of executive control. But having failed to suspend the constitution in 1839, the British Government was obliged to conciliate the Jamaican oligarchs. During the early forties, this was not difficult, for despite the problems associated with inadequate labour and drought the Jamaica planters responded favourably to the friendly overtures of their governors, and in modest fashion they voluntarily increased executive authority.[5] Both Metcalfe and Elgin complimented the energy and public service of assemblymen, and being pragmatic politicians, both discouraged any overt imperial pressure to revise the system. In prophetic terms, Metcalfe predicted that the Jamaican planters would willingly undertake constitutional reforms to enhance the power of the

[2] Ibid.

[3] In 1850, for example, a committee of the Assembly assigned to study the question of rum duties estimated that revenue from that source would produce £28,600. When the committee report was taken up by the whole House, the estimate was arbitrarily increased to £32,000 and a motion to raise it another £3,000 was narrowly defeated. In fact, the rum duties for the year returned only £24,600; consequently, a deficiency in the revenue which might have been only £4,000 had the committee's report been accepted, was increased to £8,000 and narrowly missed being £11,000. Barkly to Grey, 30 Dec. 1854, C.O. 137/324, no. 130.

[4] C. E. Grey to Earl Grey, 31 Dec. 1851, C.O. 137/311, no. 115.

[5] In 1844 the Assembly relinquished its sole right to appoint persons to the various Boards established for the administration of government affairs, extending the Governor the privilege of naming some members. Lord Elgin regarded this as a major step forward for the executive. Elgin to Stanley, confidential, 3 Aug. 1845, C.O. 137/284.

executive whenever their control of the Assembly was threatened by the popular, or coloured, party.[6]

Although the so-called popular party—apart from its racial composition—endangered the long-standing domination of the planter class over local economic affairs, this peril to the planter interests paled before the blow struck by the British Parliament in 1846. The Sugar Duties Act and the depression which followed shattered relations between the planters and the Governor and, momentarily, unified all political elements in Jamaica against the British Government. Rather than relinquish any of their prerogatives in favour of the colonial executive, assemblymen of all factions chose to exploit their power to close off supplies in hope of defeating free trade or, at the very least, reducing the costly government establishment created during the preceding decade.

In the retrenchment crisis of 1848–9, Governor Sir Charles Grey repeatedly called for parliamentary intervention, like that attempted in 1839, to correct 'distortions' in the Jamaica constitution.[7] The Colonial Office sympathized with Grey, but it refused to carry the issue to Parliament.[8] Having been badly burned in 1839, it distrusted the wisdom of Parliament on colonial matters, and it was unwilling to risk rebuff from a House of Commons deeply occupied with distressing economic conditions at home. The Colonial Office no longer felt anxiety for the emancipated people: they had proven their ability to protect their own interests. As for the Assembly, it would, in the Secretary of State's view, either vote supplies and undertake necessary reforms itself or it would be left to suffer the consequences of its own irresponsibility.[9]

Those consequences became increasingly apparent as the crisis wore on. The planters were at the forefront of the retrenchment battle. Suffering grievous losses, they hoped to pare public costs to the bone in order to permit general island revenues to

---

[6] Metcalfe to Russell, 12 Feb. 1841, C.O. 137/255, no. 187.

[7] C. E. Grey to Earl Grey, confidential, 21 Feb. 1849, C.O. 137/301; C. E. Grey to Earl Grey, confidential, 21 Apr., 7 May, 21 May, C.O. 137/302.

[8] Taylor's draft dispatch, not sent, bound in C. E. Grey to Earl Grey, 21 Feb. 1849, C.O. 137/301; Minute by Earl Grey, bound in C. E. Grey to Earl Grey, 21 Apr. 1849, C.O. 137/302.

[9] Copy of a dispatch, Earl Grey to C. E. Grey, 16 Apr. 1849, bound in C.O. 137/301, no. 21.

be used to subsidize government in the parishes where they were most heavily taxed. Several times Sir Charles Grey referred to the planters—especially those directly connected with the metropolitan West Indian interest—as being determined to create financial havoc in order to achieve their objectives.[10] But when the central aim of the Assembly—the restoration of protection—was firmly and consistently denied by the Russell Government the solidarity of the House began to dissolve. The Assembly's refusal to vote supplies during 1849 had left office-holders in the colony without salaries. The great majority of lower and middle ranking officials were men of colour,[11] and though some of them may have been in sympathy with the principle of retrenchment, they were the main victims of the Assembly's policy. Widespread discontentment caused by the protracted struggle against the mother country became manifest in the elections of mid-1849 which weakened planter forces in the legislature.[12] The Governor made it clear that unless the Assembly voted supplies, he would dissolve the legislature again and call for new elections which might destroy the planters' majority.[13] Rather than risk political defeat at the hands of the popular party, the planters renewed supplies.[14]

In Jamaican politics, the word 'party' was used for want of a better term. No organized or disciplined political parties existed in the Assembly, though everyone employed such designations as country party, popular party, King's House party, and town party to describe interest groups which tended to cohere on various issues. In fact, political attachments in Jamaica were fragile and fluctuating, and assemblymen prided themselves on their independence of outlook. Nevertheless, some basic combinations were apparent by the early fifties, and these combinations—although they lacked organization—tended to

[10] C. E. Grey to Earl Grey, 19 June 1848, C.O. 137/296, no. 57; C. E. Grey to Earl Grey, 19 Sept. 1848, C.O. 137/297, n). 78.
[11] Bigelow claimed that four-fifths of all public offices in the colony were held by blacks or people of colour; this may well have been an exaggeration. See his, *Jamaica in 1850*, p. 51.
[12] C. E. Grey to Earl Grey, 7 Sept. 1849, C.O. 137/303, no. 79.
[13] In spite of the difficulties occasioned him by the planters, Sir Charles Grey declared himself 'very far from wishing that the representatives of the English and planting interest should be at once made entirely subordinate to a coloured or indigenous party'. C. E. Grey to Earl Grey, 8 Oct. 1849, C.O. 137/303, no. 94.
[14] C. E. Grey to Earl Grey, 31 Dec. 1851, C.O. 137/311, no. 115.

reflect distinctions of race, creed, and economic interest. Sir Charles Grey identified four groups in the Assembly. The first and largest was comprised 'of planters and of proprietors of impoverished estates, and of merchants closely connected with the planting interest'.[15] A second group, gaining ground on the first, was that of coloured members. Jewish merchants, numbering seven or eight, constituted a third element, and the rest were 'almost all practising lawyers'.[16]

The planting interest—referred to as the country party—was frequently at odds with coloured and Jewish factions on economic matters. With one or two exceptions, there were no political figures among the coloured population of the island who earned a large income from the land,[17] and Jewish traders who had limited dealings with the estates disliked import duties and other commercial taxes which the planters advocated as a means of relieving landowners from direct taxation.[18]

Race and religion tended to reinforce economic divisions. Most coloured Jamaicans were dissenters, and in company with the Jewish population they disapproved the expensive Anglican establishment. Normally, racial distinctions were muted in Jamaica. Barkly observed that outward manifestations of prejudice were considered 'repugnant to the spirit of the age' and that distinctions of race and creed were politely veiled under the nomenclature of party or faction.[19] But those distinctions continued to exist: Grey believed that the most persistent divisions in the Assembly were occasioned by race,[20] and Barkly referred to race as the deep seated cause of disunity in the legislature.[21] In trying times, the veneer of courtesy which usually concealed racial animosity was thrust aside—as in the debates over constitutional reform in 1853—exposing

[15] C. E. Grey to Newcastle, 10 May 1853, C.O. 137/316, no. 40.

[16] Ibid. Grey's successor, Sir Henry Barkly, described the Assembly in similar terms, although he designated the fourth element as the King's House Party, a group especially interested in the patronage commonly bestowed by the governor. Barkly to Newcastle, 10 Dec. 1853, *Newcastle Papers*, 9,553; Barkly to Sir George Grey, 19 Oct. 1854, C.O. 137/324, no. 107.

[17] Barkly to Russell, confidential, 7 June 1855, C.O. 137/326.

[18] Grey to Newcastle, 10 May 1853, C.O. 137/316, no. 40.

[19] Barkly to Sir George Grey, 19 Oct. 1854, C.O. 137/324, no. 107.

[20] C. E. Grey to Earl Grey, 31 Dec. 1851, C.O. 137/311, no. 115.

[21] Barkly to Sir George Grey, 19 Oct. 1854, C.O. 137/324, no. 151.

the bitterness and resentment which divided men of colour from their white colleagues.[22]

The planters, themselves, represented several shades of political opinion. Some were firmly attached to the metropolitan West Indian interest; others identified strongly with the local community. The planting interest may have held the largest share of House seats, but even when they were united they had difficulty retaining an active majority throughout a legislative session. After emancipation, annual sessions of the legislature, beginning in October or November, were frequently protracted into the early months of the following year, a period which coincided with crop time on the estates. Planters who lived at great distance from Spanish Town were obliged to absent themselves for extended periods; during their absence, rump sessions of the Assembly were dominated by a combination of their rivals designated the town party—coloured members, Jewish merchants, and a few doctors, journalists, or lawyers not connected with the planting interest. Jamaican politics had a kaleidoscopic quality. Writing in 1853, Henry Barkly indicated that the Assembly was 'so evenly balanced, or rather subdivided into so many variously influenced and slightly cohering sections, as almost to baffle conjecture as to the side on which a majority will be found in respect of any question that arose'.[23]

The main question confronting the colony in the early fifties was its suffocating public and private[24] indebtedness. Between 1843 and 1853, annual expenditures had consistently exceeded revenue, and the island's public debt had mounted

---

[22] Reporting on the discussions which occurred on constitutional reform, Barkly declared that the contention between coloureds and whites was so intense in some instances as to beggar description. Barkly to Newcastle, 10 Dec. 1853, *Newcastle Papers*, 9553.

[23] Barkly to Newcastle, 23 Nov. 1853, C.O. 137/319, no. 18.

[24] The private debt of Jamaica planters was incalculable, but some notion of their inability to repay it can be gleaned from the fate of £244,100 in loans made by the British Government to proprietors whose estates had been damaged during the slave rebellion of 1831. Only 11 of 58 plantations that had received loans remained in cultivation; of those, only three were fully cultivated. The remaining eight exported merely 400 hogsheads in 1853, a crop which some of them might individually have made in better times. Dense forest grew over those properties which had ceased cultivation, none of which could be sold for more than a trifle, and then only in parcels to local peasants. Barkly to Newcastle, 14 Jan. 1854, C.O. 137/322, no. 8.

from £447,000 to £771,000.[25] Slightly more than £200,000 of that amount (including arrears of interest) was owed the British Government for a loan made after the destructive slave insurrection of 1831. Much of the rest consisted of unredeemed island cheques.

For three years, January 1850 to January 1853, the Jamaica Assembly tried to raise a loan from the imperial Government to permit the consolidation of a portion of its public debt. But the Colonial Office refused to countenance such measures until the colony overhauled its financial machinery, established permanent taxes to meet fixed expenditures, and transferred financial administration to responsible government officers.[26] A Bill to achieve these objectives was submitted in the 1851 session, but the Assembly refused to relinquish its extraordinary fiscal prerogatives.[27] All parties in Jamaica hoped that a return of the Tories to power in Britain would bring a restoration of protection[28] and with it a partial revival of the island's prosperity. In that event, some thought, the Assembly might overcome its financial difficulties without constitutional adjustments.

To the colonists' delight the Tories came to power in 1852. They weathered a general election in the summer, but as a minority government they confronted a formidable opposition coalition of Whigs, Radicals, and Peelites. Irish members held a balance between protectionists and free traders in the House of Commons which assembled in November 1852, making return to protection politically impossible. When Disraeli suffered defeat on his budget in December, the Tories resigned and were speedily replaced by a free-trade coalition under

[25] Barkly to Labouchere, 16 Mar. 1856, C.O. 137/331, no. 44.

[26] Minutes by Taylor and Earl Grey, bound in C. E. Grey to Earl Grey, 6 Feb. 1850, C.O. 137/306, no. 13.

[27] C. E. Grey to Earl Grey, 1 Mar. 1852, C.O. 137/313, no. 16.

[28] In combination with the most respectable planters, clergymen, and missionaries, the Governor—who was, himself, an advocate of constitutional reform—made repeated appeals for renewed protection, arguing that without tariff relief most of the remaining estates would cease operations, thereby destroying the base on which a large proportion of the colony's taxation depended. Memorial, enclosed in C. E. Grey to Earl Grey, 2 Mar. 1852, C.O. 137/313, no. 19; C. E. Grey to Earl Grey, 1 Mar. 1852, C.O. 137/313, no. 18; C. E. Grey to Pakington, 10 June 1852, C.O. 137/313, no. 51; C. E. Grey to Pakington, 26 June 1852, C.O. 137/313, no. 53.

Lord Aberdeen.[29] These events shattered the colonists' hopes for tariff relief and the Assembly proceeded directly to a second retrenchment struggle.

It resolved to reduce government salaries by 20 per cent, while limiting its intake of revenue by a similar percentage.[30] As before, the Council rejected these measures, and the Assembly withheld supplies. Losing up to £1,000 a day in rum and import duties, the colony was unable to maintain its institutional establishments. Police served only on a voluntary basis; prisons were emptied; widows and orphans who relied on endowed charities were greatly distressed.[31] Why, it must be asked, did an Assembly that had suffered defeat in a similar struggle three years before renew its encounter with the British Government?

The motives of Assemblymen varied.[32] Those members of the country party most firmly attached to London were, by 1853, desirous of provoking imperial intervention to rid the island of its Assembly and establish in its place a Crown colony system. This group, clearly a minority, deplored the political instability of the Assembly, a condition which they believed discouraged capital investment in the island. They feared the rising power of the coloured faction; and they were convinced, by reference to Trinidad and British Guiana where immigration was stimulating economic recovery, that the great estates would benefit from authoritarian government. A majority of assemblymen considered a stoppage of supplies the only effective means of demonstrating the colony's complete impoverishment. Their objective was to achieve financial relief from London in the form of a remission of debt, a public loan, a reduction of the colonial establishment, or possibly all three. Coloured members tenaciously defended the assembly system: they expected to dominate the House in the foreseeable future, and they wanted its vast powers left intact. This group was anxious to reduce government salaries, not only as a measure of relief, but because lower salaries, being less attractive to Euro-

[29] Robert Stewart, *The Politics of Protection. Lord Derby and the Protectionist Party* (Cambridge, 1971), pp. 206–15.
[30] Grey to Newcastle, 10 May 1853, C.O. 137/316, no. 40.
[31] Grey to Newcastle, 26 May 1853, C.O. 137/316, no. 50.
[32] Most of the material in this paragraph is drawn from a single dispatch by C. E. Grey to Newcastle, 10 May 1853, C.O. 137/316, no. 40.

peans, would give men of colour easier access to high office. Jewish members welcomed any form of fiscal relief, and some of their number profited greatly from an interruption in tariffs which permitted them to stock up on foreign supplies without payment of duty. Rumours circulated widely in the colony that mercantile members of the Assembly, in anticipation of a stoppage, had placed heavy orders with American firms.[33]

Once again, Sir Charles Grey invoked parliamentary intervention to reform the Assembly, but the Duke of Newcastle who had assumed the seals of office in the Aberdeen coalition was unwilling to seek parliamentary action on the Jamaica constitution. For a decade the trend in colonial affairs had been running against imperial intervention in the dependencies. Grey's views on the Empire at large and upon Jamaica in particular were out of step with the times—'utterly opposed to ordinary views and current opinions and therefore . . . wholly impracticable', wrote Henry Taylor.[34] Canada had enjoyed responsible government since 1840. Responsible government had come to Nova Scotia and New Brunswick in 1848, to Prince Edward Island in 1851. Representative institutions were extended to most of the Australian colonies by an Act of 1850, and a large measure of self-government was granted to New Zealand two years later. Even the Cape Colony with its manifold problems shed the Crown colony system in favour of representative institutions in 1853. The Colonial Reform Union continued to seek greater self-government in the colonies; the Manchester School advocated colonial economic self-sufficiency; and individuals, like the Radical Sir William Molesworth, persistently demanded investigations into colonial government, insisting that inefficiency, extravagance, and colonial discontentment were the consequence of too much central power.[35] Even Henry Taylor, who was noted for his attachment to the Crown colony principle during much of his extended career, commented in 1852: 'My own view is that the Colonies will be best retained in amity with the Mother Country by the utmost practicable separation of their political

---

[33] Gardner, *History of Jamaica*, p. 447.
[34] Minute of Taylor, bound in Grey to Pakington, 26 June 1852, C.O. 137/313, no. 53.
[35] *Cambridge History of the British Empire* (Cambridge, 1940), II, 383.

transactions, & that with most of the Colonies the Govt has already closer relations than it has strength or competence to manage.'[36] A suspension by Parliament of the Jamaica constitution would have produced great alarm in all those dependencies which had recently secured a release from authoritarian rule.[37] Newcastle's concern over that prospect, his anxiety regarding Parliament's reaction to any proposal for intervention in Jamaica, and his frame of mind concerning imperial affairs at large deterred him from a forcible policy.

Instead, the Secretary of State offered Jamaica a compromise. If the Assembly would undertake reform—that is, vote permanent taxes to the colonial Government, place financial administration in the hands of responsible salaried officers, and allow proper auditing of accounts—then the metropolitan Government would extend the colony a low interest loan of £500,000. Furthermore, the Colonial Office would attempt to decrease the number of government servants in Jamaica, pay most of the Governor's salary, and seek a general reduction in salaries commensurate with the depressed state of the colony. In his exposition of this policy, Newcastle warned the planters: unless they accepted his compromise, they must anticipate being overwhelmed in the Assembly by representatives of the coloured and black population.[38] Newcastle appointed Henry Barkly, former Governor of British Guiana, to succeed Sir Charles Grey, trusting that his vaunted conciliatory powers would produce a fruitful arrangement. He did not equip Barkly with specific instructions for remodelling the Jamaican constitution. Responsible government of a Canadian variety was considered, but it was thought unsuitable for an island in which only 3,000 people, many of whom were uneducated, exercised the franchise. In effect, the details of reform were left up to Barkly and the Assembly.[39]

The House grappled with the problem from October to

[36] Taylor's minute, bound in Grey to Pakington, 24 Sept. 1852, C.O. 137/314, no. 84.

[37] In a minute on a similar situation in St. Vincent, Taylor wrote: 'it may well be doubted with what feelings the N. American & Australian Colonies (or at least the latter—the former perhaps feel sufficiently secure to be indifferent) wd regard the exercise by Parliament of a power to revoke grants of Colonial Constitutions.' Taylor to Merivale, 15 Aug. 1855, bound in C.O. 28/182, Windward Islands, no. 9.

[38] *Hansard*, CXXVIII, 3rd Series, Lords, 947–57, 30 June 1853.

[39] Draft to Henry Barkly, 16 Aug. 1853, bound in C.O. 137/319.

March 1854: contention between factions was fierce, and Barkly expressed astonishment at 'the inveterate hatred and jealousy which prevail[ed] on the subject of colour'.[40] From the outset, the planters' fear of the coloured party inclined them to extend weighty power to the executive. Initially, coloured members were willing to accept a plan by which the Governor would acquire a number of agents in the Assembly to propose money votes, but in committee sessions C. H. Jackson, their spokesman, insisted that men of his class must dominate those positions. They would not, he declared, tolerate a 'white ministry'.[41] Bryan Edwards, a planter and leader of the Bar, drafted a Bill during the January recess which greatly empowered the Legislative Council and provided for an Executive Committee to serve as a vehicle for the Governor in the legislature. In February, with the planters absent taking crop,[42] the coloured party patched and carved the Bill without altering its basic structure. They pared the number of Council members (predominantly whites involved in the sugar industry) who would be permitted to hold government office. Likewise, they insisted that officers receiving emoluments be disqualified from serving as members of the Executive Committee. The salaries to be paid to executive committeemen were reduced from £1,000 to £800, a tactic intended to discourage the most prominent Europeans from serving on the Committee.[43] In spite of these modifications in Edward's Bill, coloured members expressed serious second thoughts about the measure at the eleventh hour. Barkly wrote:

The fact is the coloured Party have found out on calmer reflection, that, in aiming a great blow at the Council by diminishing official influence in it, and in creating as they imagined at the same time a number of smug ministerial berths for themselves, they have given up far more than they are likely to gain, by having included in the measure a cession of the powers of misappropriating the Revenue, and a great increase of the power of the Representative of the Crown.[44]

[40] Barkly to Newcastle, 10 Dec. 1853, *Newcastle Papers*, 9553.
[41] Ibid.
[42] When the measure passed through committee, eleven coloured members controlled a House numbering seventeen, with only two planters present. Barkly to Newcastle, 26 Feb. 1854, *Newcastle Papers*, 9553.
[43] Barkly to Newcastle, 10 Apr. 1854, C.O. 137/323, no. 46.
[44] Barkly to Newcastle, 10 Mar. 1854, *Newcastle Papers*, 9553.

In late March, coloured assemblymen tried to torpedo the Bill by attaching amendments to it—including a reduction of judicial salaries—which were calculated to evoke opposition in the Council. At that point, however, Governor Barkly out-manoeuvred Edward Jordan and the Chief Justice in the Upper House, securing a majority of one to pass the Bill.[45]

The 'Act for the Better Government of this Island' was signed by the Governor in April. It separated the Legislative Council from the Privy Council,[46] increasing membership in the former from 12 to 17. Only persons who paid £30 a year in taxes or enjoyed an annual income of £300 from freehold property were eligible for appointment to the Council. This excluded almost all coloured men in the colony. The Council regained the right to initiate legislation which did not involve the appropriation of money. An Executive Committee, not to exceed three members from the Assembly and one from the Council, was to serve as the Governor's liaison with the legislature. It was responsible for placing annual estimates before the Assembly and it assumed the administration of executive matters formerly entrusted to legislative boards. The composition of the Assembly was not changed, but that body was prohibited from initiating money Bills. The Act established a permanent Civil List of £25,000 and assigned £30,000 per year from import duties to repay the £500,000 loan which was subsequently voted by Parliament.[47]

Although the new system favoured the planting interest no one was entirely happy with it. The Governor and the Secretary of State complained that the fixed Civil List did not meet all permanent government charges. The coloured party was apprehensive that the Legislative Council, dominated by leading planters, would exert a heavy hand in legislation. Although many of the larger planters would have preferred outright

---

[45] W. P. Morrell, *British Colonial Policy in the Mid-Victorian Age* (Oxford, 1969), p. 386.

[46] Thereafter the Privy Council, appointed by the Governor, became an advisory body to the Governor. Some members of the Legislative Council also served in the Privy Council; most did not. The number of Privy Councillors in 1856 was 16. Barkly to Labouchere, confidential, 25 Jan. 1856, C.O. 137/330.

[47] Barkly to Newcastle, 10 Apr. 1854, C.O. 137/323, no. 46; Ronald V. Sires, 'Constitutional Change in Jamaica, 1834–1860', *Journal of Comparative Legislative and International Law*, 3rd Ser., XXII (1940), 185.

abrogation of the Assembly they were generally heartened by the Act, believing that the enhanced power of the executive would offset the growing influence of the coloured faction and better serve their economic interests. No one was quite certain how the Executive Committee would function or to whom precisely it owed responsibility, the Governor or the House, and this matter—deliberately left vague—subsequently became a source of considerable controversy. In the last analysis, the Assembly had been lured to reform only by the promise of a reduced government establishment and an imperial loan, and the British Government had been induced to extend those concessions only as a result of the embarrassment and disorder occasioned by the stoppage of supplies. For all parties it was an expedient and experimental arrangement.

Perceiving that assemblymen elected under the new law were about 50 per cent Anglo-Saxon, 30 per cent of African extraction, and 20 per cent Jewish, Barkly chose to draw his executive committeemen from the largest two groups.[48] Accordingly, he appointed Henry Westmoreland, a prominent planter, to superintend agricultural affairs, public works, and finance. Bryan Edwards, who had a seat in the Legislative Council, assumed leadership in judicial matters, and Edward Jordan was given special charge over matters pertaining to the social and educational well-being of the community. These men, moderate in their views and widely respected, were able to compromise their differences and preserve commendable harmony in administration. But they were less successful in managing the passage of legislation through the Assembly. That body retained all its former factiousness. Assemblymen not only rejected the spirit of compromise exhibited by executive committeemen, they variously accused them of subservience to the Governor, of sacrificing principle to tranquillity, or of betraying the cause of class or faction. Bills were thwarted or mutilated for reasons which the Governor described as political and personal, not philosophical or ideological. In spite of the Executive Committee's successive defeats on major Bills, committeemen did not resign, nor did the Assembly seek their resignation. A mild state of anarchy reigned in the House: no one was asking probing questions about ministerial responsibility, and it was

[48] Barkly to Sir George Grey, 19 Oct. 1854, C.O. 137/324, no. 107.

generally conceded that no other combination of men could have managed the business of the House more effectively.

Although the new constitutional system worked indifferently in a political sense, it achieved important administrative success. This was especially true in the area of public finance. By 1855 revenues were brought into line with expenditures and the dizzy spiralling of colonial debt was arrested.[49] In the following year, the Executive Committee assumed the administration of parish finances which for many years had been ineptly and corruptly managed.[50] The hereditaments tax, an inequitably levied and inefficiently collected impost was abolished in 1858 in favour of a duty on exports.[51] An improvement in sugar prices during the last years of the decade aided island revenues, and reductions in the judicial and ecclesiastical establishments relieved expenditures. Nevertheless, the colony was perpetually crippled by the enormous weight of debt incurred in former years. When the popular party sought larger sums for education, the planters denied them on grounds of economy; likewise, the planters' opponents rejected publicly supported immigration with similar arguments. In many cases economy was used as an excuse for inaction or retribution; but, on the whole, Jamaicans of all classes were compelled to suffer for the Assembly's earlier transgressions.

The Jamaican reforms prompted similar constitutional adjustments in the Lesser Antilles. Sir William Colebrooke, Governor-General at Barbados, explained the Jamaican plan to his lieutenants in the Windwards, indiscreetly suggesting that those impoverished islands might also receive a loan from the mother country if they initiated similar constitutional changes.[52]

[49] Barkly to Labouchere, 16 Mar. 1856, C.O. 137/331, no. 44.

[50] Hall, *Free Jamaica*, p. 179; Gardner, *History of Jamaica*, p. 451.

[51] Darling to Labouchere, 10 Mar. 1858, C.O. 137/336, no. 37. The hereditaments tax was a levy on property. In many cases, assessments had been made many years in the past and the real value of property after extended depression did not coincide with the basis on which it was taxed. The rate of tax varied from parish to parish, as did favouritism and corruption in its collection. The impost extended to small landowners as well as large, many of whom were so remote that tax collectors never reached them. Collectors were generally of low calibre and their unscrupulous treatment of peasants and small farmers—forcing the sale of a few sticks of furniture and overcharging—rendered the tax as disagreeable to the poor as to the planters.

[52] Colebrooke to Sir George Grey, 1 Nov. 1854, C.O. 28/181, Windward Islands, no. 13. Colebrooke had hoped to consolidate the Leewards and the Windwards

The legislatures of Tobago, St. Vincent, and Grenada immediately passed resolutions endorsing the principles of the Jamaican reform, but their illusions regarding an imperial loan were promptly dismissed by a Colonial Office disclaimer. Nevertheless, the need for reform was manifest in these islands.

St. Vincent may be taken as an example. Although the colony had a large debt, it had no specific plan for its repayment. Annual expenditures exceeded revenues, and public money was being disbursed without legal sanction. There was no provision for education; the hospital was closed; the jail was dilapidated—in fact, all public facilities were thoroughly decrepit. The Assembly, controlled by a half dozen people who lived in or about Kingstown, met infrequently, and their business was months in arrears. There was 'no public opinion, no public spirit, no unity of action, no identity of personal interest with the general interests and welfare . . .'[53] There was little hope for economic recovery, but successive Governors, chafing with frustration, condemned the old legislative system which reserved power to a degenerate Assembly and prevented the executive from effectively communicating his views and objectives to the legislature. When Edward John Eyre assumed executive responsibilities in the colony in 1855, he thought it virtually ungovernable without reform and incapable, by itself, of effecting necessary changes.[54] Like Sir Charles Grey in Jamaica, he urged the British Government to intervene to save the colony. But the Colonial Office minimized the problem: 'Lt. Govr Eyre,' wrote Henry Taylor, 'has described very truly and distinctly a state of things which is new to him, because he is new to these colonies, and which appears to him . . . impossible to continue but in reality it is only the old & general state of things throughout the Chartered W. Indian Islands.'[55] This was not exactly true. Conditions had severely deteriorated, but a Colonial

into political unions with each having a general legislature. He considered a constitutional reform in each of the islands preliminary to such a legislative union, and he expected that an imperial loan would be contingent on the establishment of a general assembly of the Windwards as well as specific reforms in the several island legislatures.

[53] Eyre to Colebrooke, 8 June 1855, enclosed in C.O. 28/182, Windward Islands, no. 8.

[54] Ibid.

[55] Taylor to Merivale, 15 Aug. 1855, enclosed in C.O. 28/182, Windward Islands, no. 8.

Office that would not seek parliamentary intervention in Jamaica would certainly not recommend it for an insignificant dependency like St. Vincent. Sir William Molesworth, the Secretary of State, concluded that nothing saving a massive reform would bring decent government to the small legislative colonies; but, he argued, jobbing, bankruptcy, and the diminution of the white population would have to continue until some momentous crisis could 'satisfy the Imperial Parliament of the necessity of interfering'.[56] For the moment, it was up to the colonists, indolent and apathetic as they were, to undertake their own reforms.

Two models for constitutional reform were current in the islands: the Jamaican plan and a proposal by Colebrooke that executive councils comprising several members from each legislative House be formed as an advisory body through which a governor could communicate directly with his legislators.[57] Lack of communication was a key problem in the old system, and both plans were designed to relieve it. Between 1855 and 1859, one of these plans or a mutation of the two was adopted in six of the Lesser Antilles: Tobago (1855), St. Vincent (1856), Grenada (1856), St. Kitts (1858), Antigua (1859), and Nevis (1859). Because Barbados was functioning with unique success under the old system, it refused to adjust its mode of operation.

Both Grenada and St. Vincent set up executive councils comprising five members from each House. Subcommittees of these bodies, working with their lieutenant-governors, prepared preliminary estimates, but the assemblies continued to control expenditures through their initiation of money Bills. When, in 1859, measures were introduced for adopting the Jamaica plan involving three-man executive committees that would have the sole right to introduce money Bills and administer various government departments in co-ordination with the executive, St. Vincent approved the plan and Grenada rejected it. At the same time, the Grenada Assembly discarded its ten man Executive Council and returned to the old legislative system. This miscarriage of reform was attributed to rancorous feelings in the Assembly and the personal enmity generated by

[56] Minute by Molesworth, 24 Aug. 1855, enclosed in C.O. 28/182, Windward Islands, no. 8.
[57] Colebrooke to Newcastle, 20 Mar. 1854, C.O. 28/180, no. 15.

individuals who had served on the Executive Council.[58] Like St. Vincent, three Leeward colonies adopted both the large executive councils that drew numerous representatives from each House and the smaller ministerial committees which assumed responsibility for financial administration. In each case, these reforms improved administrative procedures and facilitated liaison between the governor and legislature. But they left the question of control unresolved. Was the executive committee —that small body preparing budgets and administering public finances—the servant of the legislature, subject to dismissal when it lost the confidence of the assembly? Or was it a tool of the Crown, impervious to the displeasure of the assembly and, indeed, the constituency that elected it? When real political strife arose in the Caribbean, these questions could not be avoided. If the former applied, then the legislature would exercise ultimate control over the executive through the small ministerial committee; if the latter were the case, the Crown would have to enforce its policies or suffer deadlock with the elected House. The first of these meant responsible government; the second, either a Crown colony system or impasse. The Colonial Office wanted none of these. It hoped to steer a course between them by employing an arrangement which no one could adequately define—or, more correctly, which everyone defined differently.

Executive committees functioned admirably as long as governors and legislative majorities were in agreement on basic issues. When they were not—when confidence was lost between the two branches of government—the position of the committees became confused, if not impossible, and the machinery of state broke down. Antigua provides an example of this. The executive committee system worked fairly well until 1862 when Governor K. B. Hamilton and the planters came into conflict over immigration policy. The House demanded that the Executive Committee, implicated with the Governor, resign. It did, but when the Governor requested the opposition leader, Charles Elridge, to serve in a new Executive Committee, Elridge insisted upon naming his own colleagues. Enjoying House support, Elridge considered himself a type of prime minister entitled to a cabinet

[58] Morrell, *British Colonial Policy*, pp. 393–4.

of his own, not of the Crown's, choosing.[59] The Governor objected, creating an impasse which was only relieved by the departure of Hamilton and the arrival of a new Governor, S. J. Hill, who brought with him an imperial endorsement of the planters' immigration programme in exchange for a moderation of Elridge's position on the constitution. The character of the constitution in Antigua was not decided in 1862; it was merely negotiated.

The role of the Executive Committee was heatedly debated in Jamaica. There, most curiously, the Governor insisted that the Committee constituted a form of ministry responsible to the legislature and the committeemen argued that ultimate responsibility for their actions resided with the Governor. The Committee, then comprising Edward Jordan,[60] George Price,[61] and William Hosack,[62] had spent £17,000 above the amount authorized for road improvements in 1860. When Governor C. H. Darling declared the Executive Committee responsible to the Assembly for that transaction, the committeemen argued that they were merely agents of the Governor and that he, not they, must assume final responsibility for the administration of public money. Despite his enormous experience in colonial government[63] and his considerable abilities, Darling was a stiff, aloof man, extremely sensitive to criticism. Since his appointment to Jamaica in 1857 he had been abused, often outrageously, by the least circumspect members of the Assembly. In

[59] The executive committee was considered by many in Antigua as a ministry. Committeemen were addressed on occasion as Mr. Prime Minister or Chancellor of the Exchequer. For the substance of this material on Antigua, I am indebted to Professor Howard Aston Rogers. See his, 'The Fall of the Old Representative System in the Leeward and Windward Islands, 1854–1877' (unpublished Ph.D. Dissertation, University of Southern California, 1970), pp. 117–27.

[60] Jordan was the most distinguished coloured politician in the island. He was Custos and Mayor of the City and Parish of Kingston, member of the Privy Council, formerly member of the old Legislative Council, and member of the Executive Committee since its founding.

[61] Price was the proprietor and manager of Worthy Park Estate, a former member of the Assembly, a current member of both the Legislative and the Privy Councils.

[62] Hosack was a proprietor, Custos of St. George, assemblyman and member of the Privy Council.

[63] Darling had been assistant private secretary to the Governor of New South Wales, military secretary to Sir Lionel Smith in Barbados and Jamaica, Agent-General for Immigration in Jamaica, Lt. Governor of St. Lucia, Lt. Governor of Cape Colony, and he had introduced responsible government in Newfoundland before returning to Jamaica as Governor in 1857.

1859 a resolution of no confidence in the Governor was proposed in the House, and two years later Darling was accused
of breaching the Assembly's privileges.[64] In each case, the
Governor and his Executive Committee had been in agreement on those issues which evoked hostile resolutions. Seeking a
shelter from abuse and concerned that the credibility of the
executive was being endangered, Darling argued that the
Assembly's resolutions of no confidence should have been directed against the Committee, not himself. By drawing upon his
experience in North America, quoting from Colonial Office
dispatches and the Act of 1854, and acknowledging that in no
instance had he acted against the advice of his Executive
Committee, Darling prepared an elaborate case contending
that Jamaica was, after all, constituted under the responsible
government system.[65]

The executive committeemen in Jamaica argued just as
vehemently that the Act of 1854 intended that the Governor
alone was responsible for colonial administration and that they
were nothing more than 'his assistants in conducting the public
affairs of the colony, and the medium of communication between him and the other branches of the legislature'.[66] The
committeemen argued pragmatically, not theoretically. Rendering the Executive Committee responsible to the Assembly
would prove chaotic, they insisted: since there were no disciplined parties in Jamaica, shifting majorities would occasion a
rapid turnover of committees and, with it, the loss of coherence
in fiscal administration.[67] The stability achieved between 1854
and 1860 would be sacrificed, they argued, and capitalists
who had begun to show interest in the island would again take
flight.[68] Or, they conjectured, responsible government might
lead to a more rigid definition of parties which would heighten
distinctions of race and might, as one anxious planter observed,
'result in a war of Races'.[69]

---

[64] Minute of C. H. Darling for the Executive Committee, 18 Sept. 1860, bound
in C.O. 137/351, no. 156.
[65] Minute of Darling, 15 Oct. 1860, bound in C.O. 137/351, no. 156.
[66] Minute of Jordan, Hosack, and Price, 25 Sept. 1860, bound in C.O. 137/351.
[67] Ibid.
[68] Minute of Hosack, 25 Sept. 1860; Minute of Price, n.d., bound in C.O.
137/351, no. 156.
[69] The language 'war of Races' was used by Benjamin Vickers in a letter ad-

The Colonial Office was chagrined by this controversy. It defended the view of the Executive Committee in every particular, and it censured Darling for having raised a troublesome constitutional issue without a major crisis. The Secretary of State held that the Governor was responsible for all administrative actions and for all legislation introduced in the Assembly by members of the Executive Committee. He deplored the prospect of a rapid turnover in committees, but with some degree of self-contradiction he declared that a committee which was unable to obtain a majority on measures of vital importance should be replaced by one that could.[70] What the Colonial Office failed to consider—or perhaps refused to consider—was what action the Governor must take when no Executive Committee could be found capable of obtaining a majority on measures of cardinal importance to the Crown. This was a critical question, for an Assembly in collision with the Governor was still capable of preventing the conduct of public business. In raising the question of ultimate responsibility, Darling exposed the Achilles heel of the reformed Jamaican constitution and threatened the tranquillity of a Colonial Office that was trying to muddle through with a hopelessly imprecise system.

Executive committee government tended by its nature to evoke strong opposition elements in the Assembly. In their administration of public works, their granting of contracts for road maintenance and other public services, and their regulation of vestry finances, executive committeemen were continually dealing with men who occupied seats in the House. Inevitably they alienated more people than they patronized, and in so doing they aroused a great deal of political opposition.[71] Because there were no disciplined political parties, the Executive Committee could not enjoy a secure majority in the House, and it perpetually faced a floating body of discontented people who hoped to benefit personally from a change. Possession of executive office, in itself, became an important political objective for leading figures in the Assembly. The £800 stipend

dressed to Messrs. Thomson Hankey & Co., London, 24 Nov. 1860, bound in Darling to Newcastle, 24 Nov. 1860, confidential, C.O. 137/351.

[70] Draft, Newcastle to Darling, 29 Jan. 1861, bound in C.O. 137/351, no. 156.

[71] Jordan, Price, and Hosack to Newcastle, 6 Dec. 1860, C.O. 137/352.

extended to committeemen was no mean reward in a colony shorn of its prosperity. In Antigua, Nevis, and St. Vincent, where the salaries awarded executive committeemen were a fraction of those given in Jamaica, payments were discontinued because the competition among legislators to acquire them had produced bitter factionalism and political disorder.[72] This same factionalism was characteristic of Jamaica in the early sixties. When the Executive Committee of Jordan, Hosack, and Price resigned at the height of the constitutional controversy (Nov. 1860), Darling replaced them with three planters—Raynes Smith,[73] Maximilian Augustus Baron von Ketelhodt,[74] and George Soloman.[75] The displaced Committee—supported by Henry Westmoreland, a former committeeman, and the coloured faction which no longer enjoyed representation—set up a withering personal opposition against Darling and his new executive agents.[76] After a year Darling obtained a leave of absence which turned out to be a permanent withdrawal.[77] The Smith–Ketelhodt committee stumbled through a second year under the administration of his successor, Lt.-Governor Eyre, before it resigned in disgust at the abusiveness and obstructionism of the opposition.

During the tenure of this ill-fated Committee, 1861–3, several important political conditions became apparent. Residing at great distance from the seat of government and preoccupied with the conduct of their estates, the committeemen were unable to spend enough time in Spanish Town to keep abreast of their administrative responsibilities. Furthermore, because they represented the country party, they confronted a large opposition majority in the House during those periods when their allies were busy taking crop. From the point

[72] Rogers, 'Fall of the Old Representative System', p. 126.

[73] Smith was a proprietor and a member of an old Jamaican family.

[74] Ketelhodt, a member of the Legislative Council, was a planter and the Custos of St. Thomas in the East where he was killed during the Morant Bay uprising.

[75] Soloman, a Jew, was a planter and merchant. He left the committee in a short time and was replaced by a planter, Whitelocke.

[76] Darling to Newcastle, 1 Mar. 1861, C.O. 137/353, no. 31. Robert Osborn co-proprietor with Jordan of the *Morning Journal*, a newspaper that scathingly denounced the Governor, had a running battle with Darling. On 5 Sept. 1861, he wrote the Governor an insulting letter accusing him of ignoring the people and behaving tyrannically. Letter enclosed in Darling to Newcastle, 17 Sept. 1861, C.O. 137/356, no. 130.

[77] Newcastle to Eyre, n.d., *Newcastle Papers*, 10,887.

of administrative efficiency alone, it became evident that the colony would best be served by an Executive Committee whose members resided close to the capital. It was equally clear that the Executive Committee could not function without a coloured member.[78] An awareness of these factors affected the character of political combinations. Whereas Governors Grey and Barkly, writing in the fifties, described their assemblies as being divided, basically, between the planter interest on one side and Jews and coloured members on the other, Governor Eyre acknowledged that 'proprietors who live principally at or near Spanish Town or Kingston' had come to constitute an important element of the town party.[79] These near-dwelling proprietors, interested in Executive Committee positions and capable of rendering continuous administrative service, were induced to ally themselves with the coloured faction as a means of securing a firm political base in the Assembly. This is evident in the behaviour of Price and Westmoreland. Furthermore, it was apparent that no Executive Committee could function for long without a majority in the House. In the last days of the Smith–Ketelhodt committee, Henry Taylor determined that changes in the Executive Committee should not be made 'in deference to an opposition which is manifestly personal in its motives & interests, & factious in its manner of proceeding'.[80] Obstructionists should be disqualified from seats on the Committee, he contended, and the British Government should be prepared to endure a stoppage of supplies rather than concede this point. Although these views were conveyed to Eyre in early 1863, they had no bearing on the course of events. A dissolution of the legislature and a general election in March did not reduce the opposition's ability to obstruct public business. After one week of wrangling with the new House which passed a resolution of no confidence in the Executive Committee, Smith, Ketelhodt, and Whitelocke resigned. Even had they weathered the confidence vote, they were determined not to continue, for

[78] In December 1862, Eyre declared that it was impractical for the government to go through another session without appointing Jordan, the most stable member of the coloured group, to the Executive Committee. Eyre to Newcastle, confidential, 23 Dec. 1862, C.O. 137/368.

[79] Eyre to Newcastle, separate, 18 Mar. 1864, C.O. 137/380.

[80] Minute by Taylor, bound in Eyre to Newcastle, 31 Jan. 1863, C.O. 137/370, no. 36.

they had no hope of carrying on the affairs of government against so determined an opposition.[81] It was one thing for Henry Taylor to insist on retaining the Committee in the face of a hostile majority, but in practice no group of committee-men could long endure the anguish, frustration, and personal distress resulting from perpetual stalemate in the legislature.

Jamaican politics became even more complicated, unproductive, and factious under the next Executive Committee. The Lt.-Governor appointed the leaders of the opposition—Jordon, Westmoreland, and Price[82]—to executive office, but he concurrently alienated their following in the Assembly. Messrs. Espeut and March, assemblymen who held salaried offices, had voted against the Smith–Ketelhodt committee on the confidence resolution. Believing that officers receiving emolument should support the executive, Eyre abruptly informed the two men that they must either relinquish their seats or resign their salaried offices.[83] This action was denounced as tyrannical, being contrary to the principle of individual independence which was supposed to motivate members of the House. After a year of haggling, the issue was resolved by the Law Officers of the Crown in favour of Espeut and March.[84] Of greater significance, however, was Eyre's dismissal of David Ewart, the Agent-General of Immigration who was guilty of negligence in failing to investigate a case of high mortality among immigrants on Low Layton Estate.[85] Like March, Ewart was a man of colour; in fact, he was married to the coloured daughter of Alexander Barclay, the aged and respected Receiver-General. When he was replaced by a white man, coloured members of the Assembly expressed offence.[86] Dismissed with Ewart was a sub-agent, Mr. Lindo, a Jew whose father held a seat in the Assembly.[87] These dismissals alienated Eyre from both the

[81] Eyre to Newcastle, 8 Apr. 1863, C.O. 137/371, no. 78.

[82] A planter, Mr. Phillips, who had not been involved with the opposition was first appointed to the committee in order that Eyre could give the impression that he was not bowing to party government. But Phillips, who lived 120 miles from Spanish Town, resigned after a few months, to be replaced by George Price. Eyre to Newcastle, 1 July 1863, C.O. 137/373, no. 164.

[83] Eyre to Newcastle, 9 May 1863, C.O. 137/372, no. 105.

[84] Minutes by Taylor, bound in Eyre to Newcastle, 24 Mar. 1864, C.O. 137/380 no. 112. Espeut recovered his seat in May 1864.

[85] Eyre to Newcastle, 24 Aug. 1863, C.O. 137/374, no. 202.

[86] Eyre to Newcastle, confidential, 27 Jan. 1864, C.O. 137/378.

[87] Eyre to Newcastle, 8 Feb. 1864, C.O. 137/379, no. 54.

coloured and Jewish groups at a time—February 1864—when representatives of the country party were away from the capital. Consequently, a resolution censuring the Governor passed the House by a vote of 13–4.[88] Eyre prorogued the Assembly, but upon its recall in March, the town party continued to obstruct business, inducing the Governor to undertake further prorogations throughout the year.[89] During the whole sordid affair, the position of the Executive Committee was exceedingly anomalous. It was the committeemen's allies in the House who obstructed business and attacked the Governor, and though they supported Eyre with their own votes they made little effort to repress the excesses of their friends.[90]

Eyre was thoroughly disenchanted with the Jamaican system of government. He advised his superiors that the time had come for the Crown either to defend its prerogatives or consent to a system of responsible government. Considering the latter alternative potentially disastrous, he declared that most of the Legislative Council, half the Assembly, and 'a large majority of the most intelligent and influential inhabitants'—by this he meant most of the European planters and their mercantile associates—would welcome a change in the constitution which produced strong executive government.[91] It was apparent to all that the country party could not control public affairs under the prevailing system. In May 1865 Dr. Lewis Bowerbank, an assemblyman who had exposed corruption in the public hospital and lunatic asylum, openly condemned the Assembly as the 'curse of Jamaica'.[92] In accord with a number of magistrates, clergymen, and private individuals,[93] he called for constitutional change to restore decency, order, and confidence in a community devastated by political licence and individual profiteering. By June 1865 the Colonial Office candidly favoured constitutional change. The Assembly of Dominica had voted to abolish itself in April of that year,

---

[88] Eyre to Newcastle, confidential, 9 Feb. 1864, C.O. 137/379. Eleven of the thirteen affirmative votes were cast by Jewish and coloured members.

[89] Eyre to Newcastle, 9 Mar. 1864, C.O. 137/380, no. 98.

[90] Eyre to Newcastle, 17 Mar. 1864, C.O. 137/380, no. 105.

[91] Eyre to Newcastle, confidential, 9 Feb. 1864, C.O. 137/379.

[92] Bowerbank to Austin, 15 Mar. 1865, bound in C.O. 137/390, no. 90.

[93] In May 1865 a public meeting in Montego Bay denounced the corruption and profligacy of the Assembly and urged reform. Eyre to Cardwell, 6 June 1865, C.O. 137/391, no. 137.

and the Colonial Office hoped without much confidence that Jamaica would do the same.[94]

Dominica had established a precedent in the islands. After 1838 its Assembly had been dominated by men of colour under the leadership of the flamboyant, self-educated newspaperman George Charles Falconer. Political battles between the white planter–merchant minority and the coloured majority (drawn mainly from small proprietors, minor civil servants, and artisans) had been fought with a degree of scurrility extraordinary even by West Indian standards. Attempts by the executive to achieve constitutional reform in the fifties had been blocked in the House, but the exposure of extensive corruption involving the Falconer group led to their defeat in the elections of 1862. Lt.-Governor Price immediately proposed the establishment of a unicameral legislature having both appointed and elected members. After two years of brutal political warfare and an unvarnished stacking of the Legislative Council, Price secured his reform. In 1865 the Dominica House, comprising nine appointed and nineteen elected members, voted to transform their body into a chamber of seven elected and seven nominated members.[95] Before the final vote was taken a wild scene occurred in the legislature. An irate body of Falconer's supporters invaded the chamber in a last ditch effort to intimidate offending members, but the chance arrival of H.M.S. *Aurora*, and the dispatch of a marine guard to clear the House, prevented serious incident and permitted the passage of the Act.[96] Engineered by the Lt.-Governor, with full support from the Colonial Office, the measure was clearly a victory for the planting interest and their allies.

Similar reform projects were contemplated in other islands during the early sixties. In Antigua, fiscal solvency was shattered after 1863 by two years of drought which reduced sugar exports by more than 50 per cent.[97] Metropolitan capitalists made it clear that constitutional reforms designed to enhance executive authority would afford them greater security of

[94] Minute by Taylor, 30 May 1865, bound in C.O. 137/390, no. 90.
[95] Rogers, 'Fall of the Old Representative System', pp. 180–212.
[96] Morrell, *British Colonial Policy*, p. 436.
[97] According to Deerr, sugar exports from Antigua, 1862–5, were: 12,920 tons in 1862; 10,124 tons in 1863; 2,618 tons in 1864; and 7,906 tons in 1865. *History of Sugar*, II, p. 195.

capital, and their opinion carried authority in a community of debtors desperately in need of credit. In 1861 Lt.-Governor Benjamin Pine recommended the establishment of a unicameral legislature at St. Kitts. That Island was comparatively prosperous and well governed, but Pine could envisage the time when planter oligarchs, whose interests he favoured, would be challenged from below.[98] In Nevis, Tobago, and St. Vincent, disorder served as an impetus to change. Between 1862 and 1865, no Executive Committee in Nevis survived longer than several months, and there were eleven changes in the Executive Committee in Tobago during a period of eight years.[99] St. Vincent suffered a major riot in 1862 which occasioned widespread damage to property and badly frightened the upper and middle classes.[100] Anthony Musgrave, the Lt.-Governor, made an impassioned appeal for imperial intervention to destroy the Assembly and reform a polity which had mismanaged public affairs to the serious detriment of the masses and planters alike.[101] Everywhere except Barbados, the legislative system was in jeopardy.

The reforms of the 1850s had not resolved political and constitutional difficulties in the islands. The executive committee system had confused rather than clarified the respective powers of governors and legislatures, and disorder and factionalism reigned in the assemblies. Colonial executives reinforced by the metropolitan West Indian interest and a substantial body of resident planters, sought further reforms to strengthen the authority of the Crown and provide greater security to the sugar industry. The Colonial Office, having lost patience with Caribbean legislatures, waited its opportunity to destroy the legislative system. That opportunity came with the tragic rebellion at Morant Bay in 1865.

[98] Rogers, 'Fall of the Old Representative System,' p. 236.
[99] Ibid., pp. 116, 128.
[100] P.P. 1863, XXXVIII (509). Although the riot began as a protest against wage reduction, it quickly assumed racial overtones. Whites and coloureds took refuge in the capital as bands of blacks, especially inflamed against whites, travelled about seizing and beating their victims.
[101] Rogers, 'Fall of the Old Representative System', p. 266.

CHAPTER 13

Morant Bay: The End of an Era

THE Morant Bay uprising, its brutal repression, and the reaction to those events in England and the colonies brought into focus the great divisions, animosities, and anxieties which permeated West Indian society and affected British attitudes toward the Caribbean colonies during the thirty years following emancipation. Though the rebellion was confined to one district of Jamaica, its ramifications were deeply felt throughout the Caribbean. The Morant Bay rising and its aftermath serves as a monument to human frailty and frustration. If one abjures the search for heroes and villains in this sad episode it is possible to see a society divided against itself with its people fragmented into separate social, racial, and economic groups struggling for incompatible objectives under consistently eroding physical and material circumstances. Although most of the conflicts which bedevilled the great experiment were brought into bold relief by the crisis of 1865, few if any of them were resolved—indeed, many of them remain unresolved. Nevertheless, the catharsis of Morant Bay constitutes a major watershed in the history of the Caribbean colonies.

There was severe distress in many areas of the British Caribbean during the 1860s. Serious riots occurred in St. Vincent; there was disorder in Barbados; drought created great hardship and social tension in Antigua. In fact, most of the problems which troubled Jamaica were apparent in other colonies. Sugar prices which had risen briefly between 1856 and 1860 slid downward reaching their lowest level for the century in 1863.[1] Wages on the estates were trimmed in response to the fall in market prices. At the same time, the cost of clothing

---

[1] Prices had risen from 25s. in 1855 to 36s. 11d. in 1857; they held around 27s. until 1860, falling to 24s. 5d. in 1861, 22s. 3d. in 1862, and 21s. 7d. in 1863. In 1865 the average London price for West Indian muscovado was 22s. P.P. 1866, LXVI (193).

rose from 30 to 100 per cent as a result of an interruption in American trade during the Civil War. For the same reason imported foodstuffs were scarcer and dearer. In Jamaica, two years of drought in the early sixties damaged provision grounds, drove up the price of locally produced food, and occasioned an increased demand for wage work on the estates. Because of poor seasons the estates were hiring fewer people, and the job market for Creole workers was further damaged by the immigration of 4,645 Indians to the island during the short-lived revival of that programme in 1860–3. In January 1865 Dr. Edward Underhill, Secretary of the Baptist Missionary Society, having received numerous letters of lamentation from his subordinates in Jamaica, wrote the Secretary of State, Edward Cardwell, declaring that the lower classes in the colony were naked, starving, overtaxed, and underemployed.[2] Since there was no capital in the island to give them honest employment, he insisted, they were compelled to steal to survive. The contents of Underhill's letter circulated widely in the island, provoking angry cries of 'exaggeration!' from some parties, including the Governor, and equally vociferous affirmations from others. Governor Eyre instituted an informal inquiry, requesting custodes, ministers, stipendiaries, and jurists from all parts of the colony to respond to a list of questions concerning the social and economic condition of the people. The evidence they produced, though varied and somewhat contradictory, was considerably less alarming than Underhill's statement, but their reports offered ample proof that privation was widespread: the physical decay of the colony was well advanced, and its moral condition was deplorable. A bastardy law was desperately needed; parental discipline was negligible and parental example pernicious; according to the Governor's summation of the evidence, many lower class people seemed to have little discernment for what was right or wrong: 'the youth of the present generation', he charged, 'are more idle, more immoral, more wanting in anything like principle and more vicious than at the time of emancipation . . .'[3]

While Eyre was collecting data on conditions in the island, meetings—called Underhill meetings—were held throughout

[2] Underhill to Cardwell, 5 Jan. 1865, bound in C.O. 137/390, no. 90.
[3] Eyre to Cardwell, 19 Apr. 1865, C.O. 137/390, no. 90, with enclosures.

the colony for the purpose of galvanizing sentiment among the poor, dramatizing their distress, and preparing appeals for relief to the Governor and Queen. At large meetings held in Savanna-la-Mar and in Clarendon it was resolved that the abandonment of estates had undermined the interests of the people by withdrawing opportunities for employment.[4] Similarly, a meeting in Spanish Town determined that the deplorable state of the common people was caused by the 'want of employment, in consequence of the abandonment of a large number of Estates and the Staple of the Country being no longer remunerative . . . by being brought into unequal competition with slave-grown produce'.[5] A petition from the people of St. Ann's complained of their inability to obtain jobs: most of the sugar estates were abandoned and the price of pimento was so low that it did not pay to harvest it.[6] Declaring their provision grounds to be exhausted from continuous replanting, the St. Ann's memorialists asked the Queen to rent them Crown lands at minimal rates.

The St. Ann's petition is the most important of many formulated in 1865, for it was in response to that appeal that the Colonial Office returned its well known Queen's Advice which intensified unrest among the poor. Furthermore, the petition is important because it exposed once again the economic dilemma that confounded Jamaicans in the free period. The people needed the estates and deplored their passing. But they prized their independence and since 1838 they had withheld from the planters the continuous and careful labour required to keep the estates going. Under a system of protective tariffs, sugar planters could tolerate some of the inefficiencies occasioned by irregular labour, but free trade imposed a competitive pressure on the estates that rendered such inefficiencies the kiss of death.

During the free-trade controversy of the late forties, James Matthew Higgins, a planter journalist, had claimed that the equalization of duties on British and slave-grown sugar would either destroy the colonial planters or reduce their wage labourers to the material level of slavery. His remarks con-

---

[4] Enclosure in Eyre to Cardwell, 23 May 1865, C.O. 137/391, no. 142.
[5] Enclosure in Eyre to Cardwell, 6 June 1865, C.O. 137/391, no. 143.
[6] Enclosure in Eyre to Cardwell, 25 Apr. 1865, C.O. 137/390, no. 117.

tained a large element of truth. Under free trade, British West Indian workers were caught between a rock and a hard place. Whether they worked regularly for low wages to keep up the estates or failed to work regularly and let them fail, they were bound to suffer injury. They could always fall back on their provision grounds for subsistence, but for many that subsistence was becoming increasingly meagre. As the St. Ann's petitioners noted, their small holdings had become exhausted from continuous cultivation.[7] If, in response to the people's appeal, the Government had permitted them the right to use unoccupied Crown land, the old dilemma would merely have been extended. The peasants, having taken up new land, would have perpetuated their exhaustive agricultural techniques and withheld their labour entirely or in part from remaining sugar estates. The petitioners of 1865 were seeking contradictory aims—more provision land and more wage labour opportunities. The hard reality of life in Jamaica was that sugar estates offering wages could barely survive in the era of free trade unless a substantial body of workers, at a sacrifice to their independence, were prepared to provide continuous cane labour at modest remuneration.

Successive governors, Richard Hill,[8] William Sewell,[9] and a host of others of lesser renown and authority had argued that the restoration of prosperity in Jamaica, and the rebuilding of its civic life depended on a revival of the sugar industry. This was clearly the Crown's position, and the imperial Government expressed its view in response to the St. Ann's petition:

. . . the prosperity of the Labouring Classes as well as of all other classes depends in Jamaica, and in other Countries, upon their working for Wages, not uncertainly or capriciously, but steadily and continuously, at the times when their labour is wanted, and for so long as it is wanted, and that if they would use this industry, and thereby render the Plantations productive, they would enable the

[7] Witnesses before the Jamaica Royal Commission declared that an objective of the Morant Bay rioters was to secure backlands at no cost for their cultivation. Report of the Jamaica Royal Commission, P.P. 1866, XXX [3683], Part I, pp. 12, 40.

[8] See p. 412, n. 15.

[9] After observing conditions in Jamaica in 1860, Sewell thought it an undisputable fact that the colony depended for a return to prosperity on the extension of sugar cultivation. See his *Ordeal of Free Labor*, p. 258.

Planters to pay them higher Wages for the same hours of work than are received by the best Field Labourers in this Country; and as the cost of the necessaries of life is much less in Jamaica than it is here, they would be enabled, by adding prudence to industry, to lay by an ample provision for seasons of drought and dearth; and they may be assured that it is from their own industry and prudence, in availing themselves of the means of prospering that are before them, and not from any such schemes as have been suggested to them, that they must look for an improvement in their condition.[10]

Historians have severely criticized this statement, none more devastatingly than Douglas Hall.[11] As he argues, the address acknowledged but failed to appreciate the complex seasonal character of the West Indian labour market, and in holding out to West Indian workers a promise of higher wages than those offered to their British counterparts, it did not account for the impact of declining sugar prices on estate wages. It was futile for the Government to have advised the people of St. Ann's to work continuously on sugar estates, most of which had already ceased to exist. At the same time, it is clear that the Colonial Office expected the Queen's Advice to reach much farther than St. Ann's, as the release of 50,000 copies of the document suggests. Supercilious as the message may have been, it was intended to impress working people that in their distressing circumstances they must recognize that the best of their apparently unfavourable alternatives was to keep the remaining estates afloat. The hope of the Colonial Office for a resurgence of the Jamaica sugar industry was based heavily upon the Encumbered Estates Act. That measure, it was thought, would permit the revival of many depressed properties if they could command disciplined labour. Whether in view of depressed sugar prices, Jamaican estates could hope to pay better wages for better work was uncertain, but reference to other colonies convinced imperial authorities that this was the case. Barbados proprietors had entered the free period with the same kind of encumbrances common in Jamaica, but by virtue of reliable labour they had been able to make consistent profits. Admittedly, wage rates were low in Barbados, but the cost per worker of

---

[10] This response was composed by Henry Taylor in a minute attached to Eyre's correspondence of 25 Apr. 1865, C.O. 137/390, no. 117; it was dispatched in a letter to Eyre, 14 June 1865.

[11] Hall, *Free Jamaica*, p. 245.

producing sugar was higher in that island than one would have expected it to be on good Jamaican properties which commanded ample labour. Barbados planters could not ratoon; they were compelled to replant every year and to spend large amounts on fertilizer. Their unit costs of production were high because their properties were comparatively small. In Trinidad and British Guiana where ratooning was possible and estates were large—as indeed they were in Jamaica—the cost per worker of producing sugar was comparatively low and the wages paid to labourers were the highest in the West Indies.

For Jamaica's working people, the Queen's Advice offered no solace. It was meaningless, if not insulting, to those isolated from active estates. For others, it conflicted with their innermost desires. Their aims were what they had always been—to preserve their independence from the planters and to retain the estates as supplementary sources of income. What they wanted was relief from the Government to facilitate that objective. When relief was not forthcoming, disaffection mounted. Reports of conspiracies, of blacks collecting arms and refusing to pay taxes were relayed to Spanish Town, prompting Eyre to request the dispatch of warships to Black River and Montego Bay in the summer of 1865.[12] Outspoken persons, long alienated from the Government and commonly designated 'demagogues' by the forces of order, exploited the situation by circulating among the poor and employing language which can only be described as inflammatory.

The most notable of these was George William Gordon, an assemblyman, Baptist preacher, and inveterate enemy of Governor Eyre. Born a slave, the son of a Scottish planter and a woman of colour, Gordon had educated himself, secured his freedom, and launched his career as a produce-broker in Kingston. In time, he purchased numerous properties in the island, none of which prospered, and by 1865 he laboured under mortgage liabilities of £35,000.[13] Sensitive, energetic, flamboyant, and erratic, Gordon was possessed by religious fervour. His search for a satisfying spiritual environment had

[12] Morrell, *British Colonial Policy*, p. 410.
[13] Report of the Jamaica Royal Commission, P.P. 1866, XXX [3683], Part I, p. 35. For a highly sympathetic account of Gordon, recently published, see Ansell Hart, *The Life of George William Gordon* (Kingston, Jamaica, n.d.).

carried him from the Church of Scotland to the Congrega-
tionalists, and finally, in 1861, to the Native Baptists, among
whom he assumed a position of authority. In the Assembly he
was a vitriolic opponent of successive governors and the
planter class, a member of no faction, being chastised with
equal vehemence by white and coloured assemblymen for his
abusive proceedings, his mob oratory, and his deliberate cultivation of a large following among the black population. While
there was a clear streak of fanaticism and a fondness for power
and notoriety in his nature, Gordon was one of the few consistent spokesmen for poor disenfranchised blacks. He denounced immigration schemes and advocated increased expenditure on education, sanitation, and asylums for orphans and
the infirm. He condemned corruption and jobbery, called for
tax relief for the poor, and in 1865 he excoriated the Government's decision to resume corporal punishment.[14] In his view,
the resources of colony were misdirected, especially in the case
of the Anglican establishment. It was not, however, his political
views which gave offence, for in the main those views were held
by other, well-respected members of the Assembly. It was his
manner, his emotional revilings of opponents in the House, and
his readiness in public forum 'to do any and everything that will
lead to his popularity, with the greasy, unwashed, mobocracy
of the island', as one coloured assemblyman, the editor of the
Falmouth Post, put it.[15]

The circumstances of 1865 provided a fertile field for Gordon's
talents. In response to the Queen's Advice, he prepared an
address to those whom he designated the poor people, the
starving people, the naked people of St. Ann's: 'come forth',
he wrote, 'and protest against the unjust misrepresentations
made against you by Mr. Governor Eyre and his band of
custodes'.[16] He urged the black poor of St. Thomas in the East

---

[14] G. W. Gordon to Cardwell, 24 Mar. 1865, bound in C.O. 137/390, no. 89.
Several years earlier Gordon had expressed his own views on the problems of
Jamaica and its needs. Gordon to Newcastle, 7 May 1862, enclosed in C.O.
137/367, no. 59.

[15] This description of Gordon was rendered by Mr. Castello in January 1864
after Gordon had harangued the Assembly for two hours on a motion to censure
Governor Eyre, a motion which no other member would second. Eyre to Newcastle,
18 Jan. 1864, C.O. 137/378, no. 14.

[16] Report of the Jamaica Royal Commission, P.P. XXXI [3683-1], Part II,
evidence of Governor Eyre, 31 Jan. 1866, p. 89.

to shake off their sloth, to speak and act: 'The Government have taxed you to defend your own rights against the enormities of an unscrupulous and oppressive foreigner—Mr. Custos Ketelhodt.'[17] Baron von Ketelhodt, a former executive committeeman, whom Gordon labelled an enemy of the people's peace, had been one of his principle targets since 1862, when the Baron was party to Gordon's dismissal from the magistracy.[18] Gordon had his largest following in St. Thomas, and there, it would appear, the parish vestry with whom he had a running battle was either corrupt, inefficient, or both.[19]

Disturbances began in Morant Bay on 7 October, when a body of peasants descended upon the town in an attempt to intimidate justices who were hearing a case of assault.[20] When the Court ordered the arrest of a disruptive spectator, the assembled peasantry rescued the man and beat the police. Several days later several policemen were dispatched to the neighbouring village of Stoney Gut to apprehend the alleged ringleader of the affair, Paul Bogle, a Native Baptist preacher, friend of Gordon, and a small property-owner of considerable influence among the local peasantry. The police were met by several hundred of Bogle's followers who forced them upon oath to desert the whites and 'cleave to the black'. On 11 October Bogle and a group numbering about 400 marched into Morant Bay carrying sticks and cutlasses. They plundered the local police station of its fire-arms and presented themselves at the Court House where the vestry were meeting. The Custos, von Ketelhodt, who, on the preceding evening had written the Governor appealing for troops, appeared on the stairway calling for peace. He was answered by threats of violence. When he began reading the Riot Act, militiamen who had stationed themselves before the Court House were hemmed in by the mob and pelted with stones. Under order, they fired into the crowd only to be swarmed under by the peasants. Those who escaped took refuge in the Court House with terrified parish magistrates. The building was set on fire and shortly

[17] Ibid.
[18] See p. 413, n. 16.
[19] Hall, *Free Jamaica*, p. 252; also, see testimony of T. W. Jackson before the Jamaica Royal Commission, P.P. 1866, XXXI [3683-1], Part II, pp. 357–63.
[20] This account is taken from the Report of the Jamaica Royal Commission, P.P. 1866, XXX [3683], Part I, pp. 10–18.

thereafter its besieged inmates were forced into the open where many of them, including von Ketelhodt, were beaten to death. In succeeding days, rebellious blacks fanned out in several directions. Bogle led a party up the Blue Mountain Valley; others proceeded to Bath, looting and beating;[21] and insurgents appeared within twelve miles of Port Antonio. Whites and coloureds fled their homes, many of them seeking refuge on ships which conveyed them to Kingston. Panic swept the island, and Governor Eyre declared martial law in the county of Surrey, except for Kingston.

Troops were dispatched from Newcastle through the interior passes to cut off Bogle; others were transferred by sea to Morant Bay, Port Antonio, and intervening points. The Maroons were called down from their mountain villages to aid the repression, and Eyre wrote to Barbados requesting all the troops they could spare. Government forces gave no quarter, and within five days the insurrection was contained. Blacks who fled the oncoming troops were shot; 1,000 cottages and other buildings were destroyed. Courts martial imposed summary punishment during and after the fighting. In fact, the known statistics tell a grim tale: at least 85 people were killed without trial, 354 were executed after trial, and about 600 were flogged, some with disgusting cruelty.[22] The intent of the authorities was plain: to crush the rebellion by swift and terrible action, thereby preventing its spread to other districts of the island.[23]

The Morant Bay uprising, though essentially a local action taken against unpopular parish authorities, was rooted in

[21] T. W. Jackson, a coloured stipendiary magistrate who had served in St. Thomas from 1860 until his transfer shortly before the Morant Bay uprising, hastened to the troubled district in the hope that he could have a quieting influence upon the people. He stopped at Amity Hall Estate for refreshment, and shortly thereafter rioters attacked the main house. Jackson went out to meet them confident that he could reason with them. They assaulted him, leaving him in a pool of blood. He survived; his host was killed. Jackson to Jordan, 16 Oct. 1865, enclosed in C.O. 137/394, no. 271.

[22] Report of Jamaica Royal Commission, P.P. 1866, XXX [3683], Part I, p. 25. At Bath, a local magistrate ordered men to be whipped with the cat after 'wires twisted round the cords, and the different tails so constructed were knotted'.

[23] In defence of his actions, Eyre wrote: 'It was necessary to make an example which by striking terror might deter other districts from following the horrible example of St. Thomas in the East.' Eyre continued to believe that the swiftness and severity of the Government's action prevented a general rebellion. Eyre to Cardwell, 8 Dec. 1865, C.O. 137/396, no. 321.

grievances which were common to blacks throughout the island. Had the insurrection in St. Thomas achieved an appearance of success, it might, under the circumstances of 1865, have ignited similar outbreaks in other parishes creating widespread conflagration. Although there was no organized conspiracy to transform Jamaica into a second Haiti as Eyre and a large portion of the white and coloured population believed,[24] the Underhill meetings and the agitation of 1865 had produced a strong sense of solidarity among the black population and afforded them a conspicuous political leadership which they had not previously possessed. The implications of the Morant Bay rising were broad and dangerous, and it serves no purpose to minimize them simply because the disturbances were quickly contained. Riots had occurred before—in Westmoreland in 1859 and at Falmouth in 1860—but those disturbances had neither the territorial nor psychological range of the St. Thomas affair.[25] Not since the slave rebellion in 1831-2 had any group of rioters so deliberately combined acts of terror with quasi-military operations. Though the suppression of the rising was inexcusably savage, the gravity of the crisis was vastly greater than anything experienced in Jamaica since emancipation.[26]

[24] Gordon was reported by many parties to have made reference in public meetings to Haiti, and Eyre was very sensitive on that point. In a letter to Cardwell defending his actions, he wrote, 'it must be borne in mind that the success which attended the efforts of the Haytians against the French, and more recently of the St. Domingans against the Spanish, afforded examples and encouragement which from the vicinity of those republics to Jamaica, were constantly before the peasantry of this country . . .' Eyre to Cardwell, Jan. 1866, P.P. 1866, XXX [3682], p. 3.

[25] In his *Free Jamaica* (pp. 248–9), Hall argues that 'the Falmouth Riot of 1859 and the Morant Bay Riot of 1865 were not dissimilar, except in the reactions of the governors and the means employed to subdue the rioters'. The great weight of evidence produced for the Jamaica Royal Commission suggests that conditions in the colony were very different from what they had been in 1859, and the actions taken by the rioters themselves took more lives, extended over much more territory, and were more clearly planned than anything which had previously occurred. Hall expresses great contempt for Eyre, but the fact that two governors would react as differently as Eyre and Darling did to the Morant Bay and Falmouth riots suggests that the circumstances of the two events were substantially different unless, of course, one believes Eyre to have been an utterly bloodthirsty character.

[26] It was the verdict of the Jamaica Royal Commissioners that 'such was the state of excitement prevailing in other parts of the island that had more than a momentary success been obtained by the insurgents, their ultimate overthrow would have been attended with a still more fearful loss of life and property.' P.P. 1866, XXX [3683], Part I, p. 40.

The action which aroused greatest controversy during this tragic episode was the arrest and execution of George William Gordon. Gordon had not been in Morant Bay at the time of the rising, but his close association with Bogle (who was captured by Maroons and executed), his opposition to the St. Thomas authorities, and his inflammatory rhetoric and political activity during preceding months implicated him in the affair. Few people in authority doubted his involvement, but the Custos in Kingston was reluctant to seek his arrest for fear of triggering disorder in the city. Eyre insisted on it, and Gordon gave himself up. He was transported to Morant Bay,[27] tried before a military court, and hanged for high treason. In a subsequent investigation of the trial, Royal Commissioners declared the evidence against Gordon insufficient to prove his complicity in the outbreak.[28] At the same time, they did not find him guiltless. He had aroused a passionate following among embittered but ignorant peasants. For his own part, he could draw the line between agitation and insurrection; his followers could not.[29]

The Morant Bay uprising was not simply a conflict of race, but in that affair as in all aspects of life and struggle in the West Indies, race was a significant factor. Black men were killed and beaten by the rioters; and from the opposite side, black troops, Maroons, black militiamen, and black magistrates were mobilized to secure order. While acknowledging this, one must not deny importance to the slogans and rallying cries of Bogle's men, or ignore the seething animus which separated the races in the years preceding the tragedy. C. A. Price, a black man who had represented St. Thomas in the Assembly, was beaten to death: his fate was determined in the streets when one rioter, spurning the order to refrain from killing black people, asserted that Price had a black skin but a white heart.[30]

[27] It was an action of the most dubious legal rectitude to remove Gordon from an area where civil law persisted to try him in a district under martial law.
[28] Report of the Jamaica Royal Commission, P.P. 1866, XXX [3683], Part I, p. 38.
[29] Eyre commented upon this when defending his arrest of Gordon, 'considering it right . . . that whilst the poor black men who had been misled were undergoing condign punishment, the chief instigator of all the evil should not go unpunished . . .' Eyre to Cardwell, 20 Oct. 1865, C.O. 137/393, no. 251.
[30] Report of the Jamaica Royal Commission, P.P. 1866, XXX [3683], Part I, p. 14.

'Colour for colour' was the pervasive cry of the rioters. They spared growing crops, trash houses, and fine homes: whites were to be humbled; particular white men were to be destroyed; and the land was to revert with its cane-fields and buildings intact to the poor black people to whom it rightfully belonged. These sentiments, though they did not represent a carefully defined long-range strategy, were widely uttered during the crisis. If they only constituted the inchoate desire, the passionate remarks of peasant people during the uninhibited mêlée of Morant Bay, they connoted an anguish, a hatred, a deep feeling of injustice, which had become a fixture of life in St. Thomas in the East—and, we may presume, in the rest of Jamaica and in other island colonies as well. One recalls the description of Morant Bay in 1862 written by P. A. Espeut, an assemblyman who had his own trials with Governor Eyre:

> The town of Morant Bay and its immediate vicinity is like many other small towns both in this Island and elsewhere, but perhaps preeminently in this Island, the nest of a set of characters whose principal occupation is that of *'half inch Lawyers'* and village politicians, some of them possessing scarcely means of livelihood and others with no visible means of subsistence, but professing to be Mechanics in a small way, while the town and its vicinity are also the hotbed of prejudices against *white persons in particular* and all respectable persons in general, their position in society being regarded by the characters alluded to as the greatest *crime* of which they could be guilty.[31]

Espeut's remark distinguishing the blacks' particular feeling against whites and their more general prejudice against 'all respectable persons' suggests that wealth and social status, not just race, were key factors bearing upon the animus of the Negroes. This was clearly the case. But in the West Indies, race, wealth, social status, and religious and cultural connections were mutually reinforcing. Wealth and high social standing tended to belong to those who were either white or who had white progenitors.

---

[31] Espeut was reporting on a public meeting involving George William Gordon held at the Native Baptist Meeting House near Morant Bay, 27 Aug. 1862. 'The negroes', he wrote, 'are taught to consider the Planters (of whom the Magistracy is principally composed) as their greatest enemies and by none more than Mr. George Wm Gordon . . .' Report of P. A. Espeut, bound in Eyre to Newcastle, 23 Sept. 1862, C.O. 137/367, no. 84.

In private, whites may have considered people of colour their social inferiors; but the colour line between the two groups had been relaxed in the free period, and in all forms of public intercourse relations between whites and coloureds had become thoroughly entwined. Blacks were not excluded from this intercourse, but in island societies which were predominantly black, comparatively few people of pure African origins could be numbered among the so-called 'respectable' classes.

In the West Indies, respectability implied a European cultural affinity, a level of education, a manner of speech, and a certain approach to religious or spiritual concerns. In the latter case, a hierarchy of preference prevailed. All groups who carried the Christian faith to the rural poor were commended and encouraged, but some were commended more than others. Of the various European sects active in the islands, the Jamaican Baptists enjoyed lowest esteem among the generality of 'respectable' persons. The Baptists had too strong an identification with the rural peasantry and too much contempt for propertied elements. The Native Baptists were even less revered in the view of the upper classes, for their dubious social and political identities were further soiled by doctrinal divergencies and antinomianism.

At the risk of affording excessive emphasis to the role of George William Gordon, one can appreciate that under the tense circumstances of 1865 his greatest social sin was to betray his class. He ignored the established conventions of political propriety—lax as they might have been in the island—and he coveted the loyalty of poor Negroes. His attachment to the Native Baptists was considered by his critics to be no more than an ignoble means of gratifying his lust for power. In all his proceedings he endangered the security of the 'respectable' classes—the element of society to which he rightly belonged by virtue of property, position, manners, and station. In so doing, he invited supreme victimization, for in the West Indies the well-being of the upper and middle classes, however they might quarrel among themselves, depended upon stability, whether that stability was grounded in the perpetuation of plantation culture or the gradual and peaceful displacement of it.

There was always more talk than action in advancing the

interests of the emancipated class. Sir Henry Barkly had divided vocal Jamaicans into two categories: the planting interests and the Negrophils.[32] Although the latter contended that the future of the island belonged to people of African descent, they did little to hasten the death of the old order and little more to advance the prospects of the new. What small farmers and the most ambitious peasants needed was better secondary roads linking their properties with main roads. They required more effective law enforcement to protect their growing crops, and they could have benefited from tax relief or from measures designed to stimulate their productivity. That they secured none of these is not surprising in view of the impoverishment of the island Government. But it is puzzling that the town party, with its substantial Negrophil elements, did not initiate more legislation on behalf of farmers and peasants during those times when planting members were predictably absent from Spanish Town. In fact, legislation continued to favour the sugar interest. Export taxes established in 1858 fell with proportionately more weight on the producers of minor crops than upon the sugar planters. Small farmers needed marketing assistance—better systems for transporting their products to port and selling them overseas—but they received no encouragement from the Government and little aid from private parties. One is compelled to speculate that the town party, which might logically have been expected to support a revised marketing system for small farmers, would have been the very group most threatened by it. On the question of educational appropriations, the Negrophils were certainly more demanding of colonial revenue than the planters, but the scale of their demands was only modestly greater when one considers the magnitude of the educational problem in the colony. There was a growing need for prompt and equitable justice at the local level, for the peasantry had little or no faith in the prevailing system and lawlessness was growing. Nevertheless, judicial reform received no serious consideration. Much of the legislature's inaction was the result of economic difficulties; part of it may be attributed to its unflattering preoccupation with personal bickering; but one cannot avoid the conclusion

[32] Barkly to Newcastle, 21 May 1855, C.O. 136/326, no. 59.

that all parties in the Assembly were primarily interested in advancing their own narrow class interests and that no group, despite protestations to the contrary, was profoundly committed to pursuing the interests of small farmers and peasants. This was certainly the conclusion reached by rural blacks.

In the wake of the Morant Bay disturbances, Eyre appealed to the legislature to make 'a great and generous sacrifice' for the sake of the colony—to abolish itself in favour of a strong executive government.[33] Both the nature of his appeal and the conciliatory response it evoked merit consideration. Speaking on 7 November, one month after the initial disturbance at Morant Bay, the Governor described the colony as existing on the edge of a volcano: 'disloyalty, sedition, and murderous intentions' were everywhere to be found, he said. He expressed contempt for the peasantry, whom he considered 'less under an obligation to work for subsistence than any peasantry in the world'. If they had failed to achieve prosperity, he asserted, it was because of their 'indolence, improvidence, and vice'. Claiming that a spirit of insurrection was deeply rooted in the colony, he declared that only a strong-minded government could preserve the island from further violence.

The Assembly took no exception to the Governor's remarks. It may be assumed, of course, that Eyre's critics in the Assembly had been humbled, if not silenced, by the catastrophe in St. Thomas and that the planters enjoyed a commanding numerical and moral position in the House. Notwithstanding that, the response of the Assembly to Eyre's address seems nothing short of remarkable in view of that body's earlier history. Thanking the Governor for his vigorous action in quelling the rebellion, it concurred with him that the disturbances had threatened the lives of the white and coloured inhabitants of the colony. It concluded that 'nothing but the existence of a strong Government [could] prevent the Island from lapsing into the condition of a second Haiti . . .'[34]

There was much hysteria in the island and the Assembly's response to Eyre provides some evidence of it. But, there is

[33] Address of Governor Eyre to the Legislature, 7 Nov. 1865, enclosed in C.O. 137/394, no. 284.
[34] Response of the Assembly to Governor Eyre, 8 Nov. 1865, enclosed in C.O. 137/395, no. 286.

little reason to presume that the House, in a panic, surrendered to the Governor and accepted, without independent inquiry, his assessment of the situation. Whatever may be said about the Jamaica Assembly, it was not a naïve body of easily led men capable of being deceived into a voluntary cessation of its authority by a Governor to whom many of its members had shown little respect during preceding years. The Assembly had weathered many crises, and despite its internal critics it would certainly have tried to weather this one had it not been convinced that its moral force was spent and its legislative competence dubious, that the security of the 'respectable' classes continued to be in danger, and that economic, political, and social stability could best be achieved under a different constitutional arrangement. There was some resistance to an elimination of the Assembly, especially among coloured members who had achieved equal status with whites through that institution, but even had the House been opposed to constitutional change, the British Government was determined to have it. The Morant Bay rising had provided the Colonial Office the momentous crisis which authorities there had long considered to be a necessary preliminary to parliamentary intervention. Secretary of State Cardwell informed Eyre in a letter of 1 December that if the Assembly would not accept constitutional change, the Government would secure it by appropriate action in Parliament.[35]

The Assembly was divided three ways. One group preferred a single legislative house consisting of elected and nominated members. Another wanted Crown colony government. A third group—though it acknowledged the rising threat of the 'lower orders'—wished to retain the old legislative system.[36] Although a compromise Bill was passed providing for a unicameral system having 12 elected and 12 nominated members, there was considerable dissatisfaction with that plan. When Eyre received

---

[35] Draft, Cardwell to Eyre, 1 Dec. 1865, bound in C.O. 137/394.

[36] Eyre to Cardwell, 7 Dec. 1865, C.O. 137/396, no. 313. In a speech to the Assembly, the aged coloured leader, Robert Osborn, declared that in years to come the colony's government would fall into the hands of blacks. 'We may strive to prevent it,' he argued, 'but I think our struggle will be in vain.' The old representative system, for all its shortcomings, was the only means by which the 'lower orders' could be trained for self-government, Osborn believed. A portion of his speech and the heated reaction to it is printed in Hart's *Life of Gordon*, pp. 122–3.

notice from London that the Crown would welcome the opportunity to alter the constitution and to assume responsibility for the government of the island, the Assembly discarded its newly devised programme, and extended a reforming prerogative to the Colonial Office.[37] Without delay, Jamaica was transformed into a Crown colony, and the ancient Jamaica Assembly ceased to exist.

It was well that it did, though the change was not without costs. The Assembly had provided an avenue through which non-white Jamaicans could achieve high social standing: it had been the focus of journalistic attention; and its proceedings had afforded colonists a source of excitement and titillation not easily replaced in the island. Its abolition meant the surrender of political initiative to a distant power, and this involved various liabilities, not least of which was the loss of self-esteem. Authoritarian government, no matter how efficient, is never a suitable nursery for self-government, and under the Crown colony system the reduced number of administrative appointments were usually given to whites and frequently to whites from Great Britain. In spite of these drawbacks, constitutional change at that juncture offered more advantages than disadvantages. The Assembly had functioned well when comparative prosperity and a climate of hope pervaded the island, but it succumbed to wilful obstructionism and personal feuding in difficult times. The Assembly's constructive periods coincided with years of high sugar prices—the early forties and late fifties—but lean years greatly outnumbered constructive ones. The 1860s were marked by unproductive and utterly divisive quarrelling. While Crown colony government eliminated representative institutions, by no means could the Assembly be considered a truly representative body. Less than one per cent of the population exercised the franchise, and if the disenfranchised black population was to gain the consideration in legislation which its numbers demanded, it was more likely to receive it under the patronizing power of the Crown than through the good offices of the colonial élite. The unpredictable nature of government under the old system discouraged capital investment in Jamaica, and everyone suffered from that. The Crown colony plan simplified administrative procedures,

[37] Eyre to Cardwell, 22 Dec. 1865, confidential, C.O. 137/396.

permitted swift legislative action, and afforded an impression of orderly, stable, and purposeful government which the wrangling Assembly had not. The Assembly may not have been the curse of Jamaica as one of its disillusioned members had asserted, but neither was it an asset to an impoverished community divided by strife and hostility. Even those who lamented its passing could not deny its panoramic imperfections.

The West India interest in Britain warmly endorsed the change to Crown colony government believing that it provided greater security for their investments. Alarmed by events in Jamaica, absentees encouraged similar constitutional changes in other islands. The Leewards were especially ripe for such change. The system of executive committees had not functioned smoothly, and the Crown was in the position of having to assume pre-eminent power, concede a form of responsible government to the assemblies, or revert to the pre-1854 assembly system. Since the latter two alternatives were unthinkable in 1865, the Colonial Office encouraged a change to authoritarian government.[38] Sir Benjamin Pine, the Acting Governor-General of the Leewards, was a superlative manipulator and a strong advocate of authority. Commending the smoother operation of an authoritarian system and assuring leading political figures in the Leewards that their interests would be protected by a change, he provided the impetus to reform. In St. Kitts and Antigua he urged planter oligarchs to terminate the old system before a large and articulate coloured element had arisen to challenge their authority. In Nevis, where the Assembly was already dominated by people of colour, he insisted that the flow of investment capital would be tied to reform. Within a year of the Morant Bay rising, Pine had orchestrated the destruction of the assembly system throughout the Leeward Islands. It was supplanted by single legislative councils having both elected and nominated members.

Constitutional change was not so easily achieved in the Windwards. The sugar interest was weaker in those communities, and consequently economic pressure from London had less

---

[38] For the material in this and the succeeding paragraph I have relied upon Morrell, *British Colonial Policy*, ch. XIV, and Rogers, 'Fall of the Old Representative System', chaps. VIII, IX.

impact. St. Vincent was an exception. The Morant Bay affair struck fear into the island's upper classes, evoking grim recollections of their 1862 riots and equally grave fears that they might be repeated. A movement was launched to establish a garrison of British troops in St. Vincent on a permanent basis, and in April 1866 it was suggested in the House that the island become a Crown colony. Opposition to that status was strong, but in the following year the Assembly abolished itself in favour of a single chamber on the Leeward Island plan. Tobago and Grenada were much slower to yield, but consistent pressure from London had its effect in the mid-1870s, producing unicameral and subsequently Crown colony government in those islands. Only Barbados withstood pressure to change.

The events at Morant Bay had enormous impact in England. Having become a forgotten backwater of empire, Jamaica suddenly captured the attention of a public fascinated and appalled by dreadful accounts of the death and dismemberment of whites and the awful retribution on riotous blacks. Exeter Hall again resounded with protest, and the radical press demanded an official inquiry. Acceding to these pressures, the Government appointed a Royal Commission of three men[39] to investigate the tragedy. The commissioners visited scenes of the disturbances, and heard 730 witnesses in a period of 51 days. In April 1866 they issued their report. Eyre was commended for the promptness and vigour with which he responded to disturbances, but the commissioners deplored his continuance of martial law for several weeks after the insurrection had been effectively reduced. They asserted that executions had been excessive and corporal punishments recklessly administered.[40]

Before this report was published, a group of radical politicians and middle-class philanthropists had formed a 'Jamaica Committee' to seek the judicial punishment of Eyre and other persons guilty of criminal excesses and to obtain just compensation for the victims of official abuse.[41] This group, led by John

[39] Major General Sir Henry Knight Storks; Russell Gurney, Queen's Counsel, Recorder of the City of London; John Blossett Maule, Barrister and Recorder of the Town of Leeds.

[40] Report of the Jamaica Royal Commission, P.P. 1866, XXX [3683], Part I, pp. 40–1.

[41] For the British reaction to the Morant Bay episode, see Bernard Semmel, *Jamaican Blood and Victorian Conscience* (Cambridge, Mass., 1963).

Stuart Mill, included Charles Buxton, Thomas Hughes, John Bright, Professor Goldwin Smith, and a large and illustrious body of middle-class industrialists and academicians. They were confronted immediately by an Eyre Defence Committee headed by John Ruskin and Thomas Carlyle. The Defence Committee drew support from the great literary names, Tennyson and Dickens, from Sir Roderick Murchison, President of the Geographical Society, and from a large portion of the aristocracy and the Anglican clergy. On the one side, Eyre was denounced as a murderer (the case of George William Gordon being prominent) who vindictively employed his power to brutalize and destroy people whom he deemed inferior by virtue of their colour. On the other side, the ex-Governor's defenders applauded his vigilance and mocked the absurdity of punishing the man who saved Jamaica. The Eyre controversy became entangled with domestic issues. Eyre's most vocal detractors were leaders of the movement for franchise reform, and the case against the ex-Governor was damaged by their participation in demonstrations at Hyde Park and Trafalgar Square. Apart from these events, the tactics of Irish Fenians convinced many Britons that disorder and terrorism must be met by forceful action—a conclusion which indirectly commended the behaviour of Eyre. When in 1868 an indictment against the ex-Governor for high crimes and misdemeanours was brought into the Court of Queen's Bench, the Grand Jury threw it out on insufficient grounds.[42] The Eyre controversy had raged for more than two years, and without question the vast majority of the nation supported the ex-Governor.[43]

After the Eyre case, the *Spectator*, a Liberal weekly, angrily commented: 'We pardon Eyre because his error of judgement involves only Negro blood . . .'[44] There was much truth in that remark. It was inconceivable that so brutal a suppression would have been launched, let alone countenanced, had the victims of it been European. The racism of whites was still a

[42] Attempts by the Jamaica Committee to secure an indictment for murder failed. Before the Eyre case was heard, the indictments against two officers who had sat on Gordon's court martial were thrown out. Semmel, *Jamaican Blood*, p. 155.

[43] The unpopular cause of the Jamaica Committee probably lost John Stuart Mill his parliamentary seat. He was the only Liberal defeated in metropolitan London in the election of 1868.

[44] Semmel, *Jamaican Blood*, p. 171.

firm fixture in their treatment of dependent peoples, and Eyre's prejudice was little different from that of his counterparts throughout the islands. His description of Negroes as creatures 'of impulse and irritation, easily misled, very excitable . . . little removed in many respects from absolute savages'[45] echoed sentiments which continued to appear in the executive correspondence of many sugar colonies.

Not many years before, strong language of that type had been used to describe the English working class. But that was much less the case in 1865. The character of the British working class, like the character of Britain, had changed demonstrably during the period encompassed by this study. The value of British trade had nearly trebled; the population of England and Wales had risen from 14,000,000 to 21,000,000; cities had grown rapidly, and their industries had produced a vigorous middle class, whose spokesmen had altered the character of Parliament and whose disposition had impressed a new morality and a vigorous self-confidence on the nation. In the sixties Britain was animated by evangelical religion and a sublime faith in progress. At the root of progress lay productivity: industry was deemed a virtue, lassitude a vice. With diligence, energy, careful abstinence, and a good measure of 'self-help', men could raise themselves above their peers: the businessman could expand his markets and increase profits; the working man could enhance his purchasing power and reap the rewards of self-respect. Respect was the by-product of virtue, and respectability was the universal goal of the nation. Conscious of their accumulated refinements, 'respectable' Britons impugned those who rejected their formula for salvation, their commitment to neatness, their dedication to industry, to discipline, and to self-control. It was a nation, wrote G. M. Young, 'easily shocked, more ready to spurn, to flaunt, to admire, and, above all, to preach.'[46]

No people seemed in greater need of preaching to than the black multitudes of the West India colonies. Had they not squandered their freedom in ignorance and idleness, scorning missionaries and rejecting planters? Had they not forsaken progress and embraced immorality? Where was the diligence,

[45] Eyre to Cardwell, 8 Dec. 1865, C.O. 137/396, no. 321.
[46] G. M. Young, *Victorian England: Portrait of an Age* (New York, 1964), p. 14.

the discipline, the subordination and foresight which rendered men virtuous and nations prosperous? In a word, to the Victorian Englishman of the mid-sixties, the West Indies were a sad disappointment. The once-proud colony of Jamaica had come to ruin: its physical infrastructure was decayed, its planters impoverished, and its people, by virtue of their own improvidence, poor, demoralized, and rebellious. Such was the state of British thinking when Henry Taylor prepared a reply to the people of St. Ann's. If his remarks were callous, they reflected the sentiments of an imperial bureaucracy whose expectations had been influenced by the remarkable changes in English society, whose attitudes were governed by evangelical propriety, and whose notions of progress were inextricably tied to productivity, trade figures, accumulating property, and the refinements which these entailed. In the fullness of their self-esteem, Victorians had grown less tolerant of diversity, of the peculiar aspirations of those who rejected their codes and worshipped at different altars. Their contempt for West Indian peasants was not merely racial—although race was an ingredient of their thinking—it was the disdain that a people who had discovered the true principles of individual and national life inevitably felt for those who had deliberately rejected them.

At the base of British social change was the nation's extraordinary economic growth. While free trade had nurtured that growth, it had shattered the West Indian economy. Where the plantations survived, the wages of workers fell. In low-density colonies, planters could not attract a numerous and disciplined agrarian proletariat which would work regularly for low wages at the call of proprietors, while accepting estate housing and provision grounds. In Trinidad and British Guiana where land was fertile, estates relatively unencumbered, and government dominated by planters, the required working force was only secured through immigration. In Jamaica and the Windwards, political complications and planter indebtedness had rendered immigration less promising and therefore less desirable.

The psychological legacy of slavery accentuated the fundamental incompatibility between planters and peasants. Apart from its physical rigour, cane labour was perceived as the work of slaves, and contracts for plantation service were despised because they smacked of the dependence and subordination of slavery. Planters and peasants were in competition for the land: the former desirous of withholding it from the emancipated class in order to compel their wage service, the latter anxious to obtain it as a means of perpetuating their independence. Committed to the preservation of a plantation system with its social hierarchy and its related civic institutions, the Crown supported the planters. From the beginning of the free period, imperial authorities had tried to reproduce in the West Indies the social and economic conditions which prevailed in rural England. Though they failed, they did not relent, and the combination of failure and relentlessness was evident in the Queen's Advice of 1865.

In the English rural system, the squire administered the law, the Anglican parson preached religion, and both served as guardians of a proper moral order. By and large, free West Indian society possessed neither the homogeneity nor the human equipment to succeed with this paternalistic model.[47] The planter-squire, usually a manager, not a proprietor, of the land, was a deeply interested party at odds with a peasantry which enjoyed vastly more independence than its British counterpart. The parson represented the planter's faith, if only his nominal faith, and his brand of worship afforded no inspiration to the emancipated class. For all its shortcomings, the English rural system had a civilizing influence on the English lower classes, but that influence was the result of general social acceptance. Because the West Indian peasantry did not acquiesce in the English system its civilizing influence was comparatively meagre.

Though it is easy to find fault in the social and institutional structure of the free West India colonies, some of the faults of the dependencies mirrored those of the metropolis. We have

---

[47] The following passage appears in the evidence of Alexander Heslop, the Attorney-General of Jamaica, delivered before the Jamaica Royal Commission. 'Q: Is the state of society in Jamaica such as to cause very great difficulty in the appointment of honest and intelligent magistrates, who from position should be above that suspicion?—Oh, very difficult, it is impossible to do it, you have not the class of people here which you have in England, representing the country gentry . . . No man in this island has any spare time to give to the public, we live from hand to mouth in all classes of life.' P.P. 1866, XXX [3683], Part I, p. 329.

criticized the Barbados planters for failing to provide adequate sanitation in Bridgetown before the onslaught of cholera, but it took a cholera epidemic in England to produce a central board of health in 1848. If public support to education was insufficient in the West Indies, it received no strong impetus in Britain until the 1850s, a time when the dual devastation of depression and free trade had stricken the sugar colonies. In the Caribbean, as in England, religious controversies were as great an impediment to educational funding as were ungenerous legislators. *Laissez-faire* had its paralysing effects upon both societies. West Indian legislatures normally took their cues from Westminster, but in the Caribbean economic adversity was an even greater impediment to collective measures of social reform than was economic philosophy. If civic order, fine roads, improved port facilities, and well-preserved public buildings were the mark of a well-regulated society, then no district of England was better regulated than Barbados.

Barbados and Jamaica have been presented as contrasting cases in this study, the former having fulfilled to a large extent the aspirations of the metropolitan emancipators of 1833, the latter having confirmed many of their apprehensions. Anti-slavery zealots may have beguiled themselves with universal pronouncements about the superior efficiency of free labour over slave labour in the production of tropical staples, but the authors of the Emancipation Act had suffered no such illusions. Officials at the Colonial Office in the early thirties had read enough Ricardo and Wakefield to foresee the perils that might beset the sugar industry in low-density colonies. What imperial authorities feared in 1833 and deplored thereafter was the loss of control by Europeans over a large portion of the emancipated population. In this regard they perceived better than the missionaries that the preservation of the sugar estates and the progress of European religion and culture were largely inter-dependent. By way of contrast, modern students of the Caribbean, expressing different biases and aspirations, have commended rather than condemned the rise of an independent peasantry in low density colonies. Whatever view one might take, it is clear that for the ex-slave there was no easy avenue to the good life. His every gain was offset by a corresponding loss. Where civic refinements were most abundant, he enjoyed little independence; where he gained his independence he sacrificed civic amenities of every description. Even the peasants of Trinidad and Guiana who acquired their own lands without losing access to wage labour on the plantations were compelled to pay for their convenience by sharing their patrimony with tens of thousands of alien East Asians.

Though great changes were wrought in the sugar colonies in the decades following emancipation, old social and economic problems lingered. The people were divided culturally, and race continued to be an important element in that division. Sugar was still king—even though its sway was severely restricted—and the well-being of the colonial population depended to an uncomfortable extent on market prices in Europe and America. The routine brutality of slavery was gone, but the conditions which breed brutality were not. Though freedom had been achieved, the poverty and ignorance in which most West Indians had their being and against which no government could effectively contend severely circumscribed the benefits as well as the uses of that freedom.

END NOTES

1. (See p. 119.) In the House of Commons, Buxton managed debate in behalf of the anti-slavery movement; in the Lords, this duty fell to Lord Suffield. These men had been spokesmen of the abolitionist position in their respective Houses for ten years. Their willingness to entertain compensation for the planters represented a position taken by the moderate side of the anti-slavery movement, essentially the old guard. The Agency Committee, representing the more zealous and radical elements of the movement, opposed compensation. It was the Agency Committee which had accelerated the movement, given it a popular dimension, and attracted tens of thousands of fresh adherents. The old leadership feared that the popular thrust of the Agency Committee might pressure them into adopting a more radical posture in Parliament. On the eve of the compensation vote, Buxton was visited by a delegation representing the more strident popular side of the movement. These men, including Sturge, Cropper, and George Stephen, urged him to oppose compensation. Buxton refused, insisting that he retain his liberty to act as the parliamentary situation required. When Buxton acquiesced to both monetary compensation and an apprenticeship, numerous persons representing a very large segment of the anti-slavery movement chastised him severely. See, Buxton, *Memoirs*, pp. 336–43. For an analysis of the changing relations between the two wings of the anti-slavery movement, see D. Eltis, 'Dr. Stephen Lushington and the Campaign to Abolish Slavery in the British Empire', *The Journal of Caribbean History*, I (1970), 47–56.

2. (See p. 143.) Magistrates who fraternized excessively with planters were transferred to other districts, not suspended. Smith to Glenelg, 9 Dec. 1835, C.O. 28/116, no. 51. In January 1836, S. M. Grindlay sentenced a Trinidad cooper to 20 stripes and a month's hard labour for impudence toward his overseers. When the cooper was cut down he threatened to complain to the Governor. Grindlay gave him another 19 stripes and a second month of hard labour. The case shocked the Colonial Office but the Governor recommended that Grindlay be retained because his record was otherwise satisfactory. The Colonial Secretary agreed. C.O. 295/110, no. 18; C.O. 295/111, no. 73. In 1835 S. M. Delafons sentenced 19 apprentices on Rome and Houston Estate in Guiana to 20 stripes each for damaging the property of the proprietor by failing to keep the boiling fires alive although those labourers had been at work for an average of 15 hours a day during the preceding 8 days. The Governor, who strongly opposed the whip, rebuked Delafons rather than suspend him, largely on grounds that the magistrate had 12 children who required his support. C.O. 111/139, no. 45. Numerous examples of this kind can be recited.

3. (See p. 183.) Circular to the Governors of the British West India and North American Colonies, Sept. 1838, C.O. 318/133. The languid and unresponsive reaction of the Treasury to the pressing needs of the planters is best illustrated by reference to Trinidad where the shortage of agricultural workers increased the planters' desire to hire wage labourers. In May 1836 Sir George Hill appealed to the imperial Government to send out small coin worth £10,000 sterling, promising to pay an equivalent value in doubloons into the British Treasury. Hill explicitly recommended that the money sent out from England should constitute fractional parts of the dollar. There were no British coins in circulation in the colony, and the dollar (or fractional parts of it) was the only coinage with which either apprentices of the island or petty merchants of the Spanish Main who conducted a large volume of business in Trinidad were acquainted. It was generally acknowledged by planters that subdivisions of the English shilling could not be circulated in Trinidad as payment of wages. The Treasury disregarded the Governor's recommendation and transmitted a mere £1,500 in the form of 1½d. and 3d. pieces. Deeply angered and disappointed, the Council of Government voted overwhelmingly to return these coins to Britain, declaring them of no value in the colony. See Hill's correspondence, C.O. 295/111, nos. 64, 81; C.O. 295/114, no. 9.

4. (See p. 212.) Popular attention was focused on the mode of power used to propel sugar mills when it might have been directed with greater prudence to the crushing apparatus. Reporting from Guiana, Dr. John Shier asserted that the average extraction rate from Guiana mills— although powered by steam—did not exceed 45 per cent of the juice of the cane. Even though the three-roller English mills generally in use were inferior to American four-roller mills, the existing apparatus would have been capable of more efficient crushing if adequate attention had been given to regular feeding and to periodic resetting of rollers which became worn and uneven. Shier obtained a 58 per cent extraction rate during a series of experiments which he conducted, and with ample justice he upbraided the planters for their failure to do as well. Memorandum of Dr. John Shier to Michael McChlery, 3 Feb. 1848, P.P. 1847–8 XXIII (245), Appendix to the Seventh Report of the Sel. Comm. on Sugar and Coffee Planting, no. 2. Writing at about the same time as Shier's report, John Davy claimed that Guiana planters had increased their extraction rate from about 50 per cent to 'in many instances . . . as much as 65 percent.' Either Davy exaggerated the advances made in Guiana or Shier underestimated them. See, Davy, *The West Indies*, p. 361.

5. (See p. 219. In addition to precipitating a substantial decline in the marketable value of his estate, the transition from coerced labour was alleged to have cost Barkly a total of £44,390. He calculated those losses in the following manner:

Losses at Highbury Estate, 1839–1847
(£ sterling)

	Credit	Debit
Deprivation of profit, calculated at £5,080 per year (based on average annual earnings, 1826–1838) for nine years of free labor.		45,720
Actual loss to Property, nine years of free labor .		6,170
Interest (4 per cent) received on compensation grant of £18,850	7,500	
TOTAL CALCULATED LOSS, NINE YEARS OF FREE LABOR		44,390

Source: Sel. Comm. on Sugar and Coffee Planting, P.P. 1847–8 XXIII (206), evidence of H. Barkly.

6. (See p. 225.) In their memorial of 1842, cocoa planters offered this accounting of expenditures on a plantation yielding 300 fanegas of cocoa:

Manufacturing and Agricultural Expenses	$920.00
Interest on this amount for six months	27.60
Road assessment	50.00
Commission on sale of produce	45.00
Manager's salary	480.00
Incidental expenses, repairs, buildings, etc..	200.00
	$1,722.60
Revenue from 300 fanegas at $6	1,800.00
Net Revenue	77.40

Memorial of Cocoa Planters, enclosed in MacLeod to Stanley, 10 June 1842, C.O. 295/136, no. 62.

7. (See p. 237.) It was commonly asserted that managers, attorneys, and leaseholders in the colonies deliberately misrepresented conditions on the plantations, exciting panic among absentees in order to depreciate the value of property and enable them to purchase estates at reduced prices. Anton Long makes this point, noting that Richard Barrett, Speaker of the House of Assembly made a number of shrewd purchases during the apprenticeship. See his *Jamaica and the New Order*, pp. 10, 25–56. Jelly repeats the charge in his *A Brief Enquiry*, p. xxi. Samuel Prescod, a Barbados liberal, expressed the same view at the General Anti-Slavery convention in London in 1840. Bigelow refers to it in his *Jamaica in 1850*, p. 87: 'It is a common thing', he wrote 'for the overseers to keep down the returns, and to increase the expenses of estates, by devices perfectly familiar here, until the owner becoming anxious to rid himself of the cares of a property which yielded nothing but anxiety and expense, should send out authority to sell

it for what it would bring. These overseers would then buy it in themselves at a ruinous sacrifice.'

8. (See p. 243.) Retrenchment was intended to affect every aspect of colonial life, and many of the cuts were deeply painful to the legislators who proposed them. £1,738 was to be shaved from road and bridge maintenance; £3,867 from immigration; £7,363 from construction projects on the lunatic asylum, public hospital, and penitentiary; and the medical dispensary programme, recently adopted, with an anticipated cost of £2,750 was to be scrapped. The salaries of officers of the Assembly (Speaker, Clerk, Sergeant at Arms, Chaplain) were to be halved; salaries of clerks of the vestries were to end, saving nearly £2,000. The reduction in salaries to which the Council objected (those of customs officers, Anglican clergymen, judicial officers, prison officers, official assignees, the Registrar in Chancery and head clerk, the Attorney General, Governor's Secretary, and Governor) involved an anticipated saving of £14,837 on what had been a salary bill of £77,220 in 1848. *Votes of the Jamaica Assembly*, 24 Jan. 1849, enclosed in C. E. Grey to Earl Grey, 5 Feb. 1849, C.O. 137/301, no. 15.

9. (See p. 270.) This decision, frequently questioned by historians, has been attacked most recently as an unsound and merely expedient measure by Dr. J. U. J. Asiegbu in his book, *Slavery and the Politics of Liberation, 1787–1861* (New York, 1969). Regrettably, Asiegbu's position is based on a limited understanding of West Indian affairs. His assertion (pp. 35–6) that West Indian colonists defied the will of the metropolitan Government by unilaterally abolishing apprenticeship in 1838 is manifestly mistaken, and his further contention that they did this in order to force the imperial Government to acquiesce in a system of labour immigration compounds his error. He contends that by late 1839 the continued refusal of the British Government to sanction free and unrestricted African immigration to the West Indies had produced 'dark threats of revolution' among colonists in British Guiana and Jamaica, the former threatening to withhold the civil list and the latter breathing secession. In fact, by the end of 1839, the Jamaican constitution crisis—presumably the dispute to which Asiegbu refers—had ended, and at no time was African immigration an important feature of that controversy. Threats to withhold the civil list were almost an annual affair in British Guiana between 1837 and 1842, but immigration was only one of many problems dividing the Court of Policy and the Colonial Office. The major issue of disagreement on immigration involved methods of financing it, not whether Africa would become a free and unrestricted source of labour. Asiegbu's assertion that a timid Colonial Office was forced into accepting African immigration to sugar colonies by the 'danger of West Indian secession' (p. 42) is absolutely groundless. At no time after emancipation did the planters of any West India colony seriously consider an act of secession. They were powerless to accomplish it; their reliance before 1846 on the protected home market rendered such considerations altogether idle; and the black freedmen would not have permitted it. Secessionist sentiment in Jamaica during the early 1830s when the issue at

stake was emancipation constituted little more than the ravings of a lunatic fringe. To presume that a greatly weakened planter class seriously contemplated secession if it did not secure emigration from Africa—the potential size of that immigration was commonly estimated to be small—is neither reasonable nor correct. It is equally mistaken to suggest that the Colonial Office would have taken such threats, had they been made, seriously (p. 42). Contrary to Asiegbu's position, the decision to permit African emigration was made after careful consideration of the risks and rewards of that action. As a policy, it was calculated to enhance the objectives of the Crown, naïve as they may have been, in Africa; to strengthen the plantation economies of the Caribbean colonies in their competition against the forces of slavery; to undermine, thereby, the institutions of slavery and the slave trade; to provide recaptives with what their liberators considered a more beneficial social and economic environment; and to accomplish all this at a saving to the imperial Treasury. Recognizing that foreign states would misrepresent British action as a form of slave-trading, the Government determined nevertheless that African emigration was more likely to advance than retard its over-all objectives. Whatever its consequences, the decision to permit African labour migration to the sugar colonies was not a temporary expedient. Indeed, subsequent ministers enlarged upon Russell's immigration policy. At the same time, James Stephen continued to oppose African emigration to the West Indies for fear of foreign reaction, but Asiegbu (pp. 40–1) misrepresents Stephen's position by quoting him out of context and giving the impression that he was willing to appease the planters on this issue. Stephen's opposition to African emigration is explicitly stated in a memorandum 3 Nov. 1840, C.O. 318/148. In fairness to Asiegbu, his book offers an excellent account of the international ramifications of British emigration policy (pp. 48–63).

10. (See p. 276.) A group of Guiana planters led by Sir John Gladstone had obtained the right to transport Indians to Guiana under five-year contracts, promising a return passage for all who sought it at the expiration of that time. This migration, involving 406 Indians, raised a storm of protest among evangelicals in England. Even *The Times,* normally friendly to the planters, attacked the procedure. John Scoble toured Guiana in 1839 dredging up unseemly incidents involving Indian workers, which he broadcast in speeches and pamphlets. In Calcutta there was criticism of Indian emigration, but that criticism focused upon Mauritius to which over 7,500 Indians had been transported. Responding to public pressure, the Council of India suspended emigration pending an investigation of the question. Although inquiries conducted in Calcutta and Mauritius uncovered a number of abuses, there was little which would confirm the vociferous claims of Exeter Hall. Nevertheless, emigration from India was not renewed until the imperial Government had assumed full responsibility for the conduct of African emigration. I. M. Cumpston, *Indians Overseas in British Territories* (London, 1953), pp. 19–27.

11. (See p. 302.) Prices were determined by a number of variables—

population density, wage rates, availability of land, location, fertility—and they fluctuated widely from one district or colony to another. In Antigua, where land was scarce, freedmen paid £6 for plots only 30 by 40 feet in size. Under such circumstances they had no chance of becoming independent peasants. A few Jamaican planters sold property for as much as £30 an acre, and on rare occasions a stipendiary magistrate would report sales as high as £80 an acre. Ordinarily, peasants obtained plots for £5 or £10 an acre. Where land was abundant and population scanty, prices fluctuated widely, according to proximity to public roadways. A Trinidad proprietor in the Naparima district sold numerous lots along the public road, 50 by 100 feet in size, for £24 each. At the highest rate, proprietors were gleaning between £130 and £200 an acre, but backland plots normally brought only £4 to £6 an acre. Mrs. Flanders, *Antigua*, II, p. 131; Metcalfe to Russell, 30 Mar. 1840, C.O. 137/248, no. 50; Precis of Reports of S.M.s bound with C.O. 137/274, no. 140; Report of R. Daly, enclosed in C.O. 137/257, no. 18; Evidence of Higgins and Lee before Subcommittee of Agricultural and Immigration Society of Trinidad, 1841, enclosed in C.O. 295/134, no. 85; Report of A. David, enclosed in C.O. 295/146, no. 56.

12. (See p. 327.) As part of the amelioration strategy, Canning's Government established two dioceses in the West Indies with bishops at Barbados and Jamaica. The Anglican clergy of Jamaica was enlarged by 50 per cent in the decade before emancipation. Alfred Caldecott, *The Church in the West Indies* (London, 1898), pp. 90–2.

Comparative Statement of Clergymen and Charity Schools

Colony	Clergy			Schools		
	1812	1825	1834	1817	1825	1834
Barbados	14	15	29	2	8	155
Trinidad	0	2	2	0	2	4
Tobago	1	1	1	0	0	13
St. Lucia	0	1	1	0	0	3
St. Vincent	1	2	3	0	1	14
Bequia	0	0	1	0	0	2
Grenada	2	2	4	0	1	18
Carriacou	1	1	1	0	0	9
Guiana	1	7	10	0	2	37
Antigua	6	8	12	0	8	32
Montserrat	1	1	12	0	0	19
Barbuda	0	0	0	0	0	4
St. Kitts	5	5	7	0	6	64
Nevis	3	3	3	0	6	19
Anguilla	0	0	1	0	0	2
Virgin Is.	1	1	2	0	0	6
Dominica	1	1	2	0	0	4
Total	37	50	81	2	34	405

Source: Schomburgk, *History of Barbados*, p. 99.

13. (See p. 329.) Methodist historians have acknowledged that their missionaries 'were under strict injunctions to inculcate submission and diligent labor upon bondsmen', a policy which they pursued with equal commitment after emancipation. G. G. Findlay and W. W. Holdsworth, *The History of the Wesleyan Methodist Missionary Society* (London, 1921), II, pp. 301–2. The action of one Presbyterian missionary in Jamaica at the outset of freedom fairly represents the position taken by the majority of his colleagues of every denomination. In the company of a stipendiary magistrate, and at the pleasure of the planters, he admonished his people against extravagant wage demands which would jeopardize the estates, against idleness, rambling about, or excessive spending on fancy clothes, horses, and other items of display. Waddell, *Twenty-nine Years*, p. 145. Militant pro-freedmen elements of the Baptist Missinary Society in Jamaica were, in some respects, an exception to this. Whereas Waddell considered 1*s*. a reasonable daily wage, they urged the freedmen to insist on 1*s*. 6*d*.; however, like all other missionaries they encouraged habits of thrift and industry characteristic of Protestant social ethics.

14. (See p. 342.) In spite of perpetual attempts at raising a 'native agency' the London Missionary Society singularly failed. After 40 years, the Georgetown mission had produced two such persons. The missionaries were unreasonably demanding in their moral code, but they bitterly resented charges from their London superiors that they were not attentive to training native pastors, answering that tireless efforts had ended with prospective agents succumbing to the temptations of their environment. Believing that those who were to be trained as teachers and pastors 'must *first* be truly *pious* persons', the missionaries argued that the only way to cultivate such piety was to educate prospective black pastors in England or North America. The temptations of an immoral and licentious West Indian society inevitably defeated their efforts. Wallbridge to Tidman, 1 Feb. 1848; Henderson to Tidman, 8 Feb. 1848; Wallbridge to Tidman, 26 Jan. 1852; Rattray to Tidman, 6 Jan. 1855, *L.M.S. Papers, British Guiana*.

15. (See p. 384.) In a long report on Jamaica, written in 1854, Richard Hill argued, 'the prosperity of sugar cultivation is the pivot on which the stability of practical usefulness, or principles of right thrifty conduct emanating from right social precepts, among our population depend . . .' Taking the example of the valley of the Rio Minho, he described the river basin and its tributary vales cultivated in cane. The surrounding mountains were dotted with the cottages and villages of settlers. Each depended on the other. Hill proceeded: 'The seaward plantations in the rich Plain of Vere, have resident bodies of labourers whose cottages have no gardens, the demands of cultivation not permitting the surface to be applied to any growth but sugar. This population is wholly fed from mountain settlements about the tributaries of the Rio Minho. Now touch but the price of sugar as it is here cultivated under all the conditions natural and artificial by which it can bear a minimum value in the home market, and reduce the relation between profit and expenditure to a balanced account, and all this industry is immediately extinguished, and the subsisting dependence of the

mountain settler on the wages earned by the labourer in the valley and the plain is annihilated at once. This would obviously end in the ruin of the colony; but in this way two-thirds of the staple agriculture have been obliterated already.' Report of R. Hill, July 1854, enclosed in C.O. 137/324, no. 101. Hill's statement was an elegant comment on two points: the interdependence of two forms of agriculture—peasant and plantation—and the heavy dependence of both on the price which sugar fetched in British markets.

16. (See p. 388.) Gordon was shabbily treated in the incident involving his dismissal from the ordinary magistracy. In May 1862 Gordon had lodged a complaint against fellow justices in St. Thomas in the East whose non-attendance at court occasioned long detention of accused persons in the Morant Bay lock-up, a place which Gordon characterized as 'the most disgusting and revolting to human nature that can be imagined! want of cleanliness, stench eno' to produce immediate sickness, and nasty, it is indeed a sink hole'. He also accused the parish Rector of having unlawfully committed a person to this lock-up. On the first charge, Gordon was perfectly correct. Prisoners, confined at night to a single room, had no sanitary facilities; they simply relieved themselves on the floor. The place was rarely, if ever, whitewashed. On the second charge, it appears, Gordon was less than accurate. The Rector whom he had accused claimed to have committed a sick and dying pauper to the lock-up as a place of shelter while he supplied him with money for his support. In fact, neither the Rector, local doctor, churchwarden, nor anyone else had offered much human succour to the dying man, whose last days were spent in disgusting filth. Gordon was accused of misrepresenting the action of the Rector. A Board of Magistrates sitting at Morant Bay found him guilty of misrepresentation, without permitting Gordon to examine eight of eleven witnesses who were prepared to give evidence regarding the state of the lock-up. On the substance of the Board's judgement, Eyre dismissed Gordon from the magistracy (he held a commission in seven parishes). While the Colonial Office upheld this judgement, it chastised Eyre for not having censured the Custos and justices for their failure to receive evidence on the state of the lock-up and their apparent neglect of duty as well as equity. Gordon was justifiably irate. He declared Eyre's action 'as insulting as it is *unconstitutional, unworthy, unenglish,* and *undeserved*'. Subsequent to these events, Gordon, a Baptist, was elected churchwarden in St. Thomas. The churchwarden of the parish was responsible for managing the affairs of the lock-up, and it would appear that Gordon's intent was to eliminate the former corrupt office-holder and set things right. His right to hold that office was disputed because he was not a member of the Established Church. The dispute occasioned three actions at law involving Gordon and the Custos, Baron von Ketelhodt. Two of them had been resolved in the Baron's favour; the third was pending when the rebellion erupted at Morant Bay. Eyre to Newcastle, 8 July 1862, C.O. 137/367, no. 41; Gordon to Austin, 5 July 1862, bound in C.O. 137/367, no. 52; Gordon to Austin, 9 July 1862, bound in C.O. 137/367, no. 52; minute of Henry Taylor, bound in C.O. 137/367, no. 52; Gardner, *History of Jamaica,* p. 467.

Wholesale Prices of British West Indian Muscovado Sugar, 1800–1865

(shillings per cwt.)

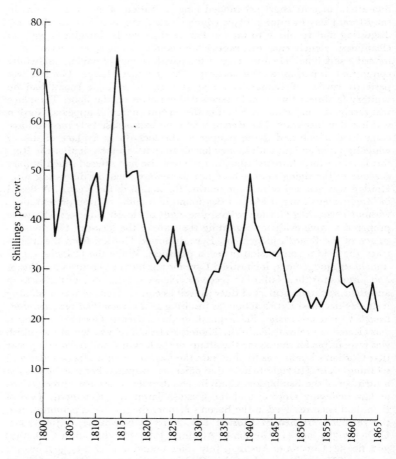

* Based on Tables printed in P.P. 1852–3 XCIX (461); P.P. 1866 LXVI (193).

British Sugar Duties, 1830–1865

(per cwt.)

Date	COLONIAL MUSCOVADO		FOREIGN MUSCOVADO		ALL REFINED	
	s.	d.	s.	d.	s.	d.
1830	24	0	66	2	168	4
1841	25	2	66	2	176	5

			Foreign Free Grown		Foreign Slave Grown			
	s.	d.	s.	d.	s.	d.	s.	d.
1844 (Nov.)	25	2	35	9	66	2	176	5

	E.W.C.		N.E.W.C.		Foreign E.W.C.		Foreign N.E.W.C.					
	s.	d.	s.	d.	s.	d.	s.	d.	s.	d.	s.	d.
1845 (Mar.)	16	4	14	0	28	0	23	4	63	0	166	0

	FOREIGN MUSCOVADO											
	E.W.C.		N.E.W.C.						E.D.R.		N.E.D.R.	
	s.	d.	s.	d.	s.	d.	s.	d.	s.	d.	s.	d.
1846 (Aug.)	16	4	14	0	24	6	21	0			31	6	28	0

1847–54   Annual decreases until discrimination ended, 5 July 1854.

	ALL SUGARS ENTERING THE UNITED KINGDOM							
	N.E.B.C.				N.E.W.C.		E.W.C.		Refined	
	s.	d.			s.	d.	s.	d.	s.	d.
1854 (5 July)	11	0			12	0	14	0	17	4
1855 (Apr.)*	13	9			15	0	17	6	20	0
1857 (Apr.)	12	8			13	10	16	0	18	4

	N.E.B.M.		E.B.M.							
	s.	d.	s.	d.	s.	d.	s.	d.	s.	d.
1864 (Apr.)	8	2	9	4	10	6	11	8	12	10

Source: Noel Deerr, *History of Sugar*, II, pp. 430–42.

E.W.C.	Equal to White-Clayed
N.E.W.C.	Not Equal to White-Clayed
E.D.R.	Equal to Double-Refined
N.E.D.R.	Not Equal to Double-Refined
N.E.B.C.	Not Equal to Brown-Clayed
N.E.B.M.	Not Equal to Brown-Muscovado
E.B.M.	Equal to Brown-Muscovado

* Tariff increases in mid-fifties occasioned by need to finance the Crimean War.

BIBLIOGRAPHY

THE most extensive bibliography for materials published on the West Indies in the twentieth century is *Caribbeana 1900–1965: A Topical Bibliography* (Seattle and London, 1968) compiled by Lambros Comitas. Lowell Joseph Ragatz's *A Guide for the Study of British Caribbean History, 1763–1834* (Washington, 1932) is a thorough and invaluable work. Its extensive annotated list of pamphlet literature on the slavery question is, in itself, a remarkable piece of scholarship. Ragatz has also published two lists of Parliamentary Papers on pre-emancipation: *A Check List of House of Commons Sessional Papers Relating to the British West Indies and to the West Indian Slave Trade and Slavery, 1763–1834* (London, 1923); *A Check List of House of Lords Sessional Papers Relating to the British West Indies and to the West Indian Slave Trade and Slavery, 1763–1834* (London, 1931). For Jamaica, Frank Cundall's *Bibliographia Jamaicensis* (Kingston, 1902) is valuable for early writing on the colony. It includes pamphlets, magazine articles, and lists of newspapers and maps. Cundall's *Bibliography of the West Indies* (Kingston, 1909) does not list works on Jamaica. Jerome S. Handler's *A Guide to Source Materials for the Study of Barbados History, 1627–1834* (Carbondale, 1971) is an important collection. Also, there is *Barbadiana: A List of Works Pertaining to the History of the Island of Barbados: Prepared in the Public Library to Mark the Attainment of Independence* (Bridgetown, 1966). The printed catalogues of special libraries provide important lists of West Indian publications. Among them are the *Catalogue of the Library of the West India Committee* and E. Lewin's *Subject Catalogue of the Royal Empire Society*, vol. III. For doctoral dissertations on the West Indies, consult Enid M. Baa's *Theses on Caribbean Topics* (Rio Piedras, 1970). A brief statement, 'Public Records in British West India Islands', *Bulletin of the Institute of Historical Research* (1930) was written by Richard Pares. The second volume of the *Cambridge History of the British Empire* (Cambridge, 1940) offers an extensive list of Parliamentary Papers dealing with the British West India colonies.

I. MANUSCRIPT SOURCES

Public Record Office
  Colonial Office records have provided the principal manuscript sources for this study. The following series have been examined for the period 1830–65:

C.O. 318 West Indies General, Immigration
C.O. 323 Colonies General, Law Officer's Reports, Miscellaneous.
C.O. 320 Miscellanea, including material on education, the military, and plans for the abolition of slavery.
C.O. 854 Circulars.
C.O. 28 Original Correspondence, Barbados.
C.O. 111 Original Correspondence, British Guiana.
C.O. 137 Original Correspondence, Jamaica.
C.O. 295 Original Correspondence, Trinidad.

The series consulted selectively were:

C.O. 441 Encumbered Estates Commission.
C.O.   7 Original Correspondence, Antigua.
C.O. 239 Original Correspondence, St. Kitts.
C.O. 29 Entry Books, Barbados.
C.O. 112 Entry Books, British Guiana.
C.O. 138 Entry Books, Jamaica.
C.O. 142 Blue Books of Statistics, Jamaica.
C.O. 300 Blue Books of Statistics, Trinidad.
C.O. 33 Blue Books of Statistics, Barbados.

Missionary Archives
London Missionary Society Papers:
Diary of John Wray, 1811–15.
General Missionary Correspondence, British Guiana.
General Missionary Correspondence, Jamaica.
Methodist Missionary Society Papers:
General Missionary Correspondence, Leeward Islands.
Baptist Missionary Society Papers:
Phillippo Papers. Included among these is the missionary's manuscript autobiography which constitutes a compilation of letters held together by a narrative.
Knibb Papers. This is a small collection of Knibb's correspondence dating from 1825.
General Missionary Correspondence, Jamaica.

Private Papers
Newcastle Papers, University of Nottingham.
Russell Papers, Public Record Office, 30/22.

II. PRINTED SOURCES

Parliamentary Papers
In addition to the statistical data and the reports of various commissions and select committees, the Parliamentary Papers

contain a considerable portion of the original correspondence which passed between colonial governors and the Colonial Office. That correspondence was printed for Parliament either at the discretion of the Secretary of State or as a result of requests made by members of either House. It is important to observe, however, that the original correspondence which flowed in and out of the Colonial Office was occasionally edited to remove sensitive material before it was printed for Parliament. For a check list of papers pertaining to the British West Indies, consult the *Cambridge History of the British Empire*, vol. II.

Public General Statutes of the United Kingdom.

Hansard's Parliamentary Debates, third series.

Votes of the Honorable House of Assembly. Jamaica (Selected volumes in the holdings of the Institute of Historical Research, London.)

The London Gazette

This publication was the official newspaper of the British Government. Orders in Council were printed in it, as were legal notices of West Indian estates being probated. Each issue printed the average price of muscovado in the London market.

III. NEWSPAPERS AND PERIODICALS

In the documents of every colony maintained at the Public Record Office there is a series which includes newspapers among other miscellanea forwarded from the colonies. The British Museum's Collindale Periodicals Library has a limited collection of West Indian newspapers, and there is a large holding of Jamaican newspapers and scattered collections from other islands at the Institute of Jamaica, Kingston. One of the most varied collections of newspapers for the Lesser Antilles in the mid-nineteenth century is held by the American Antiquarian Society, Worcester, Massachusetts. For a check-list of that holding, see Waldo Lincoln, 'List of Newspapers of the West Indies and Bermuda', *Proceedings of the American Antiquarian Society* (1926), 139–55.

The newspapers most consistently consulted for this study were:

The Times [London].

The Falmouth Post.

The Port of Spain Gazette.

The Guiana Chronicle.

The Anti-Slavery Monthly Reporter, 1825–36 is a valuable source of data and opinion on the West Indies and abolitionism. The title of the journal was shortened to *The Anti-Slavery Reporter* in the course of its publication.

IV. CONTEMPORARY BOOKS, PAMPHLETS, ETC.

An Abstract of the British West Indian Statutes for the Protection and Government of Slaves, London, 1830.

ALLEN, Grant. *In All Shades.* 3 vols. London, 1886.

ANDERSON, James. *Report on Mechanical Improvements in Tropical Agriculture and the Manufacture of Sugar, Addressed to the President and Council of the Royal Agricultural Society of Jamaica*, Kingston, 1845.

ANDERSON, James S. *The History of the Church of England in the Colonies and Foreign Dependencies of the British Empire.* 3 vols. London, 1856.

ANDERSON, William Wemyss. *A Description and History of the Island of Jamaica, Comprising an Account of its Soil, Climate, and Productions, Shewing its Value and Importance as an Agricultural Country, and a Desirable Place of Residence for Certain Classes of Settlers*, Kingston, 1851.

ANDREWS, E. W., and ANDREWS, C. McLean. *Journal of a Lady of Quality: Being the Narrative of a Journey from Scotland to the West Indies, North Carolina, and Portugal in the Years 1774 to 1776.* New Haven, 1921.

BAKER, John. *An Essay on the Art of Making Muscovado Sugar.* London, 1775.

BARCLAY, Alexander. *A Practical View of the Present State of Slavery in the West Indies.* London, 1826.

——. *Remarks on Emigration to Jamaica, Addressed to the Coloured Class of the United States.* New York, 1840.

BARRETT, William Garland. *Immigration to the British West Indies. Is it the Slave-Trade Revived or Not?* London, 1859.

BAYLEY, F. W. N. *Four Years Residence in the West Indies.* London, 1833.

BEAUMONT, Augustus H. *The Jamaica Petition for Representation in the British House of Commons or for Independence.* London, 1831.

BECKFORD, William A. *A Descriptive Account of the Island of Jamaica.* 2 vols. London, 1790.

BELL, John. *A Practical Treatise on the Culture of Sugarcane.* London, 1831.

BESSEMER, Henry. *On a New System of Manufacturing Sugar from the Cane and its Advantages as Compared with the Method Generally Used in the West Indies.* London, 1852.

BICKELL, R., Revd. *The West Indies as They Are; Or a Real Picture of Slavery.* London, 1825.

BIGELOW, John. *Jamaica in 1850: Or the Effects of 16 Years of Freedom on a Slave Colony.* New York, 1851.

Biggs, J. *Observations on the Manufacture of Sugar and Rum in Jamaica.* London, 1843.

Bleby, Henry. *Death Struggles of Slaves: Being a Narrative of Facts and Incidents which Occurred in a British Colony During the Two Years Immediately Preceding Negro Emancipation.* London, 1853.

Blyth, George, Revd. *Reminiscences of a Missionary Life with Suggestions to Churches and Missionaries.* Edinburgh, 1851.

Brassey, Annie. *In the Trades, The Tropics and the Roaring Forties.* London, 1885.

Breen, Henry H. *St. Lucia: Historical Statistical, and Descriptive.* London, 1844.

Bridgens, R. *West India Scenery, with Illustrations of Negro Character, the Process of Making Sugar, etc.* London, 1839.

Bridges, George W., Revd. *The Annals of Jamaica.* 2 vols. London, 1827–8.

Bronckhurst, H. V. P. *The Colony of British Guiana.* London, 1883.

Buchner, J. H. *The Moravians in Jamaica. History of the Mission of the United Brethren's Church to the Negroes in the Island of Jamaica from the Year 1754 to 1854.* London, 1854.

Burchell, William F. *Memoir of Thomas Burchell, 22 Years a Missionary in Jamaica.* London, 1849.

Burge, William. *A Reply to the Letter by the Marquis of Sligo to the Marquis of Normanby, Relative to the Present State of Jamaica.* London, 1839.

Burnley, W. H. *Observations on the Present Condition of the Island of Trinidad.* London, 1842.

Buxton, C. *Slavery and Freedom in the British West Indies.* London, 1860.

Caines, Clement. *Letters on the Cultivation of the Otaheite Cane, etc.* London, 1801.

Capadose, Henry. *Sixteen Years in the West Indies.* 2 vols. London, 1845.

Carbery, Edward. *Inducements to the Colored People of the United States to Emigrate to British Guiana.* Boston, 1840.

Carmichael, A. C. *Domestic Manners and Social Condition of the White, Coloured and Negro Population of the West Indies.* 2 vols. London, 1834.

Chandler, John. *Extracts from the Journal of John Chandler, Whilst Travelling in Jamaica.* London, 1841.

Clark, John, Dendy, Walter, and Phillippo, James Mursell. *The Voice of Jubilee. A Narrative of the Baptist Mission, Jamaica from its Commencement.* London, 1845.

Clarke, John. *Memoir of Richard Merrick, Missionary in Jamaica.* London, 1850.

CLARKSON, Thomas. *A Letter to the Clergy of Various Denominations and to the Slave-Holding Planters in the Southern Parts of the United States of America.* London, 1841.

———. *Not a Labourer Wanted for Jamaica: to Which is Added, an Account of the Newly Erected Villages by the Peasantry There and Their Beneficial Results, and the Consequences of Re-Opening a New Slave Trade, as it Relates to Africa.* London, 1842.

COLERIDGE, Henry Nelson. *Six Months in the West Indies in 1825.* London, 1826.

COX, F. A., Revd. *History of the Baptist Missionary Society from 1792 to 1842.* 2 vols. London, 1842.

CUNDALL, Frank, ed. *Lady Nugent's Journal.* London, 1934.

DALTON, Henry G. *The History of British Guiana.* 2 vols. London, 1855.

DAVY, John. *The West Indies, Before and Since Slave Emancipation.* London, 1854.

DAY, Charles W. *Five Years Residence in the West Indies.* London, 1852.

Debates in Parliament—Session 1833—on the Resolutions and Bill for the Abolition of Slavery in the British Colonies. London, 1834.

DENMAN, Joseph, Capt. R.N. *West India Interest, African Emigration, and the Slave Trade.* London, 1848.

DeVERTEUIL, L. A. A. *Three Essays on the Cultivation of the Sugar Cane in Trinidad.* Port of Spain, 1848.

———. *Trinidad: Its Geography, Natural Resources, Administration, Present Condition, and Prospects.* London, 1884.

DUNCAN, Peter, Revd. *A Narrative of the Wesleyan Mission to Jamaica.* London, 1849.

EDWARDS, Bryan. *The History, Civil and Commercial, of the British Colonies in the West Indies,* 3rd ed. 3 vols. London, 1801.

EMERY, Robert. *About Jamaica: its Past, Present, and its Future.* London, 1859.

EVANS, H. B. *Our West India Colonies: Jamaica, A Source of National Wealth and Honour.* London, 1855.

EVANS, W. J. *Sugar Planter's Manual: Being a Treatise on the Art of Obtaining Sugar from the Sugar Cane.* London, 1847.

FERGUSSON, W. *A Letter to Thomas Fowell Buxton, Esq.* London, 1839.

[FLANDERS, Mrs.]. *Antigua and the Antiguans.* 2 vols. London, 1844.

FOSTER, Henry B., Revd. *Rise and Progress of Wesleyan Methodism in Jamaica.* London, 1881.

FROUDE, James Anthony. *The English in the West Indies.* London, 1888.

GAMBLE, W. H., Revd. *Trinidad, Historical and Descriptive.* London, 1866.

GARDNER, W. J. *History of Jamaica.* London, 1873.

GODWIN, Benjamin. *On the Essential Sinfulness of Slavery, and its Direct Opposition to the Precepts and Spirit of Christianity: Papers Presented to the General Anti-Slavery Convention.* London, 1840.

GOMM, Sir William. *The Story of Newcastle, Jamaica.* London, 1863.

GRAINGER, James, M.D. *An Essay on the More Common West-Indian Diseases: to Which are Added, Some Hints of the Management, etc., of Negroes.* Edinburgh, 1802.

GREY, Henry George, 3rd Earl. *The Colonial Policy of Lord John Russell's Administration.* 2 vols. London, 1853.

GURNEY, Joseph John. *A Winter in the West Indies, Described in Familiar Letters to Henry Clay of Kentucky.* London, 1840.

HALLIDAY, Sir Andrew, M.D. *The Natural and Physical History of the Windward and Leeward Colonies.* London, 1837.

HARVEY, Thomas, and BREWIN, William. *Jamaica in 1866. A Narrative of a Tour Through the Island with Remarks on its Social, Educational and Industrial Condition.* London, 1867.

HENNEY, T. *Eight Treatises on the Cultivation of the Sugar Cane.* Spanish Town, 1843.

HILL, Richard. *Lights and Shadows of Jamaica History.* Kingston, 1859.

HINTON, John H. *Memoir of William Knibb, Missionary in Jamaica.* London, 1847.

HODGSON, Studholme, Capt. *Truths from the West Indies.* London, 1838.

HORSFORD, John, Revd. *A Voice from the West Indies: Being a Review of the Character and Results of Missionary Efforts in the British and Other Colonies in the Caribbean Sea.* London, 1856.

HOVEY, Sylvester. *Letters from the West Indies.* New York, 1838.

JELLY, T. *A Brief Enquiry into the Condition of Jamaica.* London, 1847.

JENKINS, J. E. *The Coolie, His Rights and Wrongs: Notes of a Journey to British Guiana.* London, 1871.

JOSEPH, E. L. *Warner Arundell: The Adventures of a Creole.* 3 vols. London, 1838.

KALLEY, Robert Reid. *An Account of the Recent Persecutions in Madeira.* London, 1844.

KAYE, Sir J. W. *The Life and Correspondence of Charles, Lord Metcalfe.* 2 vols. London, 1858.

KERR, Thomas. *A Practical Treatise on the Cultivation of the Sugarcane and the Manufacture of Sugar.* London, 1847.

KINGSLEY, Charles. *At Last: A Christmas in the West Indies.* 2nd ed. London, 1889.

LAIRD, MacGregor. *The Effect of an Alteration in the Sugar Duties on the Condition of the Negro Race Considered.* London, 1844.

LEVI, L. *On the Sugar Trade and Sugar Duties*. London, 1864.

LEWIS, Matthew Gregory. *Journal of a West India Proprietor, Kept During a Residence in the Island of Jamaica*. London, 1834.

LUCKOCK, B., Rev. *Jamaica, Enslaved and Free*. London, 1846.

MACRAE, Alexander. *A Manual of Plantership in British Guiana . . . With Some Suggestions for Improvement of the Present Practice*. London, 1856.

MCDONNELL, Alexander. *Considerations on Negro Slavery with Authentic Reports Illustrative of the Actual Condition of the Negroes in Demerara*. London, 1824.

MCKINNEN, Daniel. *Tour Through the British West Indies in the Years 1802 and 1803*. London, 1804.

MCMAHON, Benjamin. *Jamaica Plantership*. London, 1839.

MCQUEEN, James. *The West India Colonies: the Calumnies and Misrepresentations Circulated Against Them by the Edinburgh Review, Mr. Cropper, etc., etc*. London, 1824.

———. *The Colonial Controversy*. Glasgow, 1821.

———. *A Letter to the Right Hon. Lord Glenelg on the West Indian Currency, Commerce, African Slave Trade, etc*. London, 1838.

MADDEN, Richard R. *A Twelvemonth's Residence in the West Indies During the Transition from Slavery to Apprenticeship*. 2 vols. Philadelphia, 1835.

———. *A Letter to W. C. Channing, on the Subject of the Abuse of the Flag of the United States in Cuba, and the Advantage Taken of its Protection in Promoting the Slave Trade*. Boston, 1839.

———. *Address on Slavery in Cuba, Presented to the General Anti-Slavery Convention*. London, 1845.

———. *The Island of Cuba: its Resources, Progress, and Prosperity Considered in Relation Especially to the Influence of its Prosperity on the Interests of the British West India Colonies*. London, 1853.

———. *Memoirs, Chiefly Autobiographical from 1798 to 1886, ed. by T. M. Madden*. London, 1891.

Marly; or, a Planter's Life in Jamaica. Glasgow, 1823.

MARTIN, R. Montgomery. *History of the West Indies*. 2 vols. London, 1836.

MARTIN, Samuel. *An Essay upon Plantership*. Spanish Town, 1821.

MATSON, H. J. *Remarks on the Slave Trade*. London, 1848.

MERIVALE, Herman. *Lectures on Colonization and Colonies*. London, 1861.

MILLS, Arthur. *Colonial Constitutions*. London, 1856.

MOISTER, William, Revd. *Memorials of Missionary Labours in Western Africa and in the West Indies*. London, 1850.

———. *Conversations on the Rise, Progress, and Present State of Wesleyan*. London, 1869.

——. *A History of Wesleyan Missions in all Parts of the World.* London, 1871.

——. *The West Indies, Enslaved and Free.* London, 1883.

ORDERSON, J. W. *Directions to Young Planters for the Care and Management of a Sugar Plantation in Barbados.* London, 1800.

PARRY, Thomas. *Codrington College, in the Island of Barbados.* London, 1847.

——. *A Charge Delivered in the Church of the Holy Trinity, Port of Spain, Trinidad, February 10, 1852.* Barbados, 1852.

PECK, Nathaniel, and PRICE, Thomas S. *Report of Messrs. Peck and Price Who Were Appointed at a Meeting of the Free Colored People of Baltimore, held on the 25th November, 1839, Delegates to Visit British Guiana and the Island of Trinidad for the Purpose of Ascertaining the Advantage to be Derived by Colored People Migrating to These Places.* Baltimore, 1840.

[PHILIP, John Baptista]. *An Address to the Right Honourable Earl Bathhurst Relative to the Claims which the Coloured Population of Trinidad Have to the Same Civil and Political Privileges with their White Fellow Subjects.* London, 1824.

PHILLIPPO, James M., Revd. *Jamaica: its Past and Present State.* Philadelphia, 1843.

PORTER, George R. *The Nature and Properties of the Sugarcane; with Practical Directions for the Improvement of its Culture, and the Manufacture of its Products.* London, 1830.

PREMIUM, Barton. *Eight Years in British Guiana, 1840–8.* London, 1850.

PRICE, George E. *Jamaica and the Colonial Office: Who Caused the Crisis?* London, 1866.

PRINGLE, Hall. *The Fall of the Sugar Planters of Jamaica, with Remarks on their Agricultural Management and on the Labour Question in that Island.* London, 1869.

PRINGLE, J. W. *The West Indian Colonies. Remarks on their Present State and Future Prospects.* London, 1839.

Proceedings of the General Anti-Slavery Convention, Called by the Committee of the Society, and Held in London, from June 12 to June 23, 1840. London, 1841.

REED, William. *The History of Sugar and Sugar Yielding Plants, Together with an Epitome of Every Notable Process of Sugar Extraction and Manufacture, from the Earliest Times to the Present,* London, 1866.

Report of the Agency Committee of the Anti-Slavery Society, London, for the Purpose of Disseminating Information by Lectures on Colonial Slavery. London, 1832.

RILAND, John, Revd. *Memoirs of a West India Planter Published from* an *Original Manuscript with a Preface and Additional Details*. London, 1827.

ROUGHLEY, T. *The Jamaica Planters Guide*. London, 1823.

ROUNDELL, C. S. *England and Her Subject Races: With Special Reference to Jamaica*. London, 1866.

SAMUEL, Peter, Revd. *The Wesleyan-Methodist Missions in Jamaica and Honduras Delineated*. London, 1850.

SARGENT, George E. *The Jamaica Missionary: A Memoir of William Knibb*. London, n.d., *c.* 1850.

SCHOMBURGK, Robert H. *A Description of British Guiana, Geographical and Statistical*. London, 1840.

——. *The History of Barbados*. London, 1848.

SCOBLE, John. *British Guiana. Speech Delivered at the Anti-Slavery Meeting in Exeter Hall, on Wednesday, the 4th of April, 1838*. London, 1838.

——. *British Guiana. Facts! Facts! Facts!* London, 1840.

——. *Hill Coolies. A Brief Exposition of the Deplorable Condition of the Hill Coolies in British Guiana and Mauritius*. London, 1840.

SEWELL, W. G. *The Ordeal of Free Labor in the British West Indies*. London, 1861.

SHIER, John. *Report on Thorough Drainage with Special Reference to its Application to the Colony of British Guiana*. Demerara, 1847.

Sketches and Recollections of the West Indies, by a Resident. London, 1828.

SLIGO, Howe Peter, Marquis. *A Letter to the Marquis of Normanby Relative to the Present State of Jamaica, and the Measures Which are Rendered Necessary by the Refusal of the House of Assembly to Transact Business*. London, 1839.

——. *Jamaica Under the Apprenticeship*. London, 1838.

SPEDDING, James. *Reviews and Discussions, Literary, Political, and Historical, Not Relating to Bacon*. London, 1879.

STEPHEN, James. *The Crisis of the Sugar Colonies*. London, 1802.

——. *The Slavery of the West India Colonies Delineated*. 2 vols. London, 1824.

STEWART, John. *An Account of Jamaica and its Inhabitants by a Gentleman Long Resident in the West Indies*. London, 1808.

——, *A View of the Past and Present State of the Island of Jamaica; With Remarks on the Moral and Physical Condition of the Slaves, and on the Abolition of Slavery in the Colonies*. Edinburgh, 1823.

STOLLMEYER, C. F. *The Sugar Question Made Easy*. London, 1845.

STURGE, Joseph, and HARVEY, Thomas. *The West Indies in 1837*. London, 1838.

SWINTON, J., and SWINTON, J. *Journal of a Voyage with Coolie Emigrants from Calcutta to Trinidad*. London, 1859.

426   BIBLIOGRAPHY

TAYLOR, Henry. *Autobiography.* 2 vols. London, 1878.

THOME, James A., and KIMBALL, J. Horace. *Emancipation in the West Indies. A Six Month's Tour in Antigua, Barbados and Jamaica in the Year 1837.* New York, 1838.

The Traveller's Guide to Madeira and the West Indies. Haddington, 1815.

TROLLOPE, Anthony. *The West Indies and the Spanish Main.* New York, 1860.

TRUMAN, George; JACKSON, John; and LONGSTRETH, Thomas B. *Narrative of a Visit to the West Indies, in 1840 and 1841.* Philadelphia, 1844.

TURNBULL, David. *Travels in the West. Cuba: With Notices of Porto Rico and the Slave Trade.* London, 1840.

[TURNBULL, David, ed.]. *The Jamaica Movement, for Promoting the Enforcement of the Slave-Trade Treaties, and the Suppression of the Slave Trade.* London, 1850.

UNDERHILL, Edward B. *The West Indies: Their Social and Religious Condition.* London, 1862.

——. *Life of James Mursell Phillippo, Missionary in Jamaica.* London, 1881.

——. *The Tragedy of Morant Bay: A Narrative of the Disturbances in the Island of Jamaica in 1865.* London, 1895.

VERNON, B. J. *Early Recollections of Jamaica, with the Eventful Passage Home via New York and Halifax, at the Commencement of the American War in 1812.* London, 1848.

WADDELL, Hope M., Revd. *Twenty-nine Years in the West Indies and Central Africa: A Review of Missionary Work and Adventure, 1829–1858.* London, 1863.

WALKER, S. A. *The Church of England Mission in Sierra Leone.* London, 1847.

WALLBRIDGE, Edwin A. *The Demerara Martyr: Reverend John Smith, Missionary to Demerara.* London, 1848.

WALLER, John Augustine, R.N. *A Voyage in the West Indies Containing Various Observations Made During a Residence in Barbados and Several of the Leeward Islands.* London, 1820.

WENTWORTH, Trelawny. *The West India Sketch Book.* 2 vols. London, 1834.

WHITEHOUSE, W. F. *Agricola's Letters and Essays on Sugar Farming in Jamaica.* Kingston, 1845.

WILLIAMS, Cynric R. *A Tour Through the Island of Jamaica from the Western to the Eastern End, in the Year 1823.* London, 1827.

WILLIAMSON, John, M.D. *Medical and Miscellaneous Observations, Relative to the West India Islands.* 2 vols. Edinburgh, 1817.

WILSON, W. Carus. *The Madeira Persecutions.* London, 1856.

WOODCOCK, Henry Isles. *A History of Tobago.* London, 1867.

WRAY, Leonard. *The Practical Sugar Planter.* London, 1848.

V. SECONDARY WORKS

ADAMS, Donald R., Jr. 'Some Evidence of English and American Wage Rates, 1709–1830', *Journal of Economic History*, XXX (1970), 499–520.

ADAMSON, Alan H. *Sugar Without Slaves: The Political Economy of British Guiana, 1838–1904.* New Haven, 1972.

ADAMSON, J. W. *English Education, 1789–1902.* Cambridge, 1930.

ARMYTAGE, F. *The Free Port System in the British West Indies.* London, 1953.

ASIEGBU, Johnson U. J. *Slavery and the Politics of Liberation 1787–1861: A Study of Liberated African Emigration and British Anti-Slavery Policy.* New York, 1969.

ASPINALL, A. *The British West Indies.* London, 1912.

——. *West Indian Tales of Old.* London, 1912.

AUGIER, F. R. *The Making of the West Indies.* London, 1961.

AKYROYD, Wallace`R. *Sweet Malefactor: Sugar, Slavery and Human Society.* London, 1967.

BAKER, W. 'William Wilberforce on the Idea of Negro Inferiority', *Journal of the History of Ideas, XXXI (1970)*, 433–40.

BARNARD, Howard C. *A Short History of English Education from 1760 to 1944.* London, 1947.

BEACHEY, Raymond W. *The British West Indies Sugar Industry in the Late Nineteenth Century.* Oxford, 1957.

BENNETT, J. H., Jr. *Bondsmen and Bishops: Slavery and Apprenticeship on the Codrington Plantations of Barbados, 1710–1838.* Berkeley, 1958.

BEAGLEHOLE, J. C. 'The Colonial Office, 1782–1954', *Historical Studies, Australia and New Zealand, I (1941)*, 170–89.

BETHELL, Leslie. 'Mixed Commissions for the Suppression of the Trans-Atlantic Slave Trade in the Nineteenth Century', *Journal of African History, VII (1966)*, 79–93.

——. *The Abolition of the Brazilian Slave Trade.* Cambridge, 1970.

BIRCHENOUGH, Charles. *History of Elementary Education in England and Wales from 1800 to the Present Day.* London, 1930.

BLACK, Clinton V. *History of Jamaica.* London, 1961.

——. *Spanish Town: The Old Capital.* Spanish Town, 1960.

BOLT, Christine. *Victorian Attitudes to Race.* Toronto, 1971.

BOYCE, Sir Rupert W. *Health Progress and Administration in the West Indies.* New York, 1910.

BRATHWAITE, Edward. *The Development of Creole Society in Jamaica, 1770–1820.* Oxford, 1971.

BRIGGS, Asa. *Victorian People: Some Reassessments of People, Institutions, Ideas, and Events.* London, 1954.

——. *The Age of Improvement, 1763–1867.* London, 1959.

BROWN, Lucy. *The Board of Trade and the Free Trade Movement, 1830–1842.* London, 1958.

BURN, W. L. *Emancipation and Apprenticeship in the British West Indies.* London, 1937.

——. *The British West Indies.* London, 1951.

BURNS, Sir Alan. *History of the British West Indies.* 2nd ed. New York, 1965.

BURROW, J. W. *Evolution and Society: A Study in Victorian Social Theory.* Cambridge, 1966.

BUXTON, Charles, ed. *Memoirs of Sir Thomas Fowell Buxton.* London, 1866.

CALDECOTT, A. *The Church in the West Indies.* London, 1898.

CAMPBELL, Carl. 'Social and Economic Obstacles to the Development of Popular Education in Post Emancipation Jamaica, 1834–1865', *Journal of Caribbean History*, I (*1970*), 57–88.

——. 'Denominationalism and the Mico Schools in Jamaica', *Caribbean Studies*, X (*1971*), 152–72.

CAMPBELL, Persia Crawford. *Chinese Coolie Emigration to Countries Within the British Empire.* London, 1923.

CARMICHAEL, Gertrude. *The History of the West Indian Islands of Trinidad and Tobago.* London, 1961.

CELL, John W. *British Colonial Administration in the Mid-Nineteenth Century: The Policy Making Process.* New Haven, 1970.

CHECKLAND, S. G. 'Finance for the West Indies, 1750–1815', *Economic History Review*, 2nd ser., X (1958), 461–9.

——. *The Gladstones: A Family Biography 1764–1851.* Cambridge, 1971.

CLEMENTI, Cecil. *The Chinese in British Guiana.* Demerara, 1915.

——. *A Constitutional History of British Guiana.* London, 1937.

COLLINS, E. J. T. 'Harvest Technology and Labour Supply in Britain, 1790–1870', *Economic History Review*, 2nd ser., XXII (1971), 453–73.

CORWIN, Arthur F. *Spain and the Abolition of Slavery in Cuba, 1817–1886.* Austin, 1968.

COUPLAND, Reginald. *Wilberforce: A Narrative.* Oxford, 1923.

——. *The British Anti-Slavery Movement.* London, 1933.

COURTENAY, P. P. *Plantation Agriculture.* New York, 1965.

COWEN, D. W., and GREENE, J. P., eds. *Neither Slave Nor Free: The Role of the Free Black and the Free Mulatto in American Slave Societies.* Baltimore, 1972.

CRATON, Michael. 'Jamaican Slave Mortality: Fresh Light from Worthy Park, Longville and the Tharp Estates', *Journal of Caribbean History*, III (1971), 1–27.

CRATON, Michael, and WALVIN, James. *A Jamaican Plantation. The History of Worthy Park, 1670–1970*. Toronto, 1970.

CUMPSTON, I. M. *Indians in Overseas British Territories*. London, 1953.

CUNDALL, Frank. *Studies in Jamaica History*. London, 1900.

———. *Political and Social Disturbances in the West Indies*. London, 1906.

———. *Historic Jamaica*. London, 1915.

CURTIN, Philip. 'The British Sugar Duties and West Indian Prosperity', *Journal of Economic History*, XIV (1954), 157–64.

———. *Two Jamaicas: The Role of Ideas in a Tropical Colony*. Cambridge, Mass., 1955.

———. *The Image of Africa: British Ideas and Action, 1780–1850*. Madison, 1964.

———. *The Atlantic Slave Trade: A Census*. Madison, 1969.

CURTIS, Stanley J. *History of Education in Great Britain*. 5th ed. London, 1963.

CUST, R. J. *A Treatise on the West Indian Incumbered Estates Acts*. London, 1865.

DAVIS, David Brion. 'James Cropper and the British Anti-Slavery Movement, 1821–1823', *Journal of Negro History*, XLV (1960), 241–58.

———. 'James Cropper and the British Anti-Slavery Movement, 1823–1833', *Journal of Negro History*, XLVI (1961), 154–73.

———. *The Problem of Slavery in Western Culture*. Ithaca, 1966.

———. 'The Emergence of Immediatism in British and American Anti-Slavery Thought', *Mississippi Valley Historical Review*, XLIX (1962–63), 209–30.

———. 'New Sidelights on Early Anti-Slavery Radicalism', *William & Mary Quarterly*, XXVIII (1971), 585–94.

DEERR, Noel. *A History of Sugar*. 2 vols. London, 1949–50.

DUTTON, Geoffrey. *The Hero as Murderer: The Life of Edward John Eyre*. London, 1967.

EISNER, Gisela. *Jamaica 1830–1930: A Study in Economic Growth*. Manchester, 1961.

ELLIS, Alfred B., Major. *The History of the First West India Regiment*. London, 1885.

ELTIS, D. 'Dr. Stephen Lushington and the Campaign to Abolish Slavery in the British Empire', *Journal of Caribbean History*, I (1970).

———. 'Traffic in Slaves Between the British West Indian Colonies, 1807–1833', *Economic History Review*, 2nd ser., XXV (1972), 55–64.

ERICKSON, Edgar L. 'The Introduction of East Indian Coolies into the British West Indies', *Journal of Modern History*, VI (1934), 127–46.

ERNLE, Rowland E. Prothero, Baron. *English Farming, Past and Present*. 6th ed. London, 1961.

FARLEY, Rawle. 'The Rise of a Peasantry in British Guiana', *Social and Economic Studies*, II (1954), 87–103.

FELDSTEIN, Stanley. *Once a Slave: The Slaves' View of Slavery*. New York, 1970.

FINDLAY, G. G., and HOLDSWORTH, W. W. *The History of the Wesleyan Methodist Missionary Society*. Vol. II. London, 1921.

FLADELAND, Betty. *Men and Brothers: Anglo-American Anti-Slavery Co-operation*. Urbana, 1972.

FRASER, Lionel M. *History of Trinidad from 1781 to 1839*. 2 vols. Port of Spain, 1891–6.

FUSSELL, George E. *The Farmer's Tools, 1500–1900: The History of British Farm Implements, Tools, and Machinery before the Tractor Came*. London, 1952.

FYFE, Christopher. *A History of Sierra Leone*. London, 1962.

GALBRAITH, John S. 'Myths of the Little England Era', *American Historical Review*, LXVII (1961), 34–48.

GALLAGHER, J. 'Fowell Buxton and the New African Policy, 1838–1842', *Cambridge Historical Journal*, X (1950–2), 36–58.

GANGULEE. *Indians in the Empire Overseas*. London, 1947.

GAYER, Arthur; ROSTOW, W. W.; and SCHWARTZ, Anna Jacobson. *The Growth and Fluctuation of the British Economy 1790–1850*. Oxford. 1953.

GHOSH, R. N. *Classical Macro-Economics and the Case for Colonies*. Calcutta, 1967.

GORDON, Shirley, 'The Negro Education Grant, 1835–1845: Its Application to Jamaica', *British Journal of Educational Studies*, VI (1958), 140–50.

——. *Report and Repercussions in West Indies Education 1835–1933*, London, 1968.

GORDON, Shirley, ed. *A Century of West Indian Education*. London, 1963.

GOVEIA, Elsa V. *Slave Society in the British Leeward Islands at the End of the Eighteenth Century*. New Haven, 1965.

GREEN, William A. 'The Apprenticeship in British Guiana, 1834–1838', *Caribbean Studies*, IX (1969), 44–66.

——. 'The Planter Class and British West Indian Sugar Production, Before and After Emancipation', *Economic History Review*, 2nd ser., XXVI (1973), 448–63.

——. 'The West Indies and British West African Policy in the Nineteenth Century—A Corrective Comment', *Journal of African History*, XV (1974), 247–59.

GRIGGS, Earl L. *Thomas Clarkson: The Friend of Slaves*. London. 1936.

GUILLEBAUD, C. W. *West Indian Sugar Crises, 1800–1930*. London, 1930.

HALL, Douglas. 'Apprenticeship Period in Jamaica, 1834–1838', *Caribbean Quarterly*, III (1953), 142–66.

——. 'Sir Charles Metcalfe', *Caribbean Quarterly*, III (1953), 90–100.

——. *Free Jamaica 1838–1865: An Economic History*. New Haven, 1959.

——. 'Slaves and Slavery in the British West Indies', *Social and Economic Studies*, II (1962), 305–18.

——. *Five of the Leewards, 1834–1870: The Major Problems of the Post-Emancipation Period in Antigua, Barbuda, Montserrat, Nevis, and St. Kitts*. St. Lawrence, Barbados, 1971.

HALL, Douglas, and MINTZ, Sidney. 'The Origins of the Jamaican Internal Marketing System', in Mintz, ed., *Papers in Caribbean Anthropology*. New Haven, 1960.

HALL, Henry. *The Colonial Office, a History*. London, 1937.

HALL, Neville. 'Law and Society in Barbados at the Turn of the Nineteenth Century', *Journal of Caribbean History*, V (1972), 20–45.

HAMILTON, T. J. *History of the Missions of the Moravian Church During the Eighteenth and Nineteenth Centuries*. London, 1900.

HANDLER, Jerome S. 'The History of Arrowroot and the Origin of Peasantries in the British West Indies', *Journal of Caribbean History*, II (1971), 46–93.

HANDLER, Jerome S., and FRISBIE, Charlotte J. 'Aspects of Slave Life in Barbados: Music and its Cultural Context', *Caribbean Studies*, XI (1972), 5–46.

HART, Ansell. *The Life of George William Gordon*. Kingston, n.d.

HENRIQUES, Fernando. *Family and Colour in Jamaica*. London, 1953.

——. *Jamaica. Land of Wood and Water*. New York, 1964.

HERSKOVITS, M. J. *Trinidad Village*. New York, 1947.

HIGHAM, C. S. S. 'The General Assembly of the Leeward Islands', *English Historical Review*, XLI (1926), 190–209, 366–88.

——. 'Sir Henry Taylor and the Establishment of Crown Colony Government in the West Indies', *The Scottish Historical Review*, XXIII (1926), 92–6.

HIGMAN, B. W. 'The West India Interest in Parliament 1807–1833', *Historical Studies*, XIII (1967), 1–19.

HITCHENS, Fred. H. *The Colonial Land and Emigration Commission*. Philadelphia, 1931.

HOETINCK, Harmannus. *Caribbean Race Relations: A Study of Two Variants.* Oxford, 1971.

HOWSE, Ernest Marshall. *Saints in Politics: The 'Clapham Sect' and the Growth of Freedom.* Toronto, 1952.

HURT, John. *Education in Evolution: Church, State, Society and Popular Education, 1800–1870.* London, 1971.

JENKS, Leland H. *The Migration of British Capital to 1875.* New York, 1927.

JOHNSON, R. 'Educational Policy and Social Control in Early Victorian England', *Past and Present*, no. 49 (1970), 96–119.

JOHNSTON, H. J. M. *British Emigration Policy, 1815–1830.* Oxford, 1972.

JONES, W. D. 'Lord Mulgrave's Administration in Jamaica, 1832–33', *Journal of Negro History*, XLVIII (1963), 44–56.

JORDAN, W. D. *White over Black: American Attitudes Toward the Negro, 1550–1812.* Baltimore, 1969.

KAY-SHUTTLEWORTH, Sir John. *Four Periods of Public Education.* London, 1862.

KERR, Madeline. *Personality and Conflict in Jamaica.* London, 1952.

KLINGBERG, Frank J. *The Anti-Slavery Movement in England.* New Haven, 1924.

KONDAPI, C. *Indians Overseas 1838–1949.* Madras, 1951.

KNAPLUND, Paul. 'Mr. Oversecretary Stephen', *Journal of Modern History*, I (1929), 40–66.

——. 'Sir James Stephen: the Friend of the Negroes', *Journal of Negro History*, XXXV (1950), 368–407.

——. *James Stephen and the British Colonial System, 1813–1847.* Madison, 1953.

KNORR, Klaus E. *British Colonial Theories, 1507–1850.* Toronto, 1944.

KNOX, Graham. 'British Colonial Policy and the Problem of Establishing a Free Society in Jamaica, 1838–1865', *Caribbean Studies*, II (1963), 3–13.

LAURENCE, K. O. 'The Evolution of Long Term Labour Contracts in Trinidad and British Guiana, 1834–1863', *The Jamaican Historical Review*, V (1965), 9–27.

——. 'The Establishment of the Portuguese Community in British Guiana', *The Jamaican Historical Review*, V (1965), 50–74.

LEVY, C. 'Barbados: the Last Years of Slavery, 1823–1833', *Journal of Negro History*, XLIV (1959), 308–45.

——. 'Slavery and the Emancipation Movement in Barbados, 1650–1833', *Journal of Negro History*, LV (1970), 1–14.

LIVINGSTONE, W. P. *Black Jamaica.* London, 1900.

LLOYD, Christopher. *The Navy and the Slave Trade.* London, 1949.

LOBDELL, Richard A. 'Patterns of Investment and Sources of Credit in the British West Indian Sugar Industry, 1838–97', *Journal of Caribbean History*, IV (1972), 31–53.

LONG, A. V. *Jamaica and the New Order, 1827–47*. Mona, 1956.

LOVETT, R. *History of the London Missionary Society, 1795–1895*. 2 vols. London, 1895.

LOWE, Robson. *The Codrington Correspondence, 1743–1851*. London, 1957.

LOWENTHAL, David. *West Indian Societies*. New York, 1972.

McPHERSON, James M. 'Was West Indian Emancipation a Success? The Abolitionist Argument During the American Civil War', *Caribbean Studies*, IV (1964), 28–34.

MANNING, Helen Taft. *British Colonial Development after the American Revolution, 1782–1820*. New Haven, 1933.

——. 'Who Ran the British Empire, 1830–1850?', *Journal of British Studies*, V (1966), 88–121.

MARSHALL, Woodville K. 'Notes on Peasant Development in the West Indies Since 1838', *Social and Economic Studies*, III (1968), 252–63.

——. 'The Termination of the Apprenticeship in Barbados and the Windward Islands: An Essay in Colonial Administration and Politics', *The Journal of Caribbean History*, II (1970), 1–45.

MASON, Philip. *Patterns of Dominance*. New York, 1970.

MATHEW, W. M. 'Peru and the British Guano Market, 1840–1870', *Economic Historic Review*, 2nd ser., XXIII (1970), 112–28.

MATHIESON, William Law. *British Slavery and its Abolition, 1828–38*. London, 1926.

——. *British Slave Emancipation, 1838–49*. London, 1932.

——. *The Sugar Colonies and Governor Eyre, 1848–66*. London, 1936.

MATTHEWS, R. C. O. *A Study in Trade Cycle History: Economic Fluctuations in Great Britain, 1833–42*. Cambridge, 1954.

MELLOR, G. R. *British Imperial Trusteeship, 1783–1850*. London, 1951.

MINTZ, Sidney. 'Labor and Sugar in Puerto Rico and in Jamaica, 1800–1850', *Comparative Studies in Society and History*, I (1959), 273–80.

——. 'The Question of Caribbean Peasantries: a Comment" *Caribbean Studies*, I (1961), 31–4.

——. 'Slavery and the Slaves', *Caribbean Studies*, VIII (1969), 65–70.

MOOHR, Michael. 'The Economic Impact of Slave Emancipation in British Guiana, 1832–1852', *Economic History Review*, 2nd ser., XXV (1972), 588–607.

MORRELL, W. P. *British Colonial Policy in the Age of Peel and Russell*. Oxford, 1930.

434 BIBLIOGRAPHY

——. *British Colonial Policy in the Mid-Victorian Age.* Oxford, 1969.

MORRIS, Sir Daniel. *Reports on the Economic Resources of the West Indies.* London, 1898.

MOTTRAM, R. H. *Buxton the Liberator.* London, 1946.

MURRAY, D. J. *The West Indies and the Development of Colonial Government, 1801–34.* Oxford, 1965.

NATH, D. *A History of Indians in British Guiana.* London, 1950.

NIEBOER, H. J. *Slavery as an Industrial System, Ethnological Researches.* The Hague, 1900.

O'LOUGHLIN, Carleen. *Economic and Political Change in the Leeward and Windward Islands.* New Haven, 1968.

OLIVER, Vere Langford. *The History of the Island of Antigua.* 3 vols. London, 1894–99.

OLIVIER, Sydney Haldane, Lord. *Jamaica: The Blessed Island.* London, 1936.

——. *The Myth of Governor Eyre.* London, 1933.

PAGET, E. 'Land Use and Settlement in Jamaica', in Steel, R. W. and Fisher, C.A., eds. *Geographical Essays on British Tropical Lands.* London, 1956.

PAGET, H., and R. FARLEY. 'The Growth of Villages in Jamaica and British Guiana', *Caribbean Quarterly*, X (1964), 38–61.

PAGET, H. 'The Free Village System in Jamaica', *Jamaican Historical Review*, I (1945), 31–48.

PARES, Richard. *Yankees and Creoles.* London, 1956.

——. *Merchants and Planters.* London, 1960.

——. *A West India Fortune.* London, 1968.

PARRY, J. H. 'Salt Fish and Ackee', *Caribbean Quarterly*, VII (1962), 30–6.

——. 'The Patent Offices in the British West Indies', *English Historical Review*, LXIX (1954), 200–25.

PATTERSON, Orlando. *The Sociology of Slavery.* Cranbury, New Jersey, 1967.

PENSON, Lillian M. 'The London West India Interest in the Eighteenth Century', *English Historical Review*, XXXVI (1921), 373–92.

——. *Colonial Agents of the West Indies.* London, 1924.

PETERSON, John. *Province of Freedom: A History of Sierra Leone, 1787–1870.* Evanston, 1969.

PHILLIPS, Ulrich Bonnell. 'A Jamaica Slave Plantation', *American Historical Review*, XIX (1914), 543–59.

——. 'An Antigua Plantation, 1769–1818', *The North Carolina Historical Review*, III (1926), 439–45.

PINNINGTON, J. E. 'Anglican Problems of Adaptation in the Catholic

Caribbean: The C. M. S. in Trinidad, 1836–44', *Journal of Caribbean History*, I (1970).

PITMAN, Frank Wesley. *The Development of the British West Indies, 1700–63*. New Haven, 1917.

——. 'The West Indian Absentee Planter as a British Colonial Type', *Proceedings of the Pacific Coast Branch of the American Historical Association*, (1927), 113–27.

——. 'The Settlement and Financing of British West India Plantations in the Eighteenth Century', in *Essays in Colonial History*, presented to Charles McLean Andrews by his Students. New Haven, 1931.

RAGATZ, Lowell Joseph. *The Old Plantation System in the British Caribbean*. London, 1925.

——. *Absentee Landlordism in the British Caribbean, 1750–1833*. London, 1928.

——. *The Fall of the Planter Class in the British Caribbean, 1763–1833*. New York, 1928.

RAIN, Thomas. *The Life and Labours of John Wray, Pioneer Missionary in British Guiana*. London, 1892.

RECKORD, Mary. 'The Colonial Office and the Abolition of Slavery', *Historical Journal*, XIV (1971), 723–34.

RICE, C. Duncan. '"Humanity Sold for Sugar!" The British Abolitionist Response to Free Trade in Slave Grown Sugar', *Historical Journal*, XIII (1970), 402–18.

RICHARD, H. *Memoirs of Joseph Sturge*. London, 1864.

RIVIERE, W. Emanuel. 'Labour Shortage in the British West Indies After Emancipation', *Journal of Caribbean History*, IV (1972), 1–30.

ROBERTS, G. W. 'Immigration of Africans into the British Caribbean', *Population Studies, a Journal of Demography*, XX (1966), 125–34.

ROBERTS, W. Adolphe. *Six Great Jamaicans*. Kingston, 1952.

RODWAY, J. *History of British Guiana*. 3 vols. Georgetown, 1922–3.

SCHUYLER, R. L. 'The Constitutional Claims of the British West Indies', *Political Science Quarterly*, XL (1925), 1–36.

——. *Parliament and the British Empire*. New York, 1929.

——. *The Fall of the Old Colonial System, a Study in British Free Trade, 1770–1870*. New York, 1945.

SEMMEL, Bernard. *Jamaican Blood and Victorian Conscience*. Boston, 1963.

——. *The Rise of Free Trade Imperialism: Classical Political Economy, the Empire of Free Trade and Imperialism, 1750–1850*. New York, 1970.

SHERIDAN, Richard B. 'Samuel Martin, Innovating Sugar Planter of Antigua, 1750–75', *Agricultural History*, XXXIV (1960), 126–39.

——. 'West India Sugar Crisis and British Slave Emancipation, 1830–33', *Journal of Economic History*, XXI (1961), 539–51.

——. 'The Wealth of Jamaica in the Eighteenth Century', *Economic History Review*, 2nd ser., XVIII (1965), 296–306.

——. 'The Plantation Revolution, 1625–1775', *Caribbean Studies*, IX (1969), 5–26.

——. 'Simon Taylor, Sugar Tycoon of Jamaica, 1740–1813', *Agricultural History*, XLV (1971), 285–96.

——. 'Planters and Merchants: The Oliver Family of Antigua and London, 1716–84', *Business History*, XIII (1971), 104–13.

SIMON, Brian. *Studies in the History of Education, 1780–1870*. London, 1960.

SIMPSON, G. E. *Religious Cults in the Caribbean: Jamaica, Trinidad, and Haiti*. Rio Piedras, 1970.

SIRES, Ronald Vernon. 'Sir Henry Barkly and the Labor Problem in Jamaica, 1853–56', *The Journal of Negro History*, XXV (1940), 216–35.

——. 'Constitutional Change in Jamaica, 1834–60', *Journal of Comparative Legislation and International Law*, 3rd ser., XXII (1940), 178–90.

——. 'Negro Labor in Jamaica in the Years Following Emancipation', *Journal of Negro History*, XXV (1940), 484–97.

——. 'The Jamaica Slave Insurrection Loan, 1832–63', *Journal of Negro History*, XXVII (1942), 295–319.

——. 'Governmental Crisis in Jamaica, 1860–66', *Jamaican Historical Review*, II (1953), 1–26.

SMITH, Goldwin. *The Empire*. Oxford, 1863.

SMITH, M. G. *The Plural Society in the British West Indies*. Berkeley, 1965.

SOLOWAY, Richard Allen. *Prelates and People: Ecclesiastical Social Thought in England, 1783–1852*. Toronto, 1969.

STARKEY, Otis P. *The Economic Geography of Barbados: a Study of the Relationships Between Environmental Variations and Economic Development*. New York, 1939.

STEPHEN, Caroline Emelia. *The Rt. Hon. Sir James Stephen . . . Letters with Biographical Notes*. Gloucester, 1906.

STEWART, Robert. *The Politics of Protection: Lord Derby and the Protectionist Party, 1841–52*. New York, 1971.

SWINFEN, David B. *Imperial Control of Colonial Legislation, 1813–65: A Study of British Policy Towards Colonial Legislative Powers*. New York, 1970.

TAUSSIG, Charles William. *Rum, Romance, and Rebellion*. New York, 1928.

TEMPERLEY, Howard. *British Antislavery, 1833–70*. London, 1972.

THOMPSON, Edward. *The Life of Charles, Lord Metcalfe*. London, 1937.

THORNTON, A. P. *The Imperial Idea and its Enemies*. London, 1959.

——. *The Habit of Authority: Paternalism in British History*. Toronto, 1966.

WARD, John M. 'Retirement of a Titan: James Stephen, 1847–50', *Journal of Modern History*, XXXI (1959), 189–205.

WARD, W. E. F. *The Royal Navy and the Slavers*. London, 1969.

WARDLE, David. *English Popular Education, 1780–1970.* Cambridge, 1970.

WARNER, Aucher. *Sir Thomas Warner, Pioneer of the West Indies: A Chronicle of his Family*. London, 1933.

WELLER, Judith Ann. *The East Indian Indenture in Trinidad*. Rio Piedras, 1968.

WESLEY, Charles H. 'The Emancipation of the Free Coloured Population of the British Empire', *The Journal of Negro History*, XIX (1934), 137–71.

WEST, E. G. 'Resource Allocation and Growth in Early Nineteenth Century British Education', *Economic History Review*, 2nd ser., XXIII (1970), 68–95.

WILLIAMS, E. T. 'The Colonial Office in the Thirties', *Historical Studies, Australia and New Zealand*, II (1943), 141–60.

WILLIAMS, Eric. *Capitalism and Slavery*. Chapel Hill, 1944.

——. *History of the People of Trinidad and Tobago*. Port of Spain, 1962.

——. *British Historians and the West Indies*. Port of Spain, 1964.

WILLIAMS, Joseph J., S.J. *Voodoos and Obeahs, Phases of West India Witchcraft*. New York, 1932.

——. *Psychic Phenomena of Jamaica*. New York, 1934.

WINCH, Donald. *Classical Political Economy and Colonies*. Cambridge, Mass., 1965.

WOOD, Donald. *Trinidad in Transition, the Years After Slavery*. London, 1968.

WOODWARD, E. L. *The Age of Reform, 1815–70*. Oxford, 1938.

WRONG, Hume. *Government of the West Indies*. Oxford, 1923.

WYNDHAM, H. A. *The Atlantic and Slavery*. London, 1935.

——. *The Atlantic and Emancipation*. London, 1937.

YOUNG, D. M. *The Colonial Office in the Early Nineteenth Century*. London, 1961.

YOUNG, G. M. *Victorian England: Portrait of an Age*. London, 1964.

VI. UNPUBLISHED THESES

ELDRIDGE, Colin Clifford. 'The Colonial Policy of the Fifth Duke of Newcastle, 1859–64', University of Nottingham, Ph.D., 1966.

FORD, Trowbridge Harris. 'The Era of Lord Brougham', Columbia University, Ph.D., 1967.

HIGMAN, B. W. 'Slave Population and Economy in Jamaica at the Time of Emancipation', University of the West Indies, Ph.D., 1970.

ROGERS, Howard Aston. 'The Fall of the Old Representative System in the Leeward and Windward Islands, 1854–77', University of Southern California, Ph.D., 1970.

Index

Abandonment (plantations), 221, 223, 249, 250, 252, 300
Aberdeen, Lord, 150, 361
Abolitionists, 99, 127, 151
Absentee proprietorship, 59, 62, 63, 132, 324
Africa, 126, 234, 265, 267, 268, 318, 347, 352
Africans, 265, 266, 268, 274, 275
African cultural legacies, 4, 26, 328, 344
African immigration: To West Indies, 265–276; Crown responsibility for, 271; high cost, 272; extent and importance, 273–5
Afro-creole culture group, 309, 317, 326
Agency Committee, 112, 406
Agricultural machinery, 193
Agricultural shows, 200
Allen, J. A., 141
American Anti-Slavery Society, 265
American Civil War, 316, 325, 382
American Colonization Society, 264 n.
Anglican Church: see Established Church
Antigua: colour prejudice, 17; pasturage, 56; rejection of apprenticeship, 124–5; cane acreage, 201; encumbered estates, 257; asylums, 309; constitutional reform, 369; Executive Committee, 370–1, 374; drought, 378
Anti-Slavery Society: strength in Parliament, 100; views of, 103; political activism, 111, 114; opposition to apprenticeship, 119
Appraisement, 133–4
Apprentices: classification of, 132–3; purchase freedom, 134; corporal punishment, 153
Apprenticeship: terms of, 121; prospects, 130; weaknesses, 131; labour relations, 131; improper classification, 133; appraisement, 133; working conditions, 135; punishments, 135–6; abolition of, 156 ff
Arima, Trinidad, 301

Arrowroot, 226
Asiegbu, J. U. J., 409
Assemblies, West Indian: finance, 68; executive powers, 68; sessions, 70; elections, 70; variations in quality, 75; initiatives, 90; annual Acts, 91; independence, 92; response to amelioration, 104 ff.; Emancipation Acts, 122–3; hostilities to governors, 146; post-apprenticeship legislation, 164, 165; reforms, 369–70; elimination of, 398; cues from Parliament, 404
Asylums, 254, 309
Austin, J. G., 289

Bahama Islands, 105, 263
Baltimore Clippers, 262
Banbury, R. Thomas, 344
Bank of Jamaica, 181
Banks, 180, 235
Baptist Missionaries: Jamaica, 29 n; attacked by Governor, 171–2; popularity with freedmen, 172; advice on wages, 197; declining contributions (1844–59), 309; attacked by other missionaries, 333; declining congregations, 341; demoralization, 342; rioting, 342–3; oppose state subsidy to education, 346, 348; relatively low esteem, 393
Baptist Western Union, 171
Barbados: colour prejudice, 17, 64; use of plough, 53; pasturage, 56; energetic assembly, 75; Emancipation Act, 124; free children, 134; prison, 166 n.; judicial reform, 179; increased public expenditures, 183; agricultural society, 200; land use, 201; agricultural methods, 201, 202; railroad, 214–15; production costs, 222; sugar production, 245–6, 257 ff.; land values, 257; public solvency, 258; import duties, 258; tax rate, 258; resident management, 258; labour relations, 259, 323; free villages,